Community-Based Corrections

EIGHTH EDITION

Leanne Fiftal Alarid
University of Texas, San Antonio

Rolando V. del Carmen
Sam Houston State University

WADSWORTH
CENGAGE Learning

Australia • Brazil • Japan • Korea • Mexico • Singapore • Spain • United Kingdom • United States

Community-Based Corrections,
Eighth Edition
Leanne Fiftal Alarid, Rolando V. del Carmen

Acquisitions Editor: Carolyn Henderson-
Meier

Development Editor: Tricia Louvar

Assistant Editor: Megan Power

Editorial Assistant: John Chell

Technology Project Manager: Andy Yap

Marketing Manager: Michelle Williams

Marketing Assistant: Jillian Myers

Marketing Communications Manager:
Tami Strang

Project Manager, Editorial Production:
Matt Ballantyne

Art Director: Maria Epes

Manufacturing Buyer: Linda Hsu

Permissions Editor Text: Bob Kauser

Permissions Editor Image: Leitha
Etheridge-Sims

Production Service: Pre-Press PMG

Photo Researcher: Pre-Press PMG

Cover Designer: Yvo Riezebos

Compositor: Pre-Press PMG

Text and Cover Printer: Edwards Brothers

For product information and technology assistance, contact us at
Cengage Learning Customer & Sales Support, 1-800-354-9706

For permission to use material from this text or product,
submit all requests online at **cengage.com/permissions**
Further permissions questions can be emailed to
permissionrequest@cengage.com

Library of Congress Control Number: 2009938856

ISBN-13: 978-0-495-81242-5

ISBN-10: 0-495-81242-0

Wadsworth
20 Davis Drive
Belmont CA 94002
USA

Cengage Learning is a leading provider of customized learning solutions
with office locations around the globe, including Singapore, the United
Kingdom, Australia, Mexico, Brazil, and Japan. Locate your local office at:
international.cengage.com/region

Cengage Learning products are represented in Canada by
Nelson Education, Ltd.

For your course and learning solutions, visit **academic.cengage.com**

Purchase any of our products at your local college store or at our
preferred online store **www.ichapters.com**

Printed in the United States of America
1 2 3 4 5 6 7 13 12 11 10 09

DEDICATION

*To my mentor Crazyhorse—the absolute coolest person—to my
loving family, and to the Mojos—ride on!*
Leanne F. Alarid

To my wife, Josie, and daughter, Jocelyn.
Rolando V. del Carmen

Brief Contents

Preface   xv

PART I: PRINCIPLES OF COMMUNITY CORRECTIONS, DIVERSION, AND SENTENCING   1

Chapter 1 • An Overview of Community Corrections: Goals and Evidence-Based Practices   2

Chapter 2 • Pretrial Release and Diversion   21

Chapter 3 • Sentencing and the Presentence Investigation Report   42

PART II: PROBATION   77

Chapter 4 • How Probation Developed: Chronicling Its Past and Present   78

Chapter 5 • Classification and Supervision: Techniques of Evidence-Based Practices   95

Chapter 6 • The Career Pathway of a Community Supervision Officer   136

Chapter 7 • Probation Modification and Termination   157

PART III: SPECIALIZED CASELOADS AND INTERMEDIATE PROGRAMS   177

Chapter 8 • Residential Community Supervision Programs   178

Chapter 9 • Nonresidential Community Supervision Programs   208

Chapter 10 • Economic and Restorative Justice Reparations   230

PART IV: PRISONER REENTRY   255

Chapter 11 • The History of Parole: From Its Origin to the Present   256

Chapter 12 • Preparing for Prisoner Reentry: Discretionary Parole and Mandatory Release   274

Chapter 13 • Parole Conditions and Revocation   297

PART V: SPECIAL ISSUES IN COMMUNITY CORRECTIONS   323

Chapter 14 • Juvenile Justice, Probation, and Parole   324

Chapter 15 • Collateral Consequences of Conviction, Pardon, and Restoration of Rights   349

Glossary   380

References   387

Table of Cases   404

Name Index   406

Subject Index   409

Contents

Preface   xv

PART I: PRINCIPLES OF COMMUNITY CORRECTIONS, DIVERSION, AND SENTENCING   1

Chapter 1 • An Overview of Community Corrections: Goals and Evidence-Based Practices   2

The Correctional Dilemma   3
Indeterminate Sentencing   7 • Origins of Modern Determinate Sentencing   8

The Paradox   9
Public Perceptions of Community Corrections   10 • Correctional Budgets   10

The Role of Corrections at Three Major Decision Points   12
Pretrial and the Bail Decision   12 • Sentencing Decision   13 • Reentry Decision   13

How Community Corrections Fits Correctional Goals   14
Protection of the Public   15 • Rehabilitation   15 • Restorative or Community Justice   16 • Deterrence through Shaming   16

Evidence-Based Practices in Community Corrections   17
Evaluating Effectiveness   18 • Outcome Measures in Evaluation   18

summary   *19*

Discussion Questions   *20*

Web Sites   *20*

Chapter 2 • Pretrial Release and Diversion   21

Introduction   22

Pretrial Services   22
History of Pretrial Release   23 • The Pretrial Release Decision   24 • Pretrial Supervision   27 • Failure to Appear   28

Diversion   30
Candidates for Diversion   31 • Drug Courts   32 • Characteristics of Drug Courts   33 • Gender and Drug Court Treatment Strategies   34 • Evaluating Drug Courts   35 • Mental Health Courts   37 • Criticisms of Diversion Programs   39

Summary   *39*

Discussion Questions   *39*

Web Sites   *40*

Case Study Exercise   *41*

Chapter 3 • Sentencing and the Presentence Investigation Report   **42**

Sentencing   43
Factors That Affect Granting a Community Sentence   43   •   Sentencing
Guidelines   44   •   Sentencing Commissions   47

Conditions of Community Corrections   47
Standard Conditions   47   •   Special Conditions   49   •
Supervision Conditions and the Constitution   51

The Presentence Investigation Report   52
Purposes of the PSI Report   52   •   Contents of the PSI Report   53   •
Preparing the PSI Report   55   •   The Initial Interview   55   •
Investigation and Verification   56   •   The Evaluative Summary   56   •
The Sentence Recommendation   57

Legal Issues Concerning the Presentence Report   58
Disclosure of the PSI Report   58   •   Inaccuracies in the PSI
Report   59   •   Hearsay in the PSI Report   59   •   Does the Exclusionary
Rule Apply?   60   •   *Miranda* Warnings and the PSI Interview   60   •
Right to a Lawyer during the PSI Interview   60

Summary   *61*

Discussion Questions   *61*

Web Sites   *62*

Case Study Exercise 1   *63*

Case Study Exercise 2   *65*

Case Study Exercise 3   *72*

PART II: PROBATION   **77**

Chapter 4 • How Probation Developed: Chronicling Its Past and Present   **78**

Precursors to American Probation   79
Procedures Related to Modern Probation   80   •   The Founders of
Probation   81   •   Development of Federal Probation   84   •   History
of Juvenile Probation and the Juvenile Court   84   •   Early Probation
Legislation in Other States   86

Organization of Probation Departments   86
Community Corrections Acts   88   •   Models of Supervision Over
Time   90

Who Is on Probation?   91

Summary   *93*

Discussion Questions   *94*

Web Sites   *94*

**Chapter 5 • Classification and Supervision: Techniques
of Evidence-Based Practices**   **95**

Introduction   96

Classification: The First Step in Supervision   96
Risk Assessments   97   •   Identifying Treatment Needs   98

The Supervision Case Plan   98
Implementing the Case Plan: Surveillance   101   •   Levels of
Supervision   103   •   Caseload and Workload Standards   103   •
Implementing the Case Plan: Treatment   104   •   Evaluation of
Neighborhood-Based vs. Traditional Probation   107

Specialized Caseloads   110
   Supervising Sex Offenders   110   •   Strategies for Supervising Known
   Gang Members   112   •   Working with Women Offenders   113

Summary   *114*

Discussion Questions   *114*

Web Sites   *115*

Case Study Exercise   *116*

Chapter 6 • The Career Pathway of a Community Supervision Officer   **136**

Introduction   137

Selection and Appointment of Probation Officers   138
   Appointment System   138   •   Merit System   139

Officer Qualifications, Training, and Salary   139
   Education and Experience   140   •   Adult Basic Training   141   •
   Juvenile Preservice Training   142   •   In-service Training   144   •
   Officer Salary   144

Firearms Policies for Probation and Parole Officers   144

Probation Officer Job Stress   148
   Sources of Stress   149   •   Decreasing Stress: Types of Immunity   150

Private Probation   151
   Statutes Authorizing Private Probation   152   •   Criticisms of Probation
   Privatization   153

Interstate Compacts on Probation   154
   The Interstate Compact for Adult Offender Supervision   154   •
   Revocation and the Interstate Compact   155

Summary   *155*

Discussion Questions   *156*

Web Sites   *156*

Chapter 7 • Probation Modification and Termination   **157**

Introduction   158

Modifying Probation Conditions   159
   Early Termination of Probation   159   •   In-House Administrative Options
   before Filing a Revocation   159

The Decision to Revoke   161

Types of Probation Violations   162
   Law Violations   163   •   Technical Violations   163

Revocation Procedure   164
   The Power to Arrest Probationers   166   •   Time on Probation or Parole Is
   Usually Not Credited if Revoked   166

Revocation Rights of Probationers and Parolees   167
   The Right to a Hearing   167   •   The Right to a Lawyer   168   •
   Level of Proof and Evidence Required   168   •   Other Revocation
   Situations   169

Probation Outcomes   170
   Probation Recidivism Rates   170   •   Who Is More Likely to Succeed or
   Fail on Probation?   171   •   Probationers Compared with Parolees   171

Summary   *173*

Discussion Questions   *173*

Web Sites   174

Case Study Exercise   175

PART III: SPECIALIZED CASELOADS AND INTERMEDIATE PROGRAMS   **177**

Chapter 8 • Residential Community Supervision Programs   **178**

Introduction   179

Residential Community Corrections Facilities   180

Halfway Houses/Community Corrections Centers   181
History of Halfway Houses in the United States   182 •
Program Components   183 • Worker Perspectives and Role
Orientation   184 • Evaluations of RCCFs   185

Shock Incarceration   186
Correctional Boot Camps   186 • Juvenile Probation
Boot Camps   189 • Offender Perspectives   189 •
Criticisms of Boot Camps   192 • Evaluations of Boot
Camp Programs   192

RCCFs Serving Specific Offenders and Specialized Caseloads   193
Supervising Offenders Who Are Mentally Ill   193 • Supervising
Offenders Who Have Abused Drugs and Alcohol   195 • Treatment
Modalities for Substance Abusers: Therapeutic Communities   196 •
RCCFs for Women Offenders   200

Supervising Working Offenders Outside of Jail   201
Jail-Based Work Release   201 • Community-Based Work Release:
Restitution Centers   203 • Work Ethic Camp   204

Summary   205

Discussion Questions   205

Web Sites   206

Case Study Exercise   207

Chapter 9 • Nonresidential Community Supervision Programs   **208**

Introduction   209

History of Intensive Supervision and Specialized Caseloads   209
Evaluations of ISP   210

House Arrest   211
Purposes of Home Detention   211 • Criticisms of House Arrest   212
• Effectiveness of House Arrest   213

Electronic Monitoring and Global Positioning Systems   213
History of Electronic Monitoring   214 • Global Positioning
Systems   216 • Empirical Evaluations of EM and GPS   220

Day Reporting Centers   221
Treatment-Oriented versus Supervision-Oriented DRCs   223 •
Evaluations of DRCs   224

Summary   226

Discussion Questions   226

Web Sites   227

Case Study Exercise   228

Chapter 10 • Economic and Restorative Justice Reparations   **230**

Introduction   231

Restorative Justice Principles   232
Forms of Restorative Justice   233   •   Effectiveness of Restorative Justice
Methods   236

Restitution   237
Restitution in History   237   •   Losses Eligible for Compensation   239   •
Problems Associated with Restitution   239   •   Effectiveness of
Restitution   242

Community Service   242
History of Community Service   243   •   Purpose of Community
Service   243   •   Prevalence of Community Service   243   •
Effectiveness of Community Service   244

Fines   246
Prevalence of Fines   246   •   Revoking Probation for Fine
Nonpayment   247   •   Forfeitures   248   •   Day Fines   248

Fees and Court Costs   249

Summary   *251*

Discussion Questions   *251*

Web Sites   *251*

Case Study Exercise   *253*

PART IV: PRISONER REENTRY   **255**

Chapter 11 • The History of Parole: From Its Origin to the Present   **256**

Introduction   257

The Origins of Parole   258
Manuel Montesinos   258   •   Georg Michael Obermaier   259   •
Alexander Maconochie   259   •   Sir Walter Crofton and the Irish
System   261

The Development of Parole in the United States   261
Four Justifications of Parole   261   •   The Medical Model:
1930–1960   263   •   A Philosophical Change   263   •
From Discretionary Parole to Mandatory Release   264

Parole Today   264
Characteristics of Parolees   267   •   Functions of Parole   270

Summary   *273*

Discussion Questions   *273*

Web Sites   *273*

**Chapter 12 • Preparing for Prisoner Reentry: Discretionary Parole
and Mandatory Release**   **274**

Introduction   275

Issues in Reentry   275
The Prisoner's Family   277   •   The Victim's Role in Reentry   277   •
Reentry and the Community   278   •   Community-Based Reentry
Initiatives   279

Eligibility for Parole   279
Time Sheets and Eligibility Dates   280   •   Prerelease Preparation within
the Institution   280

The Parole Board and Releasing Authority   282
Term and Qualifications of the Parole Board   284   •   The Parole
Hearing   284   •   Parole Hearing Attendees   285   •   The Parole Board
Decision   287

Models of Parole Release Decisions   287
The Surveillance Model   287   •   The Procedural Justice Model   288   •
The Risk Prediction Model   288

Legal Issues in Parole Hearings   291
No Due Process Protections   291   •   Use of Hearsay, DNA, and No Right
to an Attorney   292

Prisoner's Perceptions of Parole Selection   292

Summary   *293*

Discussion Questions   *293*

Web Sites   *294*

Case Study Exercise   *295*

Chapter 13 • Parole Conditions and Revocation   **297**

Introduction   298

Prisoner Perspectives on Getting   298
California Study   299   •   Iowa Study   300

The Field Parole Officer   301
The Officer's Perspective   301

Conditions of Parole   303
Limited Rights of All Parolees   304   •   Legal Issues in Parole Conditions
for Sex Offenders   304

Violating Parole   305
Warrants and Citations   308

Characteristics of Parole Violators   308
Parole Revocation Rate   309   •   Attitudes on Revocation   310

Parole Absconders   311
Why Do Parolees Leave?   312   •   Locating and Apprehending
Fugitives   312   •   Predicting Absconding Behavior   313

Parole Effectiveness   314
Recidivism Studies   316   •   Predicting Parole Outcomes   316

Summary   *318*

Discussion Questions   *319*

Web Sites   *319*

Case Study Exercise   *320*

PART V: SPECIAL ISSUES IN COMMUNITY CORRECTIONS   **323**

Chapter 14 • Juvenile Justice, Probation, and Parole   **324**

Introduction   325
In Re Gault: The Decline of Parens Patriae   326

Juvenile Justice and Adult Justice Systems Compared   327
Differences from Adult Courts   327   •   Jurisdiction of Juvenile
Courts   329   •   Transfer from Juvenile Courts to Adult Courts   331

An Overview of The Juvenile Justice Process   332
Procedure before Adjudication   332   •   Blended Sentences   336

Juvenile Probation   336
    Conditions of Probation   337   •   Change as an Integral Process   337
        •   Juvenile Probation Officers as "Superheroes"   339   •   Intensive
    Supervision Probation   340   •   School-Based Probation   340   •
    Fare v. Michael C.   341   •   Are Juvenile Records Confidential?   342

Juvenile Parole/Aftercare   343
    Juvenile Parole Boards and Parole Officers   343   •   Revocation of
    Juvenile Probation or Parole   344   •   Evaluating Juvenile Parole
    Programs   344

The Future of Juvenile Justice   345

Summary   *345*

Discussion Questions   *346*

Web Sites   *346*

Case Study Exercise   *347*

Chapter 15 • Collateral Consequences of Conviction,
Pardon, and Restoration of Rights   **349**

Introduction   350
    Civil and Political Rights Defined   351   •   Background of Civil Disabilities   351

Civil Disabilities Today   352
    Differences by State   352   •   Rights Lost through Discretion   353

Civil and Political Rights Commonly Affected by Conviction   354
    Loss of Right to Vote   354   •   Loss of Employment-Related Rights   356
    Loss of Right to Own or Possess a Firearm   359   •   Loss of Welfare
    Benefits   360   •   Loss of Parental Rights   360   •   Loss in Court   361
    Loss of the Right to Hold Public Office   361   •   Problems With Civil
    Disability Laws   362

Effects of Conviction for Sex Offenders   362
    Sex Offender Registration Laws   362   •   Community Notification
    Laws   364   •   Residency Restrictions   366   •   Involuntary Civil
    Commitment of Sexual Predators   366

Pardon   367
    The Power to Pardon   368   •   Kinds of Pardon   368   •   Procedure for
    Obtaining a Pardon   368   •   Legal Effects of a Pardon   369   •   Effects of
    a Pardon on Occupational Licensing   369

Restoration of Rights   370
    Restoration upon Application   370   •   Automatic Restoration   371
        •   Restoring Good Moral Character   371   •   Expungement of Arrest
    and Conviction Records   372   •   Sealing of Records Not Resulting in a
    Conviction   373

Summary   *375*

Discussion Questions   *375*

Web Sites   *375*

Case Study Exercise   *377*

Glossary   380

References   387

Table of Cases   404

Name Index   406

Subject Index   409

Preface

A dramatic shift is occurring in the way that offenders are supervised and prepared for release in corrections. With over four million offenders being supervised in the community, coupled with an emphasis on public safety, there is an increase in the use of correctional technology and an efficient use of rehabilitation programs. Through the principles of effective correctional intervention, more is known about what works with certain types of offenders. There is also a broader array of choices available as alternatives to incarceration than ever before. Evidence-based practices are changing the way that many agencies operate to an acceptance of empirical research and evaluation to determine what improvements they can make.

This book operates on two assumptions. First, most people who are diverted from a conviction or who are convicted of a crime are supervised in the community. This means that most people in the corrections system are on a form of community-based corrections and not in jail or prison.

A second assumption is that while some people should be incarcerated for their crimes, the reality is that few are kept for the remainder of their natural lives. Estimates range between 95 percent and 97 percent of people in jail or prison today will be released at some point and return to the community. This book examines programs that operate to fit the needs of both types of offenders.

The goal of the eighth edition of *Community-Based Corrections* is to provide students with comprehensive, up-to-date, evidence-based practices and research for probation, release from prison, and other community-based alternatives. We have sought to present community-based correctional programs in their historical, philosophical, social, and legal context and to integrate real-life practice to the greatest extent possible.

Because we want this book to be of practical use, we have provided many examples of community-based programs, laws, and procedures from state and federal jurisdictions. In this edition, as in previous ones, we wrestled with the problem of using examples and laws from as many states as possible to make the materials relevant to a broad audience. However, the states' systems vary widely in their programs, laws, and sophistication. We decided we would not do students justice if we included laws and examples from only the large, populous states, and we could not possibly incorporate examples and laws from every jurisdiction. We therefore decided to use the federal system as our primary point of reference. We have cited state laws and programs throughout the book nonetheless.

New Updates and Organization of the Eighth Edition

The most significant changes to note with this edition are the incorporation of evidence-based practices and specialized caseloads throughout the text. One brand new feature is called "Field Notes" and consists of a series of six opinion-based essays written by practitioners addressing a topic of importance, such as a judge's perspective of drug court or how a juvenile officer feels about carrying a firearm.

Some exciting chapter-by-chapter changes from the previous edition that we wish to highlight include: Chapter 1 provides a new diagram from which students can obtain a broad view of community corrections programs within the justice system. Annual costs of prison and community sentences are provided in a new table. The student is introduced to evidence-based practices, which remains a theme throughout the text. The "what works" debate is moved to earlier in the chapter for better flow when discussing the move from indeterminate to determinate sentencing. The public perception of community corrections section has been completely rewritten.

Chapter 2 chronicles the purpose of pretrial release and addresses why the most recent trend in the federal system has been to increase pretrial detention. This chapter provides a thorough update on mental health courts.

Federal sentencing guideline information has been updated in Chapter 3 to correspond with changes that occurred as a result of *U.S. v. Booker*. More detail is added to the text to better explain the North Carolina sentencing grid. As presentence investigation reports are streamlined, another major change in this chapter was to update the federal presentence investigation report used in previous editions with one where the defendant has been convicted of tax evasion. Case Study No. 3 has been added as an instructional guide to conducting and writing a Full Version PSI that is used in states allowing more judicial discretion. This case study includes the arrest report, criminal background check, and collateral interviews. The student can then create a client or the class can engage in a mock interview of a client in class.

Chapter 4 includes a few new sections that were moved from other chapters. The sections on "Organization of Probation Departments" and community corrections acts (previously in Chapter 5 of the seventh edition) were moved as part of chronicling how probation departments developed. Current probationer characteristics round out the concluding section of Chapter 4 (previously in Chapter 6 of the seventh edition) to show how probationers have changed over the last decade.

We thought it was important to discuss the foundation of community supervision—classification and supervision—earlier in the book, so we moved part of the seventh edition's Chapter 6 to the new edition's Chapter 5. We tie in classification and supervision methods to tools used in evidence-based practices. We introduce specialized caseloads here, and discuss sex offenders, gang members, and a brand new section on women offenders. We update the chapter with a different assessment instrument that links in an exercise for the student to complete an assessment interview, score a risk/needs classification, and make a supervision case plan all for the same client. This exercise can be completed individually or in groups of two to four students as a small group project.

The chapter containing topics relevant to officers, such as salaries, firearms, stress, etc. is now in Chapter 6. The section on private probation has been newly expanded and revised. The topic of interstate compacts (transfer of supervision to another state) follows the section on private probation to conclude this chapter.

Chapter 7 includes more information on in-house administrative options that are tried before a community supervision officer files a revocation, as well as supervisory strategies to reduce the occurrence of technical violations. If a revocation is filed in the federal system, a new table shows the revocation guidelines that U.S. probation officers follow. The chapter also addresses what happens to offenders who revoke while on deferred adjudication.

Chapter 8 has incorporated more supervision strategies for specialized caseloads and clients with special needs, to include clients with mental health issues and those with alcohol and drug dependency problems. The section on work release has been expanded to include both jail-based and community-based uses of work capable offenders in the community. There is also a small section that discusses community options for women arrested for prostitution.

Specialized caseloads are frequently more intensive than regular community supervision and can include electronic monitoring, substance abuse treatment, and day reporting centers which are discussed in Chapter 9 relative to the supervision of high-risk offenders. This chapter also contains a brand new case study (Case C: Jonas Knight) for specialized caseloads—an offender who is convicted of a sexual offense and who also has a learning disability.

Chapter 10 has expanded information on family group conferencing and other restorative justice programs that were gathered through a restorative justice conference held at the University of Texas-San Antonio in May 2009. There are updated sections on presentence restitution to increase restitution collection rates and a further distinction between fines and fees.

Chapter 11 contains an update of the "Parole Today" sections to include recent information on parolee characteristics and the latest information on the use of medical parole.

Chapter 12 includes various new reentry programs and an updated section of court cases for legal issues in parole board hearings. Graduated sanctions and options in lieu of arrest were added to Chapter 13 for parole violators to address what is being done as an alternative to filling county jail and prison beds.

Chapter 14 includes updated information on trends continuing in juvenile justice with respect to community-based programs. In the final chapter, there were quite a few updates with regard to civil disenfranchisement and employment-related criminal background checks. Many additions can be found in rights lost for sex offenders with respect to residency restrictions and how the Adam Walsh Act affected national registries. We clarified the distinction between expungement and sealing, not only with revised definitions, but we hope with better examples. We have updated all of our web sites at the end of each chapter. As in the previous edition, the case studies were prepared for in-class discussion or for out-of-class written exercises to initiate critical thinking.

PEDAGOGICAL FEATURES AND LEARNING TOOLS

The most notable teaching pedagogical tool available in this edition allows the student to apply kinesthetic learning and case study methods to examine an arrest report, criminal background check, and collateral interviews to create a client or engage in a mock interview of a client in class in order to complete a presentence investigation interview and report, score a risk/needs classification, and create an individualized supervision case plan for a client. All of these tools are placed in the appropriate chapters, so the student can engage in the writing process as they read.

Chapter Learning Objectives   Here is a bulleted outline of key concepts and learning objectives. Key terms are boldfaced in the text, with their accompanying definitions in the margins, and are defined in the glossary.

Boxed Features   Some of the chapters have boxed material. One box theme is titled: "Technology in Corrections" and illustrates how advancements in equipment and knowledge about data have impacted aspects of corrections programs. Another theme is "Corrections Up Close." This theme investigates a particular topic in more detail as it pertains to the chapter material.

Chapter Review   Each chapter is followed by a summary and discussion questions that will encourage students to think critically about the materials presented in the chapter. The discussion questions could also serve as written exercises in many cases or as topics for essays or research papers. Each chapter has updated Internet sites for more information on topics found within that chapter. The book contains numerous case studies for in-class discussion or written assignments. Photographs, tables, and figures will help students to visualize the concepts under discussion.

Ancillaries

FOR THE INSTRUCTOR

eBank Instructor's Resource Manual with Test Bank. The electronic manual, prepared by Elmer Polk of the University of Texas at Dallas, includes learning objectives, key terms, a detailed chapter outline, a chapter summary, discussion topics, student activities and a test bank. Each chapter's test bank contains questions in multiple-choice, true false, fill-in-the-blank, and essay formats, with a full answer key. The test bank is coded to the learning objectives that appear in the main text, and includes the page numbers in the main text where the answers can be found. Finally, each question in the test bank has been carefully reviewed by experienced criminal justice instructors for quality, accuracy, and content coverage. The manual is available for download on the password-protected website and can also be obtained by e-mailing your local Cengage Learning representative.

eBank PowerPoint Slides   These handy Microsoft PowerPoint slides, which outline the chapters of the main text in a classroom-ready presentation, will help you in making your lectures engaging and in reaching your visually oriented students. The presentations are available for download on the password-protected website and can also be obtained by e-mailing your local Cengage Learning representative.

Criminal Justice Media Library   This engaging resource provides students with more than 300 ways to investigate current topics, career choices, and critical concepts.

FOR THE STUDENT

CL eBook   CLeBook allows students to access Cengage Learning textbooks in an easy-to-use online format. Highlight, take notes, bookmark, search your text, and, in some titles, link directly into multimedia: CLeBook combines the best aspects of paper books and ebooks in one package.

Course360   Online Learning to the Next Degree. Course360 from Cengage Learning is a complete turnkey solution that teaches course outcomes through student interaction in a highly customizable online learning environment. Course360 blends relevant content with rich media and builds upon your course design, needs, and objectives. With a wide variety of media elements including audio, video, interactives, simulations and more, Course360 is the way today's students learn.

Careers in Criminal Justice Website   Available bundled with this text at no additional charge. Featuring plenty of self-exploration and profiling activities, the interactive Careers in Criminal Justice Website helps students investigate and focus on the criminal justice career choices that are right for them. Includes interest assessment, video testimonials from career professionals, resume and interview tips, and links for reference.

Acknowledgments

This book could not have been written without the generous assistance of many colleagues and corrections professionals. We wish to express our appreciation to Kent and Terri Sisson for preparing many of the case studies that follow the chapters. We appreciate the professionals who wrote personal "Field Notes" essays that added more personality to the book: Judge Al Alonso, Eladio Castillo, Ralph Garza, Mark Masterson, Tess Price, and Abel Salinas. Our thanks to Richard Russell for his contribution, "A Day in the Life of a Federal Probation Officer." Other colleagues who so kindly provided us with information and referrals to use in our text include William Barton, Indiana University; Dan Beto, now retired from the Correctional Management Institute of Texas; and Trey Williams, University of Houston-Downtown.

Special thanks to Carolyn Henderson-Meier of Wadsworth Cengage for her support throughout the process. Project development editor Tricia Louvar, and our copy editor Carol Alexander significantly improved our book through their keen eyes and attention to every detail.

We express our special appreciation to our colleagues who reviewed drafts of earlier editions of the book. Their insightful comments and suggestions proved invaluable. In particular, we appreciate the work of Joseph Apiahene, University of Texas-Pan American; Lincoln Chandler, Florida Memorial College; Dana DeWitt, Chadron State University; Teresa Hall, Sandhills Community College; Charles Hinman, Kirtland Community College; G. G. Hunt, Wharton County Junior College; David Jaso, Austin Community College; J. H. Koonce, Edgecombe Community College; Sheri Short, Navarro College; David Stumpf, Central Lakes College; and Ron Walker, Trinity Valley Community College. For the seventh edition we would like to thank Rodney Henningsen, Sam Houston State University; Patrice Morris, Rutgers University-Newark; Gaylene Armstrong, Sam Houston State University; Denny Langston, Central Missouri State University; and Thomas Allen, University of South Dakota. For the eighth edition, we acknowledge Megan Cole, Brown College, 1st Lt. Gary F. Cornelius, George Mason University, Cathryn Lavery, Iona College, Jeffrey O'Donnell, Point Park University, and George Alexander, Buffalo State University.

Finally, we would like to personally thank the following individuals for their pictorial contributions to the text: Ray Alarid, Bob Goodson, Mike "Twinkie" Hicks, Alex Holsinger, Kristi Holsinger, LaShaun Lars, Wayne Lucas, Eric Myers, Dolly Owen, Donnie Turner, "Chopper" Dave Vargo, Jennifer "Pinky" Vargo, and Jim Wuster. This text is more interesting because of you.

Leanne Fiftal Alarid
Rolando V. del Carmen

PART I

Principles of Community Corrections, Diversion, and Sentencing

The idea behind community corrections programs is that most offenders can be effectively held accountable for their crimes at the same time that they fulfill legitimate living standards in the community. Most offenders do not pose an imminent danger to themselves or to others and can therefore remain in the community to maintain relationships. Punishing offenders in the community confers several benefits.

First, the offender remains in the community where he or she has responsibilities. With legitimate employment, offenders can continue supporting themselves and their family of origin, and they will pay taxes. Second, offenders in the community are more likely than prison-bound offenders to compensate their victim through restitution or to pay back the community through community service. Finally, community corrections programs do not expose offenders to the subculture of violence that exists in many jails and prisons.

Chapter 1 introduces the basic goals and programs of community corrections and explains why the study of community corrections is important, while introducing the student to the concept of evidence-based practices. Chapter 2 examines the bail decision as the first major decision point and includes information on diversionary programs and specialty courts such as drug and mental health courts. Chapter 3 focuses on sentencing as the second major decision point, and it explains the presentence investigation report to aid judges.

An Overview of Community Corrections: Goals and Evidence-Based Practices

CHAPTER LEARNING OBJECTIVES

- Describe how correctional agencies and programs carry out the conditions or sentence imposed by the court judge.
- Define corrections and its purpose.

- Examine sentencing policies and how they have contributed to correctional growth in institutional and community-based corrections.
- Identify various types of community corrections programs.

This supervised work crew from a community center spends their day clearing ditches as a part of their community service.

CHAPTER OUTLINE

The Correctional Dilemma
Indeterminate Sentencing
Origins of Modern Determinate Sentencing

The Paradox
Public Perceptions of Community Corrections
Correctional Budgets

The Role of Corrections at Three Major Decision Points
Pretrial and the Bail Decision
Sentencing Decision
Reentry Decision

How Community Corrections Fits Correctional Goals
Protection of the Public
Rehabilitation
Restorative or Community Justice
Deterrence through Shaming

Evidence-Based Practices in Community Corrections
Evaluating Effectiveness
Outcome Measures in Evaluation

Summary

KEY TERMS

community corrections
probation
indeterminate sentencing
presumptive sentence
determinate sentencing
bail

pretrial supervision
intermediate sanctions
prisoner reentry
prerelease program
parole
institutional corrections

restorative justice
evidence-based practices
net widening
recidivism

The Correctional Dilemma

In the United States approximately 7 million people, equivalent to about 3 percent of the total adult population, are currently under some form of correctional supervision. Our nation's crime control policies over the last three decades have resulted in a steady increase of convicted misdemeanants and felons in the correctional system today. Yet, our country's recent economic troubles and military spending have required a reallocation of resources. Corrections departments, among many other government agencies, have found it quite challenging to do more with less financial support.

This text focuses exclusively on community-based corrections. **Community corrections** are any sanctions in which offenders serve all or a portion of their entire sentence in the community. A community sentence seeks to repair the harm the offender may have caused the victim or the community and to reduce the risk of re-offending in the future. Figure 1.1 shows the wide variety of community-based sanctions available, including residential programs (e.g., halfway houses and therapeutic communities), economic sanctions (e.g., restitution, fines, and forfeitures), and nonresidential or outpatient options (e.g., probation, parole, and electronic monitoring).

The most common form of community supervision is **probation.** Probation is defined as the release of a convicted offender under conditions imposed by the court for a specified period during which the court retains authority to modify the conditions or to resentence the offender if he or she violates the conditions. Probation forms the base of the community supervision, and most of the other sanctions introduced in Figure 1.1 are programs or conditions of probation.

Community Corrections
A nonincarcerative sanction in which offenders serve all or a portion of their sentence in the community.

Probation
The community supervision of a convicted offender in lieu of incarceration under conditions imposed by the court for a specified period during which the court retains authority to modify the conditions or to resentence the offender if he or she violates the conditions.

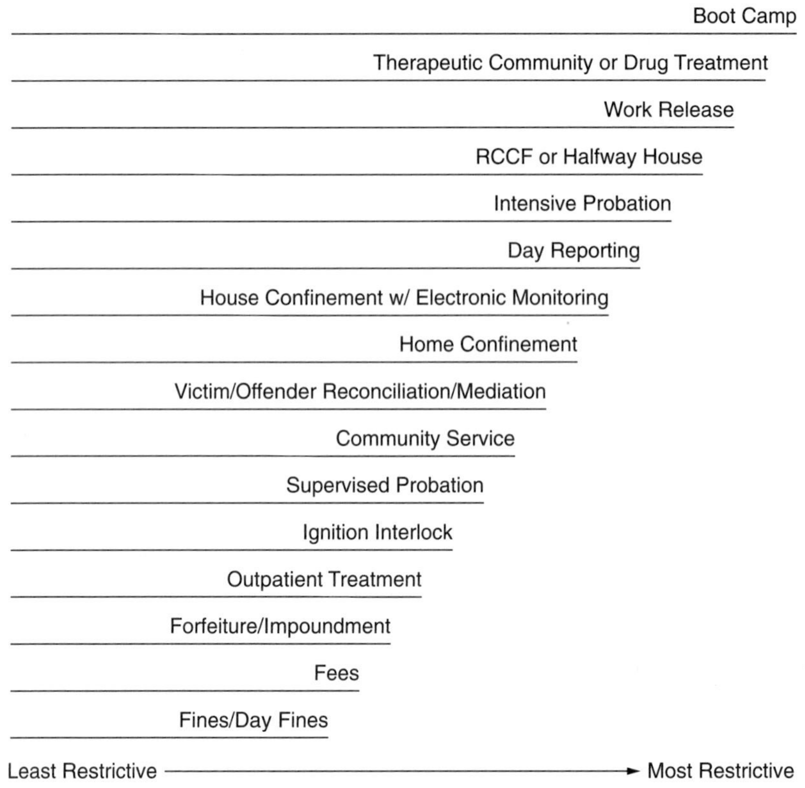

FIGURE 1.1   Community Corrections by Restrictiveness.

Adapted From: Center for Community Corrections (1997). *A Call for Punishments that Make Sense,* p. 37 Washington, DC: Bureau of Justice Assistance. Retrieved From: www. communitycorrectionsworks.org/ steve/nccc/punishments.pdf

Boot Camp

Therapeutic Community or Drug Treatment

Work Release

RCCF or Halfway House

Intensive Probation

Day Reporting

House Confinement w/ Electronic Monitoring

Home Confinement

Victim/Offender Reconciliation/Mediation

Community Service

Supervised Probation

Ignition Interlock

Outpatient Treatment

Forfeiture/Impoundment

Fees

Fines/Day Fines

Least Restrictive ──────────────────────────────▶ Most Restrictive

Due to the combination of many of these sanctions, it is helpful to understand community corrections as having many alternatives from which sanctions can be applied to different offenders to achieve individualized results. The American Probation and Parole Association (APPA) was created to bridge these alternatives. The APPA is an international policy and educational organization for practitioners who work with adults and juveniles in the field of community corrections. The APPA serves to educate and train members and develop standards for the discipline. The APPA's policy statement explains the purpose of probation in Box 1.1. This policy statement is broadly applicable to the function of all programs and agencies in community corrections.

Table 1.1 shows the latest government statistics regarding the number of people currently on some form of correctional supervision. As of December 31, 2006 there were 4.2 million offenders on probation, and nearly 800,000 on parole, which is considerably more than the 2.3 million offenders incarcerated in jail and prison. Over the last 7 years, there was an average increase of 2.4 percent of prisoners and 1.7 percent of those on community supervision *each year* in the corrections system (Bonczar 2008; Glaze and Bonczar 2008). The number of female offenders has grown as well, although women have always been underrepresented in the criminal justice system in comparison to their numbers in the general population. Sources say that in the last 15 years, the number of women on probation and parole has doubled. While this sounds like a lot, women still comprise only 12 percent of all parolees and 23 percent of probationers today. Most women are eligible for a community corrections sentence, because they tend to have shorter criminal records and commit less violent crimes than do men.

BOX 1.1   COMMUNITY CORRECTIONS UP CLOSE

What Is the Purpose of Probation?

The purpose of probation is to assist in reducing the incidence and impact of crime by probationers in the community. The core services of probation are to provide presentence investigation and reports to the court, to help develop appropriate court dispositions for adult offenders and juvenile delinquents, and to supervise those people placed on probation. Probation departments in fulfilling their purpose may also provide a broad range of services including, but not limited to, crime and delinquency prevention, victim restitution programs, and intern/volunteer programs.

POSITION

The mission of probation is to protect the public interest and safety by reducing the incidence and impact of crime by probationers. This role is accomplished by:

- assisting the courts in decision making through the probation report and in the enforcement of court orders;
- providing services and programs that afford opportunities for offenders to become more law-abiding;
- providing and cooperating in programs and activities for the prevention of crime and delinquency; and
- furthering the administration of fair and individualized justice.

Probation is premised upon the following beliefs:

- *Society has a right to be protected from persons who cause its members harm, regardless of the reasons for such harm.* It is the right of every citizen to be free from fear of harm to person and property. Belief in the necessity of law to an orderly society demands commitment to support it. Probation accepts this responsibility and views itself as an instrument for both control and treatment appropriate to some, but not all, offenders. The wise use of authority derived from law adds strength and stability to its efforts.
- *Offenders have rights deserving of protection.* Freedom and democracy require fair and individualized due process of law in adjudicating and sentencing the offender.
- *Victims of crime have rights deserving of protection.* In its humanitarian tradition, probation recognizes that prosecution of the offender is but a part of the responsibility of the criminal justice system. The victim of criminal activity may suffer loss of property,

emotional problems, or physical disability. Probation thus commits itself to advocacy for the needs and interests of crime victims.

- *Human beings are capable of change.* Belief in the individual's capability for behavioral change leads probation practitioners to a commitment to the reintegration of the offender into the community. The possibility for constructive change of behavior is based on the recognition and acceptance of the principle of individual responsibility. Much of probation practice focuses on identifying and making available those services and programs that will best afford offenders an opportunity to become responsible, law-abiding citizens.
- *Not all offenders have the same capacity or willingness to benefit from measures designed to produce law-abiding citizens.* Probation practitioners recognize the variations among individuals. The present offense, the degree of risk to the community, and the potential for change can be assessed only in the context of the offender's individual history and experience.
- *Intervention in an offender's life should be the minimal amount needed to protect society and promote law-abiding behavior.* Probation subscribes to the principle of intervening in an offender's life only to the extent necessary. Where further intervention appears unwarranted, criminal justice system involvement should be terminated. Where needed intervention can best be provided by an agency outside the system, the offender should be diverted from the system to that agency.
- *Punishment.* Probation philosophy does not accept the concept of retributive punishment. Punishment as a corrective measure is supported and used in those instances in which it is felt that aversive measures may positively alter the offender's behavior when other measures may not. Even corrective punishment, however, should be used cautiously and judiciously in view of its highly unpredictable impact. It can be recognized that a conditional sentence in the community is, in and of itself, a punishment. It is less harsh and drastic than a prison term but more controlling and punitive than release without supervision.

(Continues)

BOX 1.1   COMMUNITY CORRECTIONS UP CLOSE (*Continued*)

What Is the Purpose of Probation?

- *Incarceration may be destructive and should be imposed only when necessary.* Probation practitioners acknowledge society's right to protect itself and support the incarceration of offenders whose behavior constitutes a danger to the public through rejection of social or court mandates. Incarceration can also be an appropriate element of a probation program to emphasize the consequences of criminal behavior and thus effect constructive behavioral change. However, institutions should be humane and required to adhere to the highest standards.
- *Where public safety is not compromised, society and most offenders are best served through community correctional*

programs. Most offenders should be provided services within the community in which they are expected to demonstrate acceptable behavior. Community correctional programs generally are cost-effective, and they allow offenders to remain with their families while paying taxes and, where applicable, restitution to victims.

Source: American Probation and Parole Association. 1987. "APPA Position Statement: Probation." Accessed: http://www.appa-net.org/about%20appa/probatio.htm. Reprinted with permission.

TABLE 1.1   Adults on Probation, on Parole, in Jail, and in Prison: 1980–2007

| Year | Total Estimate in Millions | COMMUNITY SUPERVISION | | INCARCERATION | |
		Probation	Parole	County Jail	State Prison
1980	1.84	1,118,097	220,438	182,288	319,598
1981	2.01	1,225,934	225,539	195,085	360,029
1982	2.19	1,357,264	224,604	207,853	402,914
1983	2.48	1,582,947	246,440	221,815	423,898
1984	2.69	1,740,948	266,992	233,018	448,264
1985	3.01	1,968,712	300,203	254,986	487,593
1986	3.24	2,114,621	325,638	272,735	526,436
1987	3.46	2,247,158	355,505	294,092	562,814
1988	3.74	2,356,483	407,977	341,893	607,766
1989	4.06	2,522,125	456,803	393,303	683,367
1990	4.35	2,670,234	531,407	403,019	743,382
1991	4.54	2,728,472	590,442	424,129	792,535
1992	4.76	2,811,611	658,601	441,781	850,566
1993	4.94	2,903,061	676,100	455,500	909,381
1994	5.14	2,981,022	690,371	479,800	990,147
1995	5.34	3,077,861	679,421	507,044	1,078,542
1996	5.49	3,164,996	679,733	518,492	1,127,528
1997	5.73	3,296,513	694,787	567,079	1,176,564
1998	6.13	3,670,441	696,385	592,462	1,224,469
1999	6.34	3,779,922	714,457	605,943	1,287,172
2000	6.44	3,826,209	723,898	621,149	1,316,333
2001	6.58	3,931,731	732,333	631,240	1,330,007
2002	6.76	4,024,067	750,934	665,475	1,367,547
2003	6.92	4,144,782	745,125	691,301	1,392,796

(Continues)

TABLE 1.1   Adults on Probation, on Parole, in Jail, and in Prison: 1980–2007 (Continued)

		COMMUNITY SUPERVISION		INCARCERATION	
Year	Total Estimate in Millions	Probation	Parole	County Jail	State Prison
2004	7.00	4,151,125	765,355	713,990	1,421,911
2005	7.05	4,189,456	772,967	747,529	1,496,013
2006	7.18	4,237,023	798,202	766,010	1,570,115
2007	7.33	4,215,361	799,058	780,581	1,595,034

Notes: Counts for probation, prison, and parole populations are for December 31 of each year; jail population counts are for June 30 of each year. Counts of adults held in facilities for 1993–1996 were estimated and rounded to the nearest 100. Totals in 1998 through 2002 exclude probationers held in jail or prison. Data for jail and prison are for inmates under custody under public and private facilities. These data have been revised based on the most recently reported counts and may differ from previous editions of SOURCEBOOK.

Sources: U.S. Department of Justice, Bureau of Justice Statistics. *Correctional Populations in the United States* 1994, (Washington, DC: U.S. Department of Justice). Lauren E. Glaze and Seri Palla. 2005. *Probation and Parole in the United States, 2004.* (Washington, DC: U.S. Department of Justice); Lauren E. Glaze and Thomas P. Bonczar. 2008. *Probation and Parole in the United States, 2007.* (Washington, DC: U.S. Department of Justice).

Although the increase is showing signs of slowing down, the rise of convicted offenders is directly related to a number of factors, including: changes in sentencing laws, an increase of probation and parole violators returning to prison, a decreased rate of release on discretionary parole, and differential police responses to drug offenses (Beck 2000).

INDETERMINATE SENTENCING

From the 1930s to the mid-1970s, **indeterminate sentencing** was the primary sentencing philosophy in the United States. Under the indeterminate sentencing model, judges decided who went to prison, and parole boards decided when offenders were rehabilitated and ready for release on parole (Forst 1995). The release date was unknown by the offender, and subject to the decision of the parole board, who by majority decision decided if the offender was making sufficient progress toward rehabilitation and was ready to rejoin the larger society. While incarcerated, offenders were able to enroll in a variety of programs aimed at self-improvement and skill building to demonstrate readiness for the parole board.

Parole was also used as a backdoor strategy for controlling the prison population. When prisons became too crowded, the parole rate increased to make room for incoming prisoners. Under indeterminate sentencing, offenders who did not go to prison were, for the most part, placed on probation. Few intermediate sentencing options existed other than prison or probation, and those that did, such as halfway houses and intensive probation, were used infrequently (Tonry 1997).

Support for indeterminate sentencing declined in the 1970s as people questioned whether prison rehabilitation worked and whether parole boards could accurately determine when offenders were ready for release. This lack of confidence in correctional programming peaked in 1974 with Robert Martinson's publication concluding that "with few and isolated exceptions, the rehabilitative efforts that have been reported so far had no appreciable effect on recidivism" (p. 25). Martinson's findings were poorly stated, criticisms were lodged against the methodology used,

Indeterminate Sentencing
A sentencing philosophy that encourages rehabilitation and incorporates a broad sentencing range where discretionary release is determined by a parole board based on the offender's remorse, insight into his or her mistakes, involvement in rehabilitation, and readiness to return to society.

and he later recanted those statements. In the complete report published the next year, Douglas Lipton, Robert Martinson, and Judith Wilks (1975) concluded:

> While some treatment programs have had modest successes, it still must be concluded that the field of corrections has not as yet found satisfactory ways to reduce recidivism by significant amounts (p. 627).

Both of these publications began a national debate about the efficacy of treatment programs. Ironically, the original intent of Martinson's article was an attempt to decrease the use of *prisons*, not treatment programs, so unbeknownst to his co-authors, Martinson published the solo piece and was ill-prepared for the catastrophe that followed.

Martinson's study was a prelude to one of the most conservative eras in American politics, one in which policy makers in many political jurisdictions were looking for reasons to repudiate the putative liberal policies of previous decades. The study confirmed what a cadre of reactionary policy makers wanted to hear, at a time in which the sentiments within the professional corrections community still ran toward a philosophy of rehabilitation rather than retribution (Locke 1998, p. 257).

In addition to questions about rehabilitation, indeterminate sentences had another problem. Most indeterminate sentences were structured with no maximum ending date. With an unknown or ambiguous release date, some offenders spent many more years behind bars than their crimes warranted, whereas others—who may have convinced the parole board that they were "cured"—were released after only a few years. This issue became a question of fairness.

ORIGINS OF MODERN DETERMINATE SENTENCING

A working group called American Friends Service Committee denounced prisons and called for a repeal on all indeterminate sentencing laws so that offenders convicted of similar crimes served roughly equal terms in prison. The committee's final report was published in 1976 under the title *Doing Justice: The Choice of Punishments* (von Hirsch 1976). The book's main premise was that punishment should be commensurate with the gravity of the last offense or series of offenses. The committee recommended the adoption of a **presumptive sentence** for each crime or category of crimes, with the presumptive sentences graded according to the severity of the crime. The severity of the crime would be graded on two scales: the harm done by the offense and the offender's culpability. The judgment of the degree of culpability would be based partly on the offender's prior record. Having proposed punishment as the main goal of sentencing, the committee then ruled out prison as the punishment for all but the most serious offenses, those in which bodily harm is threatened or done to the victim. The committee proposed alternatives such as periodic imprisonment, increased use of fines, and other lesser sanctions.

At about the same time, another **determinate sentencing** model emerged. David Fogel (1979), author of *". . . We Are the Living Proof . . .": The Justice Model for Corrections,* is considered by many to be the "father of determinate sentencing." As early as 1970, he had actively urged a narrowing of sentencing and parole discretion and had been among the most influential determinate sentencing advocates in drafting legislation in various states. One of the main goals was to disconnect the release date from prison program participation. He advocated abolishing parole boards and establishing "flat-time" sentencing for each class of felonies.

Maine became the first state in 1975 to return to determinate sentencing where the minimum and maximum sentence range is predefined and release is determined by legislative statute (Forst 1995). The sentence length is therefore determined by criminal behavior rather than by how long it takes for the offender to become

Presumptive Sentence
A statutorily determined sentence that offenders will presumably receive if convicted. Offenders convicted in a jurisdiction with presumptive sentences will be assessed this sentence unless mitigating or aggravating circumstances are found to exist.

Determinate Sentencing
A sentencing philosophy that focuses on consistency for the crime committed, specifying by statute or sentencing guidelines an exact amount or narrow range of time to be served in prison or in the community, which mandates the minimum amount of time before the offender is eligible (if at all) for release. Also known as a presumptive, fixed, or mandatory sentence.

rehabilitated behind bars. With less sentencing options for judges, personal and social variables played less of a role in the sentencing process. The slogan "you do the crime, you do the time" became more popular, and funding for prison treatment programs diminished. In determinate sentencing, judges have less discretion, but are able to deviate slightly (higher or lower) from the prescribed sentencing guidelines, but must provide justification for doing so. Parole board decision making has also been limited in many states to only certain types of offenders or abolished altogether in 16 states (Petersilia 2003).

Examples of determinate sentencing policies included mandatory minimums, truth in sentencing, three strikes laws, and sentencing guidelines. All states adopted mandatory minimum sentencing laws requiring certain types of offenders, such as violent or repeat offenders, to serve a certain amount of time before release can be considered. "Truth in sentencing" laws are a type of mandatory minimum requiring that offenders serve at least 85 percent of the original sentence length before becoming eligible for release (Petersilia 2003). Three strikes laws mandate long prison terms for the third felony conviction. Some states require a life sentence for violent third-time felons, while other states might count any felony.

Sentencing guidelines are typically a matrix for the judge based on the offender's prior criminal record and the current conviction. Some guidelines are voluntary, while others are mandatory. The most controversial set of mandatory sentencing guidelines is at the federal level. Proponents contended that the guidelines decreased judicial disparity and potential for discrimination and created accountability for sentencing decisions. Opponents said that the federal guidelines were developed with little thought as to how sentence length would affect burgeoning prison populations, and that they decreased the use of community correctional alternatives. Federal parole was abolished and prisoners are now allowed one year of mandatory release. The federal guidelines have since been revised and allow for judges to consider more mitigating and aggravating circumstances to adjust the sentence.

Most states have retained aspects of both indeterminate and determinate sentencing structures. In comparison to federal judges, state-level judges seem to have more discretion and more alternatives to incarceration.

The Paradox

> We are used to thinking of community safety as contingent upon who is allowed to live in the community. Justice seems separationist because formal justice processes remove offenders from everyday life for accusation and conviction ceremonies, and they often result in penal removal, as well. The idea that communities are made safe by eliminating unsafe residents is equally an ingrained idea in American traditions (Clear and Corbett 1997, p. 2).

Correctional policy is in many ways a paradox, because it shifts according to the tide of public perception and what is important to vocal constituents and public interest groups. Maruna and King (2008, p. 338) note a shift away from expert-driven decisions in penal policy to one based ". . . more explicitly by symbolic and expressive concerns . . . [and] emotionalization of public discourse about crime and law." Measuring broad public perceptions is typically conducted via telephone opinion polls or with social science research surveys. Opinion polls have been criticized for asking crime policy questions in too simplistic a manner to be valid indicators, and some of the larger opinion poll companies are directly tied to mass media. The media has long been criticized for sensationalizing violence and atypical crimes, while downplaying average or common crimes that never result in a prison sentence. The average American citizen as a result is only exposed to a very small percent of the overall crime picture and may be less informed about what should be done in response to crime.

PUBLIC PERCEPTIONS OF COMMUNITY CORRECTIONS

Average public perceptions about crime and punishment are based more on emotional reaction more so than on logic or rational thinking. We rely on survey research trends and generalizations that the public has recently held about community corrections and rehabilitation of offenders. The body of research in this area (Cullen, Fisher, and Applegate 2000; Roberts and Hough 2002) found a number of observations that include:

- The public is interested in both punishment and rehabilitation, as long as strategies lead to safer communities.
- People realize that harsh punishment without treatment is an ineffective strategy.
- While the public is supportive of prison alternatives for nonviolent offenders, there is a low tolerance for failure of people who have been to prison.

Proposed strategies to increase the level of public support for community corrections involve appealing to the public on an emotional level. The thinking here is that if emotions can lead to fear (of crime), which can lead to punitiveness, then emotions can also work to decrease beliefs in harsh sentencing for some offenders. For example, retribution has emotional roots in anger and feelings of injustice. The opposite of retribution is the compassionate side of forgiveness, which is considerably much harder to accomplish, but can be viewed as a process to work toward as individuals and communities heal. Another idea appealing to one's emotional side is the idea of "redeemability"—that is, convincing others that people can change their ways if they are given the tools and the means to do so (Maruna and King 2008, p. 345). But this is only half of the solution.

Experts also suggest that the level of public trust in politics and media sources needs to be raised by informing the public in an open and honest manner, and by presenting a broader view of the issues and not just the atypical cases. Politicians need to acknowledge the limits of public knowledge (e.g., people often think first and only of prison) and attempt to remedy the problem (Roberts and Hough 2002). Public opinion research on sentencing preferences demonstrated higher validity when the public was given diverse sentencing options and adequate information, such as program descriptions and detailed information about an offense or an offender. However, readers are cautioned that exposure to information may have only short-term effects rather than lasting effects, since many beliefs about crime and punishment are based on emotional rather than rational arguments (Maruna and King 2008).

CORRECTIONAL BUDGETS

It is important to continue monitoring public opinion, because of the other side of the correctional paradox: the funding source for corrections is driven almost completely by public tax dollars. Billions of dollars are spent annually to support correctional agencies in the United States. In 2003, for example, a total of $36.1 billion was spent nationwide just on operating adult state and federal *prison* institutions, with a median of $368 million per state (Camp, Camp, and May 2003). This amount did not include budgets for jails, juvenile facilities, and community corrections. In comparison to prisons, probation and parole agencies, whether combined or separate, had an average annual budget of $82.9 million for the entire state. This means that about 18 cents of every correctional dollar is directed to community corrections programs to supervise more than 70 percent of all people under correctional supervision.

Table 1.2 shows annual costs per person for selected forms of correctional supervision in the federal system and a sampling of three different states with moderate living costs. Jail and prison incarceration in these areas ranged between $22,000 and nearly $28,000 per year. Incarceration is significantly more expensive than community supervision, especially considering that the offender shares some of the costs. For example, probation supervision costs between $866 and $3,535 per person per

TABLE 1.2 Annual Costs per Person for Selected Forms of Correctional Supervision[a]

Supervision Type	Federal (FY 06)	Colorado (FY 07)	Ohio (FY 07)	North Carolina (FY 08)
Prison	$24,443	$27,558	$24,641[c]	$27,911
Jail	$22,899	$22,000	$25,082	N/R
Pretrial Services	$2,061	N/R	N/R	N/R
Residential Community Facility (RCCF)	$21,558	$18,662[b]	$22,206	N/R
Probation	$3,535	$1,121	N/R	$866
Intensive Probation	N/A	$3,275	$1,799	$6,099
Parole	N/A	$3,401	N/R	N/R
Intensive Parole	N/A	$8,319	N/R	
Additional Services				
Day Reporting	N/A	N/R	$8,708	N/R
Electronic Monitoring using:				
Radio Frequency	$1,161	N/R	$1,982	$3,077[d]
Global Positioning Systems	N/R	N/R	N/R	$9,432

Notes:

FY= Fiscal year of that particular budget

N/A = Program not available in that area

N/R = Program likely available, but cost not reported

a = These costs are averaged for supervision of general population offenders. Costs for special needs offenders and those in maximum security institutions are significantly higher.

b = The cost of all RCCFs to taxpayers are actually lower. In Colorado, the total cost above includes $12,457 of taxpayer money + $6,205 ($17/day) that offenders are expected to pay. The average collection rate is $14/day.

c = This estimate is for a non-violent first-time offender at a minimum security level prison.

d = This is the reported cost for "electronic house arrest"

Sources: U.S. Probation and Pretrial Services System (2007). "OPPS releases new incarceration and supervision costs." *News and Views*, 32 (12), 3; Division of Probation Services, DOC, and DCJ Office of Community Corrections (2008). Table 1 of annual placement costs in Colorado in FY 2007. Retrieved from: http://www.ccjrc.org/pdf/cccjj_2008_report.pdf; Ohio Department of Rehabilitation and Correction (2007). North Carolina Department of Corrections (2008). "Cost of supervision ending June 30, 2008." Retrieved from: http://www.doc.state.nc.us/dop/cost/

year, but the offender subsidizes these costs with monthly fees ranging between $25 and $40. Parole, electronic monitoring, day reporting, and residential facilities are all partially subsidized by the offender.

Correctional budgets have been hit hard these last few years due to the economic recession in 2009 and continued war in Iraq. Budgets were cut drastically, forcing hiring freezes to avoid layoffs of government employees. We discuss in the next section the three main decision points in the corrections system.

The Role of Corrections at Three Major Decision Points

The criminal justice system is guided by formal written laws, codes, and statutes, and also by informal discretion. Discretion is a form of subjective decision-making that begins when a victim or witness decides whether to report a crime to the police. Some would argue that discretion plays as important, if not more important, a role than formal law. Another decision point early in the process is the arresting decision made by a law enforcement officer. As you can see in Figure 1.2, community corrections plays a pivotal role at three major decision points that follow the arrest: bail, sentencing, and reentry.

PRETRIAL AND THE BAIL DECISION

After a police officer makes an arrest, the suspect is booked in jail, and the prosecutor's office decides whether to charge the suspect with a crime. If the prosecutor chooses not to charge, the suspect is automatically released. If the prosecutor opts to

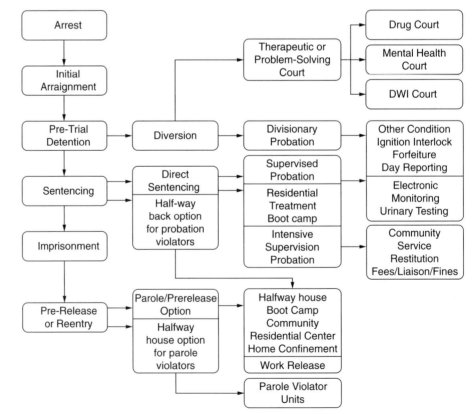

FIGURE 1.2 The Three Main Decision Points: How Cases Are Referred to Community Corrections.

Adapted From: Center for Community Corrections (1997). *A Call for Punishments that Make Sense*, p. 35 Washington, DC: Bureau of Justice Assistance.

charge, the suspect officially becomes a defendant and goes before a judge, magistrate, or other official authorized to inform the defendant of the charges, determine whether the defendant is requesting appointed counsel, and ascertain whether the defendant is eligible for release from jail. Although most defendants are released on their own recognizance with the promise to appear at their next court date, some defendants must secure their next appearance with **bail,** or monetary payment deposited with the court to ensure their return. When the conditions of the bond have been satisfied, the defendant is released on a bond. Many times, particularly in the federal system, the defendant is released on **pretrial supervision,** which is a form of correctional supervision of a defendant who has not yet been convicted. Forms of pretrial supervision may include client reporting, house arrest, and electronic monitoring. Pretrial supervision accounts for the defendant's whereabouts to keep the community safe, it allows the defendant to prepare for upcoming court appearances, it allows the defendant to continue working and supporting dependents, and it keeps bed space in the jail available for another defendant who may not be eligible for release. We discuss bail and pretrial decision points in Chapter 2.

Bail
Monetary payment deposited with the court to ensure the defendant's return for the next court date in exchange for the defendant's release.

Pretrial Supervision
Court-ordered correctional supervision of a defendant who has not yet been convicted whereby the defendant participates in activities such as reporting, house arrest, and electronic monitoring to ensure appearance at the next court date.

SENTENCING DECISION

Community corrections agencies and programs perform the important function of implementing the sentence imposed by a judge. At a basic level, a correction is a social control mechanism for convicted offenders, and it also keeps others law abiding through general deterrence. We recognize the importance of incarcerating offenders who are dangerous to the public or who have committed violent crimes so heinous that incarceration is a deserved punishment. However, the vast majority of people who commit a crime can be punished in ways that do not warrant imprisonment. Judges and prosecutors need a variety of "front-end" punishments from which to choose, and community corrections offer a diversity of sentencing options.

The community-based punishments shown earlier in Figure 1.1 are known as **intermediate sanctions** because they offer graduated levels of supervision. They provide rewards for positive behavior with gradually less supervision when offenders achieve and maintain desired program outcomes. Intermediate sanctions can also impose greater levels of surveillance, supervision, and monitoring than probation alone, but less supervision than that provided in jail or prison. A full range of sentencing options gives judges greater latitude to select punishments that closely fit the circumstances of the crime and the offender (DiMascio 1997). We discuss the sentencing decision in Chapter 3, and then devote seven chapters to the forms community corrections takes, beginning with probation and the various graduated residential, monetary, and nonresidential sanctions.

Intermediate Sanctions
A spectrum of community supervision strategies that vary greatly in terms of their supervision level and treatment capacity, ranging from diversion to short-term duration in a residential community facility.

REENTRY DECISION

Over forty years ago, the President's Commission on Law Enforcement and Administration of Justice (1967) introduced the term *reintegration*. Its report stated that

> institutions tend to isolate offenders from society, both physically and psychologically, cutting them off from schools, jobs, families, and other supportive influences and increasing the probability that the label of criminal will be indelibly impressed upon them. The goal of reintegration is likely to be furthered much more readily by working with offenders in the community than by incarceration. (p. 165)

In this report, the commission called on the community to provide needed employment and educational opportunities, while community correctional workers act as advocates to link offenders to programs and monitor their progress. This statement still holds true today, though instead of "reintegration" we use the term "reentry." Reentry requires the offender to participate in programs that develop legitimate accomplishments and opportunities as they adapt to a community setting, but there seems to be less emphasis on the role of the community in assisting in the offender's return. (We would argue that quite the opposite has happened with some offenders—an issue we will discuss in greater detail in Chapter 15.)

Approximately 95 to 97 percent of prisoners incarcerated today will one day leave prison and rejoin the larger society. A community correction serves an important purpose by assisting prisoners in community reentry after they have spent time in prison. **Prisoner reentry** is any activity or program "conducted to prepare ex-convicts to return safely to the community and to live as law abiding citizens" (Petersilia 2003, p. 3). Prisoner reentry applies to prisoners who are released automatically based on mandatory statutes as well as prisoners released early at the parole board's discretion.

Prisoner Reentry
Any activity or program conducted to prepare ex-convicts to return safely to the community and to live as law-abiding citizens.

Prerelease Program   A **prerelease program** is a minimum-security institutional setting for imprisoned offenders who have already done some time in prison and are nearing release. Prerelease offenders are chosen by corrections officials and transferred to a different type of residential program that the offenders can complete in a shorter duration than if they served their full prison sentence. Prerelease programs are considered to be more treatment oriented than prison. Examples of these programs are halfway houses, boot camps, and therapeutic communities that are located inside a prison, separate from the general prisoner population. The purpose of back-end programs is to save money and prison space while also providing program participants with a specialized treatment regimen. Examples of prerelease programs are fully discussed in Chapters 8 and 9.

Prerelease Program
A minimum-security community-based or institutional setting for offenders who have spent time in prison and are nearing release. The focus of these programs includes transitioning, securing a job, and reestablishing family connections.

Parole   **Parole** is the discretionary release of an offender before the expiration of his or her sentence under conditions established by the paroling authority. Parole is in many ways similar to probation. Both involve supervised release in the community and the possibility of revocation should the parolee or probationer violates the conditions of release. Although some technical differences do exist, the primary difference is that probation is supervision in the community instead of incarceration, and parole is supervised release after a portion of the prison sentence has been served. (See Chapters 11 through 13 for more coverage of parole.)

Parole
Early privileged release of a convicted offender from a penal or correctional institution, under the continual custody of the state, to serve the remainder of his or her sentence in the community under supervision.

How Community Corrections Fits Correctional Goals

The goals of community corrections complement the overall goals of **institutional corrections**, which is an incarcerative sanction where offenders serve their sentence away from the community in a jail or prison institution. Community corrections attempts to punish offenders while at the same time protecting the public, addressing victims' needs, and preventing future criminal behavior through one or more of the following objectives: rehabilitation, community reentry, restorative justice, and shaming.

Institutional Corrections
An incarcerative sanction in which offenders serve their sentence away from the community in a jail or prison institution.

PROTECTION OF THE PUBLIC

Most offenders have shown by their offenses that they cannot easily conform to the norms of society. One of the goals of community-based corrections, therefore, is to help offenders conform to behavioral expectations and to monitor their progress toward that goal. Perhaps the major criticism of traditional probation and parole has been their perceived failure to protect the public from further criminal acts by individuals under supervision in the community. For probation or any other community-based program to be effective and accepted by policy makers and the public, it must first demonstrate that the offenders under supervision are adequately monitored and that the public has nothing to fear from their actions.

Control may be accomplished in a variety of ways. First, as is discussed in Chapter 5, offenders should be assessed to determine the degree of risk posed by their participation in community programs. Second, those who supervise offenders in community-based programs must accept responsibility to protect the public by monitoring compliance with court orders and conditions of release. Finally, violations of supervised conditions must be taken seriously. If the programs are to become credible sanctions, courts and paroling authorities must be willing to revoke probation or parole for those who cannot or will not comply with the conditions of release. (The procedures and reasons for violating probation and parole are covered in Chapters 7 and 13.)

REHABILITATION

A second goal of community corrections programs is to correct some of the inadequacies of offenders that may be linked to their criminal behavior and their continued involvement in the criminal justice system. Some of these problems include, but are not limited to, drug or alcohol addiction, lack of emotional control, inadequate education or vocational training, lack of parenting skills, and mental illness or developmental disability.

Correctional treatment or "programming" is the means by which offenders can receive assistance for their problems to reduce further criminal behavior. The basis of effective rehabilitation is that the offender has to have the genuine desire to change and has to want to complete the mental, emotional, and sometimes spiritual work to promote this transformation. This is an important point, because some offenders refuse to adequately respond to treatment. Offenders who pose an immediate and serious danger to society or to themselves may be better served in a more secure program.

Another point is that oftentimes offenders receive more treatment outside of prison than they do in prison. This results in part because programs in prison have been trimmed as correctional budgets have tightened. Also, taxpayers bear less of the cost for offender treatment in the community because employed offenders usually pay for either a portion or all of their treatment. DiMascio (1997) wrote that community-based sanctions provide a means for offenders who are not dangerous to repay their victim and their communities. Intermediate sanctions also promote rehabilitation—which most citizens want, but most prisons are no longer able to provide—and the reintegration of the offender into the community. And, once the programs are in place, they do this at a comparatively low cost (p. 41).

Most offenders can reduce their likelihood of future criminal behavior by changing other behaviors, such as abstaining from drugs or alcohol or controlling their emotions. Proponents of rehabilitation believe that for certain types of offenders, if the issues that are related to recidivism are addressed, the likelihood of future criminal behavior may be reduced between 10 and 60 percent. The Corrections Program Assessment Inventory (CPAI), designed by Andrews and Gendreau (Gendreau 1998), indicates that currently only 10 to 20 percent of all correctional rehabilitation programs are of "high quality." A high-quality treatment program contains elements indicating that an effective correctional service is being provided. Offenders are all different, and different treatment approaches must be used to address unique problems. Some advances have been made, and more is now known about what works (and what does not) with different types of offenders. The key is to replace ineffective programs with those that work and to fill the treatment programs with appropriate offenders who will respond to the type of treatment offered (Palmer 1992).

RESTORATIVE OR COMMUNITY JUSTICE

Restorative Justice
Various sentencing philosophies and practices that emphasize the offender taking responsibility to repair the harm done to the victim and to the surrounding community. Includes forms of victim offender mediation, reparation panels, circle sentencing, and monetary sanctions.

A different philosophy of justice has emerged in recent years known as **restorative justice** or community justice. Restorative justice is centered on the victim throughout the whole process and emphasizes offender responsibility to repair the injustice that offenders have caused their victims (Karp 1998; Van Ness and Strong 1997; Wright 1996).

When a crime is committed, the offender harms both the individual victim and the community at large. Through a variety of techniques such as community boards, mediation, and face-to-face meetings with the individual victim, restorative justice attempts to strengthen community life by drawing on the strengths of the offenders and the victim instead of focusing on their deficits (Umbreit 1999). Local volunteers and the faith community agree to mentor or assist in the supervision of the offender's reparation. The offender must repair the damage by remaining in the community and performing community service, providing victim restitution, and participating in victim impact panels and other educational programs.

Restorative justice is most effective for nonviolent crimes, particularly those committed by juveniles or first-time adult felony offenders, because the victim is compensated for property losses. What many victims may not realize is that incarcerating offenders for property crime will provide a loss of temporary freedom, but the victim will rarely, if ever, be compensated. When given a choice between compensation and incarceration, 75 percent of respondents to a study conducted in Minnesota indicated that they would rather be compensated for a property crime than demand the offender be incarcerated (Umbreit 1999). Thus, community-based corrections programs are necessary and important to guide the restorative justice process. At this time, however, restorative justice is less likely to be endorsed for violent crimes. (Reparations based on the restorative justice model are discussed in Chapter 10.)

DETERRENCE THROUGH SHAMING

Another way that is thought to deter offenders is by using shaming penalties, or scarlet-letter sanctions, to shame offenders publicly. The idea behind shaming is to integrate a punishment that is consistent with affecting an offender's dignity. Examples of shaming sentences include forcing offenders to issue public apologies, obligating offenders to place a bumper sticker on their car or a sign on their front yard acknowledging their crime, or forcing a slumlord to live in one of his rat-infested apartments (Reske 1996). According to Kelly (1999), for shaming to be effective, five conditions must be present:

1. The offender must belong to an identifiable group, like a religious or an ethnic community.
2. The form of the shaming penalty must be sufficient to compromise the offender's social standing in this group.
3. The punishment must be communicated to the offender's community, and the community must in fact withdraw or shun him.
4. The offender must actually fear being shunned.
5. There must be some method for regaining social status by bringing the offender back into her community, unless the offense is so grave that the offender must be permanently shunned (pp. 806–807).

Although used only rarely by a small number of judges, shaming is quite controversial because commentators question whether it violates the Eighth Amendment of the Constitution. In an analysis of the constitutionality of scarlet-letter sanctions, one researcher recommended that the duration be short and that it not endanger the offender's safety in any way. Kelly (1999) suggested that we need "to create a more objective test that asks whether a reasonable person would consider the particular scarlet-letter probation condition severely humiliating and shameful" (p. 860). Currently, very little empirical evidence exists on the effectiveness of shaming punishments (Reske 1996).

In sum, community corrections is important because the sanctions can provide many options for individuals who have committed a crime but do not pose a serious threat to community safety. Community-based corrections seeks to sanction offenders through punishment while also attempting to improve individual life circumstances. Decreasing risk, increasing rehabilitation, and restorative justice are important components in changing offenders' attitudes and behaviors, leading to the prevention of future criminal behavior. Community corrections also serves to ease institutional crowding in jails and prisons by drawing from the population of convicted offenders those who are predicted to be at less risk to the outside community.

Evidence-Based Practices in Community Corrections

Part of the challenge therein lies in public recognition of the importance of community corrections, as this approach serves to increase public safety and multiplies methods of choice for those who break the law. One of the ways to accomplish such an image change is through evidence-based practices.

Evidence-based practices (EBP) involves using current best practices or interventions for which there is consistent and solid scientific evidence of success. Assessment must show that such practices work to meet the intended outcomes and are open to periodic measurement, evaluation, and dissemination of practices and interventions. EBP is used in a number of fields, including medicine, education, social work, mental health, and criminal justice. Within the criminal justice system, EBP is used in police departments, courts, and correctional departments.

EBP is not based on intuition, speculation, anecdotal evidence, or tradition (e.g., "that's the way we've always done it around here"). Rather, EBP is grounded in empirical data and research in studying what works. The idea behind EBP in corrections is that agencies should use only the most successful programs. The best programs are those that are effective in changing offender behavior—whether that

Evidence-Based Practices
"Integrating into everyday practice the correctional programs and techniques that have been shown to be the most effective with offenders using evaluation results from systematically evaluated research studies."

behavior is reducing re-arrest, reducing technical violations, increasing the number of drug-free days, or the number of days offender is working or employed while on supervision. Each goal must be measured empirically—meaning accurate data needs to be recorded electronically for later evaluation.

EVALUATING EFFECTIVENESS

For citizens to view community corrections as the preferred punishment option, agency leaders need to be open about research and program evaluations. To measure both the process of going through a program and the impact a program had after its completion, it is necessary to conduct and report empirical research in a way that makes sense to the average citizen (MacKenzie 2000).

Regarding methodology, it is important to determine the rigor and sophistication of the research to know what does and does not work. If the treatment does work, the research must be able to identify for which type of offenders and under what conditions the treatment works the best. Although more is now known about what works, continuing to evaluate community-based programs and other offender treatment efforts is important (Latessa and Holsinger 1998).

When evaluating the effectiveness of a program, it would be ideal to compare offenders who are randomly selected to receive the "treatment" (for example, the community corrections program) with matched "control" groups (those on regular probation, in prison, or both). Then the groups can be compared on a number of outcome measures. This ideal situation is hard to come by in reality because sentencing guidelines prevent it, and many judges cannot be persuaded to randomly assign offenders to programs.

Furthermore, many offenders are sentenced to multiple types of programs. Thus, it is difficult to isolate one treatment effect from another and to evaluate which program had the intended effect. It is also difficult to assess which of the program elements were responsible for positive or negative effects.

A final difficulty with evaluating the effectiveness of intermediate sanctions, in particular, is determining whether the sanction has participants that were diverted from probation (a front-end strategy) or prison (a back-end strategy). In other words, suppose that the only two sentencing choices were probation or prison (control group). The intermediate sanction (the program to be measured) that targets criminals who would have gone to prison anyway, but are being given one last chance, is taking more serious offenders than if the intermediate sanction recruited offenders who were not prison bound. Intermediate sanctions would be an increased penalty for offenders who would have been sentenced to probation had that intermediate sanction not existed. This is called **net widening,** or "widening the net," and it usually results in a cost increase instead of a cost savings. We revisit the net widening issue throughout the book when we apply this term to diversion, boot camps, and intensive supervision probation.

Net Widening
Using stiffer punishment or excessive control for offenders who would have ordinarily been sentenced to a lesser sanction.

OUTCOME MEASURES IN EVALUATION

The most commonly used measure of program or treatment effectiveness is the rate of **recidivism.** Recidivism is defined as the repetition of or return to criminal behavior, measured in one of three ways: re-arrest, reconviction, or re-incarceration. Some studies separate out return to criminal behavior from technical violations committed while on community supervision. Other studies lump violations together

Recidivism
The repetition of or return to criminal behavior, variously defined in one of three ways: rearrest, reconviction, or reincarceration.

as a single category. The way recidivism is defined is determined by agency access and methods of data collection. Determining success or failure is difficult, because researchers define recidivism in a variety of ways; hence, there are no universally accepted means by which to measure it.

Recidivism as the primary (or sometimes the only) outcome measure has caused concern among criminal justice researchers. Reasons for not including other outcome measures are that programs keep poor records of other measures or that available measures are buried within an officer's handwritten "chrono" notes deep within offender files. As more programs go paperless, data becomes easier to collect and measure.

Other variables of importance will of course depend on the type of program being evaluated. Variables that can be measured during supervision include: the number of days employed; the amount of restitution collected compared to the amount ordered; the percent of fines and/or fees collected; the number of community service hours performed, the number of clients enrolled in school; the number of drug-free days; the types of treatment programs completed, and the number of times client attended each treatment program. Type of termination is critical as to whether the client completed supervision successfully or unsuccessfully. The number and types of technical violations and/or new arrests would be vital, particularly for unsuccessful clients. Finally, effectiveness could also be measured based on the impact that community corrections programs have in reducing the institutional crowding problem or on the total cost savings they incur.

Community corrections programs have been encouraged to develop evidence-based practices that incorporate sound diagnostic and classification testing of risks and needs, as well as cognitive-behavioral treatment paired with community supervision techniques, all of which will be discussed later in the text.

SUMMARY

- Community corrections can provide many options for individuals who have committed a crime, but do not pose a serious threat to community safety.

- Community-based corrections seeks to sanction offenders through punishment, while also attempting to improve individual life circumstances. Reintegration, rehabilitation, and restorative justice are important components in changing offenders' attitudes and behaviors, leading to the prevention of future criminal behavior.

- Community corrections also serves to ease institutional crowding in jails and prisons by drawing from the population of convicted offenders those who are predicted to be at less risk to the outside community.

- Providing a range of community-based sanctions allows the rewarding of positive behavior by increasing freedom or the sanctioning of negative behavior by increasing the sanction.

- The public demands correctional programs that satisfy both punishment and public safety objectives. Evidence-based practices is a step in the direction to further professionalize and transform the image of community-based corrections to the method of choice for lasting offender change.

- The effectiveness of community supervision programs depends on the following factors: how recidivism is defined and how long after supervision it is measured; how other outcomes variables are measured during supervision; whether there is a comparison group; how the groups are selected; and if net widening occurred.

DISCUSSION QUESTIONS

1. Has the purpose of corrections changed again recently?

2. What recent factors have contributed to correctional growth?

3. How does community corrections fit the general correctional goals as you perceive them?

4. What is the value in public opinion poll research compared to social science research?

5. What does a "continuum of sanctions" mean in the sentencing process? If you were a judge, how would you apply this continuum?

6. Will evidence-based practices be just another passing fad?

7. To measure effectiveness of community corrections, are there any other outcome measures that could be used?

WEB SITES

National Center on Institutions and Alternatives
www.ncianet.org

Community-Based Corrections
www.co.clark.wa.us/corrections/index.html

U.S. Department of Justice, Bureau of Justice Corrections Statistics
www.ojp.usdoj.gov/bjs/correct.htm

The Official Home of Corrections
www.corrections.com

Fortune Society
www.fortunesociety.org

Doble Research Company
http://www.dobleresearch.com

The Pew Center on the States

What Works in Community Corrections
http://www.pewcenteronthestates.org/
uploadedFiles/Petersilia-Community-
Corrections-QandA.pdf

Pretrial Release and Diversion

CHAPTER LEARNING OBJECTIVES

- Distinguish the difference between pretrial release and diversion.
- Explain the factors involved in the decision to release one from detention.
- Determine eligibility for diversion.

- Summarize the challenges that pretrial programs face in offenders appearing for their next court date.
- Understand how drug courts and mental health courts are a form of diversion.

Judge Hutson listens to a recently arrested defendant before rendering a pre-release decision.

CHAPTER OUTLINE

Introduction

Pretrial Services
History of Pretrial Release
The Pretrial Release Decision
Pretrial Supervision
Failure to Appear (FTA)

Diversion
Candidates for Diversion
Drug Courts
Mental Health Courts
Criticisms of Diversion Programs

KEY TERMS

pretrial release
delegated release authority
pretrial supervision

failure to appear
diversion
drug courts

completion rates
retention rates
mental health courts

Introduction

Upon arrest, a felony offender is typically booked in a local jail. Within a 24-hour period (maximum of 72 hours if arrest takes place on a weekend), defendants are interviewed by a pretrial officer to assist the court in making decisions about the bond, or the way the defendant will be released from jail, if at all. Most people who are accused of a crime do not need to be held in jail while waiting for their next court date; holding them there disrupts their employment, family life, and ability to prepare and aid in their own defense (Miyashiro 2008). Although some defendants are detained in jail, most people are released on some kind of bond, which is a general term for a method of release from detention.

This chapter discusses the release and community supervision of individuals who have been *accused* of a crime but not necessarily convicted. We begin first with pretrial services.

Pretrial Services

Pretrial services is a department that has two overlapping functions. First, it assists the court in deciding who to release and who to detain (the release decision). Second, pretrial services attempts to improve the efficiency of the courts through helping to supervise released defendants so they appear at their next court date (pretrial supervision). Ultimately, the pretrial defendant's case will likely result in one of four options: dismissal, diversion, a conviction as a result of a plea agreement, or the defendant requesting to go to trial. We discuss the pretrial release and pretrial supervision separately.

Pretrial release is defined as the defendant's release from jail while awaiting his or her next court appearance. The pretrial release decision is one of the first decisions judges make following an arrest so that defendants who qualify can be effectively released, whereas other defendants are released pending supervision in the community prior to their next court date. Pretrial release allows defendants who have not yet been convicted the opportunity to live and work as productive citizens until their next scheduled court date.

Pretrial Release
A defendant's release in the community following arrest as an alternative to detention while the defendant prepares for the next scheduled court appearance.

© Marmaduke St. John/Alamy

Bail bond companies help provide the means of release for pretrial detainees who do not have the money to pay the full bail amount.

HISTORY OF PRETRIAL RELEASE

The first pretrial release program began in 1960 as the Manhattan Bail Project to assist judges in identifying defendants who could be released on their own recognizance (ROR) before their next scheduled court date. This led to the Bail Reform Act of 1966 to establish guidelines on appropriate bail amounts and alternatives to detention for those unable to afford bail. The act was a reminder that the law favors *release,* unless there is a substantial risk that the defendant may not appear at the next court hearing. Pretrial programs became so successful that within two decades more than 200 cities had developed such programs. A Federal Pretrial Services Act was passed in 1982 to authorize pretrial supervision for federal defendants accused of felony and class A misdemeanors. Growing concern about the risks posed by some pretrial defendants led to the passage of a second Bail Reform Act in 1984 that included the safety of the public as an important criterion in the decision to release a pretrial defendant. When this act was challenged in the courts, the U.S. Supreme Court reaffirmed that pretrial detention was for defendants who posed a threat to themselves or to others, and was not for the purpose of punishment (*U.S. v. Salerno* 1987). So, community safety and the risk of flight are two appropriate considerations in any bail decision (VanNostrand and Keebler 2007).

Only three nationwide studies on pretrial release programs have been conducted since their inception in 1960. The most recent one comprehensively reviewed more than 200 programs in terms of services offered, how they were administered and budgeted, staff training issues, and how each program measured up against national standards set by the American Bar Association and the National Association of Pretrial Services (Clark and Henry 2003). The researchers found that most programs were funded by the county level of government, and increasingly there were significantly more pretrial release programs managed by probation (34 percent) than administered by jails (27 percent) or the courts (24 percent). Newer pretrial release programs tend to be smaller in size, with an average staff size of 18. Only 2 percent of pretrial programs in the sample had a staff with more than

200 people, and 10 percent of pretrial programs (usually in rural areas) had a staff size of one person.

THE PRETRIAL RELEASE DECISION

The pretrial release decision at the state level typically consists of a quantitative point system of the potential risk posed, whereas the federal system relies on a pretrial investigation interview and scoring a Risk Prediction Index (RPI). The RPI was approved for use as an estimate of the likelihood that a defendant will fail to appear for his or her next court hearing or commit a new crime if released. The RPI ranges from 0 to 9 and considers these factors: the number of arrests; the use of a weapon in the most recent offense; defendant's employment; history of illegal drug use/alcohol abuse; previous escapes while on supervision; education level, and living situation (Administrative Office of the U.S. Courts 2005a).

In both the state and federal systems, pretrial services recommends the "least restrictive option" available to the court, taking into consideration the safety of the community and the defendant's likelihood of reappearance in court. This approach requires judges to consider all possible alternatives and to detain only if none are appropriate. In this way, jails will be less likely to become overcrowded; defendants can better prepare for their defense and also return to work or school while their case is pending. However, not every defendant placed on pretrial release is supervised by a pretrial program. Defendants on supervised pretrial release in the federal system may remain in this condition for one to two years (Wolf 1997).

When recommending the least restrictive measure and possible release of a suspect from custody, pretrial services officers examine whether the defendant poses a danger to the community and the likelihood that the defendant will appear for the next court date (Newville 2001). The National Association of Pretrial Services recommends that all defendants be interviewed by a pretrial services officer before the initial court appearance. The pretrial officer collects information on:

- the defendant's character,
- mental condition,
- local address,
- time spent in the area,
- employment,
- prior convictions,
- prior incidents of failure to appear (FTA) for court,
- financial resources, and
- comments from the arresting officer and victims.

The defendant is not required to answer any questions about the pending crime, nor does the pretrial services officer consider the weight of the evidence against the defendant (Wolf 1997).

In practice, not every individual supervised by pretrial services obtains a bond interview before a releasing decision is made. In one Illinois county, for example, just over half of defendants on pretrial supervision were evaluated by a bond officer (Cooprider, Gray, and Dunne 2003). One-fourth of all programs nationwide waited to conduct the bond interview until after the first court appearance (Clark and Henry 2003). Programs that interviewed the defendant before the initial court appearance and that used objective risk assessment instruments in their release decision were less likely to have an overcrowded jail than programs that subjectively assessed defendants and interviewed them following the first court appearance. Most pretrial services officers made a release/detain recommendation to the court

(88 percent), but 21 percent of these programs had **delegated release authority**, which allowed the pretrial services officer to release the defendant before the initial court appearance (Clark and Henry 2003). An eight-question pretrial assessment is currently being validated to determine its utility in predicting new arrests and future incidents of FTA in court. The items include defendant's age at first arrest, any previous times the defendant has failed to appear in court, number of jail incarcerations, employment status, self-reported use of illegal drugs, and stability of residence (Lowenkamp, Lemke, and Latessa 2008).

> **Delegated Release Authority**
> Statutory authority that allows pretrial services officers to release the defendant before the initial court appearance in front of the judge.

Types of Bonds   The judge ultimately makes both the release (in/out) decision and sets the type of bond or bail. Table 2.1 identifies and defines the ways a defendant can be released. Financial bonds require cash or property assets deposited directly with the court; a *surety bond* is available when the defendant uses the services of a bail company or other corporation to assure the next appearance. Unsecured bonds do not require any money up front, but only require the full bond amount if the defendant refuses to appear. A ROR requires only the signed agreement by the defendant that he or she will appear. If a defendant with a ROR fails to attend the next hearing, there is no bond amount to pay, but a warrant is still issued for the defendant's arrest. Finally, a conditional release is most often used for traffic offenders, specifying their driving conditions until their next hearing. The table percentages do not include defendants who were denied bail (about 6 percent) or those who could not afford their set bail amount.

Bail amounts are set according to the severity of the offense. Figure 2.1 shows that bail amounts for felony offenders vary from under $5,000 to well above $50,000. Surety bonds (such as those procured through a bond company, corporate,

TABLE 2.1   Types of Federal Pretrial Releases from Jail

Release Type	Percent of Released Defendants[a]	Definition
Unsecured bond	42%	Defendant pays no money to the court, but is liable for the full bail amount if fails to appear (FTA).
Release on recognizance	34%	Defendant signs an agreement to appear; no money is paid or owed to the court for FTA.
Conditional release	5%	Defendant is released with specific court-ordered conditions (third party, elec monit).
Surety bond	10%	Use of a bail bond company where the bail company is liable if the defendant FTA; bail company charges a 10–15% fee for taking the risk.
Deposit/Collateral	9%	Defendant deposits bail amount in cash or property collateral with court; money is returned after all court dates; bond is forfeited for FTA.

[a]Percentages include released defendants only and do not include defendants who were denied bail or who could not afford their set bail amount.

Source: Compendium of Federal Justice Statistics. 2007. Type of pretrial release for cases terminated October 2003 to September 2004, Table 3.2. Washington, DC: U.S. Department of Justice.

FIGURE 2.1   Bail Amounts Set for Felony Defendants

Source: Thomas H. Cohen and Brian A. Reaves. 2006. *Felony Defendants in Large Urban Counties, 2002.* Washington, DC: U.S. Department of Justice, p. 18.

Percentages may not add up to 100% because of rounding.

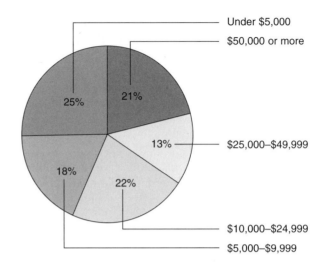

or insurance company) have declined among federal defendants (Cadigan 2007). Considering the overall socioeconomic status of most defendants and their families, a significant proportion of defendants remain in detention if they cannot meet the financial conditions of their bail amount.

Recent Trends in the Federal Release Decision   Despite the changes that were made to reform bail in the 1960s and keep people out of the system, once again there seems to be a growing trend toward an increase in federal pretrial detention. According to Figure 2.2, pretrial detention rates have been steadily *increasing* in the federal system since 1992 to the present time, and now comprise over 60 percent of defendants. In contrast, state court detention rates (overall average) have fluctuated from 34 to 38 percent of defendants between 1992 and 2002 (Van Nostrand and Keebler 2007).

One explanation might be the increase in immigration cases that necessitates detention if the defendant cannot show community ties and may be a flight risk. However, no evidence existed for detaining defendants based on their offense, particularly with drug offenses and weapons charges. With immigration cases, the FTA rate is a little bit higher than other crimes (4.3 percent for immigration offenses vs. 2.8 percent for violent crimes), but the likelihood of committing a new crime on release is less (2.3 percent for immigration offenses vs. 6.9 percent for weapons-related offenses). Researchers are hinting at the possibility of racial disparity in federal pretrial decision making (Byrne and Stowell 2007). When immigration cases were excluded, less than half of defendants were released on average (47 percent) nationwide—with the districts varied widely from a low of 24 percent to a high of 76 percent of arrested defendants released. If immigration cases were included, then the most recent numbers show that 61 percent of all federal defendants were detained prior to sentencing or trial (VanNostrand and Keebler 2007).

Another explanation of rising pretrial detention rates might be that the individual situations related to the release decision have changed over time, impacting the "score" defendants receive, regardless of dangerousness. Have defendant characteristics changed? Is how we measure "flight risk" relevant to today's defendants? We do know that individuals more likely to be released pretrial tended to have no prior convictions or had only one misdemeanor conviction, were employed at arrest, had some college education, were more than 40 years of age, or were female (Cohen

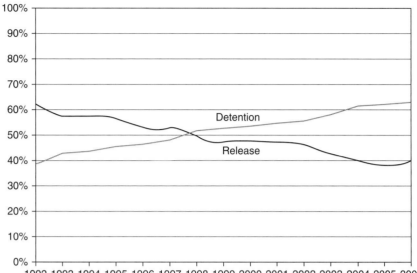

FIGURE 2.2   Federal Release and Detention Rates

Source: Cadigan, Timothy P. 2007. Pretrial services in the federal system: Impact of the Pretrial Services Act of 1982. *Federal Probation* 71(2): 10–15.

and Reaves 2006). Also, pretrial defendants with mental illnesses were considered for pretrial release because they could obtain the necessary services in the community more often than in a jail environment (Clark and Henry 2003).

But if we compare defendant characteristics with those of 20 years ago, we see that fewer defendants are employed – 31 percent of defendants today compared with 57 percent in 1987. Also, more defendants are transient. For example, in 1987, two-thirds of defendants lived in the same area for 5 years or more. Today, that rate has diminished to one-third of defendants, leading one to question whether the pretrial decision favors release or detention (Cadigan 2007). One consistent trend is that most pretrial defendants, whether they are supervised or not, appear in court and do not commit new offenses, suggesting the overuse of pretrial supervision in the federal system (Byrne and Stowell 2007). Perhaps it is time to revisit how the federal system makes the detention/release decision for "flight risk," or to redefine necessary vs. unnecessary pretrial detention.

PRETRIAL SUPERVISION

Once a decision has been made to release a defendant, a certain percent of defendants are supervised on what is known as **pretrial supervision**. Most felons in the federal system are on some form of pretrial supervision for between six and seven months, or an overall average of 203 days until sentencing. If a defendant requests a trial, he or she remains on pretrial supervision until the trial's conclusion, which reportedly takes twenty months from arrest (Cadigan 2003). Apparently, some federal districts find it difficult to release defendants from supervision even if their behavior has been positive and not shown signs of being a flight risk.

In the state system, the number of those evaluated for pretrial supervision is significantly less than those who receive it. For example, for every 10 defendants evaluated, only 2 are recommended for supervision. This is primarily because many clients on pretrial supervision are directly referred by judges without an evaluation. Direct referrals are primarily misdemeanor and traffic defendants, 60 percent of whom are accused of DUI and misdemeanor domestic battery (Cooprider, Gray, and Dunne 2003).

Pretrial Supervision
Court-ordered correctional supervision of a defendant who has not yet been convicted whereby the defendant participates in activities such as reporting, house arrest, and electronic monitoring to ensure appearance at the next court date.

When a defendant is not in compliance with the pretrial supervision conditions set by the court (for example, the client has not called or has not attended treatment programs), 89 percent of programs will give the defendant a warning the first time. Most programs will report the second act of noncompliance to the court with a recommendation for specific action. Officers may recommend to the court that either no action be taken or that more restrictive action be taken, such as increasing telephone contact with the defendant (Clark and Henry 2003). More serious acts of noncompliance, such as absconding or a rearrest, may result in the court's issuance of a bench warrant, the detention of a suspect, or bail revocation.

Little is known about how many conditions are necessary to keep track of people, without detriment to the whole purpose of pretrial supervision—that is, to keep offenders out of jail. Clients on pretrial supervision were required to call in weekly until their scheduled court date, comply with curfew, submit to drug testing, maintain employment, and avoid contact with victims and any complaining witnesses. One trend is certain—the more rules a person has to follow, the greater the chance that the person will violate one or more of the conditions. The jury is still out, however, on which offenders may pose a risk to public safety. On the one hand, defendants in the state system who were on bond for murder, burglary, or motor vehicle theft were more likely than other types of felony offenders to appear for court, but were also more likely to commit new felony crimes while on pretrial release (Cohen and Reaves 2006). On the other hand, in the federal system, Byrne and Stowell (2007) found that even though technical rule violations increased there was no overall change in new crimes committed. They conclude: "This certainly suggests that setting multiple release conditions and identifying technical violators of these release conditions does not improve community safety and the appearance of defendants at subsequent court dates." (p. 32)

FAILURE TO APPEAR

Failure to Appear
A situation in which a defendant does not attend a scheduled court hearing.

The whole purpose of pretrial supervision is to ensure the defendant appears for court and the public is safe while the defendant is out on bond. Defendants who **failed to appear** did not attend their scheduled court date, and seemed most likely to flee the day before their trial, sentencing hearing, or just prior to surrendering themselves for incarceration (Henry 2007). Clark and Henry (2003) found that the number of jurisdictions nationwide that issue warrants and conduct other forms of follow-up for FTA has actually decreased in recent years. According to Figure 2.3, federal pretrial defendants are a good bet—they appeared in court 98 to 99 percent of the time, and FTA rates are actually declining.

Of the federal offenders who were released pretrial, those who had used a bail company (surety bond) had the highest FTA rate (3.8 percent), which was nearly twice that of release on recognizance. The rates for local jurisdictions were much worse—one out of every four defendants was unsuccessfully terminated from pretrial supervision, mostly for repeated nonappearance (Cooprider, Gray, and Dunne 2003).

The way to decrease FTA rates is to remind clients of their upcoming court dates. Clark and Henry (2003) found that 87 percent of pretrial programs reminded defendants of their upcoming court date, but that may not be enough to reduce the high FTA rates. Over half of pretrial programs reminded the defendant with a courtesy phone call, 25 percent sent a letter, and 12 percent conducted a home visit (see Table 2.2). About 21 percent of pretrial programs provided no follow-up or reminders whatsoever. Many pretrial programs lack the funding to track FTA rates,

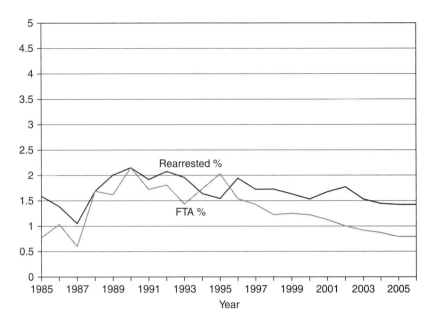

FIGURE 2.3 Failure to Appear and Rearrest Rates for Federal Defendants

Source: Cadigan, Timothy P. 2007. Pretrial services in the federal system: Impact of the Pretrial Services Act of 1982. *Federal Probation* 71(2): 10–15.

TABLE 2.2 Failure to Appear (FTA) Follow-up by Pretrial Programs

	PERCENTAGE OF PRETRIAL PROGRAMS		
FTA Follow-up Action	**2001** ($N = 191$)	**1989** ($N = 155$)	**1979** ($N = 117$)
Send letter to defendant urging return	25	43	55
Call defendant urging return	52	64	80
Make home visit to defendant urging return	12	17	45
Have arrest authority with FTA warrant	19	13	14
Assist police in locating defendant	35	52	57
Attempt to locate defendant who left jurisdiction	24	33	32
Seek to have warrant quashed when defendant returns	20	22	N/A
Place defendant's case back on court calendar	19	27	N/A
No FTA follow-up action taken	21	N/A	14

Source: John Clark and D. Alan Henry. 2003. *Pretrial Services Programming at the Start of the 21st Century: A Survey of Pretrial Services Programs*. Washington, DC: Bureau of Justice Assistance.

and most (71 percent) have no means by which to track the rearrest rates for their jurisdiction.

Reducing FTA Rates   Goldkamp and White (1998) wanted to measure the degree to which various pretrial notification and deterrence services made a difference in the rate of participation in orientation sessions, FTA rates, and rearrest rates of pretrial releases. They conducted an experiment that included random assignment of four different experimental groups, which were compared with a baseline group that received none of these services.

- Group 1 received an orientation session and was required to call in once per week.
- Group 2 received the same services as Group 1, along with a personal phone call to remind them the night before the court date.
- Group 3 was a higher-risk group than Groups 1 and 2. They received the same services as Group 1, and they made phone contact twice per week and had to meet in person three days before the court date.
- Group 4 (also a higher-risk group) received the same services as Group 3, and a warrant officer visited the residence for any noncompliance during the pretrial period.

Groups 1 and 2 showed no significant differences; phone contact the night before the court date had no significant effect on FTA and rearrest rates, largely because few defendants could actually be reached by phone (not home, wrong numbers, answering machine, and so forth). The small number of defendants who were successfully contacted had high rates of attendance/compliance (Goldkamp and White 1998).

No significant differences were found for Groups 3 and 4, showing that the threat of a warrant officer had no significant deterrent impact on FTA and rearrest rates. Issuing a warrant or threat letter did not seem to increase compliance. When all four experimental groups were compared simultaneously with the baseline group that received none of the pretrial services, there were no significant differences on rate of orientation session attendance (56 percent experimental and 51 percent baseline), FTA (18 percent experimental and 19 percent baseline), fugitive status (20 percent experimental and 21 percent baseline), and rearrest rates (6 percent experimental and 8 percent baseline). This experiment raised serious questions about the impact of notification and deterrence, since the "do nothing" approach was no better or worse than any service provided by a pretrial program (Goldkamp and White 1998).

Diversion

Thus far, we have talked about pretrial release and supervision, under the assumption that an offender is ultimately going to enter a plea of guilty or not guilty at the arraignment. Following the pretrial release decision, the prosecutor or defense attorney can suggest **diversion**, which is the suspension or removal of a case from further court action provided the defendant successfully completes the terms of supervision. Diversion can occur prior to arrest (by police) or it can occur "post-booking," which is after arrest, but before formal prosecution. In this section, we discuss post-booking diversion since it most directly influences community-based supervision and reduces the time spent in jail.

The idea of diversion began in the mid-1960s with programs such as Treatment Alternatives to Street Crime (TASC) for drug abusers and the Manhattan Court Employment project for vocationally disadvantaged offenders. Diversion attempts to keep offenders from the negative effects of incarceration, while at the same time providing rehabilitation programs in the community that address challenges the offender may face.

Prosecutors and defense attorneys in many jurisdictions are able to recommend defendants for diversion programs before the arraignment or plea. In considering

Diversion
An alternative program to traditional criminal sentencing or juvenile justice adjudication that provides first-time offenders with a chance or addresses unique treatment needs, with the successful completion resulting in the dismissal of the current charges.

BOX 2.1   COMMUNITY CORRECTIONS UP CLOSE

Can Risk Assessment Instruments Determine Diversion Eligibility?

Objective risk assessment instruments are being used more often—such as to identify offenders who may qualify for diversion or to determine which pretrial defendants can be released prior to their next court date. A new 6-item risk assessment instrument has been developed as a pretrial screening tool (Lowenkamp, Lemke, and Latessa 2008). The researchers used age at first arrest, prior FTAs, employment status at arrest, number of previous jail incarcerations, movement of residence in last 6 months, and drug use as indicators of who presented the greatest likelihood of rearrest for a new crime upon release.

Using history of prior juvenile contact with authorities, adult criminal history, current offense, and offender characteristics, one instrument in Virginia was designed to complement the state's sentencing guidelines. The instrument was tested in six pilot sites and saved $1.2 million in these sites during the study, with an estimated net savings of between $2.9 million and $3.6 million annually (Ostrom et al. 2002).

However, for diversion eligibility, risk assessment instruments may be more accurate for adults than for juveniles. When examining diverted youths with higher risk scores against a comparison group, Shelden (1999) found that youths with the higher risk scores actually had lower recidivism rates than a comparison group. More long-term studies need to follow diverted and nondiverted youths into adulthood.

---

which factors were important in their decision, the defendant's probation/parole history, mental health, substance abuse history, community ties, and evaluative needs were all viewed as either most important or important by both the prosecutor and defense. The defendant's adult criminal record, gang affiliation, official version of the offense, and pending cases were all ranked significantly higher in the diversion decision by prosecutors than by defense attorneys (Alarid and Montemayor 2009). The defendant's situation and offense must qualify for this alternative to traditional criminal sentencing. Offenses that qualify for diversion include theft, possession of controlled substances, driving while intoxicated, domestic violence assault, and prostitution. Defendants whose situations qualify for diversion might be juveniles, first-time offenders, or those with mental health problems. Upon the successful completion of diversion, the charges are dismissed. For this reason, many jurisdictions consider diversion a type of pretrial program (Ulrich 2002). Box 2.1 discusses how risk assessment instruments have been developed to further predict candidates for diversion.

CANDIDATES FOR DIVERSION

Diversion programs attempt to provide problem-solving courts and community services for three types of individuals. First, diversion helps youthful offenders in an attempt to avoid the criminal label or deviant stigma that results from having a conviction. Diversion can help first-time adult offenders who do not pose a risk to public safety and who, upon completion of the program, are unlikely to return to criminal behavior (Alarid and Montemayor 2009). In the federal system, white-collar criminals such as those accused of fraud, larceny theft, and embezzlement are eligible for pretrial diversion. Offenders who are ineligible include those with 2 or more prior felony convictions, addicts, public officials, or those accused of a crime violating national security (Ulrich 2002).

A second candidate for diversion is a person with special needs such as a mental illness that is related to the individual's criminal behavior. Most offenders in this situation have committed minor offenses and are better suited for rehabilitative functions such as medication stabilization and counseling (Castillo and Alarid 2009). We address the issue of mental health courts as a means to attain stability later in the chapter.

A third candidate for diversion is a person who requires treatment for a problem, such as drug or alcohol abuse, that may be related to the arrest. These types of diversionary programs involve specialty courts for common crimes, such as drug courts or DUI courts, to which we now turn.

DRUG COURTS

Drug courts are a proactive way for a court judge, prosecutor, and defense attorney to use diversion or a suspended sentence for monitoring people with a substance abuse problem who have not yet been convicted (see Figure 2.4). The drug court concept integrates outpatient substance abuse treatment with criminal justice case

Drug Courts
A diversion program for drug addicts in which the judge, prosecutor, and probation officer play a proactive role and monitor the progress of clients through weekly visits to the courtroom, using a process of graduated sanctions.

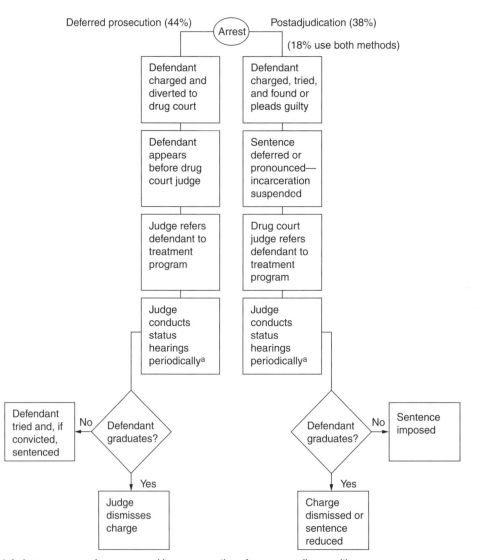

FIGURE 2.4 Flowchart of Two Drug Court Approaches

Source: Daniel C., Harris et al. 1997, *Drug Courts: Overview of Growth, Characteristics, and Results.* Washington, DC: U.S. General Accounting Office, p. 92.

a Judges may reward progress and impose sanctions for noncompliance with program requirements.

processing. Upon successful completion of the drug court program, charges are dismissed. If offenders withdraw or are terminated from the program without successfully completing it, they are charged and tried for the original offense, and sentenced accordingly. Figure 2.4 also shows that drug courts are used as a "post-adjudication proceeding," which means that following a plea of guilty the sentence is deferred. Provided individuals remain crime free for a certain amount of time, they can get their offense reduced or dismissed by the court. There are approximately 1,600 drug courts for adults and juveniles operating, with another 400 in the planning stages (Galloway and Drapela 2006).

CHARACTERISTICS OF DRUG COURTS

The idea of drug courts began in 1989 in Dade County, Florida, under the assumption that treatment interventions of first-time drug offenders or low-level drug users would be more likely to curb future drug use than punishment without treatment. A second assumption was that the sooner the treatment intervention began after arrest, the less time the offender would spend in jail in a negative environment where drug use could continue (Alonso 2009).

The drug court concept was much different than traditional criminal courts. The judge, prosecutor, defense attorney, and probation officer all work together noncompetitively to allow more informal and direct interaction between the defendant and the judge. It allows the team to work for the client and not in a game, with each other to see "who wins." The entire team monitors the progress of each client through staffing and court hearings every 2 weeks. Promoting the idea of a drug court from within is sometimes difficult, as attorneys trained in traditional courtroom practices may resist change, as Judge Alonso's essay in "Field Notes" will attest (see Box 2.2).

A process of graduated sanctions is used as behavior improves or worsens. For example, as a defendant moves through the program, the public recognizes his or her efforts. Clients who relapse may have to repeat certain segments of the program. Repeated relapses may mean short-term incarceration. Thus, judges intervene before the pattern of technical violations occurs as in regular probation, and the court collaborates with the drug treatment specialists. A final assumption about drug courts is that with any addiction, relapse is to be expected, but participants are also expected to prevent relapse from becoming a pattern.

Drug courts are specifically for nonviolent drug offenders with at least "moderate substance usage." The offenders may be misdemeanants or felons, and they must voluntarily agree to participate. An initial substance abuse assessment determines eligibility for program participation (Listwan et al. 2003). This assessment examines history of drug use and/or results of drug screening. A system of levels varies the intensity of the program balanced against freedoms and privileges. Treatment is one year in length and typically begins with an intensive two weeks of inpatient treatment. Treatment involves detoxification through acupuncture, drug testing through urine screenings, and group and individual counseling. Clients are also referred to Narcotics Anonymous and Alcoholics Anonymous (Alonso 2009). As the client progresses through the program, the levels gradually taper to day treatment and then to outpatient, which is the most common status. Most clients relapse during treatment, but a continuous pattern of drug use is not acceptable and results in program failure. Drug court completion rates for those who successfully finish the one-year program vary from 29 percent to 43 percent (Taxman and Bouffard 2003).

FIELD NOTES

What were the challenges and rewards you faced introducing the concept of drug courts?

As a judge handling criminal cases, I was frustrated at the large number of probationers testing positive for alcohol and illegal drugs. While working on my Masters at the National Judicial College in 2001, I shared my frustration with one of my professors. He introduced me to drug courts and their existence in many cities. That year, I returned home and began implementing the rudimentary steps of drug courts following the ten key components. Since this was a new concept in our jurisdiction, I was met with incredible resistance from probation officers, defense attorneys, and the district attorney's office. Even our legislators informed me that this was a rehabilitative program not supported by the public. The public, they said, supported the "tough on crime, lock them up and throw away the key" concept.

My first obstacle was the opposition of our ten probation officers who had been trained on being "tough." In a traditional court, if a defendant tested positive for illegal drugs, in most cases, they recommended revocation and incarceration. If a judge ordered treatment instead of jail, the judge was considered weak and ineffective. One of the probation officers even asked to be transferred out of my court.

Our district attorney's office would not agree to pretrial diversion and did not buy into the non-adversarial approach of drug courts. The DA advised me their prosecutors were not "social workers." And the attorneys, who were trained in law school to be advocates for the adversarial approach, also had a difficult time

Judge Al Alonso *Bexar County Court No. 1, San Antonio, Texas*

representing a client within a team approach fostered by the drug court program.

All the members in the drug court team—probation officer, treatment therapist, drug court coordinator, defense attorney, prosecutor – work together toward supporting defendants (drug court participants) in their recovery.

After studying the drug court program and reading the research, I knew drug court was the best program we had in our criminal justice system in addressing non-violent drug abusers and alcoholics. I realized the answer to all resistance was to educate all members on drug courts, including our county elected officials and state legislators.

In 2002, I obtained a U.S. Department of Justice grant. The grant provided for drug court training for a ten member team, plus one state legislator. We were the first court in the county to be certified by the National Drug Court Institute, a major step in beginning to turn back the resistance. Slowly, attitudes began to change.

The next challenge was communication with the program participants. Team members had to learn the technique of "motivational Interviewing," a non-confrontational, non-argument, sympathetic approach. Each participant is treated with fairness, dignity, and respect. Some change of personnel took place.

Today, we have four drug courts. In my 40-year professional career, board certified in criminal law, and 15 years as a judge, this is the criminal justice program that changes lives, saves money, and lowers crime. It is the most satisfying work I have done in my legal career.

GENDER AND DRUG COURT TREATMENT STRATEGIES

One of the ongoing issues in drug court research is that some drug courts do not effectively address gender differences. Women and men have different reasons for abusing drugs, different drugs of choice, and different drug use patterns. Women are more likely to be primary caretakers of dependent children, have lower education levels, and be impoverished, all of which may affect their ability to complete treatment programs. Research shows that women use drugs to cope with traumatic situations, such as domestic violence, mental illness, sexual abuse, and physical abuse. In this manner, women are likely to self-medicate alone and need to be drawn out of the despair they feel. Women also use to maintain a relationship with a significant other who also uses (Dannerbeck, Sundet, and Lloyd 2002).

Men who participate in drug court tend to abuse alcohol or marijuana. Men use in a more social and public context that involves establishing or maintaining a reputation, or gaining a sense of control. Men have better completion rates, perhaps because drug courts were modeled to better address their needs, patterns, and reasons that they drink (Dannerbeck, Sundet, and Lloyd 2002).

Although drug courts address other problems in conjunction with substance abuse treatment, such as housing, employment, food, transportation/bus passes, and health screenings, gender-specific and cultural issues need to be addressed. States such as Michigan, California, and New York have developed separate drug court programs for men and women. Programs for women can be directed more specifically at reasons why women use in the context of trauma and significant relationships. Furthermore, the programs may be able to spend more time on parenting, abuse, and domestic violence. This allows women to establish closer relationships with other drug court participants and the judge, and should increase completion rates. Another benefit of a single-sex environment is that women (and men) are less distracted by the opposite sex and thus take the program more seriously (D'Angelo 2002).

EVALUATING DRUG COURTS

Drug courts reportedly saved money over traditional court processing in Multnomah County, Oregon, when the costs for arrest, booking, court time, treatment, jail time, and probation were summed for 120 people, some of whom went through drug court and some of whom did not. When the 120 people were tracked to determine recidivism, the drug court participants were less likely to be rearrested than those in the control group. The cost of obtaining drug court treatment was $5,928 per year per offender, whereas it cost $7,369 for traditional processing of one drug offender for one year (Carey and Figgin 2004). Other researchers disagree that drug courts

© AP Photo/Steven Senne

A Rhode Island drug court Magistrate listens to the defendant's treatment progress as she holds her one-year-old daughter. The defendant's defense attorney is present for these bi-weekly meetings, while the drug court program coordinator organizes the docket.

save money. Although drug court clients did indeed spend less time behind bars prior to court disposition, they spent twice as long in jail for noncompliance of drug court sanctions than a randomized control group who were eligible but did not go through drug court (Gottfredson, Najaka, and Kearley 2003; Gottfredson, Kearley, Najaka and Rocha 2007).

Related to the concern of overuse of incarceration for noncompliance, a General Accounting Office (GAO) study found that completion and retention rates varied widely by program, and they were lower than expected. **Completion rates** represent individuals who are favorably discharged as a percentage of the total number admitted and not still enrolled. According to Figure 2.5, only 31.2 percent of those enrolled had graduated, whereas 30.2 percent were still actively enrolled. Nearly 21 percent had been terminated for violations, and an additional 3.5 percent voluntarily withdrew. **Retention rates** are a combined total of the successful completers and those actively enrolled compared to the total number admitted (GAO 1997, p. 50). Later retention rates have remained between 40 and 60 percent. It is a disappointment that half of those who are eligible cannot or do not wish to complete the full phase of treatment (Fischer 2003).

The best method of testing effectiveness is random assignment to drug court and to regular supervision (either probation or prison). Sites where this has been done found that drug courts had a positive effect on reducing recidivism. The control group was rearrested at nearly three times the rate of the drug court participants (Gottfredson and Exum 2002), and the difference between the two groups remained apparent two years later (Gottfredson, Najaka, and Kearley 2003). After three years, the judicial hearings and drug testing had a direct effect against reducing future

Completion Rates
Individuals who are favorably discharged from drug court as a percentage of the total number admitted and not still enrolled.

Retention Rates
The combined total of the successful completers and those actively enrolled compared to the total number admitted to drug court.

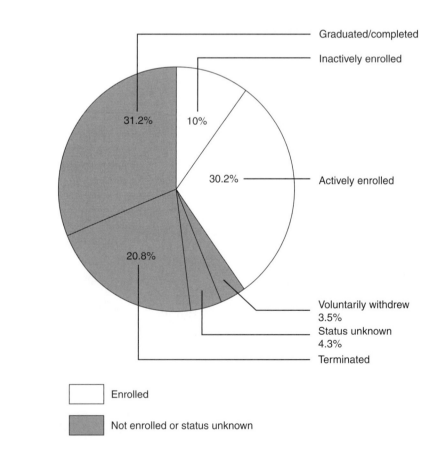

FIGURE 2.5 What Happened to Drug Court Participants?

Source: Daniel C. Harris et al. 1997. *Drug Courts: Overview of Growth, Characteristics, and Results.* Washington, DC: U.S. General Accounting Office, p. 55.

crime and a return to drug use—participants who had more judicial contact and who felt that they received fair treatment, even if they didn't like the outcome, were more likely to follow the contract and less likely to commit crime and return to drug use than offenders who had less or no judicial contact (Gottfredson, Kearley, Najaka, and Rocha 2007). Drug treatment had an indirect effect for participants in this same study.

A nationwide study of 95 drug courts (a total of 2,020 participants in one year) over a two-year period revealed an average rearrest rate (where a charge was filed) of 16 percent after the first twelve months following graduation, and 27 percent after twenty-four months (Roman, Townsend, and Bhati 2003). Recidivism rates varied widely among the different programs, making comparison across programs difficult. Programs serving felony offenders and offenders who had a more severe drug problem had higher recidivism rates than programs that treated only misdemeanor clients. Access to other community services, program size, police practices, prosecutor decisions, program duration, and violation policies affected the recidivism rate as well. Researchers caution against the use of recidivism as the sole determiner of program success, and also against making too many program comparisons across programs that should not be compared. Two consistent conclusions were drawn when comparing program participants. First, when drug court graduates were compared with drug offenders who went to prison without treatment, drug court graduates were rearrested at significantly lower rates over a three-year period (Galloway and Drapela 2006; von Zielbauer 2003). A second conclusion is the difference in recidivism by gender. Moreover, women had lower rearrest rates than men. Also, Caucasian individuals had lower recidivism rates than minority drug court participants (Roman, Townsend, and Bhati 2003). These findings may be due to drug court participant behavior, the justice system response, or a combination of both factors. The drug court model does seem most applicable to offenders who are motivated to change (Listwan et al. 2003).

MENTAL HEALTH COURTS

Many of the people suffering from mental illnesses who come to the attention of the criminal justice system are appropriate candidates for a diversion program if their criminal charges involve a nonviolent offense. An indigent person who is mentally ill but poses no danger to public safety may benefit more from mental health and social services than from the criminal justice system (Ulrich 2002). Due to the deinstitutionalization of the mentally ill and the lack of community mental health providers to serve clients without health insurance, indigent people with mental illnesses have limited resources and come to the attention of the criminal justice system, which has become the largest mental health institution in the country (Slate and Johnson 2008). The Council of State Governments (2008, p.2) reported that "nearly two-thirds of boys and three-quarters of girls detained in juvenile facilities were found to have at least one psychiatric disorder, with approximately 25 percent of these juveniles experiencing disorders so severe that their ability to function was significantly impaired." While a small number of offenders with mental illnesses need to be separated from the rest of society, incarceration is overly stressful and not the best situation for stabilizing the clear majority of mentally ill individuals who are best served in the community. Many jail diversion programs exist for mentally ill offenders; where police, prosecutors, and jails work together, these have been shown to produce cost savings and to free jail space (Bexar County Diversion Program 2006; Gordon, Barnes, and VanBenschoten

2006). Mental health courts began in 1997 as a second diversion option for this purpose.

Like the drug courts, **mental health courts** use a team problem solving approach in lieu of traditional case processing to supervise and treat mentally ill offenders in the community. Participants are initially identified during the jail booking process through mental health screenings or assessments. For example, a jail diversion coordinator receives an instant message when a client with certain criteria is booked in jail. Within 24 hours, the diversion coordinator notifies the courts that an eligible diversion case should be considered. Eligibility criteria are long-term Axis 1 disorders that have affected daily functioning, such as schizophrenia, anxiety or obsessive-compulsive disorder, bipolar disorder, or severe depression. Participants must be competent and be able to voluntarily participate on their own. The eligible Axis 1 disorders do not include substance abuse as the *primary* diagnosis. The Axis 1 disorder must be the primary problem, but substance abuse is frequently a *secondary* diagnosis. The high rate of co-occurring disorders in this population—people with both a mental illness and who have a substance abuse problem—are treated simultaneously for both.

Another way of identifying eligibility bypasses pre-approval of a prosecutor, relying instead on mental health specialists, along with the jail medical screener, to make a group decision about appropriateness for the program; the decision is then presented to the court for final approval. Once the judge agrees, the group can create a transition plan while the client is stabilizing on medications in jail, separated from the regular jail inmate population.

Once a client is accepted into the mental health court program, a mental health court team is made up of a judge, prosecutor, defense attorney, mental health providers, and a pretrial services officer with specialized training in mental health (Slate 2003). Defense attorneys assist offenders who are unable to fully understand their circumstances because of their disorder or chemical dependence. The same team members meet twice a month with each participant in court in a "status hearing" to discuss progress through the program. The status hearing takes place in the courtroom where the daily docket is specifically for mental health court clients. Prior to each status hearing, the team members "staff" each person's situation, which means they meet as a group without the participant present, to update and share information about each person in the program. Each team comes to a decision on what actions to take at the next status hearing: whether to increase or decrease medication, treatment exposure, sanctions, or to graduate the participant to the next level or in some way reward the participant with a gift certificate. Specially trained probation officers have "specialized caseloads," which are smaller caseloads that use a more unique case management style specific to the needs and challenges that people with mental illnesses face. We discuss specific strategies and types of specialized caseloads in more detail in Chapters 5 and 8.

There are approximately 175 mental health courts nationwide, with another 18 for juveniles. The more successful mental health courts seem to have a solid community partnership and availability of community services for homelessness, transportation, and medication stability. Outcome evaluations of various courts found that participants in mental health courts had less new charges/arrests and as a result, fewer new jail bookings and days in jail than non-participants who had a mental illness. Participation in mental health court also increased the rate at which clients received services as compared to what would happen if they were court-ordered through the traditional process to attend treatment (Council of State Governments 2008).

CRITICISMS OF DIVERSION PROGRAMS

One criticism of diversion programs overall, whether they are youth programs, drug courts, or mental health courts, stems from a lack of clarity about the best course of action if a participant fails to complete the necessary requirements of the program. Some diversion programs, such as drug courts, use the threat of a criminal record if a participant relapses. But incarceration would not work for mentally ill offenders, as it would likely exacerbate the problem. In theory, this may lead to net widening , which makes it possible that other programs may gain control over individuals who otherwise would not have been in the system in the first place. Net widening defeats the true purpose of diversion—to keep the offender out of the system—so flexibility for the change process is important. A second critique of diversion programs is that they may be perceived by the average citizens as absolving the defendant of responsibility. Diversion programs still require all defendants to be accountable for their actions; furthermore, they strive to use community resources more effectively and improve the defendant's quality of life.

SUMMARY

- Pretrial services consist of the pretrial release decision from jail and pretrial supervision of defendants as a condition of their release.

- Pretrial release can consist of either a quantitative point system (as in state and local cases) or professional subjective assessment (for the federal system) to determine risk of flight.

- The purpose of pretrial supervision is to ensure that the defendant appears for court and the public is safe while the defendant is out on bond.

- Diversion focuses on offenders who voluntarily agree to enter a contractual agreement with the courts, jail, or probation office whereby the offender is supervised in the community.

- Upon completion of the period of diversion supervision, the offender will not have a formal record of conviction. If the offender on diversion supervision does not comply with the conditions, a formal execution of the sentence ensues.

- Drug court is a type of diversion program that integrates substance abuse treatment in a coordinated and ongoing interactive team approach of judges, prosecutors, and probation officers.

- Mental health courts are organizationally similar to other problem-solving courts, except that they deal with offenders who are mentally ill and link with a variety of community service providers.

DISCUSSION QUESTIONS

1. What kinds of individuals do you think are best suited for pretrial release?

2. Agree or disagree with the following statement: "The increased number of federal defendants who are being detained is necessary for public safety."

3. What rate of failures to appear is acceptable to you in the normal business of the courts?

4. How can bail be made more affordable for indigent offenders who cannot afford to bond out of jail?

5. Are drug courts a good idea for higher-level drug dealers?

6. How many chances (how much leeway and in what types of offenses) should be given to defendants in diversion programs before they are considered to have "failed" the program?

7. Should mental health courts be expanded for juveniles with mental illnesses? Why or why not?

8. Other than drug courts and mental health courts, what other offenses or types of persons who would benefit from a specialized diversionary-style court?

WEB SITES

American Bar Association: Steps in a Trial
    http://www.abanet.org/publiced/courts/
    pretrial_appearances.html

San Francisco Pretrial Diversion Project, Inc.
    http://www.sfpretrial.com/community.html

Minnesota (Clay County) Pretrial Diversion
Programs for Juveniles
    http://www.co.clay.mn.us/Depts/Attorney/
    PJDivPro.htm

Louisiana (Baton Rouge) Parish Attorney Pretrial
Diversion Division
    http://brgov.com/dept/parishattorney/pretrial.htm

Adult Drug Court Programs
    http://www.judiciary.state.nj.us/criminal/
    crdrgct.htm

National Estimates of Recidivism Rates for Drug
Court Graduates
    http://www.ncjrs.org/pdffiles1/201229.pdf

Florida Drug Courts
    http://www.flcourts.org/gen_public/family/
    drug_court/index.shtml

The CMHS National GAINS Center
    www.gainscenter.samhsa.gov

Policy on Mental Health Courts
    http://www.youthlaw.org/policy/advocacy/
    juvenile_mental_health_court_initiative/

Anchorage, Alaska, Mental Health Court
    http://www.state.ak.us/courts/mhct.htm

King County District Court, Mental Health Court
    www.kingcounty.gov/courts/districtCourt.aspx

CASE STUDY EXERCISE

The Diversion Decision

This chapter discussed factors that affect the decision to grant a diversionary sentence. The following case examples are before the court, and you are tasked with deciding if the case should or should not be diverted. You must justify your decision in writing.

CASE A

Defendant Smith has been arrested for possession of ecstasy—enough for two hits. Smith has no criminal history and has been employed as a laborer with a construction company for two years, excluding a brief layoff period. He has a good work record with the company. He admits that he uses alcohol and had been drinking and using ecstasy the night of the offense. Smith has used marijuana and cocaine, but indicates all of the usage has been in the past and not recent. Smith lives by himself; he has never been married and has one child from a previous relationship. Smith is two months behind on his child support payments and does not see the child very often. Smith's defense attorney argues that his client has never been in any form of mental health counseling or substance abuse treatment/counseling, and would agree to go to drug court as a diversionary measure. The state's attorney is opposed to drug court for Defendant Smith because of the type of drug—ecstasy. The police have recently been trying to rid the streets of the supply of ecstasy and believe that Smith may be tied somehow to a major ecstasy drug ring in the area, but they need more time to prove the allegations, which right now, are "shaky" at best.

CASE B

Defendant Thompson has been arrested for a felony crime, "throwing objects from an overpass," which resulted in injury to a passenger of a vehicle. Thompson is a 19-year-old college freshman. He and another college friend had prepared shredded paper in their school colors for the homecoming football game. While walking across an overpass over the interstate highway, he and another student decided to throw some of the shredded paper, which was in black plastic trash bags. They proceeded to cut open a bag and pour the paper down on the vehicles. When they cut into a second bag and poured the contents onto the passing vehicles, they were unaware that a brick had been put into the bag for weight. The brick struck the windshield of a vehicle, causing the windshield to break and chip; a piece of the glass flew into the eye of the victim, causing permanent loss of vision.

Defendant Thompson has a prior misdemeanor for theft when he was 17, for which he received a one-year diversionary sentence, which he completed just six months ago. Thompson is not employed and is a full-time college student. He makes passing grades and has not had any student violations at the university. Thompson denies any illegal drug usage and admitted to drinking in the past, but denies drinking at all since his prior misdemeanor arrest. Thompson's attorney proposes diversion once again to the court; he will continue to attend school, and he will participate in community service by helping the victim and her family at their farm without pay. The state's attorney is adamantly opposed to diversion, as this is Thompson's second arrest in less than two years. Due to the seriousness of the victim's injuries, the state's attorney feels that this offense should become part of the court record. The district attorney feels that diversion would trivialize the victim's injuries and appeals to you not to grant diversion.

3

Sentencing and the Presentence Investigation Report

CHAPTER LEARNING OBJECTIVES

- Define the legal factors in granting community sentences.
- Explain the purpose and contents of the presentence investigation report.
- Determine how the presentence investigation report is prepared by way of an investigation

interview, verification, and evaluative summary.

- Summarize the legal issues and criticisms regarding the presentence investigation report.

© Lew Long/CORBIS

The sentencing decision reflects a balance between the severity of the offense, and the individual circumstances of each situation.

CHAPTER OUTLINE

Sentencing
Factors that Affect Granting a Community Sentence
Sentencing Guidelines
Sentencing Commissions

Conditions of Community Corrections
Standard Conditions
Special Conditions
Supervision Conditions and the Constitution

The Presentence Investigation Report
Purposes of the PSI Report
Contents of the PSI Report
Preparing the PSI Report

The Initial Interview
Investigation and Verification
The Evaluative Summary
The Sentence Recommendation

Legal Issues Concerning the Presentence Report
Disclosure of the PSI Report
Inaccuracies in the PSI Report
Hearsay in the PSI Report
Does the Exclusionary Rule Apply?
Miranda Warnings and the PSI Interview
Right to a Lawyer During the PSI Interview

KEY TERMS

sentencing
reflective justice
presumptive sentencing grids
sentencing commission
standard conditions
special conditions
clear conditions

reasonable conditions
presentence investigation
   (PSI) report
post-sentence report
indeterminate sentence
offender-based presentence report
presentence investigation

determinate sentence
offense-based presentence report
victim impact statement
disclosure
hearsay evidence
exclusionary rule

Sentencing

Sentencing has long been considered the most difficult decision in the criminal justice process. **Sentencing** can be defined as the post-conviction stage in which the defendant is brought before the court for formal judgment pronounced by a judge. The judge is influenced by the presentence investigator's report as well as the wishes of the prosecutor and the defense attorney. Sentencing demands choosing among a number of alternatives and involves an examination of public safety, rehabilitation, deterrence, and retribution.

The philosophy behind community sentences is that an offender can best learn how to live productively in a community by remaining in free society under supervision, as opposed to being transferred to the setting of a jail or prison.

Sentencing
The postconviction stage, in which the defendant is brought before the court for formal judgment pronounced by a judge.

FACTORS THAT AFFECT GRANTING A COMMUNITY SENTENCE

The judge's decision to allow a defendant to serve a community corrections sentence depends on the offender's eligibility, the sentencing conditions fixed by statute, and the availability of community-based services.

Offender Eligibility for Community Corrections   A community corrections sentence is discretionary and a privilege, not a right. All eligible defendants must at least be considered for probation or some other intermediate sanction. States sometimes legislate restrictions against the use of probation for crimes of violence, or for those defendants with too many prior felony convictions. However, more serious felony offenders are being punished in the community due to plea bargaining and institutional crowding.

Conditions of Probation Fixed by Statute   The ability of the defendant to meet the statutory conditions of probation and other types of intermediate sanctions must be considered in the decision. If the presentence information about the defendant shows that he or she cannot meet the statutory conditions that must be imposed, then services will not be sought and probation conditions not met. For example, if restitution is required by statute, and a defendant is ordered to pay restitution in the amount of $700 per month but has a job that pays minimum wage, the defendant is barely able to meet his or her own bills, let alone be expected to make payments of an additional $700 per month. To avoid confronting the defendant and the court with dilemmas of this sort, many authorities recommend that statutes refrain from describing specific conditions, leaving the matter open for the judge to decide based on the most up-to-date information that can be obtained by competent presentence investigations about the defendant and the available treatment facilities and programs.

Availability of Community-Based Services   Granting a sentence in the community also depends on the availability and quality of other sentencing dispositions for that defendant. Availability is defined largely by whether a state has an existing community corrections act (see Chapter 4). A range of sentencing alternatives, including drug and alcohol counseling, day reporting centers, electronic monitoring, restitution, community service, home confinement, and intensive supervision programs, are widely utilized. The court may also be influenced by knowledge of institutional crowding or deplorable conditions in the adult prison system or of lack of treatment in youth institutions.

Reflective Justice
Each defendant's case is considered in total according to its subjectivities, harms, wrongs, and contexts, and then measured against concepts such as oppression, freedom, dignity, and equality.

Other Factors   When determining whether to grant probation, judges engage in a process of **reflective justice**, which means that each individual case is considered in terms of ". . . its subjectivities, harms, wrongs, and contexts, and then measured against concepts such as oppression, freedom, dignity, and equality" (Hudson 2006, p. 39). With reflective justice, judges consider the social stability of the defendant, defined by family ties, marital status, employment length, and drug abuse history. Judges also take into account whether the case was plea bargained or a trial, the political nature of the offense, and how their own decision may affect public opinion (Wicharaya 1995). Because judges can take so many factors into account, there was fear that individual judges would inconsistently apply their own philosophy, resulting in disparity, particularly with probation-eligible sentences. Many states opted to control judicial discretion through sentencing guidelines, which we discuss next.

SENTENCING GUIDELINES

Among the goals of sentencing guidelines and the determinate sentencing movement are to reduce or eliminate perceived sentencing disparity, increase judicial accountability for sentences, increase punishments for violent offenders, and provide a basis for population projections and resource allocation (Lubitz and Ross 2001). About half of all states have adopted some form of sentencing guidelines. Although these guidelines vary greatly from jurisdiction to jurisdiction, they generally establish a sentence based on the severity of the offense and the offender's prior criminal history.

Presumptive Sentencing Grid
A narrow range of sentencing guidelines that judges are obligated to use. Any deviations must be provided in writing and may also be subject to appellate court review.

With **presumptive sentencing grids,** judges are obligated to use the guidelines, and they must provide written reasons for any deviation from the guidelines.

These departures may also be subject to appellate court review. North Carolina and Pennsylvania have "structured presumptive sentencing zones"; that is, these states have integrated intermediate sanctions directly into both their felony and misdemeanor sentencing guidelines. Violent offenders in these states receive lengthier prison sentences, whereas nonviolent offenders can receive intermediate sanctions or other forms of community-based or even restorative justice sanctions (Lubitz and Ross 2001). We discuss North Carolina sentencing guidelines as an effective model.

North Carolina Sentencing Guidelines   How do you increase sentence lengths for only the most serious offenses *without* building new prisons? North Carolina has done so by incarcerating only the most serious offenders—so violent prisoners must serve 100 percent of their time in prison without early release. Violent offenders must also serve an automatic nine-month post-release community supervision, while sex offenders serve five years after prison. So far, this sounds like what many states did, except that sentencing guidelines in many states did not authorize community options. The difference between North Carolina and other states can be seen in their sentencing grid, which allows for more classes of crimes to be eligible for community-based corrections and builds that expectation right into the grid (see Figure 3.1). As a result, sentence lengths for violent offenders increased, but the *percent of sentenced offenders going to prison decreased*. The state instead increased its use of pretrial release programs, work release, day-reporting centers, and community substance abuse treatment programs for drug and nonviolent offenders.

"Sentence type" is listed for each class of crimes. North Carolina's sentencing grid (see Figure 3.1) has three types of sentences: (1) *Prison*; (2) residential intermediate sanctions/intensive supervision such as boot camps, and day reporting (*Res CC*); and (3) nonresidential punishments (*Probation*), which can include community drug treatment, community service, restitution, and fines. Prior record points are calculated as follows: 1 point per Class 1 or A1 misdemeanor, 2 points per property or drug felony, 4 points for each voluntary or involuntary manslaughter, 6 points for kidnapping/robbery/second-degree murder, 9 points for each rape, and 10 points for each first-degree murder (Wright 1998).

Within each class of crimes, you will also see an "aggravating" sentence, a "presumptive" sentence, and a "mitigating" sentence. The sentence may not deviate from the "presumptive," except in a predefined list of aggravating and mitigating circumstances. For example, if there was a firearm used in the crime (an aggravating circumstance), sixty months are added to the minimum. If "substantial assistance" is rendered for helping the prosecutor arrest or prosecute other criminals, judges may reduce or even suspend a mandatory sentence for drug defendants (a mitigating situation). Only sentences where a deviation occurred based on an aggravating or mitigating circumstance can be appealed, or if the prior record score was miscalculated. Research shows that North Carolina has been effective in differentiating the type of offenders sent to prison versus those who serve time in the community (Wright 1998). Any modifications of the grid must also show how the changes would impact the current number of prison beds or community resources. This sentencing grid and the subsequent changes tied to resources is the reason we chose this as a model of rational sentencing policy.

United States Sentencing Guidelines   The original United States Sentencing Guidelines set narrow, mandatory ranges of punishment based on the instant offense, the offender's prior criminal history, and facts that, if proven by a preponderance of the evidence, could potentially enhance an offender's sentence above the range in the guidelines. If the prosecutor could show aggravating facts to the sentencing judge, the court would be obligated to enhance the punishment even further.

FIGURE 3.1   North Carolina Felony Sentencing Grid (Numbers Represent Months)

PRIOR RECORD LEVEL

CURRENT FELONY CRIME CLASS		I 0 Pts	II 1–4 Pts	III 5–8 Pts	IV 9–14 Pts	V 15–18 Pts	VI 19+ Points
Class A: Murder		Death or Life Without Parole ONLY					
Class B1: Agg Sexual Battery	Sentence Type Aggravating	Prison 240–300	Prison 288–360	Prison 336–420	Prison 384–480	Prison Life Without Parole	Prison Life without Parole
Agg Child Molestation	Presumptive	192–240	230–288	269–336	307–384	346–433	384–480
Rape, Agg Sodomy	Mitigating	144–192	173–230	202–269	230–307	260–346	288–384
Class B2: Second-Deg. Murder	Sentence Type Aggravating Presumptive Mitigating	Prison 135–169 108–135 81–108	Prison 163–204 130–163 98–130	Prison 193–238 152–190 114–152	Prison 216–270 173–216 130–173	Prison 243–304 194–243 146–194	Prison 270–338 216–270 162–216
Class C: Kidnapping Second-Deg. Rape Agg Assault	Sentence Type Aggravating Presumptive Mitigating	Prison 63–79 50–63 38–50	Prison 86–108 69–86 52–69	Prison 100–125 80–100 60–80	Prison 115–144 92–115 69–92	Prison 130–162 104–130 78–104	Prison 145–181 116–145 87–116
Class D: Armed Robbery Burglary First-Deg. Arson	Sentence Type Aggravating Presumptive Mitigating	Prison 55–69 44–55 33–44	Prison 66–82 53–66 40–53	Prison 89–111 71–89 53–71	Prison 101–126 81–101 61–81	Prison 115–144 92–115 69–92	Prison 126–158 101–126 76–101
Class E: Child Molestation Drug Trafficking Drug Manuf/Selling	Sentence Type Aggravating Presumptive Mitigating	Res CC or Prison 25–31 20–25 15–20	Res CC or Prison 29–36 23–29 17–23	Prison 34–42 27–34 20–27	Prison 46–58 37–46 28–37	Prison 53–66 42–53 32–42	Prison 59–74 47–59 35–47
Class F: Involun. Manslaughter Att Rape, Incest, Cocaine 200–400 g	Sentence Type Aggravating Presumptive Mitigating	Res CC or Prison 16–20 13–16 10–13	Res CC or Prison 19–24 15–19 11–15	Res CC or Prison 21–26 17–21 13–17	Prison 25–31 20–25 15–20	Prison 34–42 27–34 20–27	Prison 39–49 31–39 23–31
Class G: Vehicular Homicide Second-Deg. Arson Robbery	Sentence Type Aggravating Presumptive Mitigating	Res CC or Prison 13–16 10–13 8–10	Res CC or Prison 15–19 12–15 9–12	Res CC or Prison 16–20 13–16 10–13	Res CC or Prison 20–25 16–20 12–16	Prison 21–26 17–21 13–17	Prison 29–36 23–29 17–23
Class H: Forgery, Theft Sale/Distribution LSD or Cocaine	Sentence Type Aggravating Presumptive Mitigating	Probation or Res 6–8 5–6 4–6	Res CC 8–10 6–8 4–6	Res CC or Prison 10–12 8–10 6–8	Res CC or Prison 11–14 9–11 7–9	Res CC or Prison 15–19 12–15 9–12	Prison 20–25 16–20 12–16
Class I: Poss Control. Sub Bad Checks Agg Stalking	Sentence Type Aggravating Presumptive Mitigating	Probation 6–8 4–6 3–4	Probation or CC 6–8 4–6 3–4	Res CC 6–8 5–6 4–5	Res CC or Prison 8–10 6–8 4–6	Res CC or Prison 9–11 7–9 5–7	Res CC or Prison 10–12 8–10 6–8

Source: North Carolina Sentencing and Policy Advisory Commission, Structured Sentencing for Felonies—Training and Reference Manual. (Raleigh: North Carolina Sentencing and Policy Advisory Commission, 1994).

Note: For each class of crimes, there is a disposition that directs the judge where the offender is to go (prison, residential community corrections, or probation), and then the judge selects the presumptive row, unless aggravating or mitigating circumstances warrant a deviation.

OFFENSE CLASS

U.S. vs. Booker (2005) ruled that this practice was unconstitutional, but there were two distinct majority opinions that followed. One majority opinion said that to enhance the punishment, the defendant must admit the aggravating circumstances or the prosecutor must prove to a jury beyond a reasonable doubt. The second majority opinion said that the Guidelines should be advisory rather than mandatory. This served to give federal judge's discretion in sentencing once again.

A small number of states (Arkansas, Delaware, Missouri, and Virginia) have voluntary guidelines that are suggestions that the judge may or may not accept. In Minnesota, sentencing guidelines are advisory, but departures from the established presumptive sentences should occur only when substantial, compelling circumstances exist.

SENTENCING COMMISSIONS

A **sentencing commission** is an independent body that monitors how the sentencing guidelines and judicial departures are used. The purpose is to use trend data over time to gauge whether sentencing disparities exist, restructure sentencing policies when needed, and make recommendations to the legislature. Sentencing commissions exist at the federal level and in about half of all states. Commission members are political appointees and have previous experience as prosecutors, defense attorneys, judges, academics, and probation or parole officers. At times, the group's diversity makes consensus difficult, and the commission is only an advisory body rather than a policy or rule-making one. Voting members number between 7 and 27, and a small number of commissions have both voting and non-voting members.

Sentencing Commission
A governing body that monitors the use of the sentencing guidelines and departures from the recommended sentences.

Conditions of Community Corrections

The authority to impose conditions of a community corrections sentence is vested with the courts. Although conditions may be recommended by the presentence investigator or probation officer, the judge has the final say regarding the conditions imposed on an offender. Box 3.1 shows the conditions of federal probation.

STANDARD CONDITIONS

Standard conditions are imposed on all community sentences in a jurisdiction, regardless of the nature of the offense committed. Standard conditions (also called "mandatory" conditions in the federal system) are either prescribed by law or set by court or agency practice and require any offender sentenced to a community corrections sanction to:

Standard Conditions
Conditions imposed on all offenders in all jurisdictions.

- Obey all federal and state laws and municipal ordinances
- Follow all directives of the supervising officer
- Work and/or attend school regularly
- Refrain from use of all controlled substances except those prescribed by a licensed medical practitioner
- Submit to drug testing
- Obtain permission from the probation officer before changing residence or employment, or leaving the jurisdiction
- Report regularly to the probation officer
- Report police contact or arrests to probation officer
- Refrain from associating with people who have criminal records unless permission is granted by the supervising officer

BOX 3.1   CONDITIONS OF FEDERAL PROBATION

Mandatory Conditions

The court shall provide, as an *explicit condition* of a sentence of probation that the defendant:

1. not commit another Federal, State, or local crime during the term of probation;
2. not unlawfully possess a controlled substance, refrain from any unlawful use of a controlled substance and submit to one drug test within 15 days of release on probation and at least 2 periodic drug tests thereafter;
3. will make restitution;
4. will pay the assessment imposed;
5. will notify the court of any material change in economic circumstances that might affect ability to pay restitution, fines, or special assessments;
6. will report the address where the person will reside and any subsequent change of residence to the probation officer;
7. if the court has imposed and ordered execution of a fine and placed the defendant on probation, payment of the fine; and
8. (only for a domestic violence crime)—attend a rehabilitation program that has been approved by the court, in consultation with a State Coalition Against Domestic Violence or other appropriate experts.

Discretionary Probation Conditions

The court may provide, as further conditions of a sentence of probation, to the extent that such conditions are reasonably related, that the defendant:

1. support his dependents and meet other family responsibilities;
2. make restitution to a victim of the offense;
3. work conscientiously at suitable employment or pursue conscientiously a course of study or vocational training that will equip him for suitable employment;
4. refrain from engaging in a specified occupation, business, or profession bearing a reasonably direct relationship to the conduct constituting the offense;
5. refrain from frequenting specified kinds of places or from associating unnecessarily with specified persons;
6. refrain from excessive use of alcohol, or any use of a narcotic drug or other controlled substance without a prescription by a licensed medical practitioner;
7. refrain from possessing a firearm, destructive device, or other dangerous weapon;
8. undergo available medical, psychiatric, or psychological treatment, including treatment for drug or alcohol dependency, as specified by the court, and remain in a specified institution if required for that purpose;
9. remain in the custody of the Bureau of Prisons during nights, weekends, or other intervals of time, totaling no more than the lesser of one year or the term of imprisonment authorized for the offense, during the first year of the term of probation;
10. reside at, or participate in the program of, a corrections facility (including a facility maintained contract to the Bureau of Prisons) for all or part of probation;
11. work in community service as directed by the court;
12. reside in a specified place or area, or refrain from residing in a specified place or area;
13. remain within the jurisdiction of the court, unless granted permission to leave by the court or a probation officer;
14. report to a probation officer as directed by the court or the probation officer;
15. permit a probation officer to visit him at his home or elsewhere as specified by the court;
16. answer inquiries by a probation officer and notify the probation officer promptly of any change in address or employment;
17. notify the probation officer promptly if arrested or if questioned by a law enforcement officer;
18. remain at his place of residence during nonworking hours and, if the court finds it appropriate, that compliance with this condition be monitored by telephonic or electronic signaling devices;
19. comply with the terms of any court order requiring payments by the defendant for the support and maintenance of a child or of a child and the parent with whom the child is living;
20. be ordered deported by a U.S. district court, if, after notice and hearing, the Attorney General demonstrates by clear and convincing evidence that the alien is deportable; and
21. satisfy such other conditions as the court may impose.

Source: U.S. Code, Title 18, Part II, Chapter 227, Subchapter B, Sec. 3563. *Conditions of Federal Probation*.

SPECIAL CONDITIONS

Special conditions (also known as discretionary conditions in the federal system) are additional stipulations tailored to fit the problems and needs of the offender. As such, the judge imposes them consistent with the crime committed or the offender's deficits in skill or ability. For example, the defendant may be required to:

- Attend literacy classes if the offender does not know how to read or write
- Obtain a GED if the offender did not finish high school
- Participate in drug or alcohol treatment if the offender is addicted
- Attend parenting classes if there are issues with dependent children
- Pay victim restitution if damage was caused
- Refrain from entering designated areas if the offense involves crimes against children
- Seek mental health treatment if the offender suffers from mental dysfunction

Limitations of Special Conditions   Special conditions of community supervision must be specific and **clear conditions**. Unclear conditions are invalid because they are unfair to the offender and, therefore, violate the offender's right to due process.

Second, the condition must be reasonable. **Reasonable conditions** result in compliance; conversely, unreasonable conditions lead to failure because the probationer cannot possibly comply with them. The definition of reasonable depends on an offender's circumstances and is decided on a case-by-case basis. For example, requiring an employed offender with a good salary to pay $500 each month in restitution may be reasonable, but the same condition would be unreasonable if it were imposed on an indigent probationer with a sixth-grade education.

Third, the supervision condition must either protect society or rehabilitate the offender, and it must be related in some way to the offense of conviction. For example, a state court invalidated a condition that a probationer be ordered to attend sex offender treatment because the treatment was not related to the offender's non-sexual offense (*State v. Bourrie* 2003).

Even a probationer who has never had a drinking problem and whose crime is unrelated to use of alcohol can be ordered to refrain from the use of alcoholic beverages. The Federal Court of Appeals held that the trial court could require that a defendant totally abstain from using alcohol during probation because in this case the defendant's *family* at the same residence had an active history of alcohol abuse and the defendant had a serious problem with illegal drugs (*United States v. Thurlow* 1995).

On the other hand, a defendant was placed on probation for tax-related offenses. One of the conditions imposed prohibited the defendant from leaving the judicial district without the permission of the court or the probation officer. The defendant thrice sought permission to travel to Russia, but permission was denied. The Federal Court of Appeals concluded that the denial of the travel request was not reasonably related to the defendant's rehabilitation or the protection of the public; thus the probationer was allowed to go to Russia (*United States v. Porotsky* 1997).

There is controversy over whether conditions known as "scarlet letter" conditions, with their public shaming qualities, do or do not serve a rehabilitative purpose (see Box 3.2). If a condition of probation is found to be unclear, unreasonable, or unrelated to rehabilitation or public safety, that particular condition is voided, but the community sentence as a whole remains valid.

Special Conditions
Conditions tailored to fit the needs of an offender.

Clear Conditions
Conditions that are sufficiently explicit so as to inform a reasonable person of the conduct that is required or prohibited.

Reasonable Conditions
Probation conditions that the offender can reasonably comply with.

BOX 3.2   COMMUNITY CORRECTIONS UP CLOSE

Are Scarlet Letter Probation Conditions Rehabilitative or Unnecessary?

Scarlet letter conditions of community supervision involve publicly shaming an offender by notifying the community of the nature of the offender's conviction. For example, notification laws inform the public of the identity and residence of sex offenders. These laws vary from state to state, with some laws requiring information regarding the residence of a sex offender to be published in a local newspaper and others requiring residents living near a convicted sex offender to be individually notified of the offender's residence. Although the legislative purpose was to protect the community by informing people of potentially dangerous offenders living in their midst, these laws also make it extremely difficult for a sex offender to become rehabilitated. Oftentimes the identity of these offenders, including their photograph, and a description of the crime committed, are made public on the Internet (Zevitz and Farkas 2000). We discuss these laws in more detail in Chapter 15.

A more controversial condition of probation is one that requires an offender to personally proclaim guilt to the public. Appellate courts in the country are sharply divided on the validity of such a condition. For example, in *Goldschmitt v. State* (1986) a trial court ordered a probationer, convicted of drunken driving, to place a bumper sticker on his car reading "Convicted D.U.I.—Restricted Licensee" as a condition of probation. The appellate court upheld the imposition of this condition, stating that it served a sufficient rehabilitative purpose and that it did not constitute cruel and unusual punishment. In *Ballenger v. State* (1993), a Georgia appellate court upheld the imposition of a condition requiring a probationer to wear a fluorescent pink plastic bracelet imprinted with the words "D.U.I. CONVICT."

Critics of shaming sentences say that it is inappropriate for the government to become involved in degradation practices; others believe that some offenders will use this opportunity as a "publicity stunt" (Reske 1996). A number of jurisdictions, however, have disallowed the imposition of scarlet letter conditions. In *People v. Heckler* (1993), the trial court imposed a condition on a probationer, convicted of shoplifting, that he wear a T-shirt bearing a bold, printed statement of his status as a felony theft probationer whenever he was outside his living quarters. The appellate court, relying on state constitutional grounds, found that this condition impinged on his inalienable right to

privacy. The court further noted that this condition, which required him to wear this T-shirt whenever he was outside his home, would undermine certain other aims of his probation, such as procuring gainful employment and staying employed.

In *People v. Meyer* (1997), a trial court ordered a defendant to erect at his home a 4-foot by 8-foot sign with 8-inch high lettering that read "Warning! A Violent Felon Lives Here. Enter at Your Own Risk!" The Illinois Supreme Court found that the purpose of this sign was to inflict humiliation on the probationer. The court further noted that the statutory provisions for probation in Illinois did not include humiliation as a punishment. Thus, the court disallowed this condition.

A California court, however, has disallowed the imposition of a scarlet letter condition on state, not federal, constitutional grounds. Challenging the constitutionality of scarlet letter or shaming conditions based on a violation of federal constitutional rights is more difficult, but it may raise First Amendment violations of free speech if the condition requires probationers to "speak their own shame" (P. Kelly 1999, p. 863).

Finally, in *People v. Letterlough* (1995), the New York Court of Appeals rejected the imposition of a condition that the defendant affix to the license plate of any vehicle he drove a fluorescent sign stating "convicted DWI" on the grounds that this condition was not reasonably related to the defendant's rehabilitation.

These cases indicate a split in court decisions. Courts that have disallowed the imposition of scarlet letter or shame conditions usually do so on the grounds that the trial court exceeded its statutory authority. They thus leave open the question to the U.S. Supreme Court on whether a state legislature can amend its laws and authorize a trial court to impose a scarlet letter condition.

Jurisdictions that have upheld scarlet letter or shaming conditions have done so on the grounds that the condition furthers the rehabilitation aims of probation by deterring the offender from committing similar crimes in the future. These courts have also held that shaming conditions do not violate the Eighth Amendment prohibition against cruel and unusual punishment. The U.S. Supreme Court has yet to rule on this matter, so the issue has not been conclusively resolved.

SUPERVISION CONDITIONS AND THE CONSTITUTION

By virtue of a criminal conviction, offenders have diminished constitutional rights, but they nonetheless retain rights that are considered basic and fundamental. When fundamental constitutional rights are limited or infringed upon by a condition of probation, the government must establish a "compelling state interest" that would justify keeping the condition.

First Amendment Rights   First Amendment rights of religion, speech, assembly, press, and petitioning the government for redress of grievances are considered basic, fundamental rights that deserve protection by the courts. For example, much of the literature of Alcoholics Anonymous (A.A.) refers to monotheistic principles and encourages prayer, leading the court to conclude that, although not a religion per se, the elements of A.A. infringed on a person's First Amendment rights of religion. Therefore, requiring A.A. meeting attendance as a condition of probation was ruled unconstitutional (*Warner v. Orange County Department of Probation* 1997). Multiple courts have reaffirmed this ruling, with the most recent Federal Appellate ruling allowing a parolee to sue a parole officer or department for ordering the parolee (who was a Buddhist) to attend A.A. and recommending revocation for failure to attend (*Inouye, V. Kemna 2007*).

Searches and Seizures   The Fourth Amendment right against unreasonable searches and seizures is not as highly protected for probationers as other constitutional rights. In *Griffin v. Wisconsin* (1987), the U.S. Supreme Court ruled that a warrantless search of a probationer's home is valid as long as reasonable grounds exist to believe contraband is present in violation of the conditions of probation. The Court also found that the departmental policy regulation permitting the search, on which the probation officer had relied, was consistent with the Fourth Amendment's "reasonableness" requirement and was therefore valid.

When a police officer or a probation officer has reasonable suspicion that a probationer has violated one or more probation conditions, or if a search may yield evidence that a probationer has been engaged in criminal activity, the Supreme Court ruled that the police officer can conduct a warrantless search of a probationer's home (*United States v. Knights* 2001).

The Privilege Against Self-Incrimination   The Fifth Amendment guarantees the privilege against self-incrimination. Does a probation condition that compromises this right violate the Constitution? The answer is probably "no." In *McKune v. Lile* (2002), the U.S. Supreme Court held that a sex offender treatment program inside a Kansas prison that required an acknowledgment of all prior sex offenses does not violate the Fifth Amendment's privilege against self-incrimination. The Court justified its decision by stating that acknowledging past crimes in the treatment program was the beginning of rehabilitation, because doing so meant that the prisoner accepted responsibility for his or her actions. According to the Supreme Court, acknowledging past crimes for rehabilitation purposes (even if the state offered no immunity and made no promises not to prosecute) for convicted offenders is different from the Fifth Amendment protection used when the state gathers information for investigatory purposes for criminal prosecution. It is likely that this case would extend to convicted probationers who are ordered to attend treatment, but the future for probationers is uncertain at this point.

The Presentence Investigation Report

Presentence Investigation (PSI) Report
A report submitted to the court before sentencing describing the nature of the offense, offender characteristics, criminal history, loss to the victim, and sentencing recommendations.

Prior to the judicial sentencing decision, many probation departments provide the judge a **presentence investigation (PSI) report**. The PSI is a document prepared by a probation officer to aid judges in the felony sentencing decision, or for offenders who have violated probation and are facing a potential incarceration sentence. The PSI is also used by prosecutors, defense attorneys, parole boards, and probation or parole officers in carrying out their tasks and making decisions. Although U.S. probation officers are involved in both case supervision and conducting five or six presentence investigations per month (Quinn 2002), most state and local probation agencies separate the investigation and supervision duties—designating some probation officers to only conduct presentence investigations and write PSI reports, whereas other officers supervise cases.

The probation officer submits the presentence investigation report to the court before sentencing. The PSI report describes the nature of the offense, offender characteristics, criminal history, loss to the victim, and sentencing recommendations. In juvenile court, the judge is furnished with a social history, or predispositional report, prior to the disposition hearing. Presentence reports are seldom required in sentencing for misdemeanor crimes. In practice, the judge who sentences for a misdemeanor relies on the police officer for information about the defendant's criminal history and the circumstances of the offense.

Although the PSI has been used since the early 1900s, the U.S. Supreme Court declared the PSI report to be a valid instrument in 1949 (*Williams v. New York*). The original function of presentence investigation reports was to assist the court in resolving the issue of whether to grant probation. Over the years, however, the PSI report has been used for the entire range of correctional punishments and programs. The PSI report's content and prevalence of use have changed with the philosophical shift from rehabilitation to punishment, and the statutory shift from indeterminate to determinate sentencing.

PURPOSES OF THE PSI REPORT

The primary purpose of the presentence investigation report is to provide the judge with timely, relevant, and accurate data on which to base a rational sentencing decision. The PSI report also assists jail and prison institutions in their classification of inmates, and in suggesting types of institutional programming that would fit the offender's needs while incarcerated. Paroling authorities use the PSI report to obtain information that is pertinent to resources upon release, such as family support, employment opportunities, and the like. Probation and parole supervisors use the PSI report when assigning offenders to caseloads. Field officers use the PSI report when writing a treatment or program plan (Petersilia 2002; Norman and Wadman 2000). Another purpose of the PSI report is to enable probation officers to establish and maintain credibility with judges, prosecutors, and probation supervisors. Probation officers are not seeking to change a judge's mind—they are merely attempting to summarize the case before them and provide sufficient and reasonable evidence (Kittrie, Zenoff, and Eng 2002).

About 64 percent of all felony cases nationwide included a PSI prior to sentencing. About half of all states require a presentence investigation in all felony cases, whereas a PSI is discretionary in 16 states, and nonexistent in about 10 states (Petersilia 2002). In the federal system, PSIs have increased in significance because federal probation officers are considered to be experts on federal sentencing guidelines. In one year in the federal system alone, federal probation officers wrote 65,156 presentence and post-sentence reports and completed an additional 52,047 collateral presentence investigations for another district and 27,117 prerelease investigations for military defendants (U.S. Department of Justice 2005a). This expertise has been bestowed on probation officers out of convenience, and some scholars believe that this new responsibility conflicts with the original philosophical intent of probation (Kittrie, Zenoff, and Eng 2002).

A **post-sentence report** may be written after the defendant has pled guilty and waived the presentence report, and the court proceeds directly to sentencing in accordance with the plea agreement. In such cases, the post-sentence report serves to aid the probation or parole officer in supervision efforts during probation or parole or supervised release and to assist the prison system in classification, programming, and release planning (Stinchcomb and Hippensteel 2001). It is estimated that half of all investigation reports written at the state level are post-sentence reports.

With the introduction of sentencing guidelines, sentencing has become less discretionary, and the importance of the PSI has declined in some states. For example, in some jurisdictions where sentencing guidelines are used, probation officers no longer write presentence reports. Instead they complete a "guidelines worksheet" and calculate the presumptive sentence. This short form deprives other agencies in the criminal justice system of valuable information about the offender.

CONTENTS OF THE PSI REPORT

For jurisdictions that do conduct a PSI, what are the essentials of a presentence report? The philosophy guiding the preparation of presentence reports may be characterized as either offender-based or offense-based.

Offender-based PSI reports: 1920s–1980s   During the era of **indeterminate sentencing**, presentence investigation reports were **offender-based** and focused on rehabilitation. That is, probation officers were guided in their **presentence investigation** by a philosophy that attempted to understand the causes of an offender's antisocial behavior and clinically evaluated the offender's potential for change. By learning about the character of the person under consideration, and the external influences that surrounded him or her, an offender-based PSI suggested alternatives for sentencing beyond incarceration that were specific to that offender.

Offense-based PSI reports: 1980s–present   The content of the presentence investigation reports changed to reflect the change to determinate sentencing. An **offense-based presentence report** focuses primarily on the crime committed. The sentencing court is concerned with the offender's culpability in the offense, whether anyone was injured, whether a firearm was used, the extent of loss to the victim(s), and other aspects of the offense. Secondary information about the offender is considered relevant, such as prior criminal record, employment history, family ties, health, and drug use. An instruction for how to conduct and write an offense-based presentence report is provided in Case Study No. 3 at the end of this chapter.

In jurisdictions where the court uses sentencing guidelines to determine appropriate sentences, the emphasis of the PSI report is on applying the particular guidelines to the facts of the case. This means that all presentence reports should be factually accurate, objective, nonjudgmental, and ideally verified by the presentence officer. The report's length and content should be appropriate to the seriousness of the offense. The greater the consequences of a judgment, the more likely it is that the court or a subsequent decision-making body will need more information.

Post-Sentence Report
A report written by a probation officer after the defendant has pled guilty and been sentenced in order to aid probation and parole officers in supervision, classification, and program plans.

indeterminate sentencing
A sentencing philosophy that encourages rehabilitation and incorporates a broad sentencing range where discretionary release is determined by a parole board based on the offender's remorse, insight into his or her mistakes, involvement in rehabilitation, and readiness to return to society.

Offender-Based Presentence Report
A presentence investigation report that seeks to understand the offender and the circumstances of the offense and to evaluate the offender's potential as a law-abiding, productive citizen.

Presentence Investigation
An investigation undertaken by a probation officer for the purpose of gathering and analyzing information to complete a report for the court.

Offense-Based Presentence Report
A presentence investigation report that focuses primarily on the offense committed, the offender's culpability, and prior criminal history.

Probation officers have often noted that judges frequently only skimmed their lengthy reports and skipped to the end of the report where the officer recommends a sentence. In response to this reality, some jurisdictions have moved to shortened versions that focus only on certain relevant variables. In some cases, these brief versions of the PSI report are presented to the court in a "fill-in-the blanks" format. This practice places a duty on the probation officer to present the most critical information in a concise, yet complete, manner. Others are open-ended and in paragraph format, analogous to an essay.

Victim Impact Statement
A written account by the victim(s) as to how the crime has taken a toll physically, emotionally, financially, or psychologically on the victim and the victim's family. Victim impact statements are considered by many states at time of sentencing and at parole board hearings.

Federal and some state presentence reports also require a **victim impact statement**. The use of victim impact statements stems from renewed interest in victims' rights and mitigating the harm the offender caused. The victim impact statement identifies the name of the victim and his or her relationship to the offender. This statement informs the judge about the physical injury the victim may have suffered, whether the victim sought medical attention, whether he or she endured physical rehabilitation, and the permanency of the injuries. A victim impact statement includes the emotional and psychological toll the offense had on the victim and the victim's family. A breakdown of the victim's financial costs that were not covered by the victim compensation fund are also provided. An example of a victim impact statement is shown in Box 3.3.

BOX 3.3   A SAMPLE VICTIM IMPACT STATEMENT

A male defendant, age 34, was charged with Assault First Degree, two counts Assault Second Degree, Armed Criminal Action, Kidnapping, two counts of Burglary and Felonious Restraint.

The male defendant followed the female victim when she moved from South Carolina to Missouri. They had two young boys together, ages 8 and 10. Based on the defendant's previous arrests for domestic violence in South Carolina, the victim obtained a full order of protection upon arriving in Missouri, with the court giving her full custody of their children and prohibiting him from having any contact with her. She chose not to list her residence since she was attempting to keep that information confidential. She did allow for him to call their sons on weekends; however, she indicated that he never called to speak to their children.

On Valentine's Day, he broke into her apartment, ripped out the lining of her couch, and hid inside of it. Upon her arrival home with their sons, he woke up (he had fallen asleep waiting for her). She sat on the couch, and he popped out of it and began to assault her. She was beaten severely around her face, arms, and stomach area. The entire assault was in front of their two sons. Finally, she was able to get to a gun, which she kept loaded in her bedroom closet. He managed to rip the gun from her hands, and he shot her point blank in the forehead.

The victim survived the attack and attempted murder. She chose to give the following victim impact statement at the sentencing hearing:

"In front of our boys, you tried to kill their mother. It has always been about you. I had to move six states away from you, to another time zone, and it wasn't far enough. You have cost me two jobs and a lifetime of self-esteem. The bullet is lodged in my forehead. Would you like to feel it? You put it there. I know that it wasn't smart of me to have a loaded gun in my house with two young children. Does everyone see now what choice I had? I didn't have any choices. You made all of my decisions for me. I told you that I wanted to live near my family again someday. I did not take the children away from you, and I did not move for any man. Although, that is what you want to believe.

The funny thing is, I forgive you. Even though I have $100,000 dollars in medical expenses to pay, the state was only able to cover the first $15,000, I would rather be stuck with that debt, than stuck with you. Tell me again that you will pay for my hospital bills as long as I don't testify against you. Well, you always said that you wanted to live in Missouri, congratulations, now you have your chance."

Source: State of Missouri v. Anthony Williams CR2000-00704.

A probation officer interviews an offender to prepare a presentence investigation report before the sentencing hearing.

PREPARING THE PSI REPORT

Preparing the PSI report requires many important skills, including interviewing, investigating, and writing. The probation officer's responsibility is to gather the facts about the offense and the offender, verify the information received, and present it in an organized and objective format.

The preferred practice is to conduct the presentence investigation and prepare the presentence report after adjudication of guilt, but before the sentencing hearing (Storm 1997). The presentence investigation should not be undertaken until after a finding of guilt because none of the material in the presentence report is admissible at the trial or during plea negotiation, and the investigation represents an invasion of privacy.

Exceptions to this rule are allowed when the defendant's attorney consents to the preparation of the report before conviction and plea. When this happens, it is called a "pre-plea report." Attorneys are generally not open to a pre-plea or pre-arraignment document over a regular PSI (Alarid and Montemayor forthcoming).

THE INITIAL INTERVIEW

The first task in preparing any type of PSI report is to interview the newly convicted offender. This meeting usually occurs in the probation officer's office or, if the defendant has not been released on bail, in jail. In some cases the initial interview takes place at the defendant's home, which provides the officer the opportunity to observe the offender's home environment and thus offers an additional dimension to the officer's understanding of the defendant. The home visit may also allow the probation officer to verify information gained from the offender with family members. The officer may also assess the offender's standard of living and relationships with family members.

The initial interview is devoted to completing a worksheet that elicits information about the offender: his or her criminal history, education, employment, physical and emotional health, family, and other relevant data. The officer also uses this

BOX 3.4	**TECHNOLOGY IN CORRECTIONS**

The PSI Report for the Cybercriminal

A "cybercriminal" uses the computer to commit a wide array of crimes, from sex crimes such as child solicitation and child pornography to identity theft, fraud, and computer hacking. When writing a presentence investigation report for a cybercriminal, it is recommended that the probation officer "determine the offender's computer knowledge and motive for participation in the offense [whether it be greed, anger, or mental illness]" (p. 8).

The PSI officer should conduct a home visit to determine what type of computer equipment and access are present. In addition, the officer should recommend special conditions such as anger management, mental health counseling, restitution, and limiting the offender's usage of a computer. Such conditions include disallowing access to a computer or a connected device, Internet or Intranet access, bulletin boards, and the use of encryption (p. 8).

Source: Brian J. Kelly. 2001. Supervising the Cyber-Criminal. *Federal Probation* 65(2): 8–10.

---

time to develop some initial sense of the offender's character, personality, needs, and problems. It is important that the presentence investigator understand a wide variety of crimes so that each PSI report is tailored to the particular crime committed (for example, see Box 3.4 for factors that a presentence probation officer must consider when writing a PSI for a cybercriminal).

INVESTIGATION AND VERIFICATION

Following the initial interview, the probation officer begins the task of investigating and verifying information supplied by the offender and obtaining employment, military, education, and criminal history records from local, state, and federal agencies. Many of these records are protected by state and federal privacy laws, and obtaining them may require the defendant's written permission. A presentence officer may need to review "court dockets, plea agreements, investigative reports from numerous agencies, previous probation or parole records, pretrial services records, criminal history transcripts, vital statistics records, medical records, counseling and substance abuse treatment records, scholastic records, employment records, financial records, and others" (Storm 1997, p. 13).

If time permits, the officer should also interview the defendant's family and friends, the prosecutor of the case, the defense counsel, the arresting police officer, the victim and/or victim's family, and the defendant's present employer or school officials. The probation officer is interested in information that might influence the sentencing decision but which is omitted during the trial, particularly any aggravating or mitigating circumstances. When obtaining information from any source—particularly from relatives, friends, acquaintances, and employers—the probation officer must be careful to distinguish facts from conclusions. As a general rule, the report should contain only information the probation officer knows to be accurate. In some cases, information may be presented that the officer has been unable to verify. When that is necessary, the officer should clearly denote the information as "unconfirmed" or "unverified."

THE EVALUATIVE SUMMARY

In writing the evaluative summary, probation officers must practice their analytical ability, diagnostic skills, and understanding of human behavior. They must

BOX 3.5   TECHNOLOGY IN CORRECTIONS

Telecommuting for Presentence Officers

Probation office budgets have not kept pace with the increased numbers of probationers being supervised in the community. Many probation officers across the country must share office space, which makes officer rapport and confidentiality difficult to maintain. As a result, many federal probation offices have experimented with telecommuting. Telecommuting allows presentence officers to complete the presentence investigation report from home using laptops, telephone calling cards, electronic computer access, and remote system linkages. Telecommuters are home two or three days out of every workweek and reportedly are more satisfied with their jobs than when they were working strictly out of the office. In addition, presentence officers who telecommuted were more productive from home than they had been before the telecommuting program began. One federal probation office in Florida found that telecommuting was more successful for officers who wrote presentence investigation reports than for officers who supervised a caseload full of clients. Telecommuting was so successful that the Middle District of Florida now allows officers with at least two years of presentence experience and "above average performance evaluations" to apply.

Source: Christopher Hansen. 2001. The Cutting Edge: A Survey of Technological Innovation: Where Have All the Probation Officers Gone? *Federal Probation* 65(1): 51–53.

bring into focus the kind of person that is before the court, the basic factors that brought the person into trouble, and the special assistance the defendant needs for resolving those difficulties. Part of the evaluative summary should include the offender's probability of risk to the community, the amount of harm the offender caused the victim and/or the community, the defendant's ability to pay restitution and court fines, and the defendant's need for treatment (Storm 1997). Writing the presentence report can actually be conducted while telecommuting from home (see Box 3.5).

THE SENTENCE RECOMMENDATION

The probation officer's recommended sentence to the judge largely depends on the sentencing guideline system or statutory equivalent. It is important to note that presentence officers recommend a sentence type, but *not* a sentence length. "Probation officers can play in the ball park but they don't make the rules" (Kittrie, Zenoff, and Eng 2002, p. 125).

One study in Ohio demonstrated that the sentencing judge adopted the probation officer's recommendation in 66 percent of the cases when prison was recommended and in 85 percent of the cases when probation was recommended. Another study in Utah found that the court agreed with the probation officer's recommendation about 91 percent of the time in felony and misdemeanor cases. Of the 9 percent of cases that resulted in a departure, half resulted in a more severe sentence and the other half in a less-severe sentence than originally recommended (Norman and Wadman 2000).

When judges, prosecutors, and public defenders were surveyed on their attitudes about the PSI, judges and prosecutors were in higher agreement than were public defenders that the sentencing recommendation should be retained as a part of the PSI report, and that the recommendations made by probation officers were appropriate. Most judges, prosecutors, and public defenders surveyed believed that the appropriate use of sentencing guidelines facilitated the reduction of sentencing disparity (Norman and Wadman 2000).

Alarid and Montemayor (forthcoming) found that legal factors such as the defendant's criminal history, previous times on probation and parole, pending cases, and the police version of the offense were more important to attorneys than extra-legal factors. Important extra-legal factors for both prosecutors and defense attorneys included social support systems, mental health issues, and substance abuse items. While legal factors may be used to control sentencing disparity, extra-legal factors were seen as valuable to aid practitioners in identifying treatment intervention services.

Legal Issues Concerning the Presentence Report

Various courts concerning the PSI report have addressed several legal issues. The most important questions raised are these: Does the defendant have a constitutional right to disclosure of the PSI report? Are inaccuracies in the PSI report legal grounds for resentencing? Is hearsay information in the PSI report allowable? Does the exclusionary rule apply to the PSI report? Must the *Miranda* warnings be given when a defendant is asked questions by the probation officer for the PSI report? Does the defendant have a right to counsel during the PSI report interview?

DISCLOSURE OF THE PSI REPORT

Disclosure
The right of a defendant to read and refute information in the presentence investigation report prior to sentencing.

Disclosure is the opportunity for the defendant (and/or the defendant's attorney) to view a draft of the presentence report. In the federal system, the defendant can view the PSI draft at least 35 days prior to sentencing, and then has 14 days to refute any statements prior to the final report submission to federal court. The U.S. Supreme Court held that there is no denial of due process of law when a court considers a presentence investigation report without disclosing its contents to the defendant or giving the defendant an opportunity to rebut it (*Williams v. Oklahoma* 1959; *Williams v. New York* 1949). A defendant may have such right, however, if disclosure is required by state law or court decisions in that jurisdiction. The PSI is not, however, a public document, so disclosure is limited to the defendant, the defendant's attorney, and the prosecutor.

After the final report has been submitted to the court, the probation officer may have to verbally answer questions about the report for the judge, and in some cases, maybe asked to testify in court on how he or she arrived at the sentencing recommendations (Storm 1997).

Compulsory disclosure has generally been opposed by judges and probation officers because third parties having knowledge about the offender may refuse to give information if they know that they can be called into court and subjected to cross-examination and that the defendant will have access to their statements (Kittrie, Zenoff, and Eng 2002). In the words of one court, the fear is that disclosure of the report "would have a chilling effect on the willingness of various individuals to contribute information that would be incorporated into the report" (*United States v. Trevino* 1996).

A second concern is that permitting the defendant to challenge the presentence report could unduly delay the proceedings. The defendant may challenge everything in the report and transform the sentencing procedure virtually into a new trial.

A third concern is protecting the confidential nature of the information in the report. To safeguard these concerns, the federal system requires withholding various parts of the PSI from the defendant when:

- Disclosure might disrupt rehabilitation of the defendant (such as psychiatric reports addressing future dangerousness).
- Information was obtained on a promise of confidentiality.
- Harm may result to the defendant or to any other person from such disclosure.

The opposite view—advocating disclosure of the presentence report—is rooted in due process, meaning fundamental fairness. Because the PSI report might have a significant influence on the type and length of sentence to be imposed, due process demands that convicted people should have access to the information on which their sentence is to be based so that they can correct inaccuracies and challenge falsehoods. Furthermore, in jurisdictions where the accused has access to the reports, the sentencing hearings have not been unduly delayed.

In sum, federal rules represent an intermediate position between complete disclosure and complete secrecy. In jurisdictions that practice disclosure, the release of the presentence report has not resulted in the problems that have been anticipated by the opponents of the practice. Instead, it seems to have led the probation services to develop skills for analyzing the offense and the offender more objectively. With greater objectivity has come greater reliance on the reports by the courts and a resultant increase in the number of reports requested and people granted probation.

INACCURACIES IN THE PSI REPORT

Disclosure policies attempt to minimize errors in the final PSI report submitted to the court. Two federal circuit courts ruled that detected inaccuracies in the PSI report are not grounds for automatic revocation of the sentence imposed (*United States v. Lockhart* 1995; *United States v. Riviera* 1996). Both courts based their decisions on a determination of whether the inaccuracies were harmless or harmful. If the error is harmless (meaning that the error would *not* have affected the sentencing outcome), then reversal is not justified. If the inaccuracies would have changed the sentencing outcome, the defendant has the burden of establishing that the error was harmful. If a defendant is sentenced on the basis of a report that is materially false or unreliable, that person's due process rights are violated (*Moore v. United States* 1978; *United States v. Lasky* 1979). The remedy in these cases is vacating the original sentence and remanding the case to the trial court to prepare a new PSI report prior to resentencing.

HEARSAY IN THE PSI REPORT

Hearsay evidence is information that does not come from direct knowledge of the person giving the information but from knowledge that person received from a third party. Although hearsay is not admissible in trial, hearsay is not in and of itself constitutionally objectionable in a PSI report. The reason for this is that the purpose of the report is to help the judge determine an appropriate sentence for the defendant. It is important that the judge be given every opportunity to obtain relevant information during sentencing without rigid adherence to rules of evidence. Because the report is usually not compiled and written by a person with legal training, the judge

Hearsay Evidence
Information offered as a truthful assertion that does not come from the personal knowledge of the person giving the information but from knowledge that person received from a third party.

must exercise proper and wise discretion as to the sources and types of information he or she might want to use.

DOES THE EXCLUSIONARY RULE APPLY?

Exclusionary Rule
A rule of evidence that enforces the Fourth Amendment's prohibition against unreasonable search and seizure, whereby illegal police searches are not admissible in a court of law. The purpose is to deter police misconduct.

The **exclusionary rule** provides that evidence seized in violation of the Fourth Amendment prohibition against unreasonable searches and seizures is not admissible in a court of law. The exclusionary rule does not apply to PSI reports. Courts have consistently resisted efforts to extend the exclusionary rule to proceedings other than the trial itself and only in instances in which the misconduct was by the police. Some might argue that sentencing is so closely related to the trial that the use of illegally obtained evidence should not be allowed to influence the sentencing proceedings. Courts, however, have rejected this argument.

Another issue that has arisen is whether the exclusionary rule applies in cases in which the illegally obtained evidence is acquired by the probation officer or the police solely for use in a PSI report and not in connection with an investigation for a criminal act. Local courts likely will decide based on state rules rather than on a possible violation of a constitutional right. Evidence illegally seized cannot be used in the PSI report if its use is prohibited by state or case law.

MIRANDA WARNINGS AND THE PSI INTERVIEW

Miranda v. Arizona (1966) held that warnings must be given whenever a suspect is under "custodial interrogation." These warnings are as follows:

1. You have a right to remain silent.
2. Anything you say can be used against you in a court of law.
3. You have the right to an attorney.
4. If you cannot afford an attorney, one will be appointed for you prior to questioning.

Appellate courts held that *Miranda* warnings do not need to be given by the probation officer when interviewing a defendant in connection with the PSI report. The presentence investigation does not trigger the defendant's right to be free from self-incrimination even if the defendant is in custody and facing serious punishment (*United States v. Allen* 1993; *United States v. Washington* 1993).

RIGHT TO A LAWYER DURING THE PSI INTERVIEW

The Tenth Circuit court held that a defendant does not have a Sixth Amendment right to have an attorney present during the PSI report interview (*United States v. Gordon* 1993; *United States v. Washington* 1993). During the interview the probation officer acts as an agent of the court charged with assisting the court in arriving at a fair sentence, not as an agent of the prosecution. In most cases, guilt has already been determined; hence, the adversarial situation that requires the assistance of a lawyer is absent.

However, a Massachusetts court disagreed, saying the defendant has a right to counsel at the PSI interview because this interview plays a crucial role in the officer's sentencing recommendation to the judge and therefore has "due process implications with respect to a defendant's interest in a fair and even-handed sentence proceeding" (*Commonwealth of Massachusetts v. Talbot* 2005). Defense counsel can, in fact, be helpful in clarifying legal terms for the defendant and assist in articulating the defendant's views for the probation officer so that revisions of the initial draft will be minimal. The legal issues of the PSI continue to be clarified over time.

SUMMARY

- Granting a community sentence to an individual offender depends primarily on the severity of the current offense and prior criminal history.

- Community values and the individual judge's philosophy of sentencing contribute to the decision. Sentencing philosophy can be based on one or more of the following: retribution, incapacitation, deterrence, rehabilitation, and "just deserts."

- The needs of the offender, the risk the offender poses in the protection of society, and the maintenance of social order must all be carefully weighed. The balancing of the best interests of both the offender and society is the crux of sentencing.

- The use of sentencing guidelines has reduced some sentencing inequality at the expense of reducing judicial discretion to sentence on a case-by-case basis.

- Supervision conditions are both standard conditions (imposed on all probationers in a jurisdiction) and special conditions (tailored to fit the offender and offense).

- Each community condition must be clear, reasonable, related to the protection of society and the rehabilitation of the offender, and constitutional.

- The presentence investigation report is a confidential document written by a person with a social science background rather than a strictly legal background.

- The primary purpose of a presentence report is to examine and expose the factors that will mitigate for or against successful community supervision.

- The legal issues in the PSI include: the offender has the opportunity to refute information contained in the PSI, hearsay evidence is allowed, and the presentence interview does not require Miranda warnings, nor the presence of an attorney.

DISCUSSION QUESTIONS

1. What should be the purpose of sentencing for first-time felony offenders—rehabilitation, deterrence, incapacitation, or retribution? What about for repeat offenders?

2. Is it more important that sentences be consistent to all offenders of a similar class of crimes or that sentences be individualized to the characteristics and needs of each offender?

3. How might sentencing guidelines affect the sentencing decision?

4. How might the availability and quality of other sentencing dispositions affect the decision to grant a sentence in the community?

5. What are the ways a judge obtains sentencing information? Which do you believe is the most useful way to establish just and fair sentences? Why?

6. Argue for or against the proposition that probation conditions should be left solely to the discretion of judges and should not be prescribed by law.

7. What are the limitations on the power of courts to impose conditions? Why are these limitations important?

8. Argue for or against scarlet letter conditions for a person convicted of Driving While Intoxicated for the first time.

9. Does a condition that dictates participation in a treatment program that requires admission of guilt as a prerequisite violate a probationer's right against self-incrimination? Justify your answer.

10. Given the time and effort it takes to complete a PSI interview and report, is the effort worth it? Why or why not?

11. How have sentencing guidelines affected the content of the PSI report?

12. What is the purpose of the victim impact statement in a PSI report? What factors brought about the use of this statement?

13. What is the federal rule regarding disclosure of the PSI report? What are the arguments for and against disclosure? What is the middle-ground approach to disclosure?

14. What factor(s) might explain why probation officers' recommendations are so highly correlated with actual sentences imposed by judges?

15. What suggestions do you have for improving the content of the PSI report?

WEB SITES

Families against Mandatory Minimums
    http://www.famm.org

Executive Summary of the Risk Assessment Used in Virginia Sentencing
    http://www.ncsconline.org/WC/Publications/
    Res_Senten_RiskAssessExecSumPub.pdf

U.S. Sentencing Commission
    http://www.ussc.gov

History of the Presentence Investigative Report
    http://www.cjcj.org/files/the_history.pdf

Kansas Guidelines for the Presentence Investigation Report
    http://www.Kywp.uscourts.gov/prob.html

California Court Guidelines for the Presentence Investigation Report
    www.courtinfo.ca.gov/rules

Colorado Attorney Advice for Offenders Regarding the PSI
    http://www.hmichaelsteinberg.com/
    thepresentencereport.htm

Conditions of Probation in Alaska
    http://touchngo.com/lglcntr/akstats/Statutes/
    Title12/Chapter55/Section100.htm

Intensive probation conditions in Arizona
    http://www.superiorcourt.maricopa.gov/
    AdultProbation/AdultProbationInformation/
    Supervision/IntensiveProbationSupervision.asp

Terms and conditions of probation in Benton County, Indiana
    http://www.in-map.net/counties/BENTON/
    probation/terms.html

Conditions of Probation in Maine
    http://www.mainelegislature.org/legis/statutes/
    17-A/title17-Asec1206.html

Conditions of Probation in Missouri
    http://www.doc.missouri.gov/division/prob/
    prob.htm

Conditions of probation in Washington, DC
    http://prop1.org/legal/840385/850124a.htm

CASE STUDY EXERCISE 1

The Sentencing Decision

The following two cases assume that the judge has granted probation. Discuss what probation conditions would be appropriate and an appropriate length for the term of probation supervision.

CASE A

Defendant Green devised a scheme to pass fictitious payroll checks. He recruited other individuals to pass the fictitious checks in exchange for money. Mr. Green would open a bank account using a fictitious check he had produced. Green would then produce additional fictitious payroll checks using the bank's logo, routing number, and account number. Mr. Green would recruit individuals who had valid identification from homeless shelters. Upon receiving checks from Green, the individuals would go to area stores to pass the fictitious payroll checks. Green gave a portion of the money to the individual passing the check and kept the remainder. When Green's residence was searched subsequent to his arrest for the offense, an electronic typewriter, 29 payroll checks matching those previously passed, a computer, marijuana, and drug paraphernalia were confiscated. Upon further examination of the computer, evidence of payroll check counterfeiting was discovered on it. Nine retail stores were victimized in the offense as the stores had cashed the payroll checks. A total loss of $14,503 was determined through documentation and investigation.

Mr. Green's prior criminal history includes a conviction for misdemeanor possession of marijuana and disorderly conduct. He was raised in two-parent home. Neither of his parents has a criminal record, and it appears they provided Green with appropriate structure and discipline. Green revealed he has used marijuana for the past 12 years. He is currently 28 years of age. He has a high school diploma and a sporadic work history. His personal finances reveal his only asset to be an automobile valued at $4,500. He has four credit card accounts. Two of the accounts are current with combined balances of $670. The other two accounts are in collection status and their balances total $6,210. The defendant is eligible for not less than one nor more than five years probation by statute.

CASE B

Police officers stopped Defendant Tuff after they observed his vehicle stopping and starting at an accelerated speed. They subsequently arrested him on several charges.

Police observed Mr. Tuff's vehicle accelerate at an unsafe speed after stopping at a yield sign. Tuff's vehicle had come to a stop at the yield sign, although there was no traffic requiring the stop. Police stopped Tuff. They smelled the odor of alcohol on Mr. Tuff, and a breath test showed Tuff had a blood alcohol content of .162. Tuff was arrested. Found on his person were a .38 caliber handgun and a small amount of marijuana. An open container of beer was inside the vehicle. Police reports reveal Tuff became angry and violent during the arrest. He had to be placed in restraints.

Tuff was convicted of Driving Under the Influence, Transporting an Open Container, and Carrying a Concealed Weapon. All were misdemeanor charges. Mr. Tuff has a prior arrest for Disorderly Conduct. The prior offense involved police responding to a disturbance where shots had been fired. Upon arrival, officers saw the defendant throw a pistol up onto a roof. He was chased and appeared to be intoxicated when apprehended. Tuff told officers he had called police because someone had shot at his home. Tuff was irate, shouting profanities and screaming he was going to kill someone. When attempts to calm him were unsuccessful, Tuff was taken into custody and charged with Disorderly Conduct.

Defendant Tuff is 21 years of age. His parents were divorced when he was born. At the age of 6, he began living with his maternal grandparents because his mother worked nights at a tavern. Tuff reports going to the Job Corp when he was 16 years old. He was terminated early from the two-year program with the Job Corp after assaulting a security guard for not being allowed a pass into town. Tuff has been employed as a laborer for three different firms. The longest term of employment in any of the positions was eight months. He was terminated from two of the positions due to absenteeism. He states he resigned from the third job due to personal problems with his spouse and a dispute with his employer over pay. Mr. Tuff completed one year of high school before the Job Corp. Tuff completed his GED as a condition of a previous term of probation.

Mr. Tuff states he was referred for anger management classes when in junior high school. He acknowledged he has had prior thoughts of suicide and, on one occasion played Russian roulette. On another occasion he tried to shoot himself in the head and pulled the trigger; however, a friend pulled the gun away causing the bullet to miss him. He states he was "depressed with life" at the time. Tuff explains he does not currently feel a desire to commit suicide and does not desire counseling. Mr. Tuff began using marijuana when he was in high school. He has also reported use of crack cocaine and methamphetamine. A urine specimen submitted by Tuff during the presentence phase revealed the use of marijuana.

The defendant was married two years ago. He has a daughter. The marriage lasted only a short period of time, and Tuff states the couple has been separated for more than a year. He does not have contact with his wife or child and is court ordered to pay $250 monthly in child support. His personal finances reveal his only reported asset to be a pickup he estimates to be valued at $8,000. His only outstanding debt is $3,600 in child support owed to the county in which his daughter resides. The defendant is eligible for not more than five years probation by statute.

CASE STUDY EXERCISE 2

Federal Presentence Investigation Report

Below, you will find an example of a federal presentence investigation report where all the names and places are fictitious. After reading the report, you may wish to discuss the case in class, or you may wish to use the sample PSI to construct your own.

IN THE UNITED STATES DISTRICT COURT FOR THE WESTERN DISTRICT OF ATLANTIS UNITED STATES OF AMERICA *VS.* FRANK JONES PRESENTENCE INVESTIGATION REPORT DOCKET NO. CR 09-002-01-KGG

Prepared for:	The Honorable Kelly G. Green U.S. District Judge
Prepared by:	Craig T. Doe U.S. Probation Officer Breaker Bay, Atlantis (123) 111-1111
Assistant U.S. Attorney	Mrs. Sharon Duncan
Defense Counsel	Mr. Arthur Goodfellow
Sentence Date:	June 5, 2009
Offense:	Count One: Tax Evasion (26 U.S.C. § 7201)
Release Status:	At liberty on a $50,000 personal recognizance bond with pretrial supervision (no pretrial custody)
Detainers:	None
Codefendants:	None
Related Cases:	Nancy Oscar CR 09-002-01; Vincent St. James CR 09-005-01
Date Report Prepared:	5/15/09
Date Revised:	5/25/09

Identifying Data:

Date of Birth:	3/19/78
Race:	White
Sex:	Male
S. S. #:	222-22-2222
FBI #:	222-22-22B
USM #:	22222-222
Education:	11th grade
Dependents:	two
Citizenship:	U.S.
Legal Address:	1430 Bird Avenue, Breaker Bay, AT 10101
Aliases:	None
Tattoos:	None
Gang Affiliation:	None known

PART A. THE OFFENSE

Charge(s) and Conviction(s)

1. Frank Jones was named in a three-count indictment filed by a Western District of Atlantis grand jury on November 1, 2008. Counts one through three charge that the defendant attempted to evade income tax due and owed by him and his wife for calendar years 2005, 2006, and 2007, respectively, in violation of 26 U.S.C. § 7201. On November 15, 2008, a superseding information was filed by the United States Attorney's Office in the Western District of Atlantis. The Information charges that on October 15, 2007, Jones evaded income tax due and owed by him and his wife for the calendar year 2007 by writing a check to the American Medisearch Organization in the amount of $20,000 for which he received 90 percent back in cash, and by filing a false tax return in which he deducted as a charitable contribution the entire amount of $20,000, in violation of 26 U.S.C. § 7201.

2. On November 21, 2008, Jones appeared before a U.S. Magistrate Judge and pled not guilty to all of the charges. He was released after posting bond and was ordered to report to the Pretrial Services Agency. On December 1, 2008, in accordance with the terms of a written plea agreement, the defendant pled guilty as charged in the superseding information. The parties entered into a plea agreement per F.R.Crim.P. 11(c)(1)(A), which calls for the dismissal of the original indictment. Jones is scheduled to be sentenced on June 5, 2009.

3. According to his supervising pretrial services officer, Jones made satisfactory adjustment while under pretrial services supervision and reported as directed. Additionally, Jones maintained employment, and there were no substance-related issues with the defendant.

The Official Version

4. The American Medisearch Organization is a not-for-profit national corporation that supervises fungus research. Across the country, the American Medisearch Organization derives its funds from 50 charter divisions, which are separately incorporated not-for-profit organizations. The American Medisearch Organization, Atlantis Division, Inc., is located in Breaker Bay, Atlantis. In late 2007, the Atlantis Medisearch Organization began to raise funds through an annual fall dinner dance, casino night.

5. Nancy Oscar began employment with the Atlantis Medisearch Organization in 1999 as a field services representative. Oscar, who created the dinner dance fund-raising event, was responsible for the fund-raising activities of the Atlantis Medisearch Organization. Three schemes developed from the dinner dance, all of which were aimed at enabling various "contributors" to inflate or falsify the "charitable" donations that could then be reported and deducted on personal, corporate, partnership, or private foundation Federal income tax returns.

6. At the dinner dance, which was usually held in October, guests were permitted to write checks, payable to the American Medisearch Organization, to purchase gambling chips. Ten percent of the value of each check was retained by the Atlantis Medisearch Organization as a donation, but 90 percent was returned to the "contributor" in the form of gambling chips.

7. Although the Atlantis Medisearch Organization raised money from other fund-raising events, its major source of income was from the annual dinner dance. Over the years, the number of people attending the dinner dance increased, the amount of advance "check-cashing" increased, the amount of

checks written for gambling chips increased, and the amount of money Atlantis Medisearch Organization raised for the American Medisearch Organization increased. In 2004 the organization raised $73,000, and in 2007 the organization raised $360,000.

8. This scheme was in essence a "check cashing" operation, allowing "contributors" to draw checks to the American Medisearch Organization several weeks before the dinner dance affair.

9. After the checks cleared the account, Oscar and other employees at her direction would arrange for the bank to ship cash to the dinner dance site. Oscar and some of the officers and members of the Atlantis Medisearch Organization would meet in rooms at the dinner dance site where they took the cash and placed it in envelopes in amounts corresponding to 90 percent of the face value of the checks sent in advance of the dinner dance by the "contributors." Oscar also arranged for additional cash to be available at the dinner dance for those members who chose to redeem their chips for cash. The scheme was able to continue and flourish not only because of the greed of the "contributors," but also due to Oscar's bookkeeping methods.

10. In support of their income tax submissions, "contributors" often attached to their tax returns copies of the fraudulent checks they wrote to the American Medisearch Organization, and during routine audits "contributors" furnished the original copy of the fraudulent check to agents of the Internal Revenue Service and directly or indirectly misrepresented that the full amount of the checks were charitable contributions to the American Medisearch Organization.

11. Over the years, the number of participants in this scheme substantially increased. According to available records, while the dinner dance attendees increased from approximately 65 in 2000 to approximately 650 in 2004, the Government has only sought prosecution of those "contributors" who participated in the various kickback schemes and filed fraudulent tax returns when the total amount of the checks written to the American Medisearch Organization was $30,000 or more over several years or $20,000 in one given year. To date, the Government has prosecuted Nancy Oscar, who was the organizer and creator of this scheme. She has recently pled guilty to a three-count indictment charging her with mail fraud, income tax evasion, and wire fraud, along with five "contributors," namely the defendant, Frank Jones, together with Samuel James, Brian McDonald, Vincent St. James, and Donald Goodman. In total, the Government expects to obtain indictments for approximately 37 additional "contributors." Although the value of the checks written to the American Medisearch Organization varied from "contributor" to "contributor," the check writers are equally culpable.

12. Frank Jones participated in this false deduction scheme involving the Atlantis division of the American Medisearch Organization and filed fraudulent income tax returns for the years 2005, 2006, and 2007. During each of the years, Jones made contributions of $20,000, but received 90 percent of the contribution (or $18,000) back in cash or in gambling chips, some of which he used to gamble with, but the majority of which he redeemed for cash. However, on each of his individual income tax returns, filed jointly with his wife, Jones deducted the full amount of $20,000 as "charitable contributions," even though he was only entitled to deduct $2,000 in each tax year, which represents the 10 percent retained by the Atlantis Medisearch Organization as a contribution to the American Medisearch Organization.

Victim Impact Statement

13. The Internal Revenue Service is the victim. In each tax year, Frank Jones deducted $20,000 as a charitable contribution from his taxable income when in fact he was only entitled to deduct a total of $2,000 as a charitable contribution during each of the tax years. As a result, Jones underreported his taxable income by $54,000. According to the results of an Internal Revenue Service audit, Jones had outstanding tax liabilities, not including interest and penalties, in the amount of $27,000, which he has paid in full.

Adjustment for Defendant's Acceptance of Responsibility

14. During an interview with Internal Revenue Service agents, and later during an interview with the probation officer, Jones readily admitted his involvement in this offense. Jones explained that he falsely claimed the charitable deductions on his personal tax returns because everyone else who attended the dinner dance was claiming the deductions.

15. Jones added that his involvement in this offense has had an adverse effect on his career and in retrospect he never envisioned the potential impact such wrongdoing would have on his life. He expressed feelings of both embarrassment and regret, and assumes full responsibility for his criminal conduct, as supported by his recent tax payment to the Internal Revenue Service in the amount of $27,000. Jones indicates that he will immediately pay the balance of his tax liabilities once the IRS has assessed interest and penalties.

Offense Level Computation

16. The 2005 edition of the *Guidelines Manual* has been used in this case.

17. **Base Offense Level:** In this offense, the total amount of evaded taxes is $27,000. According to USSG. §2T4.1(D), the base offense level for tax losses of more than $12,500 but less than $30,000 is twelve.   12

18. **Specific Offense Characteristics:** Pursuant to the provision found in USSG. §2T1.1(b)(1) since the defendant failed to report or to correctly identify the source of income exceeding $10,000 in any year from criminal activity, the offense level is increased by two levels.   +2

19. **Adjustment for Role in the Offense:** None.   0

20. **Adjusted Offense Level (Subtotal):**   14

21. **Adjustment for Acceptance of Responsibility:** The defendant has shown recognition of responsibility for his conduct and a reduction of two levels for acceptance of responsibility is applicable under USSG. §3E1.1(a).   −2

22. **Total Offense Level:**   12

PART B. THE DEFENDANT'S CRIMINAL HISTORY

Juvenile Adjudications

23. None

Criminal History Computation

24. A check with the FBI and the local police authorities reveals no prior convictions for Frank Jones. Therefore, Jones has a criminal history score of zero. According to the sentencing table (chapter five, part A), 0 to 1 criminal history points establish a criminal history category of I.

PART C. OFFENDER CHARACTERISTICS

Personal and Family Data

25. Frank Samuel Jones was born on March 19, 1978, in Breaker Bay, Atlantis, to the union of Samuel and Patricia Jones. Jones is an only child and was raised by his parents in the upper river section of Breaker Bay in an upper-middle-class socio-economic setting. Jones has fond memories of his developmental years, advising that he was reared under Roman Catholic traditions by concerned, loving parents who emphasized hard work, respect, and honesty.

26. The defendant's father was a partner in the Atlantis Tallow Company, a refinery and exporting company which manufactured tallow, the main ingredient in soap. When the defendant was 17 years old, his father became critically ill with tuberculosis and was not expected to recover. Jones withdrew from school and worked at his father's company. According to the defendant, his father died following a massive heart attack. While reporting a positive relationship with his father, Jones advised us that he felt much closer to his mother, who died of natural causes at the age of 80.

27. Jones married Nancy Lipson Smith. This union produced two children: Frank, Jr., and Melissa, ages 13 and 15, respectively, For the past 13 years, the defendant and his family have resided at 1701 Seagull Lane, in a rather reclusive, wooded, upper-class area in Breaker Bay. A home investigation found this 5-bedroom bi-level, ranch-style home to be impeccably maintained.

28. Mrs. Jones describes her marriage in harmonious terms and states that the defendant is a kind, considerate, and devoted husband and father. Jones, for the most part, is a private person, and has suffered embarrassment as a result of the publicity in this case. The defendant's wife believes that her husband's actions "were not very well thought out," adding that "he never thinks about the impact his actions may have on his life or family." Mrs. Jones considers the defendant's conduct in this offense as an isolated incident contrary to his otherwise "law-abiding lifestyle." According to Mrs. Jones, her husband has been described by his children as a "workaholic," but he never allows himself to neglect the needs or concerns of his family.

Physical Condition

29. The defendant is 5'10" tall and weighs 180 pounds. He has brown eyes and slightly graying brown short hair. At our request, the defendant's private physician, John W. Brown, M.D., provided a summary of Jones' overall health, which was described as excellent and free from hospitalizations.

Mental and Emotional Health

30. The defendant states that he has never been seen by a psychiatrist and describes his overall mental and emotional health as good. We have no information to suggest otherwise. Jones was polite and cooperative during the presentence process and presented himself as a professional and soft-spoken businessman, voicing normal stress and concerns affiliated with pending legal difficulties.

Substance Abuse

31. Jones states that he rarely drinks alcohol and has never used narcotics. A urine specimen collected by the probation officer tested negative for illicit drug use.

Education and Vocational Skills

32. The defendant later received his GED and continued his education at Atlantis University, where he received a Bachelor of Science degree in marketing. This was confirmed by the registrar's office at Atlantis University.

Employment Record

33. For the last 5 years, Jones has been employed by Greater Life Securities, Inc., in Breaker Bay, where he earns approximately $80,000 a year. Prior to that, Jones was employed by the Marshall, Jones, and LaBelle securities firm. Jones also worked at his father's business for several years.

Financial Condition: Ability to Pay

34. A review of the defendant's amended personal income tax returns for 2005 through 2007 (which now reflect the $57,000 in additional income previously reported as charitable deductions) reveals that he earned approximately $121,000 adjusted gross income.

35. Equity in Other Assets 1701 Seagull Lane Breaker Bay, Atlantis (family residence) $ 280,000

36. Unsecured Debts- Auto Loan $17,000; Credit cards- $ 3,000

37. Monthly Cash Flow: $4,500

Based on the defendant's financial condition, he has the ability to pay a fine within the guideline range.

PART D. SENTENCING OPTIONS

38. Guideline Provisions: Based on an offense level of 12 and a criminal history category of I, the guideline range of imprisonment is 10 to 16 months.

39. Statutory Provisions: The defendant is eligible for a term of probation in this offense, pursuant to 18 U.S.C. § 3561(a). The authorized term for a felony is not less than one nor more than five years, pursuant to 18 U.S.C. § 3561(c)(1).

Impact of Plea Agreement

40. Under the plea agreement, Jones has entered a plea to one count of tax evasion, in return for the dismissal of two other tax evasion counts.

Fine

41. According to USSG §5E1.2(c)(3), the minimum fine for this offense is $3,000 and the maximum fine for this offense is $30,000.

Restitution

42. Pursuant to 18 U.S.C. § 3663, restitution may be ordered. In this case, the $57,000 + interest and penalties= $62,500 are outstanding to the Internal Revenue Service, and can be forwarded to the following address:
Internal Revenue Service
Attention: Mr. Sam Claim
111 IRS Tower
Breaker Bay, Atlantis 11111

43. In accordance with the provisions of USSG §5E1.1, restitution of $62,500 shall be ordered.

PART E: FACTORS THAT MAY WARRANT DEPARTURE

44. The probation officer has no information concerning the offense or the offender which would warrant a departure from the prescribed sentencing guidelines.

SENTENCING RECOMMENDATION
U.S. DISTRICT COURT FOR THE WESTERN DISTRICT OF ATLANTIS
DOCKET. # CR 05-002-01-KGG

Total Offense Level 12
Criminal History Category: I

Frank Jones is a successful businessman who appears to be a situational offender, having been motivated by opportunistic greed. While his acceptance of responsibility and remorse are reflected in the guideline calculation, a sentence within the guideline range is recommended. As such, a split sentence of five months in a federal community correctional facility followed by five months of home confinement as a condition of supervised release is the recommended sentence in order to reflect the seriousness of the defendant's conduct and to provide just punishment. The defendant earns a considerable income and is employed with a reputable commodities firm. In view of Jones' financial profile, restitution of $62,500, a fine of $20,000 in addition to the $100 penalty assessment, is also recommended to be paid immediately. Inasmuch as he does not appear to pose a risk to the community nor to be in need of correctional treatment, the minimum term of supervised release of two years will be sufficient. Since the defendant will owe interest and penalties to the Internal Revenue Service as soon as they are calculated, it is recommended that collection of these monies be a condition of supervised release. A restriction against incurring any new debts until the criminal sanctions are paid is an additional recommended condition. Disclosure of financial information is also recommended. As this is a felony conviction, Jones must submit to DNA testing. Within 72 hours of sentencing, the defendant shall report in person to the Atlantis Federal Community Corrections Center, 123 Willow Lane. While on supervised release the defendant shall not commit any federal, state, or local crimes, and he shall be prohibited from possessing a firearm or other dangerous device. The defendant shall not possess a controlled substance and he shall comply with the standard conditions of supervised release as recommended by the United States Sentencing Commission.

Respectfully submitted,

Craig T. Doe
U.S. Probation Officer

CASE STUDY EXERCISE 3

Instructions on How to Conduct and Write a Full Presentence Investigation Report

You will need to create a client named Sue Steel OR your instructor can create a mock interview where the class interviews Sue Steel. Prepare a list of questions and organize your responses according to the 10-part guide below to writing a detailed presentence investigation report that is used in states allowing more judicial discretion. The section ordering below is a bit different from that of the federal PSI, but it includes all the necessary information that you would find representing a state-level PSI. For each section, and for each piece of information, be sure to state which parts of the PSI have been verified or are verifiable vs. which ones were self-reported by the defendant.

TO: Judge Name
FROM: Probation Officer Name
RE: Defendant's Name

1. Defendant's Personal Characteristics
   - Name and aliases
   - Case number
   - Gender
   - Date of Birth
   - Education level
   - Employment history and skills
   - Vocational skills
   - Military
   - Mental health history: Any psychotropic medications
   - Physical health: major illnesses, current prescription meds
   - Drug history, dependency, and/or current addiction
   - Known gang affiliation
2. Current Offense
   - Facts of the crime from the police report
   - Initial charge(s) and final plea agreement or conviction(s)
   - Defendant's version of the offense and circumstances leading up to it
   - Accomplices and/or role in current offense
   - Defendant's acceptance of responsibility for crime
   - Level of cooperation or terms of the agreement upon which a plea of guilty was based
3. Defendant's Prior Criminal History
   - Juvenile adjudications (Case numbers, offense type, dates, and dispositions)
   - Adult diversions or convictions (Case numbers, offense type, dates, and dispositions)
   - Previous time spent in custody
   - Pending charges or outstanding warrants

4. Family History and Background
- Family of origin (parents, upbringing, siblings)
- Criminal history of family members
- Marital status/evidence of domestic violence or abuse?
- Dependent children
- Current family ties and responsibilities (e.g., child support?)
- Stable living arrangements

5. Victim Impact Statement: contact victims and request statements or interviews
- Any statements made by the victim to police or the probation officer
- The type of harm done to the victim as a result of the offense: physical, emotional, psychological, financial, property
- The monetary amount of the victim's loss

6. Collateral Information from People Who Knew the Defendant
- Former employers
- Former educators and teachers
- Former probation or parole officers
- Former neighbors
- Interviews with family members
- Written recommendation letters if applicable

7. Sentencing Options and the Defendant's Suitability for Each Option
- Custody
- Intermediate sanctions
- Probation

8. Fines and Restitution
- Mandatory and recommended restitution and/or fines to be assessed against the defendant
- Defendant's ability to pay restitution and fines
- Does defendant have any other debts (credit card debt, auto loans, mortgage, etc.)

9. Factors Warranting Departure from Sentencing Guidelines
- *Using the North Carolina sentencing grid in Chapter 3,* figure the prior criminal history score based on 1 point per misdemeanor and 2 points for each felony. Then, figure the presumptive sentence for both charges. Finally, decide if there are mitigating or aggravating circumstances that warrant departure from the presumptive sentence.

10. Summary Sentencing Recommendation to the Court
- Summarize the main points from Sections #1–8—do not present any new information—just the highlights should be used as a justification.
- Recommend the sentencing type for each offense (in the current situation) and any financial penalties.
- Recommend any special conditions of probation that are related to the current offense

ENCLOSED DOCUMENTS YOU WILL NEED TO COMPLETE THE PSI:
POLICE ARREST REPORT:

Officer Briggs responded to a disturbance call at the JC Penney at the Anytown Mall at 3:15 pm on July 12, 2009. The call was placed by Mall Security Officer Washington at 2:53 pm. Officer Briggs interviewed the JC Penney clerk who notified mall security. The clerk said that Defendant Steel became agitated and irate because the clerk refused to accept her check without proper identification. As Steel angrily tried to leave the mall, she was approached for questioning by private security. One of the private security officers *happened to notice a "shiny metal object" in her waistband that appeared to be a weapon of some sort. Private security conducted a frisk and recovered a .38 caliber weapon from her waistband and a book of checks for "Janine Smith" when she was arrested. Private security detained Steel at the mall until police arrived. Defendant booked in county jail at 4:25 pm Officer Briggs phoned the bank and the victim. Bank research conducted the next business day on this account revealed that four checks were written to retail stores that totaled $975 over a period of three days. The signature of all four checks did not match the signature on file at the Bank. The four checks were written out of order— in different numerical sequence than the rest of the checks in the account. Victim Janine Smith confirms never receiving said checks in the mail, and confirms that she did not write these checks nor authorize anyone else to sign checks on her account.*

NCIC Criminal Background Check

NAME: Steel   Sue   M.   White   Female
DOB: 6/30/85   SS# 123-45-6789   FBI: 98765US43
Aliases: Harris, Cherlyn   DOB: 6/30/85
   Steel, Suzanne   DOB: 3/20/81
1679   S. Madison   Anytown, NC 01234
Prints on file
Finger Print Class: PO   PI   09   CO   18
                          15   PM   12   23   19

Adult Arrest record
2008 MISD 123- Theft by deception- Bench warrant issued.
2002CV 5967422496- Credit Card Abuse- disposition unknown.
2001CV 283845067- Simple Felony Fraud. Probation completed after 14 months.
Juvenile Arrest record
1999JV 16412345- Juvenile Records sealed.

Victim Impact Statement by Janine Smith

Janine Smith made the following statement to the prosecutor:
   "Ms. Steel is a neighbor that lives down my street. I have said "hi" to her once or twice but never expected that she would be the kind of person to do anything like this. I was just shocked when the police called me. Although the Bank knows that I didn't write the checks, my checking account is still short $975.00, which is a lot of money for me to lose in one month. That is nearly all I have—now I am unable to cover my rent and pay my utility bills. I may be able to work something out with some of the companies under the circumstances, but I am not sure if my landlord will go for it. If I could just get my money back, that's all I want. I don't know what I'm going to do."

Collateral Interviews

Former employers: Mrs. Juanita Medina, the defendant's most recent employer, was contacted by phone to verify that Sue Steel had employment at a janitorial service cleaning office buildings. Steel worked at this firm prior to detention in this case. Mrs. Medina was willing to rehire Steel upon her release from custody because her "work habits were good." Her employer is aware of her conviction and supervision. No other job history could be verified.

Former neighbor: One neighbor, who wishes to remain anonymous, says he remembered the defendant as "quiet and kept to herself."

Family members:

Defendant's sister (Mary Sparks) has one child of her own and has agreed for Steel to reside there if Steel is granted community supervision. The home was checked and it seems to be acceptable and close to a bus route.

Defendant Steel has one dependent child who is currently in the temporary custody of her mother. Steel's mother could not be reached despite repeated calls.

PART II

Probation

Probation is the most frequently used and possibly the most misunderstood sentence in corrections. Two out of every three convicted offenders are on probation, yet probation budgets account for only 10 percent of the entire correctional budget. As a result of a severe shortage of probation personnel over the years, caseloads have become larger, the time spent per client has diminished, and face-to-face contacts are slowly being been replaced altogether by correctional technology.

Chapter 4 chronicles the history of probation from the early 1800s to the present, including a section on how supervision philosophies have changed over time, and ends with a comparison of who is on probation. Chapter 5 is the foundation chapter in the contemporary supervision of probationers, including classification of risk and needs and the specialized supervision of offenders with higher risks and special needs. Chapter 6 pays particular attention to how officers are selected and trained, along with nuances in supervision, such as privatization and interstate supervision. Chapter 7 discusses probation condition modification and both successful and unsuccessful termination. Revocation is an unsuccessful termination that occurs when conditions of probation are not followed.

4

How Probation Developed: Chronicling Its Past and Present

CHAPTER LEARNING OBJECTIVES

- Recall the social and legal history of probation in England and the United States.
- Discuss the founders of probation.
- Restate how supervision philosophies have changed in the United States.
- Describe how probation is organized and operates.

- Examine how Community Corrections Acts contribute to community supervision programs.
- Characterize how a probation officer's working style has changed.

© Colorado Historical Society

The historical state capitol building in Denver, Colorado where probation was later allowed as an alternative to prison.

CHAPTER OUTLINE

Precursors to American Probation
Procedures Related to Modern Probation
Founders of Probation
Development of Federal Probation
History of Juvenile Probation and the Juvenile Court
Early Probation Legislation in Other States

Organization of Probation Departments
Community Corrections Acts
Models of Supervision Over Time
Who Is on Probation?

KEY TERMS

amercement	suspended sentence	brokerage of services
security for good behavior	conviction	community resource management
filing	John Augustus	team model
motion to quash	parens patriae	justice model
surety	Community Corrections Acts	neighborhood-based supervision
recognizance	casework	

Precursors to American Probation

Probation, as it is known and practiced today, evolved out of ancient precedents in England and the United States devised to avoid the mechanical application of the harsh penal codes of the day (Rotman 1995). Early British criminal law, which was dominated by the objectives of retribution and punishment, imposed rigid and severe penalties on offenders. The usual punishments were corporal: branding, flogging, mutilation, and execution. Capital punishment was commonly inflicted on children and animals as well as men and women. At the time of Henry VIII, for instance, more than 200 crimes were punishable by death, many of them relatively minor offenses against property.

Methods used to determine guilt—what today is called *criminal procedure*—also put the accused in danger. Trial might be by combat between the accused and the accuser, or a person's innocence might be determined by whether he or she sank when bound and thrown into a deep pond—the theory being that the pure water would reject wrongdoers. Thus, the choice was to drown as an innocent person or to survive the drowning only to be otherwise executed. Sometimes the offender could elect to be tried "by God," which involved undergoing some painful and frequently life-threatening ordeal, or "by country," a form of trial by jury for which the accused first had to pay an **amercement** to the king. The accepted premise was that the purpose of criminal law was not to deter or rehabilitate but to bring about justice for a past act deemed harmful to the society.

Early legal practices in the United States were distinct from British common law in a number of ways. First, **security for good behavior,** also known as *good abearance,* was a fee paid to the state as collateral for a promise of good behavior. Much like the modern practice of bail, security for good behavior allowed the accused to go free in certain cases either before or after conviction. Under **filing,** the indictment was "laid on file" in cases in which justice did not require an immediate sentence. However, the court could impose certain conditions on the defendant. The effect was that the case was laid at rest without either dismissal or final judgment and without the necessity of asking for final continuances.

Amercement
A monetary penalty imposed arbitrarily at the discretion of the court for an offense.

Security for Good Behavior
A recognizance or bond given the court by a defendant before or after conviction conditioned on his or her being "on good behavior" or keeping the peace for a prescribed period.

Filing
A procedure under which an indictment was "laid on file," or held in abeyance, without either dismissal or final judgment in cases in which justice did not require an immediate sentence.

Motion to Quash
An oral or written request that the court repeal, nullify, or overturn a decision, usually made during or after the trial.

Surety
An individual who agrees to become responsible for the debt of a defendant or who answers for the performance of the defendant should the defendant fail to attend the next court appearance.

Recognizance
Originally a device of preventive justice that obliged people suspected of future misbehavior to stipulate with and give full assurance to the court and the public that the apprehended offense would not occur. Recognizance was later used with convicted or arraigned offenders with conditions of release set.

Suspended Sentence
An order of the court after a verdict, finding, or plea of guilty that suspends or postpones the imposition or execution of sentence during a period of good behavior.

Conviction
A judgment of the court, based on a defendant's plea of guilty *or nolo contendere,* or on the verdict of a judge or jury, that the defendant is guilty of the offense(s) with which he or she has been charged.

Massachusetts's judges also often granted a **motion to quash** after judgment, using any minor technicality or the slightest error in the proceedings to free the defendant in cases in which they thought the statutory penalties inhumane. Some early forms of bail had the effect of suspending final action on a case, although the chief use of bail then (as now) was for the purpose of ensuring appearance for trial, such as using the assistance of **sureties.**

All of these methods had the common objective of mitigating punishment by relieving selected offenders from the full effects of the legally prescribed penalties that substantial segments of the community, including many judges, viewed as excessive and inappropriate to their offenses. They were precursors to probation as it is known today. The procedures most closely related to modern probation, however, are recognizance and the suspended sentence.

PROCEDURES RELATED TO MODERN PROBATION

In the 1830 case of *Commonwealth v. Chase,* often cited as an example of the early use of release on **recognizance,** Judge Peter Oxenbridge Thacher found the defendant (Jerusha Chase) guilty on her plea, suspended the imposition of sentence, and ruled that the defendant was permitted to be released upon her word that she would reappear at a later date for her next court appearance. Recognizance came to be used in Massachusetts as a means of avoiding a final conviction of young and minor offenders in the hope that they would avoid further criminal behavior. The main thrust of recognizance was to humanize criminal law and to mitigate its harshness. While recognizance was illegal in 1830, it is used today to ensure a defendant's presence at court and is *neither* a disposition nor a form of supervision in itself.

A **suspended sentence** is a court order, entered after a verdict, finding, or plea of guilty, that suspends or postpones the filing, imposition, or execution of sentence contingent on the good behavior of the offender. Suspended sentences grew out of efforts to mitigate the harsh punishments demanded by early English law.

There are two kinds of suspended sentence—suspension of *imposition* of sentence and suspension of *execution* of sentence. In the case of suspension of imposition of sentence, a verdict or plea may be reached, but no sentence is pronounced, and there is no conviction. This means that there is no criminal record and no loss of civil rights provided law-abiding behavior continues for a specified period of time (for example, for three years). The withholding or postponement of sentence is revoked or terminated if the offender commits a new crime.

In the case of suspension of execution of sentence, the defendant is placed on probation and the **conviction** remains on record. A conviction is followed by the execution of criminal sanctions and loss of civil rights and privileges. The suspended sentence can thus be either a separate disposition or a sentencing alternative connected with probation.

The Power to Suspend Sentence   English common law courts had the power to suspend sentence for a limited period or for a specified purpose. Handing down suspended sentences and calling it "probation" was a common practice in the federal courts. In a case known as the "Killits" case, Judge Killits refused to vacate the suspended sentence even when the victim did not wish to prosecute. This case went all the way to the U.S. Supreme Court, and in 1916 the Court held that federal courts had no power to suspend indefinitely the imposition or execution of a sentence (*Ex parte United States* 242 U.S. 27, 1916). This aspect—the recognition of legislative authority to grant the power of indefinite suspension to the courts—made probation as now defined and practiced in the United States largely statutory. As a result of the Killits case, the president pardoned approximately 2,000 people. The Court as a remedy to an indefinite suspension suggested probation legislation.

The early controversy about the court's authority to suspend sentence has also resulted in differing ideas about the relationship between probation and suspended sentence. In some jurisdictions, probation was not a sentence in itself but was a form of a suspended execution of sentence. In 1984 the Federal Sentencing Reform Act recognized probation as a bona fide sentence (18 U.S.C.A. 3561).

THE FOUNDERS OF PROBATION

Volunteers and philanthropists were instrumental in the development and acceptance of probation in practice long before probation became law. The development of the probation idea can be credited to two co-founding individuals: John Augustus and Matthew Davenport Hill.

John Augustus   The credit for founding probation in the United States is reserved for **John Augustus,** a Boston bootmaker. Augustus (1939) was committed to bailing out offenders that he deemed would return to court. The offenders would be ordered to appear before the court at a stated time at which Augustus would accompany each to the courtroom. If the judge was satisfied with Augustus's account of his stewardship, the offender, instead of being committed to the House of Correction, would be fined one cent and court costs and Augustus paid the fine. See Box 4.1 detailing Augustus' commitment for nearly two decades until his death in 1859.

Followers of John Augustus included John Murray Spear, who served as a "voluntary public defender, lecturer, and traveler, a tract distributor, and a worker with discharged prisoners" (Lindner and Savarese 1984b, p. 5). The settlement movement, a group of university students and professors, was also prominent in the establishment of probation in New York. The University Settlement was a grassroots social reform organization that advocated for the poor people of the community, including those on probation. In protest of materialism, industrialization, and

> **John Augustus**
> A Boston bootmaker who was the founder of probation in the United States.

Library of Congress

Early juvenile courts focused on rehabilitation rather than punishment. Here, an 8-year old boy appears with his parents in 1910. The boy has been accused of stealing a bicycle, and the court is weighing what is in the boy's best interests.

BOX 4.1   COMMUNITY CORRECTIONS UP CLOSE

John Augustus—Massachusetts Bootmaker and Probation Co-Founder (1785–1859)

John Augustus was born in Burlington, Massachusetts (then part of Woburn), in 1785. About 1806 he moved to Lexington and operated a shoe manufactory in part of his home. His first wife and child died when his daughter was an infant. Augustus married again and had four children, one of whom died at age 10. He apparently prospered, as he owned a large tract of land on both sides of Bedford Street. Augustus had four or five employees working for him. His old home, now renovated and restored at One Harrington Road and known as the Jonathan Harrington House, faces the Lexington Common.

It was in his shop at 5 Franklin Avenue near the police court, now only an alley, that Augustus received frequent calls from those who sought his help. His business there suffered owing to the time he spent away from it bailing people in the courts. All of Augustus's residences are of particular interest because as soon as he began his work in the courts, his home became a refuge for people he had bailed until more permanent plans could be made for them. From 1845 until his death in 1859, Augustus lived at 65 Chambers Street, in the West End of Boston. Nothing remains today of this old house.

Augustus was influenced by the formation of the Washington Total Abstinence Society in Boston on April 25, 1841, of which he was also a member. Its members pledged not only to abstain from intoxicating liquors themselves, but to assist alcoholics in the belief that they could be saved through understanding and kindness, rather than through commitment to prison. Augustus (1852) describes in his own words the moving story of his first probationer:

"In the month of August 1841, I was in court one morning when the door communicating with the lockroom was opened and an officer entered, followed by a ragged and wretched looking man, who took his seat upon the bench allotted to prisoners. I imagined from the man's appearance that his offence was that of yielding to his appetite for intoxicating drinks, and in a few moments I found that my suspicions were correct, for the clerk read the complaint, in which the man was charged with being a common drunkard. The case was clearly made out, but before sentence had been passed, I conversed with him a few moments, and found that he was not yet past all hope and reformation, although his appearance and his looks precluded a belief in the minds of others that he would ever become a man again. He told me that if he could be saved from the House of Correction, he never again would taste intoxicating liquors; there was such an earnestness in that tone, and a look expressive of firm resolve, that I determined to aid him; I bailed him, by permission of the Court. He was ordered to appear for sentence in three weeks from that time. He signed the pledge and became a sober man; at the expiration of this period of probation, I accompanied him into the courtroom; his whole appearance was changed and no one, not even the scrutinizing officers, could have believed that he was the same person who less than a month before, had stood trembling on the prisoner's stand. The Judge expressed himself much pleased with the account we gave of the man, and instead of the usual penalty—imprisonment in the House of Correction—he fined him one cent and costs, amounting in all to $3.76, which was immediately paid. The man continued industrious and sober, and without doubt has been, by this treatment, saved from a drunkard's grave." (pp. 4–5)

With this encouragement, Augustus continued to appear in court to assist alcoholics who appeared likely prospects for reformation, to rehabilitate them, and then to return with them to court for a report on their progress. By January 1842, he began accepting donations from private philanthropists to carry on his work. From this time on, Augustus's record is one of dedication to a cause to which he devoted the remainder of his life, much of his own financial resources, as well as the money contributed by Boston people.

By 1858, John Augustus had assisted a total of 1,946 people (1,152 males and 794 females). He had acted as a bondsman for them to the amount of $19,464, and he paid $2,417.65 for fines and costs. Augustus faced opposition, misunderstanding, and even physical abuse, especially from court officers.

For every person bailed out, the jailer lost a fee of between 62 and 75 cents; the clerk lost 25 cents, and the turnkey was out 40 cents. Although the opposition of the court officers was discouraging, the judges and the press were friendly, and influential people in the community continued to give him both moral and financial support of between $750 and $1,700 annually.

Augustus varied his answers to his critics. To some he said that for each person bailed to him, a commitment to a house of correction was prevented. To those who understood social progress and justice only in terms of a dollar saved, he pointed out that the public was saved the greater expense of caring for the person in jail. When he was charged with cheating the jails of their rightful tenants, he

(Continues)

BOX 4.1   COMMUNITY CORRECTIONS UP CLOSE (*Continued*)

John Augustus—Massachusetts Bootmaker and Probation Co-Founder (1785–1859)

replied that his form of treatment was more effective, that it saved the offender for his family and for society and did not disgrace him forever as a commitment would.

Augustus dedicated his life to being both a bail bondsman and a probation officer in charge of reforming the lives of the wayward, until his death on June 21, 1859.

Sources: John Moreland, an unpublished paper presented at the 35th Annual Conference of the National Probation Association, Boston, Massachusetts, May 29, 1941; Augustus, John. 1972. *A report of the labors of John Augustus, for the last ten years, in aid of the unfortunate.* Montclair, NJ: Patterson Smith. (Originally published 1852)

---

widening gaps between social classes, settlement residents lived and worked in the poorest sections of the city and resolved to teach and learn from the local residents (Lindner and Savarese 1984c, 1984d).

In 1878, almost 20 years after the death of John Augustus, adult probation in Massachusetts was sanctified by statute. A law was passed authorizing the mayor of Boston to appoint a paid probation officer to serve in the Boston criminal courts as a member of the police force. Three years later this law was changed so the probation officer reported to the prison commissioner. Due to corruption, the law was revised again to disallow police officers from becoming probation officers (Panzarella 2002). Statewide probation did not begin until 1891 when a statute transferred the power of appointment from the municipalities to the courts and made such appointment mandatory instead of permissive. For the first time, the probation officer was recognized as an official salaried agent of the court.

Matthew Davenport Hill   Matthew Davenport Hill was less known in the United States, but he deserves equal credit alongside John Augustus as a co-founder of probation. Hill laid the foundation of probation in England where he lived and worked. Born to Reverend Thomas Wright Hill in 1792 and the eldest of eight children, Matthew Davenport Hill was a member of a family intricately involved in politics and the movement for social change (Lindner 2007). While in Parliament, Hill was deeply concerned with equality of all people and worked toward ending transportation of English convicts, among other causes. According to criminal justice historian Charles Lindner:

> His contribution to helping develop a probation system may have evolved from his early experiences as a lawyer, during which time he witnessed a number of cases in which young offenders were sentenced to a term of imprisonment of only one day... [Hill] also required that there be persons willing to act as guardians of the young offender (Lindner 2007, p. 40).

The guardians would be required to report back to Hill's court on the juveniles' behavior. Police had the power to enforce the court reporting process and to provide social service assistance. Hill kept court records of the offender's behavior, which included early accounts of recidivism, measured by reconviction rate. Apparently, over a 12-year period, 80 offenders out of 417 were reconvicted, many because they returned to similar circumstances that contributed to the previous crimes in the first place (Lindner 2007, p. 40). Hill was a close personal friend of a number of other justice reformers, including Jeremy Bentham, Sir Robert Peel, Dr. Enoch Wines, a prison reformer; and Captain Alexander Maconochie (who will be discussed in Chapter 11 as influential in the development of parole). Matthew Davenport Hill died in 1872 at the age of 80.

DEVELOPMENT OF FEDERAL PROBATION

Historical accounts of federal probation suggest that federal judges were extremely resistant to enacting probation legislation. Between 1909 and 1925, 34 unsuccessful attempts were made to pass a law authorizing federal judges to grant probation. The Volstead Act (the Prohibition Amendment) and the intense lobbying that the prohibitionists conducted convinced judges not to support probation because prohibitionists were afraid that judges would place violators of the Volstead Act on probation (Evjen 1975). The bill was finally passed in 1925 and sent to President Coolidge, who was formerly governor of Massachusetts and understood how probation worked. Since probation in Massachusetts had been successful for nearly five decades, Coolidge had no problem signing the National Probation Act. The act authorized each federal district court to appoint one salaried probation officer with an annual income of $2,600.

Between 1927 and 1930, eight probation officers were required to pass the civil service examination. In 1930, the original law was amended to empower judges to appoint without reference to the civil service list, and the limitation of one officer to each district was removed. At the same time, the Parole Act was amended to give probation officers field supervision responsibility for federal parolees and probationers. Thus, the average caseload was 400 probationers per probation officer. Officers relied heavily on as many as 700 volunteers (Evjen 1975).

Between 1930 and 1940, the Federal Bureau of Prisons (FBP) administered the federal probation system, and Colonel Joel R. Moore became the first federal probation supervisor. The number of officers increased from 8 to 233, but the appointments remained largely political.

In 1940, the U.S. probation system had increased so dramatically that the administration of probation was moved from the FBP to the Administrative Office of the U.S. Courts. The era from 1940 to 1950 concentrated on initial qualifications, standardized manuals, and in-service training. Initial qualifications for federal probation officers were that they be at least 25 years old, but preferably 30–45 years of age; have a baccalaureate degree; possess two years of experience in social work; and be mature, intelligent, of good moral character, patient, and energetic (Evjen 1975).

In 1984, the Comprehensive Crime Control Act abolished federal parole and brought all supervised prison releases under the auspices of federal probation. Federal probation is administered as an appendage of the federal courts.

HISTORY OF JUVENILE PROBATION AND THE JUVENILE COURT

From the 1700s to the early 1800s, children were disciplined and punished for crimes informally by parents and other adults in the community. Most children contributed to the family income, but there were no formal mechanisms to care for children whose parents died or were left homeless. Between 1817 and the mid 1840s, middle-class female reformers or "child savers" institutionalized runaway or neglected children in houses of refuge to provide them a family environment, but the good intentions of the child savers were not fully realized in practice. Although some institutions were humane, most children were further exploited for labor, abused, and victimized.

To protect children from this exploitation, the New York Children's Aid Society shipped children to farmers in the West to keep them from being committed to the House of Refuge. In 1890 the Children's Aid Society of Pennsylvania offered to place in foster homes delinquents who would otherwise be sent to reform school. Known as *placing out*, this practice was an early form of juvenile probation (Binder, Geis, and Bruce 1997).

The Illinois Juvenile Court Act of 1899 legally established a juvenile system different from the adult system to stop the exploitation of children. The court was anchored on the belief that a child's behavior was the product of poor family background and surroundings. It operated informally, was civil in nature, and was geared toward rehabilitation. Initially, there were those who believed that juvenile courts were created to coddle young criminals (Butts and Harrell 2003). This is likely an oversimplification. Indeed, although "some reformers were motivated by a desire to save growing numbers of poor and homeless children from the streets of America's cities, [others such as judges, prosecutors, and police were] mainly interested in removing the legal obstacles that prevented criminal courts from dealing effectively with young hoodlums" (Butts and Harrell 2003, p. 4). Before the advent of the juvenile court, intervention did not occur until after youths were convicted for a crime, so the thinking was that the juvenile system could intervene at an earlier point in time well before a conviction. "The trick was to create a new type of court that would have the power to intervene but would not have to abide by the restrictions of criminal procedure and due process rights" (Butts and Mears 2001, p. 172). In doing this, the state could intervene in cases where the juvenile needed protection from an abusive home or neglect.

Another observer said that "the 1899 Illinois Juvenile Court Act was, in part, yet another response to the growing incidence of jury nullification, concern about the dominance of sectarian industrial schools in Chicago filling with immigrants, and reform-based opposition to confining youth with adults" (Shepherd 1999, p. 16). Whatever the motivation, the idea of a separate court for juvenile offenders caught on and spread quickly. By 1925, 46 states, 3 territories, and the District of Columbia had juvenile courts (Shepherd 1999). Two concepts that formed the backbone of the original juvenile justice system were the recognition that level of intent for youth is different than adults, and that the state might have to intervene as a protector in the best interest of the child.

John Augustus also had volunteer successors who were influential in the development of juvenile probation in the United States. These volunteers included Rufus R. Cook, Miss L. P. Burnham, and Lucy L. Flower, among others. Rufus "Uncle" Cook provided supervision to juveniles while he also served as chaplain of the Suffolk County Jail in Boston. Miss L. P. Burnham was credited with being "the first career woman in the probation field" (Lindner and Savarese 1984b, p. 5). Lucy Flower, wife of a prominent Chicago attorney, was responsible for the creation of juvenile probation services in Illinois. She obtained support from the Chicago Bar Association to draft and pass the necessary legislation to provide a separate court and detention system that was different from the adult system (Lindner and Savarese 1984b).

Juvenile probation was formed under English common law and the doctrine of **parens patriae,** which is a Latin term for the doctrine that "the state is parent" and therefore serves as guardian of juveniles who might not be able to fend for themselves. The state intervened as a substitute parent in an attempt to act in the best interest of the child by using four principles. First, the court appointed a guardian to care for the child. The second principle was that parents of offenders must be held responsible for their children's wrongdoing. Third, no matter what offense children have committed, placing them in jail was an unsuitable penalty. The fourth principle stated that removing children from their parents and sending them even to an industrial school should be avoided, and

Parens Patriae
Latin term meaning that the government acts as a "substitute parent" and allows the courts to intervene in cases in which it is in the child's best interest that a guardian be appointed for children who, through no fault of their own, have been neglected and/or are dependent.

> that when it [a child] is allowed to return home it should be under probation, subject to the guidance and friendly interest of the probation officer, the representative of the court. To raise the age of criminal responsibility from seven or ten to sixteen or eighteen without providing for an efficient system of probation, would indeed be disastrous. Probation is, in fact, the keynote of juvenile court legislation. (Mack 1909, p.162)

Mack further related,

> Whenever juvenile courts have been established, a system of probation has been provided for, and even where as yet the juvenile court system has not been fully developed, some steps have been taken to substitute probation for imprisonment of the juvenile offender. What they need, more than anything else, is kindly assistance; and the aim of the court, appointing a probation officer for the child, is to have the child and the parents feel, not so much the power, as the friendly interest of the state; to show them that the object of the court is to help them to train the child right, and therefore the probation officers must be men and women fitted for these tasks. (p. 163)

A detailed discussion of the contemporary juvenile court and other types of community corrections for juveniles can be found in Chapter 14. For now, we return to a discussion of early probation laws in the adult system at the time when probation first began in the northeastern region of the United States.

EARLY PROBATION LEGISLATION IN OTHER STATES

New York's probation law allowed for police officers to be probation officers, but one of the two positions was occupied by three different University Settlement members (Lindner and Savarese 1984d). Later probation legislation in other states had a provision that the probation officer should not be an active member of the regular police force. Although this early legislation provided for the appointment of probation officers, most legislation did not provide money for salaried positions. According to Lindner and Savarese (1984a), this omission was deliberate because there was a feeling that the probation legislation would not have passed at all if there were appropriations and costs attached. Thus, probation workers in many areas were volunteers, paid from private donations, or they were municipal workers and other court officers who supervised probationers in addition to their regular jobs.

Organization of Probation Departments

After Massachusetts, Vermont was the second state to pass a probation statute, adopting a *county* plan of organization in 1898. Each county judge was given the power to appoint a probation officer to serve all of the courts in the county. California enacted a probation statute in 1903 following the Vermont pattern of county-based probation administration. The California law provided for adult as well as juvenile probation (U.S. Department of Justice 1974).

On the other hand, Rhode Island in 1899 adopted a *statewide* and state-controlled probation system. A state agency, the Board of Charities and Correction, was given the power to appoint a probation officer and assistants. States such as New York ultimately followed a state-controlled system (U.S. Department of Justice 1974). As various states enacted probation legislation, they did not do so uniformly. Initial probation legislation followed either Vermont's local organizational pattern or Rhode Island's state organizational pattern. Initial probation development in the U.S. resembles a "patchwork quilt" in many ways.

Over time, changes occurred in the way that probation departments are structured. Smaller, more localized departments found themselves at a disadvantage when trying to compete fiscally with larger agencies, such as state prisons and county jails that may send representatives to the state capitol during key budget times. For that reason, many probation and parole departments have merged. It has been only recently that some probation departments have combined adult and juvenile probation services. The three main structural differences pertain to:

- the branch of government: this may be executive/state or judicial/local
- the autonomy of probation agencies: these may be combined with parole, or can each be stand-alone departments
- age factors: agencies may combine their adult and juvenile supervision together, or be separate

In Table 4.1 the states with one or more asterisks (about half of all states) are ones in which the adult and juvenile systems are each administered differently. In most of the differences, the juvenile system is more fragmented and local, or a combination of both judicial and executive, depending on the county. However, juvenile

TABLE 4.1   Organizational Structure of Adult and Juvenile Probation/Parole Services

	ADULT		JUVENILE	
State	**Level/Branch**	**Combined or Separate Adult Probation & Parole**	**Level/Branch**	**Combined or Separate Juvenile w/Adult**
Alabama	State/Executive	Combined	County/Judicial	Separate
Alaska	State/Executive	Combined	State/Executive	Separate
Arizona	County/Judicial	Both	County/Judicial	Both
Arkansas	State/Executive	Combined	County/Judicial	Separate
California	County/Judicial	Separate	County/Judicial	Combined
Colorado	State/Judicial	Separate	County/Judicial	Combined
Connecticut	State/Judicial	Separate	State/Judicial	Separate
Delaware	State/Executive	Combined	State/Executive	Separate
Florida	State/Executive	Combined	State/Executive	Separate
Georgia	State/Executive	Separate	Mixed/Exec & Judicial	Separate
Hawaii	State/Judicial	Separate	State/Judicial	Separate
Idaho	State/Executive	Combined	County/Judicial	Separate
Illinois	County/Judicial	Separate	County/Judicial	Combined
Indiana	County/Judicial	Separate	County/Judicial	Combined
Iowa	County/Executive	Combined	State/Judicial	Separate
Kansas	State/Judicial	Separate	County/Judicial	Combined
Kentucky	State/Executive	Combined	State/Executive	Separate
Louisiana	State/Executive	Combined	Mixed/Exec & Judicial	Separate
Maine	State/Executive	Separate	State/Executive	Separate
Maryland	State/Executive	Combined	State/Executive	Separate
Massachusetts	State/Judicial	Separate	State/Judicial	Separate
Michigan	State/Executive	Combined	County/Judicial	Both
Minnesota	Mixed/Exec &Judicial	Both	Mixed/Exec & Judicial	Separate
Mississippi	State/Executive	Combined	Mixed/Exec & Judicial	Separate
Missouri	State/Executive	Combined	Mixed/Exec & Judicial	Separate
Montana	State/Executive	Combined	State/Judicial	Separate
Nebraska	State/Judicial	Separate	State/Judicial	Combined
Nevada	State/Executive	Combined	County/Judicial	Separate
New Hampshire	State/Executive	Combined	State/Executive	Separate
New Jersey	State/Judicial	Separate	State/Judicial	Combined
New Mexico	State/Executive	Combined	State/Executive	Separate
New York	County/Executive	Separate	County/Executive	Combined
North Carolina	State/Executive	Combined	State/Executive	Separate

(Continues)

TABLE 4.1   Organizational Structure of Adult and Juvenile Probation/Parole Services (Continued)

| State | ADULT | | JUVENILE | |
	Level/Branch	Combined or Separate Adult Probation & Parole	Level/Branch	Combined or Separate Juvenile w/Adult
North Dakota	State/Executive	Combined	State/Exec & Judicial	Separate
Ohio	Mixed/Exec &Judicial	Both	County/Exec & Judicial	Both
Oklahoma	State/Executive	Combined	Mixed/Exec & Judicial	Separate
Oregon	County/Executive	Combined	Mixed/Executive	Both
Pennsylvania	Mixed/Exec &Judicial	Both	County/Judicial	Both
Rhode Island	State/Executive	Combined	State/Executive	Separate
South Carolina	State/Executive	Combined	State/Executive	Separate
South Dakota	State/Judicial	Separate	State/Judicial	Combined
Tennessee	State/Executive	Separate	Mixed/Exec & Judicial	Separate
Texas	County/Judicial	Combined	County/Judicial	Both
Utah	State/Executive	Combined	State/Judicial	Separate
Vermont	State/Executive	Combined	State/Executive	Separate
Virginia	State/Executive	Combined	Mixed/Exec & Judicial	Separate
Washington	State/Executive	Combined	County/Exec & Judicial	Separate
West Virginia	County/Judicial	Separate	State/Judicial	Combined
Wisconsin	State/Executive	Combined	County/Exec & Judicial	Separate
Wyoming	State/Executive	Combined	Mixed/Exec & Judicial	Separate

Executive = Administered under the executive branch of government

Judicial = Administered under the courts/judicial branch

Source: Barbara Krauth and Larry Linke. 1999. *State Organizational Structures for Delivering Adult Probation Services.* Longmont, CO: LIS, Inc. for the National Institute of Corrections, U.S. Department of Justice.

and adult probation services are fully integrated in at least 10 states and partially integrated in select jurisdictions in another 6 states (Krauth and Linke 1999).

COMMUNITY CORRECTIONS ACTS

Community Corrections Act
Formal written agreement between the state government and local entities for the state to fund counties to implement and operate community corrections programs on a local level.

To address concerns about local community differences and the lesser ability of local government to render political pull, community corrections acts were developed to expand local sentencing options in lieu of imprisonment. **Community Corrections Acts** (CCAs) are statewide agreements through which funds are granted to local governments to develop and deliver community correctional sanctions and services (McManus and Barclay 1994). CCAs decentralize correctional sanctions, so that they more closely reflect community values and attitudes. The first community corrections act was enacted in Minnesota in 1973, and they now exist in 28 states.

State-run programs do not qualify as CCAs, only those that are operated locally or through private agencies. In this way, local governments benefit from the greater revenue-generating capacity of state government. An example of a recently revised CCA can be found in Box 4.2. Oregon is a good example of a CCA that shares characteristics found in other state agreements. Harris (1996) found that most CCAs are legislatively authorized statewide to provide state funding for local initiatives, decentralization of program design and delivery, and provides for citizen participation and/

BOX 4.2 COMMUNITY CORRECTIONS ACT IN OREGON

423.475. The Legislative Assembly finds and declares that:

(1) Passage by the voters of chapter 2, Oregon Laws 1995, has created mandatory minimum penalties for certain violent offenses, and the probable effect thereof will be a significant increase in the demands placed on state secure facilities.

(2) The state recognizes that it is in a better position than counties to assume responsibility for serious violent offenders and career property offenders.

(3) Counties are willing, in the context of a partnership with the state, to assume responsibility for felony offenders sentenced to a term of incarceration of 12 months or less.

(4) Under the terms of the partnership agreement, the state agrees to provide adequate funding to the counties if the counties agree to assume responsibility of those offenders.

423.505 Legislative policy on program funding. Because counties are in the best position for the management, oversight and administration of local criminal justice matters and for determining local resource priorities, it is the legislative policy of this state to establish an ongoing partnership between the state and counties and to finance with appropriations from the General Fund statewide community correction programs on a continuing basis. The intended purposes of this program are to:

(1) Provide appropriate sentencing and sanctioning options including incarceration, community supervision and services;

(2) Provide improved local services for persons charged with criminal offenses with the goal of reducing the occurrence of repeat criminal offenses;

(3) Promote local control and management of community corrections programs; and

(4) Promote the use of the most effective criminal sanctions necessary to protect public safety, administer

punishment to the offender and rehabilitate the offender. [1977 c.412 §1; 1989 c.607 §1; 1995 c.423 §2]

423.520. The Department of Corrections shall make grants to assist counties in the implementation and operation of community corrections programs. The department shall require recipients of the grants to cooperate in the collection and sharing of data necessary to evaluate the effect of community corrections programs on future criminal conduct. [1977 c.412 §5; 1987 c.320 §221; 1995 c.423 §3; 1997 c.433 §10]

(1) The county may contract with public or private agencies including, but not limited to, other counties, cities, special districts and public or private agencies for the provision of services to offenders. [1977 c.412 §13; 1987 c.320 §224; 1989 c.613 §2; 1995 c.423 §7]

423.570 Monthly fee payable by person on supervised release; use; payment as condition of release; waiver. (1) A person sentenced to probation or placed by an authority on parole, post-prison supervision or other form of release, subject to supervision by a community corrections program established under ORS 423.500 to 423.560, shall be required to pay a monthly fee to offset costs of supervising.

(3) The fee shall be determined and fixed by the releasing authority but shall be at least $25.

(4) Fees are payable one month following the commencement of supervision and at one-month intervals thereafter. Each county shall retain the fee to be used for funding of its community corrections programs.

Source: Oregon Legislative Assembly, Legislative Counsel Committee. Adapted from the 2003 Oregon Revised Statutes, Chapter 423—Corrections and Crime Control Administration and Programs. Retrieved on February 21, 2009 from: http://www.oregon.gov/DOC/TRANS/CC/orsite_map.shtml

or privatization. This is important because it allows local communities the opportunity to develop programs to fit their needs. For example, Ohio and North Carolina developed day-reporting centers, while Iowa and Indiana developed victim offender dialogue meetings. Jurisdictions that want to initiate a new program, such as a drug court or mental health court, must agree to contribute matching funds (Center for Community Corrections 1997). Note that Oregon's act includes the provision for a monthly fee while on supervision, so that offenders help subsidize their own costs to taxpayers.

States that do not have CCAs (e.g., Arkansas, Idaho, Illinois, Louisiana, Nevada, New Hampshire, North Dakota, Rhode Island, Utah, Vermont) still subsidize and contract out to public and private agencies, but the funding mechanism is not formalized and appears less consistent than in states that have CCAs in place.

MODELS OF SUPERVISION OVER TIME

As community corrections acts were established, they helped create stability in the idea of correctional supervision in the community as the primary mode of social control. In this section, we review how probation supervision styles have changed over the last 100 years.

Casework
A community supervision philosophy that allowed the officer to create therapeutic relationships with clients through counseling and directly assisting in behavior modification to assist them in living productively in the community.

The Casework Model: 1900–1970. When probation began, the supervision process was oriented toward casework, providing therapeutic services to probationers or parolees (often referred to as clients) to assist them in living productively in the community. Probation and parole officers frequently viewed themselves as "caseworkers" or social workers, and the term "agent of change" was a popular description of their role. The literature of probation and parole supervision during this period was replete with medical and psychiatric terminology, such as *treatment* and *diagnosis*. Casework stressed creating therapeutic relationships with clients through counseling and directly assisting in behavior modification (National Advisory Commission on Criminal Justice Standards and Goals 1973). The probation officer was thus viewed as a social worker engaged in a therapeutic relationship with the probationer "client."

Brokerage of Services
Supervision that involves identifying the needs of probationers or parolees and referring them to an appropriate community agency.

Brokerage of Services Model: 1970–1980. In the early 1970s the casework approach began to break down. Many services needed by probationers and parolees could be more readily and effectively provided by specialized community agencies that provide mental health, employment, housing, education, private welfare, and other services. The National Advisory Commission on Criminal Justice Standards and Goals (1973) reported: "Probation also has attempted to deal directly with such problems as alcoholism, drug addiction, and mental illness, which ought to be handled through community mental health and other specialized programs" (pp. 107–108). This alternative strategy for delivering probation and parole services is referred to as the **brokerage of services** approach. The "service broker" type of probation or parole officer does not consider him- or herself the primary agent of change as in the casework approach. Instead, the officer attempts to determine the needs of the probationer or parolee and locates and refers the client to the appropriate community agency. Thus, an unemployed parolee might be referred to vocational rehabilitation services, employment counseling, or the state employment office. Instead of attempting to counsel a probationer with emotional problems, the service broker officer would locate and refer the probationer to agencies whose staff is skilled in working with problems such as those faced by the probationer. In this supervision strategy, developing linkages between clients and appropriate agencies is considered one of the probation or parole officer's most important tasks.

Community Resource Management Team (Crmt) Model
A supervision model in which probation or parole officers develop skills and linkages with community agencies in one or two areas only. Supervision under this model is a team effort, each officer utilizing his or her skills and linkages to assist the offender.

Closely allied to the brokerage approach was the **community resource management team model.** Individual probation and parole officers became specialists by developing skills and linkages with community agencies in one or two areas. For example, one officer might be designated the drug abuse specialist and another, the employment specialist, whereas a third developed expertise with women offenders. This approach recognized that the diverse needs of the probation or parole caseload cannot be adequately satisfied by one individual. Thus the caseload is "pooled," and the probationer might be assisted not by one officer but by several.

The Justice Model: 1980–2000. By the mid-1980s, the **justice model** dominated probation and parole supervision. The justice model advocates an escalated system of sanctions corresponding to the social harm resulting from the offense and the offender's culpability. The justice model regards a sentence of probation not as an alternative to imprisonment, but as a valid sanction in itself. When viewed as an alternative to incarceration, the public tends to regard probation as an expression of leniency. The justice philosophy regards probation as a separate, distinct sanction requiring penalties that are graduated in severity and duration corresponding to the seriousness of the crime.

Advocates of the justice model hold that practices of counseling, surveillance, and reporting accomplish very little and have minimal impact on recidivism. They favor probation that consists of monitoring court orders for victim restitution or community service and that ensures that the imposed deprivation of liberty is carried out. Thus, this model primarily assists offenders in complying with supervision conditions. Other services such as mental health counseling, alcohol and drug treatment are available, but brokered through social agencies in the community.

> **Justice Model**
> The correctional practice based on the concept of just deserts and even-handed punishment. The justice model calls for fairness in criminal sentencing, in that all people convicted of a similar offense will receive a like sentence. This model of corrections relies on determinate sentencing and/or abolition of parole.

Neighborhood-Based Supervision. A philosophical change has unfolded yet again to rethink the way that probation supervision is implemented to encompass both the offenders and the communities in which they reside. This supervision strategy is more visible in the community and is known by a variety of terms such as **neighborhood-based supervision** (the term we will use in this text), "community justice" or "broken windows probation." (Beto 2000).

In neighborhood-based supervision (NBS), the probation officers are in the community more than the office and engage community groups as partners and collaborators in offender supervision. By making probation more visible and establishing leverage with community groups, NBS aims to make probation a more respected punishment in the community. The strategies of NBS would in turn help improve the overall quality of life in the community and contribute to decreasing crime. The elements of NBS include holding probation administrators and line officers accountable for achieving specific outcomes, such as:

> **Neighborhood-Based Supervision**
> A supervision strategy that emphasizes public safety, accountability, partnerships with other community agencies, and beat supervision.

- Emphasis on public safety
- Partnerships with police, treatment providers, and faith-based initiatives
- Supervision in field beats
- Strong and consistent enforcement of probation conditions
- Use of satellite tracking and geographic information systems technology
- Rational allocation of resources using offender assessments
- Measuring program effectiveness by establishing performance-based initiatives (Beto 2000, p. 12)

This philosophy has required a paradigm shift in how probation officers and supervisors currently think and operate. Even with all these changes, the dual role as therapeutic change agents and enforcers who see to it that their clients do not threaten public safety is a constant challenge.

In Chapter 5, we discuss how neighborhood-based community supervision is implemented. For now, we end this chapter with a brief overview of who is on probation.

Who Is on Probation?

Table 4.2 shows that probationer demographics have stayed fairly stable over time. About 60 percent of probationers nationwide have a direct sentence to probation, 30 percent have some type of suspended sentence (such as diversion), and 9 percent have a split sentence (a short time in jail, followed by a longer period of probation). The vast majority of probationers have been sentenced for a drug or alcohol violation, followed by property offenses, with less than 20 percent of probationers sentenced for a violent offense. About 77 percent of all adult probationers are men, and 23 percent

TABLE 4.2   Characteristics of Adults on Probation Over Time: 1995, 2000, and 2007

	1995	2000	2007
Gender			
Male	79%	78%	77%
Female	21	22	23
Race/Hispanic Origin			
White	53	54	55
Black	31	31	29
Hispanic	14	13	13
American Indian/Alaska Native	1	1	1
Asian/Pacific Islander[a]	**	1	1
Status of Probation			
Direct imposition	48	56	54
Split sentence	15	11	9
Sentence suspended	26	25	27
Imposition suspended	6	7	8
Other	4	1	2
Status of Supervision			
Active	79	76	70
Inactive	8	9	7
Absconded	9	9	9
Supervised out of state	2	3	3
Warrant status	*	*	7
Residential Program	*	*	1
Financial conditions remaining	*	*	2
Other	2	3	2
Type of Offense			
Felony	54	52	47
Misdemeanor	44	46	51
Other infractions	2	2	3
Most Serious Offense			
Sexual assault	*	*	3
Domestic violence	*	*	6
Other assault	*	*	10
Burglary	*	*	5
Larceny/theft	*	*	12
Fraud	*	*	5
Drug law violation	*	24	26
Driving while intoxicated	16	18	15
Minor traffic offenses	*	6	7
Other	84	52	10
Adults Entering Probation			
Without incarceration	72	79	76
With incarceration	13	16	14
Other types	15	5	10

(*Continues*)

TABLE 4.2   Characteristics of Adults on Probation Over Time: 1995, 2000, and 2007 (Continued)

	1995	2000	2007
Adults Leaving Probation			
Successful completions	62	60	60
Returned to incarceration	21	15	15
With new sentence	5	3	8
With the same sentence	13	8	6
Unknown	3	4	1
Absconder[b]	*	3	4
Other unsuccessful[b]	*	11	10
Death	1	1	1
Other	16	11	9

Notes: For every characteristic there were people of unknown status or type.
*Not measured. **Less than 0.5 percent. [a]Includes Native Hawaiians. [b]In 1995 absconder and other unsuccessful were reported as "other."

Sources: Lauren E. Glaze and Seri Palla. 2005. *Probation and Parole in the United States, 2004.* Washington, DC: U.S. Department of Justice, Bureau of Justice Statistics; Lauren E. Glaze and Thomas P. Bonczar. 2008. *Probation and Parole in the United States, 2007.* Washington, DC: U.S. Department of Justice, Bureau of Justice Statistics.

are women. The race/ethnic group composition for probationers varies by region of the country, but on a nationwide scale more than half (56 percent) of probationers are white, 30 percent are African American, 12 percent are of Hispanic origin, and 2 percent are either Native American or Asian/Pacific Islander (see Table 4.2).

SUMMARY

- In the American colonies, where English law prevailed, distinct American practices developed. Precursors to American probation included filing, security for good behavior, recognizance, and suspension of imposition of sentence. American judges exercised discretion to reduce the severity of punishment in cases in which the circumstances of the crime or characteristics of the offender warranted leniency.

- The increasing awareness that prisons were not accomplishing their stated purpose of reforming the offender and that suspension of sentence without supervision was not a satisfactory alternative brought about the development of probation as it is known today.

- With the foundation laid by judges, volunteers, and the University Settlement movement, John Augustus brought about the practice of probation as it is known today.

- The concept that crimes committed by children should be dealt with differently, with special courts and special facilities for juveniles, was formalized by the creation of the first juvenile court in Illinois in 1899.

- There are two kinds of suspended sentence—suspension of *imposition* of sentence and suspension of *execution* of sentence. Imposition of sentence means that there is no conviction, and it will be dropped if the defendant completes probation successfully. Execution of sentence means the defendant is placed on probation and the conviction remains on record.

- Probation organizational patterns have little uniformity in the United States.
  - Probation services may be combined with parole or kept separate.
  - Adult and juvenile probation may be combined or entirely separate.
  - Probation may be administered by the executive branch of government or by the judiciary.

- Community corrections acts provide state funding to local probation agencies for development of a wider range of community supervision and treatment programs.

- The four eras of community supervision that have influenced probation as we know it were: case work, brokerage of services, justice model, and neighborhood probation.

DISCUSSION QUESTIONS

1. What was the significance of the decision in *Commonwealth v. Chase?*

2. What are the two kinds of suspended sentence? Why is the distinction critical to an understanding of modern probation?

3. What was the Killits case? What was its impact on modern probation?

4. Who were John Augustus and Matthew Davenport Hill, and how did they assist in creating support for probation as we know it today?

5. Why are community corrections acts advantageous to local-level supervision?

6. How has the concept of supervision changed over the past century? What factors have brought about these changes?

7. Which of the models of supervision do you view as the most effective for use today?

WEB SITES

History of New York Corrections, N.Y. Corrections Society
http://www.correctionhistory.org/

History of U.S. Probation Office
http://www.nmcourt.fed.us/web/PBDOCS/FIles/history.html

Hampshire Probation Service, United Kingdom
http://www.hampshire-probation.gov.uk

American Probation and Parole Association
http://www.appa-net.org/

Federal Probation
http://www.uscourts.gov/library/fpcontents.html

Classification and Supervision: Techniques of Evidence-Based Practices

CHAPTER LEARNING OBJECTIVES

- Identify the importance of caseload classification in identifying risk and needs.
- Describe classification techniques that lead to defining the level of supervision and development of a treatment plan.
- List the principles of effective correctional intervention in offender treatment.
- Recall how workload allocation is important to keep caseloads manageable.
- Explain how neighborhood-based supervision probation officers are involved with the community.
- Provide examples of offenders on specialized caseloads.

© Andrew Ramey/PhotoEdit

The foundation of supervision is getting into the field to meet with clients in their own neighborhoods.

CHAPTER OUTLINE

Introduction

Classification: The First Step in Supervision
Risk Assessments
Identifying Treatment Needs

The Supervision Case Plan
Implementing the Case Plan: Surveillance
Levels of Supervision
Caseload and Workload Standards

Implementing the Case Plan: Treatment
Evaluation of Neighborhood-Based vs. Traditional
    Probation

Specialized Caseloads
Supervising Sex Offenders
Strategies for Supervising Known Gang Members
Working with Women Offenders

Summary

KEY TERMS

classification
risk assessment
static factors
dynamic factors
case plan

supervision
surveillance
field contact
collateral contact
caseload

principles of effective intervention
cognitive-behavioral therapy
motivational interviewing
penile plethysmograph

Introduction

Probation departments provide both an investigatory and a supervisory function in the criminal justice system. While Chapter 3 addressed the presentence investigatory function, in this chapter, we discuss the classification and supervisory functions of probation and parole officers as they pertain to management of offenders in the community. Evidence-based practices (EBP) that have been shown to improve the supervision of offenders are classification assessments, case planning, having different levels of supervision, motivational interviewing, cognitive-behavioral treatments, and using the principles of correctional intervention.

Much of this chapter applies to both probation and parole supervision because the mechanics of the supervision process and the condition terms are similar. In many states and in the federal system, the officers supervise a mix of both probationers and parolees on the same caseload.

Classification: The First Step in Supervision

Classification
A procedure consisting of assessing the risks posed by the offender, identifying the supervision issues, and selecting the appropriate supervision strategy.

Each new client on community supervision must first be classified. **Classification** consists of the supervising officer using an objective assessment scale to compute the risks posed by the offender, identifying offender needs requiring intervention, and selecting the appropriate supervision and treatment strategies. Researchers indicate that objective actuarial prediction models, if used by a trained officer, are more reliable and efficient than subjective methods. Highest priority is placed on identifying risks that would likely jeopardize public safety if not addressed. Risk variables also determine the level of supervision required by the offender. At the same time, a priority is placed on identifying needs that, if not addressed, will likely lead to a return to criminal behavior (Lowenkamp, Latessa, and Holsinger, 2006).

Drug and alcohol testing is common while on probation supervision.

RISK ASSESSMENTS

Risk assessment provides a measure of the probationer or parolee's degree of dangerousness to the public and also measures the offender's propensity to engage in future criminal activity. Probation and parole jurisdictions have developed some form of risk prediction scale to assist them in developing supervision plans and in caseload classification. These instruments differ in some respects, but all of them place offenders in groups with a known statistical probability of committing new crimes or violating the conditions of supervision.

The first-generation assessments relied on interviewing the offender and using case-by-case anecdotal information to make the decision about risk. Although professional judgment and intuition can be accurate, different questions were asked of each offender and comparisons among cases was difficult. Many types of assessment tools were later developed, some of which are more sophisticated than others. The second-generation assessments include Client Management Classification (CMC), the Correctional Offender Management Profiles for Alternative Sentences (COMPAS), the Wisconsin Client Management Classification, and the Salient Factor Score. These assessments primarily use **static** questions about previous behavior, which has already happened and cannot be altered.

More recent third-generation assessments are the Offender Inventory Assessment (OIA) and the Level of Service Inventory-Revised (LSI-R). These assessments include both static and **dynamic** factors, which aid in measuring both negative and positive offender change over time. Dynamic factors include family relations, friends, emotional health, housing, leisure, and financial situation. The LSI-R is a 54-item scale that assigns a numerical value to many of the same factors identified in the presentence report. The officer completes the LSI-R by interviewing the offender and scoring one point for every affirmative answer.

The LSI-R has been validated for use with male and female adult offenders and some juvenile offender populations. The risk score of the LSI-R can accurately predict future criminal activity, in that the higher the risk score, the more likely that

Risk Assessment
A procedure that provides a measure of the offender's propensity to further criminal activity and indicates the level of officer intervention that will be required.

Static Factors
Correlates of the likelihood of recidivism that (once they occur) cannot be changed (age at first arrest, number of convictions, and so forth).

Dynamic Factors
Correlates of the likelihood of recidivism that can be changed through treatment and rehabilitation (drug and alcohol abuse, anger management, quality of family relationships, and so forth).

the offender will recidivate (Lowenkamp and Bechtel, 2007). For this reason, the high-risk offenders should receive the "lion's share" of the treatment services to counteract that risk. A meta-analysis of 47 different studies of the LSI-R shows that it accurately targets high-risk clients who are at greatest need of intervention, but that it more accurately predicts adult men and is less accurate at predicting recidivism for women offenders (Vose, Cullen, and Smith, 2008). There is apparently a fourth generation risk/needs assessment called the LSI Case Management Inventory that integrates assessment with case planning (VanBenschoten, 2008).

No matter whether the programs were treatment oriented or supervision oriented, mixing low-risk offenders with high-risk offenders in the same program later *increased* recidivism. These findings have led to one risk principle, which is to reserve the most intensive treatment programs for the highest-risk offenders, in part, because this target population will benefit exponentially more from the intervention than the low-risk offenders (Hanley, 2002).

Copyright protection does not allow reproduction of the LSI-R, so we provide examples of other instruments currently used. Figure 5.1 shows the Wisconsin Risk and Needs sheet. The Client Management Classification assessment instrument (known as the "Strategies for Case Supervision" in Texas) is used by many community supervision departments nationwide and can be found at the end of this chapter. The Salient Factor Score (SFS-98) is the assessment version for the federal system, and that instrument can be found in Chapter 12.

IDENTIFYING TREATMENT NEEDS

The officer must also identify those characteristics, conditions, or behavioral problems that limit the offender's motivation or may lead to a return to criminal behavior. Such treatment needs include drug or alcohol abuse, mental illness, anger management issues, or deficiencies in education or vocational skills. Treatment activities are defined as actions taken by the supervising officer intended to bring about a change in the offender's conduct or condition for the purpose of rehabilitation and reintegration into the law-abiding community. Together, both risk and needs assessments can (and should) define the types of correctional services that are made available to offenders (Andrews, Bonta, and Wormith, 2006).

Sources of information that may be used to identify treatment needs include the presentence report, prison disciplinary records and the prerelease plan, physical or medical health evaluations, records of drug or alcohol abuse and other related criminal conduct, financial history, and residential history. Because the federal PSIs are so detailed, they capture most of the information in the risk and needs assessment of the LSI-R. In these cases, case managers use the LSI-R to gauge client honesty (or consistency) by comparing their responses to the PSI and the LSI-R. The importance of carefully gathering and evaluating the offender's history cannot be overstated, for past behavior is, at the moment, the best predictor we have of future behavior.

The Supervision Case Plan

After reviewing the court-ordered conditions of probation, assessing the offender's risk by calculating a risk score, and determining treatment concerns, the officer identifies specific supervision issues and selects the appropriate strategies for addressing them (Storm, 1997). In other words, the officer is developing a **case plan,** which is an individualized, written document that clarifies how each court-ordered condition is to be fulfilled by the offender and the supervising officer in the context of the risks

FIGURE 5.1

RISK ASSESSMENT

Defendant: _____   Date: _____

			Risk Score

1. Number of address changes in the last 12 months............................
    0 None
    2 One
    3 Two or More   _____(1

2. Percentage of Time Employed in the last 12 months.......................
    (Adult or Juvenile—include deferred)
    0 60%
    1 40%−59%
    2 Under 40%
    0 Not Applicable   _____(2

3. Alcohol Usage...………..............
    0 Alcohol use unrelated to criminal activity ex., no alcohol-related arrest, no evidence of use during offense.
    1 Probable relationship between drug involvement and criminal activity.
    2 Definite relationship between alcohol use and criminal activity; ex., pattern of committing offenses while using alcohol   _____(3

4. Other drug usage..….........................
    0 No abuse of legal drugs; no indicators of illegal drug involvement, ie., use, possession or abuse.
    1 Probable relationship between drug involvement and criminal activity.
    2 Definite relationship between drug Involvement and criminal activity; ex., pattern of committing offenses while using drugs, sale or manufacture of illegal drugs.   _____(4

5. Attitude...…….......
    0 Motivated to change; receptive to assistance
    3 Somewhat motivated but dependent or unwilling to accept responsibility
    5 Rationalizes behavior; negative; not motivated to change.   _____(5

6. Age at first adjudication of guilt...
    0 24 or older
    2 20−23
    4 19 or younger   _____(6

7. Number of prior periods of Probation / Parole Supervision.................
    (Adult or Juvenile)
    0 None
    4 One or more   _____(7

8. Number of Prior Probation / Parole Revocations.............................
    (Adult or Juvenile)
    0 None
    4 One or more   _____(8

9. Number of Prior Felony Adjudications of Guilt................…................
    (or Juvenile commitments – include deferred)
    0 None
    2 One
    4 Two or more   _____(9

10. Adult or Juvenile adjudications for.................................…..............
    (Select applicable and add for score include current offense, Maximum score: 5)
    0 None
    2 Burglary, Theft, Auto Theft or Robbery
    3 Worthless Checks or Forgery   _____(10

11. Adult or Juvenile Adjudications for.............................…….....…....…......
    Assaultive Offense within the last FIVE years
    (An offense, which is defined as Assaultive or one in which involves a use of a weapon, physical force or the threat of force)
    0 No
    8 Yes   _____(11

Sum of Items 1–11: _____(12

Risk Level: _____(13

> RISK
> 1 — Maximum (15+)
> 2 — Medium (8 − 14)
> 3 — Minimum (0 − 7)

(Continues)

FIGURE 5.1 (Continued)

NEEDS ASSESSMENT

1. ACADEMIC/VOCATIONAL SKILLS

| −1 High school or above skill level | 0 Adequate skills, able to handle everyday requirements | +2 Low level causing minor adjustment problems | +4 Minimal skill level causing serious adjustment problems | _____(1 |

2. EMPLOYMENT

| −1 Satisfactory employment for one year or longer | 0 Secure employment, no difficulties reported; or homemaker, student or retired | +3 Unsatisfactory employment or unemployed but has adequate job skills | +6 Unemployed and virtually unemployable; needs training | _____(2 |

3. FINANCIAL MANAGEMENT

| −1 Long-standing pattern of self-sufficiency e.g., good credit | 0 No current difficulties | +3 Situational or difficulties | +5 Severe difficulties; may include overdrafts, bad checks or bankruptcy | _____(3 |

4. MARITAL/FAMILY RELATIONSHIPS

| −1 Relationships and support exceptionally strong | 0 Relatively stable relationship | +3 Some disorganization or stress but potential for improvement | +5 Major disorganization or stress | _____(4 |

5. COMPANIONS

| −1 Good support and influence | 0 No adverse relationships | +2 Associations with occasional negative results | +4 Associations almost completely negative | _____(5 |

6. EMOTIONAL STABILITY

| −2 Exceptionally well adjusted; accepts responsibility for actions | 0 No symptoms of emotional instability; appropriate emotional responses | +4 Symptoms limit but do not prohibit adequate functioning; e.g. anxiety | +7 Symptoms prohibit adequate functioning; e.g., lashes out or retreats into self | _____(6 |

7. ALCOHOL USAGE PROBLEM

| | 0 No use; use with no abuse no disruption of functioning | +3 Occasional abuse; some disruption of functioning | +6 Frequent abuse; serious disruption of functioning | _____(7 |

8. OTHER DRUG USAGE PROBLEM

| | 0 No disruption of functioning | +3 Occasional abuse; some disruption of functioning | +5 Frequent abuse; serious disruption of functioning | _____(8 |

9. MENTAL ABILITY

| | 0 Able to function independently | +3 Some need for assistance; potential for adequate adjustment; possible retardation | +6 Deficiencies severely limit independent functioning; possible retardation | _____(9 |

10. HEALTH

| | 0 Sound physical health; seldom ill | +1 Handicap or illness interferes with functioning on a recurring basis | +2 Serious handicap or chronic illness; needs frequent medical care | _____(10 |

11. SEXUAL BEHAVIOR

| | 0 No apparent dysfunction | +3 Real or perceived situational or minor problems | +5 Real or perceived chronic or severe problems | _____(11 |

12. S.O.'s IMPRESSION OF DEFENDANTS NEEDS

| −1 Well adjusted | 0 No needs | +3 Moderate needs | +5 High needs | _____(12 |

```
            NEEDS
1 – Maximum (30+)
2 – Medium (15–29)
3 – Minimum (14 & below)
```

Sum of Lines 1–12: _____(13

RISK LEVEL: _____(14

and needs posed. A case plan is negotiated and signed by both parties. Progress on the case plan is reviewed during each appointment and can be modified as circumstances change (Lerner, Arling, and Baird, 1986).

A **supervision** issue is an identified problem, offender characteristic, or pattern of conduct that requires intervention to overcome or change. An issue is identified and the officer develops strategies to deal with or monitor that issue. Interviewing the offender can be done using a structured assessment interview called a Client Management Classification (CMC), which can be found at the back of this chapter following the case study. The CMC contains 56-questions to ask the offender, followed by "Behavioral Patterns" and "Impressions" sections that are completed about the offender immediately afterwards. The risk/needs assessments and the CMC interview are used to identify strengths and weaknesses of various life issues. The weaknesses are linked to the current offense or have occurred so often that they are serious problems that need to be changed or addressed. Implementation of this case plan occurs through surveillance and the development of prosocial behaviors.

Supervision
The oversight that a probation or parole officer exercises over those in his or her custody.

IMPLEMENTING THE CASE PLAN: SURVEILLANCE

Surveillance is an important element of supervision that provides a means of ascertaining whether probationers and parolees are continuing to meet the conditions imposed by the court or the parole board. Surveillance can be a good tool for reducing an offender's access to crime opportunities (Cullen, Eck, and Lowenkamp, 2002). The most common form of surveillance is maintaining contact through face-to-face meetings with each client in the office setting. Offenders also check in through phone and/or mail verification. A **field contact** is considered to be the most time consuming, but is also the most valuable type of contact. In a field contact, the officer visits the offender's home or place of employment to monitor progress.

Surveillance
Community monitoring methods of ascertaining offender compliance through one or more of the following means: face-to-face home visits, curfew, electronic monitoring, phone verification, and drug testing.

Field Contact
An officer's personal visit to an offender's home or place of employment for the purpose of monitoring progress under supervision.

© AP/Wide World Photos

Claude Allen, a former aide to President Bush, pleaded guilty to theft for making false returns at discount department stores while working for the White House. Allen pleaded guilty in Montgomery County Circuit Court to one misdemeanor count of theft under $500 and was sentenced to two years of supervised probation with a $500 fine.

BOX 5.1   TECHNOLOGY IN CORRECTIONS

Virtual and Mobile Community Supervision Techniques

Technology has enabled community supervision officers to rethink day-to-day supervision methods. In the past, officers used to spend most of their day in their offices responding to calls and visits from probationers who came to them. Now, technology has afforded low-risk probationers the opportunity to check in with their officer using centrally located kiosk machines. A kiosk machine is an interactive computerized touch screen machine that allows offenders on probation or parole to receive and send personal messages back and forth to their supervising officer at any time of day. A kiosk machine can be set up anywhere that is monitored, such as in a lobby of a police station or in a grocery store that is open 24 hours a day. Each probationer's password is his or her fingerprints, which is also the password to each touch screen. Offenders can use kiosk machines to notify the probation officer of a change of address or employment, and the probation officer can use them to ask the individual client questions, to which the client can type a response. Kiosks also store information on bus routes, job postings, and schedules for services such as treatment programs, employment offices, and driver's license bureaus. In some jurisdictions, kiosks have replaced face-to-face meetings (Ogden and Horrocks 2001).

For offenders in remote areas or probationers who cannot afford telephones, special pagers are provided in lieu of a kiosk that allow a supervision officer to beep the client with a directive, such as to call the officer immediately or to submit a urine sample within a designated period of time. Clients do not know the number to their personal pagers, so no one else can beep them with personal calls (Ogden and Horrocks 2001).

With less time spent on low-risk clients, probation and parole officers can then spend more time out in the field seeing their higher-risk clients in person. To document their visits while in the field, probation officers have a portable office that consists of a cell phone, pager, and laptop computer. Some jurisdictions have already replaced laptop computers with tablet PCs, Blackberrys, or PDAs equipped with wireless internet capabilities. All of these devices are handheld so they are lighter weight and allow the officer more mobility. Most tablet PCs have either a handwriting or voice recognition feature so there is no keyboard. Internet access allows officers to retrieve GPS coordinates of offenders, retrieve client information from protected databases, and check public record databases through SmartLinx with the same level of security they enjoy through their office.

Source: Thomas G. Ogden and Cary Horrocks. 2001. Pagers, Digital, Audio, and Kiosk: Officer Assistants. *Federal Probation* 65(2): 35–37.

Collateral Contact
Verification of the probationer or parolee's situation and whereabouts by means of the officer speaking with a third party who knows the offender personally (such as a family member, friend, or employer).

On a quarterly basis, supervision officers make at least one **collateral contact**, which means that the officer contacts employers, teachers, and/or or relatives to verify that each offender is adhering to probation conditions. Few offices, however, specify the quality of the contact. Other ways that probationers have to contact their probation officer include kiosk machines in the community (see Box 5.1).

Methods of surveillance included unannounced and announced home visits, curfew, electronic monitoring, and collection of urine samples for drug testing (Taxman, 2002).

In addition to surveillance by probation officers, police watch probationers and parolees, warrantless searches of probationers' homes can be conducted by *police* if the search was based on the police's "reasonable suspicion" that the probationer was also thought to be engaged in criminal activity (*United States v. Knights*, 2001). Reasonable suspicion is a lower standard of proof than "probable cause," which is needed for most residence searches. However, the U.S. Supreme Court said that the probationer has a diminished expectation of privacy while on probation, and the probationer is more likely to violate the law than a citizen not on probation. Public support and cooperation are difficult to obtain for any probation or parole system that does not assure the community of at least minimum protection against potential criminal activities by those under supervision.

LEVELS OF SUPERVISION

One of the principles of effective supervision is developing various levels of supervision to differentiate offenders who need closer supervision from those who require less. Although various names are used, there are typically three or four levels of supervision. A three-level supervision is maximum, medium, and minimum supervision, while a four-level probation system like that found in Table 5.1 is max (sex offenders), high, standard, and administrative.

At the lowest level of supervision, there may be no requirement that the probationer personally visit or contact a probation officer. Rather, the probationer may be required to call in and leave a message on a voice-recorded line, or mail-in a verification of address and employment. This level of supervision is known as administrative supervision and in California as "banked probation." Over 60 percent of all Los Angeles probationers were tracked solely by computer and had no contact with an officer. Administrative probation is for offenders who have committed minor crimes, who have satisfied their financial obligations, or have been in compliance for two years, and can be transferred down to this level.

Regular or standard probation supervision includes an endless variety of contact types. For example, Offender A on medium supervision may expect two face-to-face contacts per month and verification of residence and employment once every twelve months. Offender B on medium supervision may only have one quarterly face-to-face contact but weekly mail-in and quarterly home visits. The frequency and intensity of contacts increases with the supervision level, such that an offender on the highest level can expect one weekly face-to-face or field contacts, one monthly collateral contact, verification of residence and employment every three months, and a criminal history check every twelve months.

CASELOAD AND WORKLOAD STANDARDS

Central to the concept of evidence-based practices is a manageable caseload. A probation or parole officer's **caseload** is defined as the number of individuals or cases one officer can supervise effectively. In practice, caseloads vary widely because not every offender requires the same amount of supervision. The more intensive the supervision, the lower the caseload number. U.S. probation officers supervise 50 to 60 cases and conduct five or six presentence investigations per month, so they are involved in both supervision and investigation (Quinn, 2002). For stand-alone local probation departments where the investigation function is separated from the supervision function, the average caseload of regular probationers is 127 adults, with a high of 239 in Rhode Island. In contrast, a single caseload of parolees on regular supervision is 70 per officer. Intensive supervision probation and parole caseloads average 18 to 29 offenders, and offenders with special needs average 35 to 55 offenders per officer nationwide (Camp, Camp, and May, 2003).

Caseload
The number of individuals or cases for which one probation or parole officer is responsible.

TABLE 5.1   Differences for Each Supervision Level

Supervision Level	Minimum Monthly Contacts	Maximum Caseload Cap	Percent on Each Level
Max	4	40	3.3%
High	2	80	8.3%
Standard	1	250	46.5%
Administrative	0	No Cap	41.8%

Source: Georgia Department of Corrections. 2009. Retrieved from: http://www.dcor.state.ga.us/

Concerns about increased caseload size possibly has led some states to place statutory limits on the number of people that one officer should supervise. For example, the New Jersey Supreme Court limited specialized (or maximum level) caseloads to no more than 50 offenders per officer, but placed no limits on standard supervision. In contrast, Maryland does not cap any caseloads, so the state can (in theory) continue to increase the number of offenders supervised.

The American Probation and Parole Association has long recommended a "workload standard" of about 120 hours per month. The workload standard is more accurate, particularly if an officer has offenders of varying supervision levels. Workload is calculated by first assuming the number of hours required to supervise each client based on their level of supervision (maximum, medium, or minimum). A maximum supervision case may require, for example, four hours of the officer's time per month. A medium supervision case may require two hours per month, whereas a minimum supervision case may only require one hour or less per month of the officer's time. Given these calculations, one officer could effectively supervise 30 maximum supervision cases, 60 medium cases, and as many as 120 minimum cases. Development of a workload standard would allow for comparison between jurisdictions and improve the next step of case planning.

IMPLEMENTING THE CASE PLAN: TREATMENT

Thus far, we have discussed how implementing the case plan is achieved through contact and surveillance, and how the form each takes depends on the level of supervision. Along with reducing opportunities for crime, implementing the case plan must also be directed toward removing or reducing barriers that may result in recidivism, as well as assisting the offender in positive behavioral change, which may involve placing offenders into treatment programs (Cullen, Eck, and Lowenkamp, 2002).

The Principles of Effective Correctional Intervention   For the last few decades, researchers and treatment specialists have sought to figure out what type of treatment is most effective with which types of offenders. Paul Gendreau (1996) published the **principles of effective intervention,** which is currently considered the basis by which correctional treatment programs should operate and is a theoretical perspective of evidence-based correctional practices. There are a total of eight principles, which indicate that treatment services should:

Principles of Effective Intervention
Eight treatment standards that, if practiced, have been shown to reduce recidivism above that of other methods and constitute a theory behind evidence-based correctional practices.

1. Be intensive, occupying 40 to 70 percent of each day for three to nine months;
2. Contain cognitive-behavioral components to prepare the mind for the behavioral change;
3. Match the program level with client abilities or what the client can relate to according to gender, age, cultural background, and risk level. Higher risk level clients will make greater strides;
4. Have positive reinforcements that should exceed punishments by a ratio of 4:1;
5. Have minimum education and experience requirements for staff;
6. Teach clients to replace criminal networks with prosocial ones;
7. Provide relapse prevention and aftercare;
8. Evaluate the program and assess the compliance of programs to the previous seven principles by using the Correctional Program Assessment Inventory (CPAI). The CPAI examines each program in terms of its implementation, leadership, staff quality, and level of available funding to operate a quality program.

Many agencies, such as the Federal Probation District in Hawaii and jurisdictions in Maryland, are using these principles as they discover the true meaning of evidence-based practices (see Davidson, Crawford, and Kerwood 2008; Taxman 2008).

Evidence-based practices begins with a staff mindset that embraces the principles and sees the value in collecting data that will later be important to the evaluation.

Cognitive-Behavioral Therapy   One of the principles of correctional intervention is the use of **cognitive-behavioral therapy** (CBT) with offenders. CBT is an effective method of helping a person change, and it is a blend of two different types of therapies: cognitive therapy that prepares the mind, and behavioral change that conditions the body. CBT is used to overcome phobias, quit habitual behaviors such as smoking, drinking, or drug use, and to change old thinking patterns such as those linked to criminality. Box 5.2 discusses six different types of cognitive-behavioral therapy used with offenders.

> **Cognitive-Behavioral Therapy**
> A therapeutic intervention of helping a person change, that is a blend of two different types of therapies: cognitive therapy which prepares the mind, and behavioral change which conditions the body.

CBT has the offender replace both unhealthy thinking processes and criminal behaviors with responsibility, empathy, and prosocial behaviors. One CBT called "Thinking for a Change" was evaluated over one year using a treatment/control group of medium to high-risk offenders who had stable mental health and were neither substance abusers nor sex offenders. Although the technical violation rate

---

BOX 5.2 **COMMUNITY CORRECTIONS CLOSE UP**

Six Examples of Cognitive-Behavioral Therapy for Offenders

Cognitive-behavioral programs are a general category of group therapy programs that are more effective for people who might be resistant to change. The cognitive component centers around reducing narcissistic traits of self-hatred and self-centeredness and preparing the mind for the behavioral change that occurs. The behavioral component links the mental processes to acting out. These therapy modules are delivered in group sessions of 6 to 12 offenders by a trained group facilitator. We briefly discuss six examples below:

1. *Moral Reconation Therapy (MRT)*—Developed by Little and Robinson in the mid 1980s, this therapy program is 32 hours long and based on the assumption that people who have higher moral development skills are less likely to repeat criminal behavior. MRT is useful for offenders during residential treatment or for offenders who need to learn how to think more abstractly and take another person's perspective.

2. *Reasoning and Rehabilitation* (R&R)—Developed in the mid 1980s by Ross and Fabiano, this therapy assumes that offenders are egocentric and lack cognitive skills of self-control and interpersonal problem solving. It is similar to MRT, but with less focus on morals.

3. *Thinking for a Change* (T4C)—Developed in the mid 1990s by Bush, Glick, and Taymans and adopted for use and dissemination by the National Institute of Corrections, this program has 22 lessons lasting 1 to 2 hours each. This program is classified as a "cognitive restructuring" program in which offenders examine

their attitudes, beliefs, and thinking patterns so that they can more fully consider the consequences of their actions. Change is through social skills and problem-solving techniques and two sessions per week is the optimal dosage.

4. *Strategies for Self-Improvement and Change* (SSC)—This year-long program was developed by Wanberg and Milkman for adult substance abusers engaged in a long-term community treatment program. This therapy examines thoughts and behavior patterns that contribute to substance abuse, and involves being committed to change and taking responsibility for oneself.

5. *Relapse Prevention Therapy* (RPT)—After intensive residential treatment, RPT is a good aftercare program that follows the SSC program discussed above. RPT is also good for relapse prevention of any obsessive thoughts and/or compulsive or habitual behavior. RPT was developed in 2000 by Parks and Marlatt and teaches coping skills when the habitual thoughts surface.

6. *Aggression Replacement Training* (ART)—For youth and adult offenders with anger management problems, this therapy uses cognitive-behavioral techniques to recognize and appropriately deal with anger. Developed by Goldstein and Glick in the mid 1990s, this is a 30-hour program.

Source: Hansen, Chris. 2008. Cognitive-Behavioral interventions: Where they come from and what they do. *Federal Probation* 72 (2): 43–49.

and the rate of rearrest was not significantly different between the two groups, the treatment group had better interpersonal problem-solving skills compared to the people who did not complete treatment (Golden, Gatchel and Cahill, 2006). Cullen and Gendreau (2000) had more positive results, as they were able to show, through examining multiple studies, that cognitive-behavioral treatment programs that followed Gendreau's principles were able to reduce recidivism by 25 percent for the treatment group compared to the control group (those not involved in the treatment regimen). Correctional treatment programs that did not follow these principles either had no effect or were able to reduce recidivism by only about 10 percent.

Motivational Interviewing   Think of community supervision as a two-way relationship between the officer and the offender that is affected by the offender's motivation to change, coupled with the way the officer responds to and encourages that change. A different way of looking at offender change could be a "strength-based" or "asset-building" approach that rewards offenders with oral or written praise, certificates of completion, vouchers with small monetary rewards, or special privileges to encourage certain positive behaviors. At the same time, removing privileges would be expected for negative behavior, but simultaneously incorporating a reward system is more of a motivating factor for the probationer to change (Alexander, VanBenschoten, and Walters, 2008).

> **Motivational Interviewing**
> A communication style in which the community supervision officer creates a positive climate of sincerity and understanding that assists the offender in the change process

This communication style has also been called **motivational interviewing,** in which the community supervision officer creates a positive climate of sincerity and understanding that will assist the offender in changing (Clark, 2005). An honest, direct relationship, along with good communication skills, is an effective means of promoting change and ensuring successful completion of the term of probation. The key in motivational interviewing is to get the offender to recognize the problem, rather than to argue why he or she hasn't made strides toward change pointed out by others. Effective techniques include asking open-ended questions of the offender, demonstrating empathy, and taking a genuine interest by follow-up statements and positive recognition (Taxman, 2008). Statements such as

"How can we come together on this?" and

"It's your choice, but is there anything we can do to help you avoid those consequences?" (Clark, 2005, p. 26) are less confrontational than mandates, threats, and a "deficit-focused" approach in which the officer responds to negative rule-breaking behavior with punitiveness and graduated sanctions. Recent research has shown the effectiveness of motivational interviewing techniques with finding employment, paying probation fees, offender recognition of drinking behaviors, and preparing offenders for substance abuse treatment (Alexander, VanBenschoten, and Walters, 2008). Similar techniques have even been shown to reduce arrests and technical violations (Taxman, 2008).

Employment Assistance   Employment is likely the single most important element in preventing recidivism for probationers and parolees (Petersilia, 2003). Not only does employment provide financial support for the offender and his or her family, but it is also crucial for establishing and maintaining self-esteem and personal dignity—qualities that are seen by most authorities as essential to successful reintegration into the community. Experienced probation and parole officers know this to be true, and most probation and parole conditions require the offender to maintain employment during the period of supervision. However, finding and maintaining employment are not simple. Offenders are often the last to be hired and the first to be terminated. Many of them are unskilled, and many have poor work habits. Some are barred from employment in their chosen fields as a result of regulatory and licensing laws that preclude people with a criminal conviction (we discuss these issues in Chapter 15).

Because of the critical relationship between success on parole or probation supervision and meaningful employment, probation and parole officers must assess the employment status of each person under their supervision and work with him or her to locate a job. In many cases, the probationer or parolee will require a vocational assessment to determine his or her employability, interests, and capabilities, as well as any barriers to employment. Many will require vocational or job-readiness training before they can seek a job. Ideally, these services are obtained from external agencies and organizations such as state employment offices or vocational rehabilitation services. The probation or parole officer's job is to locate the existing service, assist the probationer in obtaining the service, and monitor progress and participation. This requires networking and connections with community agencies.

Appealing to Informal Social Controls Informal social controls such as family members and community agencies are also significant resources that officers can access to help probationers develop prosocial behaviors. Probationers were significantly more likely to succeed on probation if they had the support of family or friends than if they did not have such support (Taxman, 2002). Neighborhood-based supervision uses these techniques to aid in supervision.

Read one federal probation officer's view (see Box 5.3) about a typical day on the job, and see if you are able to determine which activities are surveillance functions and which are oriented toward treatment.

EVALUATION OF NEIGHBORHOOD-BASED VS. TRADITIONAL PROBATION

Recall from Chapter 4 that in neighborhood-based supervision (NBS), the probation officers conduct the supervision and implement the case plan by being more visible and having a strong community presence. The elements of NBS include assignment

---

BOX 5.3 COMMUNITY CORRECTIONS UP CLOSE

A Day in the Life of a Federal Probation Officer

It's Tuesday, and I've got my work cut out for me on this cold January day in West Texas. On the way in to work I mentally review the upcoming scheduled events for the day: 8:30 A.M. meet with assistant U.S. attorney regarding a probation revocation hearing on John D.; 9:00 A.M. revocation hearing in Judge B's court—contested; thereafter, head for the counties to do field supervision and collateral work. This will be an overnighter, so I'll be back in the office on Thursday—another court day.

I'm almost at the office, but I need to make a quick stop at Joe R. to collect a random urinalysis (UA). He's been out a month now and seems to be doing all right. He's working, home is stable, and the UA will address the primary supervision issue in this case—history of drug abuse. I'm almost ready to complete an initial supervision plan in this case. Although he participated in drug treatment in the institution, he may need treatment in the community. Time will tell; but for right now random UAs will do.

Well, I caught him before he left for work, and things seem solid. The wife seemed happy, the job is stable, and there was no problem with the UA. It's going to be a great day! I love this job! On to the office.

Oops, I spoke too soon. Telephone voice mail—David S. got arrested for DWI [driving while intoxicated]—he's still locked up at County. I'll swing by the county jail on the way out of town. Other than that, no other emergencies.

The assistant U.S. attorney is ready for a contested hearing. That's fine; five dirty UAs and failure to participate in drug treatment will get you every time. The supervision file is well documented, and I'm prepared to testify as to chain of custody on the dirty UAs. Our contract provider was subpoenaed and will testify on the failure to participate violation. We're in Judge B's court, and the AUSA [assistant U.S. attorney] tells me the defendant has decided to plead true and throw himself on the mercy of the court—good luck. Sure enough, the judge revokes

(Continues)

BOX 5.3   COMMUNITY CORRECTIONS UP CLOSE (*Continued*)

A Day in the Life of a Federal Probation Officer

John D.'s probation and sentences him to twenty-four months' custody. John takes it all right, but his mother doesn't. If he had taken the judge's advice and "lived at the foot of the cross," he'd still be on probation—instead, he's locked up, and his mother is crying in court. It's always harder on the family. I'll talk to her—maybe it will help. John couldn't do it on the street, so maybe he will get the help he needs inside. [The federal correctional institution in] Fort Worth has an excellent treatment program—I'll tell her that and maybe she will feel better. I hate this job!

Well, it's midmorning and time to hit the road. Fort Stockton is 100 miles down the road, but I've got to stop at the county jail on the way out of town. I'll check out the government vehicle with the four-wheel drive in case the roads get bad; cellular phone 1; pepper spray; sidearm; and laptop in case I have time to do chronos. Gosh times have changed; in the good old days I'd be leaving town in my personal vehicle with a smile on my face.

At the county lockup David S. advises he was arrested by the P.D. [police department] for DWI—but he really only "had a couple." Of course, he forgot he was supposed to abstain completely from alcohol. When I get back in town I'll get the offense report, staff the case with the boss, and decide what type of action to take. David has been on supervision for over a year and has done exceptionally well. Graduated sanctions may be in order, and if so, I'll ask the court to place him in the halfway house with a required treatment condition.

On the road again. This is what I've got to do in Fort Stockton: check in with the sheriff—he knows everything that is going on in his county; go by our drug contractor's office and visit with the therapist regarding Mary J.; go by the county clerk's office and finish this collateral request out of the Northern District; and conduct home inspections on Bob S. and Joe R. Talk about time management—the boss will love this! Sheriff B. is in a great mood, and he says all my people have been behaving themselves. Over coffee I advise him John D. will be getting out on parole—for the second time—and will be coming back home to Fort Stockton. That didn't make his day. At the drug treatment facility the contractor gives me a good report on Mary J. She's keeping all her appointments and has not submitted any dirty UAs. Her participation in treatment is good, and her mother has also attended a couple of counseling sessions. Great report!

The county clerk was busy, but she did have the judgments I had called ahead about—that was a quick and easy collateral, not like the last one that took two hours to find an old judgment. These people in Fort Stockton are great to work with; they really know how to help you. Man I love this job!

Well, there's Bob S.'s house. I think I'll drive past and around the block—just in case. Everything looks cool, and his car is in front, so he should be home.

Bob was surprised to see me, advising it was his day off since the day before he had pulled a double on the rig he works. Oil field work is steady, but the cold weather is hard, and it shows on Bob's face. The wife seems to be doing well, and the house is neat and clean. Things look solid, but I know better than to start bragging. This offender has a history of drug violations, which presents certain risk control issues. Risk control issues never go away!

At Joe R.'s no one comes to the door, but I thought I heard someone inside. I leave my card, drive around the block, and call Joe on the cellular phone. It amazes me how sneaky I can get when I have to. Sure enough, Joe's girlfriend answers the phone and advises Joe is still at work. Work is 15 miles out of town at a ranch, so I'll try to catch him first thing in the morning.

I'm running a little ahead of schedule, so I'll stop by and see Mary J. She should be home from work; if she's not her mother will be, and she'll let me know how her daughter is really doing. The supervision issues here are enforcing court-ordered sanctions and drug treatment. Sure enough, Mary J. is there and seems to be doing really well. She gives me her community service hours documentation and discusses her progress in the drug treatment program. Her mother is obviously very satisfied with her daughter's progress and is a good supervision resource to me.

Before I check into the motel, I call the office on the cellular to check my voice mail. David S. called to advise he bonded out of jail. I call him back and set up an appointment for him to come in on Thursday. We'll staff him at that time. I'm glad now that I brought the laptop—I can catch up on some chronos. Since I lucked out and saw all the people I needed to, I won't need to go out tonight—it's getting too cold out here in West Texas anyway. What a day—win a few, lose a few. Gosh I love this job!

The next morning comes early, and I catch breakfast before I hit the road. I figure I'll work my way back to the office and try to catch Joe R. at the ranch before he gets busy. I'm positive his girlfriend told him I was by the house, so he should be expecting me. I'm not quite comfortable

(Continues)

BOX 5.3   **COMMUNITY CORRECTIONS UP CLOSE (*Continued*)**

A Day in the Life of a Federal Probation Officer

with this offender because he does have some violence in his background. Therefore, officer safety and risk control are the primary supervision issues I am addressing. Wouldn't you know it, he locked the main gate on me—but what he doesn't know is the rancher previously gave me a key to the gate. As I drive up to the ranch headquarters, I can see my man out by the horse corral. He seems surprised to see me. We visit, and he convinces me he is making a "good hand." I try not to be too obvious, but I'm looking for any signs of contraband or a weapon. Ranch hands and rifles seem to go hand in hand—no pun intended. Nothing is obvious, although Joe just seems to be nervous. As I drive back down the road to the main gate, I call the Border Patrol sector

headquarters and check in with the duty agent. Joe is clean as far as they know, but they agree to drive by in the next few days. They'll let me know. The agent advised they have received recent intelligence of illegal aliens working in the area where Joe works.

Well, I'm almost home, and it's a beautiful day. In fact, it looks like it will warm up. The only pressing issue I know of is the staffing on David S. You know what, I really do love this job!

Source: The author, Richard V. Russell, was supervising U.S. probation officer for the Western District of Texas. He is now retired and resides in Midland, Texas. Reprinted with permission.

---

of offenders according to zipcode or type of offense (or both), developing community partnerships with police, treatment providers, and faith-based initiatives. Cases are assigned to officers according to geographic beat areas in a community (Reinventing Probation Council, 1999), which is ideal for using geographic information systems (GIS) technology (see Box 5.4).

BOX 5.4   **TECHNOLOGY IN CORRECTIONS**

Using Geographic Information System Technology in Probation and Parole Supervision

Geographic information system (GIS) mapping uses special computer software to visually diagram locations in a neighborhood, or the entire city, of individuals and/or events. GIS mapping enables a probation or parole agency to obtain a full picture of who is on probation and where probationers live. By "parsing" and "geocoding" the data, probation supervisors have detailed information to use when assigning new cases to their officers. Available data includes number of police calls for service, the number and location of orders of protection, and access to treatment venues from probationers' residence. An officer who supervises an entire caseload of offenders in the same area can achieve a higher level of field surveillance than the officer who must drive all over the city. GIS technology can also overlay information on bus routes, employer locations, locations of alcohol establishments, and schools to determine feasibility of probationer success and how travel time can be minimized when probationers move from one location to another. This technology gives probation officers more details about their jurisdiction or the "beat" in

which their clients live, and information can be shared with police departments, who already use GIS to locate suspects and investigate new crimes.

GIS technology is also helpful to supervisors when assigning new clients to a caseload. The supervisor can examine where the offender lives and assign offenders in the same neighborhood to the same officer, such as in neighborhood-based supervision. In this way, officers can supervise their caseload in a small area of town where they can be more likely to visit them in the neighborhood, rather than driving haphazardly all over town. Using GIS mapping, routes from one house to the next can be planned for a series of home visits. The possibilities of GIS applications for corrections are still being discovered and linked to other agencies within the broader criminal justice system.

Sources: Keith Harries. 2003. Using Geographic Analysis in Probation and Parole. *National Institute of Justice Journal* 249: 32–33; Jaishankar Karuppannan. 2005. Mapping and Corrections: Management of Offenders with Geographic Information Systems. *Corrections Compendium* 30(1): 7–9, 31–33.

NBS sites started in Boston, Phoenix, Tucson, Dallas/Ft. Worth, Waco, Texas, and Spokane, Washington. Preliminary evaluations of these sites compared probationers supervised in the NBS program, which had smaller caseloads, with probationers supervised using traditional probation. An evaluation of one site indicated that probationers supervised in the NBS program perceived more support and help from their probation officer in finding employment and in making connections to treatment providers than did probationers supervised on traditional caseloads (Lutze, Smith, and Lovrich, 2004). NBS officers had more autonomy and a closer connection with police and the community than traditional probation officers, but relationships with treatment service providers were similar for both groups. NBS probationers were more likely to be violated for technical violations than traditional probationers, yet both groups committed a similar number of new crimes while on supervision. Overall recidivism rates between the two groups were not significantly different (Lutze, Smith, and Lovrich, 2004). Evaluations of the other sites need to be completed to obtain a more complete picture of NBS.

Specialized Caseloads

Standard probation techniques provide sufficient monitoring for most sentenced offenders, but there are some offenders who have different needs, or may need a more intensive form of monitoring, and also may require a particular kind of treatment. Between 5 to 10 percent of probationers and parolees are classified as being in a specialized caseload, which may include probationers in a boot camp or a substance abuse residential treatment program (Camp, Camp, and May, 2003). The use of specialized caseloads means that a supervising officer becomes an expert in working with a particular subpopulation of offenders. Specialized caseloads are effective in improving supervision quality and effectiveness for offenders such as those who are gang members, addicted to drugs, offenders with a mental illness, and those convicted of a sex offense.

There are many forms that supervision can take with specialized caseloads that likely require an intensive form of probation or a more structured residential program. In this chapter, we discuss strategies for two different specialized caseloads: gang members and sex offenders on probation. We also include a section on working with women probationers. In Chapter 8, offenders with mental illnesses and drug abuse problems are discussed alongside more structured residential programs.

SUPERVISING SEX OFFENDERS

The term *sex offender* refers to a wide range of behaviors ranging from exposing oneself in a public place to rape. Some sex offenders are aggressive and violent, while others are quite the opposite—passive and compliant. Many people may be surprised to find out that 60 percent of all convicted sex offenders are under conditional supervision in the community (Jenuwine, Simmons, and Swies, 2003), but typically the period of supervision is significantly longer than for other types of offenders. Sex offenders generally have lower recidivism rates than other types of offenders but they are generally feared and regarded with disdain by the public. Public contempt and political pressures have caused more laws to be passed that regulate sex offenders than perhaps any other type of offender, with the exception of death row prisoners. These laws include mandatory treatment, polygraphs, increased supervision, public notification, and the possibility of civil commitment and/or chemical castration.

Polygraph Tests   Polygraph tests have been recognized as a tool to reduce the secrecy and deceit that sex offenders typically use with their victims and supervising probation officers. Many sex offenders are motivated by gaining power over their victims in a calculating way that minimizes detection. As a result, some jurisdictions require that sex offenders, when initially placed on community supervision, submit to a baseline polygraph examination that explores previous sexual behaviors and current deviant thoughts. Polygraphed sex offenders "reported many more victims [especially male victims], far less history of being sexually abused themselves, and a much higher incidence of having offended as juveniles" than did the nonpolygraphed sex offender group (Hindman and Peters, 2001, p. 10). If used properly, the baseline test can then be shared with treatment providers to measure treatment progress and law enforcement if necessary to compare against any later polygraph tests given throughout the period of probation.

Probation and parole officers in sex offender units are specially trained in the area of sex offenses and in recognizing secrecy and deceit, which frequently characterize crimes against children. Payne and DeMichele (2008) discuss how to work with sex offenders without compromising the officer's own mental health. One of the ways is to separate the person from what they have done. Working with sex offenders does not mean condoning their behavior. The mark of a true professional is and the ability and willingness to supervise and talk to a person who has behaved badly, along with the capacity to view the person and the behaviors in a nonjudgmental way without being manipulated or conned.

Sex Offender Treatment   Sex offenders are typically court mandated to attend intensive treatment specific to the type of sex offense. Aggressive rapists require an entirely different treatment approach than do more passive pedophiles. The assumption about inappropriate sexual behaviors is that there is no "cure" in the medical sense, but offenders learn how to control their urges and replace them with appropriate behaviors. A **penile plethysmograph** is used to measure the gender and ages of victims in which the sex offender is attracted. This device also tracks how the treatment is progressing and whether a different approach needs to be used. Treatment is conducted in both individual and group settings and the duration is typically for 1 to 2 years. Therapy can be supplemented with a hormone called medro oxyprogesterone acetate, otherwise known as Depo Provera. Depo provera changes the hormone levels to decrease sexual urges and increase responsiveness to treatment. The use of hormones is a form of chemical castration (Payne and DeMichele, 2008).

Penile Plethysmograph
A device that measures erectile responses in male sex offenders to determine level of sexual arousal to various types of stimuli. This device is used for assessment and treatment purposes.

Increased Supervision   Supervising sex offenders in the community involves more frequent contacts and more frequent searches. Sex offenders who are most at-risk of recidivism are increasingly being monitored using global positioning systems (GPS) technology to quell the concerns. Currently, 44 states authorize the use of GPS or electronic monitoring for sex offenders; 10 of these states require lifetime monitoring for the highest-risk sex offenders (Armstrong and Freeman, 2009). We discuss GPS in more detail in Chapter 9, including how the technology works.

For the vast majority, a "containment approach" with the following guidelines is recommended (English et al. 1996):

- Two to four face-to-face contacts between officer and probationer per month
- Two probationer home and computer searches per month
- Weekly cognitive–behavioral group therapy and individual counseling
- Sharing of information on a regular basis between probation officers and treatment providers

Special conditions required of sex offenders may also include submission of a blood sample for DNA recording, prohibition of any pornography, restricting Internet access to certain chat rooms and web sites, prohibition of patronizing sex-oriented businesses, and child safety zones. A child safety zone condition means that the offender is not allowed within a certain range of places where children typically congregate. These places include schools, day care centers, and playgrounds (McKay, 2002).

Two laws that affect sex offenders even after their sentence is completed are civil commitment and public notification laws. Civil commitment allows for the indefinite commitment of a sex offender who has been deemed to be a sexual predator and who has a mental illness linked to his or her behavior. If the mental illness can be shown to be linked to a continual threat to others, offenders can be held against their will. Public notification laws require sex offenders to register with law enforcement for a certain period of time (e.g., 10 years or indefinitely), and if a high risk, require the neighboring community to be notified. Both of these laws will be discussed in more detail in Chapter 15.

STRATEGIES FOR SUPERVISING KNOWN GANG MEMBERS

Most gang members are young offenders, either juveniles between 12 and 17 years, or young adults in their early to mid-20s. Gang members pose a challenge for probation and parole officers. While on supervision, gang members are significantly more likely than non–gang members to be rearrested for drug and violent crimes (Olson, Dooley, and Kane, 2004). Gang members have more extensive criminal histories and associate with other people who were themselves involved in criminal activity. This situation creates a high propensity for recidivism, making it necessary to assign active gang members to intensive supervision caseloads. A number of different strategies are used in the intensive supervision of probationers and parolees in the federal system.

Prepared Profiles for Officers   An information clearinghouse such as the Sacramento Intelligence Unit (SIU) has detailed information on gang history, activity, and interpretation of tattoos and gestures. SIU staff prepares profiles of gang members for community supervision officers just before a prisoner is released. Nearly 4,000 profiles at SIU are compiled annually for this purpose and can be used in any jurisdiction (Administrative Office of the U.S. Courts, 2006).

Information Exchange with Law Enforcement   Probation officers should routinely interact with local law enforcement as a second source of information gathering and education. Some officers attend workshops and are members of gang task forces to further specialize and keep current as new groups emerge and as codes and signs change.

Drug Education and Mentoring for at-Risk Youth   Officers in one federal district in Massachusetts visit local high schools and juvenile detention centers to present a drug education program to educate at-risk youth on legal consequences of criminal conviction. Young offenders are also provided with mentors, some of whom are former offenders who have succeeded in the reentry process (Administrative Office of the U.S. Courts, 2006).

Checking the Chat Rooms   Gang members are savvy users of technology with their own cell phones, Blackberrys, personal web sites, and Facebook pages. Probation and parole officers must keep current within the online community and social networks with discussion boards and chat rooms to determine information about gang activity, parties, and drugs (Bennish, 2008).

WORKING WITH WOMEN OFFENDERS

Most supervision techniques and treatment programs were developed to serve characteristics of people for which there are greater numbers. In terms of gender, men have always outnumbered women by a ratio of 3:1, thus, supervision and treatment have had men's backgrounds, risk level, and individual needs in mind. What this means is that some of these strategies work for women and others require a deeper understanding of the finer distinctions to formulate an approach that works with them. Understand that this section will not apply to all women, as it is written as general guidelines regarding the differences between most men and most women under correctional supervision.

Women probationers originate from all walks of life, but many have typical backgrounds. Women on community supervision have typically entered the system because of a crime they committed alongside a male partner (boyfriend, husband, or brother) or acting alone out of financial need. The typical female probationer has not completed high school and lacks skills for employment above the minimum wage. Three out of four women have dependent children. The low wages and the presence of children mean that many women are living below the poverty line with little perceived means and opportunities to change their situation. There is a disproportionate number of women who have been physically or sexually abused and/or neglected as children. The abuse oftentimes continues into adulthood through male partners and is sometimes passed on to children as women remain in a submissive and dependent role. Although more women may act in leadership crime roles, far more of them act in secondary traditional roles (Alarid et al., 1996). The early experiences with abuse and disempowerment later affects a woman's self-esteem, emotional and mental states, and rate of substance abuse, all of which are linked as various pathways to crime (Alarid and Cromwell, 2006). Since many women define themselves by their relationships rather than by their careers, they tend to seek out partners that will provide them what they feel they deserve.

This link between early experiences and criminality is important because women typically are more at-risk of harming themselves than others. All else being equal, women generally pose less risk than men to the community at large. This is partially due to the way that risk is currently defined by classification instruments.

Practitioners who have worked with men and women have noted that women on supervision seem to be more open to sharing their feelings and thoughts than men, in part, because women value relationships and recognize the value of establishing rapport to further that relationship. Men on supervision, on the other hand, value independence and will tend to withhold information (not always intentionally), because they have been socialized not to share their problems with others (Festervan, 2003). Taken together, these gender differences may contribute to the view of women offenders as having more needs than men—in fact, women are just more open about them.

Festervan (2003) operates a female community facility and recommends that during the time women offenders are addressing prior abuse and problems with drugs and alcohol, they be allowed to do so in an environment they perceive as safe from sexual harassment and that doesn't involve posing for men that they may have only perceived or related to in a sexual way. This involves non-confrontational therapy modalities best supervised by women staff, and also kept separate from men offenders. While Festervan believes men can be effective officers, anyone who works with women offenders must be well-versed in issues such as pregnancy, parenting/childcare, domestic violence, sexual abuse, mental health, educational opportunities, and substance abuse. Supervising a woman involves the ability to empathize with her past, while simultaneously aiding her in changing her victim mentality to becoming more responsible and empowered.

SUMMARY

- Use of a valid classification is important to assess risk and identify treatment needs, which in turn lead to developing the case plan and appropriate level of supervision.

- Various techniques of evidence-based practices include risk and needs assessments, case planning, motivational interviewing, cognitive-behavioral treatment, and principles of correctional intervention.

- Merely observing conditions of release or managing not to be arrested for a new offense does not indicate that an offender has been rehabilitated. The personality, training, and experience of the supervisory officer determine the outcome just as much as the offender's motivation.

- Implementing the case plan is achieved through monitoring and treatment. Monitoring is through performed through contact and surveillance, with the form depending on the level of supervision.

- The treatment aspect is about removing or reducing barriers that may result in recidivism, as well as assisting the offender in positive behavioral change, which may involve placing offenders into treatment programs. Adequate supervision must deal with all phases of offenders' lives, including family and the community in which they live and work.

- Neighborhood-based probation supervision (NBS) seeks to change the operation and accountability to make probation a more respected and more visible part of the corrections system. The effectiveness of NBS rests in part on the officer being able to secure the assistance and cooperation of community agencies and individuals within his or her beat.

- Sex offenders and gang members pose a challenge for probation and parole officers as both groups are seen as at-risk groups in a different way. While sex offenders are less likely than gang members to be rearrested for violent crimes, sex offenders are more despised by the public. A variety of strategies have been developed to reduce the risk that each group poses.

- Working with women offenders requires knowing about potential pathways to crime that involve domestic violence, sexual/physical abuse, mental health, lack of educational opportunities/skills, and substance abuse problems. Supervising women involves empathizing with her past, while simultaneously aiding her in changing her victim mentality to becoming more responsible and empowered.

DISCUSSION QUESTIONS

1. Argue for the use of neighborhood-based probation supervision over traditional methods. In what situations might NBS be most useful?

2. How does assessing client needs in education, employment, treatment, and so on help develop the program plan? How much should a client be expected to do while on supervision?

3. Discuss the use of various risk prediction scales. How might risk assessment best be used in community supervision?

4. Discuss the concept of caseload and workload computation. Why might workload be a better method of allocating probation or parole officer resources?

5. How does a specialized caseload differ from a traditional caseload?

WEB SITES

Center for Evidence-Based Practices, University of California-Irvine
> http://ucicorrections.seweb.uci.edu

General Information about Risk and Needs Assessments, Inc.
> http://www.riskandneeds.com

Information on Case Management and Risk Assessment
> http://www.justiceconcepts.com/

Applying EBP to Offender Supervision
> http://www.nicic.org/library/020095

Role Playing Scenarios on Video: Two PO/Offender contact Sessions- 24 minutes
> http://www.nicic.org/library/022005

"Thinking for a Change" Lesson Plans- An example of a Cognitive-Behavioral Program
> http://www.nicic.org/library/016672

The Change Companies®, Changing Offender Behavior System
> http://www.changecompanies.net

Empirical Validation of the Arizona Risk/Needs Assessment
> http://www.nicic.org/library/018821

Using Risk/Needs to Improve Decision Making in the Maryland Juvenile Justice System
> http://www.ncjj.org/stateprofiles/profiles/MD06.asp

A Study of the Efficiency and Effectiveness of Juvenile Risk/Needs Assessment in Texas
> http://www.la.utexas.edu/research/cccjr/research/intakerib.htm

A Research Study of Assessments and Conditional Releases in Canada
> http://www.csc-scc.gc.ca/text/rsrch/reports/r133/r133-eng.shtml

Motivational Interviewing
> http://www.motivationalinterviewing.org

Evidence-Based Practices that Work in Florida
> http://www.dc.state.fl.us/pub/recidivismWSIPP/index.html

The special needs of women in the justice system
> www.gainscenter.samhsa.gov (click on the "Publications" link on the "Resources" tab)

CASE STUDY EXERCISE

Classification and Supervision in Probation and Parole

There are two new clients on your caseload. Below is the information that you have received on each person. Using the risk and needs classification instrument (Figure 5.1 in this chapter), complete the following:

1. Assess the risks posed by the offender and select the appropriate supervision assignment based on the risk score.
2. Score out the "needs" level of the client.
3. If you're able to interview the offender use the CMC Assessment interview in the Appendix on page XX, and complete the 56 questions, followed by the "Behavioral Patterns" and the ""Impressions" sections. Then, go on to complete the "Case Planning" and "Program Plan" part of the assignment. If an interview is not possible, turn directly to the "Case Planning" and "Program Plan" part of the assignment and consider the factors that have placed the client at risk and which of these factors are related to the offense.
4. Choose the top ranked three to four problems to develop goals that the client will strive to achieve and action items for what the client needs to do to reach each goal.

CASE A: THOMAS USER, THE SUBSTANCE ABUSER

Thomas User, age 18, has been placed on probation for possession of methamphetamine and ecstasy. There were no known victims in the current offense. Police reports indicate that Mr. User was stopped by a police cruiser because he had been standing on the same corner for hours. An outer pat search revealed that he had eight tablets that were confirmed by drug testing to be ecstasy, and he had enough methamphetamine for up to 12 hits.

Mr. User has two previous misdemeanor convictions as a juvenile, one for possession of paint huffing material and one for minor in possession of alcoholic beverages. He has one misdemeanor conviction as an adult for menacing in the second degree.

Mr. User has a spotty employment record, having only been employed at one fast-food restaurant for four months out of the last two years. The rest of the time, Mr. User says he sold and used drugs. He has a drug habit that is related to his arrest but has not yet been assessed for drug treatment. It is unclear how motivated Mr. User is to attend treatment.

Mr. User has an IQ of 68, which defines him as developmentally disabled. Although there are no apparent signs, it is unclear whether Mr. User is also mentally ill. He is a high school dropout, having only completed the tenth grade. He does not have his GED. He reports himself to be in good physical health. You notice he seems underweight, and he has two teeth missing.

Mr. User reports that he has fathered one child, but he does not know the whereabouts of the child or the mother. The child is approximately 2 years of age, and there is no claim by the mother for child support.

CASE B: SUE STEEL, THE FORGER

Sue Steel was convicted of two charges—criminal possession of a weapon and passing bad checks. Ms. Steel stole a box of checks from the mailbox belonging to Janine Smith. Posing as Ms. Smith, Client Steel wrote a total of four checks to retail stores that totaled $975 over a period of three days. A JC Penney clerk notified mall security when Steel became agitated and irate because the clerk refused to accept a check without proper identification. As Ms. Steel tried to leave the mall, she was approached for questioning by private security. One of the private security officers happened to notice a "shiny metal object" in her waistband that appeared to be a weapon of some sort. Private security detained Steel at the mall until police arrived to conduct a frisk. She was carrying a .38 caliber weapon and a book of checks for "Janine Smith" when she was arrested.

She is 25 years of age and has a history of criminal conduct; her prior convictions began at age 15, with one juvenile conviction for simple robbery and two adult convictions involving forms of fraud. Her simple robbery conviction involved one victim who was injured, reportedly by Steel's codefendant. Records indicate she successfully completed juvenile probation by age 17.

Her first conviction as an adult was at age 19 for felony fraud. She completed probation and was released from supervision after fourteen months. Her current conviction, passing bad checks, resulted in a confinement sentence of six months. The jail uncovered a pending misdemeanor case for "theft by deception." As she had been in detention prior to sentencing, she was given "time served" for the misdemeanor conviction, which ran concurrently with her other two current charges. She was incarcerated for three months and 22 days, and the sentencing court ordered her to serve the remaining two months and eight days on home confinement with electronic monitoring, and then transfer out to probation supervision for another two years.

Ms. Steel has a high school diploma, and she has a "transient" job history—moving from job to job. She has employment at a janitorial service cleaning office buildings. Ms. Steel worked at this firm prior to detention in this case, and her employer was willing to rehire her upon her release from custody. Her employer is aware of her conviction and supervision. Ms. Steel was ordered to pay $975 in restitution for her current offense. She has not yet made any payments toward her restitution. She is living with her sister and her sister's child, and has one dependent child who is currently in the temporary custody of her mother.

Client Steel reports a prior history of child abuse at the hands of her father, who died of cirrhosis of the liver when Steel was 15 years old. Steel says her father abused her and her mother, but this cannot be confirmed through any police records. She reports to be in good medical health and there is no evidence indicating otherwise. There is no evidence of drug use in any previous offenses or the current offense, and Steel has never attended drug treatment.

Client Management Classification Assessment Instrument

The purpose of the CMC is to provide the probation professional with an efficient and effective case management system. CMC includes procedures for developing individualized strategies for the quality supervision of adult offenders. This process is accomplished through the completion of the three system components: an assessment procedure, a supervision planning process, and supervision according to one of five distinct strategies, depending on individualized case needs. It is not to be used with juveniles nor for any other than its stated purpose.

CMC Instructions

There are four parts to the CMC assessment instrument. Whenever possible, the following sequence (A to D) should be followed.
   a. Attitude Interview (45 items)
   b. Objective History (11 items)
   c. Behavioral Observations (8 items)
   d. Officer Impressions of contributing factors (7 items)

The Attitude Section

Column One   A SEMI-STRUCTURED INTERVIEW with suggested questions has been developed to elicit attitude information about the offense, the offender's background, and about present plans and problems. The average interview takes about forty-five minutes and the scoring about five minutes.

Use a natural, open conversational style of interviewing that is comfortable for both you and the probationer. If the probationer presents some important or interesting information requiring follow-up, feel free to do so before returning to the structured sequence. While stressing free-flowing communication, some structuring is required to ensure the reliability and validity of the instrument. Therefore, make every effort to preserve the meaning of the questions when transposing them into your own words.

In the interview, each section is introduced by one or two open-ended questions, which are intended to encourage discussion on a particular subject. If the information needed to score the items is not obtained from the open-ended questions, one or two specific questions are provided for each item. If those questions fail to elicit the needed information, continue to inquire with increasingly direct questions unless you see the word –stop-. "Stop" means to discontinue inquiry (except to repeat or clarify a misunderstood question).

For some items "a" and "b" questions are included. If the "b" question is asterisked (*), always ask it unless the answer to the "a" question makes the "b" questions meaningless (e.g., "no" to question 10a). If question "b" is not asterisked, ask it if the needed information was not elicited from question "a."

Column Two   THE ITEM OBJECTIVES AND RESPONSES are listed in column two. Many times the suggested questions will approach the item objective in an indirect manner in order to elicit the most valid response.

Column Three   A SCORING GUIDE is included to provide criteria and assistance in scoring ambiguous responses. When scoring, you must choose only on alternative for each item. If you cannot choose an alternative, do not rate the item.

ATTITUDES ABOUT OFFENSE: Could you tell me about the offense that got you into trouble?

Questions

1a. How did you get involved in this offense?

1b. (if denied) What did the police say that you did?

1. Motivation for commiting the offense:
   a. Emotional motivation (e.g.,anger, sex offense, etc)
   b. Material (monetary) motivation
   c. Both emotional and material motivation

1. a.
   –Using drugs
   –Assault (not for robbery)
   b.
   –Prostitution
   –Car theft
   –Selling drugs
   c.
   –stealing from parents for revenge
   –stealing primarily for peer acceptance
   –man who won't pay alimony primarily because he is angry with his ex-wife

2a. How did you decide to commit the offense?

2b. Could you tell me more about the circumstances that led up to the offense?

2. Acceptance of responsibility for current offense
   a. Admits committing the offense and doesn't attempt excuses.
   b. Admits committing the offense but emphasizes excuses (influence by friends, drinking, etc)
   c. Denies committing the offense

2. a. explains circumstances but takes responsibility
   b. blames circumstances doesn't take responsibility
   c. probationers who deny any significant aspect of the offense are scored "c" (probationer admits he helped to jimmy car window but denies responsibility for removing valuables because friends removed them).

3. Looking back at the offense, what is your general feeling about it? –STOP–

3. Expression of guilt about current offense:
   a. No prior offenses (skip 5,6,7,8)
   b. Mainly misdemeanor
   c. No constant pattern
   d. Mainly felonies

3. a. Probationer must feel some personal shame and regret (not just to impress officer)
   b. "I feel bad because now I have a record"; "people are disappointed in me"; "I know it was wrong"
   c. Using drugs or sexual activities between consenting adults

4a. What prior offenses have you been convicted of?

4b. Were you ever in trouble as a juvenile? (list below)

4. Offense and severity
   a. No prior (skip 5,6,7,8)
   b. Mainly misdemeanor
   c. No constant pattern
   d. Mainly felonies

4-8 include juvenile and serious traffic offenses (drunk driving) don't count dismissals
4. Use only prior offenses
   a. Should not be used if probationer has more than two serious felonies
   b. Over 50% of probationer's offenses are felonies

5a. Have you ever been armed or hurt someone during these offenses?

5b. Did you ever threaten anyone?

5. Was probationer ever involved in an offense where he (she) was armed, assaultive or threatened injury to someone?
  a. yes
  b. no

5-8 Use current and prior offense factors to score 5-8

6a. How did you decide to commit these offenses?

6b. Did you plan these offenses beforehand?

6. Offenses were generally
  a. Planned
  b. no consistent pattern
  c. impulsive

6. Officer's judgment based on all factors
  a. Exhibitionist who drives around in a car looking for a girl to whom to expose himself
  b. Person who decides to commit an offense, then drinks to build courage
  c. Exhibitionist who is driving to work, suddenly sees a girl and pulls over and exposes himself
  d. Person who gets drunk and into a bar fight

7. Were you drinking or on drugs when you committed this offense?

7. Percent of offenses committed while drinking or on drugs.
  a. never
  b. 50% or less
  c. over 50%

7. Count offenses where there any chemical use regardless of whether person was intoxicated or not.

8. Did you do the offense alone or with others?

8. Offenses were generally committed
  a. alone
  b. no consistent pattern
  c. With Accomplices

Offense	(Item 4) Fel./Misd.	(Item 5) Assaultive	Circumstance of Offense	(Item 6) Planned?	(Item 7) Chemicals?	(Item 8) Accomplices?

School and Vocational Adjustment: Now, I'd like to find out some things about your background. Let's begin with school. How did you like school?

9. What was your favorite subject in school? –STOP-

9. Favorite subject
   a. Vocational
   b. Academic
   c. Gym
   d. No favorite

9. a. Business Course
   b. Music or Art

10a. Did you have a favorite teacher in high school?

10b. What did you like about him/her?

10. Attitude toward teachers
   a. no favorite
   b. teacher chosen because of certain qualities that the probationer admired
   c. teacher chosen because of close personal relationship with the teacher

10. a. "She would help kids"
   b. "she would help me"

11a. How far did you go in school?

11b. Did you have any problems with school work? (if didn't graduate why not?)

11. Probationer's school performance
   a. no problems
   b. learning problems
   c. lack of interest, behavior or other problems

11. a. Don't use for probationer who didn't complete high school.
   b. for probationer whose learning problems result from a lack of capacity. If probationer has both lack of capacity and behavioral problems, score b. Lack of capacity take precedence when scoring.

12. Now, I'd like to know about your work history. What kind of jobs have you had?

12. Primary vocation
   a. unskilled labor
   b. Semiskilled labor
   c. skilled labor or white collar
   d. no employment history (homemaker skip to 13 & 14)
   e. student or recent graduate (skip 13 & 14)

12. Average person could do job without training. Probationer's been in the job market for over 6 months but has no employment history.
   a. Job requires some training or experience.
   b. for homemaker, use prior vocational history if any. If none check "d" and skip 13 & 14.
   c. Probationer was recently a student and hasn't had opportunity to establish employment pattern (skip 13 & 14).

13a. How long did you work on your most recent job?

13b. How long between that job and your previous job? (start w/most recent and work backwards until pattern emerges).

13. Percent of working life where probationer was employed fulltime:
   a. over 90%
   b. over 50%–90%
   c. 50% or less

13. "Working life. . . i.e. time period society would expect one to be working, subtract time in school.

14a. What was your reason for leaving your most recent job?

14b. Have you had any trouble getting jobs?

14. Primary vocational problem
  a. none
  b. problems due to lack of skills or capacity
  c. attitude or other problems

14. a. Don't use "a" if working less that 90%
  b. "Because of my drinking problem.
  c. has essentially not been self supporting

(Item 12) (Start with most recent) Jobs & Job Responsibilities	(Item 13a) Duration	(Item 14a) Reason for Leaving
(Item 13b) Unemployment Interval		
(Item 13b) unemployment Interval		
(Item 13b) Unemployment Interval		

15a. Where do you live now?

15b. Have you moved around much? (deal with time after age 18)

15. Living stability background:
  a. essentially stable living arrangements
  b. Some unstable periods
  c. essentially unstable living arrangements

15. Consider what is stable for the probationer's age group.

16a. Have you had any trouble supporting yourself or received welfare?

16b. (If applicable) How did you support yourself when you were unemployed?

16. History of being self-supporting:
  a. Probationer has usually been self-supporting
  b. probationer has had several periods where he/she wasn't self-supporting.

16. Illegal activities and welfare are not counted as self-supporting. For probationer who has not had the opportunity to support him/herself(homemaker or living with relative) estimate the likelihood of his/her being able to support her/himself.

17a. How do (did) you get along with your father?

17b. How do you feel about your father?

17. Present feelings toward father:
  a. Close
  b. Mixed or neutral
  c. Hostile

17. a. In multi-father families, use the person whom the probationer identifies as father
  b. "we get along" (without implication of closeness)

18a. If you did something wrong as a teenager, how did your father handle it?

18b. What kind of discipline did he use?

18. Type of discipline father used (during teen years)
    a. verbal or privilege withdrawal
    b. permissive (let do as he/she pleased)
    c. physical

18. a. If the probationer didn't live with father or father figure during at least part of teenage years, do not rate item 18.
    b. "He always left it to mom"

19a. How do (did) you get along with your mother?

19b. How do you feel about your mother?

19. Present feelings toward father:
    a. Close
    b. Mixed or neutral
    c. Hostile

19. a. In multi-mother families, use the person whom the probationer identifies as mother.
    b. "we get along" (without implication of closeness

20a. If you did something wrong as a teenager, how did your mother handle it?

20b. What kind of discipline did she use?

20. Type of discipline father used (during teen years)
    a. verbal or privilege withdrawal
    b. permissive (let do as he/she pleased)
    c. physical
    -STOP-

20. a. If the probationer didn't live with mother or mother figure during at least part of teenage years, do not rate item 18.
    b. "He always left it to dad"

21a. Were you ever abused by either of your parents?

21b. Did either of them ever go overboard on the punishment? -STOP-

21. Was probationer ever physically abused by a biological, step or adoptive parent?
    a. yes
    b. no

21. Item 21 should be based on facts described and not whether the client felt abused
    a. cuts on face, severe body bruises, sexual abuse, locked in closet or starved for unusual amount of time.

22a. How would your parent's have described you as a child (before you were a teenager)?

22b. Did both of your parents see you the same way?

22. Parental view of probationer:
    a. good child
    b. problem child
    c. parents differed

22. a. no special problem "like anybody else"
    b. "my parents were always complaining about me" seen as "strange kid"

23. How would you describe yourself as a child?

23. As a child, probationer describes self as:
    a. good child (normal or average)
    b. problem child

23. Accept what the probationer says even his/her behavior doesn't match his/her perception (ex from item 22 apply here).

24a. How do you get along with your brothers and sisters?

24b. How do you feel about them?

24. General feelings toward siblings:
    a. Close
    b. Neutral or mixed
    c. hostile
    d. no siblings

24. a. Include half-siblings; exclude step-siblings.
    b. "like some, not others."

25. Would you describe your early childhood as happy or unhappy?

25. General attitude toward childhood
    a. happy
    b. not happy

25. Accept the probationer view.

26. If you could change anything about your childhood, what would you change?

26. Satisfaction with childhood
   a. basically satisfied
   b. dissatisfied with material aspect
   c. Dissatisfied with self, family or emotional climate.

26. "I should've gone to school."

27. Can you describe your father's personality? (if the answer is unclear, ask probationer to describe another person he/she knows well.)

27. Probationer's description of personality
   a. multi-facedted
   b. Superficial (e.g., "good," "nice," "bad," etc.)

27. The focus of this item is the complexity with which the probationer views people. The ability to describe attributes, or explain the reasons for behavior, is being measured. "Superficial" indicated a lack of capacity to perceive depth of personality and not just an evasion of the question. One or two complex statements are sufficient for an "a" score.
   a. –"ambitious and honest"
      –"sensitive to others"
      –"dad was strict because that is the way he was brought up"
   b. –"no good drunk" (with no further explanation)
      –"kind"
      –"don't know"

28a. What are your friends like?

28b. Have any of them been in trouble with the law?

28. Probationer's associated are:
   a. essentially non-criminal
   b. Mixed
   c. Mostly criminal

28. Don't count marijuana use (alone) as criminal
   a. don't use "a" if probationer committed offense with accomplices

29a. How do you get along with your friends?

29b. How do they act toward you?

29. In interaction with friends probationer is:
   a. used by others
   b. withdrawn
   c. other problems
   d. normal

29. This item should be based on officer's judgment of the quality of the probationer's interactions. If the officer is used by friends even though the probationer thinks he/she get along "ok" check choice "a".

30a. Do you have a closest friend?

30b. What do you like best about him/her?
   -STOP-

30. Description of probationer's relationship with his/her closest friend:
   a. talk or help each other
   b. do things together (less emphasis on talking or sharing feelings)
   c. has none

30. a. –"we do things for each other"
      –"we're like brothers"
   b. –"he's a hunter too"

31. Are you satisfied with the way you get along with people?

31. Satisfaction with interpersonal relationships:
   a. feels satisfied
   b. feels dissatisfied

31. Accept the probationer's statement.

32. In general, do you tend to trust or to mistrust people? -STOP-

32. General outlook toward others:
   a. basically trusting
   b. mixed or complex view
   c. basically mistrusting

32. A complex view of people (trust some situations and not in others)
   −"I trust people too much."
   −"It takes a while to get to know them."

33a. Can you tell me about your relationships with women (men)?

33b. Do you generally go out with a lot of women/men or date the same person for long periods?

33. Probationer's opposite sex relationship pattern generally is:
   a. long term or serious relationships (over six months)
   b. short and long term relationships
   c. short term less emotionally involved relationships, or little dating experience

33. short term relationships with no solid commitments to persons of the opposite sex

34. In your relationship with your wife/girlfriend (husband/boyfriend), who tends to make the decisions?

34. In opposite sex interactions, probationer generally:
   a. dominates
   b. is average or adequate
   c. is nonassertive or dominated

34. Officer's judgment: Do not accept the probationer's response without exploring his/her relationships or seeing how some specific decisions are made (who decides what to do or with whom to socialize; who controls the money).

35. Do you consider yourself to be a nervous (or anxious) person? -STOP-

35. Does probationer view self as a nervous person?
   a. yes
   b. no

35. Accept the probationer's statement
   a. −"I worry a lot"
      −"I'm hyperactive."

36a. What kinds of things get you depressed?

36b. What do you do when you're feeling depressed? (If denies, find out how he/she keeps from getting depressed.)

36. What does probationer do when feeling depressed?
   a. seeks someone to talk to. Or tries to figure it out
   b. seeks an activity to distract self
   c. drinks or uses drugs
   d. isolates self

36. **a.** −"Forget about them"
      −"watch TV"
   b. −"I pray"
      −"I go to sleep"

37a. Have you ever thought seriously about hurting or killing yourself?

37b. (If probationer says yes to above) Have you ever tried it?

37. Self-destructive behavior
   a. never seriously contemplated suicide
   b. has had definite thoughts of suicide
   c. has attempted it

37. requires overt action that resulted in self-harm or clear intent toward suicide.

38a. What do you do when you are feeling angry with people?

38b. Have you ever hurt anybody when you were angry?

38. In handling anger, probationer
   a. is physically aggressive
   b. avoids expression to others or has trouble expressing anger appropriately
   c. Responds appropriately

38. a. Based on all sources of reliable information and not just on probationer's statement: Physically aggressive problems should take precedence in scoring. IF probationer says, "I Leave," find out if/how he/she deals with the anger later.
   b. "I break things"

39a. Can you describe your personality?

39b. What do you like and what do you dislike about yourself?
-STOP-

39. In describing self, probationer
   a. emphasized strength
   b. emphasizes in adequacy (probationer tends to downgrade self)
   c. can't describe self

39. a. If the probationer gives both positive and negative statements about himself/herself, choose the one emphasized most. If the positive and negative have equal emphasis, choose the first response given.
   b. Choice "c" is designed to identify the probationer who is incapable of showing insight or complexity into himself/herself; "I'm okay"; "I'm nice"; "I get into too much trouble"; etc.

40. (No question asked. Rate your impression of probationer's openness in discussing feelings.)

40. Openness in discussing feelings
   a. discusses as openly as able
   b. is evasive or superficial

40. a. If the officer felt that the probationer was fairly straightforward in talking about his/her feelings.
   b. If the officer thought the probationer was evasive or superficial.

41. Aside from your legal problems, what is the biggest problem in your life right now?
-STOP-

41. What does the probationer view as his/her most important problem area right now?
   a. Personal
   b. Relationships
   c. Vocational-Educational (including employment)
   d. Financial
   e. no big problems presently (score item 42 as "a")

41. a. Probationer names several important problems
   –drinking or drugs
   –"Get my head together"
   b. –"get things straightened out with my fiancée"
   –"try to get along better with my parents"

42. How do you expect this problem to work out?

42. Attitude toward solving problems:
   a. optimistic; expects to succeed (include 41e)
   b. Unclear
   c. Pessimistic; expects to fail

42. a. "OK because I've got a better paying job"
   b. "OK I hope"
   "I'll be okay if I get a better paying job."
   c. Probationer is pessimistic about outcome or can't figure out a solution.

43a. What goals do you have for the future?

43b. What are your plans for achieving your goals? -STOP-

43. Future Plans
  a. Short term goals (most of which can be fulfilled within 6 months)
  b. unrealistic goals
  c. realistic, long term goals (well developed beyond 6 months)

43. a. "Just live day to day." Poorly developed goals with no plans for achieving them.
  b. Strange, way-out, or impossible to achieve goals.
  c. Probationer is able to (1) set a goal within the realm of possibility and (2) list the steps necessary to achieve the goal.

44. (no question asked. Rate the item based on follow-through on jobs, education, training programs, treatment programs, etc., based on all sources.)

44. Probationer usually sticks with, or completes, things he/she begins.
  a. yes
  b. no

44. Compare to the average probationer.

45a. How will being on probation affect your life?

45b. What do you expect to get from being on probation? -STOP-

45. Probationer's general expectations about supervision
  a. no effect
  b. monetary, counseling, or program help
  c. hopes supervision will keep him/her out of trouble
  d. negative expectations
  e. mixed or unclear expectations

46. Age of earliest court appearance:
  a. 14 or younger
  b. 15–17
  c. 18–22
  d. 23 or older

46. Include juvenile offenses and serious traffic offenses (drunk driving, hit and run). Including divorce, custody proceedings, etc.

47. Number of prior offenses:
  a. None
  b. 1–3
  c. 4–7
  d. 8 or more

47. Exclude the probationer's present offense when rating this item. Include juvenile and serious traffic offenses.

48. Number of commitments to state or federal correctional institutions:
  a. None
  b. 1
  c. 2 or more

48. Include juvenile commitments.

49. Time spent under probation or parole supervision:
  a. None
  b. 1 year or less
  c. Over 1 year; up to 3 years
  d. Over 3 years

49. Include juvenile supervision.
  a. Use "a" for new probationer.

50. (Circle all applicable choices.)
  a. Frequent head aches, back or stomach problems
  b. Serious head injuries
  c. Prior psychiatric hospitalization
  d. Outpatient psychotherapy
  e. None of the above

50. a. Vague complaints not diagnosed by a physician.
  b. Skull fractures/head injuries that required treatment (beyond X-ray)
  d. Professional inpatient or outpatient drug/alcohol treatment.

51. Highest grade completed:
  a. 9th or below
  b. 10th to 12th
  c. High school graduate (exclude GED)
  d. Some post-high school training leading toward a degree

52. Did probationer ever receive special education or remedial help in school?
  a. Yes
  b. No

52. Include special programs for learning deficiencies (rather than behavior problems). Do not include English as a Second Language.

53. Probationer was raised primarily by:
  a. Intact biological family
  b. Other

53. Choice "a" requires both natural parents in an intact home until probationer reached about 16 years of age.

54. Did either parent have a history of (circle all applicable choices):
  a. Being on welfare
  b. Criminal behavior
  c. Psychiatric hospitalization
  d. Suicide attempts
  e. Drinking problems
  f. None of the above

54. Includes step and adoptive parents.

55. Have siblings (including half and step siblings) ever been arrested?
  a. None
  b. Some
  c. Most
  d. Not applicable

56. Currently probationer is:
  a. Single (never married)
  b. Single (separated or divorced)
  c. Married (including common-law)

BEHAVIORAL PATTERNS

Rate the following behaviors as observed during the interview. Use (b) for the average offender. Use (a) and (c) for distinct exceptions to the average offender.

1. Grooming and dress
   a. Below average   **b.** average   **c.** above average
2. Self-confidence
   a. Lacks confidence   **b.** average   **c.** overly confident
3. Attention span
   a. Easily distracted   **b.** average   **c.** very attentive
4. Comprehension
   a. Below average   **b.** average   **c.** above average
5. Thought process
   a. Sluggish   **b.** average   **c.** driven (accelerated)
6. Affect
   a. Depressed   **b.** average   **c.** elated
7. Self disclosure
   a. Evasive   **b.** average   **c.** very open
8. Cooperation
   a. Negativistic   **b.** average   **c.** eager to please

OFFICER IMPRESSIONS

On the continuum below, rate the significance of each factor with regard to the probationer as it contribute to the probationer's legal difficulties CIRCLE ONE NUMBER PER ISSUE.

1 = **Highly significant** to probationer's legal difficulties
2 = **Significant** to probationer's legal difficulties
3 = **Somewhat Significant** to probationer's legal difficulties
4 = **Minor Significance** to probationer's legal difficulties
5 = **Not Significant** to probationer's legal difficulties
At least one item must be rated a "1" and at least on item must be rated a "5."

A. **Social inadequacy:** Socially inept. Unable to perceive the motives and concerns of others. Unable to survive in society and care for self.
(1) (2) (3) (4) (5)

Socially adept. Able to assert self and to perceive the motives and concerns of others. Able to survive in society and care for self.

Do not merely rate performance on social situations. RATE ABILITY.

_____   _____   _____

B. **Vocational Inadequacy:** Lacks the capacity to obtain and maintain relatively permanent and reasonably paying employment.
(1) (2) (3) (4) (5)

Has the capacity to obtain and maintain relatively permanent and reasonably paying employment.

Do not merely rate job performance. RATE CAPACITY.

_____   _____   _____

C. **Criminal Orientation:** Criminal behavior is an acceptable and common part of the probationer's life and he/she attempts to live off crime without trying to make it in a pro-social way.
(1) (2) (3) (4) (5)

Criminal behavior is not an acceptable nor common part of his/her life, nor does he/she attempt to live off of crime without trying to make it in a prosocial way.

Do not merely rate the frequency of offenses. RATE VALUES AND ORIENTATION.

D. **Emotional Factors:** Emotional problems (chemical dependency, sex, fear, depression, low self-esteem, anxiety) contributed highly to the offense.
(1) (2) (3) (4) (5)

Emotional factors did not contribute significantly to the offense.

E. **Family History Problems:** Parental family problems in childhood and adolescence contributed significantly to the offense (pattern).
(1) (2) (3) (4) (5)

Parental family problems of childhood and adolescence did not contribute significantly to the offense (pattern).

F. **Isolated Situational** (Temporary Circumstances) Unusual or temporary circumstances in the probationer's life, which are unlikely to be repeated, contributed significantly to the offense.
(1) (2) (3) (4) (5)

Offense is not a result of unusual or temporary circumstances (offense is part of a continuing pattern).

Do not merely rate infrequency of offenses. RATE OVERALL PATTERN.

G. **Interpersonal Manipulation:** Uses, controls, and/or manipulates others to gain his/her own ends with little regard for the welfare of others.
(1) (2) (3) (4) (5)

Misuse of others, manipulation, and control did not contribute significantly to offense (pattern).

Area	Rank	Strength/Resource	Problem/Weakness	Rank
Present Offense				
Offense Pattern				
Education/learning				
Mental Health				
Employment Record				
Vocational Skills				
Financial Mgmt				
Residential Stability				
Family History				
Interpersonal Skills				
Companions/Peers				
Intimate Marital Relationships				
Life Skills				
Drugs & Alcohol				
Plans & Goals				
Sexual Behavior				
Physical Health				
Values & Attitudes				

Case Planning: For each area, first Identify the strengths and weaknesses, being very specific.

Step 2: **Then rank order each of the areas that need (or don't need) intervention.**

Step 3: **Develop the Program Plan**
Choose the top ranked 3-4 problems from the "case planning" table above. Re-state the problem, and for each problem, develop one long range goal that the client will strive to achieve. Then, develop specific action items (2-3) for the probationer to achieve in a step by step process to reach each goal.

Problem Statement #1:

_____

Long-range Goal for Problem #1: _____

_____

_____

Probationer Action Item A to Meet Goal 1:

_____

_____

_____

_____

Probationer Action item B to Meet Goal 1:

_____

_____

_____

_____

Probationer Action item C to Meet Goal 1:

_____

_____

_____

_____

Officer Action Plan to Help Client Reach Goal 1:

_____

_____

_____

Problem Statement #2:

_____

Long-range Goal for Problem #2:

_____

_____

Probationer Action Item A to Meet Goal 2:

_____

_____

_____

_____

Probationer Action item B to Meet Goal 2:

_____

_____

_____

_____

Probationer Action item C to Meet Goal 2:

_____

_____

_____

_____

Officer Action Plan to Help Client Reach Goal 2:

_____

_____

_____

Problem Statement #3:

_____

Long-range Goal for Problem #3:

_____

_____

Probationer Action Item A to Meet Goal 3:

_____

_____

_____

_____

Probationer Action item B to Meet Goal 3:

_____

_____

_____

_____

Probationer Action item C to Meet Goal 3:

_____

_____

_____

_____

Officer Action Plan to Help Client Reach Goal 3:

_____

_____

_____

Problem Statement #4:

_____

Long-range Goal for Problem #4:

_____

_____

Probationer Action Item A to Meet Goal 4:

_____

_____

_____

_____

Probationer Action item B to Meet Goal 4:

_____

_____

_____

_____

Probationer Action item C to Meet Goal 4:

_____

_____

_____

_____

Officer Action Plan to Help Client Reach Goal 4:

_____

_____

_____

Signed,

_____   _____

Client   Supervising Officer

6

The Career Pathway of a Community Supervision Officer

CHAPTER LEARNING OBJECTIVES

- Identify the types of educational and character qualifications needed to manage a caseload of offenders.

- Discuss important issues to the orientation of a department, such as firearms policies and reducing stress.

- Analyze the perspectives and criticisms of private probation agencies.

- Recall how offenders are supervised when they want to go to a different jurisdiction than where they committed their crime.

© Spencer Grant/Stock, Boston Inc.

Case management involves a balance between helping offenders get through their supervision, and communicating consequences of their actions.

CHAPTER OUTLINE

Introduction

Selection and Appointment of Probation Officers
Appointment System
Merit System

Officer Qualifications, Training, and Salary
Education and Experience
Adult Basic Training
Juvenile Preservice Training
In-service Training
Officer Salary

Firearms Policies for Probation and Parole Officers

Probation Officer Job Stress
Sources of Stress
Decreasing Stress: Types of Immunity

Private Probation
Statutes Authorizing Private Probation
Criticisms of Probation Privatization
Attorney Views on Privatization

Interstate Compacts on Probation
New Interstate Compact for Adult Offender Supervision
Revocation and the Interstate Compact

Summary

KEY TERMS

preservice training
Peace Officer State Training
In-service training
role ambiguity
role conflict

negligence
absolute immunity
qualified immunity
private probation
private service provider

Interstate Compact
sending state
receiving state
Interstate Compact for Adult
   Offender Supervision

Introduction

There are about 93,000 probation/parole officers and correctional treatment specialists nationwide. While most officers in the federal system supervise offenders after conviction (62 percent), the remainder work is in the pretrial process with presentence investigations (21 percent), pretrial supervision (12 percent), and pretrial activations (Hughes, 2008). State and local officers work primarily with post-conviction supervision. People are initially attracted to probation and parole careers because of simultaneous emphases on helping people and protecting the community. You will find that over the course of such careers, particularly in local jurisdictions, staff turnover is high. We explore reasons for this phenomenon, one of which might be a difference by gender. Women represent 54 percent of line staff, but only 13 percent of probation and parole supervisors (Camp, Camp, and May, 2003).

Carl Klockars (1972) developed a classic typology of probation officers that defined four basic types of supervision officers: the law enforcer, the time-server, the therapeutic agent, and the synthetic officer. Most officers are characterized as either law enforcers or therapeutic agents, but the two styles can work together to become more like the synthetic officer. (Steiner, 2004). The synthetic officer is involved in evidence-based practices such as those we read about in Chapter 5—holding offenders accountable for their behavior while being engaged in problem solving. As you read this chapter, think about how these styles may vary according to each person's own beliefs about crime causation, the kind of training he or she receives, and each department's orientation. These work styles explain how supervision officers ultimately deal with offenders (see Box 6.1).

This chapter will discuss the selection process, desired qualifications, and training involved in working in probation and parole, or any community corrections position involving the supervision of offenders.

BOX 6.1 COMMUNITY CORRECTIONS UP CLOSE

Carl Klockars's Typology of Work Styles

Law Enforcers stress the legal authority and enforcement aspects of their job, dictating firmness and obeying the laws as essentials. Of prime importance to such officers are the court order, authority, and decision-making power.

Time-Servers have similar philosophies as law enforcers, but time-servers have little aspiration to improve their skills or change their ways. Their conduct on the job is to abide by the rules and meet minimal job responsibilities, but they do not strive to excel. Rules and regulations are upheld but unexamined. They do not make the rules; they just work there.

Therapeutic Agents see their role as administering a form of treatment, introducing the probationer or parolee to a better way of life and motivating constructive patterns of behavior. They give guidance and support to those who are unable to solve their problems by themselves and provide their clients with an opportunity to work through their ambivalent feelings. The philosophy of the therapeutic

agent includes respecting clients, demonstrating concern, and helping individuals perceive the degree to which their old ways of behaving have been problematic.

Synthetic Officers are distinguished by their recognition of the balance between both treatment and law enforcement components of probation officers' roles. Thus, they frequently encounter role conflict while combining the paternal, authoritarian, and judgmental with the therapeutic roles. Duffee (1984) talks about this role conflict when he states: "It is this officer who wraps his client in a warm hello hug, bruising him with his gun butt as he does so" (p. 191).

- Which working style will tend to have a higher revocation rate compared to other officers?
- Which style will tend to take more time and have longer client sessions?
- How does working style of an officer affect the success or failure of an offender?

Selection and Appointment of Probation Officers

The initial selection of probation officers is similar to the system used to select other public employees; for instance, California requires that its officers be American citizens. (See Box 6.2 for a discussion on whether requiring probation officers to be U.S. citizens is unconstitutional.) Probation and parole officers are also prohibited from having any felony convictions and must undergo a criminal background check. Officers are either appointed, selected on merit, or some combination of the two.

APPOINTMENT SYSTEM

Jurisdictions that appoint probation officers have a judge or selection committee that appoints a chief probation officer, who in turn selects assistants subject to the approval of the advisory body. Salary scales are fixed, and the judicial body that holds the power to select the chief probation officer determines broad policy matters.

In the federal system, for example, the judges of each federal district court appoint a chief probation officer. The chief probation officer selects the subordinate probation officers, who are all classified as law enforcement personnel. There are more than 4,000 U.S. probation officers in 94 judicial districts, supervising offenders under mandatory supervised release and those on military parole. (See Box 6.3 for the responsibilities of a federal probation officer.) Where juvenile and adult probation services are administered locally, the court judges may choose the chief probation officer.

BOX 6.2   COMMUNITY CORRECTIONS UP CLOSE

Is the U.S. Citizenship Requirement to Become a Probation Officer Unconstitutional?

The issue of employment rights for immigrants remains a central concern today, with state laws protecting people who have a legal right to work in the United States from being refused a job. However, there are some jobs or functions that require that the employee be a citizen of the United States, such as positions with political or peace-keeping functions. This requirement excludes permanent residents who are legally able to be in the United States, but who are not citizens or who have not sought "naturalization."

The state of California mandated that its probation officers be American citizens. A lawsuit was filed by a group of permanent resident aliens saying that the citizenship requirement was unconstitutional in that it violated the equal protection clause of the Fourteenth Amendment. The lower court of California agreed that this was unconstitutional. The state appealed the decision, and the case went to the U.S. Supreme Court.

The state of California argued that all of its probation officers were by law, "peace officers." In other words, by definition probation officers were authorized to carry and use a firearm, and exercise broad discretion in the potential use of coercive force and removal of freedom of probationers on community supervision. Second, all peace officers in California were required to be U.S. citizens, including local and state police. The state argued that they were merely extending to probation officers the requirement already in place for the police. The U.S. Supreme Court reversed the lower court decision and sided with the state of California. In upholding the citizenship requirement, the Supreme Court recognized that

> ". . . the probation officer acts as an extension of the judiciary's authority to set the conditions under which particular individuals will lead their lives and of the executive's authority to coerce obedience to those conditions. From the perspective of the probationer, his probation officer may personify the State's sovereign powers; from the perspective of the larger community, the probation officer may symbolize the political community's control over, and thus responsibility for, those who have been found to have violated the norms of social order. From both of these perspectives, a citizenship requirement may seem an appropriate limitation on those who would exercise and, therefore, symbolize this power of the political community over those who fall within its jurisdiction." (*Cabell v. Chavez-Salido* [1982] 454 U.S. 432).

MERIT SYSTEM

Merit or civil service systems were developed to remove public employees from political patronage. In a merit system, applicants who meet minimum employment standards are required to pass a competitive exam. People who score above a specified minimum grade are placed on a ranked list. Candidates are selected from the list according to their order of rank. In some systems, applicants are also graded on the basis of their education and employment history. The merit system is used in some states to determine promotions and is required in 4 states (Delaware, Indiana, Rhode Island, and Wisconsin). Elements of both appointment and merit systems may also be used. Applicants are initially screened through a merit exam, and candidates are selected by the agency in a process similar to the appointment system.

Officer Qualifications, Training, and Salary

As former adult probation officer Eladio Castillo can attest, probation and parole officers should possess good oral and written communication skills to be able to interview offenders, provide testimony to judges, sympathize with victims, and correspond with offenders' employers and family members. It is desirable for officers

FIELD NOTES

What types of knowledge, skills, and abilities do you believe are important for students to acquire before looking for a job [or develop shortly after being hired] as a probation officer?

The most important knowledge, skills, and abilities that I believe are important for students to acquire before looking for a job involve the use of practical work techniques. Although the theoretical aspects learned as a student are important, one must understand critical thinking and professional interpersonal relationships. The ability to identify and analyze information and observations swiftly to determine the validity of a judgment is a skill used on a daily basis. Students must learn to condition their mind to set aside assumptions, mindsets, and biases, and evaluate evidence to substantiate which hypothesis of a question has the least amount of inconsistencies.

Furthermore, working professionally with others is a skill that must be acquired when entering the field. When working in a group, individual creativity, uniqueness, and autonomous thinking are still important; however, you must learn to collaborate in order to obtain and maintain the cohesiveness of the structure to accomplish the goal.

Knowing how to work with different offenders is important. You must learn to identify problems by focusing on the risk and needs of each individual. Understanding

Eladio D. Castillo, *M.S.*
Former Adult Probation Officer

social learning, social bonding, mental disorders, substance abuse, finances, and criminal tendencies will facilitate your decision on how much time you should spend on the individual, whether in treatment or socioeconomic assistance. Whatever the problem(s) may be, you must learn to identify it at the initial appointment or early in the probation term to avoid potential noncompliance.

Also, time and stress management are important skills one must acquire. As is the case in many jobs, the number of offenders on a probation officer's caseload is often more than policy recommends. Nonetheless, you must learn to manage your time to accomplish specific tasks, projects, or goals. Time management depends on the individual, and you must learn to prioritize activities. ou will feel the weight of stress over time, but adapting and coping with the stress is key.

Lastly, understanding and communicating in a secondary language is an asset. Executives consider secondary languages when hiring, and some agencies even provide incentive pay. When working with offenders, you can use their primary language, if it is not English, to better communicate and understand them. If the offenders feel comfortable with you, their compliance increases from my experience. Although a secondary language is not required, it would be beneficial to acquire the skill, not only for probation, but in any of your future aspirations.

to know how to treat people fairly, consistently, firmly, and with respect. It is helpful for officers to be knowledgeable about different cultures and to be good time managers. (See Box 6.4 for examples of job postings found online.) These skills are gained by education, experience, and training.

EDUCATION AND EXPERIENCE

Most adult probation and parole officers must have a minimum of a baccalaureate degree, and at least 86 percent of states hiring juvenile probation officers require that they possess a degree (Reddington and Kreisel, 2003). Traditionally, probation officers were recruited out of the social work and psychology fields. As the emphasis of probation changed from treatment to public safety and control, a preference has emerged to recruit individuals with degrees in criminal justice, criminology, and sociology. This is because knowledge of crime causation and criminal law are important. It is an advantage for applicants who work with juveniles to have knowledge of development and adolescent psychology and juvenile justice. In addition to

BOX 6.3   COMMUNITY CORRECTIONS UP CLOSE

Duties of a Federal Probation Officer

A probation officer shall—

1. Instruct a probationer or a person on a supervised release, who is under his supervision, as to the conditions specified by the sentencing court, and provide him with a written statement clearly setting forth all such conditions;
2. Keep informed, to the degree required by the conditions specified by the sentencing court, as to the conduct and condition of a probationer or a person on supervised release, who is under his supervision, and report his conduct and condition to the sentencing court;
3. Use all suitable methods, not inconsistent with the conditions specified by the court, to aid a probationer or a person on supervised release who is under his supervision, and to bring about improvements in his conduct and condition;
4. Be responsible for the supervision of a probationer or a person on a supervised release who is known to be within the judicial district;
5. Keep a record of his work, and make such reports to the Director of the Administrative Office of the United States Courts as the Director may require;
6. Upon request of the Attorney General or his designee, assist in the supervision of and furnish information about, a person within the custody of the Attorney General while on work release, furlough, or other authorized release from his regular place of confinement, or while in the prerelease custody pursuant to the provisions of section 3624c;

7. Keep informed concerning the conduct, condition, and compliance with any condition of probation, including the payment of a fine or restitution of each probationer under his supervision and report thereon to the court placing such person on probation and report to the court any failure of a probationer under his supervision to pay a fine in default so that the court may determine whether probation should be revoked;
8. (A) when directed by the court, and to the degree required by the regimen of care of treatment ordered by the court as a condition of release, keep informed as to the conduct and provide supervision of a person conditionally released under the provisions of section 4243 or 4246 of this title, and report such person's conduct and condition to the court ordering release and to the Attorney General or his designee; and
9. (B) immediately report any violation of the conditions of release to the court and the Attorney General or his designee;
10. If approved by the district court, be authorized to carry firearms under such rules and regulations as the Director of the Administrative Office of the United States Courts may prescribe; and
11. Perform any other duty that the court may designate.

Source: United States Sentencing Commission. 2002. *Federal Sentencing Guidelines* Chapter 3603, 1–10:1001–1002. Accessed: http://www.ussc.gov/2002guid/TABCON02.htm

---

educational requirements, some jurisdictions may also require psychological evaluations, weapons qualification, and drug screening.

ADULT BASIC TRAINING

Once an officer has been selected and hired, he or she begins training. **Preservice training** provides the basic knowledge, skills, and abilities that newly hired officers need before they begin working independently. Combined probation and parole departments require an average of 208 hours of preservice training before officers assume their duties. However, probation and parole offices that are separate require significantly less training for probation officers (84 hours on average) and 182 hours for parole officers. Preservice training requirements range from 0 hours for probation officers in West Virginia to 600 hours for parole and probation officers in North Dakota (Camp, Camp, and May, 2003). Table 6.1 lists a typical training curriculum for probation and parole officers in North Carolina, which provides 160 hours of basic training.

Preservice Training
Fundamental knowledge and/or skills for a newly hired officer in preparation for working independently.

BOX 6.4   COMMUNITY CORRECTIONS UP CLOSE

Sample Job Advisements

U.S. PROBATION OFFICER

A career position for presentence and investigation /supervision officer in U.S. Probation. Minimum requirements: BS/BA social sciences and at least 3 yrs related experience. Computer skills required. MA/MS preferred. Under age 37 (OPM Reg. SCRF842.803A)

Starting salary $55K. Send cover letter, resume and AO78 application (available at www. ohsp.uscourts.gov)

MICHIGAN PAROLE/PROBATION OFFICER 9/10/11

Wages: $17.81 − $28.32 /hr (depends on grade)
Union: United Auto Workers
Job Description: Employee of this position follows the policies, procedures, Directors Office Memorandums (DOMs), and guiding principles of the Department of Corrections to provide background information to the courts on offenders convicted in Circuit Court and to supervise those convicted.
Minimum Education: Possession of a bachelor's degree in criminal justice, correctional administration, criminology, psychology, social work, counseling and guidance, child development, sociology, school social work, social work administration, education psychology, family relations, human services, or theology.

Minimum Experience:

- *PPO 9:* None required.
- *PPO 10:* One year of professional experience working with adult offenders equivalent to a Parole/Probation Officer 9.
- *PPO 11:* Two years of professional experience working with adult offenders equivalent to a Parole/Probation Officer, including one year equivalent to a PPO 10.

Special Requirements: Possession of a valid driver's license and the availability of an automobile for business. Possession of a cell phone listed in the name of the employee. Residence is required in the area where employed. Passing a criminal background check and substance abuse test.
How to Apply: Interested applicants must submit a cover letter, resume, copy of official college transcript and Reference Authorization form. All required forms must be submitted at the time of application for further consideration. Application materials must be postmarked by the deadline date.

Source: http://www.careerbuilder.com Retrieved on March 1, 2009

Peace Officer State Training Specialized and standardized training that officers are required to complete before they may carry a firearm on the job.

In many states where probation and parole officers carry firearms, they must complete **Peace Officer State Training** (POST). POST topics include strategies of case supervision, record keeping, legal liability, professional ethics, arrest and detention procedures, firearms handling, defensive tactics, and stress reduction. During the training process, POST instructors use metaphors and stories from their own field experiences that greatly influence how new recruits perceive the organizational culture. POST trainers thus shape the attitudes and values of the probation and parole officer subculture, which affect their work role orientation (Crank, 1996).

JUVENILE PRESERVICE TRAINING

For the supervision of juveniles, the American Correctional Association recommends that juvenile probation officers receive 40 hours of preservice training, whereas the American Bar Association suggests 80 hours of preservice training with an additional 48 hours within the first six months. Reddington and Kreisel conducted a nationwide survey to determine trends in juvenile probation officer training. They found that 20 states certified juvenile probation officer positions with an average of 100 hours of preservice training. Most other states mandated orientation training where the officer does not go through an academy, but strictly learns on the job, with between 8 and 200 hours of training within the first year of employment. Compared to adult probation officers, who average 125 training hours, juvenile probation officers averaged

TABLE 6.1   Probation/Parole Officer Basic Training Program Course Topics and Hours

I.	ORIENTATION ORGANIZATION, POLICY AND PROCEDURES: 12 Hours		
	300	Division of Community Corrections Employee	4
	301	Overview of Community Corrections	3
	306	Community Corrections Administration	1
	307	Targeting Offender Needs	4
		Total	12
II.	LEGAL CONSIDERATIONS: 20 Hours		
	302	Introduction to the Legal System	2
	303	Legalities of the Pre-Sentence/Diagnostic Investigations	4
	304	Probation Law—Part I—Violations, Sanctions, Hearings	4
	304	Probation Law—Part II—Arrest, Search, Seizure	6
	315	Parole Law	2
	317	Processing New Parole Cases	2
		Total	20
III.	OFFICER-PROBATIONER/PAROLEE RELATIONS: 28 Hours		
	320	Understanding Offender Behavior	4
	324	Counseling Methodologies—Parts IA (CBI)	2
	324	Counseling Methodologies—Part IB(Nonverbal/Verbal Intervention)	2
	324	Counseling Methodologies—Part II – Gangs	4
	325	Crisis Interventions and Domestic Disputes	4
	330	Counseling Substance Abuse Cases	2
	331	Interview Techniques	4
	336	Offender Supervision	6
		Total	28
IV.	PROBATIONER/PAROLEE MANAGEMENT: 32 Hours		
	311	Case Management	6
	313	Unlawful Workplace Harassment	2
	318	Parole Violations and Revocations	4
	326	Community Resource Management	2
	327	Processing Probation Cases—Part I/II	16
	329	Closing Cases	2
		Total	32
V.	DEFENSIVE PROTECTION: 30 Hours		
	328	Arrest Procedures	8
	333	Controls, Restraints, Defensive Techniques	18
	334	Personal Protection	4
		Total	30
VI.	COURTROOM PREPARATION AND DEMEANOR: 8 Hours		
	305	Public Speaking	2
	314	Moot Court	4
	332	Role of the Probation/Parole Witness	2
		Total	8
VII.	OTHER: 30 Hours		
	312	Drug Identification	4
	335	Basic Life Support	8
	337	Employee Wellness	4
	338	Professional Ethics	2
	339	Personal Conduct	6
	000	Review and Testing	6
		Total	30
		Course Total	**160**

Source: North Carolina Department of Correction Office of Staff Training. For a full listing of topical descriptions of each topic. Retrieved on March 5, 2009 from: www.doc.state.nc.us/OSDT/Forms/Syllabus_PPO.DOC

just over 77 hours (Reddington and Kreisel 2000, 2003). The main reason for this difference is that there are no national training standards for juvenile probation.

IN-SERVICE TRAINING

In-Service Training
Periodic continuing education training for seasoned officers.

In-service training is continuing education training that occurs annually for seasoned officers following the first year of employment. This allows officers to keep current with new laws or new developments in the field, or to repeat important topics from the initial training. Training topics may include evidence-based practice principles, cognitive-behavioral treatment principles, motivational interviewing, and supervision techniques with special needs offenders. In at least one jurisdiction, probation officers are exposed to empathy training, which aims to sensitize probation officers to what juvenile probationers endure during arrest and detention (Rainey, 2002).

The American Correctional Association recommends that seasoned officers receive 40 hours of annual training. Forty hours annually appears to be the most common requirement for adult probation and parole departments, with the average ranging between 33 for probation and 42 hours for parole (Camp, Camp, and May, 2003). For officers supervising juveniles, only 30 states require annual training—a median of 30 hours per year (Reddington and Kreisel, 2000).

OFFICER SALARY

Based on the positions advertised nationwide in 2009 (www.payscale.com), an entry- level probation officer or correctional treatment specialist with less than one year of experience can expect a median salary of $32,859. With five to nine years of experience, the median salary for the same job is $37,843; with 10 to19 years, the salary is $43,456, and with 20 years or more on the job, the salary rises to $56,000. Another salary web site reported that the overall average for probation and parole officers was $46,000, which averaged the following three jobs: parole officer at $33,000; court services officer at $42,000; and deputy probation officer at $54,000 (www.indeed.com/salary/). Probation officers in urban areas working for local government agencies tended to earn higher salaries than where the department was situated in a state government.

Another general trend is that parole officers in stand-alone departments had a higher starting salary. They also had higher salaries over their career than did parole or probation officers in combined departments. The differences in salary could be due to there being fewer turnovers of probation officers in stand-alone departments, or their earning better raises over time than those provided by combined departments or by stand-alone parole departments.

Probation and parole administrators earned considerably more than field officers. The average salary for parole administrators was $161,435, and for probation administrators, $101,109. For combined departments, probation and parole administrators earned an average of $84,442 (Camp, Camp, and May, 2003). As officers' job expectations have risen, so have the amount of training and their salaries. One example of increased responsibility is the authorization to carry weapons.

Firearms Policies for Probation and Parole Officers

One of the strongest indicators of a department's philosophy is its stance on firearms. One study found that as the percent of armed officers increases, the more enforcement-oriented the department (Roscoe et al., 2007). In the federal system,

TABLE 6.2   Number of States with Firearms Policies for Probation and Parole Officers

Firearms Policy	PROBATION		PAROLE	
	Adult	**Juvenile**	**Adult**	**Juvenile**
Officers Not Armed Statewide	17	40	12	43
Mandatory Arming Statewide	17	4	25	3
County Specific	6	5	2	2
Optional Choice	9	2	9	2
Job Specific (Intensive)	3	2	4	1

Source: American Probation and Parole Association. 2006. *APPA Adult and Juvenile Probation and Parole National Firearm Survey 2005–2006.* Lexington, KY: APPA. Accessed: http://www.appa-net.org/information%20clearing%20house/survey.htm.

85 out of 94 judicial districts allow federal probation officers to carry firearms of .40 caliber and above. As of October 2006, the American Probation and Parole Association reported that officers in 35 adult probation jurisdictions and 40 adult parole jurisdictions carry firearms (see Table 6.2). About half of all firearm-carrying jurisdictions in the adult system are mandatory, whereas other jurisdictions depend on the type of clients supervised. In California, 60 percent of counties are authorized to use firearms, but wide variation existed on who was authorized. Some counties allowed only officers who supervised a specialized caseload, such as violent or other high-risk offenders, to carry a firearm, whereas other counties allowed any officer the option (Nieto, 1996).

In comparison to those officers supervising adults, the vast majority of juvenile officers do not carry firearms. In the juvenile system, 13 states allow firearms for officers, 2 give officers the option, and 2 states narrow firearms to only certain counties or to officers who supervise serious juvenile offenders. Juvenile probation officer Teressa Price provides her professional opinion about carrying a firearm on the job in Field Notes.

Courtesy of Leanne F. Alarid

As the community supervision officer's role focuses increasingly on public safety, more officers now carry firearms and handcuffs.

Probation and parole officers who become licensed to carry firearms participate in such training known as Firearms Training System or FATS, a more realistic decision-making test in potential uses of deadly force.

The firearms policy for the Eastern District of Missouri states that "officers should avoid the use of a firearm except in self-defense or in defense of a fellow probation officer. The officer may not use a firearm unless the officer believes he/she, or a fellow officer, is in imminent danger of death or serious bodily injury and there is no means of a safe retreat" (Scharr, 2001, p. 47). This firearm policy, as written, does not allow a probation officer to use a firearm to come to the aid of any other third party. Federal officers receive two weeks of training that includes qualifying with at least 80 percent accuracy and passing a written exam.

Advocates of officers carrying firearms contend that as officers are expected to make more late-night home visits and be present out in the field, their time away from the office diminishes, as does their safety. Probation officers in specialized units who supervise gang members and violent offenders have been the most assertive. Officers favoring the carrying of firearms while on duty tended to be younger and more likely to practice law-and-order case management strategies rather than casework or treatment-oriented approaches (Sluder, Shearer, and Potts, 1991). Guns seem to satisfy a philosophical need for safety, independent of the actual perceived threat (Roscoe et al., 2007).

Jurisdictions where probation is under the judicial branch have tended to oppose the carrying of firearms, contending that carrying firearms is a function under the executive branch of powers, and not appropriate for employees of the judicial branch. The New Jersey Supreme Court upheld this, saying that judicial officers performing an executive branch function unconstitutionally violated the separation of powers (*Williams v. State of New Jersey*, 2006), and may conflict with rehabilitation objectives and traditional casework strategies (Small and Torres, 2001).

Those opposed to officers carrying a firearm question whether the threat to probation officers is real or perceived. Opponents argue that not every probation officer may need to carry a deadly weapon, especially if that officer supervises misdemeanants or juveniles. Furthermore, an officer's safety or life may be at greater risk if a probationer or parolee is carrying a weapon, because a greater chance exists that the offender may use a gun against an armed officer than an

FIELD NOTES

Has carrying a firearm changed the way you approach community supervision of juveniles? If so, how has it changed, and what has not changed? Do you think the policy is a good idea?

As a juvenile probation officer (JPO), I feel it is important that I am equipped with everything necessary to maintain my safety, as well as the safety of those around me. I was a JPO for eight months before becoming certified to carry a firearm. For those eight months, I was stationed at a local high school and was required to visit the homes of juveniles on my caseload on a weekly basis from 6pm to10pm. I had to be out after dark, wearing a visible vest with "Probation Officer" in big letters on the back. Anyone could spot me easily and all I had was mace and a baton, not enough to protect myself from a kid with a gun.

I received my certification on a Friday and began carrying my firearm the following Tuesday. I would not say that it necessarily changed how I supervised the juveniles on my caseload, but it did change my comfort level in that I knew that I had the training and ability to react in the unfortunate situation that anyone, not a just a juvenile, should open fire either at the school or in the community.

Detaining juveniles, sending them to placements, and boot camps or treatment centers, along with placing them on electronic monitoring sometimes are a part of supervising juveniles. All of the above things came at a monetary cost to the parents who, often times, could not afford the burden of paying child support to a placement for their child resulting in the

Teressa Price *Juvenile Probation Officer, Dauphine County, Pennsylvania.*

government garnishing their wages. And I was the one making the decision to recommend these things to the court. All it would take is one upset juvenile, or parent for that matter, to get their hands on a firearm and see me as a target.

With violence among juveniles increasing, I believe it is a good policy that juvenile probation officers have all the equipment necessary to protect them. If someone opens fire randomly, or at me specifically, I would not be able to do much with a can of mace. With being stationed at a school, it is especially important because I, along with the school resource officer, would also have the ability to protect the students and faculty of the school. While I would not say that school shootings are the norm, I would say that these things do happen occasionally. Juveniles are receiving charges for bringing a weapon on school property--anything from a small baseball bat to an AK-47. In the crucial minutes it would take for someone to call 911 and the police to respond, many could be wounded or dead. School probation officers and school resource officers could respond immediately to the threat whether that threat is another student, or an intruder in the school.

I know that juvenile probation officers carrying firearms is a controversial subject and that not everyone agrees that it is a necessary part of supervising children in the community. I, however, am grateful to have every protection possible, along with the knowledge and training on how and when to use it in the event that I need it.

unarmed officer (Scharr, 2001). An early study found that probation officers who carried a firearm experienced more confrontation incidents than officers who did not carry a firearm. In addition, male probation officers were significantly more likely to be confronted and/or physically assaulted than female probation officers (Parsonage and Bushey 1989). Since that study, officer confrontations have greatly decreased as officers pay more attention to safety issues by conducting home visits in pairs, wearing body armor, and training in self-defense techniques. Of the serious incidents that have occurred, over half occurred in the field, and only 28 percent occurred in the probation office. The three most common incidents were threats, animal attacks, and other situations defined as "dangerous" (Small and Torres, 2001).

Due to these concerns, not all officers want to carry a firearm. Other options should be provided if an officer is philosophically opposed to carrying a firearm.

BOX 6.5   TECHNOLOGY IN CORRECTIONS

Interactive Firearms Video Training

The Firearms Training System (or FATS) is the use of interactive video technology to enhance firearms training for any peace officer, including probation, parole and pretrial services officers. FATS training is different from shooting at traditional fixed targets. In FATS training, a video image is projected onto a screen, and this image is connected to a computer, speakers, and firearm replicas that spray a harmless liquid peppermint when the trigger is pulled. Each different scenario requires the trainees to choose what action to take. After a variety of scenarios, the trainees discuss and justify their actions to the instructor.

An evaluation of FATS training found that 32 percent of probation officers reported that the training had altered their perceptions "to a great extent" of the value of a firearm for self-defense, and another 34 percent said that their perceptions changed "to some extent." The training helped clarify the meaning of the firearms policy, as well as the moral issues and liability that accompany the use of potentially deadly force. Scharr concluded: "After the training, officers clearly indicated they were surprised at how quickly a critical incident could occur, how likely it is that they will be perceived as law enforcement officers during a critical incident, how difficult it can be to work in teams and communicate during a critical incident. . . . This suggests that the training was effective in heightening officer awareness of danger and the necessity for continued training in mental preparedness and self-defense proficiency" (p. 49).

Source: Timothy M. Scharr. 2001. Interactive Video Training for Firearms Safety. *Federal Probation* 65(2): 45–51.

These options include chemical agents, stun guns, pressure points training, and field visits with two officers.

From a more practical viewpoint, carrying firearms involves ongoing liability and training costs. One jurisdiction in which adult probation officers did carry firearms later placed a moratorium on them, prohibiting all officers from carrying weapons. The moratorium was the result of concerns about training costs and the department's inability to pay for proper training within their budget (Chasnoff, 2006). Some jurisdictions may favor the idea, but simply can't afford to implement the policy.

The American Probation and Parole Association (1994) neither supports nor opposes the carrying of weapons by probation and parole officers. The association argues that, should officers be authorized to carry weapons, decisions should be made according to actual need, proper training, liability issues, and selection procedures that minimally include a physical and psychological examination. All probation officers who choose to carry a firearm receive training, such as the interactive video Firearms Training System (see Box 6.5).

Probation Officer Job Stress

Probation and parole supervision is a job centered around people, rather than around information and data. Building professional relationships with offenders from which change takes place is an art, and result in a great deal of satisfaction and reward when officers can impact the lives of their clients. As one federal probation officer said, "If you can help someone lead a stable and productive life, then it is worth all the effort. You can't explain the rewards of helping someone else. To see someone make it through that system and lead a productive life is a reward" (Quinn, 2002, p. 265). Another revealed that satisfaction resulted when "achieving successful outcomes with offenders who have managed to make changes in their life" (Annison, Eadie, and Knight, 2008, p. 266).

Jobs that are people centered also tend to have higher levels of risk and burnout than jobs that are data centered. Although most jobs are stressful to some degree, being a probation and parole officer can be stressful because of its unpredictability. One of the purposes of this section is to inform readers of the realistic concerns of community corrections supervision, so that people interested in this profession are aware of the potential concerns this line of work may present. Studies of probation officer stress can certainly apply to any position in the area of community corrections supervision.

Most studies of probation officer stress do not compare the job with other types of employment, so it is difficult to say whether being a probation officer is a "high-stress" or "low-stress" job overall. One study found that state probation officers endured significantly more stress than federal level probation officers (Slate and Johnson, 2008).

SOURCES OF STRESS

Researchers have uncovered the following sources of stress for line probation officers (Slate, Johnson, and Wells, 2000; Wells, Colbert and Slate, 2006):

- Excessive paperwork
- Lack of time to accomplish the job (must take work home)
- Inadequate salary
- Lack of promotional opportunities
- Role ambiguity
- Role conflict (treatment and law enforcement)
- Lack of participation in decision making
- Court leniency on offenders
- Failure to recognize accomplishments

Sometimes feeling overly stressed may simply mean that the job is not a good fit for the person. In criminal justice, written documentation is an important part of taking legal responsibility for the supervision of another person. Federal officers in particular spend a lot of time documenting everything on every client they supervise, and that is what some officers may refer to as "excessive paperwork" (Slate and Johnson, 2008). Time spent on paperwork and heavy caseloads led to the feeling that there is not enough time for the actual supervision part.

Role ambiguity refers to the idea that community supervision officers have discretion and can choose whether or not to exercise it. This is why common sense, ethics, and consistency are so important. Officers also have to manage their time because they may be out in the field. People who are accustomed only to following the lead of others and who cannot manage their time well may experience a sense of uneasiness because they may not feel comfortable acting on their own.

Role conflict, a common source of stress, refers to the idea that officers must be empathetic, understanding, and objective enough to help offenders who have broken the law. At the same time, they must also be able to revoke or terminate clients who are not following the conditions of their supervision (as we will discuss in the next chapter).

Lack of participation in decision making is a complaint of line officers who make recommendations to their supervisors, judges, and parole boards, but who do not actually get to make the final decision. The decision is, therefore, made by a third party who does not have daily interactions with the offender; the officer may at times feel a sense of betrayal by a court that does not agree with the officer's recommendations. One recommendation to reduce this problem is to allow officers the opportunity to participate in workplace decision making (Slate and Johnson, 2008).

Finally, supervising offenders all too often ignore the basic principles of behavior modification: reward positive behavior and discourage negative behavior. Community corrections supervision frequently takes action on negative behavior and ignores or downplays positive or prosocial behavior. This would make a

Role Ambiguity
The discretion that exists in the role of the probation and parole officer to treat clients fairly and consistently and according to individual circumstances.

Role Conflict
The two functions of a probation and parole officer, that of enforcing the rules and laws, and providing support and reintegration, that are sometimes contradictory and difficult to reconcile.

behavioral psychologist shudder and might explain in part, at least, why so many offenders "fail" on supervision. Despite these problems, many people find this line of work very rewarding and have spent their entire career in community corrections.

DECREASING STRESS: TYPES OF IMMUNITY

One of the ways to decrease probation and parole officer stress is for officers to know general limits of the law regarding actions or inactions on the job. It is important for officers to minimize risk by keeping track of the people they are supervising and to respond professionally to inappropriate behaviors. No matter how accomplished and organized the officer, the probationer or parolee may at times injure or victimize the general public. What happens if the victim feels the injury could have been prevented if only the officer had "properly supervised" the client?

Negligence
The failure of an officer to do what a reasonably prudent person would have done in like or similar circumstances.

Given that it is impossible for officers to control the actions of their clients at all times, the best that officers can do is to follow department policy, follow the orders of the court or the parole board, and justify their actions with accurate paperwork. **Negligence** is the failure to do that which a reasonably prudent person would have done in like or similar circumstances. For example, if an officer finds out through credible sources that one of her probationers is planning to commit a crime, and the officer could have prevented it but failed to do so, the officer is likely negligent. A person may be held liable (or responsible) if the negligence was gross or willful. All of these terms are subjective according to the meaning assigned by a judge or jury, but gross or willful negligence generally means that a person must have intentionally or maliciously failed to act (del Carmen et al., 2001).

Since probation and parole officers are government officials (as are police, judges, and prosecutors), probation and parole officers are entitled to different types of legal protection so that they may feel comfortable exercising discretion without fear of being personally sued over actions of clients under their supervision. The type of immunity officers have depends on what *function* they are performing (del Carmen et al., 2001).

Absolute Immunity
Protection from legal action or liability unless workers engage in discretion that is intentionally and maliciously wrong.

Absolute Immunity **Absolute immunity** protects government officials from any legal action unless they engage in acts that are intentionally and maliciously wrong. Absolute immunity provides the highest level of protection. In *King v. Simpson* (1999), the court ruled that parole board officials have absolute immunity in adjudicatory decisions to grant, deny, or revoke parole. Probation and parole officers have absolute immunity only when acting in a quasi-judicial or prosecutorial function, such as when probation officers are preparing and submitting a presentence investigation report (*Spaulding v. Nielsen*, 1979). The Spaulding case affirmed that probation officers who are preparing presentence investigation reports are acting in a quasi-judicial role, and even if there are errors later found in the PSI, the probation officer is fully protected from getting sued by the defendant. As discussed in Chapter 3, every defendant has the opportunity to review and make changes to any errors in his or her PSI before it is submitted to the judge. State statutes, however, must define PSI reports as a quasi-judicial function—otherwise the probation officer is eligible for qualified immunity.

Qualified Immunity
Protection from liability in decisions or actions that are "objectively reasonable."

Qualified Immunity Qualified immunity is much more narrow and limited to those in the executive branch or to workers performing administrative functions. In **qualified immunity,** workers are not liable for wrongdoing when their actions are found to be "objectively reasonable" and within the scope of employment. This standard is also subjective. Given that most functions of probation and parole officers are administrative rather than quasi-judicial/adjudicatory, probation and parole officers have qualified immunity (del Carmen et al., 2001).

Parole officer functions are defined differently from jurisdiction to jurisdiction. In New York, parole officers have only qualified immunity when recommending the issuance of a revocation warrant. This is because under New York law, issuing a revocation warrant is considered an investigatory, not a prosecutorial, function (*Best v. State*, 1999). In another state, the same activity—initiating a parole revocation proceeding and presenting the case during parole revocation hearings—was identified as a quasi-judicial function and therefore subject to absolute immunity.

As probation and parole officers are increasingly carrying firearms on the job, they are also a type of law enforcement officer, particularly if they have completed peace officer training. With this training also comes more liability and responsibility, making the decision to carry very much a personal and individual choice that should be carefully considered. We recommend that applicants find out in advance what kind of firearms policy exists (mandatory, optional, none, and so forth) and determine what situation is most suitable.

Private Probation

As state and local government look to trim costs in their budgets, they have increasingly turned to private companies for a wide array of services from drug testing to electronic monitoring. **Private probation** agencies contract with the local or state government to provide misdemeanor probation supervision. According to Alarid and Schloss (2009), private probation refers to the supervision side, but it is frequently the case that a private probation company will also provide treatment services, so a more generic term for a private probation company is a **private service provider**. A private service provider is "any for profit or non-profit private organization that contracts with county-level or state-level government to provide probation supervision, independent probation treatment services, or both probation supervision and treatment under one roof" (Alarid and Schloss, 2009, p. 5).

The privatization debate is centered around two main arguments, the first of which assumes that continued growth in the correctional system ensures survival of the agency which depends on outside referrals and fees collected from offenders. Another theory suggests that the government cannot adequately function as effectively as private companies, so services have been redistributed out of necessity, particularly to lower-risk individuals (Garland, 2001).

Private, nonprofit entities have been involved in community supervision of offenders for quite a long time—since the 1800s. The Salvation Army has a long history of providing such services. Over time, state codes and statutes were formulated to permit the use of private agencies for ancillary treatment services such as mental health, driving while intoxicated classes, drug treatment, and anger management (see Figure 6.1) to be provided for state and local probationers, or for private agencies to provide direct probation supervision. Because of the growing number of probationers for the number of staff available to supervise them, states are increasingly contracting with private probation agencies to assist with supervision.

At least 18 states currently use the private sector for some form of supervision, 10 of whom rely on private agencies for the sole responsibility of supervising misdemeanor and low-risk clients, while the state agency focuses on felony probationers (Schloss and Alarid, 2007). In the 10 states that rely on the private sector for misdemeanor supervision, it is estimated that over 300,000 probationers are being supervised by private agencies, which is three times more than the number of offenders in private jails and prisons. This number does not include the thousands of probationers

Private Probation
An agency that is owned and operated by a private business or nonprofit organization, and contracts with the state, local, or federal government to supervise clients convicted of a misdemeanor.

Private Service Provider
Any for profit or non-profit private organization that contracts with county-level or state-level government to provide probation supervision, independent probation treatment services, or both probation supervision and treatment.

FIGURE 6.1 Pie chart of Private Treatment Services

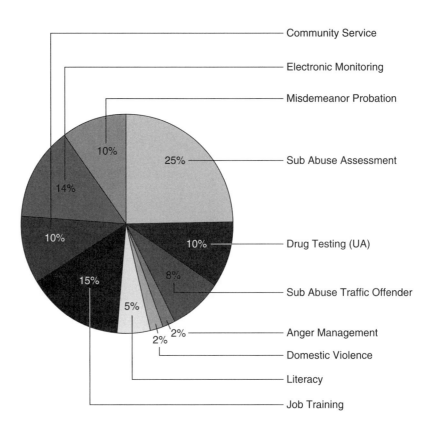

who are court-ordered to attend outpatient treatment centers (many of which are private) and the thousands of offenders in residential community correction facilities.

The adult probation office in Connecticut contracted with a private probation service to take on cases that required a lower level of supervision. The private contractor had no face-to-face contact with any low-level probationers, but assisted the state in monitoring compliance of community service via phone calls and the mail and by completing paperwork for each case. The state probation office was able to concentrate its efforts on the supervision of high-risk cases (Bosco, 1998). One such private company in the area of private misdemeanor probation services is Providence Community Corrections, which operates in Florida, Georgia, South Carolina, Tennesse, and Washington. Providence Community Corrections is a subsidiary of Providence Service Corporation, which is involved in a number of private contracts with substance abuse treatment, drug courts and adult community corrections (see www.provcorp.com).

STATUTES AUTHORIZING PRIVATE PROBATION

Regulating the private sector has generally been slow, with some jurisdictions operating in the grey area of unclear or non-existent standards for awarding contracts to private providers, staff hiring requirements, and curriculums for outpatient treatment services (Schloss & Alarid, 2007). Statutes examined by Schloss and Alarid (2007) in 7 states that authorized private probation (Alabama, Arkansas, Florida, Georgia, Missouri, Utah, and Tennessee) found that most states required agencies to sign a formal contract with the government that outlined the scope of services to be provided, the responsibilities of the contractor, and the obligations of the court. For example, private agencies in Missouri wishing to provide services must make application to provide services with the Circuit Judge, and must be able to prove financial ability and liability insurance to operate a probation office. However, Missouri has few standardized guidelines for private agency approval other than that the agency cannot be related in any way to the judge. Once agencies are approved for a three-year term, there are no requirements to provide verification of fees collected.

CRITICISMS OF PROBATION PRIVATIZATION

Critics of privatization say that the need to provide effective correctional services seems to be at odds with the prerequisite of making a profit for the business. Private sector probation is seen as intruding and competing with the government's traditional and ultimate responsibility to carry out punishment in a fair manner (Bosco, 1998). Furthermore, the private sector is usually not equipped to be a full-service organization, and thus it might only be able to take low-risk offenders who require little if any monitoring. Private-sector services have no uniform method of monitoring probation conditions or ensuring that victim restitution is collected (Leznoff, 1998).

State statutes also uncovered broad requirements for hiring officers as employees. Some states, such as Georgia, provided specific requirements for ongoing training and education of private probation officers. Georgia required officers to have completed two years of college, have no felony convictions, and be a minimum age of 21. Other states have no educational or training requirements for hiring individuals who wish to become private probation officers (Schloss and Alarid, 2007).

Another concern relates to the lack of standardization for agencies that wish to become program providers for probation agencies. Some states have no requirement that providers demonstrate qualifications such as licensing and experience. Ethical questions arise if private probation agencies are also treatment providers and require their ancillary services as a part of probation supervision. Schloss and Alarid (2007) argue for more stringent and standardized requirements for the supervision of offenders by private probation agencies, and believe that Georgia, Utah, Colorado, and Tennessee provide good examples in this endeavor.

Attorney Views on Privatization   Recommendation of community supervision as a sanction is partly dependent on the perceptions of courtroom attorneys: whether they accept probation as a viable alternative. During the case screening process, prosecutors decide whether sufficient evidence exists to charge a defendant with a crime. If enough evidence exists, prosecutors also decide the level or severity of the offense. Prosecutors are in a unique position to assess defendant eligibility for probation, and/or to connect defendants with private probation agencies. Because of this, prosecutors and defense attorneys were surveyed to measure their beliefs about the use of private treatment providers. Private agency accountability to the courts was of primary concern for prosecutors, while defense attorneys were more concerned about the treatment cost for their clients (Alarid and Schloss, 2009).

In contrast with traditional probation where the court orders the client to report to his or her probation officer after sentencing, private service providers have a representative stationed at the court to make initial contact with the client at sentencing. In this way, the offender's initial appointment and intake has been completed immediately after sentencing rather than the 7 to 14 day time period that it takes to start traditional probation. Court attorneys generally supported having a private representative present in court (Alarid and Schloss, 2009). Attorneys also believed that qualifications for offering supervision and treatment services were important, such as utilizing identical curricula state-wide, so that treatment offered by one private provider would be the same as that offered by another.

Interstate Compacts on Probation

Prior to 1937, a probationer or parolee could not be supervised outside the state where he or she was convicted, even though many transient offenders were arrested and convicted far away from home. As a result, the offender often could not be provided with supervision in the very place that would offer the best chance for success on probation or parole. A group of states entered into a statutory agreement by which they would supervise probationers and parolees for each other. Known as the **Interstate Compact,** the agreement was originally signed by 25 states in 1937. By 1951, the interstate compact had been ratified by all the states, as well as Puerto Rico and the Virgin Islands.

The Interstate Compact on Juveniles was established in 1955 to provide for return of juvenile runaways, escapees, and absconders as well as for cooperative supervision of juvenile probationers and parolees. A survey of field staff and interstate compact administrators found that 15,000 youths in the United States were being supervised via interstate compact but that one-third of all requests submitted by the sending state were denied by the receiving state (Linke and Krauth, 2000).

The compacts identify the **sending state** (the state of conviction) and the **receiving state** (the state that undertakes the supervision). The receiving state informs the sending state on a quarterly basis of the probationer's progress, but the sending state retains ultimate authority to modify the conditions of probation, revoke probation, or terminate probation. It is also generally held that the sending state alone has authority to determine upon what basis a violator may be returned. The reasons for return cannot be challenged by the receiving state.

The offender must meet certain residence requirements of the receiving state. Ordinarily, the probationer or parolee must be a resident of the receiving state, have relatives there, or have employment there. The receiving state agrees to provide "courtesy supervision" at the same level that it gives to its own cases.

The three main problems with interstate compacts were liability, monitoring compliance, and slow processing speed. Since probation supervision styles varied from state to state, each state had different thresholds and policies for when a probationer was considered to be in violation. For example, one state might consider a probationer to be in violation even though the other state wished to continue supervision (Cushman and Sechrest, 1992). In addition, some states were asked to accept far more interstate compact supervision cases than they sent out. At times, some states sent their most noncompliant cases elsewhere, and this form of supervision became a "dumping ground." Finally, the process of obtaining approval was slow, and some offenders relocated prior to being approved for supervision. Interstate compacts were largely unorganized and inconsistent in their approaches (Linke and Krauth, 2000).

Because of these problems, the National Institute of Corrections (NIC) Advisory Board spent two years, from 1997 to 1999, studying the problem and determining the best resolution. The NIC joined with the Council of State Governments to provide a new way to administer interstate compacts (National Institute of Corrections and the Council of State Governments, 2002).

THE INTERSTATE COMPACT FOR ADULT OFFENDER SUPERVISION

The **Interstate Compact for Adult Offender Supervision** program began in 2000. This revised compact developed an interstate commission that is composed of one commissioner representative from each participating state. The commission is a national organization empowered to create and enforce the same rules for all states, collect national statistics, coordinate training and education, and notify victims for

Interstate Compact
An agreement signed by all states and U.S. territories that allows for the supervision of parolees and probationers across state lines.

Sending State
Under the interstate compact, the state of conviction.

Receiving State
Under the interstate compact, the state that undertakes the supervision.

Interstate Compact For Adult Offender Supervision
A formalized decree granting authority to a commission to create and enforce rules for member states for the supervision of offenders in other states.

public safety. The commission has annual meetings to modify rules and to deal with conflicts among states as needed.

In addition to the commission, each state has its own council, composed of a compact administrator and at least one person from each branch of government (legislative, judicial, and executive). The compact administrator is charged with administering and managing all interstate compacts for his or her own state (National Institute of Corrections and the Council of State Governments, 2002). With this new structure and oversight commission, correctional administrators are hopeful that the problems with interstate compacts will be a thing of the past. As of 2004, all states except Virginia and Mississippi were members. There are reportedly as many as 250,000 offenders nationwide on interstate compact supervision.

REVOCATION AND THE INTERSTATE COMPACT

The sending state may enter the receiving state to take custody of the probationer or parolee who has violated the terms of release without going through extradition proceedings. The probationer waives extradition prior to leaving the sending state, so the sending state may retake a person being supervised in another state simply by having its officer present appropriate credentials and proving the identity of the person to be retaken. The probation violator is usually incarcerated in the receiving state at the expense of the sending state.

The receiving state is obligated to surrender the probationer unless a criminal charge is pending against the individual in the receiving state. In such a case, the probationer cannot be retaken without the receiving state's consent until he or she is discharged from prosecution or from any imprisonment for such offense. The effect is that the sending state cannot retake the probationer into custody until all local charges are disposed of.

A national organization called the Parole and Probation Compact Administrators' Association (PPCAA) was formed so that interstate compact officers could exchange information and solve challenges that arise. PPCAA meets twice per year to address issues as they occur so that all state policies are consistently enforced.

SUMMARY

- Probation or parole officers are selected by appointment, merit, or a combination of the two. In most states, necessary qualifications include being a U.S. citizen, being at least 21 years of age, possessing a baccalaureate degree, passing a drug test, and not having a felony record.
- Issues continually evolving are the provisions for preservice and in-service training and the effect of firearms policies in probation and parole.
- Applicants should find out about the firearms policy of the department they are applying to and also determine whether carrying a firearm is suitable to them, as this is very much an individual decision.
- The future of probation aims to give line-level officers more decision-making opportunities and responsibility, which, in turn, will likely decrease job stress and burnout.

- Corrections workers have absolute immunity when acting in a quasi-judicial or prosecutorial function, but have only qualified immunity when performing administrative or other discretionary functions.
- Private service providers are growing in number and seem accepted by court attorneys who work with PSP representatives.
- Some private community corrections organizations have the potential to effectively supervise low-risk clients, but requirements range widely by jurisdiction.
- Interstate compacts are written agreements between two agencies that allow probationers and parolees to be supervised in another state.

DISCUSSION QUESTIONS

1. How are probation officers selected in your jurisdiction? What are the advantages and disadvantages of administering probation services in this way?

2. Why are college degrees required for probation and parole officers, but not necessarily for entry-level police officers?

3. What are the advantages and disadvantages of having a college education in the field of community correctional supervision?

4. Do probation officers receive enough training for the responsibilities they have? Why or why not?

5. What are the advantages and disadvantages regarding probation and parole officers carrying weapons?

6. Would you carry a weapon on the job? Why or why not? Would you carry a firearm only under certain conditions (such as supervising a certain type of individual)?

7. Out of the possible sources of stress identified, which ones can be controlled by the officer and which ones are a function of the job?

8. Discuss innovative ways that the various sources of work-related stress can be effectively managed.

9. How can probation and parole officers minimize the chances that they will lose a civil lawsuit if they are ever sued?

10. Agree or disagree with the following statement: Private probation supervision and treatment services should be expanded.

11. What limitations or controls would you place on private probation agencies? Why?

12. How might interstate compact supervision be *more helpful* for the offender than local supervision? How might interstate supervision be *more difficult* for the offender?

WEB SITES

Career Planning Resources for Probation, Parole, and Correctional Treatment Workers
  http://www.career-planning-education.com/law-criminal-justice/probation-officers.htm#outlook

U.S. Probation Office, Southern District of Ohio, Job Description
  http://www.ohsp.uscourts.gov/aboutus.html

Occupational Guide to Probation and Parole Officers in California
  http://www.calmis.cahwnet.gov/file/occguide/PROBOFF.HTM

Job Description for Probation and Parole Officer in Australia
  http://www.migrationexpert.com/australia/visa/Parole_or_Probation_Officer_jobs.asp

Oregon Juvenile Probation Officer Job Description
  http://egov.oregon.gov/DAS/HR/class/ccrt/spec/6787.pdf

Pennsylvania Practice Improvement Collaborative
  http://www.ireta.org/pic/parole_probation_training.htm

Addressing stress in corrections: Programs and strategies
  http://www.nicic.org/library/016698

California Penal Code 830.5: Carrying a Firearm
  http://law.onecle.com/california/penal/830.5.html

Pennsylvania (Carbon County) Adult Probation and Parole Officer Firearms Policy
  http://www.pabulletin.com/secure/data/vol31/31-14/584.html

Judicial Correction Services, Inc.
  www.judicialservices.com

Providence Community Corrections
  www.provcorp.com

Probation Modification and Termination

CHAPTER LEARNING OBJECTIVES

- Identify how probation conditions are modified and under what circumstances.
- List the types of in-house options available for resistant probationers before revocation.
- Explain the reasons for revoking probation as a type of unsuccessful termination.
- Analyze the rights probationers have during the revocation process.
- Decide whether probation is or is not an effective sanction.

When a probationer commits a new crime or fails to heed court-ordered conditions, a warrant is issued and the probationer eventually must return to custody.

© Bonnie Kamin/PhotoEdit

CHAPTER OUTLINE

Introduction

Modifying Probation Conditions
Early Termination of Probation
In-House Administrative Options before Filing a
   Revocation

The Decision to Revoke

Types of Probation Violations
Law Violations
Technical Violations

Revocation Procedure
The Power to Arrest Probationers
Time on Probation or Parole Is Usually Not Credited if
   Revoked

Revocation Rights of Probationers and Parolees
The Right to a Hearing
The Right to a Lawyer
Level of Proof and Evidence Required
Other Revocation Situations

Probation Outcomes
Probation Recidivism Rates
Who Is More Likely to Succeed or Fail on Probation?
Probationers Compared with Parolees

Summary

KEY TERMS

revocation	technical violations	final revocation hearing
early termination	due process	standard of proof
law violations	preliminary hearing	preponderance of the evidence

Introduction

Placing an offender on probation implies that, in the best judgment of the court, the offender is able to abide by the law and observe the conditions of release while remaining in the community under supervision. Probation is conditional, meaning that the probationer's liberty is subject to compliance with specified rules. Recall from the earlier chapters that deferred adjudication is where no formal sentence is rendered, and probation when the community sentence becomes part of one's permanent record. If the probationer is compliant with the rules, probation can be successfully terminated early, but the conviction remains. If deferred adjudication is completed successfully, there is no conviction of record. This chapter talks primarily about probation, but deferred adjudication will be mentioned for comparison.

A resistant offender has either not sufficiently met supervision conditions or may be involved in new criminal behavior. Probation violations or serious misbehavior can cause the judge to extend the period of probation, impose additional conditions, or revoke probation. When considering modifying or revoking probation, the courts assess the risk the offender poses to the community, whether the change will increase compliance, and whether the change will better serve the needs of the offender at the present time. **Revocation** is a serious matter to the probationer because most of the time, it removes a certain level of freedom at a higher cost to taxpayers (recall the cost differentials in Table 1.2 within Chapter 1). Revocation denotes a sentence to a more intensive punishment such as a residential facility, electronic monitoring (to be discussed in Chapters 8 and 9), or even jail.

When an offender is incarcerated, judges have decided that the public safety risk outweighs the goal of helping that person to be a contributing member of society. When offenders are imprisoned, they and their children may become dependent

Revocation
The process of hearings that results when the probationer is noncompliant with the current level of probation. Results of a revocation are either modifying probation conditions to a more intensive supervision level, or the complete elimination of probation and sentence to a residential community facility, jail, or prison.

on government assistance. Revocation, however, is one way to protect the community from offenders who may become a danger to public safety or who continue to commit criminal acts. Incarceration is not, however, the only viable alternative for probationers who continually fail to abide by supervision conditions. Sometimes, *modifying* probation is a more practical and cost-effective option.

Modifying Probation Conditions

The court can modify the length and conditions of probation. For offenders who are abiding by conditions, shortening the term or easing restrictions is used as a reward. Probationers who are not abiding by conditions may have their term extended or additional restrictions imposed.

EARLY TERMINATION OF PROBATION

In many states the court is given authority to reward a probationer for good behavior by terminating probation after a portion of time has been served. Some states allow felony probationers to apply for **early termination** after having satisfactorily served one-third of the probation term or two years, whichever is less. Article 3564 of the *Federal Rules of Criminal Procedure* states that the court may "terminate a term of probation previously ordered and discharge the defendant at any time in the case of a misdemeanor or an infraction or at any time after the expiration of one year of probation in the case of a felony, if it is satisfied that such action is warranted by the conduct of the defendant and the interest of justice." The authority to terminate probation early is vested in the judge, who acts on the initial recommendation of the probation officer.

> **Early Termination**
> Termination of probation at any time during the probation period or after some time has been served.

Other rewards for good behavior may include the reduction of supervision level (thus reducing the number of contacts), waiving fines, reducing curfews, or community service hours. Positive recognition may include giving the probationer completion certificates, affirmation letters, or reference letters from his or her employer or school, or from the court (Carter and Ley 2001). All of these incentives are discretionary, and the probation supervisor or judge reviews the behavioral record of the probationer before granting or rejecting the request.

In cases of deferred adjudication probation or suspended sentence, where the finding of guilt is deferred but the person still must complete conditions, if the deferred adjudication period is successful, charges are dismissed and the finding of guilt is never made. Note that in some states, the prior deferred adjudication probation can be used as a "prior" to increase the sentence if the offender commits another crime in the future.

The rate of successful termination on local and state level probation varies greatly by jurisdiction due to the lack of uniform law on when a probation revocation must be filed. A national average has been estimated showing that between 60 and 70 percent of probationers successfully complete probation. At the federal level, the rate of success is higher, with over 80 percent of federal probationers terminating probation successfully with no violations (see Figure 7.1).

IN-HOUSE ADMINISTRATIVE OPTIONS BEFORE FILING A REVOCATION

Administrative interventions are in-house approaches that take place through a probation officer, sometimes in conjunction with a supervisor's advice or approval, prior to filing a formal revocation with the courts. Through administrative interventions, the officer attempts to gain compliance for a resistant offender and

FIGURE 7.1   Federal Probation
Outcomes

Source: U.S. Department of Justice.
2008. *Compendium of Federal Justice
Statistics*, 2004. Washington, DC: U.S.
Department of Justice.

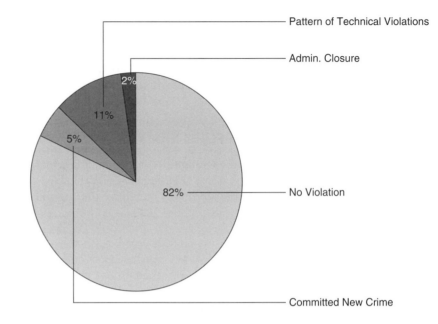

uses oral/written reprimands, staffings, motivational interviewing techniques, or a
directive (Taylor and Martin 2006). Administrative interventions are limited since
the initial conditions and length of probation is clearly a judicial function, and this
includes restitution payment schedules, and the maximum number of drug tests to
be performed. The probation officer's job is merely to ensure that these conditions
are followed. However, the distinction between a judicial "condition" and a probation officer "directive" is unclear (Barklage, Miller, and Bonham 2006).

Various guidelines have been formulated to aid probation officers in response
options available to them for resistant offenders. An example of these guidelines
can be found in Table 7.1. Note that the response depends on the severity of the
probation violation, the offender's predefined risk level defined by the risk/needs assessment (see Chapter 5), and assaultive history. Once the response range has been
determined, with or without a second opinion from a supervisor, probation officers
can choose from a variety of responses, depending on what they feel would be most
appropriate in each particular case.

To what extent can probation officers modify or interpret existing probation
conditions in response to specific violations without having to go back to court?
Some agencies have the probationer sign a waiver that he or she is agreeing to modified sanctions in lieu of going to court, and thus is waiving the right to a court hearing. This waiver is kept on file to show the court the avenues that were tried before
the probation officer requested a formal revocation proceeding. According to Jones
and Kerbs (2007), most officers preferred to use in-house intervention techniques
with probationers who made little to no effort to find employment, who failed to
report, did not appear for community service work, and for the first positive alco-
sensor test indicating the offender has ingested a substance with alcohol. Officers
favored more formal interventions with the courts for repeated positive drug tests
coupled with failure to attend treatment.

Responding to resistant probationers is not entirely the officer's decision. A substantial number of officers surveyed felt some kind of external pressure (supervisory, prosecutor, etc.) to go against their wishes by either withholding formal actions
when they wanted to file, or to take action when they wanted to work longer with

TABLE 7.1   Probation Violation Decision Guidelines

Decision-Making Level	Probation Violation Type*	Possible Responses to Probationer
Probation Officer	Failure to report	Verbal warning/reprimand
	Making false statements	Case Staffing
	Violating curfew	Home visit + 7-day curfew
	Changing residence/jobs w/o permission	Loss of travel
	Failure to pay restitution	Community service: 1–8 hrs.
	Failure to perform community service	Increase reporting
	Drug use/positive drug test	Increase drug testing
		Probationer sign waiver
Supervisor Staffing	Failure to test for drugs/take Antabuse	Drug treatment
	Failure to participate in drug treatment	Increase supervision level
	Possession of contraband	Community service: 20–40 hrs.
	Failing to register as a sex offender	Curfew (up to 30 days)
	Repeated curfew violations	Curfew (up to 30 days)
	Second positive drug test	Drug treatment
	Repeated failure to report	Increase supervision level
Court Hearing	Third positive drug test	Residential treatment
	Possession of weapons	Boot camp
	Absconding after 60 days	Electronic monitoring
	Denying access to searches	Intensive probation
	Committing new offense	Jail or prison
	Threatening victim	Day reporting center
	Deliberate pattern of noncompliance	Extension of probation

* Response also depends on level of risk probationer poses

Source: Madeline M. Carter (Ed.). 2001. *Responding to Parole and Probation Violations: A Handbook to Guide Local Policy Development.* Prepared for the National Institute of Corrections, U.S Department of Justice (Washington, DC), pp. 54, 75.

the offender (Jones and Kerbs 2007). Regardless of these pressures or perceptions, probation officers must be very careful not to impose new or different conditions without first obtaining court approval (Barklage, Miller, and Bonham 2006).

The Decision to Revoke

When probation conditions have been modified and are still not being followed, the case must ultimately come before the court so the court can make the decision whether or not to revoke. Various issues are involved in probation revocation, including revocation authority, types of probation violations, revocation procedures, and rights during revocation.

Although the probation officer or the supervising department may recommend revocation, only the court judge has discretionary authority to revoke probation. This authority remains with the court that granted probation unless the case has been transferred to another court that is given the same powers as the sentencing court (18 U.S.C. sec. 3561, sec. 3563). Discretionary revocation allows the court to (1) continue probation with or without extending the term, (2) modify the conditions of probation, or (3) revoke the sentence of probation and resentence the defendant. Stickels (2007) found that of the probationers who continued to be resistant

TABLE 7.2   Federal Revocation Table Determining Imprisonment Months

| Grade of Violation | Original Criminal History Category at Initial Sentencing | | | | | |
	I	II	III	IV	V	VI
Class A Felony Superv. Class B Felony or Below	24–30	27–33	30–37	37–46	46–57	51–63
Grade A Violation	12–18	15–21	18–24	24–30	30–37	33–41
Grade B Violation	4–10	6–12	8–14	12–18	18–24	21–27
Grade C Violation	3–9	4–10	5–11	6–12	7–13	8–14

Source: U.S. Bureau of Prisons. 2008. *Guidelines Manual* (November 1, 2008). Section 7B1.4, p. 488.

after the administrative options had been exhausted, 42 percent of those who cases went in front of the judge had their probation conditions modified or extended by the courts for noncompliance, and 54 percent went to jail or prison.

While most revocation decisions are discretionary, some jurisdictions explicitly mandate automatic revocation and resentencing for some behaviors. In the federal system, instances of mandatory revocation include: (1) committing any crime of violence or facilitating sexual contact against a child under the age of 16 (Carlie's law); (2) possession of a firearm; (3) possession of a controlled substance or positive drug test; or (4) refusal to comply with drug testing. Revocation may not always result in imprisonment, but additional conditions or stricter supervision will be imposed. Table 7.2 shows the number of months of imprisonment that federal probationers (or those on mandatory supervised release) must serve if revoked. Regardless of the severity or type of revocation, offenders who were originally convicted of a Class A felony are distinguished only by their original criminal history score that was determined at sentencing. For offenders who were originally convicted of all other types of offenses, there are essentially three violation "grades" or levels of severity of revocation behavior that determine the amount of time served. Grade A violations are new crimes, while Grades B and C violations are technical violations. For example, let's say Nadine was originally convicted of Possession of a Controlled Substance and her original criminal history category defined by her prior record was "II." Nadine was sentenced to probation. While on probation, she committed a series of technical violations (positive drug tests) that were defined as Grade B technical violations. According to Table 7.2, Nadine must serve between six and twelve months, as long as the number of months in the table does not exceed her original sentence length.

An example of a state that has mandatory probation revocation rules is Michigan. In Michigan, mandatory revocation is imposed on juveniles who have been "waived" to adult probation supervision and who subsequently commit a new misdemeanor or felony crime while on supervision. In this case, the new crime runs concurrent with the original offense—that is, the length of supervision for the new charge cannot exceed the term left on the original charge, but probation must be revoked (Michigan Judicial Institute 2003).

Types of Probation Violations

Law Violations
Violations of probation or parole conditions that involve the commission of a crime.

Technical Violations
Multiple violations that breach one or more noncriminal conditions of probation.

Revocation of probation is generally triggered in two ways: law violations and technical violations. A **law violation** occurs if a probationer commits another misdemeanor or felony crime. By contrast, **technical violations** are a pattern of infractions that breach a condition of probation. Examples of technical violations include testing positive for drugs, failure to report, failure to maintain employment, failure to attend treatment, and association with known felons.

LAW VIOLATIONS

Revocation for violating the law occurs in about 16 percent of all revocations (12 percent of revocations filed involve a felony and 4 percent involve a misdemeanor). In misdemeanors and drug use/possession, most jurisdictions simply revoke probation instead of prosecuting the offender for the new crime. Revocation for a new crime is a more convenient option that achieves the same result, which is a modification of conditions or incarceration and removal from society. Even if the offender is guilty of a new crime, however, revocation is not automatic. Instead, it is left to the discretion of the court.

On the other hand, acquittal for a new offense may lead to revocation because of the differences in standards of proof. Although conviction for an offense requires guilt beyond reasonable doubt, the standard of proof for revocation is only a "preponderance of the evidence." What may not suffice for conviction may be adequate for revocation. There is no double jeopardy because revocation is merely an administrative and not a criminal proceeding, even if it results in incarceration.

TECHNICAL VIOLATIONS

Most violations of supervision (85 to 90 percent) come under the category of technical violations, meaning they do not constitute criminal acts, but rather, a pattern of rule violations. Research in two studies on revocation motions filed provides information on what types of technical violations were most common:

Reasons for Violating Probation	Burke (1997)	Gray, Fields, and Maxwell (2001)
New crimes	16%	9.6%
Technical Violations	84%	90.4%
Positive urinalysis for drug use	27%	22.4%
Failure to participate in treatment	20%	9.0%
Failure to report	10%	33.6%
Abscond	18.5%	2.5%
All other technical violations	8.5%	22.9%

Note: These two jurisdictions show a large difference between "failing to report" and "absconding," likely due to the definition that each agency has for appointment no-shows. Filing and/or granting a revocation is subjective, so the types of technical violations and the overall revocation rates vary greatly by jurisdiction.

Absconding from probation supervision is a type of technical violation and a significant problem in many jurisdictions. Burke (1997) recorded 18.5 percent of all probation terminations nationally were because the probationer left the jurisdiction. The problem seemed less extensive at the federal level where just over 2 percent of all federal probationers are terminated because they are fugitives. What differentiates a probationer who absconds from a probationer who succeeds? One study in Michigan (Gray, Fields, and Maxwell 2001) found that after a 30-month follow-up, 2.5 percent of all probationers absconded on active supervision. Probation absconders had more extensive felony criminal histories, longer terms of probation, and more stringent conditions than probationers who terminated successfully (Mayzer and Gray 2000).

Gray et al. (2001) found that time was a factor in revocations. About 30 percent of all probation violators were terminated within the first three months of supervision, mostly with technical violations. Probationers who committed a "new crime" seemed to violate later in the probationary period, but they were also more likely to be unemployed, to have a prior criminal history, to be on probation for an assaultive offense, and to have a pattern of technical violations.

As a general rule, probation is not revoked for occasional violations of technical conditions. Probation officers are instead urged to address these violations promptly and with the least restrictive means necessary to ensure compliance. Supervisory strategies to reduce the occurrence of technical violations include a sound assessment and case plan as discussed in Chapter 5 (Sachwald, Eley, and Taxman 2006), intervention by a specially trained "technical violation" unit officer, implementing *and using* more graduated sanctions instead of incarceration, reducing the number of cases each officer supervises (Hill 2006), and using out-of-custody hearings (Andrews and Janes 2006). Because incarceration results in high costs, revocation should be the last resort for dealing with offenders having a pattern of technical violations.

Revocation Procedure

Revocation procedures are governed by a combination of constitutional rules, state law, and agency policy. Revocation proceedings begin with a violation report prepared by a probation officer. The report is passed directly to the court that originally granted probation or to the prosecutor to file a motion with the court. Should the court decide to pick up the probationer for a revocation hearing, the

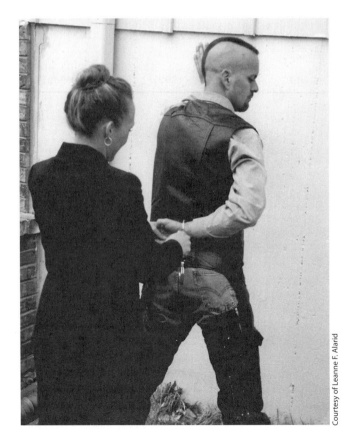

A probation officer with arrest powers locates one of her clients, and will bring him to jail to await a probation violation hearing.

Courtesy of Leanne F. Alarid

BOX 7.1   TECHNOLOGY IN CORRECTIONS

"Big Brother is Tracking" How Revocations Are Being Processed Faster

Each agency in criminal justice (e.g., law enforcement, courts, institutional corrections, and community corrections) maintained its own database, but previous databases were not compatible to readily share information with each other. Each agency stored some information on main-frame computers and other information in hard copy paper files that took one to two months to follow offenders when they transferred to another agency or institution. Offenders who were in the process of revocation hearings would sometimes sit for weeks (or even months) in jail waiting for the process to conclude. Other entities were sometimes not aware of the offender's location. Each of the older non-compatible agency databases contained much of the same information (current offense, criminal history, age, gender, and so on), so an offender was reinterviewed each time he or she entered an institution or was booked in jail for a revocation.

An offender tracking system known as "O-Track" solves the redundancy issue by automating data from six criminal justice agencies into one database. The six agencies are courts, county jails, probation, parole, community corrections centers, and state departments of corrections. The O-Track system stores eight main categories for each individual. Each category has subcategories or fields called modules. Below each of the eight categories are examples of information that O-Track stores:

Category 1: Offender Case File is the shell of the offender's file. Basic fact sheets, vital statistics, photographs, fingerprints, locations, and movements are available in this section to form summary information collected from throughout the system's database. Caseload assignments, due date reports, overdue report lists, case file audits, and workload formula statistics are performed and managed.

Category 2: Case Management is the core of the system. This section collects data about the offender and tracks his or her progress through the corrections system from presentence investigation, diagnostics, and classification, through the prison system (if applicable) and conditional release on parole. Offender data is handled as a case file to develop case reports and to support decision-making in the case management process. Included here are offender education and training, employment, treatment programs, visits, and prerelease preparation.

Category 3: Parole Board has information about previous and upcoming parole board hearings for applicable offenders.

Category 4: Offender Management focuses on security and supervision functions that manage the offender as a member of a population, such as cell assignments, gang membership, security incidents, protective custody, intelligence information, escapes, and disciplinary reports.

Category 5: Offender Administrative Systems provides accounting for inmate funds while incarcerated, commissary purchases, clothing issues, and inmate property. This system also tracks offender grievances filed against the prison system.

Category 6: Interagency Linkages provides an electronic interface to allow information to be sent and received from external databases, such as local police, Federal Bureau of Investigations (FBI), Department of Motor Vehicles, Human Services, Social Services, medical hospitals, interstate compacts, and the Bureau of Prisons.

Category 7 is for Warrants and Category 8 is for Reports and Statistics. The automated system allows all agencies to know more about how long probation violators have been sitting in jail, so that efforts can be made to process the revocation faster and re-release them to the community or conclude the hearing process and resentence them to prison. O-Track was initially developed by the Utah State Department of Corrections and sold for use by other states (such as Alaska, Colorado, Idaho, Montana, and New Mexico). It is expected that more states will automate their systems like this in the future.

Source: Utah Department of Corrections. 2009. http://corrections.utah.gov/contenthome/homepage.asp

---

court will issue a warrant for arrest (in 82 percent of cases) or a summons (in 18 percent of cases) (Burke 1997). Box 7.1 discusses how automated centralized data systems track offenders as they are rearrested or transferred to a different facility or institution.

Peggy Burke (1997) studied what happened in probation and parole revocation proceedings. She found that 60 percent of all revocations resulted in some form of incarceration, whereas 40 percent remained on probation with additional conditions. Of the incarcerative sanctions, the most frequent type was prison (36 percent) or some time in jail followed by release back out to probation (21 percent).

The state of Georgia has "probation detention centers," which are minimum-security units specifically for people who have violated probation and are either waiting for their revocation hearing or are serving time away from the community following their revocation hearing. There are 16 men's units and three women's units with approximately 3,500 probationers. Georgia officials have used these probation detention centers as an alternative to ease jail crowding.

THE POWER TO ARREST PROBATIONERS

Arrest of a probationer for a technical violation or arrest for a new crime does not automatically mean that probation will be revoked—it just means that the officer can incarcerate the offender and request that the court conduct a revocation hearing. Federal law has the following provision for federal probationers:

> If there is reason to believe that a probationer or a person on supervised release has violated a condition of his probation or release, he may be arrested, and upon arrest, shall be taken without unnecessary delay before the court having jurisdiction over him. A probation officer may make such an arrest wherever the probationer or releasee is found, and may make the arrest without a warrant (Federal Criminal Code and Rules 2004).

In states where probation officers are peace officers, they are usually authorized to make an arrest of a probationer with or without a warrant as long as the officer has probable cause. In states where probation officers are expressly prohibited from making an arrest, the probation officer must rely on the police.

These differences in the arrest powers of probation officers reflect the orientation of probation departments in the various states. Agencies with a treatment orientation, such as juvenile probation departments, do not want their officers to be viewed as law enforcement agents because it lessens their effectiveness as treatment agents, so the power to arrest is denied. By contrast, agencies with a surveillance orientation believe that law enforcement is a necessary function of probation, and thus it is not unusual for probation officers to be armed and certified as law enforcement officers.

TIME ON PROBATION OR PAROLE IS USUALLY NOT CREDITED IF REVOKED

If probation is revoked and the offender goes to prison, most courts have ruled that time served on probation or parole is not credited toward the sentence in the same way that incarceration time in jail or prison would be (*Bruggeman v. State* 1996). However, a federal court and now a Florida statute permit the court the option to credit none, some, or all time spent on supervised release toward the sentence (*United States v. Pettus* 2002; *Summers v. State* 2002). Generally, a parolee whose parole has been revoked may be paroled again, but the revoked parolee must remain in prison for a specified time before becoming eligible for another parole.

As long as the offender is abiding by the terms of parole (or probation), he or she will minimally receive credit on the sentence as straight time, that is, without the benefit of good-time credits. In other states. the parolee may receive reductions for good behavior while on parole.

Revocation Rights of Probationers and Parolees

A probation or parole revocation is an "administrative hearing" that is closer to a civil proceeding because it is seen as an extension of the existing sentence (*Hampton v. State* 2001). As such, neither is governed by the same rules as in formal criminal trials. Given that the legal rights at time of revocation are virtually identical, the rights afforded in probation revocation proceedings are extended to parole revocations and vice versa. For example, the result of a probation revocation hearing is not a conviction but a finding of either revoking or continuing probation (*Soliz v. State* 1961). If probation is revoked, the judge will modify the probation conditions or resentence the offender altogether. On the other hand, if the parole board revokes parole, the parolee returns to jail or prison (parole revocations will be discussed in Chapter 13).

In revocation proceedings, the defendant is not constitutionally entitled to a jury (*People v. Price* 1960) nor to a speedy trial. In some states, however, the law provides for a jury hearing in juvenile cases. The probationer or parolee is not entitled to the Fifth Amendment privilege against self-incrimination (*Perry v. State* 2001). Remaining silent at a revocation hearing may prejudice the outcome against the defendant, but testifying at a revocation hearing can be used as evidence at a later criminal trial unless the probationer (or parolee) has been given "immunity" on what he or she says at the revocation.

During a revocation proceeding, offenders are entitled to certain rights prior to probation being revoked. These rights were granted by the U.S. Supreme Court in the case of *Morrissey v. Brewer* (1972) and *Gagnon v. Scarpelli* (1973), arguably the two most important parole and probation cases ever to be decided by the Court. Gerald Scarpelli was on probation for a felony when he was arrested for burglary. He admitted involvement in the burglary but later claimed that his admission was coerced and therefore invalid. His probation was revoked without a hearing and without a lawyer present. After serving three years of his sentence, Scarpelli sought release through a *writ of habeas corpus*. He claimed violations of two constitutional rights: the **due process** right to a hearing and the right to a lawyer during the hearing.

THE RIGHT TO A HEARING

The Court said that probationers were entitled to a two-stage hearing consisting of a **preliminary hearing** and a **final revocation hearing**. The preliminary or "show cause" hearing is a recorded hearing to determine whether probable cause exists to believe that a probation violation has occurred. If the magistrate finds probable cause, a revocation hearing is held. If probable cause is not found, the judge must dismiss the proceeding. The total time that passes from the point the probation officer detects the violation until the court renders a decision regarding the revocation hearing is 44 to 64 days (Burke 1997). The vast majority of probation violators spend this time in the county jail waiting for the revocation proceeding decision.

Extending the same due process rights that parolees had afforded to them one year earlier in *Morrissey v. Brewer*, both probationers and parolees were now entitled to the following due process rights before and during revocation hearings:

1. Written notice of the alleged probation violation
2. Disclosure of the evidence of violation
3. The opportunity to be heard in person and to present evidence and witnesses
4. The right to confront and cross-examine adverse witnesses
5. The right to judgment by a detached and neutral hearing body
6. A written statement of the reasons for revoking probation, including evidence used in arriving at that decision

Due Process
Laws must be applied in a fair and equal manner. Fundamental fairness.

Preliminary Hearing
An inquiry conducted to determine if there is probable cause to believe that the offender committed a probation or parole violation.

Final Revocation Hearing
A due process hearing that must be conducted before probation or parole can be revoked.

THE RIGHT TO A LAWYER

A probationer is generally not entitled to a court-appointed lawyer during revocation proceedings, but there are exceptions. The first case that addressed this issue was *Mempa v. Rhay* (1967). In that case, the Court said that a defendant has a constitutional right to a lawyer during probation revocation *that is followed by sentencing*. This is because sentencing is an important phase that has always required the presence of a lawyer for the defendant. In *Gagnon v. Scarpelli* (1973), the Court said entitlement to a lawyer during revocation proceedings should be case-by-case on the basis of a "colorable claim" in which the defendant claims innocence of the allegations, or when defendants appear incapable of speaking for themselves. Given the fact that inarticulate people must voice their need for counsel in order to get legal assistance, indigence is used as a proxy, with some states routinely providing counsel to indigent probationers in revocation proceedings.

LEVEL OF PROOF AND EVIDENCE REQUIRED

Standard of Proof
The level of proof, measured by the strength of the evidence, needed to render a decision in a court proceeding.

Preponderance of the Evidence
A level of proof used in a probation revocation administrative hearing, in which the judge decides based on which side presents more convincing evidence and its probable truth or accuracy, and not necessarily on the amount of evidence.

The **standard of proof** varies widely among the states because the U.S. Supreme Court has not decided this issue. Most courts require **preponderance of the evidence** as the standard for revocation (*United States v. McCormick* 1995), which is the evidence that convinces the judge that a probationer violated the terms of his or her probation. If the state presents proof of a condition violation, the probationer has the burden of presenting evidence to meet and/or overcome prima facie proof (*State v. Graham* 2001). Preponderance of the evidence is approximately the same amount of evidence as that required to make an arrest (probable cause). However, one court case (*Benton v. State* 2003) said that arrest for a crime by itself is not enough to revoke probation, but probation may be revoked for an "indictment" by a grand jury (*Newsom v. State* 2004) or a conviction by a judge or jury. Interestingly, parole revocation is permissible even if charges are later dismissed (*Reyes v. Tate* 2001). So it seems that whether a lower burden of proof than preponderance of the evidence (such as reasonable grounds or reasonable suspicion) would suffice for revocation is being addressed by lower courts, but has yet to be addressed by the U.S. Supreme Court.

The testimony of the probation officer is crucial at a revocation proceeding. Whether such testimony—unsupported by any other evidence—is sufficient to revoke varies by state. For example, the probationer's admission to a probation officer was sufficient to support a revocation, and eliminates the need on the part of the government to present proof of the violation (*Fields v. State 2002*).

Most states admit hearsay evidence during revocation, but some do not. Reliable hearsay evidence (statements offered by a witness that are based upon what someone else has told the witness and not upon personal knowledge or observation) may be admitted in a parole (or probation) revocation hearing (*Belk v. Purkett* 1994). The court suggested using these questions to establish reliability:

1. Is the information corroborated by the parolee's own statements or other live testimony at the hearing?
2. Does the information fit within one of the many exceptions to the hearsay rule?
3. Does the information have other substantial indicia of reliability?

A "yes" answer to any of these questions signifies that the hearsay is reliable and therefore may be admitted as evidence in the revocation proceeding.

OTHER REVOCATION SITUATIONS

Other situations may involve a revocation situation that is a bit different from standard adult probation. These situations include probationers who are revoked for not fulfilling financial commitments, offenders on deferred adjudication, juvenile probation revocations, and consequences if the probation term has expired.

Revocation for an Inability to Pay? Violating a probationer largely depends on whether the behavior was willful and intentional. For example, a probationer can be revoked for refusal to pay monthly fees, restitution, or fines. An indigent probationer cannot be revoked if he or she is unable to pay a fine or restitution provided the probationer was not somehow responsible for the failure to pay (*Bearden v. Georgia* 1983). The probationer, however, has the burden of showing that the inability to pay was not willful. In other words, the defendant has to show effort and desire to fulfill financial obligations (*State v. Gropper* 1995).

On the other hand, the courts will allow revocation, even in cases where the probationer is not at fault (there is no willful violation), if it can be shown that not revoking is a risk to public safety. For example, probationers on community supervision for predatory sex offenses were not able to complete mandatory sex offender treatment programs because none were available in their community. After finding no better alternatives, the court supported incarceration over allowing these offenders to remain in the community without treatment (*People v. Colabello* 1997).

Offenders on Deferred Adjudication Offenders on "deferred adjudication" can have their cases dismissed without a record of conviction if they successfully complete a period of community supervision. If offenders on deferred adjudication violate by either committing a new crime or engaging in a pattern of technical violations, they are risking the chance that a judge will later "adjudicate as guilty" and pronounce a sentence. This sentence will also become part of the offender's permanent record. Stickels (2007) warns of the possibility that judges may bypass intermediate sanctions and sentence those adjudicated as guilty directly to prison.

Juvenile Probation Revocation In the federal system, the U.S. Code differentiates between juveniles age 17 and younger (18 U.S.C., sec. 5037(c)(1)), and juveniles between the ages of 18 and 21 (18 U.S.C., sec. 5037(c)(2)). In either case, a juvenile may not be sentenced to a prison term longer than an adult would be for the same offense (*United States v. RLC* 1992). The revocation options depend on the age of the juvenile at the time of sentencing for the original offense, not the age of the juvenile at time of revocation.

Revocation after Probation Term Expires Probation may still be revoked after the probation period has expired when the defendant is arrested for violation of probation, or when a warrant is issued for the probationer's arrest before the period of probation expires (*Jones v. State* 1996).

Federal law also authorizes delayed revocation, saying that "the power of the court to revoke a sentence of probation for violation of a condition of probation, and to impose another sentence, extends beyond the expiration of the term of probation for any period reasonably necessary for the adjudication of matters arising before its expiration if, prior to its expiration, a warrant or summons has been issued on the basis of an allegation of such a violation" (Federal Criminal Code and Rules 2004). Probation may also be revoked after the term of probation has expired if the probationer evades supervision before completing the sentence. Probation statutes usually provide that the term of probation is "tolled" if the defendant is either charged with a violation of probation or flees the jurisdiction (or cannot be found) and a warrant is issued. To toll the running of a sentence or a period of time limitation is to interrupt it, to "stop the clock." The Illinois statute, for example, provides that when a petition is filed charging a violation of a probation condition, the court may order a warrant for the offender's arrest. Meanwhile, the warrant "tolls" the probation sentence indefinitely, or until the offender "answers" a court summons or is arrested on the warrant.

Probation Outcomes

How does probation measure up? Studies of the effectiveness of probation outcomes are typically measured after the period of supervision has been completed. The studies can be divided into three main groups: research measuring recidivism rates, studies that measure characteristics of probation recidivists, and those that compare probationers with another group of offenders, such as prisoners or offenders in a different community-based program.

PROBATION RECIDIVISM RATES

As we discussed in Chapter 1, the rate of success on probation largely depends on the definition of "success" and "failure" used by researchers. A definition of failure used in one study was "non-compliance with probation conditions which results in (a) revocation; (b) absconding from supervision without notifying the probation department; or (c) being sentenced for another offense in another jurisdiction" (Morgan 1995, p. 143). Other researchers conceptualize "failure" as equivalent to recidivism, which could be the arrest, conviction, or incarceration for a new crime while on supervision. This second albeit narrower definition would not necessarily include technical violations.

The probation "success" rate, in contrast, includes individuals who have completed the term productively as well as those who may have been referred to court for a number of technical violations but were not revoked (Morgan 1995). About 35 studies have been published that measured probationer recidivism rates in the United States (see Geerken and Hayes 1993 for a review). While on probation, the rearrest rate varied from 12 percent to 65 percent, and the conviction rate fluctuated between 16 and 35 percent. The revocation rate, which for most studies included both technical violations and new crimes, varied from 14 percent to 60 percent (Morgan 1994). The various recidivism rates are likely more indicative of diverse decision-making styles and behaviors of probation officers, judges, and police officers than actual differences in a probationer's return to criminal behavior.

Keep in mind that the revocation rate will increase the longer a group of offenders are studied during the follow-up period. The revocation rate one year after probation will be lower than the rate three years later. One study of 79,000 felons placed on probation in 17 states found that 43 percent were rearrested for a felony within three years while on probation. Within the rearrested group, 46 percent of the probationers that had been sent to prison or jail had absconded within the three years. Furthermore, 71 percent had either completed their probation or were still on probation (Langan and Cuniff 1992). This is similar to a Midwestern state where 73 percent completed successfully and the others were rearrested, of which 19 percent of all probationers were incarcerated as a result of the revocation (Stageberg and Wilson 2005).

Probationers who were revoked seemed to more commonly "fail" for technical violations rather than for new crimes (Gray, Fields, and Maxwell 2001; Minor, Wells, and Sims 2003; Sims and Jones 1997). The problem with revocation for technical violations is that this is an extremely costly option for taxpayers when probationers don't follow the rules. Many states recognize this and are responding with other options for probation violators. For example, Delaware's Probation Reform Law not only shortened the term of probation to no longer than two years, but technical violators could be placed on work release or in probation violation centers for up to five days per violation, not to exceed 10 days per calendar year (Sentencing Accountability Commission and the Statistical Analysis Center 2005). It remains to be seen how this policy change in how violations are handled ultimately affects probation violation rates, as well as jail and prison admissions.

The results of these studies are not necessarily conclusive as to success or failure of probation because of methodological design flaws, such as an overreliance on official data, lack of comparison groups, deficiencies of longitudinal designs, and conditions too inconsistent to allow comparison. Other problems include seeing success or failure as an either/or concept rather than as a matter of degree (Farrall 2003). Probation is most successful with people who are eligible for diversion, misdemeanor, and first-time felony offender status.

WHO IS MORE LIKELY TO SUCCEED OR FAIL ON PROBATION?

Success on probation (or parole) seems to be predicted in part by the personal characteristics of the offender (see Table 7.3). Generally, women, offenders over the age of 30, and those with no prior adult or juvenile convictions were more likely to succeed. Also, offenders who had skills that allowed them to maintain employment, those who were high school graduates, and those who lived with their spouse or children were less likely to become recidivists. Offenders who were on probation for a misdemeanor are more likely to succeed than felony offenders (Morgan 1994, 1995; Petersilia et al. 1985; Sims and Jones 1997). It seems then that conventional ties and positive social support of friends and family significantly contribute to reintegration success. On the other hand, being young, being unmarried, having previous convictions, and lacking knowledge, skills, and abilities seem to be attributes that contribute to higher failure rates on probation. Of the federal probationers who were terminated unsuccessfully for a new crime, violent felony offenders and people convicted of immigration offenses are the most likely to commit a new crime, whereas felons who are on probation for a "public-order" offense are the least likely.

An analysis of the effectiveness of treatment for drug offenders on probation was conducted. The study compared one group of probationers who were being drug tested with a second group that was being subjected to both drug testing and drug treatment. Researchers found that the group that received both testing and treatment had a higher failure rate on probation, likely due to more surveillance, increasing the chance of revocation for technical violations (Albonetti and Hepburn 1997).

PROBATIONERS COMPARED WITH PAROLEES

Researchers comparing probationers with parolees discovered that probationers committed fewer technical violations and fewer new crimes than parolees. Of offenders on probation, about 6 percent committed a new crime (versus 15 percent of parolees). Probationers committed technical violations at a rate of 13 percent, about half that of parolees, at nearly 28 percent (U.S. Department of Justice 2005a).

TABLE 7.3　Characteristics of Federal Probationers Terminating Supervision

Characteristic	Number of probation terminations	Percent terminating supervision with:			
		Successful completion	Committed new crime	Technical Violation	Admin. Closure
Gender					
Male	10,781	81.2%	5.9%	10.9%	2.0%
Female	4,915	84.6%	4.3%	9.5%	1.5%
Race					
White	10,598	84.0%	5.3%	9.0%	1.7%
African American	3,935	78.1%	6.1%	13.6%	2.2%
American Indian	428	64.7%	4.9%	28.3%	2.1%
Asian/Pacific Islander	492	92.5%	2.6%	4.2%	0.6%
Ethnicity					
Hispanic	2,818	80.8%	8.3%	9.9%	1.0%
Non Hispanic	12,602	82.6%	4.8%	10.6%	2.0%
Age					
16-18 years	114	67.5%	7.9%	22.8%	1.8%
19-20 years	567	61.6%	11.3%	26.0%	1.1%
21-30 years	4,762	76.3%	7.4%	14.7%	1.5%
31-40 years	4,105	82.5%	6.0%	10.2%	1.3%
41 and over	6,166	89.0%	2.9%	5.8%	2.5%
Education					
Less than High School	3,642	76.2%	7.9%	14.2%	1.6%
High School Graduate	5,254	81.4%	5.1%	11.8%	1.6%
Some college	3,538	86.8%	3.8%	7.5%	2.0%
College Graduate	1,878	92.9%	1.9%	2.9%	2.3%
Drug Abuse					
None	12,664	92.6%	2.4%	3.7%	1.3%
Drug history	1,691	84.5%	1.4%	9.0%	2.5%
GROUP TOTAL	15,721	82.3%	5.4%	10.5%	1.8%

Note: Each termination was counted separately. Technical violations and terminations for new crimes are shown only if supervision terminated with incarceration or removal from active supervision for reason of a violation. The data exclude corporate offenders.

(a) Technical violations range widely from drug use, escape, quitting a job without permission, not reporting, and other probation conditions

Source: U.S. Department of Justice. 2008. *Compendium of Federal Justice Statistics, 2004.* Washington, DC: U.S. Department of Justice.

As you can see in Figure 7.2, revocation rates vary by type of offense originally committed and by type of community supervision (probation vs. mandatory supervision). This table shows that probationers were more likely to complete supervision successfully than parolees (both on discretionary parole and mandatory parole supervision), no matter what type of crime they had been convicted of.

FIGURE 7.2　Percent of Federal Offenders Completing Supervision With a New Crime or Technical Violation

Source: U.S. Department of Justice. 2008. *Compendium of Federal Justice Statistics, 2004.* Washington, DC: U.S. Department of Justice.

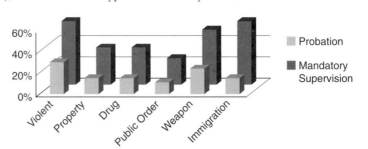

Overall, the benefits of community supervision far outweigh the costs of public safety; probationers and parolees are not responsible for as many crimes as the public thinks. One study found that people who were not on community supervision committed more than 90 percent of all burglaries and robberies. Even if parole and probation were completely eliminated, there would be very little difference in overall burglary and armed robbery rates (Geerken and Hayes 1993).

SUMMARY

- Probation costs significantly less than other forms of correctional supervision.
- Courts are empowered to terminate probation early for good behavior and to extend probation or issue more intensive conditions for noncompliance.
- The decision to revoke is initially recommended by the probation officer but left up to the judge's discretion.
- Probation violations include law violation and technical violations of conditions.
- The motion to revoke is filed by the prosecutor, and the court issues the warrant to revoke.

- For high-risk cases, the probationer is kept in detention pending an administrative hearing.
- Time served on probation is not credited as jail or prison time if the probation is revoked.
- Probationers and parolees must be given due process rights, including notice of charges and right to confront witnesses and present evidence in their favor.
- Probationers have lower recidivism rates than parolees.

DISCUSSION QUESTIONS

1. Should early termination of probation be given as a good behavior incentive or should probationers serve their entire term regardless of behavior? What are the advantages and disadvantages of each approach?

2. If you were a probation officer and your client refused to report or check in, how many times (or how long) would it take before you filed a revocation with the courts?

3. If you were a probation officer and your client could not find a job, what steps would you take with this person to help them? At what point would you consider taking them back to court to request for a modification in conditions or revocation for not having a job? Defend your answer.

4. If you were a probation officer and your client admitted to using drugs and said that his/her drug test would come back positive, what do you do?

5. How do a supervising officer's motivational interviewing techniques factor into unresponsive client behavior?

6. Which type of technical violation do you perceive as the worst kind, and why?

7. In the decision to revoke probation, what are implications for the probationer, the probation officer, and the community?

8. Do the revocation procedures in place now provide for enough due process for probationers? What, if anything, might be lacking?

9. Do probation officers have too much or not enough authority in arresting probationers? Defend your answer.

10. Is the "preponderance of the evidence" standard of proof too low, or should a different standard be used for revocation? If so, should the new standard require more or less evidence?

11. How does revocation contribute to jail crowding? What alternatives could be tried to remedy this problem?

12. Does probation continue to be a viable punishment? Why or why not?

WEB SITES

Colorado Probation Services and Revocation
  http://www.17thjudicialdistrict.com/probation_
  services.htm

Maine Probation Revocation Policy
  http://janus.state.me.us/legis/statutes/17-A/
  title17-Asec1206.html

Missouri Probation Revocation Policy
  http://doc.mo.gov/division/prob/pdf/Red%20
  book.pdf

Oklahoma Probation and Parole Cases under
Supervision: Operating and Closing Cases
  http://www.naicja.org/events/
  transferringprobationandparolecases.pdf

Texas Appellate Court Decision Regarding Juvenile
Probation Revocation
  http://www.tjpc.state.tx.us/publications/
  reviews/03/03-1-21.htm

Comparison of costs: Probation/community
corrections vs. Prisons
  http://www.drugwarfacts.org

CASE STUDY EXERCISE

Probation Modification and Termination

Chapter 7 explains the probation revocation process and the types of violations that can result in revocation. In the following two cases, list the violations of probation known to the probation officer. Would you concur with the probation officer's recommendation for revocation of probation? If not, at what point would you consider recommending revocation in this case? Are there other alternatives you might recommend?

CASE A

Probationer Conner was under supervision for possessing a destructive device. He has a history of some violent behavior (domestic violence, battery of a law enforcement officer). Special conditions of Conner's supervision require that he participate in mental health treatment and substance abuse treatment.

Shortly after Mr. Conner's supervision term begins, he tests positive for marijuana use. When confronted by his probation officer, he admits to using marijuana. However, Conner states he uses the marijuana to self-medicate and he will commit violent acts if he ceases its usage. Mr. Conner concludes his probation officer will be responsible for his violent acts toward others and himself, as the officer is instructing him to cease the marijuana usage. The probation officer reminds Conner of the condition of supervision that states he is not to use or possess illegal drugs and advises him his use of illegal substances cannot be allowed and that the sentencing court will be advised of the violation.

Mr. Conner entered treatment at the beginning of his supervision term. As a result of his response to the instruction to cease marijuana usage, the probation officer recommends to the court that Conner be referred for a psychiatric evaluation to see if he would benefit from psychotropic medications. The court concurs with the officer's recommendation and Conner is referred for the evaluation. The psychiatrist diagnoses Bipolar Affective Disorder, Type II, and prescribes Depakote. This medication requires regular lab work to evaluate its effectiveness. Mr. Conner fails to attend his next appointment with the psychiatrist. Results of a urine specimen taken from Conner a week after his evaluation with the psychiatrist are received. The specimen reveals Conner has used both marijuana and amphetamine. The probation officer petitions the court for a warrant to have Mr. Conner arrested and brought before the court for violations of his supervision.

CASE B

Probationer York is under probation supervision for simple assault. She has a history of violent behavior and anger management issues. She has no known drug or alcohol problems. She has been under probation supervision with you for the last five months and had been reporting regularly. Special conditions of York's supervision require that she complete anger management classes by the end of her term, which is supposed to end in four months if all goes well. Anger management treatment takes three months, and the program has a waiting list of clients who are court-ordered to attend treatment. Probationer York keeps saying she will go down for an anger management assessment but just never does. When you call to verify employment at the restaurant, her employer says that she quit coming three weeks ago and was replaced.

Two weeks have gone by since you called her former employer and still no sign of York. York won't return your phone calls. She misses her regular appointment with you this afternoon. What should you do?

PART III

Specialized Caseloads and Intermediate Programs

C ommunity sanctions for offenders for whom a sentence of imprisonment is excessive but for whom diversion or regular probation may be too lenient are discussed in this section. Chapter 8 considers residential sanctions in which offenders must live away from home and inside a facility within the community while completing their sentence. Residential programs include boot camps, halfway houses, and other specialized treatment facilities for offenders with substance abuse problems or mental illnesses.

Chapter 9 explores nonresidential community corrections programs in which the offender resides at home, while participating in the program under a strict set of rules and curfews. Nonresidential programs include intensive supervision probation, house arrest, electronic monitoring, and day reporting centers.

Finally, Chapter 10 discusses sanctions tied to restorative justice and economic sources. Restorative justice is a philosophy that underscores the need for offenders to repair the harm done to their victims and to the surrounding community. Community service, restitution, and fines are types of restorative justice sanctions that can be used as tools to accomplish punishment objectives for certain offenders.

8

Residential Community Supervision Programs

CHAPTER LEARNING OBJECTIVES

- Describe the function and purpose of residential community corrections facilities.
- Discuss the effectiveness of residential community corrections programs for high-risk offenders.

- List the most common types of residential facilities in the community.
- Identify the various types of residential community corrections facilities.

This minimum security residential treatment facility in California allows a variety of contacts with the community.

CHAPTER OUTLINE

Introduction

Residential Community Corrections Facilities

Halfway Houses/Community Corrections Centers
History of Halfway Houses in the United States
Program Components
Worker Perspectives and Role Orientation
Evaluations of RCCFs

Shock Incarceration
Correctional Boot Camps
Prison Boot Camps: The Case of New York State
Juvenile Probation Boot Camps
Offender Perspectives
Criticisms of Boot Camps
Evaluations of Boot Camp Programs

RCCFs Serving Specific Offenders and Specialized Caseloads
Supervising Offenders Who Are Mentally Ill
Supervising Offenders Who Have Abused Drugs
   and Alcohol
Treatment Modalities for Substance Abusers:
   Therapeutic Communities
RCCFs for Women Offenders

Supervising Working Offenders Outside of Jail
Jail-Based Work Release
Community-Based Work Release: Restitution Centers
Work Ethic Camp

Summary

KEY TERMS

intermediate sanctions
widening the net
residential community corrections
   facilities
halfway house

shock incarceration
boot camp
restitution center
therapeutic community
relapse

work release
work ethic camp

Introduction

Regular probation supervision is adequate for misdemeanor offenders and for many felony offenders. However, there are people who need closer supervision than traditional probation but who may not require the custodial nature of prison. **Intermediate sanctions** are sentencing options between prison and probation that provide punishment that fits the circumstances of the crime and the offender (DiMascio 1997). These sanctions are attempts to provide increased control over offenders within the community. Until the advent of these intermediate punishments, the courts were faced with the polarized choice of either probation or prison. Morris and Tonry (1990) contended that the United States has at times been too lenient with probationers who need tighter controls and too severe with prisoners who would present no serious threat to public safety if under supervision in the community. In the continuum of sanctions presented in Chapter 1, intermediate sanction programs are situated in the middle between probation and prison.

   The positioning over where a particular sanction lies in the continuum of sanctions often depends on who selects program participants. For example, if prosecutors and judges are the key decision makers in program selection, they tend to choose offenders who should have received probation. This decision would **widen the net,** because individuals who should have received probation are instead given a harsher sentence only because that sanction is available, and not because the offender requires more supervision. Widening the net increases costs because individuals eligible for probation receive more supervision. With more conditions to follow, their chances of violating conditions increase, so jail populations are not reduced.

Intermediate Sanctions
A spectrum of community supervision strategies that vary greatly in terms of their supervision level and treatment capacity, ranging from diversion to short-term duration in a residential community facility.

Widening the Net
When an individual who should have received probation is sentenced to a harsher intermediate sanction only because that sanction is available, not because the offender requires more intensive supervision.

On the other hand, correctional administrators select participants who are bound for jail or prison and allow a chosen few the opportunity for a reduced sentence upon completion of a less costly program, thus reducing the institutional population and costs of confinement. Some of the evaluation components to bear in mind include whether the intermediate sanction reduced prison beds, whether it produced a cost savings, and whether it reduced recidivism—or a return to criminal behavior (Tonry 1997). This chapter addresses residential community corrections programs in which offenders reside while serving time.

Residential Community Corrections Facilities

Residential Community Corrections Facilities
A sanction in the community in which the convicted offender lives at the facility and must be employed, but can leave the facility for a limited purpose and duration if pre-approved. Examples include halfway houses, prerelease centers, restitution centers, drug treatment facilities, and work release centers.

Residential community corrections facilities (RCCFs) are a popular intermediate sanction because they provide more intensive supervision than probation and parole but allow offenders to remain in the community where they have access to more treatment services than they otherwise would in prison. RCCFs cost less than jail or prison, in part, because offenders subsidize a portion of the cost through working full time. Offenders can continue to contribute to their own families as well as pay back victims for harm done. RCCFs are the most diverse type of community corrections sanction. Thus, it is difficult to describe an "average" residential facility or a typical client (Settles 2004). RCCFs do have the following commonalities:

- Residents live in the facility (not at home).
- Residents must be employed (or be working part time and going to school).
- Residents can leave the facility at any time for work at a verified job.
- Residents must be preapproved to leave the facility for any other reason, and they are limited to a certain pass duration, purpose, and curfew (Latessa and Travis 1992, p. 170).

Outside of those similarities, many differences exist, such as facility size, whether the facility is public or private, type of treatment programs offered, and type of clients selected. Halfway houses are the oldest type of RCCFs, having been around since the 1830s. But there are other, newer adaptations of residential facilities, including community corrections centers, prerelease centers, restitution centers, work ethic camps, work release centers, and residential drug treatment facilities (see Box 8.1 for a comprehensive list).

Because of the diversity of RCCFs, it is difficult to estimate their numbers. At the last known nationwide count of local facilities, there were 628 RCCFs and halfway house facilities housing nearly 19,500 offenders. Of this number, 55 (8.7 percent) facilities were operated by the department of corrections, whereas the rest

BOX 8.1

Terminology for Various Types of Residential Community Corrections Facilities

Community corrections centers	Probation violator unit
Halfway houses	Residential drug treatment facilities
Intermediate sanction facility	Restitution centers
Mentally ill offender facility	Therapeutic communities
Parole violator unit	Work ethic camps
Prerelease centers	Work release centers
Probation boot camps	

are privately owned and operated. The number of inmates in RCCFs at that time represented 4.4 percent of the total inmate population, at an average cost per day of around $43 per offender. Alaska, Iowa, Montana, and Wyoming were the most avid users of RCCFs, housing about 14 percent of their total inmate population in these facilities (Camp and Camp 1999). In the federal system, as of 2007, there were over 8,000 federal inmates in community corrections centers, an increase from just over 6,000 seven years ago (Sabol and Couture, 2008).

Halfway Houses/Community Corrections Centers

Halfway houses are residential facilities for probationers, parolees, or those under intensive supervision probation (ISP) who require a more structured setting than that would be available from living independently. Halfway houses are staffed 24 hours a day, seven days a week for various types of offenders and are also known as "community corrections centers." The term "halfway house" was used because of the two types of clients accepted—those who were halfway on their way out of prison and those who were one step away from it if they didn't make it.

"Halfway out":

a) State-level prerelease offenders who are transferred from the department of corrections (DOC or prison) to the community and anticipate receiving parole within the next one to two years
b) Paroled offenders who pose a greater community risk and need assistance in making the transition from prison to the community

Halfway House
The oldest and most common type of community residential facility for probationers or parolees who require a more structured setting than would be available if living independently.

Many residential community corrections facilities are privately owned and operated, and may be located in the middle of residential neighborhoods, such as Prosperity Recovery House in Sumner, Washington.

"Halfway in":

a) As an intermediate sanction sentence for offenders requiring more structure and control than that provided by probation, ISP, or even house arrest, but for whom prison is too severe a sanction, such as for veterans with a substance abuse or mental health problem

b) As an increased sanction for probation and parole violators

c) As a diversion program, where, upon completion, charges are dismissed

d) For pretrial individuals who are awaiting trial and/or are material witnesses who have been released on recognizance, and are not a threat to the community (Wells 1997; Settles 2004).

History of Halfway Houses in the United States

The halfway house concept has been traced back to the early 1800s in England and Ireland. In the United States, the halfway house idea originated in 1816, at the time when most penitentiaries still practiced the Pennsylvania-style system of solitude and complete silence. Prisoners were locked in their cells all day and were not allowed to interact with one another for fear that they would "contaminate" one another. Interaction would take away from the penance that prisoners must seek for full reformation (Keller and Alper 1970).

Following a tumultuous riot in a Pennsylvania prison, a commission was appointed to examine the problems with the prison system. One commission recommendation was to create temporary shelters to help prisoners get back on their feet as they were transitioning back to the community. This proposal was not adopted by the legislature because of strong feelings that prisoners, even after release from prison, should not be allowed to interact.

As penitentiaries transitioned from the solitude of the Pennsylvania system to the silent interaction of the Auburn or "congregate" system, prisoners were allowed to work outside of their cells. State support for halfway houses was still lacking, so private, nonprofit organizations opened halfway houses for the first time to provide a place for prisoners to go after release from prison.

For example, in 1845, the Isaac T. Hopper Home opened for male prisoners in New York City. In 1864, the Temporary Asylum for Discharged Female Prisoners opened in the Boston area. The Boston halfway house for women received less opposition than facilities for men. The reason for this difference was an underlying belief that, unlike male prisoners, female prisoners did not associate for the purpose of talking about criminal activity. Female prisoners were believed to contribute to their own rehabilitation (Wells 1997). At that time, halfway houses merely provided food and shelter to ex-prisoners and did not provide treatment services.

By the end of the nineteenth century, private halfway houses opened in eight other states. Criminal justice officials, such as law enforcement officers and corrections administrators, remained opposed to this idea. Funds for halfway houses dwindled, and with the Great Depression of the 1930s, many were forced to close. Only one halfway house, The Parting of the Ways in Pittsburgh, remained open (Keller and Alper 1970).

In the 1950s, private halfway houses were viewed in a brand-new light. Concern about crime and high parole revocation rates prompted halfway houses to assume a role beyond offering food and shelter. Halfway houses provided transition services to prisoners and became involved in both treatment and correctional supervision. In addition to being less expensive than prison, halfway houses protected the community because residents were more closely monitored than traditional parolees (Glaser 1995).

In the 1960s, halfway houses became more visible when they received government assistance for the first time. At the urging of then Attorney General Robert F.

Kennedy, Congress appropriated funds to open federal-level halfway houses for young offenders. Financial support increased as a direct result of emphasis placed on reintegration by the President's Commission on Crime and Administration of Justice (Latessa and Travis 1992). The Safe Streets Act of 1968 established the source of funding for halfway house expansion throughout the 1970s. A meeting of a newly formed group called the International Halfway House Association was held in Chicago in 1964. This private nonprofit policy organization later changed its name to the International Community Corrections Association and currently seeks to improve community corrections policy all over the world. The organization currently represents 250 private corrections agencies operating approximately 1,500 programs and an additional 1,000 members (International Community Corrections Association 2009).

Although government funding decreased substantially in the early 1980s, private halfway houses found a niche in the corrections market to provide alternatives to imprisonment and create an outlet for prison crowding control (Latessa and Travis 1992). That growth has continued well into the present in some states; for example, in 2007, 50 percent of California's female prisoner population was to be transferred to private community corrections facilities that would contract with the state (Schultz 2007).

Currently, no single model exists, as each halfway house is unique in structure, treatment programs offered, and type of clients it accepts. Private halfway houses can choose which clients they wish to accept on a contractual basis. Their prison case manager or probation officer refers offenders who are eligible for placement. The government pays the facility a specified amount per day per offender, and the offender is expected to assist in the per diem payment. For example, if it costs $43 per day per offender to operate a residential halfway house (Camp and Camp 1999), the state department of corrections pays the halfway house about $32 per day per offender, and each client is charged about 25 percent of the cost, or $11 per day. Each program has a different per day cost, depending on how many in-house programs are offered. For instance, Crosspoint is a center in San Antonio that has a contract with the Bureau of Prisons to accept federal clients at $65 per day (Settles 2004).

PROGRAM COMPONENTS

Offenders live in the facility, leaving to go to work, attend church, and attend school or participate in rehabilitation activities such as drug treatment. Residents are required to maintain a full-time job or be going to school full time. When not at work, residents maintain the facility through assigned chores, perform court-ordered community service, and attend classes or counseling sessions that their case manager mandates. Most halfway houses require residents to submit to regular drug testing and breathalyzers. Prison systems make extensive use of halfway houses to allow inmates a graduated release—something to fill the gap between total incarceration and absolute freedom. A six-month stay in a halfway house allows the inmate to decompress and adjust to freedom more readily.

Levels System: A Form of Behavior Modification   Increased freedom must be earned and is based on good behavior, the amount of time spent in the program, and the client's financial situation. Most halfway house programs have some kind of a behavior modification program called a "levels system," which we illustrate as a hypothetical example. In a levels system, the bottom level is the most restricted and the top level has more freedom away from the halfway house and more privileges. For example, in a five-level system, new clients start on Level 5, where there is a "hold" placed on them (they cannot leave the facility) until their case manager has completed the intake process. Once intake is complete, clients move to Level 4, where they remain until they obtain a job and get caught up on their rent. Level 4 clients are allowed passes to attend treatment (Alcoholics Anonymous and Narcotics Anonymous) and one four-hour pass per week to attend church (outside of leaving for work). Each level has its own curfew, which is not applicable to clients who work evenings or nights. In addition to treatment and church passes, Level 3 clients can take one day-time pass of no longer than eight hours, with a curfew of 10:00 P.M. Level 2 clients have Level 3 privileges, with a later curfew of 11:59 P.M. At Level 1, clients must be caught up on all restitution, community service, and rent. They must have $100 in savings. Level 1 clients have a weekday curfew of 11:59 P.M. but can take weekend passes, from Friday to Sunday, to visit preapproved friends and family. Level 1 clients can own an insured car and have driving privileges, whereas all other clients must depend on someone else for a ride or must take the bus. All clients, regardless of their level, must produce receipts and verification that the approved destination was visited. Passes are allowed to a verified address of a family member or for four hours at a time to see a movie or to go shopping. Some programs require clients to spend 14 days on each level before advancing to the next level.

Upon program completion of the residential phase, paroled clients are assigned a parole officer in the appropriate jurisdiction. Most successful probation clients are transferred to the "nonresidential" phase of the halfway house program. During the nonresidential phase, clients live at home but come to the halfway house to be tested for drugs, attend group treatment, or visit their nonresidential case manager.

Due to the program's structure, residents who completed an RCCF program successfully reported experiencing a greater internal locus of control and less loneliness. Most other residents surveyed felt the RCCF assisted in readjustment from prison, helped them find a better job, assisted in abstaining from drugs and alcohol, allowed them to financially assist their families, and allowed closer family relations than when in prison (Twill et al., 1998).

Worker Perspectives and Role Orientation

Two different types of staff work at a halfway house. One group is primarily involved in activities that are custody oriented, while the case managers and counselors take care of treatment and rehabilitation. The job of the halfway house case manager has been described as similar to that of a probation and parole officer, in the sense that the counselor must be "capable of possessing conflicting goals of rehabilitation and punishment" (Wells 1997, p. 27).

Leanne Alarid worked at a halfway house in Denver, Colorado. Alarid describes her job responsibilities working both types of positions:

I began working as a member of the client management staff, involved in security and physical accountability for over 80 males and females. In this capacity, I conducted population counts, searched people and belongings for contraband, signed clients in and out of the facility, dispensed medications and Antabuse, and conducted breathalyzers and urine screenings. When an opportunity to work as a case manager became available, I transferred within the facility from the security-oriented job to one oriented around treatment. In this position, I became occupied with treatment, programming, and revocation issues for 20 to 24 individuals. A case manager had duties very similar to a prerelease officer or a parole/probation officer in that I assessed my client's needs and risks and I devised individual program plans to meet each of their needs. I assisted my clients with adjustment problems they experienced while in the program, and I supervised their progress. I also taught drug and alcohol treatment classes for new clients, and I prepared prerelease plans and attended monthly parole board hearings.

Another perspective on working in a halfway house comes from Melodye Lehnerer (1992), who describes the different roles she played during her two-year experience conducting ethnographic research from one halfway house. Lehnerer began as a volunteer, moved to being a "peripheral member," and then became an "active member" as an assistant caseworker. As membership involvement increased, role conflict arose between staff affinity and identification as a researcher. Lehnerer did not particularly like being a caseworker because it required that she be too much of a "social control agent" for her self-identity, and it also made collecting data more difficult (p. 180). Thus, Lehnerer decided to quit being case manager and take on more of a "helping agent" role and started teaching general equivalency diploma (GED) classes and life skills to clients. As a teacher and staff member, Lehnerer explains how the clients still viewed her differently as "staff" from when she was a volunteer:

> Quite often residents would approach me after class and apologize for their or someone else's behavior. It was their way of teaching me how the game was played. Given the context, staff members and residents were protagonists. That was just the way it had to be. . . . [I]n the classroom setting there existed a pre-existing relationship based upon power differences. (p. 156)

Lehnerer discusses how residents maintained a code of secrecy from staff. She also stressed how residents and staff did not trust each other, and how information control was a valuable resource used by both parties: "Lack of trust was directly linked to staff beliefs that residents were concealing information and resident beliefs that staff were using information to further discredit them" (p. 228).

Punishment and Treatment Role Orientations   Halfway houses provide reintegration assistance, but they are primarily geared toward minimizing risk, which is a custody concern. Therefore, workers may experience role conflict, which is a clash between punishment and treatment goals. Ely (1996) stated that some staff members reduced their role conflict by detaching from their clients and suspending empathy, whereas other staff would convert, mentally retreat (do nothing), or resign. Alarid explains:

> When I moved from being involved in security issues and running facility operations to case management, I experienced more role conflict. The case manager role had two opposing sides: treatment and reprimand. The most effective case managers were the ones who could balance the two sides and who believed in both. However, some counselors were lopsided in that they invested heavily in treatment issues but could not bring themselves to put someone in jail who posed a liability risk to the community. No one ever likes sending someone back to prison, but you have to be willing to switch hats pretty readily from helping someone out one day and having to revoke them the next. Because of this difficulty, the burnout rate among staff is fairly high. The most valuable thing I learned through all this was, above all, to treat people with fairness, consistency, and respect.

EVALUATIONS OF RCCFS

As with other community-based programs, effectiveness of halfway house programs cannot be readily compared because wide variation exists in the quality of programs and the types of offenders admitted. Effectiveness has typically been measured by examining the program success or failure rates or by comparing recidivism rates of halfway house residents with a matched sample of probationers or parolees.

Latessa and Travis (1992) found that RCCF residents had more treatment needs than regular probationers or parolees, and as a result, RCCF clients received more treatment intervention. RCCF clients who completed treatment programs performed better with more structured supervision than they are under regular probation supervision, so it is likely that treatment participation might have been the critical difference.

Clients who were younger, used drugs and alcohol, had more extensive prior criminal histories, lacked employment and educational skills, and had fewer community ties were more likely to *fail* in RCCFs than individuals without substance abuse problems and with a less extensive criminal history (Hartmann, Friday, and Minor 1994).

While variables that predict a greater likelihood of success or failure can be identified, the more important question to be asked is how beneficial is it to have high-risk offenders in residential community corrections programs? Data of 53 Ohio RCCFs were used (comprising 7,306 clients) and compared with those of 5,801 parolees to analyze success rates and recidivism rates of low-risk versus high-risk clients. A risk score was calculated based on criminal history and demographic data, and scores separated low-risk and high-risk individuals in both the treatment and the control groups (Lowenkamp and Latessa 2005). The researchers found that low-risk parolees outperformed low-risk RCCF clients—in other words, low-risk RCCF had higher recidivism rates than parolees. The exact opposite results occurred for high-risk individuals—high-risk RCCF clients were more successful than high-risk parolees, suggesting that RCCFs are effective with high-risk offenders, and not as effective with low-risk offenders (Lowenkamp and Latessa 2005).

Shock Incarceration

Shock Incarceration
A brief period of incarceration followed by a term of supervised probation. Also called shock probation, shock parole, intermittent imprisonment, or split sentence.

Shock incarceration refers to a brief period of imprisonment that precedes a term of supervised probation in hopes that the harsh reality of prison will deter future criminal activity. A variety of shock incarceration formats are used, and they go by a number of names—shock probation, shock parole, intermittent incarceration, split sentence, and boot camp. The programs vary somewhat in design and organization, but all feature a short jail or prison term followed by supervised release. The target population is young offenders with no previous incarcerations in adult prisons. An estimated 10 percent of all adults on probation received a split sentence consisting of some combination of incarceration and probation (Bonczar and Glaze 1999).

In shock probation, an offender is sentenced to imprisonment for a short time (the shock) and then released and resentenced to probation. The prison experience is thought to be so distasteful that the offender will fear returning, and thereafter, avoid criminal behavior. The original shock probation program was established in Ohio in 1965. It was praised for making an unforgettable initial experience, but not allowing full immersion into the institutional subculture, assisting in reintegration into the community, and making offenders more receptive to probation (Vito and Allen 1981). Another type of shock incarceration is correctional boot camp programs.

CORRECTIONAL BOOT CAMPS

Boot Camp
A form of shock incarceration that involves a military-style regimen designed to instill discipline in young offenders.

The idea of **boot camp** programs for offenders first began in 1983 in Georgia, whereby correctional programs borrowed the military concept of breaking existing habits and thought patterns and rebuilding offenders to be more disciplined through intensive physical training, hard labor, drill and ceremony, and rigid structure. This concept

Boot camp attempts first to break down offenders and then to rebuild them to respect authority, increase their self-control, and improve personal responsibility.

Courtesy Leanne Fiftal Alarid

multiplied as the most common form of shock incarceration from 1983 to the late 1990s. Boot camp programs exist inside state prisons or local jails, within the community, and even as a small part of the Federal Bureau of Prisons (MacKenzie and Hebert 1996). However, the more successful correctional boot camps also provided therapeutic and educational activities, such as drug and alcohol education, individual or group counseling, vocational training, anger management, and academic education. Ronald Moscicki (1996), superintendent of a boot camp program in New York, stated the importance of having both military and treatment components:

> Boot camps often seem to begin with the assumption, "If it ain't rough, it ain't right." Most people think that "rough" is sweaty drills, "in your face," and bulging muscles. They never associate "rough" with inmates sitting in a circle in white shirts and ties, with counselors and drill instructors leading a treatment group or academic classes, teaching inmates how to read and write. . . . In truth, the military part is the easiest because it is constant repetition. . . . If all we expect from our inmates is that they follow orders, we will have good inmates. Inmates, even good ones, belong in jail. (pp. 287–288)

Correctional boot camp participants live in "barracks," wear military-style fatigues, use military titles, and address their drill instructors by "sir" or "ma'am." Each "platoon" is responsible for the actions of every individual, and many boot camps use group rewards and punishments to encourage people to work together. A small number of programs even use "brigs" or punishment cells for temporary solitary confinement.

In general, eligible candidates are young first-time felony offenders convicted of a nonviolent offense, and because of the physical demands, they must meet minimum physical requirements. Many eligible offenders have been involved with drugs or alcohol in the past, and most program participants volunteer to participate. Programs typically last 90 to 180 days before graduation to probation or parole supervision (depending on whether the boot camp is located in the community or the prison). The two main types of boot camp programs are:

- Prison Boot Camps. Offenders are chosen by correctional administrators to participate, and ultimately the offender volunteers for the program. The boot camp is usually within a prison correctional facility, but boot camp participants remain separate from the general population for the program duration. Offenders are paroled upon graduation from boot camp. Time served is significantly less than that with a regular prison sentence.

- Probation/Jail Boot Camps. Offenders are chosen to participate at time of sentencing by judges or jail authorities. Although the judges are directed to choose offenders who otherwise would have gone to prison, probation boot camps are criticized for widening the net—choosing offenders who otherwise would have been sentenced to probation. These boot camps are located in the community and are supervised by county sheriff departments, probation departments, or a combination of both. Offenders in probation boot camps do not go to prison but remain in a residential community facility. Following boot camp, offenders graduate to ISP or regular probation.

Prison Boot Camps: The Case of New York State   In New York, those who are accepted into the program are assigned to one of four minimum-security facilities. Male participants work in platoons of 54 to 60 men and proceed through the 180-day program as a unit. Table 8.1 shows a schedule of the daily activities of participants. About 41 percent of their time is devoted to treatment and education. Physical training and drill constitute 26 percent of the time, and hard labor on facility and community projects constitute the remaining 33 percent. For most such a rigid a schedule is new and many cannot conform to the program and drop out at a rate of 37 percent (Clark, Aziz, and MacKenzie 1994).

Those who successfully complete the six-month regimen are paroled and enter a six-month postrelease phase of the program known as AfterShock. The goal of After-Shock is to continue the close supervision that began in the institutional phase and provide opportunities and programs in the community designed to improve the parolee's chances for successful integration. Each participant has two parole officers to allow increased contacts between the officers and the parolees for home visits, curfew checks, and drug testing. AfterShock parolees have priority access to community services such as educational and vocational training. After completion of AfterShock, parolees are transferred to regular parole supervision (Bourque, Han, and Hill 1996).

TABLE 8.1   Daily Schedule for Offenders in New York Shock Incarceration Facilities

Time	Schedule
A.M.	
5:30	Wake up and standing count
5:45–6:30	Calisthenics and drill
6:30–7:00	Run
7:00–8:00	Mandatory breakfast and cleanup
8:15	Standing count and company formation
8:30–11:55	Work and school schedules
P.M.	
12:00–12:30	Mandatory lunch and standing count
12:30–3:30	Afternoon work and school schedule
3:30–4:00	Shower
4:00–4:45	Network community meeting
4:45–5:45	Mandatory dinner, prepare for evening
6:00–9:00	School, group counseling, drug counseling, prerelease counseling, decision-making classes
8:00	Count while in programs
9:15–9:30	Squad bay, prepare for bed
9:30	Standing count, lights out

Source: National Institute of Justice. 1994. *Program Focus Shock Incarceration in New York.* Washington, DC: U.S. Department of Justice, National Institute of Justice (August).

Shock incarceration programs save money by reducing costs in regular prison programs and avoiding capital costs for new prison construction. The New York State Department of Corrections estimated that it saved $2 million in prison costs for every 100 shock incarceration graduates. Recidivism rates for graduates 12 months after completion of the program were 10 percent compared with 15 percent for those who were screened but rejected and 17 percent for those who withdrew or were removed from shock incarceration before completion. After 24 months, 30 percent of graduates had returned to prison, compared with 36 percent of the considered inmates and 41 percent of those who failed to complete the program. At 36 months, shock incarceration graduates still returned to prison at lower rates, but the difference was significant only between program graduates and the considered group (Clark, Aziz, and MacKenzie 1994).

JUVENILE PROBATION BOOT CAMPS

Like prison boot camps, boot camps operated by probation departments also intend to reduce institutional crowding, provide rehabilitation, punish offenders, and reduce recidivism. There are only a small number of juvenile probation boot camps left in the United States, and most of them are in the southern region. In Texas, for example, 10 county-operated post adjudication detention facilities in Texas are registered as boot camps collectively housing over 500 teenagers, such as the Delta program near Houston, Texas, for juvenile males aged 14 to 16 years old. Delta recently decided to make drills and exercise a smaller part of the program, while increasing counseling and education programs (Peterson 2009).

An evaluation study measured attitudinal changes in coping and self-control, perceptions of boot camp staff, benefits of participating in counseling, attitudes toward program staff, perceptions of future opportunities, and the quality of relationships with family and friends. The researchers found that a probation boot camp program for young adults produced significant positive measures of attitudinal change in probationers (Burton et al., 1993; Kilgour and Meade 2004), and seemed to affect staff as well. Box 8.2 tells the story of a probationer named Mr. John from the perspective of one of the boot camp teachers at this program.

A recidivism study on probation boot camp program graduates measured them at two years and then again at four years after release to see if the attitudinal changes transferred into behavioral changes. Two years after release, 22 percent of boot camp graduates had been sentenced to prison. Four years following boot camp, 61.7 percent of graduates had been sentenced to prison, including the two-year recidivists (Anderson, Dyson, and Burns 1999). Of the juvenile boot camp programs studied, *counseling* was the program component that made the greatest difference in reducing recidivism. Programs that had counseling had lower recidivism rates than boot camp programs without this component (Wilson, MacKenzie, and Mitchell 2005).

OFFENDER PERSPECTIVES

Many participants of prison boot camps felt fortunate to have been chosen for the program because they obtain release upon boot camp program completion much faster than from a traditional prison sentence. Hank, age 23, was sentenced to prison for 18 months and provides his perspective on getting out early after participating in a Massachusetts boot camp:

> I came here to get out of jail in 4 months that is all. I've been in and out of jail for a lot of years. So I know about jail environments. This place is a positive community environment. You don't see anything like this in regular jail.

BOX 8.2 COMMUNITY CORRECTIONS UP CLOSE

A Boot Camp Teacher's Unforgettable Experience: The Story of Mr. John

Despite the troubled and violent lives students at the Harris County Boot Camp have led, the story of Derrick John still seems to catch them off guard. I drag it out and use it to get their attention just once during the few weeks that I will be their teacher. I wait for the precise moment when I feel it will be most effective—sometimes at the beginning of our time together, sometimes at the end. Most of the time, however, I tell the story when I am feeling overwhelmed by the task in front of me.

He was a nice guy with a great smile, I always start. An attractive, lean young man, 6-foot-3 or taller, I often told him he should go to Hollywood when he got out of Boot Camp. I actually looked forward to seeing him in class. This is not always true of the students I teach. While it's easy to like the students, almost all are tough and drain on any teacher caring enough to look into their eyes. Even the smart, easy learners have needs for attention that are so deep they draw energy from you. They have holes in their young lives that have made them hard and violent or else depressed and despairing.

Simple autobiographies the students write their first class take days for me to read because of the harsh existence most have had. And that's just the parts of their lives they are willing to write down. Even joking, these students have affectations that show they are covering up, trying for a resilience to bounce back from family cycles that have led them to crime.

For a while, Mr. John was one of those same draining students who spent the first half of his tenure at Boot Camp with a chip on his shoulder. "Why do we have to do this? I don't understand that," he'd say, without really ever listening or trying to understand in the first place.

When his mood was even darker, he'd just lay low and try not to call attention to himself. Those quiet students who try hard to go unnoticed are often the most troubled, I have found. On those quiet days, I worried the most about Mr. John, feeling like he was still fuming, boiling deep inside his youthful outward appearance.

Then, for whatever reason, a light went on inside Mr. John when he was about halfway through the program. I see this reaction to Boot Camp often. The program teaches discipline and respect, and the students seem to catch on at some point. Either that happens, or they realize they are here for the long haul and should take advantage of the county's services. Whichever is the case, an education immediately reduces their chances of returning to the criminal justice system.

Mr. John started caring, and then he started learning. He finished assignments quickly and made scores higher than that I even expected of him. But halfway is often too late for some probationers, especially those who quit school as early as Mr. John. Time and his Boot Camp days were running out.

Every day his schoolwork improved. He became an ideal student, working hard and offering me a respect he had never shown before. I began to joke about having him stay in the program long enough to get his G.E.D. We call it "recycling," and it means more time at Boot Camp for probationers. It's the thing they dread the most. "If I could just keep you another three months, Mr. John," I'd say, "I could help you finish this G.E.D." "I think I'll just have to talk someone into getting you recycled."

It would make him crazy when I would say this. No one wanted to be recycled. Everyone wanted to go home, even those whose home life had led them to Boot Camp.

Dodging Recycling

No one ever jokes about recycling, either. It's much too serious a subject to the probationers. I was only half joking, though. I would have loved to have kept Mr. John in Boot Camp and still think about the difference it would have made had he stayed there for another three months.

His beaming smile would fade for a moment at my attempt at humor. "You wouldn't do that to me," he'd start. "Would you?" Something in my returned look would tell him I wasn't serious, and his smile would reappear before I even needed to reassure him.

Of course, I could never have him recycled at that point. He was now the picture of a perfect student. I knew, however, he had started working too late to finish his G.E.D. in Boot Camp. I emphasized the importance of continuing his education now that he was on the right track. He could still get his G.E.D. in a few more months with the help of the continuing education program at the Harris County Adult Probation Department. He just had to take more of the responsibility on himself.

Finally, one Wednesday, as is always the case with graduations at Boot Camp, he left the program along with the other 45 members of his barracks. He marched for the crowd of parents and visitors and listened to the graduation speech of hope for the future—now with cleaned slates and new, healthier habits and minds. He was so nervous, like all the probationers are on this day, that he shook my hand quickly with little notice as to whose hand

(Continues)

| **BOX 8.2** | **COMMUNITY CORRECTIONS UP CLOSE (*Continued*)** |

A Boot Camp Teacher's Unforgettable Experience: The Story of Mr. John

it was. He never let his eyes meet mine, although I tried to impress him with one last remark. "Keep at it, Mr. John. You've come too far to stop," I said.

Nine days later, his last essay still in my briefcase, Mr. John was shot and killed by a police officer after a robbery. He had fallen back in with a peer group that had waited for him back home and outside the secure barbed wire fence of the Boot Camp. At 17 years old, Mr. John never even had a life. With little or no parenting and an unsuccessful school experience, he never had a chance. When he entered Boot Camp, he may have looked like a hardened street thug, but when he left, he looked like the boy he still was.

Story's Impact

I don't know what part of Mr. John's story reaches my other students first. Maybe they see their own vulnerability to death. Maybe they were shocked by his youth. Maybe they are just frustrated that I use him as an example of my desire to keep them out of trouble and into education.

I can't keep them alive just by keeping them locked up, which is what I wish I had done with Mr. John. I know that wouldn't be a life. I know also that if they return to their former habits and former friends, things are going to happen to them anyway. Sooner or later. Prison or death.

I run across Mr. John's math workbook when I'm searching other files. Occasionally, I see an essay he wrote tucked in with other students' school papers. Maybe I run into the newspaper article about his death. I keep all these remembrances intentionally. It always surprises me for that minute; stuns me with reality.

I see his smile and picture his long legs stretching from his desk at the back of the classroom. And his eyes; I can still see the boy that would never live long enough to be a man. I want to be reminded of Mr. John. That's why I keep his schoolwork. I also want my other students to be reminded. I want them to realize that this same probationer could be any one of them. I tell them that I can't have it happen again. The story of Mr. John has broken my heart, and it will never harden to such blows. With this, I'm telling them that I care. I want them to try. I want them out of trouble and into a happy life that does not include violence and death.

Source: Denise Bray Hensley. 1995. One Boy's Life. *Houston Chronicle* (September 17) Reprinted with permission.

My family tells me how much I've changed. I lost 25 pounds, learned to control my impulses, and learned to not drink. The program and classes are all supportive. I never expected to learn about wellness and parenting. I have a 2-year-old son and another one just 3 months old. I want to go home and do the right thing. I wanted to quit many times; for a while, every day I thought, "This is the day I quit and get out of here." The staff made me realize that I need to stick it out "one day at a time." I learned how to talk to other people, staff, and other inmates. . . . I was always a follower who got into trouble easily. I learned how to say "no" to my impulses. The first week I hated the DIs [drill instructors] . . . [but] they taught me respect. When I think of it, that was missing in my life. Today, when I leave here, I can hold my head high and be proud of my completion of the program. I also know I need a support system to keep myself from getting into negative situations. (as quoted in Ransom and Mastorilli 1993, pp. 307–318)

Another male prisoner named Wayne, an 18-year-old Native American convicted of assault and battery, was a perfect candidate for the Massachusetts boot camp. Not only does Wayne have a problem controlling his temper, but he also has a drinking problem. He talks about the changes he has experienced because of boot camp:

This was a heck of an experience. I've been in several programs and halfway houses, and this is the best program I've ever seen. . . . The 12-step classes are outstanding. They teach you how to stay sober. In addition, they teach you how to be responsible for yourself. This is, mentally, a tough program. When I first got here, I thought this place was crazy, a bunch of cops yelling. I did not know what to expect. I thought about quitting often. I've been impulsive and did what I wanted to do. One day, I was tired and when a DI was yelling at me, I told him I would not give him the pleasure of seeing me quit. I've learned to respect the DI. I can talk to the DI. They're not cops, the enemy. They made me responsible for myself. They taught me to care. . . . When I leave here Friday, I've already got plans to go to A.A. [Alcoholics Anonymous] meetings. . . . There is no negativity here like regular jail. I've tried to think about something negative . . . nope, nothing. Now don't get me wrong. I hate this place. . . . However, I love what the program has done for me. I never had plans or goals in my life. I've learned to suck it up and drive on. Open my ears and shut my mouth, otherwise, you are in the front leaning push-up position a lot. I have not found myself in that position in about a month; that's progress. (Ransom and Mastorilli 1993, pp. 313–314)

CRITICISMS OF BOOT CAMPS

One of the primary concerns is that boot camps widen the net, especially probation and juvenile boot camps. In net widening, the costs increase because offenders who should be on probation are going through a more expensive program.

Another concern is that the confrontational style of the military-style boot camp can have potentially negative outcomes because many boot camp environments are characterized by coercion, stress, and leadership styles that are likely to reduce self-esteem, increase the potential for violence, and encourage the abuse of power. Lutze and Brody (1999) suggest that the harsh environment in many boot camps may violate the Eighth Amendment prohibition on cruel and unusual punishment, which may make boot camps targets for offender lawsuits. One boot camp closed in Tampa after a 14-year-old boy died as a result of a videotaped beating by boot camp staff (Associated Press 2006). Other camps in at least four other states have closed, citing possible abuses and high recidivism rates (Milligan 2001).

Finally, some boot camps have trouble retaining good staff and have high staff turnover. This results in inconsistent standards and behavioral problems for participants, factors which in turn are likely to affect later behavioral change.

EVALUATIONS OF BOOT CAMP PROGRAMS

What happens at boot camp should *not* stay at boot camp. Boot camp graduates had higher short-term positive adjustment scores than offenders in other programs (Brame and MacKenzie 1996). However, short-term positive attitude changes did not directly translate into long-term reduced recidivism. Much of the effectiveness of boot camps depends on the comparison group. Boot camp participants had lower rates of recidivism when compared with a jail or prisoner group, but the outcome was less favorable when boot camp was compared with probation (Wilson, MacKenzie, and Mitchell 2005).

A study of eight different boot camps demonstrated that treatment mixed with discipline can reduce recidivism. The researchers found a strong focus on rehabilitation, aftercare, voluntary participation, selection from prison-bound offenders, and longer program duration (MacKenzie et al., 1995). As with the juveniles, the physical side of the boot camp experience (drills, labor, and discipline), by itself, is not enough to reduce recidivism. Recidivism reduction was seen in programs that offered three or more hours of treatment per day along with physical drills and training.

Whether boot camps reduce prison crowding depends on whether the program targets prison-bound offenders. Not surprisingly, programs that allowed departments of corrections administrators to select participants were more likely than those involving judicial selection to alleviate prison crowding because corrections administrators were more likely to select offenders who were eligible for prison (MacKenzie et al., 1995). Parent (1996) explains why many boot camps have failed to reduce costs and institutional crowding:

> Many limit eligibility to nonviolent first offenders, select offenders who otherwise would receive probation, and intensively supervise graduates, thus increasing rates of return to prison for technical violations. In most jurisdictions, boot camps appear more likely to increase correctional populations and costs rather than reduce them. (p. 263)

The high point for boot camps diminished such that by 2000, due to years of net widening and lack of counseling and educational components to significantly reduce recidivism, one-third of these boot camps had closed, and 51 programs remained in operation at a cost per day of $58 per offender (Parent 2003). Of those offenders, 553 (8.7 percent) were female and 5,836 (91.3 percent) were male. Today, fewer than 40 programs remain open in the United States, and the future of these programs remains uncertain.

RCCFs Serving Specific Offenders and Specialized Caseloads

There are many other types of RCCFs, including some that are operated by private companies and others that are operated by county jails. Private companies manage therapeutic communities and specialized residential programs for offenders in specific situations, which include women, offenders with substance abuse problems, and mentally ill offenders. County jails operate work release, work crews, and other programs where offenders are supervised outside of the jail facility, but sleep at night in the jail.

SUPERVISING OFFENDERS WHO ARE MENTALLY ILL

People with severe mental illnesses who are homeless and might be in need of stabilizing medication may eventually find themselves in jail or on probation because they will eventually draw attention to themselves. Some self medicate with illegal drugs or turn to criminal activities to support a habit and are turned away from a resource-depleted mental health system. There are also some severely mentally ill people who are not stabilized on medications, and who may act out in deviant ways, but not necessarily be criminal or dangerous. As police focus on quality-of-life issues, ordinance violations, and small-time drug offenses, people who are homeless and who have a substance abuse problem get caught up in the corrections system (Slate et al., 2003).

Responses to offenders with mental illnesses in the community vary to include mental health courts, specialized caseloads, outpatient treatment, and residential treatment. As you learned in Chapter 2, mental health courts emphasize keeping mentally ill offenders out of jail and prison unless they are a clear threat to themselves or others. However, only about 15 percent of probation and 25 percent of parole departments have staff who are specially trained to deal with specialized caseloads of mentally ill clients (Slate et al., 2003).

Community-Based Residential Facilities for Mentally Ill Offenders An inpatient residential facility is an alternative to a jail setting for offenders who need more structure and treatment intervention, but are not yet ready to be released to probation. After experiencing cognitive behavioral treatment and stabilizing on medication, offenders are transferred to probation within three to four months. These separate treatment programs are seen as more effective than those jail in their ability to reduce felony recidivism when compared to similar offender groups that received mental health treatment through other programs (Braddock, Lehman, and Maclean 2002). A more recent study highlighted the importance of incorporating substance abuse treatment into the program to address offenders who self medicate and commit crime to support the habit (Castillo and Alarid 2009).

Specialized Mental Health Probation Caseloads A disproportionate number of people with mental health issues are on community supervision. It is estimated that about 16 percent of all probationers have general mental health needs and between 5 and 10 percent of parolees have serious mental illnesses that require medication and therapy (Slate et al., 2003).

One response to supervising offenders with mental illness is to have a specially trained officer operating a caseload specializing in mental health issues. When traditional probation caseloads were compared with specialized caseloads, 90 supervisors drawn from a nationwide sample of 25 probation departments reported that training on mental health issues and a reduced caseload number were the two biggest differences (Skeem, Emke-Francis, and Louden 2006). Training allowed probation officers a more empathetic understanding of various imbalances, so that officers could learn to recognize mental health stability and deterioration prior to the time when the situation gets "past the point of no return." Training also allowed officers to understand resistance and how to gain the trust and compliance necessary to work with this population. The caseload size was less than half on the specialized caseloads compared with traditional probation—48 specialized compared with 130 regular—allowing officers on specialized caseloads the opportunity for a different style of case management and a greater focus on both treatment and supervision (Skeem, Emke-Francis, and Louden 2006).

Maintaining a positive working relationship with treatment providers was important for probation officers. The two greatest challenges when working with mentally ill probationers were coordinating treatment and ensuring compliance with medication and counseling sessions. Mentally ill individuals tend to behave in a noncompliant manner more often than probationers on traditional caseloads. Problem-solving strategies and court appearances were used much more often than revocation to address noncompliance. Community officers who work with offenders with mental illnesses are recommended that the officer be

"... patient and flexible, have a basic knowledge of mental health disorders, and be particularly skilled in firm yet non-confrontational communication strategies. . . monitoring compliance with any medication regimen and detecting signs that may indicate that the defendant is a danger to others or disoriented. . . pay attention to signs of withdrawal (such as poor hygiene, disorganization within a household or drastic changes in physical appearance). . . [and] establish a collateral network that includes treatment providers and individuals who are in daily contact with the defendant and thus in the best position to observe early signs of deteriorating and/or dangerous behavior (Administrative Office of the U.S. Courts 2007, Chapter V, p. 17).

Outpatient Community Treatment   The strongest predictors of recidivism for offenders with mental illness were prior criminal history, previous substance abuse problems, and resistance to psychotropic medication compliance (Swanson et al. 2001). Outpatient community treatment seems to be most successful when services first begin on an inpatient basis. Outpatient community treatment allows mentally impaired offenders who are stabilized on medication and no longer a danger to themselves or others a chance to avoid the harmful incarcerative environment, while improving independent functioning and continuing an ongoing treatment regimen. Offenders with mental illnesses who were released from jail were more likely to use aftercare services after release. This increased use of services was believed to have lessened the likelihood of future arrests (Swanson et al. 2001; Ventura, Cassel, Jacoby, and Huang 1998).

Based on the discussion, we recommend that mental health services be strongly connected with criminal justice agencies. Examples of programs with criminal justice collaborations are those in Milwaukee, Wisconsin, and Multnomah County, Oregon. Second, a standardized training curriculum for probation and parole officers is necessary to continually educate workers in criminal justice about mental health issues. A model program in New York incorporates elements of crisis intervention and recognizes signs of mental disorder (Slate et al., 2004).

SUPERVISING OFFENDERS WHO HAVE ABUSED DRUGS AND ALCOHOL

The majority of offenders serving community correction sentences have problems with drugs or alcohol, or their crime was drug related. A nationwide survey of a stratified random sample of more than 2,000 probationers on active supervision found nearly half of them admitted to being under the influence of drugs or alcohol during the commission of their crime. For a number of others, substance abuse contributed directly or indirectly to the crime(s) that led to their conviction. While under probation supervision, half of probationers surveyed were randomly tested for drug use, and 38 percent were treated for drug and/or alcohol abuse (Mumola and Bonczar 1998). Technological advances in drug and alcohol testing will be further discussed in Chapter 9, such as urine screenings, hair analysis, saliva analysis, skin patches that measure blood alcohol levels, and pupillometry, or measuring how a pupil responds to light.

In this section, we will discuss general supervision and treatment strategies that probation and parole officers use for clients who have a problem with drugs or alcohol. According to Steiner (2004), obstacles that probation and parole officers face in the supervision of offenders with substance abuse problems include:

- Identifying quality drug treatment programs with trained staff
- Being able to refer clients to a community-based program (due to space availability)
- Limited ability to keep offenders in mandatory treatment
- Relapse prevention after the intensive treatment ends (events, thought patterns, or stressful situations may trigger substance use)

Because of these challenges, a supervision style called the "treatment retention" model was proposed for parole officers. The model recommends that treatment begin for offenders while they are incarcerated and that, when they are released from prison, a cognitive–behavioral relapse prevention program retains offenders in treatment throughout the reentry and parole period (Steiner 2004). When offenders with substance abuse problems begin to have problems following conditions or relapse back into drug use while on supervision, Steiner argues for graduated sanctions that are tailored to a treatment plan rather than merely just revocation to prison.

Another supervision tool is the monitored use of Antabuse, a prescription medication that negatively reacts with a person's system if he or she ingests alcohol. Clients on Antabuse must take this medication every two to three days under the watchful eyes of staff, who administer the medication in community clinics or in day reporting centers. Other medications such as Methadone or Buprenorphine, are administered to clients with addictions to heroin or other opiate-based drugs. Naltrexone is an opiate antagonist that blocks opiate access from receptors in the brain. These substances are used over a long period of time to decrease dependency on opiate-based drugs.

Gender-Responsive Strategies   Treatment approaches for substance abuse should vary depending on why clients abuse substances in the first place. Bloom and McDiarmid (2000) note an important gender difference: "Men in recovery tend to emphasize the problems caused by the consequences of drug use, and women more often report the 'stressors' leading to drug use" (p. 15). Female offenders respond to strategies that incorporate their problems, and supervision of female probationers should therefore be "relational" in that they should engage the children and the spouse in the recovery process. Family group conferencing (discussed in Chapter 10) may be one tool to accomplish treatment and healing goals. Programs that use an "empowerment model of skill building to develop competencies that enable women to achieve independence" are ideal strategies for female offenders (Bloom and McDiarmid 2000, p. 13).

TREATMENT MODALITIES FOR SUBSTANCE ABUSERS: THERAPEUTIC COMMUNITIES

A variety of treatment modalities are available to treat addiction problems—for example, recall our discussion of drug courts in Chapter 2. Drug courts allowed offenders with a substance abuse problem a chance at avoiding a prison term, and upon successful completion of drug court many of them were able to avoid a conviction altogether. Clients at drug court or on probation were still expected to go either to an inpatient/ residential treatment facility or on an outpatient basis. Abel Salinas, a manager of a community-based residential substance abuse treatment facility, provides insight into the rewards and challenges in working with probationers with substance abuse problems (see Field Notes).

Therapeutic Community
A type of residential community facility specifically targeted for drug offenders, offenders who are alcoholics, and/or drug addicts who are amenable to treatment.

Another treatment modality is the therapeutic community. **Therapeutic communities** (TCs) focus on the long-term treatment of alcoholism and drug addiction and abstinence from substances for criminal offenders. This section focuses on TCs in the community with less surveillance than those in prison. TCs are generally better suited for long-term poly-drug addictions (addiction to more than one kind of drug for an extensive period of time), whereas drug courts are geared toward moderate forms of addiction. Helping an individual through change is a process and entails more stumbling blocks. Thus, a typical TC has a period of six to nine months of residential drug and alcohol treatment, with a period of aftercare as the offender transitions from the

FIELD NOTES

When working with offenders who have difficulties with substance abuse, what are the most rewarding long-term and short-term aspects? What are the greatest challenges and how do you and your staff attempt to overcome them?

There are many rewarding aspects that result from working with substance abusers. However, the single most rewarding aspect that I can see is the improvement in the quality of life for, not just the offender who successfully completes treatment, but for the immediate and extended family as well. Too many times, children and spouses suffer the residual affect of a drug user's inability to maintain employment, effectively communicate problems to their significant others, and serve as role models to children who seek the support and guidance of adult users. Children who witness this learned behavior often times fall into the same lifestyle as their using parents, and the cycle continues.

By helping to repair one person, the domino effect of ruined lives and extreme hardships for families can be stopped or broken, and in some situations, even reversed.

Seeing a former offender who spent time in the drug and alcohol treatment facility at a local grocery store, while putting gas in their car, or at a movie theater, and having them tell you that they have removed themselves from their drug-using lifestyle and are well on their way to improving their family relationships and employment status is nothing short of gratifying.

A very rewarding short-term aspect is those offenders who come into the program who, although not entirely excited to be here, nonetheless appear to have their stress level lowered somewhat by their new structured and therapeutic environment. This is often the complete opposite of the chaotic and deceitful

Abel Salinas *Manager, Substance Abuse Treatment Facility*

environment that they've left, where the threat of violence, arrest, and looking over their shoulder is the norm.

The single greatest challenge in residential services can be described as the *career criminal* vs. the *drug abuser*. The drug abuser readily admits a problem, wants help, understands the negative consequences of their drug abuse, but still feels a strong desire to use drugs. This is where the treatment staff, probation officers, and security personnel intervene to assist the individual, using cognitive behavioral therapy and motivational interviewing techniques.

On the other hand, the career criminal does not admit a problem, does not want help for a drug problem, does not understand the negative consequences of their drug abuse or drug dealing, does not have any desire to stop their anti social behavior, and sees treatment as only a way of avoiding a lengthy jail or prison term. Their only desire to is to get back into the community and neighborhoods and continue their lifestyle.

This clash of attitudes and beliefs between the career criminal and drug abuser is probably one of the most challenging aspects to deal with in residential services. Although the career criminal, in my opinion, represents only a small minority of the entire population, their manipulation of well-intentioned residents, staff, and counselors can have a detrimental impact on many of the residents.

We try our best to overcome this constant push and pull by singling out the career criminal and offering them more intensive treatment, while paying special attention to their criminogenic needs. Good quality communication between security staff, counselors, and probation officers keeps us on our toes and lessens the chances of falling for the manipulative ways of the career criminal.

therapeutic environment to dealing with stressors of daily life. Table 8.2 summarizes the differences between therapeutic communities and drug courts.

The Therapeutic Community Environment   TC candidates are thoroughly screened for suitability and readiness for treatment. If accepted, offenders with a substance abuse problem must be motivated to adhere to all rules and participate in all activities required by the TC program. A TC environment is considered to be like a supportive

TABLE 8.2   Comparing Therapeutic Communities and Drug Courts

Characteristics	Therapeutic Communities	Drug Courts
Initial point of intervention	After conviction	After arrest and before conviction
Type of program	Residential/inpatient	Nonresidential/outpatient
Where located	Community, jail, or prison	Community only
Program length	12–18 months	12–18 months
Voluntary	Yes	Yes
Estimated percent of waking hours devoted to treatment and self-improvement	100%	25–50%
People involved in defendant's progress	TC counselor, TC former addicts, TC peers in program	Judge, prosecutor, public defender, probation officer/case manager, treatment provider
Who imposes rewards and sanctions	TC participants/peers (confrontational)	Judge (nonadversarial collaborative)
Treatment and monitoring forms	Group, confrontation, individual counseling, community meetings, drug testing, shaming, extra chores	Group counseling, individual counseling, drug testing, acupuncture, community service, sitting in the jury box, case management visits
Average annual cost per client	$3200–$9000	$1600–$6000

surrogate family, except that physical fighting and sexual relations are not allowed. Each day in a TC is highly structured and disciplined. Clients have daily cleaning chores within the facility and hours of peer group sessions that focus on confronting attitudes and behavior of each resident. The goal of these sessions is for other clients in the group to tear down the defense mechanisms and excuses that addicts use to continue (or start) using drugs as a response to a desire or stressor. The sessions attempt to resocialize new thoughts, attitudes, and behavioral choices in all areas of one's life (family, friends, work, leisure time, spirituality, and so forth). Other types of counseling focus on self-worth, self-discipline, and respect for authority. There is little idle time, as even personal free time is used for some type of intellectual or creative self-improvement. Visits by friends and family are not allowed, and TC clients never mix or interact with non-TC prisoners.

The TC is also the only type of program that is largely peer-operated and peer-enforced. Though there may be a free-world staff contact person, the TC rules are enforced by the residents, and the group is run by the residents, who earn various leadership roles based on a levels hierarchy. Clients who graduate from the program are transferred to probation or parole, depending on their initial status. Clients who refuse to participate in sessions or who use drugs and alcohol while in the TC program are removed and incarcerated for the remainder of their sentence.

Challenges of the TC   One of largest challenges for TCs to overcome is the low program completion rate. Treatment programs should expect failures and relapses, but during the first 30 days, between 25 and 85 percent of new residents drop out of the program (Goldapple and Montgomery 1993). Efforts are needed to either improve retention rates (perhaps by redefining "success" and "failure") or better screen applicants' motivation to participate. For the first 30 days, new residents need to be more thoroughly educated about the process, and they may need confidence building before being confronted in group therapy (Goldapple and Montgomery 1993).

A second challenge is the use of shaming and humiliation that occurs for clients who misbehave or fail to participate. Examples include "PT" (extra chores or duties), wearing a dunce cap or a sign (stating what was done wrong) around the facility for a specified period of time, or shaving one's head. Some of the methods of punishment for disobedience have been criticized for their ineffectiveness toward changing behavior.

Types and Uses of Therapeutic Communities   A prison-based TC accepts prisoners without disciplinary reports who are within one or two years of release; acceptance is based on a rigorous application interview. Many prison-based TC participants graduate to a community-based TC for aftercare upon release.

A community-based TC is designed for clients who may have failed in various other community programs (for example, a halfway house, probation, or parole), because of either alcohol abuse or illegal substance addiction. Residential drug and alcohol treatment programs are also used as diversion from prison. For example, Florida has an 18-month Drug Punishment Program, which includes six months in a secure facility, then three months in a community facility, followed by nine months of ISP. Like the Colorado program, candidates are screened for suitability and readiness for treatment. This program targets males and females age 21 and younger. During the early phases, they are diagnosed, an individual treatment plan is developed, and clients receive group counseling (Bureau of Justice Assistance 1998).

Another similar program for nonviolent probationers exists in Dallas, Texas. This 300-bed facility provides 200 beds for clients in the first six-month residential phase of the program. Then, clients with adequate support systems enter a six-month aftercare program where they live at home and report to a probation officer. The remaining 100 beds are reserved for clients who do not have strong support systems and need an additional three months to make a successful transition through the "live-in, work-out" program. This is unique because transition from residential living to community living is seen as a prime opportunity for relapse. Probation officers work with the treatment facility staff to review clients' progress (Barthwell et al., 1995, pp. 39–47).

Sometimes community TC programs are used as a transition step for clients who graduate from prison-based therapeutic communities or other types of drug treatment programs while behind bars. For example, women in California with drug problems could attend a drug treatment program and then, upon their release, could be transferred to a residential program in the community to deal with issues of relapse and opportunity.

Evaluations of Therapeutic Communities   An evaluation of the California women's programs indicates that women who completed both the institutional treatment phase and the community residential treatment phase had lower incidences of drug use and higher levels of parole completion. Female drug offenders who participated in the institutional phase but did not enter the community phase did not fare so well. The researchers concluded that there was a shortage of facilities for female drug abusers. Many women applied but were unable to enter the community residential phase of the program because of space shortages. These women did not complete treatment, which left them vulnerable to **relapse** (Prendergast, Wellisch, and Wong 1996).

Another evaluation of a prison-based TC (Eisenberg and Fabelo 1996) found that recidivism was significantly reduced over a twelve-month period for clients who completed the TC compared to TC dropouts, even when controlling for age and education. However, for TC dropouts, recidivism rates were the same as for a comparison group of people who had never entered the TC program.

Relapse
When an offender with a substance abuse problem returns to using alcohol or drugs.

RCCFs FOR WOMEN OFFENDERS

Statistics on convicted women offenders indicate that most women are nonviolent property or drug offenders and do not pose a threat to the community (Pollock 1999). Therefore, most women felons do not require prison sentences and would be ideal candidates for community placement. One type of placement that has been developed especially for women arrested for prostitution is a Women's Recovery Center in Minnesota (see Box 8.3).

Given that women offenders also have problems with drugs or alcohol, and that many are mothers of at least one child under the age of 18, RCCFs that address gender-specific issues have grown. There are more than 65 residential treatment programs and another 70 programs resembling halfway houses for women to live with their children while they are serving a residential community sentence. Studies indicate that the children of offenders suffer emotionally, developmentally, and economically when their parents go to prison. Children of incarcerated parents stand a greater chance of following in the footsteps of their parents by becoming involved in the juvenile justice system at an early age. Because the mother is still the primary caregiver in the majority of families, the effect of incarcerating mothers with dependent children is pronounced (Mumola 2000). The question then becomes: How can women offenders be punished or sanctioned without punishing their children?

John P. Craine House   The John P. Craine House was founded in 1978 in Indianapolis, Indiana, and is designed specifically for women offenders convicted of misdemeanors or nonviolent felony offenses that are caretakers of preschool-aged children. The program teaches the women to be emotionally and economically independent as a

---

BOX 8.3   COMMUNITY CORRECTIONS UP CLOSE

A Community Alternative for Dealing with the Root Causes of Prostitution

"I had been through so much abuse that I honestly believed that I was not worth anything, and it really didn't matter if I got high because nobody gave a damn anyways."-Sheila Ayala, Graduate of the Magdalene Program (Neff 2006).

In Nashville, Tennessee, Reverand Becca Stevens started "Magdalene" as a grassroots non-profit outreach program for women involved in prostitution (Neff 2006). Ramsey County in St. Paul, Minnesota, opened a 12-bed program called the Women's Recovery Center with funding from the Minnesota legislature (Nelson 2004). Both centers are a diversion option at the front end or a postrelease option for women prisoners who have a genuine desire to get out of prostitution. Both programs address the root causes of prostitution which are childhood/young adult physical and sexual abuse, drug dependency, and mental health issues that resulted from the abuse, which include post-traumatic stress, depression, and low self-esteem. A woman in each program learns to understand how sexuality was a large part of her identity, and how drug use masked her painful past. For example, Clemmie is one Magdalene client who reported that since the time

she was 6 years old, her mother allowed other adult men to molest Clemmie and her sister. "At that time [when she was a teenager], we got introduced with an older guy that had told me about how I can make money off of selling my body, and it was like 'off to the races' because I know I can do this. . . . I already know what the mens want." A program resident learns the difference between unequal male/female relationships (such as an abusive pimp who feeds her drug habit) and relating to others in a more equal way. Most importantly, she discovers self worth and sobriety, along with learning opportunities for housing, legitimate employment, health care, and how to build a stable life to regain full parental rights of her children. The St. Paul program reports an 80 percent success rate, and the Tennessee program's success rate is unknown (Neff 2006; Nelson 2004).

Sources: Neff, Tom. 2006. *Chances: The women of Magdalene.* Video documentary, The Documentary Channel; Nelson, William F. 2004. Prostitution: A community solution alternative. *Corrections Today* (October): 88–91.

preventive intervention for their children (Barton and Justice 2000). As only one of six programs in the country Craine House holds a maximum of six adults and eight children at one time and serves 10 to 17 women and about 20 children each year.

Craine House resembles a halfway house in the sense that women pay for part of the program cost through the expectation of employment. Staff assess the needs of each woman, and formulate an individualized treatment plan. However, this facility seems to provide much more individualized and specialized attention, not only for the offender's needs, but also for her children, as described below:

> parenting skills, substance abuse treatment, job seeking skills, educational and/or job placement in the community, personal budgeting, nutrition information, and advocacy as indicated by individualized assessments. The program arranges for day care for the children at nearby locations to enable the women to work in the community. The program is staffed around the clock by counselors and family living specialists. . . . Basic goals for the Craine House program are to provide a safe, structured environment; promote the preservation of mother–child relationships; enhance the offenders' abilities to maintain economic and emotional independence while leading responsible, law-abiding lives; and prevent the neglect, abuse and potential delinquency of the offenders' children. (Barton and Justice 2000, pp. 7–8)

Because of the high level of services offered, it costs Craine House $80 per person per day. The disadvantage to this is that it costs more than incarceration. However, considering that the program is also providing prevention programs for the children, the cost may be money well spent in the long run. The average length of stay in the program is five months (six-and-a-half months for those who complete the program and two months for noncompleters). Just over 70 percent (53) of the women have successfully completed the program, whereas 22 women did not because of a technical violation or the commission of a new crime. The other five women still resided at Craine House.

Recidivism after successfully completing the program was measured by whether the women had appeared in court on a new charge or crime. Out of the 53 women who successfully completed the program, 11 committed a new crime. Most graduates were out for an average of two years before recidivating. Women who recidivated committed either a property or drug crime, but none committed a violent crime. The recidivism data for the first cohort of women extend six years. The long-term effects of Craine House as a prevention mechanism for the children who have participated would be worthwhile to determine.

Supervising Working Offenders Outside of Jail

County jails are responsible for detention of both pretrial defendants and convicted offenders. While nearly 781,000 offenders are detained inside the facility, an additional 68,000 offenders nationwide are still under care and supervision outside the jail facility in the community (Sabol and Minton 2008). One of those groups is offenders on work release. Other groups include offenders sentenced to restitution centers and work ethic camps that stress employment.

JAIL-BASED WORK RELEASE

Work release could be considered both a type of institutional corrections and a community corrections program, given that offenders reside in a facility (a community facility, jail, or prison) but are released into the community for a short duration

Work Release
A program in which offenders who reside in a facility (a community facility, jail, or prison) are released into the community only to work or attend education classes or both.

every day to work, attend education classes, or both. We discuss work release here because it is a form of prerelease program in the offender's preparation for release into the community.

The traditional use of work release is much more restrictive than the halfway house environment because offenders are not allowed to leave the facility for any other reason except work and school. This type of release is for a specified purpose and for a specific duration.

The definition of work release varies greatly, however. A broader definition of work release can include defendants or convicted offenders who spend a portion of their time in jail, and a portion of their time *working* in the community. If the broader definition is used, work release could include traditional work release, weekender programs, and some pretrial programs. Federal statistics indicate that for jails nationwide, 8,011 offenders were on traditional work release in 2000, while in 2007, the number decreased to 7,369. If the broader definition is used, an additional 10,473 offenders on a weekender program, and 11,148 on some sort of other pretrial supervision might be added (Sabol and Minton 2008). A weekend jail program involves reporting to jail only on the weekends (e.g., reporting in Friday by 7:00 P.M. and staying until Sunday at 7:00 P.M.), but living and working regularly during the week. We wish to emphasize that work release does *not* include community service work crews. Most clients on work release hold regular jobs in private businesses and are close to their release dates, by six months or less. Box 8.4 discusses the use of iris recognition to better ensure that the correct offenders exit the jail each day for work release.

We will discuss the two basic types of traditional work release which are unsupervised and supervised:

- An offender on unsupervised work release would, for example, be incarcerated in jail from 6:00 P.M. until 6:30 A.M., whereby every morning, the offender is released out the door to catch a bus to go to work. After leaving work at 5:00 P.M., the offender has 60 minutes to return back to jail each evening. Offenders on this form must submit paycheck stubs and/or documentation of hours worked to account for their time.

BOX 8.4   TECHNOLOGY IN COMMUNITY CORRECTIONS

"The Eyes Have it": Iris Recognition for Work Releasees

Given the frequent entries and exits that work releasees make each day from jail, along with the chaos that generally accompanies groups of people coming and going, it is possible that staff could mistakenly authorize the reentry of a different person, or worse yet, allow the release of the wrong person. As a result, some jails have turned to iris recognition technology to reduce identification errors, especially when people have a similar look or the same name. People who are experts in biometrics say that, unlike fingerprints, which can fade or change over the course of one's life, the iris tissue remains the same. Even within a single individual, the left iris is different than the right. The iris image is initially captured on a high-resolution digital camera and stored within a database. The area where work releasees enter and leave the jail is equipped with an iris scanner that checks whether a particular inmate can leave, and records both the exit and entry times. While no one has been wrongly released or mismatched since the new system has been in place, the National Law Enforcement and Corrections Technology Center reports that at this time, there is no national database or iris templates so the information cannot be checked against other states or other facilities within that state—yet.

Source: National Law Enforcement and Corrections Technology Center. 2006. The eyes have it. *TechBeat* (Fall). Retrieved from: http://www.justnet.org

- An offender on supervised work release would also spend the same number of hours at the jail, but would leave in a group in a county-owned van to go to a temporary or permanent work site for the day. The group would be accompanied by at least one deputy officer, and it would return together in the evening. For both types, offenders who leave the work site or do not return on time will have a warrant issued for their arrest.

The first documented uses of work release were in Vermont in the early 1900s, with work release legislation first introduced in the state of Washington in 1913. The federal system and all the states authorized work release programs by the mid-1970s, primarily for minimum-security inmates who are within six to nine months of being released from a jail or prison. In these cases, work release controls institutional crowding and simultaneously provides the offender an opportunity to find and retain employment, which is the most important factor in reintegration success and reducing recidivism.

Work release can also be a useful sentence for first-time offenders, particularly if the offender already has a job or is already going to school at the time the crime is committed, and if the offender has a high victim restitution payment but poses minimal public safety risk. In these specific cases, the judge orders that offenders must reside in jail and be allowed to continue working to pay restitution or continue working or attending school (for example, high school or college classes). This option is sometimes used when restitution centers or halfway houses are not available in the area. Work release can also be an option for physically disabled or mentally disabled offenders if program staff works with clients to help them seek gainful employment, a goal that is significantly more difficult than for the average offender (Mawhorr 1997).

The available evidence for work release programs is scant—five studies of work release from a prison setting have been conducted between 1974 and 2007. Four out of five of these studies found that participating in work release reduced recidivism compared to prisoners who were eligible but did not participate (Drake 2007; Jeffrey and Woolpert 1974; LeClair and Guarino-Ghezzi 1991; Turner and Petersilia 1996b). The fifth study which used random assignment of treatment and control groups found no difference in recidivism (Waldo and Chiricos 1977). Washington State continues to use work release facilities regularly for about one-third of all offenders exiting prison. A follow-up study reported that, compared to prison, work release yields a net future benefit to taxpayers of nearly $1,700 saved per person, and the rate of recidivism for new crimes is 1.8 percent lower (Drake 2007).

COMMUNITY-BASED WORK RELEASE: RESTITUTION CENTERS

Restitution centers are a type of residential community correctional facility specifically targeted for work capable offenders who owe victim restitution or community service. The difference between a work release/restitution center and a halfway house is that in a work release facility, the main emphasis is on gainful employment and payment of rent, child support, restitution, and other court-ordered fees. The client stays at the facility until it is time to go to work. A halfway house expects offenders to seek gainful employment, but also allows the client leisure passes to visit family, attend church, and go to the store or to treatment sessions.

Restitution Center
A type of residential community facility specifically targeted for property or first-time offenders who owe victim restitution or community service.

The first known community-based restitution center was the Bishop Lewis Center, established in 1970. The facility still accepts adult males directly from the Washington State Prison who have been sentenced for a non violent crime, are eligible for minimum custody, and have six months or less until their earliest release date (Drake 2007). Restitution centers provided some treatment, but the focus is on stable employment and paying back the victim. Some programs will release the offender when the restitution is paid in full. As a result, some jurisdictions such as Florida, Texas, and Washington consider work release *a component of an RCCF* (as well as for jails and prisons) and thus refers to clients who are sentenced to halfway houses, restitution centers, and prerelease centers (Levin 2008). Many work release facilities are co-ed, with a few in the larger cities having one for males and one for females. Festervan (2003) discusses the issues surrounding the supervision and employment opportunities for women at an all-female restitution center.

Texas Restitution Centers   Texas restitution centers serve both probationers and parolees for an average of five months. During their stay, center residents remain employed, develop restitution plans, and the centers offer GED, life skills, cognitive restructuring curriculums, and individual and family counseling as needed. They may also be required to work at community service projects on weekends and during evening hours. The offenders normally remain at the center until their restitution is completed. About 8 out of 10 offenders remain employed by the time they complete the program (Levin 2008). The average cost of a restitution placement cost taxpayers $60 per day, with an additional $10 to $25 a day paid by each offender. Across the state as a whole, restitution center clients pay over $4.5 million toward court fees/fines and victim restitution. In addition, they contribute community service hours that equal approximately $600,000 in labor costs if someone were paid for that labor (Levin 2008). One internal evaluation of various centers around the state reported that 18.4 percent of clients were revoked to prison over a two-year period (Texas Department of Criminal Justice 1999), compared with felony probationers who averaged 30 percent prison revocation rate (Texas Legislative Budget Board 2005).

Florida Work Release Centers   In Florida, state prisoners are eligible for work release when they have ten months remaining on their sentence, and they are minimum custody inmates. Inmates usually find a minimum wage job within one month despite not having any help from anyone from within the work release agency. The client is not allowed out of the facility unless he or she is going to look for work or going to an existing job. Once employed, about 75 percent of a client's paycheck is deducted for various expenses—45 percent for facility room/board, 10 percent for restitution, 10 percent for child support (if applicable), and 10 percent for savings. The remainder is provided as an allowance every two weeks (Berk 2008). Staff monitor employment closely—visiting on site weekly. Berk found that work release inmates had higher employment rates and earned about $400 more per quarter for the first year than a comparison group that did not participate in a work release program. Berk (2008) concludes:

> For prison programs, the bottom line is the recidivism effect. I find that work release participation does lower recidivism but that individuals who commit income-generating crimes [such as robbery, burglary, and drug dealing] are responsible for this change. Ex-offenders who commit non-income motivated crimes have improved employment outcomes after work release participation, but their probability of returning to prison does not change. (p. 24)

WORK ETHIC CAMP

Work Ethic Camp
A 120-day alternative to prison that teaches job skills and decision making using a cognitive–behavioral approach, followed by intensive supervision probation.

A different type of residential program is called a **work ethic camp,** which is a 120-day prison-alternative program based on a cognitive–behavioral treatment approach. One program in Nebraska allows inmates to be eligible once they have completed the 90-day intake and assessment period (Siedschlaw and Wiersma 2005). Once the participants have completed the 120-day program, they are released on ISP. The work ethic camp is considered to be a minimum-custody facility but costs nearly $44 per day per person, but the duration of the work ethic camp stay is about half that of the cost to incarcerate, which translates into a cost savings. The higher program cost is due to the assistance the program offers in developing job readiness skills, decision-making skills, and life skills such as money management.

Combined Work Release and Therapeutic Community   A program called CREST combines the therapeutic community concept (discussed previously) with work release. Clients entering the program from prison must first progress through a significant amount of drug and alcohol education, counseling, and confrontation before they are eligible for the work release phase in the community. Evaluation data indicated that CREST participants have significantly lower relapse and lower recidivism rates than a comparison group (Nielsen, Scarpitti, and Inciardi 1996). More recently, a study of nearly 20,000 Irish prisoners who participated in combined work and treatment programs (life skills, substance abuse treatment, and other therapeutic services) were significantly less likely to return to prison as a result of program participation (Baumer, Donnell and Hughes 2009).

SUMMARY

- Offenders in intermediate sanction programs had more severe criminal records and treatment needs than probationers but less severe criminal records than people incarcerated in prison.

- Offenders with intermediate community sentences were more likely than probationers and prisoners to acquire technical violations that later led to sentence revocation.

- Halfway houses remain the most common type of residential community program for offenders who have needs greater than offenders on regular probation or parole. Halfway houses are a more intensive form of supervision than probation and parole, but they are also valuable as a reentry tool for prisoners coming out of prison. Overall evaluations of halfway houses show that the benefits outweigh the costs, particularly for high-risk offenders.

- Boot camps are a type of shock incarceration program that varies in the degree of treatment programs offered. Voluntary participation, selection

from the prison population, and intensive aftercare provisions are important elements of the boot camp experience. The recidivism rates for most boot camps are no different from recidivism for prisoners, so the popularity of boot camps has declined in recent years.

- Restitution centers assist in motivating offenders to pay back victims, whereas work release and work ethic programs teach offenders job skills and allow them the ability to maintain gainful employment.

- Therapeutic communities use peer support and cognitive behavioral interventions to help individuals overcome addiction to drugs and to prevent relapse episodes so a person can maintain a life of sobriety.

- Residential programs for women offenders allow their children to live with them so that the women can learn better parenting skills and can maintain close relationships, which in turn aids in preventing recidivism.

DISCUSSION QUESTIONS

1. What are some examples of residential community corrections facilities?

2. What would working in a halfway house be like? What are some of the problems you might face?

3. What are some of the program components inherent in halfway houses?

4. Do halfway houses work?

5. Discuss the evolution and use of boot camps. What are the purposes of shock incarceration?

6. What are some of the positive and negative aspects associated with boot camps?

7. Compare a therapeutic community environment with a boot camp.

8. What goals does a therapeutic community attempt to achieve with substance abusers?

9. What are the issues with the treatment of offenders with mental illness?

10. What other types of offenders should be on specialized caseloads other than the ones mentioned in this chapter?

11. How are work release programs different from work ethic programs?

12. Should programs like the John Craine House be expanded?

WEB SITES

International Community Corrections Associations
http://www.iccaweb.org

Ohio Community Corrections Association
http://www.occaonline.org/links.asp

Community Corrections Association of Pennsylvania
http://www.cor.state.pa.us/stats/lib/stats/ccc.pdf

NIJ Publication: Lessons Learned from a Decade of Boot Camp Research
http://www.ncjrs.org/pdffiles1/nij/197018.pdf

Factsheet: Juvenile Boot Camps
http://www.nmha.org/go/boot-camps

University of Cincinnati Research Studies: Halfway Houses
www.uc.edu/ccjr/research.html

U.S. Department of Heath and Human Services, Treatment Improvement Protocol)TIP Series
http://kap.samhsa.gov/products/manuals/tips/index.htm (Note: see the appendices of TIP 42)

The Criminal Justice/Mental Health Consensus Project
www.consensusproject.org

The Criminal Justice/Mental Health Information Network
www.cjmh-infonet.org

National Institute of Corrections, Corrections Library
http://www.nicic.org/library/014000

New York State Division of Probation and Correctional Alternatives

Shared Services: Defendants with Mental Illness
http://www.dpca.state.ny.us/shared_mentally_ill.htm

John P. Craine House
http://www.crainehouse.org

CASE STUDY EXERCISE

Site Visit to One Community-Based Residential Correctional Program

Visit one community-based correctional program and use this visit to conduct your own case study. Your visit may be done individually or with a small group. You will likely need to clear the visit ahead of time with your instructor, or your instructor may suggest a facility with which he or she has some connections. If this is a group exercise, perhaps members can be assigned to each focus on a small section of the paper or presentation. There are four sections, and questions are presented so that each member can ask a few questions during the site visit. Write a paper or make a presentation to include one or more of the following areas:

SECTION 1: PROGRAM DESCRIPTION

- What are the goals of this program?
- What tools or techniques are used to meet these goals?
- What is the capacity (how many clients can be treated at one time)?
- How many contact hours/treatment hours are a part of this program?

SECTION 2: CLIENTS

- Who are the clients being served?
- What does the typical client look like (gender, age, education, and so on)?
- What are the client's perspectives of the treatment program?

SECTION 3: STAFF

- What is the client-to-staff ratio?
- What are the staff backgrounds and qualifications?
- What are the perspectives of the staff about working there (or about program effectiveness)?

SECTION 4: EVALUATION

- How many clients finish the program, (and how many drop out or do not complete it?)
- What are the reasons for not completing the program?
- What is the daily (or yearly) cost per client served?
- Have any clients been tracked after they leave the program? What were the results?

9

Nonresidential Community Supervision Programs

CHAPTER LEARNING OBJECTIVES

- Describe the conditions when offenders complete their sentence using court-mandated services on an outpatient basis.
- Explain the following sanctions when used in some combination with each other: intensive supervision probation, house arrest, electronic monitoring, and day reporting centers.
- Identify what services offenders pay for by making monthly payments to help keep the program cost down.

© Joel Gordon

Reporting kiosks such as this one in New York, are more common in public areas or in police stations to allow non–violent and low-risk offenders the convenience of checking in to their probation officer.

CHAPTER OUTLINE

Introduction

History of Intensive Supervision and Specialized Caseloads
Evaluations of ISP

House Arrest
Purposes of Home Detention
Criticisms of House Arrest
Effectiveness of House Arrest

Electronic Monitoring and Global Positioning Systems
History of Electronic Monitoring
Global Positioning Systems

How Do People Feel About EM/GPS?
Empirical Evaluations of EM and GPS

Day Reporting Centers
Treatment-Oriented versus Supervision-Oriented DRCs
Evaluations of DRCs

Summary

KEY TERMS

intensive supervision probation
house arrest
electronic monitoring
home-based electronic monitoring

remote location monitoring
real-time access
global positioning system
active GPS

passive GPS
exclusion zones
inclusion zones
day reporting centers

Introduction

Programs that require offenders to live at a residential facility during their community-based sentence were discussed in Chapter 8. Each residential program provides some form of outpatient aftercare, usually in the form of probation or parole, to further aid the transition process. This chapter examines outpatient sanctions and programs that offenders participate in while living at home. These programs can be sentences by themselves, or they can be combined with other sanctions such as probation, as a phase of aftercare or following a period of time spent in a residential facility, or following confinement in jail and prison. Types of nonresidential programs we will discuss independently in this chapter include intensive supervision, house arrest, electronic monitoring, and day reporting centers.

History of Intensive Supervision and Specialized Caseloads

Intensive supervision probation/parole (ISP) is an enhanced form of supervision that subjects offenders to closer surveillance, more conditions, and more treatment exposure than regular probationers and parolees. ISP was designed for high-risk, high-need offenders who were released from prison or those offenders who needed a more intensive community sentence in lieu of prison. *ISP is also known today as specialized caseloads.* In Chapter 5, we discussed specialized caseloads as a supervision strategy for specific types of high-risk offenders such as sex offenders and known gang members. In this section, we more fully review the history behind the concept of intensive supervision.

The use of ISP began in California in the 1950s under the assumption that increased contact would improve rehabilitation efforts and provide a viable alternative to incarceration. The focus at that time was to determine the ideal number of

Intensive Supervision Probation
A form of probation that stresses intensive monitoring, close supervision, and offender control.

probationers that one officer could effectively rehabilitate. Officers spent most of their time not out in the field with counseling and treatment efforts, but in writing reports and more detailed documentation in the office for the courts (Hanley 2002). ISP continued to be used in limited jurisdictions, but was not fully implemented until three decades later when the concept re-emerged in the 1980s.

This time, however, ISP was a way to keep tighter control on probationers and parolees and alleviate jail and prison crowding caused by abrupt changes in sentencing practices. Officers who supervised ISP clients had smaller caseloads to allow each officer greater contact in hopes that it would enhance public safety. Although smaller caseloads were found to provide increased surveillance and control, they also increased the detection for technical violations which led to a return to prison (Steiner 2004). In fact, ISP recidivism rates were no different than for parolees using traditional supervision methods. When compared to regular probationers, ISP recidivism rates were higher (Brown, 2007). Critics pointed to a net widening effect, particularly for those selected for ISP who were not necessarily chosen from a high-risk, high-need offender pool as originally purported but may have been only be medium risk or have medium-level needs (Reichel and Sudbrack 1994). All indicators pointed to a bleak outlook for ISP that was in danger of being eliminated.

EVALUATIONS OF ISP

The costs of ISP programs are definitely greater than regular probation, but the key to assessing the efficacy of ISP lies in whether it can produce a cost savings over those destined for prison. Most evaluation studies have shown that ISP, as currently administered, is not cost effective. Technical violations that sent ISP offenders to prison doubled the actual cost of ISP (Petersilia and Turner 1993a). ISP offenders were rearrested at about the same rate and posed no greater or less risk to public safety than did prisoners on work release (Deschenes, Turner, and Petersilia 1995). This study, along with dozens of others, reaffirmed the potential of ISP to widen the net and increase costs for offenders who actually pose a low risk.

ISP programs have gone the route of boot camps—that is, if the programs wanted to remain open, they had to show some type of positive result such as cost savings, reduced recidivism, and the like. Since control and surveillance alone were shown to be less effective than combining surveillance and treatment components, the programs had to adapt accordingly.

Adapting ISP for Success with Specialized Caseloads   Important changes emerged to save ISP from extinction, many of which are contained in evidence-based practices. First and foremost was to combine intensive supervision with intensive forms of cognitive-behavioral treatment to significantly lower recidivism. Second was to choose high-risk offenders as opposed to low-risk offenders for ISP. High-risk offenders, who are twice as likely to be rearrested while on supervision, can be differentiated beforehand from low-risk offenders (Hanley, 20002). Providing more treatment services to the *high*-risk clients (as opposed to the low-risk clients) is important. However, failure to comply with treatment is the primary reason for program failure; it is defined by missing sessions or testing positive for drug use (Brown 2007). There must be clear guidelines that treat change as a process and allow for a certain degree of noncompliance to allow offenders (especially those who are not dangerous) to complete the program. Direct contact with the offender in the form of personal visits and phone contact (considered more "surveillance" activity) will increase the chances of program completion (Hanley 2002). Perhaps this is why programs with a treatment philosophy had higher rates of noncompletion than programs with a focus on surveillance (Brown 2007). The important measurement is not rate of program failure from technical violations, but rate of rearrest. High-risk offenders who were exposed to appropriate services to address criminogenic needs had less new crimes and rearrests (Bonta, Wallace-Capretta, and Rooney 2000; Hanley 2002; Paparozzi and Gendreau 2005).

Moving to Specialized Caseloads   The method by which cases are initially assigned to an officer's caseload has been integral to further success. ISP officers are assigned cases based on offense type first, and then based on geographic zip code. Supervising offenders of the same type of crime allows officers to become true experts in both supervision and treatment for this particular type of client. Specialized caseloads are showing some satisfying results. Compared to regular probationers, domestic violence offenders on ISP were less likely to be arrested for any new crime over a two-year period of supervision. Sanctions for probation violators were stricter in the ISP program than on regular probation (Johnson 2001). The size of the experimental group was small (25 in the ISP and 32 in the comparison group), so the results are not conclusive.

A matched sample of 240 ISP parolees was compared with 240 high-risk, high-needs parolees on traditional supervision. The ISP group had more technical violations but fewer new convictions than the traditional parolees who received fewer treatment services. This study and the previous one on domestic violence offenders suggest that cognitive–behavioral treatment interventions can reduce recidivism in high-risk, high-need populations in the community.

House Arrest

House arrest is an intermediate sanction designed to confine pretrial detainees or convicted offenders to their homes during the hours when they are not at work, attending a treatment program, or visiting a supervising officer. Defendants who cannot afford bail and who do not qualify for release on personal recognizance may be considered for house arrest. For convicted offenders, house arrest is typically either a condition of ISP or is coupled with electronic monitoring.

PURPOSES OF HOME DETENTION

House arrest is otherwise known as home detention or home confinement; it is neither a new concept nor a U.S. innovation. Galileo (1564–1642) was placed under house arrest by church authorities for his heretical assertion that the earth revolved around the sun. House arrest programs proliferated in the United States in the 1980s as an alternative to incarceration for pretrial detainees and a means of easing jail overcrowding while ensuring appearance in court. The purpose of house arrest is not, however, to deter or to reduce recidivism (Jones and Ross 1997).

Offenders remain within the confines of their home during specified hours ranging from 24-hour-per-day confinement to imposition of late-night curfews. Most states and the federal system now operate some form of house arrest program. California, Florida, Georgia, Kentucky, Oklahoma, and Oregon all make extensive use of this option. Florida's "community controllees" (those under house arrest) are required to maintain employment and to participate in self-improvement programs, such as a general equivalency diploma (GED) program to obtain a high school diploma, drug and alcohol counseling, or other "life skills" programs. Many

House Arrest
A community-based sanction in which offenders serve their sentence at home. Offenders have curfews and may not leave their home except for employment and correctional treatment purposes. Also called home detention or home confinement.

are required to perform community service as well. When they are not participating in work, self-help programs, or community service, they must be at home.

Florida's community control officer caseloads are limited by statute to 20 offenders, and the officers work weekends and holidays. They are required to make a minimum of 28 contacts per month with each offender for a period not to exceed twenty-four months. Officers' schedules vary from day to day, resulting in regular but random visits with the offenders. If an offender is not where he or she should be at any particular time, a violation of community control is reported to the court. Some house arrest programs randomly call offenders, and a computer verifies the offender's unique voice electronically. If the voice is that of another person or a tape-recorded voice of the offender, the computer will register an unauthorized absence. Too many unauthorized absences may result in a technical violation of probation and time in jail.

CRITICISMS OF HOUSE ARREST

The first criticism directed at house arrest is that it does not seem to be a punishment. Staying at home for most people is considered a luxury and not a negative experience. The courts recognize that home confinement is not the same as jail or prison confinement, and therefore time spent on home confinement awaiting trial as a pretrial detainee cannot be counted as time served toward the conviction, as jail time is for other pretrial detainees (*People v. Ramos* 1990). In some jurisdictions, home detention is considered a part of probation, and time spent is counted. However, as with probation, if house arrest is revoked, time served on home confinement does not apply. Thus, if an offender with a one-year sentence to home confinement fails to complete the program, and his home arrest is revoked, he must begin his one-year sentence in jail and serve the full term.

Another argument is that the intrusiveness of house arrest violates a pretrial detainee's constitutional right to privacy in the home, especially one occupied by other family members. To get around this, house arrest for pretrial defendants is voluntary, so if the offender does not agree to the conditions, he or she will be resentenced to another sanctioning option. A convicted offender's privacy rights, however, are not violated by the use of house arrest and/or electronic monitoring.

Potential risks with house arrest are that offenders can still commit crimes from their residence. For example, pretrial detainees and probationers have been arrested for selling drugs out of their homes. Since customers came to the house and the detainee never left home, no violations were recorded. If it were not for suspicious neighbors calling the police, these probationers might have been able to continue selling drugs without getting caught for some time.

Another challenge of house arrest is that domestic violence incidents may erupt. Because the offender is home all the time and cannot leave the house to "cool off," some offenders take out their frustrations on family members. Several community control officers in Florida report that it is not unusual for the spouse of an individual on house arrest to complain that he or she cannot stand another day with the husband or wife at home all day. And according to the officers, several house arrestees have requested that they be sent to prison instead of continuing on house arrest. One told his supervising officer, "If I have to spend any more time with my old lady, I'll probably kill her. Send me on down to Raiford [the state prison]."

Considerable self-discipline is required to comply with house arrest, and many offenders are impulsive by nature and may be unable to sustain the required behavior for long periods.

EFFECTIVENESS OF HOUSE ARREST

Given that house arrest is an enhancement for probation or parole and has more conditions than routine supervision, house arrest suffers from many of the same problems as ISP. Offenders on house arrest are twice as likely as regular parolees to have their parole revoked for a technical violation (Palumbo, Clifford, and Snyder-Joy 1992).

For defendants awaiting trial, house arrest was paired with electronic monitoring to relieve jail overcrowding. The program accepted only 24 percent of those referred for screening, excluding people without telephones, parole violators, absconders, people with pending warrants, and those with a history of violence. Of the 256 people who were accepted, 73 percent successfully completed the program. Of those who failed to complete the house arrest program, 13 percent were technical violators and 14 percent absconded (Maxfield and Baumer 1990). If we compare failure rates and absconding rates with other pretrial programs for state offenders, the rates are comparable.

On a positive note, house arrest allows pretrial defendants the chance to keep working and supporting their families without interruption caused by incarceration. Harjit Sandhu and his colleagues (1993) conducted a unique program comparison between offenders sentenced to house arrest and another group of offenders sentenced to a residential community corrections facility (RCCF). The RCCF residents had done time in prison and were within six to nine months of being released on parole. RCCF residents lived at the facility and paid room and board, whereas house arrestees lived at home but did not wear electronic monitoring devices. The RCCF residents had to look for new jobs following their release from prison whereas those on house arrest most likely retained their present jobs. A significantly higher percent of CTC residents (51 percent) were unemployed compared with people on house arrest (17 percent). A follow-up one year later indicated that despite a significantly more serious criminal history, offenders on house arrest had lower recidivism rates than offenders sentenced to the residential community treatment center. The author attributes the differences in success rates to house arrestees having stable employment and family lives, which may have given them greater motivation to succeed in order to avoid going to prison (Sandhu, Dodder, and Mathur 1993). Although the high rate of current employment of offenders on house arrest appeared to contribute to their success, many RCCF offenders who failed were unemployed. Another important difference is that those on house arrest were helping their own household, while offenders at the RCCF facility may have had less motivation to pay rent to a facility.

Today, most house arrest programs are paired with some form of electronic monitoring, so let's examine this correctional technology.

Electronic Monitoring and Global Positioning Systems

Imagine this scenario: Samson has been in prison for the last three years, convicted of reckless endangerment. Samson was paroled from prison on the condition that for the first year he wears an electronic device that fits snugly around his ankle. The ankle device is waterproof and shock proof, and Samson must wear the device even while showering and sleeping. A transmitter in Samson's ankle bracelet emits a continuous signal to his personal receiver, which is attached to the phone lines at his residence. This receiver only transmits to Samson's ankle device and to no other. If the signal is lost for any reason—say if Samson moves

Ankle monitoring devices can transmit either to home-based receivers using radio frequencies or via global positioning satellite system to a receiver carried around the waist.

© Spencer Grant/PhotoLibrary

beyond 500 feet from his device—the transmitter is unable to communicate with the receiver, and the receiver automatically calls in to a centralized computer. The computer checks to see if the absence of the signal is authorized or unauthorized. The absence is authorized if Samson has received prior permission from his parole officer, for example, to go out looking for a job or is at work during his scheduled hours. If the absence is unauthorized, his parole officer is automatically notified. Samson has a curfew, and he still must visit his parole officer, who checks the device to make sure Samson has not tried to tamper with it or remove it in any way. Samson must get permission prior to going anywhere, so he has to plan everything in advance.

Samson's sanction is called **home-based electronic monitoring** system, as it operates from radio frequencies through phone lines. **Electronic monitoring** (EM) is a correctional technology used in intensive supervision probation, specialized parole, day reporting centers, and house arrest. EM can also be used for pretrial detainees; that is, for defendants who have not yet been convicted but require an elevated level of supervision while out on bond or pretrial supervision (see Figure 9.1). EM is a technological means of assuring that certain conditions of probation, such as curfew, are met. In the federal system, convicted EM offenders were monitored between one and six months, whereas pretrial detainees were monitored up to nine months. State offenders wore an EM transmitter for a shorter time—an average of four months (Camp, Camp, and May 2003).

Home-Based Electronic Monitoring
An intermittent or continuous radio frequency signal transmitted through a land line telephone or wireless unit into a receiver that determines whether the offender is or is not at home.

Electronic Monitoring
A correctional technology used as a tool in intensive supervision probation, parole, day reporting, or home confinement, using a radio frequency or satellite technology to track offender whereabouts using a transmitter and receiver.

HISTORY OF ELECTRONIC MONITORING

Robert Schwitzgebel at the University of California developed electronic monitoring technology in the 1960s during the deinstitutionalization movement of the mentally ill. When thousands of mentally ill patients were released from mental hospitals, some were monitored in the community as an alternative to institutionalization (Roy 1997). The idea for use of EM devices in the criminal justice system was inspired by New Mexico judge Jack Love, who saw how the comic book character Spiderman was tracked by a wrist transmitter. The judge persuaded a computer

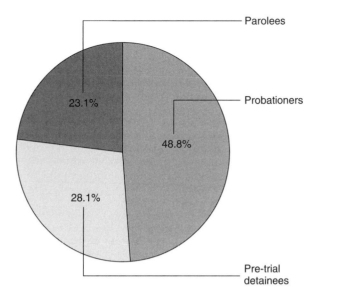

FIGURE 9.1 How Electronic Monitoring is Used

Source: American Probation and Parole Association. Accessed: http://www.appa-net.org/publications&resources/pubs/electronic_monitoring.pdf.

salesman to develop the device. The wrist device was first tried in 1983 for offenders convicted of driving under the influence (DUI) and white-collar crimes at a time when cell phones were not the norm (Vollum and Hale 2002). These wrist devices had to be worn at all times. When the probation office called the house, offenders verified their whereabouts by turning their palm up and inserting the wrist device into a receiver that sat next to the telephone. These early units are called passive radio frequency electronic monitoring systems because they only verify if the offender is or is not at home through radio waves.

Problems of Early Homebound EM   Early electronic monitoring programs required that offenders had a landline telephone—something critics asserted discriminated against indigent offenders who could not afford landline service. A second drawback was that passive EM was only able to track whether an offender was or was not within a certain number of feet of the receiver connected to the offender's telephone. Home-bound EM systems were not able to track where offenders went once they left their home. The earliest wrist systems were not unique to each offender and more than one wrist system could be used on the same monitoring system. Thus, there was no guarantee that the probation office was actually communicating with the "correct" person (Greek 2002). Technical and electric problems such as bad wiring, close proximity to radio stations, power outages, and call-waiting and call-forwarding features caused problems with the transmitter being able to send and receive the required information to central control. Certain areas could not receive transmissions, such as bathtubs or some body positions (e.g., sleeping in the fetal position) that would ultimately cause false alarms. As these problems were slowly addressed, the technology improved greatly. Home-based ankle devices are still in frequent use today and have become sturdier, with fewer problems (see Box 9.1 for the latest updates on home-based systems).

A single home-based EM transmitter and receiver system costs $50,000 for the equipment, plus operating costs. Offenders help subsidize the operating costs by paying a monthly fee of $10 per day. The cost effectiveness of electronic monitoring depends on the custody level of the comparison group and how revocations are handled.

BOX 9.1 TECHNOLOGY IN CORRECTIONS

Advances in Electronic Monitoring

Electronic monitoring (EM) is used more frequently than global positioning monitoring at this time because of cost. As a result, we will discuss four options that exist for EM. First is *voice verification monitoring.* Monitoring occurs throughout the day and/or night by means of a special pager or random calls made to particular locations at specific times to verify an offender's presence. When the pager beeps, the offender must immediately call the probation or parole office. Through voice verification, the computer ensures a positive match between the voice template (the official voice version made at the probation office) and the voice on the phone. The computer records whether or not the voice matched and the phone number from which the call originated (Gowen 2001). The offender doesn't know the number of the pager, so no one else but the computer and the officer can page the offender.

A second advancement is *group monitoring.* Individual home-based systems still exist, but now there are ways that a single receiver can monitor up to 75 clients at one time. This makes it possible for community facilities such as halfway houses and group homes to detect the presence or absence of clients out to a 300 foot range and would prevent temporary unauthorized absences and allow facilities to better detect a "walk-away"/escape (BI Inc., 2009).

A third improvement in EM is *cellular communication* that addresses an earlier criticism that EM discriminates against people who cannot afford land lines or cellular phones. Now, with BI Home Cell®, there is no need for a phone; only a single working electrical outlet is required. The company developed a modified receiver that was compatible with a cellular unit that enables data to be transmitted wirelessly (BI Inc., 2009).

Finally, **remote location monitoring systems** are handheld portable receiving devices that an officer uses to monitor offenders on his or her caseload to intercept the offender's monitor signals. This enables officers to drive by an offender's house (or work) randomly to verify where the offender is without stopping to see him or her in person. Remote monitoring reportedly increases officer efficiency by reducing data entry time and providing real-time access (Gowen 2001).

Source: BI Inc. (2009). BI products and services. Retrieved at: http://www.bi.com; Gowen, Darren. 2001. Remote location monitoring—A supervision strategy to enhance risk control. *Federal Probation* 65(2): 38–41.

GLOBAL POSITIONING SYSTEMS

Remote Location Monitoring
When a supervising officer uses a hand-held remote receiver to wirelessly verify an offender's physical location.

Global Positioning System
A system that uses 24 military satellites orbiting the earth to pinpoint the offender's exact location intermittently or at all times.

Active GPS
A real-time GPS system that transmits data through wireless networks continuously at a rate of once or twice per minute. A phone line continually calls a reporting station to update the offender's location, which is tracked by a computer.

The most sophisticated technology for monitoring offenders in the community is **global positioning systems** (GPS). GPS uses 24 military satellites that orbit the earth and 5 ground control stations to pinpoint locations anywhere in the world using data coordinates. Here's how it works: offenders wear a permanent ankle bracelet, and they also carry a GPS receiver containing a microprocessor and antennae and a battery charging unit. The external equipment is small enough to fit in a waist pack or purse, but the offender must always be within a certain distance (e.g., 50–150 feet) of the portable receiver (Greek 2002). The GPS portable receiver replaces the receiver that was plugged into the landline phone on the home-bound systems. The transmitter and receiver serves as the medium between the satellite and the central control unit that monitors offender locations. Some systems integrate the receiver and transmitter as one component on the bracelet (Armstrong and Freeman 2009).

The way the receiver records data and how often the data are transmitted determines the type of GPS system. **Active GPS** systems transmit the data through wireless networks used by cell phones. Active systems are also known as **real-time** units because data can be transmitted often with a short lag time. The offender's transmitter emits a radio frequency signal once or twice per minute. At once per minute, there are 1,400 track points in a 24-hour period. A phone line continually calls a reporting station to update the offender's location, which is tracked by a computer.

Cell phones work as a means of transmission only in areas where cell phone service is supported by a cellular network. Rural areas without good cell phone capability are limited to other options.

In a **passive GPS system**, the daytime tracking data is temporarily stored and downloaded at night through a land-line phone while the offender is sleeping. Some systems require the offender to bring in the equipment periodically for a download to an off-site monitoring center that permanently stores the data. In either case, knowledge about alerts and violations is delayed by as much as twenty-four hours later. Hybrid systems combine elements of active and passive systems, in that alert data is transmitted once every six to twelve hours, but violation data is transmitted immediately.

How Do the Zones Work? The microprocessor inside the receiver also allows the probation officer to use software to program in **exclusion zones** and/or **inclusion zones** (Gowen 2001). Thus, an offender on probation for an offense related to his compulsive gambling habit would not be allowed to enter any casino without the device sounding an unauthorized area alarm. Another exclusion zone would be the residence and workplace of an identified victim. In contrast, an inclusion zone allows the officer to program in the offender's work schedule, special appointments, and other events so that the computer can verify the location as it occurs. If necessary, the officer is alerted if the offender enters an exclusion zone, as in the case of an assaultive offender who has gone near his or her victim.

Each offender, according to his or her crime and work schedule, has personally defined restricted areas and people that constitute when a violation is committed. In each GPS system, notification methods are different. In some systems, all alerts are transmitted from in-house monitoring centers to the supervising officer's pagers; it is the responsibility of the officer to check each alert to determine what happened. Reasons for alerts vary widely, and it is not always initially apparent why the alert occurred. Serious alerts result if the offender enters an exclusion zone, enters an inclusion zone at a time other than what the schedule dictates, or attempts to tamper with or remove the unit. Other reasons for a registered alert could be battery failure or technical failure such as when through no fault of the offender, signal is blocked and cannot be received. One study reported that *each offender* averages approximately three to four alerts every month (Armstrong and Freeman 2009). If an officer is supervising twenty offenders, that averages to two alerts per day. Which system registers more false alarms, the active or passive GPS, is open to question. One study in Florida found passive GPS to register three times more false alarms than active systems (Levin 2008b), while active and passive systems in Arizona seemed to register similar numbers and types of alerts (Armstrong and Freeman 2009). One concern about the high number of alerts, particularly those for equipment failure, is the reliability and shortcomings of the equipment. With the high number of alerts, there may be a tendency for officers to become complacent over time, like the boy who cried "wolf."

Authorities can potentially use EM and GPS to solve crimes by tracing the offender's whereabouts. In a boat theft case in Tampa, police were able to prove that a suspect was at the scene of the crime at the exact same time the theft was committed. The suspect was on EM for felony grand theft (Kalfrin 2008). As an extra bonus, some units even allow officers to text message or leave a voice message directly to the receiver worn by the offender. Examples of different GPS systems are:

- VeriTracks® by Virginia-based Veridian Corporation
- SMART® (Satellite Monitoring and Remote Tracking) by Pro Tech Monitoring Inc.
- Exacutrac® by Colorado-based BI, Inc.

Real-time
Instant and immediate access via a supervising officer's internet connection to pinpoint the exact location of offenders on GPS monitoring with a 30-second delay.

Passive GPS
A GPS system that temporarily stores location data that is downloaded through a landline phone once every 24 hours or at specific times when the offender is home.

Exclusion Zones
Exact locations the offender is prohibited from being in or near.

Inclusion Zones
Exact locations, such as employment, school, or an appointment, where the offender is required to be at a certain time.

TABLE 9.1   Electronic Monitoring Techniques for Various Offender Risk Levels

Risk Level	Type of System	Contact Frequency	Verification
Low	Remote pager	Random/infrequent	Phone call/pager
Low/Medium	Home-based system	Programmed or random	Phone call/pager & voice verification
Medium/High	Hybrid (pager and home-based system)	Frequent/random	Phone call/pager & voice verification
High	GPS/satellite	Continuous	GPS signals
			Emitted exclusion/ inclusion zones
			Video camera at home

Source: Adapted from Darren Gowen. 2001. Remote Location Monitoring—A Supervision Strategy to Enhance Risk Control. *Federal Probation* 65(2): 39.

For What Types of Offenders is GPS Intended?   GPS is authorized in nearly every state in the U.S., but most states allow its use only for sex offenders. Of these, ten states require that high-risk sex offenders be monitored for *life* using GPS or EM (Armstrong and Freeman 2009). Another five states allow GPS for a wider variety of offenses—both sexual and non-sexual—although only for the term of supervision. The type of technology used, whether it is EM or GPS, depends solely on the client's offense and risk level (see Table 9.1).

Limitations of GPS   The drawbacks to GPS technology include loss of GPS signal, short battery lives, and cost. Despite the advances in technology, in more remote areas where cell phone service is weak or unavailable, radio frequency EM is a more reliable option. Even in urban areas, the receiver has trouble picking up the signal from the satellite in some locations (for example, in a basement of a high-rise office building or between buildings). In addition, in cell phone "dead spots" the offender's receiver is unable to make the repeated cell phone calls to the central station with updates (Turner et al., 2007).

GPS is not completely foolproof. For instance, a motivated offender could cut through the ankle device with specialized tools. The primary drawback, though, is cost. Real-time active GPS systems cost $10–$16 for the equipment, while passive GPS costs $5 per day, which is still less expensive than building new facilities, especially as older facilities become too expensive to repair (Levin 2008b). Greek (2002) suggests cutting costs by using passive GPS, which records data only once every 10 to 15 minutes rather than continuously and/or downloading the daily location information at night while the receiver is recharging.

Other Uses of Satellite Technology   As the cost of using GPS decreases and as cell phone service improves in rural areas, the number of offenders supervised using satellites will increase in the future. Box 9.2 discusses the issue of microchips surgically implanted under the skin of offenders under correctional supervision.

Another avenue that is currently being pursued is the use of a video camera hooked up to a computer with Internet access. Offenders under this system would be required to step in front of the camera when beeped or called. The video camera allows for interaction (for example, a weekly meeting) between a probation officer and the offender.

With the technological advances made in computers and satellites, the potential for offender tracking is limitless. Box 9.3 examines how electronic monitoring can be combined with less invasive methods to measure alcohol levels for DUI offenders.

BOX 9.2   TECHNOLOGY IN CORRECTIONS

A Microchip off the Ole Cell Block: Are Surgical Microchips a Violation of Offender Privacy?

British ministers are considering surgically implanting microchips beneath the skin of offenders supervised in the community. The chips are the same ones that are used to track pets, cattle, luggage, and cars. "The tags, injected into the back of the arm with a hypodermic needle, consist of a toughened glass capsule holding a computer chip, a copper antenna and a capacitor that transmits data stored on the chip when prompted by an electromagnetic reader" (Brady 2008. p. 1). The tags are reportedly beginning to be used with humans in limited conditions, such as tracking gang members within jails, entry into secure locations, or voluntary usage by customers of exclusive nightclubs (Brady 2008). The courts have not yet ruled on whether this practice is too invasive or violates privacy for community supervision.

Source: Brady, Brian. Prisoners to be chipped like dogs. *The Independent*, January 13, 2008. Retrieved from: http://www.independent.co.uk/news/uk/politics/prisoners-to-be-chipped-like-dogs-769977.html

BOX 9.3   TECHNOLOGY IN CORRECTIONS

Urine Trouble: Less Invasive Methods to Measuring Blood-Alcohol Content

Only about 10 percent of all offenders who used alcohol at the time of their offense were actually ordered to abstain from alcohol while on probation or parole. When clients are revoked for the use of alcohol or drugs, the courts will only accept results from urinalysis screenings. When an offender provides a urine sample, a staff member of the same sex is typically present to observe the procedure while the sample is collected, and the sample must be preserved in a cool environment so logistically it is not realistic to conduct urine tests that often. For the client who is ordered not to drink alcohol, other less invasive methods were devised to test blood alcohol (BAC) levels in the body on a more routine basis. One company developed a system they call SCRAM® (Secure Continuous Remote Alcohol Monitoring), while another device is called the Sobrietor®. SCRAM® combines EM with the use of transdermal technology to measure ethanol levels through perspiration (Kirby 2001). The measurements can occur randomly or continuously, and like EM or GPS, the ethanol readings can be communicated via a smart modem to a central monitoring station. The BI Sobrietor® is a handheld remote device that detects alcohol in the breath through a sample. The unit calibrates to the voice of the person being tested and compared to the baseline voiceprint already on file, and the individual must verify his or her voice while submitting a sample (Reuell 2008).

The ignition interlock system is a different method for testing DUI offenders, now mandatory in some states. Ignition interlocks are installed into vehicles through the ignition system and require the driver to submit to a breathalyzer before the car will start. Some require the driver to periodically blow into the interlock while driving. While the ignition interlock will disable a car if alcohol is detected, the other systems can measure alcohol levels when the offender is not driving. One concern with all of these systems is whether the correct offender is being tested. Combining the ignition interlock with image transmission and voice verification has improved the validity of the test. In either case, the offender's picture is taken or voice is recorded at the same time he or she submits to the test.

Tissue spectroscopy is the latest new technological development in measuring BAC levels by modifying a glucose monitoring device into a BAC testing device. This technique ". . . measures a person's BAC [on the inner forearm] through a sensor pad that detects light reflected from capillaries in the middle layers of the skin. The amount of infrared light wavelengths reflected through the skin is affected by alcohol consumption" (Levin 2008b, p. 6). Tissue spectroscopy is currently being developed for commercial use.

Sources: Levin, Marc A. 2008b. Five technological solutions for Texas' correctional and law enforcement challenges. *Texas Public Policy Foundation Policy Perspective* (June). Retrieved from: http://www.texaspolicy.com; Phillips, Kirby. 2001. Reducing Alcohol-Related Crime Electronically. *Federal Probation* 65(2): 42–44; Reuell, Peter. 2008. High-tech device knows when you're not sober. *The Metrowest Daily News*, February 10, 2008. Retrieved from: http://www.metrowestdailynews.com/multimedia/

How Do People Feel About EM/GPS?   Electronic monitoring has had its share of critics, from those who are concerned that the widespread use of electronic monitoring has resulted in net widening to those with ethical concerns that private companies are profiting from electronic monitoring equipment for correctional supervision technology (Lilly 2006; Nellis 2006). For the most part, as technology has become more precise in tracking the offender's whereabouts, the general public has become more confident and supportive of its use for offenders.

Probation officers supported the use of electronic monitoring as a tool for increased field supervision and visits, but also said that increased contact meant more paperwork. One officer said:

> "They're getting seen at least weekly. Sometimes, you know, if people are not compliant or doing what they're supposed to be doing, they're being seen maybe twice a week. . . There's a lot of requirements by the court. . . assessments, and get treatment, and get evaluations, and attend meetings... [and] everything has to be verified. Like grocery shopping, we need to know where they are going. It has to be the closest store. We need to see their receipts the following time. . . If they got a window [of free time], you're responsible for where they're supposed to be." (Martin, Hanrahan, and Travers 2008, p. 9).

Officers also said that because of the regulations, there is a high probability of violations. The trend now in EM is to use more graduated sanctions for technical violators and reserve jail time as a last resort.

Offenders on EM as an alternative to jail preferred EM over jail in every case, although offenders reported that they experienced limitations on spontaneity, felt a loss of control over their freedom, suffered shame from this sanction, and some experienced family problems from constantly being at home. EM was viewed as less controlling than jail and as a second chance sanction, allowing offenders to remain productive in the community (Payne and Gainey 2004). Offenders have raised legal and constitutional issues regarding electronic monitoring, but the courts have consistently rejected them or were not ready to review them (*U.S. v. Balon* 2004). Equal protection and due process arguments have also been raised without success. EM and GPS has so far passed constitutional muster and has become an often-used alternative to imprisonment.

EMPIRICAL EVALUATIONS OF EM AND GPS

EM program completion rates are quite impressive—97 percent completed the EM period of their probation successfully, and 80 percent completed the entire term of their probation (Lilly et al. 1992). Completion rates for convicted nonviolent federal offenders were higher (89 percent) than for pretrial detainees and community supervision violators (77 percent and 75 percent, respectively). The four reasons pretrial drug offenders and supervision violators were most likely to fail were unauthorized leave of the area (return later), flight/absconding (whereabouts unknown), arrest for a new crime, and tampering with EM equipment (Gowen 2000). Program completion rates decreased after 180 days, so it seems there is a threshold as to how long offenders can be under EM or GPS (Roy 1994).

Empirical evaluations support the notion that EM technology makes a difference in how offenders act *while under supervision* when compared with similar offenders on traditional probation or parole. Florida offenders ($n = 75,661$ total) who were placed under one of two types of electronic monitoring (home-based and GPS monitoring) were separated into groups by type of sentence (for example, EM as a probation violation sanction, EM as a post-prison sentence, or a direct sentence to EM) and measured while under supervision. Offenders on EM were more likely to complete the terms of supervision and less likely to commit technical violations and new crimes than those in a comparison group. In addition, home-based EM was as effective as GPS in significantly reducing the likelihood of technical violation, committing new crimes, and absconding while under supervision. A California study of high-risk sex offenders found that GPS parolees had about the same rate of recidivism as other high-risk sex offenders on traditional parole supervision (Turner et al., 2007).

Long-Term Effects   There is some support for the claim that EM widens the net of penal control for some drug offenders, but not for violent and property offenders (Padgett, Bales, and Blomberg 2006). Padgett and her colleagues suggest that EM is effective for monitoring serious offenders, but the long-term recidivism rates after supervision has ended remain unclear at this point. One study of recidivism after supervision ended found that EM tracked offenders generally had similar rates of rearrest as offenders who served their full sentence in jail or prison. When federal offenders on EM were compared with federal offenders in a halfway house, rearrest rates were similar while on supervision. Within one year of release from supervision, EM participants were less likely than halfway house clients to be rearrested. Although drug use between the two groups of program participants was similar, EM offenders maintained more continuous employment than halfway house residents (Klein-Saffran 1992).

Gender Differences   It seems that gender and family conditions play a significant role in the outcome of EM sentences. Men who lived with a significant other while on EM reported receiving positive family support and help with dependent children, but women offenders reported that significant others were a source of stress and conflict impacting their success on EM. The women offenders perceived little support from their partner in assisting them with the child care role. The lack of freedom to leave home because of EM affected women's primary caretaker role for dependent children (Maidment 2002). Clearly, with offenders spending much more time at home, some situations improve whereas other situations worsen.

Success with EM and GPS seems to depend on identifying the type of individual, home, and work situation that creates the most ideal environment for completion without a risk to the public. EM and GPS offer tremendous potential for community supervision, although some caution that perceived expectations of GPS are perhaps greater than its performance capabilities at this time (Armstrong and Freeman 2009). In a work in progress where officers were interviewed, the researchers found "Agents consistently said that GPS monitoring cannot stop sex offending behavior… [and it is still unclear] whether GPS creates a false sense of security (Turner et al., 2007, p. 19). We predict that EM and GPS technology will further improve and become more reliable in the future, but will there be a threshold at which we have to decide as a society how much invasion of our privacy are we willing to accept for that accuracy?

Day Reporting Centers

Day reporting centers (DRCs) are a type of outpatient program based on a three-phase levels system where offenders report daily for a variety of treatment programs, itinerary, and random drug testing. Day reporting centers are like a "one-stop shop" with all the resources and educational programs in one place. The staff to offender ratio is low, with about one staff member to every fourteen clients served

Day Reporting Centers
Nonresidential programs typically used for defendants on pretrial release, for convicted offenders on probation or parole, or as an increased sanction for probation or parole violators. Services are provided in one central location, and offenders must check in daily.

Day reporting centers combine education and vocational training with group counseling in a highly structured program setting, such as this evening anger management group session.

(Craddock 2009). DRCs are also open extended hours to accommodate offenders who work days and evenings. Some jurisdictions (e.g., Nebraska and Indiana) use day reporting for defendants on pretrial release (Kim et al. 2007, 2008), and other states (such as North Carolina and New Jersey) use DRCs as a reentry mechanism for prisoners coming out on parole (Craddock 2009) or as an increased sanction for probation or parole violators. Parent (1995) noted that:

> If policy makers want DRCs to reduce prison and jail crowding, they should use day reporting as an early release mechanism and should let corrections officials [or bail officers rather than sentencing judges] select inmates for DRC placement. Among inmates released early, DRCs should be used for those who pose the greatest risk to the public or who have the most serious problems that are likely to impair their adjustment. To reduce total costs, officials should use less structured and less expensive forms of supervision for low-risk, low-need inmates who are granted early release. (pp. 127–128)

"Day centres" have been popular in England and Wales since the 1970s and began to appear in the United States in 1985. Juveniles were already exposed to day treatment centers established in the United States, so the concepts were applied for adults. Connecticut and Massachusetts were among the first states to adopt day reporting centers with the goal of reducing jail or prison crowding and providing a closer level of supervision than traditional probation or parole. *Most DRC programs exist in states that do not have ISP as a sentencing option* (Parent et al. 1995). DRCs primarily provide services for felony offenders, but vary widely on what types of offenses each accepts. For example, the Maricopa County, Arizona, DRC rejected applicants for any of the following reasons: victim injury, use of a weapon, sex offense, history of violence, escape risk, pending charges/warrant/hold, prosecutorial objection, nonverifiable residence, and refusal to participate. On the other hand, one of the largest DRCs in the country in Harris County, Texas, will accept higher risk offenders such as sex offenders, stalkers, boot camp graduates, mentally ill offenders, developmentally disabled offenders, probation/parole violators, and graduates of therapeutic communities. This center processes up to 2,000 offenders

BOX 9.4   COMMUNITY CORRECTIONS UP CLOSE

A Typical Day Reporting Experience

John, 28 years old and unemployed, is arrested for possession of cocaine. He is sentenced to probation, but during that time he misses several meetings with his probation officer and tests positive for drug use. Rather than punishing John for this probation violation by sending him to the state prison, which is already 10 percent over capacity, the judge assigns him to a nearby DRC. The DRC, which the state judicial department began operating two years ago, accepts John because, based on his history and offense, he is of small risk to the community and is in need of drug abuse treatment and other services. Furthermore, by keeping John under community supervision, the judge avoids adding to the already high prison population.

John begins the first phase of the three-phase program in June. For the first three weeks, he must report to the DRC five times each week, where he twice is tested for drug use. The program is open from 8 A.M. to 6 P.M. Monday through Friday and from 9 A.M. to 1 P.M. on Saturdays. When he is not at the center, John must remain at home except to do errands that he has already planned on a weekly itinerary on record at the DRC. Program staff telephone John several times during the day to monitor his whereabouts and ensure that he is abiding by his 8 P.M. curfew. Once a week, staff also makes an unannounced visit to his home. John also begins to attend drug abuse education classes, GED classes, job skills training, and group counseling sessions, conducted on-site by program staff. In addition, twice a week he goes to a drug abuse outpatient clinic, referred by the DRC.

In the middle of his second week, John misses a counseling session and a GED class. Instead of moving to the second, more lenient, phase at the end of the third week, John must remain under the more intensive form of supervision for an additional week. Informed that another violation might land him in the state correctional facility, he subsequently commits no other violations. By the end of June, he is ready to begin the second phase, during which he must continue with his drug abuse treatment and classes but report to the DRC only twice a week. In addition, he joins many of the other 90 offenders in performing several cleanup and construction projects around the city.

After three months without violating any regulations, John begins the third and final phase of the program, during which he reports to the DRC only once a week. With assistance from a job placement agency that offers its services at the DRC, he finds employment with the state parks system. By the end of November, he has been released from the DRC. The cost to the state of his placement in the DRC has been half of what it likely would have been had he been incarcerated, and John seems on his way to making a more productive contribution to society.

Source: Dale Parent et al. 1995. *Day Reporting Centers* (vol. 1). Washington, DC: U.S. Department of Justice, National Institute of Justice, p. 23.

---

per day. Most DRCs are much smaller, with a daily capacity of between 40 to 85 offenders (Parent et al. 1995).

Box 9.4 tells the story of a typical experience at a day reporting center. Participants must report *every day* to the day center and be there from 9:00 to 5:00 P.M. While there, they participate in structured programming activities and get tested randomly for drugs. After three weeks, they can move to the second phase for one month where they can start looking for a part-time job, but they still continue to be involved in structured classes, community service, and are in touch with program staff by phone at least twice per day. By the time they get to Level 3, they must either be employed full time, be going to school full time, or a combination of both. They still visit the DRC three times per week and provide a daily itinerary (Kim et al. 2008). For probationers and parolees who do not take their supervision conditions seriously, other DRCs serve to provide enforcement or "muscle" without sending these people to jail or prison.

TREATMENT-ORIENTED VERSUS SUPERVISION-ORIENTED DRCs

The common theory behind DRCs is that offenders will stay out of trouble when they are occupied, especially with activities that will improve their chances for a more normal life—for example, by obtaining a GED or finding a job. DRCs all have the requirement of daily itinerary, attendance, and the phases (Kim et al. 2007). Because of the wide variety of clients that DRCs around the country serve, they also differ in their program goals. Some DRCs are more "treatment oriented" and others are more "supervision oriented" (Craddock 2009).

Treatment-oriented DRCs provide a wide range of services, all on an outpatient basis. The most common services were job-seeking skills/job placement, drug abuse education/treatment, psychological counseling, life skills training, and GED education classes/literacy. Other services provided by a smaller number of DRCs include parenting, anger management, vocational training, and transportation assistance. Once employed, offenders are still required to attend treatment programs at night or on weekends. Craddock (2009) noted that DRCs that focus on criminogenic needs outlined by risk assessment instruments will help increase program completion rates and reduce recidivism. Craddock found that "employment programming is the only component that predicts completion" (p. 130). Her findings also suggested that housing assistance be incorporated for parolees coming out of prison.

Supervision-oriented DRCs ensure that clients are abiding by the rules, ensure accountability through itineraries, and keep them busy so they do not have the time or opportunity to engage in criminal activity. "The itineraries state when clients are to leave home, their destinations, how they will travel (walk, drive, take the bus, or get a ride), when they are to arrive, and when they are to return home" (Anderson 1998, p. 63). Itineraries are important for two reasons. First, clients learn (some for the first time) how to plan their days in advance. Second, the DRCs can monitor where the clients are when random phone calls are placed via a computer. DRCs are authorized to give out Antabuse, a prescription medication prescribed for alcoholics that prevents the use of alcohol. Urine screenings and alco-sensor tests ensure that clients have not been using drugs. Another characteristic of DRCs is that many clients are on 24-hour electronic monitoring. As the clients remain longer in the program, DRCs may be able to give clients more freedom by removing the electronic monitoring device while they still remain on supervision. Many DRCs have a combination of both supervision and treatment orientations.

In many ways, DRCs are nonresidential versions of halfway houses because the two programs provide very similar services, except that DRC offenders live at home. Like most halfway houses, most DRCs are private facilities that contract out-to-state and local entities. Furthermore, contact between program staff and offenders in DRCs are for longer time periods than that with intensive supervision probation. ISP programs have more field visits (where the officer goes to the home or job site to visit the offender), but DRCs are actually more structured with EM, phone contact, and in-facility time because the offender comes to the center (Kim et al. 2007).

Sentences to DRCs range from forty days to twelve months, with an average of six months' duration (Parent 1995). The average daily cost per offender is $35. This would make the DRC more costly than traditional probation/parole, and even more expensive than ISP. However, DRCs cost less than residential treatment or incarceration in jail or prison (Parent et al. 1995). Much of the treatment program costs is absorbed by the DRC itself or by another agency. In one out of every four DRCs, offenders pay for their own drug treatment.

EVALUATIONS OF DRCS

Keep in mind that DRCs serve high-risk clients, and the offenders have a lot of responsibility in this program. Also remember that making it in a program is greatly influenced by local policy and practitioner decisions. Rearrest rates are more influenced by actual offender behavior.

Completion Rates   DRC programs seem notorious for lower completion rates compared to completion rates of other community-based programs. Termination rates averaged 50 percent within four to six months and ranged from 14 percent to 86 percent. Termination rates were higher for service-oriented programs than for supervision-oriented DRCs. Failure rates were also higher for programs longer than six months in duration (Craddock 2009). High fai'ure rates resulted because of the level of supervision intensity and the type of offender admitted to the program. Whereas work release programs accepted lower risk offenders, DRCs tended to accept probation and parole violators and other types of higher-risk clients (Parent 1995). As stated earlier, DRCs that focus on criminogenic needs, specifically employment and transitional housing, will help increase program completion rates (Craddock 2009).

Evaluations of European DRCs are roughly the same as those for U.S. DRCs. In one British study of more than 600 offenders in 38 DRC programs, 63 percent of offenders were reconvicted of a new crime within two years of being sentenced to a DRC (Mair, and Nee 1992). George Mair (1995) commented about this finding:

> On the face of it, this may look high, but the offenders targeted by centers represent a very high risk group in terms of probability of reconviction. Probation centers [DRCs] may be condemning themselves to what appears to be a high reconviction rate by successfully diverting offenders from custody, and this must be taken into consideration when interpreting the overall reconviction rate. (p. 137)

Perhaps it is more about who the clients are and whom they are compared against. DRC programs seem to fare well as a reentry program for prisoners, especially when compared against prisoners who are freed under no supervision and parolees under traditional parole. Even after controlling for demographics and prior criminal history, prisoners released with no supervision had a greater volume of arrests and were arrested faster than DRC clients (Ostermann 2009).

Does Time Spent in the DRC Make a Difference?   The Illinois Criminal Justice Authority tracked a treatment group of pretrial detainees who had participated in a DRC for 70 or more days and compared them with a group that had been eligible for the DRC but had participated for 10 days or less, but did not drop out of the program. Members of these two groups were tracked for three years in terms of their rearrest and reincarceration rates. The group with more time in the DRC (the 70 day and over group) was not only rearrested and reincarcerated at significantly lower rates than the control group, but they remained free for an average of 122 days longer than the control group (Martin, Lurigio, and Olson 2003).

However, researchers in Indiana and Utah found that offenders who were placed in the DRC for longer than 120 days were significantly less likely to complete the program as those who had 120 days or less in the DRC (Roy and Grimes 2002). So it seems that, while longer is better, the threshold for an ideal period of time for a DRC is more than 70 days but no longer than 120 days.

Predictors of DRC Failure   The Illinois Criminal Justice Authority was also interested in factors that predicted who would be rearrested and who would remain crime free. The researchers found that previous criminal history (more prior arrests), youth, and less time spent in the DRC program were the most significant predictors of rearrest following release from the DRC (Martin, Lurigio, and Olson 2003). Similar results in terms of age and criminal history were found elsewhere (Craddock 2009; Roy and Grimes 2002). In addition, employment was a key component that predicted program completion and reduced the likelihood of rearrest and reincarceration (Craddock 2009; Kim et al. 2007).

In sum, there is no one "right way" to operate a DRC or any of the programs discussed in this chapter. Each program has different goals and different kinds of clients. The key is to specifically define the goals of the program (for example, reduce institutional crowding, allow a graduated sanction for probationers, and the like) and then measure whether the program is achieving those goals and contributing to an improved quality of life for the society at large, for the offenders, and for the victims—a principle we discuss more in the next chapter.

SUMMARY

- ISP programs, if they operate with close supervision and little treatment intervention, will not produce cost savings and will not significantly decrease the number of prison beds.

- Technical violation rates are high with closer supervision and as a result, probation and parole enhancement ISP programs may increase the number of jail and prison commitments.

- Potential for ISP programs lies in offering significantly higher treatment intervention strategies in concert with intensive supervision to decrease the number of revocations and the number of new crimes committed while on supervision.

- House arrest by itself provides cost savings but does not deter criminal misconduct. The level of monitoring is minimal unless house arrest is combined with electronic monitoring.

- Technological advances made in the area of electronic monitoring include the use of computers and satellites to monitor offenders in the community. No matter what type of electronic monitoring system is currently used, all offenders must minimally wear an ankle-monitoring device, and they cannot tamper or remove the device without sounding an alarm to a central control station.

- Day reporting centers typically accept convicted offenders or pretrial detainees who require a higher level of supervision than clients under electronic monitoring or house arrest. Day reporting centers also provide all the services in one place and are the most costly type of nonresidential intermediate sanction, but DRCs still cost less than jail or prison.

- All forms of nonresidential programs are more effective when goals are clarified and target offender populations are more accurately defined to best meet offender needs without unduly compromising public safety.

DISCUSSION QUESTIONS

1. How does intensive supervision probation differ from regular probation?

2. What are the advantages and disadvantages of house arrest?

3. How does electronic monitoring support house arrest? What ethical and social criticisms are associated with EM?

4. How do electronic monitoring devices work? What are some of the technical problems associated with them?

5. What is at issue in the surveillance and treatment of sex offenders on probation or parole?

6. How are day reporting centers different from ISP?

7. Do day reporting centers accomplish their objectives?

8. Which of the intermediate sanctions discussed in this chapter are probation or parole enhancements, and which sanctions are true alternatives to prison?

9. Why should intermediate sanction programs have clear goals and objectives?

WEB SITES

American Correctional Association List of
Community Corrections Publications
www.aca.org/publications/home.asp

Juvenile ISP Programs
http://www.nicic.gov/library/018875

Sex Offender Risk and Needs Assessment (Canada)
http://www.csc-scc.gc.ca/text/pblct/forum/e091/
e091g-eng.shtml

Association for the Treatment of Sexual Abusers
http://www.atsa.com

Center for Sex Offender Management
http://www.csom.org

A Training Curriculum for Supervising
Sex Offenders in the Community
http://www.nicic.org/library/017636

Department of Community Justice: Adult
Sex Offender Supervision
http://www.co.multnomah.or.us/dcj/
acjsoffendersup.shtml

The Juvenile Electronic Monitoring Program of
Multnomah County
http://www.co.multnomah.or.us/dcj/jcj.shtml

Davidson County Day Reporting Center Evaluation
http://www.nicic.gov/library/period173

Evaluation of Maricopa County (Arizona) Day
Reporting Center
http://www.nhtsa.dot.gov/people/injury/alcohol/
repeatoffenders/eval_dayreport.html

Atlanta Georgia Day Reporting Center
http://www.dcor.state.ga.us/Divisions/Corrections/
ProbationSupervision/DayReporting.html

CASE STUDY EXERCISE

Intermediate Community Programs

In the following cases, you are the judge, and you must decide which form of intensive supervision community program (either any residential program from Chapter 8 or increased form of probation supervision from the options in Chapter 9) to send the offender to by considering the circumstances provided. Jail is not an option. After you have made your decision, defend your answer.

CASE A

John is a 29-year-old male who has been twice convicted of fraud by forging checks. His first conviction resulted in a sentence of five years; probation with an order to make restitution in the amount of $2,720. John made three payments of $230 each before absconding supervision. He turned up again after six months and was reinstated on probation by the Court after he promised to faithfully fulfill the terms of his supervision and to complete his restitution obligation. During his supervised release, he was in violation of probation conditions regularly and never completed his restitution payments. However, due to the fact that the state prison was seriously overcrowded, the Court did not revoke his probation and he was finally released from supervision.

The current case involves passing a forged check at a local grocery store in the amount of $624. Due to his previous failure on probation, the Court is concerned that he is not capable of following court-ordered probation conditions, yet does not want to commit him to the state prison or to a jail term. John has a wife and two small children and is their only source of support. He is currently employed as a house painter.

CASE B

Ricardo is a 23-year-old identified gang member of the Mexican Mafia, a Latino gang with roots in California and Texas. He has a history of criminal offenses including shoplifting, one motor vehicle theft, and three DUIs. Ricardo is not assaultive, but the group in which he is a member has been known to participate in assault and other violent methods. His file does not indicate his rank in the gang, but it shows he has been a member for at least six years. His current offense is larceny, involving theft from his former employer, a local carpet laying company. The probation report concludes that Ricardo needs more structure than can be gained from probation or intensive supervision but does not recommend a prison sentence due to his current nonviolent offense. The PSIR reports that Ricardo needs to learn discipline, good work habits, and respect for the rights of others and is concerned about his gang status.

CASE C

Jonas has been placed on probation for indecent sexual behavior with a 5-year-old boy. This is his first felony offense, with two prior misdemeanor offenses as an adult—1 count of indecent exposure and 1 count of misdemeanor theft. Jonas is now 20 years of age and lives with his maternal aunt, who was his guardian from the age of 12 until he turned 18.

Jonas has suffered emotional and sexual abuse as a child from his stepfather and mother for the first 6 years of his life when he became known to social services who investigated his case. This investigation resulted in his stepfather being charged with indecency with a child, and Jonas was placed in foster care. While in foster care over the next several years, he was adjudicated numerous times for fire setting and cruelty to animals, when he was finally sent to juvenile detention. While in detention at the age of 12, he tried to hurt himself and was removed to a padded cell for further assessment. Testing revealed that Jonas had attention deficit hyperactivity disorder and was prescribed Ritalin. He remained out of the system from the age of 12 until the age of 18 when he was arrested for indecent exposure.

His IQ was recently assessed using the Wechsler Abbreviated Scale of Intelligence (WASI test) and estimated to be 70 (verbal IQ was 72 and performance IQ at 73). His current communication and daily living skills are equal to that of an 8-year-old boy, and his socialization domain is equal to that of a 7-year-old child. He has a reduced capacity to learn new information and to solve problems. He has a fourth-grade education and cannot read very well. He has not yet registered as a sex offender in the state. The PSIR recommended some form of cognitive-behavioral treatment.

10

Economic and Restorative Justice Reparations

CHAPTER LEARNING OBJECTIVES

- Examine how restorative principles and practices differ from traditional criminal justice practices.
- Explain the forms that restorative justice takes, including victim–offender mediation, victim impact classes, family group conferencing, and circle sentencing.

- Discuss the economic/monetary sanctions used in both restorative and traditional criminal justice systems to include restitution, community service, fines, and forfeiture.

© Paul Conklin/PhotoEdit

Court-ordered community service can be accomplished in a variety of ways, including collection of roadside refuse.

CHAPTER OUTLINE

Introduction

Restorative Justice Principles
Forms of Restorative Justice
Effectiveness of Restorative Justice Methods

Restitution
Restitution in History
Losses Eligible for Compensation
Problems Associated with Restitution
Effectiveness of Restitution

Community Service
History of Community Service
Purpose of Community Service

Prevalence of Community Service
Effectiveness of Community Service

Fines
Prevalence of Fines
Revoking Probation for Fine Nonpayment
Forfeitures
Day Fines
Evaluation of Day Fines

Fees and Court Costs

Summary

KEY TERMS

community justice
restorative justice
restitution

community service
fine
victim compensation fund

forfeiture
day fines
fee

Introduction

When an offender is punished for a crime, the public may feel short-term satisfaction or the victim may find some closure, but many may be left wondering how the punishment will actually affect the offender's future thinking or behavior. In a traditional criminal justice system, the state acts on behalf of victims to punish the offender. It should be no surprise that even following sentencing, victims may still feel angry, unsupported, more socially isolated, and more distrustful of a system that was designed to punish on their behalf. Many come to realize that government-legitimized retribution achieves a form of justice or revenge but does not necessarily heal. Traditional criminal justice strategies and the "get tough" movement may not be as effective as we once thought in dealing with the harm caused, the resulting social isolation, and the destruction of community trust that results when crimes are committed. Separating predatory and violent offenders from the general public is necessary, but incarceration is not the magic bullet for most offenders, the majority of whom will be released one day. Incarcerating more people for longer periods of time does not necessarily make our communities safer.

The concept of **community justice** is a philosophy of using the community to control and reduce crime and to rebuild community relationships through community policing, community courts, and restorative justice. Although some authors use the terms "community justice" and "restorative justice" interchangeably, community justice is actually a broader concept that describes a philosophy overriding the whole criminal justice system (police, courts, and corrections), whereas restorative justice deals only with the sentencing and corrections component (APPA n.d.).

In Chapter 1, we introduced the concept of **restorative justice** as a sentencing philosophy and practice that emphasized the offender taking responsibility to repair the harm done to the victim and the surrounding community. Restorative justice is more victim centered than traditional methods, involving the victim and the community throughout the whole justice process (Karp 1998; Van Ness and Strong 1997;

Community Justice
A philosophy of using the community to control and reduce crime through community policing, community courts, restorative justice, and broken-windows probation.

Restorative Justice
Various sentencing philosophies and practices that emphasize the offender taking responsibility to repair the harm done to the victim and to the surrounding community. Includes forms of victim offender mediation, reparation panels, circle sentencing, and monetary sanctions.

TABLE 10.1   Roots of Restorative Justice in the U.S.

Mainstream American Justice	Indigenous Native American Justice
Imported from Anglo-American models	Indigenous, shared views of the community and victims*
Written codified laws, rules, procedures*	Unwritten/oral customs, traditions, practices
Crime is a violation of the state	Crime is a violation of one person by another
Justice is administered*	Justice is part of the life process*
Offender is focal point; privilege against self-incrimination	Victim is focal point*; offender is obligated to verbalize accountability
Adversarial (fact-finding) process; victim and offender have no contact	Communal*; victim and offender are involved in the whole process and decide action jointly
Conflict settled in court; focus on establishing guilt and blame	Conflict settled through mediation and repairing relationships*
Public defender or lawyer representation*	Extended family member representation
Retributive and deterrence	Restorative or holistic; connects everyone involved*
Incarceration, so criminal can pay debt to society	Community service, restitution, reconciliation*
Criminals who break the law deserve to be punished	Criminal acts are a part of human error, which requires correctional intervention by the community*
Church and state are separated	Spiritual realm is cohesive with justice*
Stigma is difficult to remove	Forgiveness is possible and encouraged

*Applies to restorative justice

Wright 1996). Restorative justice is practiced worldwide in both juvenile and adult systems, and the form that it takes is largely dependent on cultural factors. The form that it has taken in the United States is considered to be more akin to "western restorative justice" compared to that practiced by indigenous and Aboriginals in other countries such as Canada, New Zealand, and Australia (Cameron 2006). Canada recognizes both forms of restorative justice—western RJ and Aboriginal justice—as western RJ speaks to the dominant Canadian majority, and Aboriginal initiatives honors the traditional values and legal principles of the Aboriginal people. In the U.S., western restorative justice is community based and combines mainstream American criminal justice with indigenous justice practiced by Native Americans long before European settlers colonized North America (see Table 10.1). Let's begin by discussing restorative justice principles and comparing them with traditional criminal justice sentencing practices.

Restorative Justice Principles

Restorative justice has roots in a variety of faith traditions that moves from a philosophy of vengeance and retribution, to one of healing, reconciliation, and forgiveness. In contrast to mainstream criminal justice, which focuses on the punishment of the offender, restorative justice focuses on the victim, the offender, and the community throughout the whole process.

Restorative justice can be used for community-based sanctions or for prisoner reentry. Community-based sanctions are discussed in this chapter, and prisoner reentry is discussed in Chapter 12. The theory behind restorative justice is John Braithwaite's (1989) reintegrative shaming, which assumes that after a crime is committed, the social bonds are weakened. These bonds must be repaired in order for the offender to move on and change future behavior. The theory of reintegrative shaming, which uses the victim and the community to disapprove of the criminal behavior, also relies on them to later forgive the offender: the exact opposite of stigmatization. Stigmatization only serves to further outcast the offender and prevents him or her from becoming a fully functioning and productive societal member (Braithwaite 1989).

Rather than focusing on deficits, restorative justice attempts to strengthen community life by drawing on the participation of the victim, the victim's social support network, the offender, the offender's social support network, and the community (Umbreit 1999). Thus, community-based corrections programs are necessary and important to guide the restorative justice process.

FORMS OF RESTORATIVE JUSTICE

A variety of forms are used in restorative justice, including victim–offender mediation, reparation boards, family group conferencing, and circle sentencing. Restitution and community service are restorative in nature and are also discussed later in the chapter. All forms of restorative justice take place postconviction in the sentencing phase and have the following commonalities:

1. One or more sessions are held in the community, with the first goal to provide the victim (and/or the victim's social support networks) with the opportunity to communicate how the crime affected him or her physically, emotionally, financially, and socially.
2. The second goal is to develop a reparative plan that is accepted by both the victim and the offender in which the offender will repair the harm caused.
3. Victim participation is voluntary, and conditions of each meeting are defined on the victim's terms.
4. The parties rely on community partners and volunteers, such as Mothers Against Drunk Driving, Parents of Murdered Children, battered women's shelters, mediators, community prosecutors, school-based officers, and various faith-based organizations.
5. Offenders must accept full responsibility for their criminal behavior. This means admitting guilt and being willing to comply with restoration agreements.
6. While restorative justice efforts can take place within jails and prisons (e.g., victim impact panels), most forms are community-based as a condition of either probation or diversion.

Victim-Offender Mediation   Victim–offender mediation (VOM) has existed since the early 1980s in the United States, and there are thousands of programs around the world (Bazemore and Umbreit 2001; Umbreit, Coates, and Vos 2001). This type of mediation is different from the mediation found traditionally in civil courts because in VOM there is no dispute about liability. A mediator first meets with the offender and the victim separately to discern each party's willingness to cooperate. Assuming that both parties volunteer, the mediator is present in the same room with the victim and the offender (and if the offender is a juvenile, the parents are invited). After the facts of the offense are described, the focus becomes repairing the harm done to the victim, which is quite emotional for both sides. Shaming plays a part in releasing the hurt, the anger, and the resentment that the victim feels (Kenney and Clairmont 2009). The parties, in one or more sessions, reach a mutually desirable written agreement that is later filed with the courts.

The primary reasons victims chose to participate were to seek restitution/repayment, to oversee punishment, and to share their grief with the offender. The quality of the mediator and the face-to-face format were key variables in the victims' satisfaction. Victims of juvenile crime who participated in VOM were significantly more satisfied (79 percent) with the case outcome than a comparison group of victims who experienced traditional case processing methods (57 percent), according to a study in four states (Umbreit and Coates 1993). Other positive findings included that restitution payments were higher with VOM participants, victims reported being less fearful of being revictimized, and "[VOM] is at least as viable an option for recidivism reduction as traditional approaches. And in a good number of instances, youth going through mediation programs are actually faring better" (Umbreit, Coates, and Vos 2001, p. 32).

After six months of observing sessions involving victims, juvenile offenders, and their parents, there was a distinct difference in how mothers and fathers reacted. While fathers were generally silent and did not appear to express any apprehension about their child's misbehavior, "Mothers enter restorative conferences with their cultural scripts intact; they are presumed responsible for their children's behavior . . . Many offenders' mothers have said to me after a conference, 'I felt like everyone thought I was a bad mother' or 'I want to prove I'm a good mother'" (Cook 2006, p. 115). There was a marked difference in the participation of parents. While all the mothers were actively involved, only half of the conferences were attended by fathers; many of the latter seemed uninvolved or even uninterested.

There are some downsides of VOM. First, there is concern that the victim's perspective has been given too much "free reign whereas offenders have more limited room to maneuver. . . it lends credence to claims that offenders' perspectives are not sufficiently addressed by RJ" (Kenney and Clairmont 2009, p. 303). Solutions to this problem include a strong facilitator who can manage emotions on both sides and allow a more balanced view so as not to undermine the "restorative" part of VOM. Second, there is no strong evidence that VOM reduces recidivism. Between 40 and 60 percent of victims refused to participate because they didn't want to take the time for a perceived trivial offense, they feared meeting the offender, or they desired traditional punishment for the offender (Umbreit, Coates, and Vos 2001). Also, some VOM programs resulted in net widening.

Reparation Bonds   Otherwise known as youth panels or community diversion boards, panels consisting of members from the community have existed as a part of the juvenile justice system since the 1920s (Bazemore and Umbreit 2001). Community reparation boards function as mediators between the court and the offender and may or may not involve the victim. The board does not decide guilt or innocence; rather, it meets postconviction with the offender and the victim separately (or together if the victim wishes) to discuss and clarify how the offender will repair the harm and to identify strategies for reducing future offending (Karp and Clear 2002). Each board has a chair who manages the session, with sanctions decided by the board rather than by the judge. Local volunteers and members of faith-based organizations agree to mentor or assist in the supervision of the offender's reparation through a volunteer reparations board. Board members typically receive some training prior to serving, and the vast majority of board members serve voluntarily. The board reports back to the court monthly or quarterly on the offender's progress, or lack thereof. Should the offender fail to comply with the sanctions, the board makes a recommendation to the court (Bazemore and Umbreit 2001). Of all forms of restorative justice, this method seems to have more community than victim participation.

Family Group Conferencing   Family group conferencing is used when the victim and offender come from the same family or close-knit group. Family group conferencing assumes that, even in a domestic or family violence situation, the family and extended family should remain a major part of the decision and that the state's authority to control family matters is secondary. The goal of conferencing is to strengthen and empower families—not to tear them apart. Unlike VOM, which most directly involves just the victim and offender, family group conferencing involves supporters of all ages for both the victim and offender. A larger group of people means that there is typically a facilitator and some type of security staff present. The group meets in a location of the family's choice at a specific time to be determined in advance. The conference begins in a similar fashion as VOM, with the facts of the case. After the offender admits to the charges, each member is given a chance to speak within the group. There may be some time provided for the offender and his or her supporters to discuss solutions before reconvening in the larger group. Other times, the negotiations take place out in the open with the victim present. Victims had low attendance rates and expressed a lower level of satisfaction with family group conferencing than did offenders. This may have been due to inadequate time given victims to prepare ahead, or to the disinclination of victims to meet their offenders (Maxwell and Morris 1996).

Family group conferencing in the United States is used in cases involving a juvenile offender and juvenile victim from two different families. School resource officers or police officers organize and facilitate family meetings at school or at a community resource center after school (Bazemore and Umbreit 2001). Family group conferencing is not typically used for child abuse or neglect cases. Conferences used in domestic violence situations, like those practiced in New Zealand, have been criticized by some in the U.S. who say that keeping children in an abusive home is too soft of an approach for the severity of the situation (Walker and Hayashi 2007).

One study of family group conferencing for juvenile delinquents discovered that many eligible cases (e.g., shoplifting and runaway) were *not* selected for various reasons. In many of the shoplifting cases, retail stores refused to participate, and in the runaway cases, the juvenile was more often the victim rather than the one at fault. (Walker 2002). Like every other form of restorative justice, family group conferencing required that juveniles take responsibility for their actions, and that the victim participates. In Walker's 2002 study, 15.6 percent of the youths selected for the conference denied criminal involvement and were excluded for that reason. For the youths who participated in the conference, most sanctions consisted of a "symbolic" apology, community service, offender counseling, or some combination of the three. Recidivism did not significantly differ overall between juveniles who participated and juveniles who did not. When juveniles were divided by their adjudication offense (violent versus nonviolent), those who participated in the conferences for nonviolent offenses were less likely to be adjudicated for a violent offense compared to a matched juvenile group that did not participate in the conferences. For the time being, family group conferencing in the U.S. does not appear to be as successful as other restorative justice methods.

Circle Sentencing   Circle sentencing is based most closely on tribal justice and the use of reintegrative shaming by more parties than the victim or a single mediator. A circle group consists of the offender, the victim, family, friends, and coworkers of both the offender and the victim, social service personnel, juvenile justice personnel, and interested community members who all gather simultaneously in a circle. A "talking piece" such as a stick or feather is used to systematize who has the floor to speak. Of all four forms of restorative justice, circle sentencing involves the largest number of participants and therefore the most organization. It may be the most effective form for repeat offenders, or where offending behavior intersects with dysfunctional relationships, but it should be used sparingly with offenders convicted of minor crimes (Bazemore and Umbreit 2001). An example of a circle sentencing session is described in Box 10.1.

BOX 10.1 COMMUNITY CORRECTIONS UP CLOSE

A Circle Sentencing Session in Canada

"The victim was a middle-aged man whose parked car had been badly damaged when the offender, a 16-year-old, crashed into it while joyriding in another vehicle. The offender had also damaged a police vehicle.

In the circle, the victim talked about the emotional shock of seeing what had happened to his car and his costs to repair it (he was uninsured). Then, an elder leader of the First Nations community where the circle sentencing session was being held (and an uncle of the offender) expressed his disappointment and anger with the boy. The elder observed that this incident, along with several prior offenses by the boy, had brought shame to his family. . . .

"After the elder finished, a feather (the "talking piece") was passed to the next person in the circle, a young man who spoke about the contributions the offender made to the community, the kindness he had shown toward elders, and his willingness to help others with home repairs. . . . The Royal Canadian Mounted Police officer, whose vehicle

had also been damaged, then took the feather and spoke on the offender's behalf. The officer proposed to the judge that in lieu of statutorily required jail time for the offense, the offender be allowed to meet with him on a regular basis for counseling and community service.

"After asking the victim and the prosecutor if either had any objections, the judge accepted this proposal. The judge also ordered restitution to the victim and asked the young adult who had spoken on the offender's behalf to serve as a mentor for the offender. After a prayer in which the entire group held hands, the circle disbanded and everyone retreated to the kitchen area of the community center for refreshments."

Source: As quoted in Gordon Bazemore and Mark Umbreit. 2001. A Comparison of Four Restorative Conferencing Models. *Juvenile Justice Bulletin* (February). Washington, DC: U.S. Department of Justice, Office of Juvenile Justice and Delinquency Programs, p. 7.

EFFECTIVENESS OF RESTORATIVE JUSTICE METHODS

Measures of restorative justice include victim satisfaction with the outcome/process, payment of restitution, and cost savings. Restorative justice is most welcomed by victims of property crimes because the victim is more likely to be compensated for property losses. In traditional criminal justice, the victim is rarely compensated. When given a choice between compensation and incarceration, 75 percent of

Two staff members of a restorative justice program give youths a second chance following a first-time nonviolent offense.

respondents to a study conducted in Minnesota indicated that they would rather be compensated for a property crime than demand that the offender be incarcerated (Umbreit 1999). At this time, however, restorative justice as the only community-based sanction is less likely to be endorsed by victims of violent crimes.

Evaluations of restorative justice techniques involving juvenile offenders show that these techniques were able to reduce recidivism of program participants, compared to juveniles going through the traditional courts for similar offenses. Restorative justice techniques for adult offenders in Canada and New Zealand were less successful in recidivism reduction (Aos, Miller and Drake 2006).

Practitioners of restorative justice are still attempting to overcome some challenges relating to community education and public opinion. Any time the community plays a role, it introduces the unpredictability of public opinion, which can vary widely. Community members may be undereducated about the nature of the crime and may even blame the victim. The offender may take advantage of this by minimizing the harmful behavior. The involvement of family and friends of both the victim and offender (particularly when the victim and offender know each other) can be difficult if the family seems more supportive or even approves of the offender's behavior (Daly and Stubbs 2006).

Finally, some victims' groups are opposed to restorative justice initiatives, finding them centered around offenders, with others finding them offensive because reintegrative shaming is used over retribution and stigmatization. Some victims are not able to communicate or advocate on their own. This may exert too much pressure on victims. "The greatest challenge victims pose to restorative justice is indifference. Restorative processes depend, case by case, on victims' active participation, in a role more emotionally demanding than that of complaining witness in a conventional criminal prosecution—which is itself a role avoided by many, perhaps most victims" (Smith 2001, p. 5).

Restorative justice sanctions are primarily economic in nature (paying back losses) and labor intensive (bettering the community). Economic sanctions such as restitution, community service, and fines are used in both restorative and traditional justice systems and will be discussed next.

Restitution

Crime victims in the U.S. suffer tangible losses of over $105 billion every year. Part of that loss is returned or restored by the very people who caused the harm in the first place. **Restitution** is defined as court-ordered payment by the offender to the victim (or the victim's family) to cover tangible losses that occurred during or following the crime. Figure 10.1 depicts two different beneficiaries (the community and the victim) and two different forms of payment (money and working without pay to provide services). The money or services offered by the offender help rehabilitate the victim financially. Restitution is also designed to be an act of atonement for the criminal (see Box 10.2 for how restitution can be used in restorative justice).

Restitution
Court-ordered payment by the offender to the victim to cover tangible losses that occurred during or following the crime.

RESTITUTION IN HISTORY

Restitution has a long history around the world. The Old Testament specified five-fold restitution for stealing and then killing an ox and fourfold restitution for stealing and killing a sheep. Double restitution was mandated for stealing (Exodus 21). Leviticus commanded that restitution plus an additional fifth be made by robbers (Leviticus 6). The Code of Hammurabi, developed between 1792 and 1750 b.c., mandated thirtyfold restitution if the victim was a "god" or a "palace," and tenfold restitution if the victim was a "villein" (a low-status laborer). British philosopher

FIGURE 10.1 Typology of Restorative Justice Sanctions

Source: Burt Galaway. 1992. Restitution as Innovation or Unfilled Promise? In *Towards a Critical Victimology,* edited by Ezzat A. Fattah. New York: St. Martin's Press, p. 350.

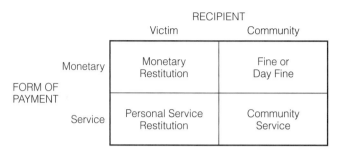

RECIPIENT

	Victim	Community
Monetary	Monetary Restitution	Fine or Day Fine
Service	Personal Service Restitution	Community Service

FORM OF PAYMENT

Jeremy Bentham (1748–1833) prescribed restitution as an essential means of making the punishment fit the crime.

Restitution was an important custom in the mid-1800s, when Quaker prison reformer Elizabeth Fry viewed repaying the victim as a step toward offender rehabilitation.

The authority of courts to grant restitution in the U.S. originates from federal statutes. From 1925 to 1982, restitution could only be imposed as a condition of probation, and it was strictly discretionary. Thus, if an offender went to prison, incarceration was used as the punishment in lieu of restitution. Stephen Schafer was a proponent of returning restitution back to the criminal justice system to elevate the victim's importance and increase victim satisfaction. Schafer believed that the criminal justice system had become too centered on the offender and the state's interests, so that the role of the crime victim was lost in the process. The victim rights movement gained momentum, and the Federal Victim Witness Protection Act (VWPA) of 1982 further broadened the use of restitution, mandating that judges provide reasons for not ordering restitution in cases with an identified victim (Davis, Smith, and Hillenbrand 1992). In the 1990s, Congress passed a series of three acts to increase the offenses for which restitution could be collected:

<u>1992</u>   Mandatory provision for courts to impose restitution for back child support

<u>1994</u>   Violence against Women Act passed to mandate restitution in cases of sexual abuse, sexual exploitation of children, domestic violence, and telemarketing fraud

---

BOX 10.2 **USING RESTITUTION IN RESTORATIVE JUSTICE**

Restitution can be used as a correctional tool in restorative justice, particularly during victim–offender mediation sessions. Five purposes of restitution include:

1. Restitution provides a less severe and more humane sanction for the offender.
2. Restitution aids the rehabilitation of the offender, and it integrates the punitive and rehabilitative purposes of the criminal law. Because the rationale incorporates the notion that punishment is related to the extent of damages done, it is perceived as just by offenders and allows them a sense of accomplishment as they complete the requirements. Restitution also provides offenders with a socially appropriate, concrete way of expressing their guilt and atoning for their offenses.
3. Restitution benefits the criminal justice system by providing an easily administered sanction that reduces demands on the system.
4. Restitution may reduce the need for vengeance in the administration of criminal law because offenders are perceived as responsible people taking active steps to make amends for their wrongdoing.
5. Restitution provides redress for crime victims.

Source: Burt Galaway. 1992. Restitution as Innovation or Unfilled Promise? In *Towards a Critical Victimology,* edited by Ezzat A. Fattah. New York: St. Martin's Press, pp. 347–371.

<u>1996</u>   Mandatory Victims Restitution Act passed to require that restitution be imposed for violent crimes and Title 18 property offenses,
and as a sentencing option in juvenile delinquency cases (Office
for Victims of Crime 2002)

As a result of these acts, victims were more likely to receive judgments in criminal
and civil cases. The remaining problem was enforcing the court order and victim collection of their restitution (Davis et al. 1992). Victims received very little information
about how to collect restitution through traditional criminal and civil courts. Through
more recent restorative justice (discussed previously in this chapter) and presentence
efforts, restitution is enforced, and collected at greater rates than in the past.

LOSSES ELIGIBLE FOR COMPENSATION

States have broadened the types of losses eligible for compensation as well as the
parties eligible to receive restitution. For example, restitution is available for the purpose of lost income as a result of physical injury or time in court, medical expenses,
transportation to and from the courthouse, necessary child care during litigation,
expenses involving the investigation and prosecution of the case, counseling sessions, sexual assault exams, human immunodeficiency virus (HIV) testing, occupational and rehabilitative therapy, moving expenses, case-related travel and meal
expenses, and burial expenses. Restitution may be ordered for psychological counseling in cases in which the victim suffered physical injury (*United States v. Laney* 1999).
Restitution is limited to the replacement value of direct or actual losses as a result of
the crime and cannot be ordered for losses defined as indirect or consequential, such
as victims' attorney fees.

Eligible parties may include the victim or the victim's family (in cases of homicide). Eligible organizations that may receive restitution include those that provided
medical care, shelter, or counseling to the victim. Many states authorize the collection of interest on the unpaid restitution amount, varying from between 6 percent
and 10 percent per year (Office for the Victims of Crime 2002).

Victims typically apply for restitution through the prosecutor's office. To receive
restitution, the victim must press charges and agree to testify if necessary. Restitution
is declared as a victim right in 19 state constitutions (AK, AZ, CA, CT, ID, IL, LA, MI,
MO, MT, NM, NC, OK, OR, RI, SC, TN, TX, and WI), even when the offender has been
incarcerated. Despite the mandatory policy, victims are more likely to get reimbursed
if the offender is sentenced to a community sanction so that he or she can work to pay
the victim back. In other states where restitution is defined as offender rehabilitation,
restitution is forfeited if the offender goes to prison.

PROBLEMS ASSOCIATED WITH RESTITUTION

Restitution remains underutilized in both misdemeanor and felony cases. Nationally,
courts ordered restitution in only 10 percent of felony convictions and 22 percent of
misdemeanors. For felony crimes, restitution was ordered in one out of four property
offenses, but in only 15 percent of all violent offenses (Durose and Langan 2007). Restitution was more often required for probationers than for people who were sentenced
to prison, most likely because people on probation have the means to pay the restitution while prisoners usually do not. About one-third of probationers are required to
pay restitution, with the average restitution ordered at $3,368 (Cohen 1995). Even
though restitution may not often be ordered even when it becomes mandatory, a
Pennsylvania study of 170,260 restitution-eligible cases determined that restitution
was ordered for the appropriate offenders and that

the odds of receiving an order of restitution were significantly greater for property than person crimes, for offenders with no or low prior records, for female offenders, and for White offenders. (Ruback, Ruth, and Shaffer 2005, p. 332)

One barrier to obtaining restitution is the victim's lack of participation in the justice process and lack of education that restitution is available. Many victims fail to request restitution or have not retained documentation showing their losses. Three other problems associated with restitution are indigence of the defendant, determining the restitution amount, and collecting restitution.

Indigent Offenders   If the defendant is indigent and cannot pay, courts generally cannot cite the defendant for contempt or send the defendant to prison. However, indigence at the time of sentencing does not entitle the offender to immunity from restitution; it is more dependent on the offender's future ability to pay (*United States v. Bachsian* 1993). If the defendant is able to pay but refuses, then incarceration is valid. In the federal system, if an incarcerated federal prisoner has restitution to pay and has the ability to pay, parole release can be contingent upon the prisoner first paying off the entire restitution amount while incarcerated (U.S. Parole Commission 2003). There are other standards in some state jurisdictions. For example, an Indiana court ruled that the decision to incarcerate a probationer for failure to pay depends solely on the type of probationary sentence. If restitution is ordered as a *suspended* probationary sentence, the defendant could be imprisoned for being unable to pay. If restitution is ordered as part of an *executed* probationary sentence, the defendant cannot be imprisoned for failure to pay (*Wooden v. State* 2001).

Declaring bankruptcy no longer excuses offenders from paying restitution. A federal statute declared that restitution orders are not dischargeable in Chapter 13 bankruptcies (11 U.S.C.A., sec 1328(a)(3)). A Texas Criminal Appeals court extended this same line of reasoning to Chapter 7 bankruptcy cases (*Cabla v. State* 1999).

Determining the Restitution Amount   In restorative justice cases, restitution amounts are determined at the victim–offender mediation session. In traditional criminal or civil cases, the court sets restitution amounts according to harm caused to the victim and the defendant's ability to pay based on full disclosure of assets and liabilities. Probation officers who complete presentence investigation (PSI) reports can suggest a restitution amount to the judge. To accurately determine a restitution amount, probation officers consider:

- Whether restitution is discretionary or mandatory (usually defined by offense of conviction)
- The victims of the offense of conviction
- The harms to the victim that are directly caused by the offense of conviction
- The harms and costs that qualify for restitution
- The effect of a plea agreement on the restitution amount (Goodwin 2001)

The offender's financial resources, existing financial obligations, and ability to pay are considered, as well as whether or not the victim was insured or was partially at fault. The defendant usually has the opportunity prior to sentencing to challenge the victim's claims or the amount of restitution recommended in the PSI.

Because it is often difficult to accurately establish a fair restitution amount, the government has the burden to prove, based on preponderance of the evidence, that the victim did suffer the harm for which the victim is requesting restitution from the offender (Goodwin 2001). The amount of restitution must be based on expenses the victim incurred by the time of sentencing and can be based only on the offense for which the offender was actually convicted.

Collecting Restitution   Collecting restitution is the responsibility of probation officers, day reporting centers, and restitution centers. The entity responsible for collecting restitution acts as both a finance officer and a collection agent by determining the weekly or monthly installment payment schedule and making sure that the victim receives the money. Offenders who get too far behind on payments, or who are able to pay but refuse to do so, might be reassigned to a formal collection agency.

How successful are agencies in collecting restitution? A Bureau of Justice Statistics study reported that 60 percent of felony offenders had paid restitution in full by the time they completed their sentence (Langan and Cunniff 1992). More recent studies were less optimistic—collection rates varied between one-third and one-half (Ruback and Bergstrom 2006).

Increasing Restitution Collection Rates   Three ways that have been used to increase restitution collection rates are notifying the offender through letters and phone calls, restorative justice techniques, and presentence efforts. Letters sent to adult probationers instructed them how to make restitution payments, how much was owed, and warned them of the consequences for failing to make payments. Probationers who received a notification letter were significantly more likely to pay restitution than probationers who did not receive such a letter or who were not employed (Lurigio and Davis 1990). This method works for offenders who are employed and wish to avoid prison.

But what about offenders who are in prison already and still have restitution payments? Some systems will not release an offender early from parole until all restitution has been satisfied. Still, there is very little incentive to pay restitution while incarcerated. Box 10.3 discusses what the federal government has been doing recently to collect restitution *before* sentencing.

But what if the offender is a juvenile? Victim–offender mediation (VOM) requires that the victim agree to meet with the offender, and restitution is made

---

BOX 10.3   COMMUNITY CORRECTIONS CLOSE UP

Can Restitution Be Collected *Before* Sentencing?

Given that offenders sentenced to prison have no incentive to make restitution payments, and that some offenders would rather go to jail to avoid making payments, the burden is largely left to parole officers who become collection agents. The officers attempt to garnish wages to collect as much restitution as possible from the offender before the sentence expires.

The federal justice system has become wiser and changed the way it administers restitution to a more effective method. Once the offender decides to plead guilty, federal plea agreements now require defendants to complete a financial affidavit, listing all assets and liabilities, including real estate, vehicles, mutual funds, and other personal property valued over a certain amount. The financial litigation unit runs a credit report and a conducts a search for assets to complete their investigation. Then, the defendant is required to pay the restitution with those assets, all *before* sentencing. The incentive of having the offender pay before sentencing is that the prosecutor has leverage at the plea agreement. If the offender has completed restitution payments in full, or at least attempted to make good, the prosecutor can make a deal with the defendant for a more lenient sentence. If the offender does not pay, sentencing will be more harsh and the attempt will be to get the restitution on the back-end—as many jurisdictions do now. The presentence restitution collection has resulted in the collection of $5.25 million in one year.

Source: Stottmann, Jonathan O. 2007. Presentence restitution: When opportunity knocks. *News and Views* 32 (19): September 10.

a large part of the incentive for victim participation. These sessions using restorative justice may show some promise of increasing the number of offenders who succeed in making all of their restitution payments. In a two-year study of VOM with juvenile property offenders in Minnesota, 55 percent of victims agreed to meet with the offender. These sessions resulted in a 93 percent completion rate (Galaway 1992). More importantly, how did VOM youth collection rates compare with youth not participating? Youthful offenders who participated in VOM sessions were significantly more likely to complete restitution payments (81 percent) than a similar group of youth offenders who did not participate in VOM (57 percent completion) (Umbreit and Coates 1993). The general public is also supportive of restitution as a community sanction, especially when informed of the cost of incarceration versus community corrections punishments.

EFFECTIVENESS OF RESTITUTION

Adult probation cases in Pennsylvania indicated that probationers who made their restitution payments were also less likely to be rearrested compared to probationers who did not comply. The researchers suggest that this is not an indicator of the effectiveness of restitution per se, but they found that people who were already integrated in the community were more likely to comply with restitution (Outlaw and Ruback 1999).

A second study assessed recidivism rates using a predefined group of prison inmates who owed restitution on their case. Out of this group, inmates were selected randomly to be released to the Minnesota Restitution Center to take part in paying the restitution. The control group remained in prison and did not pay the restitution. The study found that there was "no difference in the likelihood of return to prison between the two groups. The restitution group, however, was somewhat more likely to have been returned to prison for technical parole violations, whereas the control group was more likely to have been returned to prison for a new offence" (Galaway 1992, p. 357). The same offenders in these two groups were tracked for sixteen months after their release. Members of the restitution group had fewer convictions and were employed for more of the time than members of the control group. So it seems that inmates who owe restitution can effectively pay restitution through a restitution center. Similar results have been found with experimental studies of youths in restitution and comparison groups.

Community Service

Community Service
Unpaid labor for the public to compensate society for harm done by the offense of conviction.

Community service has been called "the most underused intermediate sanction in the United States" (Tonry 1998, p. 89). **Community service** is defined as unpaid service to the public to compensate society for harm done by the offender. Community service is typically ordered by the judge as a part of probation; the place of work is chosen by either the judge or the supervising officer. Community service might consist of working for a tax-supported or nonprofit agency such as a hospital, public park, or library, or for a poverty or public works program. The most frequent type of community service work is picking up roadside litter, doing landscape maintenance, removing graffiti, or painting buildings. Some work assignments have trucks or vans that transport work crews to the site where they are supervised for the day, but most assignments require the offender to take the initiative and report to complete the service order.

History of Community Service

Community service first began in the United States as an organized program in 1966 in Alameda County, California. This initiative was created as a substitute for paying fines for low-income female traffic offenders. The women worked without pay in lieu of their fine and avoided jail for fine nonpayment. Because of the positive attention this program received, hundreds of community service programs were established in the 1970s for juveniles and nonviolent adults. In the United States, community service developed as an alternative to fines or as an additional condition of probation (Tonry 1999a).

The English Model   Community service suffices in England and Wales as an acceptable alternative to prison for crimes considered to be minor such as petty theft or drug possession. Special community service officers administer the sanction. The English model became popular in other areas of Europe, such as Scotland, Switzerland, and the Netherlands. The United States did not follow the English model, believing instead that community service was not punitive enough to substitute for prison. It is not uncommon to see U.S. judges order between 100 and 1,000 hours of community service in addition to other probation conditions (Tonry 1999a). This difference in American perceptions of community service demonstrates that, in comparison with most other countries in the world, community corrections sanctions are more punitive (and are not just reflected in long prison sentences).

Purpose of Community Service

Like monetary restitution, community service is both punitive and rehabilitative. It is punitive in that the offender's time and freedom are partially restricted until the work is completed. It is rehabilitative in the sense that it allows offenders to do something constructive, to increase their self-esteem, to reduce their isolation from society, and to benefit society through their efforts. In comparison with restitution, community service requires neither that there be an identifiable victim nor that the victim be cooperative in the prosecution process.

Furthermore, community service provides an alternative sanction for indigent offenders who are unable to afford significant monetary sanctions or for those whose financial resources are so great that monetary restitution has no punitive or rehabilitative effect. Community service is a good example of a restorative justice program, and it can also be used to divert offenders from having a formal conviction on their record.

Prevalence of Community Service

According to Table 10.2, community service was used as a part of probation sentences for 9 percent of misdemeanants and 20 percent of felony probationers nationwide (Kyckelhahn and Cohen 2007). This nationwide estimate appears to differ widely by region. For example, community service is used in Texas as a condition of probation in 76 percent of cases, most commonly with drug and property offenders.

Although community service is used as a jail alternative, it is rarely or never used as a sole sanction (Caputo 2005). The number of hours of community service varies depending on the nature and seriousness of the offense. For example, Texas

TABLE 10.2   Most Common Probation Conditions Received by Sentenced Felony Defendants

Most serious conviction offense	Number of defendants	Percent whose sentence to probation included —		
		Community service	Restitution	Treatment
All offenses	7,834	19%	12%	26%
All felonies	6,649	20%	10%	29%
Violent offenses	741	26	15	20
Property offenses	1,813	22	26	9
Drug offenses	3,384	18	1	45
Public-order offenses	693	23	10	13
Misdemeanors	1,186	9%	22%	7%

Note: Data represent felony defendants in the 75 largest counties in 2004. Data available for 99 percent of cases. Total for felonies includes cases that could not be classified into 1 of the 4 felony offense categories. A defendant may have received more than one type of probation condition. Not all defendants sentenced to probation received probation conditions. Detail may not add to total because of rounding.

Source: Tracey Kyckelhahn and Thomas H. Cohen, 2007. *Felony Defendants in Large Urban Counties, 2004.* Washington, DC: Bureau of Justice Statistics, Table 29. Retrieved from: http://www.ojp.usdoj.gov/bjs/stssent.htm#scps

provides for the following community service hours for probation (Texas Code of Criminal Procedure, Art. 42.12 Sec. 22(a)(1)):

PUNISHMENT RANGE	MAXIMUM HOURS	MINIMUM HOURS
First-degree felony	1,000	320
Second-degree felony	800	240
Third-degree felony	600	160
State jail felony	400	120
Class A misdemeanor	200	80
Class B misdemeanor	100	24

Community service orders ranged from 20 to 600 hours, with the average number of hours at 230 for felons and 60 for misdemeanants. In most jurisdictions, the offender's employment status must be considered in determining the community service schedule, in that employed offenders must be able to work and retain gainful employment, so they are limited to 16 hours of community service per week. Unemployed offenders can perform up to 32 community service hours per week (Caputo 2005). Offenders in some jurisdictions may be able to "work off" fines by performing community service in lieu of the fine or, with judicial permission, in lieu of incarceration. In Texas, 8 hours of community service is equivalent to one day of jail confinement regardless of the offense committed (Caputo 2005).

EFFECTIVENESS OF COMMUNITY SERVICE

Many nonprofit organizations, such as churches, homeless shelters, libraries, and the U.S. Forest Service, have benefited from the labor provided by offenders. Community service seems to have positive effects on federal offenders too, according to Box 10.4. Completion rates vary from 50 percent to a high of 85 percent, depending on how community service is enforced (Anderson 1998). One main reason offenders do not complete community service orders is the lack of enforcement on completing the hours before the probation sentence is served. Rarely are probationers extended on probation because they fail to complete community service hours (Caputo 2005).

Community service has enjoyed wide public support although only one research study was found since MacDonald's study in 1986 that empirically evaluated the

BOX 10.4   COMMUNITY CORRECTIONS CLOSE UP

One Offender's Experience Doing Community Service

Carl worked as a mail carrier for the U.S. Post Office. He repeatedly threw away all third-class mail in a dumpster because he deemed it a nuisance to his customers. When his crime was detected, he was fired and prosecuted for a misdemeanor. He was ordered to pay restitution and to perform 300 hours of community service. The presentence investigation indicated that Carl was one quarter short of obtaining a B.A. degree in mathematics, and he was a nonviolent misdemeant. The community service probation officer assigned Carl to work a seven-hour shift once per week at an elementary school for 42 weeks. He was initially assigned to playground and lunchroom duties, but his knowledge and leadership qualities were so impressive that he was assigned as a math tutor for three boys in the third grade. Because part of the boys' learning problems were due to lack of parental discipline, Carl met with the parents of the boys to discuss the problem. The boys improved their math grades and overall classroom performance. At the end of his community service, Carl was offered a job as a teacher's aide. Although he turned down the offer, Carl felt he had touched the lives of a few kids and had received much more in return. Because of the success of Carl's placement, the courts have expanded community service to four other schools.

Carl's case is one example of the many federal offenders who must complete community service. In a 10-year period in the Northern District of Georgia, offenders worked 300,000 hours and finished projects valued at over $3 million. The success of community service programs depends on good agency relationships between the probation department and outside community agencies. Success also depends on the placement skills and monitoring from probation officers. The officers must be attuned to whether the court intends the community service to be punitive or rehabilitative. The placement also must match the skills and risk level of the offender.

Richard Maher, a supervising U.S. probation officer of the Northern District of Georgia, reports that over a three-year period, 5 percent of probationers who are sentenced to community service later accept paid jobs with their placement or through contacts established while doing community service work. Community service saves money, provides work for nonprofit agencies, and provides opportunities for offenders.

Source: Richard J. Maher. 1994. Community Service: A Good Idea That Works. *Federal Probation* 58(2): 20–23; and Richard J. Maher. 1997. Community Service: A Way for Offenders to Make Amends. *Federal Probation* 61(1): 26–28.

---

effectiveness of community service in the United States. Bouffard and Muftic (2007) examined 200 DUI misdemeanants who were sentenced to community service compared to another group of similar offenders who were assessed a monetary fine. Offenders who completed community service had a similar recidivism rate as the monetary fine group. Despite the lack of cost benefit analysis showing how much each program costs compared to its benefit, and considering only a 50 percent successful completion of community service compared to over 90 percent of the offenders who paid the fine, the researchers continued to believe that community service offered more benefit than fines (Bouffard and Muftic 2007).

As the search continues for less costly and more effective methods of dealing with offenders, community service has the potential to be a growing trend in U.S. corrections. One difficult problem with evaluating and expanding community service programs is that most do not have clear goals and objectives. In expanding their use, the following must be delineated:

- Is the purpose of community service to reduce recidivism, to divert offenders, or both?
- Should community service be used instead of or in addition to other sanctions?
- Should community service be expanded for prison-bound offenders?
- How is the value of community service work calculated compared to days in jail or fine amounts?

Payment of fines and fees typically accompany probation or other community sanctions. Fines tend to be underused because their collection is not well enforced. Recently, the federal system has encouraged payment of fines before sentencing to receive a lighter sentence.

Courtesy Leanne Fiftal Alarid

There are no easy answers to these questions. The potential for greater use of community service through offender labor as an alternative to jail or prison is limitless if developed without further increasing community risk.

Fines

Jeremy Bentham, the English jurist, (1748–1832) once said, "A fine is a license paid in arrears." In other words, instead of buying beforehand the permission to engage in a certain activity, the offender, if caught, pays the fine later. In modern times, a **fine** is defined as a monetary sanction imposed by the judge, with the amount depending on the severity of the offense. The modern fine is directed at the consumers of a certain illegal activity and not at the indigent (O'Malley 2008). There are three types of fines that we will discuss: fixed fines, forfeitures, and day fines.

The first type is a fixed monetary amount that is referred to in the field and in this text as a "fine." Ninety percent of fines go to victim/witness assistance programs or a general **victim compensation fund**, which is a state fund that dispenses compensation to victims of violent crime for losses not covered by restitution (Ruback and Bergstrom 2006). A fine is viewed as a punishment, with the failure to pay grounds for revocation or issuance of a warrant.

A fine can be imposed as a sole penalty, as in the case of traffic offenses, or accompanied by probation, an intermediate sanction, or incarceration. Fines have been used in European criminal justice systems as a primary sanction. For example, in Germany, more than 80 percent of all crimes committed by adults are punished by a fine as the only penalty. Compared to many other countries, fines in the United States have generally been underused and their collection not well enforced.

PREVALENCE OF FINES

Fines are used in only 25 percent of all state felony cases and in 13 percent of federal cases (Durose and Langan 2004). When fines are used, they are in addition to a probation sentence. In the federal system, fines are used as a stand-alone or sole means of punishment in nearly one-third of misdemeanor offenses, but less than 1 percent of federal felony cases (United States Department of Justice 2005a).

Fines are routinely imposed as the primary sanction for organizational or corporate defendants in cases of corporate or white-collar crime. According to the Federal Sentencing Guidelines Manual (2008, p. 510):

The base fine is determined in one of three ways: (1) by the amount based on the offense [seriousness] level... (2) by the pecuniary gain to the organization

Fine
A fixed monetary sanction defined by statute and imposed by a judge, depending on the seriousness of the crime.

Victim Compensation Fund
A state fund that dispenses compensation to victims of violent crime and is paid for by offenders who are convicted.

from the offense; and (3) by the pecuniary loss caused by the organization, to the extent that the loss was caused intentionally, knowingly or recklessly.

Whichever loss is deemed to be the greatest of these three types is the one selected. This helps to ensure that organizations will seek to detect and report such gains in the future and/or prevent intentional losses from happening again. Organizational fines using these guidelines typically range from $5,000 up to $72 million (Federal Sentencing Guidelines Manual, 2008).

When a fine is imposed in individual-level federal felony cases, they ranged from $28 to as much as $10,000, with an average of $1,000 (Vigorita 2002). Fines are assessed for offenders who are eligible for a community sentence and have the ability to pay. State-level judges rarely have information on the defendant's ability to pay, so eligibility rests largely on offense severity and prior criminal record. Employed offenders are more likely to be assessed fines than unemployed offenders. Judges who are reluctant to use fines point out that offenders tend to be poor and may have no means other than additional criminal activity to obtain the funds to pay their fines. Fixed fines may overly burden a poor person but be less consequential to an affluent offender. When the financial penalty is too high, however, offenders are significantly more likely to revoke their probation (Ruback and Bergstrom 2006). In addition, the Seventh Circuit Court of Appeals held that the federal district court was not authorized to order a defendant to pay fines to private charities because fines are paid to the government, not to private parties (*United States v. Wolff* 1996).

REVOKING PROBATION FOR FINE NONPAYMENT

O'Malley (2008) stressed that the modern fine is technically not aimed at indigent people and is not translatable into jail time. Given that fine collection rates range from 14 percent (Parent 1990) to nearly two-thirds of probationers satisfying their financial obligations in full (Allen and Treger 1994), we have a substantial number of probationers who do not satisfy their financial obligations. What happens if a defendant does *not* pay the whole fine? A defendant can avoid paying a fine, in part or in full, if he or she is demonstrably unable to pay. The U.S. Supreme Court held that probation cannot be revoked solely because of an offender's inability to pay a fine or restitution because revocation based on indigence violates the equal protection clause of the Fourteenth Amendment (*Bearden v. Georgia* 1983). The Court distinguished, however, between indigence (inability) and unwillingness (refusal) to pay. Unwillingness to pay court-ordered restitution or fines despite a probationer's ability to do so may result in revocation. Statutes in most states and the federal system provide for allowing a flexible payment schedule if the defendant is unable to pay the entire fine immediately, modifying the sentence to reduce the fine, and in some cases forgoing the fine and imposing an alternative sanction.

The federal system mandates that federal prisoners shall not be released on parole or mandatory release until the fine is paid in full (U.S. Parole Commission 2003). In contrast, many fines remain unpaid in the state system. As a result, the American Bar Association and researchers have issued recommendations over the years that include clearer payment instructions for offenders, positive motivators to encourage payments in full, designating a central officer/public official to collect the fines, and authorizing that official either to file a court order holding the offender in contempt of court or to file a civil lawsuit against the offender for the remaining fine balance (American Bar Association 1994; Ruback et al. 2006).

Increasing Payments of Fines and Restitution   One of the drawbacks of imposing any type of financial obligation is the court response if offenders fail to follow through. Traditionally, that response has been "jail therapy" (i.e., incarceration). How then do we increase the numbers of probationers who make payments of fines and restitution *without* increasing incarceration rates? "Project MUSTER" (Must Earn Restitution) was an experiment for low-risk work capable probationers who were court-ordered to pay, but who missed three months or more of payments or were 60 percent or more in arrears of the total amount (Weisburd, Einat, and Kowalski 2008). Selected probationers were assigned at random to one of three groups: (1) no change in supervision; (2) served with a violation of probation and an upcoming court date; or (3) the MUSTER group: served with a violation notice like group 2, employment training, and ordered to complete an additional 15 hours of community service *per week* that payments were missed. After six months, the researchers found that groups 2 and 3 were more likely to make court-ordered payments than probationers in the "do nothing" group. One-third of MUSTER probationers compared to 13 percent of group 1 paid in full. Over 60 percent of MUSTER (compared to 35 percent of the first group) paid at least half the obligation. It seemed that the mere threat of probation violation was enough of a motivator to increase payment in full, but extra community service did not contribute (Weisburd, Einat, and Kowalski 2008).

FORFEITURES

Forfeiture
A government seizure of property that was illegally obtained, was acquired with resources that were illegally obtained, or was used in connection with an illegal activity.

A **forfeiture** is a "government seizure of property because it is illegal contraband, was illegally obtained, was acquired with resources that were illegally obtained, or was used in connection with an illegal activity. Forfeiture can be either criminal or civil" (Ruback and Bergstrom 2006, p. 257). Whereas criminal forfeiture occurs after a conviction, civil forfeiture can occur when proof by preponderance of the evidence is met. Preponderance of the evidence is a lower standard of proof. The purposes of forfeiture are to make certain that offenders cannot keep illegal property and make a profit, and to discourage criminals from using houses and businesses to conduct criminal transactions. Unlike a traditional fixed fine, forfeiture is not considered to be a punishment by the Supreme Court. However, a forfeiture is limited in that it must not be "grossly disproportionate to the gravity of the defendant's offense [or else] the forfeiture would violate the excessive fines clause" of the Eighth Amendment (Ruback and Bergstrom 2006, p. 257). The authors estimate that 40,000 forfeitures occur every year, 80 percent of which are civil and the remaining 20 percent of which are from criminal cases.

DAY FINES

Day Fines
Fines that are calculated by multiplying a percentage of the offender's daily wage by the number of predefined punishment units (the number of punishment units depend on the seriousness of the crime).

Using fixed fines in criminal sentencing presents difficulties due to offenders' socio-economic differences. For this reason, a pilot program began in Staten Island, New York, to use fines in a different way, based on a system practiced in many European countries. **Day fines**, otherwise known as structured fines, are court fines figured as multiples of the offender's daily income. For example, a school custodian and a stockbroker, both convicted of the same offense, with the same criminal history and identical risk factors, would pay different amounts because they earn different amounts of money. The stockbroker, who makes an annual income of $100,000 per year, would pay more than the custodian, who makes $25,000 per year. Based on a day fine of 10 percent, the stockbroker would be fined $10,000 and the custodian would pay $2,500. In a day fine system, offenders would be fined the same multiple or percentage of income, determined by their crime and prior history. In this way, day fines would provide the same degree of financial hardship to each offender. Using the previous example, in a tariff or conventional fine situation, the stockbroker and the custodian may have received fines of the same amount. Thus, day fines overcome many of the shortcomings associated with fixed fines.

Evaluation of Day Fines   Day fines were first evaluated in Staten Island, New York, and Milwaukee, Wisconsin (McDonald, Greene, and Worzella 1992). In Staten Island, day fines were used only for misdemeanor cases, and fines were limited to a maximum of $1,000. Lawyers and judges alike were in full acceptance of this system. The study found that in comparison with fines assessed and collected before the study began, the average fine amount increased, as did the proportion of fines collected. Seventy percent of those assessed day fines paid in full, 13 percent were resentenced to community service or to a jail sentence averaging 11 days, and 14 percent of offenders absconded. As a result of this study, the New York legislature examined the possibility of removing the cap of $1,000 (which reflected the old tariff system) to make it possible to bring in more revenue under the day fine system (up to 18 percent more revenue). The researchers found that a workable day fine system could be developed for regular use in courts.

The Milwaukee project involved the impact of day fines on noncriminal violations. There were two groups (an experimental and a control group), and simultaneous comparisons could be made between regular fines and day fines. The results were somewhat disappointing as only 37 percent were from the day fine group and 25 percent from the conventional group paid in full. Using day fines did seem to benefit the collection of fines from the most impoverished offenders, however. Day fines did not deter future criminal conduct (nine months after sentencing) any more than conventional fines. The county treasury received less in total collections overall, which resulted in resistance to further use of day fines, and the project was abandoned.

As a result of the earlier mixed reviews, other pilot project sites were selected for evaluation in Phoenix. Day fines in Phoenix were used as diversion for low-risk, low-needs offenders who were not in need of formal supervision. Potential candidates of the Financial Assessment Related to Employability (FARE) program were identified by probation officers during the completion of the presentence investigation report. FARE offenders were supervised by a special FARE probation officer, whose primary job was fine collections. FARE was considered a success because a higher rate of day-fine offenders paid their fines compared to a matched group of offenders (Turner and Greene 1999). Total amount of fines collected by the day-fine group was $62,000 more than the comparison group and there was no increase in recidivism. Despite these encouraging results, day fines have not caught on in the United States as an alternative sanction.

Fees and Court Costs

A fee is differentiated from a fine, in that a **fee** is a court-imposed reimbursement that the offender pays directly to the courts for the administration of the criminal justice system. Fees began to be assessed in the 1980s and are also known as "court costs" in other regions of the country. The two terms have the same meaning so we will use "fees" in this text. Box 10.5 shows examples of fees including $250 for DNA testing, prosecution/court costs of $200, and corrections supervision fees of $40 per month—each of which may be itemized and may depend on the type of offense and type of sentence (Ruback and Bergstrom 2006). Offenders using electronic monitoring and global positioning system technology incur additional monthly fees.

Probation user fees are also imposed for probationers especially if they under the court structure and if the jurisdiction is fee-dependent. For example, since 40 percent of probation budgets in Texas rely on probation user fees, there is a legitimate concern as to whether probationers who are compliant in making their payments are ever released off supervision early or whether they are carried on the caseload because of the money they provide.

Fee
A monetary amount imposed by the court to assist in administering the criminal justice system by the offender's repayment of debt accrued by the investigation, prosecution, and supervision of the case.

BOX 10.5   COMMUNITY CORRECTIONS CLOSE UP

What Expenses Are Defendants Required to Pay as "Fees?"

Fees are the government's attempt to recover from individual offenders the expenses that were incurred in the investigation and prosecution of the defendant's case. Fee payment ranges greatly by jurisdiction from one state-mandated fee to up to 36 various county-based costs, not including what is mandated by the state (Ruback and Bergstrom 2006). One thing is clear: acquitted defendants do not pay fees. The lower courts are divided, however, on the legal costs for convicted offenders. Although some jurisdictions have fixed court costs, others are variable depending on ability to pay.

Examples of fees, as they apply to the case, include court clerk, crime lab, fingerprint card, bail administration, DUI testing, drug testing, psychological evaluation, drug treatment evaluation, victim impact panel, highway safety class, electronic monitoring, and community service fee. The U.S. Supreme Court authorized repayment of legal fees for attorney's fees as a probation condition (*Fuller v. Oregon* 1974), appointed defense counsel for defendants who were later found not to be indigent (*United States v. Angulo* 1988), and offender repayment of defense witness fees (*United States v. Dougherty* 1987). The high court has remained silent on the requirement of most other types of fees and court costs. To muddy the waters a bit more, most trial courts do not have any authority over parole conditions, so court costs are often assessed for probationers but not for parolees, unless the parole board is statutorily authorized to require repayment (some are, but most are not).

A fee is not considered punitive and is therefore subject to different legal standards for nonpayment than a fine. Even though probationers with fines were ordered to pay lower fees than probationers without fines, it seems likely that fees would still compete with other financial obligations such as monthly household bills, fines, victim restitution, and payment for court-ordered treatment. Courts have held that it is unacceptable to require an indigent defendant to pay court costs. Perhaps this is why Illinois probationers in higher income brackets were more likely to be ordered to pay probation fees than probationers in lower income brackets (Olson and Ranker 2001). Of the 55 percent of these probationers who were ordered to pay, nearly three-fourths conformed.

Offenders in rural areas were more likely to be assessed partial fees than offenders in urban areas. This may be due to the ideology of the court in rural areas that all offenders will contribute something to the greater whole as opposed to caseloads in urban areas, which are larger, giving officials less time to enforce their collection. Perhaps rural jurisdictions rely more heavily on reimbursement if they have a lower available tax base from which to draw (Ruback and Bergstrom 2006).

To what degree does probation serve as a collection agency? Requiring probation or parole officers to collect fees reduces officers to collection agents and diminishes the counseling role of their work (Olson and Ranker 2001). Effective collection techniques are important for restitution, fines, fees, and forfeitures. The federal government recommended that there be:

- A short time period for payment (three months), which increases the likelihood of full payment
- A convenient location to make payments (police stations, probation departments, night deposit boxes outside the court, payment by mail, and so on)
- A wide variety of payment methods (credit cards, debit cards, cash, personal checks, money orders)
- Discounts for early payment
- Surcharges for late payment
- Overdue payment reminder notices in the mail or by telephone
- Consequences for nonpayment (Bureau of Justice Assistance 1996, pp. 29–33)

SUMMARY

- Community justice is a philosophy of using the community to control and reduce crime through community policing, community courts, and neighborhood-based probation.

- Once a crime has been committed, restorative justice emphasizes the offender taking responsibility to repair the harm done to the victim and to the surrounding community.

- Restorative justice is more victim centered than traditional methods, involving the victim and the community throughout the whole justice process.

- Restorative justice programs rely heavily on community partners and volunteers to carry out mediation, reparation boards, face-to-face meetings with the victim, and victim impact classes. Present patterns in the use of restitution still vary widely

although observers predict greater emphasis on restitution in the future, particularly in conjunction with other sentences.

- Community service also holds some promise, but at present it is not well enforced.

- The use of fixed fines is still perceived as either too lenient or problematic for impoverished offenders sinking deeper into poverty.

- Forfeitures and day fines are two other types of fines.

- Although asset forfeitures have greatly increased, day fines did not catch on as an approved community sanction.

- Collection rates of the various economic sanctions remain a huge unresolved issue at present.

DISCUSSION QUESTIONS

1. How is restorative justice different from traditional justice approaches?

2. Using the restorative justice approach, what would you require as a sentence for a 17-year-old offender who forcefully broke a window to get into a house and stole property valued at $1,000 when the occupants were at work?

3. How is community service used as a correctional tool?

4. How do monetary restitution and community service differ? How are they alike?

5. Does restitution provide for integration of both offender and victim in the criminal justice system?

6. How can restitution be used for juveniles who are too young to legally work full time?

7. Is it fair to require that probationers pay court costs, but not parolees? Why or why not?

8. How specific do statutes need to be in itemizing required expenses?

9. Why is it that the collection of fines is treated differently from the collection of fees? Should they be treated the same if they are not paid in full?

10. How does a day fine overcome the problems associated with fixed fines? Why has the day fine idea *not* caught on in American criminal justice?

WEB SITES

Rethinking Crime and Punishment
 http://www.rethinking.org.uk/press/
 march03speechCSR.htm

National Center for Victims of Crime
 http://www.ncvc.org/ncvc/main.aspx

Restorative Justice
 http://www.restorativejustice.org

The Center for Restorative Justice and Peacemaking, University of Minnesota
 http://rjp.umn.edu

The Centre for Restorative Justice, Simon Fraser University, Canada
 http://www.sfu.ca/crj

Restorative Justice Ministry Network of North America
http://www.rjmn.net

Bridges to Life Faith-based restorative justice program
http://www.bridgestolife.org

Restorative Justice Initiative, Marquette University Law School
http://www.law.marquette.edu/jw/restorative

Fresno Pacific University's Center for Peacemaking and Conflict Studies

Website Links Dealing with Restorative Justice
http://fresno.edu/pacs/

The Purpose of Economic Sanctions
http://www.econlib.org/library/Enc/Sanctions.html

CASE STUDY EXERCISE

Restorative Justice

In the following scenarios, conditions of the offender's supervision will provide for a form of restorative justice. For each of the following cases, discuss one or more community service and/or restorative justice referrals or conditions that would aid the offender in complying with the community sentence.

CASE A

An 18-year-old male with no prior record has been convicted of a "hate" crime. He, with two juveniles, burned a cross in the yard of a church and painted derogatory racial messages on its front door. Most of the church congregation is African American; the offender is white and reports affiliation with a white supremacist organization. The offender states he began his involvement with the organization only recently and became involved in the offense as a part of his initiation into the organization.

CASE B

A 40-year-old woman is convicted of a drug trafficking offense. She has little prior legitimate employment history and has prior convictions for other offenses involving sales of illegal drugs. Despite her lack of legitimate earnings, this offender has acquired many assets. Most of the assets have been forfeited as the prosecutor has proven they were purchased with funds obtained through illegal activities. The offender denies illegal drug usage. She states she was involved in the sale of illegal drugs for the money. She shows no remorse for her crime and has no understanding of the harm her criminal conduct has on society. In fact, she quickly states she believes her sale of illegal drugs is a "victimless" crime.

CASE C

A college professor has been granted diversion after an arrest for driving under the influence. He states he was taking a prescription medication and had three drinks at a colleague's home before driving home. The driver realized his judgment was impaired while he was driving and pulled to the shoulder of the road. Law enforcement observed him driving erratically and nearly driving into the ditch before bringing his vehicle to a stop on the shoulder of the road. They questioned him, and he admitted he had been drinking alcoholic beverages.

PART IV

Prisoner Reentry

The next three chapters focus on different methods of release from prison. The history and philosophy of reentry began as discretionary parole, and have over time been substituted and even replaced by mandatory release. This history is the subject of Chapter 11. Chapter 12 pays particular attention to issues involved in the preparation for prisoner reentry. Chapter 13 examines parole conditions and legal aspects of community supervision as well as what happens when these conditions are not met. It also reviews the effectiveness of parole.

The History of Parole: From Its Origin to the Present

CHAPTER LEARNING OBJECTIVES

- Explain how transportation and ticket-of-leave influenced the development of parole.

- Describe how parole was inspired by the work of Alexander Maconochie on Norfolk Island.

- Discuss how parole was subsequently implemented by Walter Crofton in Ireland and by Zebulon R. Brockway in New York's Elmira Reformatory.

- Discuss the history of parole into the modern era, including the criticisms that nearly led to its demise.

- Distinguish the roles of discretionary parole and mandatory supervised release.

Norfolk Island was the destination where English convicts who were disciplinary problems were sent. This view is the way the former penal colony now looks.

CHAPTER OUTLINE

Introduction

The Origins of Parole
Manuel Montesinos
Georg Michael Obermaier
Alexander Maconochie
Sir Walter Crofton and the Irish System

Development of Parole in the United States
Four Justifications of Parole
The Medical Model: 1930–1960

A Philosophical Change
From Discretionary Parole to Mandatory Release

Parole Today
Characteristics of Parolees
Functions of Parole

Summary

KEY TERMS

unconditional release
parole
mandatory release
discretionary release
parole d'honneur
Alexander Maconochie

transportation
ticket-of-leave
marks system
Norfolk Island
Sir Walter Crofton
the Irish system

Zebulon R. Brockway
medical model
just deserts
justice model
medical parole

Introduction

Of the hundreds of thousands of prisoners who reenter the community every year, one out of five is an **unconditional release,** receiving no supervision whatsoever after they leave prison because they have served their full sentence behind bars. In prison language, this is known as "maxing out" or "killing your number." Most prisoners who reenter the community do so under some type of supervised release. With nearly 800,000 state and federal prisoners on supervision currently across the country, most will be off supervision completely within one to two years (Bonczar 2008).

There are two types of post-prison supervision: discretionary and mandatory release. Individuals on **mandatory release** enter the community automatically at the expiration of their maximum term minus credited time off for good behavior. Mandatory release is decided by legislative statute or good-time laws. In contrast to mandatory release, individuals released on **discretionary release** enter the community because members of a parole board have decided that the prisoner has earned the privilege of being released from prison while still remaining under supervision of an indeterminate sentence.

Parole is the conditional release of a convicted offender from a correctional institution, under the continued custody of the state, to serve the remainder of his or her sentence in the community under supervision. Historically, parole referred only to discretionary release. But as you will see in this chapter, as laws and release methods have changed, parole has become a more general concept incorporating mandatory supervision. *Parole is a broad concept that in this text refers to post-prison supervision of both mandatory and discretionary released offenders.* Parolees on both mandatory release and discretionary release are supervised by a parole officer and adhere to similar conditions. If these conditions are not followed, either type of parolee (mandatory or discretionary) can be returned to prison for the remainder of the sentence. Figure 11.1 shows the types of release and how their numbers have changed over the years. You can see that mandatory release has increased, whereas prisoners leaving prison on discretionary release has decreased.

Unconditional Release
A type of release from prison without correctional supervision because the full sentence has been served behind bars. Also known as "maxing out" or "killing your number."

Mandatory Release
Conditional release to the community under a determinate sentence that is automatic at the expiration of the minimum term of sentence minus any credited time off for good behavior.

Discretionary Release
Conditional release because members of a parole board have decided that the prisoner has earned the privilege while still remaining under supervision of an indeterminate sentence.

Parole
Release of a convicted offender from a penal or correctional institution, under the continual custody of the state, to serve the remainder of his or her sentence in the community under supervision, either by discretionary or mandatory release stipulations.

FIGURE 11.1   Releases from State Prison, by Method of Release, 1980–2003

Note: Data are from the National Prisoners Statistics (NPS-1) series.

Source: Lauren E. Glaze and Seri Palla. 2005. *Probation and Parole in the United States, 2004.* Washington, DC: U.S.Department of Justice.

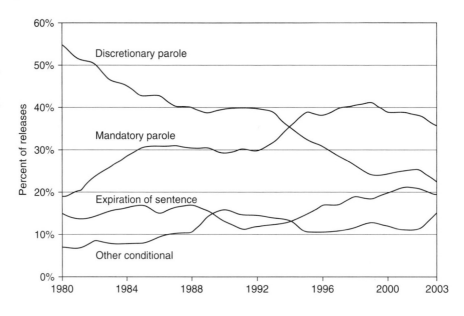

The Origins of Parole

Parole D'honneur
French for "word of honor," from which the English word parole is derived.

The English word *parole* is derived from the French **parole d'honneur,** meaning "word of honor." The French seem to prefer the term *conditional liberation* to the one borrowed from their language. In 1791, during the French Revolution, the Comte de Mirabeau (Honore-Gabriel Rigueti) published a report based on the idea of reformation, which emphasized the principles of labor, segregation, rewards under a mark system, conditional liberation, and aid on discharge. Another Frenchman, Bonneville de Marsangy, public prosecutor of Versailles, published a book in 1847 in which he discussed conditional liberation, police supervision of discharged convicts, aid upon discharge, and rehabilitation. This book was distributed by the government to the members of both chambers of Parliament (Wines 1919).

Parole as a practice originated almost simultaneously with three European prison administrators: a Spaniard, Manuel Montesinos; a German, Georg Michael Obermaier; and an Englishman, Alexander Maconochie.

Manuel Montesinos

In 1835, Col. Manuel Montesinos was appointed governor of the prison at Valencia, Spain, which held about 1,500 convicts. He organized the institution using military-type discipline, and he encouraged prisoner vocational training and education. The novelty of his plan was that there were practically no officers to watch the prisoners, who nevertheless made few, if any, attempts to escape. Each prisoner could earn a one-third reduction in the term of his sentence by good behavior and positive accomplishments. The number of prisoner recommitments while Montesinos was governor was significantly reduced. Despite all his efforts, the law that allowed this program was subsequently repealed, and Montesinos ultimately resigned. Montesinos drew the following conclusions from his experiment:

> Self-respect is one of the most powerful sentiments of the human mind, since it is the most personal; and he who will not condescend, in some degree, according to circumstances, to flattery of it, will never attain his object by any amount of chastisement; the effect of ill treatment being to irritate rather than to correct,

and thus turn from reform instead of attracting to it. The moral object of penal establishments should not be so much to inflict punishment as to correct, to receive men idle and ill-intentioned and return them to society, if possible, honest and industrious citizens. (as quoted in Wines 1919, p. 194)

GEORG MICHAEL OBERMAIER

When Georg Michael Obermaier became governor of a prison in Munich, Germany, in 1842, he found approximately 700 rebellious prisoners being kept in order by more than 100 soldiers (Wines 1919). In a short time, he gained the men's confidence, removed their chains, discharged nearly all of their guards, and appointed one of them superintendent of each of the industrial shops. His success in reforming prisoners was so great that reportedly only 10 percent of prisoners relapsed into crime after their discharge. He was aided by two favorable circumstances: Many of the men had no fixed term of imprisonment, and discharged inmates were supervised by prison aid societies.

ALEXANDER MACONOCHIE

Chief credit for developing early parole systems, however, goes to **Alexander Maconochie,** who was in charge of the English penal colony on Norfolk Island.

Transportation of English Prisoners to America The **transportation** of English criminals to the American colonies evolved from a 1597 law that provided for the banishment of dangerous criminals. The government transported convicted felons to the American colonies as a partial solution to the poor economic conditions and widespread unemployment in England. The king approved the proposal to grant

Alexander Maconochie
A British naval captain who served as governor of the penal colony on Norfolk Island, who instituted a system of early release that was the forerunner of modern parole. Maconochie is known as the "father of parole."

Transportation
The forced exile of convicted criminals. England transported convicted criminals to the American colonies until the Revolutionary War and afterward to Australia.

Courtesy Michael Maconochie, London

Alexander Maconochie served as superintendent of the penal colony on Norfolk Island, where he and his family lived with 2,000 incorrigible convicts. Maconochie was best known for his early "marks system" and as a champion of prisoner rights and privileges to encourage good behavior. Although he was successful at transforming the lives of many convicts, his humane treatment of prisoners was politically unfavorable, and he was subsequently replaced.

reprieves and stays of execution—pardons—to convicted felons who could physically be employed in the colonies.

Until 1717, the government had paid a fee to contractors for each prisoner transported. Under a new procedure adopted that year, the contractor was given "property in service," and the government took no interest in the welfare or behavior of the offender unless he or she violated the conditions of the pardon by returning to England before the sentence expired. Upon arrival in the colonies, the "services" of the prisoner were sold to the highest bidder, and thereafter the prisoner was an indentured servant.

Transportation of English Prisoners to Australia   The Revolutionary War brought an end to the practice of transporting criminals to America, but the transportation law was not repealed. Detention facilities in England became overcrowded, resulting in a more liberal granting of pardons. During a serious crime wave, the English public demanded enforcement of the transportation law, and Australia was designated as a convict settlement, with the first shipload arriving there in 1788. Transportation to Australia differed from transportation to the American colonies in that the government incurred all expenses of transportation and maintenance, and the prisoners remained under government control instead of being indentured. The governor of New South Wales granted conditional pardons—setting deserving convicts free and giving them grants of land, and even assigning newly arrived convict laborers to them. In 1811, a policy was adopted that required prisoners to serve specific periods of time before becoming eligible to receive a **ticket-of-leave** (for example, a seven-year sentence became eligible for the ticket-of-leave after four years, and those serving life sentences after eight years). However, there were no provisions for supervision of "ticket-of-leave men."

Ticket-of-Leave
A license or permit given to a convict as a reward for good conduct, which allowed him to go at large and work for himself before his sentence expired, subject to certain restrictions and revocable upon subsequent misconduct. A forerunner of parole.

Marks System   In 1837, Alexander Maconochie, a retired British naval captain and professor of geography, proposed to the House of Commons a system whereby the duration of the sentence would be determined not by time but by the prisoner's industry and good conduct. He proposed a **marks system** by which "marks" or credits would be credited daily to prisoners in accordance with their behavior and the amount of labor they performed. As prisoners demonstrated evidence of good behavior and a good work ethic, their freedom and privileges gradually increased. Marks were deducted for negative behavior. Maconochie's system allowed prisoners to move from strict imprisonment, to labor in work gangs, through conditional release around the island, and finally to complete restoration of liberty (Morris 2002).

Marks System
A theory of human motivation organized by Maconochie that granted credits for good behavior and hard work, or took away marks for negative behavior. Convicts used the credits or marks to purchase either goods or time (reduction in sentence).

Norfolk Island
The notorious British supermax penal colony 1,000 miles off the coast of Australia that housed the most incorrigible prisoners.

Norfolk Island   Maconochie was given the opportunity to test his mark system in 1840 when he was appointed superintendent of the notorious penal colony on **Norfolk Island,** 1,000 miles off the eastern coast of Australia. Norfolk Island was known to have 2,000 of the most incorrigible convicts; they had been sent there from other prisons in Britain and Ireland because they had committed crimes of violence while incarcerated (a "supermax" of the 1800s). Within a span of four years, Maconochie's system and humane treatment of the prisoners transformed their horrific lives into a peaceful orderly existence. Maconochie discontinued flogging and chain gangs and introduced adequate food, health care, disciplinary hearings, and reading material (Morris 2002).

Despite Maconochie's successes, many influential colonists in Australia who believed that convicts should be kept in irons and flogged saw Maconochie's treatment of prisoners as radical and lobbied the governor for Maconochie's dismissal. The governor was torn between his hope that Maconochie's experiment would succeed and his fear of the political power of the colonists who opposed the project. Maconochie was dismissed in 1844, and his experiment came to an abrupt end. As free settlers in Australia increased in number, they protested the use of the country as a dumping ground for prisoners. In 1867, transportation of prisoners from England to Australia was terminated (Morris 2002).

The years following saw an outbreak of crime and prison riots in England, which were attributed to poor prison administration and the lack of supervision of the ticket-of-leave men. The British public thus came to regard the ticket-of-leave system as a menace to public safety. A royal commission was appointed to investigate both areas, and the report resulted in policemen being given responsibility for supervising released prisoners. Later, a number of prisoner aid societies, supported in part by the government, were established.

SIR WALTER CROFTON AND THE IRISH SYSTEM

Sir Walter Crofton, who had studied Maconochie's innovations on Norfolk Island, became the administrator of the Irish prison system in 1854. Crofton adopted the use of the marks system inside prison. Under Crofton's administration, the **Irish system** became renowned for its three levels: strict imprisonment, indeterminate sentence, and ticket-of-leave. Each prisoner's classification was determined by the marks he or she had earned for good conduct and achievement in industry and education, a concept borrowed from Maconochie's experience on Norfolk Island.

The ticket-of-leave system was different from the one in England. The general written conditions of the Irish ticket-of-leave were supplemented with instructions designed for closer supervision and control and thus resembled the conditions of parole in the United States today. Ticket-of-leave men and women residing in rural areas were under police supervision, but a civilian employee called the inspector of released prisoners supervised those living in Dublin. The inspector had the responsibility of securing employment for the ticket-of-leave person, visiting his or her residence, and verifying employment. The Irish system of ticket-of-leave had the confidence and support of the public and of convicted criminals.

Parole was later applied to prisoners of war as a part of Articles 10, 11, and 12 of the 1949 Geneva Convention. A parole agreement is a promise that prisoners of war give their captors that they will not escape or bear arms. If a country authorizes military members to use parole, captors may choose to free a prisoner of war under certain conditions bound by the POW's word of honor. Although parole is authorized by some countries in the world, the United States does not allow any member of the armed services to enter into a parole agreement.

Sir Walter Crofton
An Irish prison reformer who established an early system of parole based on Alexander Maconochie's experiments with the mark system.

Irish System
Developed in Ireland by Sir Walter Crofton, the Irish system involved graduated levels of institutional control leading up to release under conditions similar to modern parole. The American penitentiaries were partially based on the Irish system.

The Development of Parole in the United States

In the United States, parole was first tried in New York at Elmira Reformatory in 1876. Federal parole began in June 1910 because of legislation that established the first three federal penitentiaries. In 1930, a formalized federal parole board was created under the U.S. attorney general's office. In 1950, because of a larger prison population in the federal system, the parole board expanded and was placed under the Justice Department.

FOUR JUSTIFICATIONS OF PAROLE

Four concepts justified the development of parole in the United States: (1) reduction in the length of incarceration as a reward for good conduct, (2) supervision of the parolee, (3) imposition of the indeterminate sentence, and (4) reduction in the rising cost of incarceration.

Reward for Good Conduct   Release as a result of a reduction in the time of imprisonment was always accompanied by a written agreement by which the prisoner would abide by the conditions specified by those authorizing the release. The agreement stipulated that any violation of the conditions would result in a return to the institution. The first legal recognition of shortening the term of imprisonment as a reward for good conduct in the United States was the 1817 good-time law in New York.

Post-release Supervision   Volunteers and prison society members originally supervised those released from prison. The Philadelphia Society for Alleviating the Miseries of Public Prisons recognized the importance of caring for released prisoners as early as 1822. In 1851, the society appointed two agents to assist prisoners discharged from the Philadelphia County Prison and the penitentiary. The first public employees paid to assist released prisoners were appointed by the state of Massachusetts in 1845.

Indeterminate Sentence   By 1865, American penal reformers were well aware of the reforms achieved by the conditional release programs of the Irish system. As a result, an indeterminate sentence law was adopted in 1876 in New York with the help of prison superintendent **Zebulon R. Brockway**. The system established at Elmira included grading inmates on their conduct and achievement, compulsory education, and careful selection for parole. Volunteer citizens, known as guardians, supervised the parolees. A condition of parole was that parolees report to the guardian the first day of each month. Written reports became required and were submitted to the institution after being signed by the parolee's employer and guardian. By 1944, every U.S. jurisdiction had adopted some form of parole release and indeterminate sentencing.

Zebulon R. Brockway
The American prison reformer who introduced modern correctional methods, including parole, to the Elmira Reformatory in New York in 1876.

Reducing the Cost of Incarceration   Howard Abadinsky (1978) maintained that the idea of parole was initiated in the United States primarily for economic reasons. For about one century between the 1840s and 1940s, American prisons were self-supported entirely by convict labor. Many southern penitentiaries turned a huge profit from convict labor by leasing out their convicts to private companies. The private companies benefited because they paid the prison less than they otherwise would have had to pay non-incarcerated workers for hard labor such as building railroads, making goods to sell on the open market, and growing crops. The prisons pocketed the money, given that the prisoners did not get paid. Most prisoners worked long hours "under the gun" in remote prison camps miles away from the main prison unit (Walker 1988).

Private companies liked the idea of using convict labor so much that it began to affect the employment rate of "free world" people (those who were not prisoners). Organized labor unions outside of prison began to apply pressure to limit private companies' use of convict labor. Legislation was finally passed to limit convict labor only to goods that could be sold to other government entities. Because of this legislation, prisoners in remote prison camps had to be relocated to a prison unit where they could be behind bars and work within the walls. More prisons had to be constructed to make space for these incoming prisoners. The profits decreased, and for the first time, taxpayers began to bear some of the cost of incarceration (Walker 1988). It was at this point that the idea of parole became more popular. Nearly every state had some form of discretionary release from prison by 1944—shortly after legislation was passed that limited convict labor to behind the walls.

THE MEDICAL MODEL: 1930–1960

Parole was seen as a major adjunct to the rehabilitation philosophy that dominated American corrections from the 1930s through the 1960s. This rehabilitative ideal, called the **medical model,** assumed that criminal behavior had its roots in environmental and psychosocial aspects of the offender's life and that these behaviors could be corrected. This meant that every offender would be dealt with on an individual basis to determine the causes of his or her criminal behavior.

Under the old punitive model of corrections, the question was "What did he do?" The medical model was more concerned with why criminals commit crime and what can be done to improve the convict's situation. According to the medical model, if prison staff could diagnose and treat "badness," then the lawbreaker should be released when "cured." The mechanisms for accomplishing this were the indeterminate sentence and parole. The release decision was thus shared between the court, which sets a minimum and a maximum period of incarceration, and the correctional system. The parole board's responsibility was to determine the optimal release time at which the inmate is most ready to reenter the community as a responsible citizen.

The medical model assumed that correctional specialists had the ability to diagnose an offender's problems and develop a means of curing those problems. Because one cannot know at the time of diagnosis how long it will take to effect a cure, the indeterminate sentence makes it possible, in theory at least, to confine an offender as long as is necessary and to follow up that confinement with community supervision.

Although parole has generally drawn support from many sources and has a history of consensual acceptance, it has been subject to vigorous criticism and reexamination. After World War I, various parole boards came under attack by critics who claimed that parole release failed to produce the desired lasting changes in offenders' behavior and attitudes. Other critics of the system pointed out that release was granted after only a cursory review of the inmates' records and that prison authorities had no criteria by which to measure rehabilitation as a basis for release decisions.

These criticisms led to two major changes in parole administration and organization. First, more emphasis was placed on post-release supervision, and the number of parole conditions was increased. Second, a shift occurred in parole authority from prison personnel to parole boards with independent authority and statewide jurisdiction.

> **Medical Model**
> The concept that, given proper care and treatment, criminals can be cured into productive, law-abiding citizens. This approach suggests that people commit crimes because of influences beyond their control, such as poverty, injustice, and racism.

A PHILOSOPHICAL CHANGE

In the 1970s, individualism, rehabilitation, sentence indeterminacy, and parole all seemed to fall from grace and appeared to be on their way out. A national commission stated, "One of the movements we are currently witnessing in the criminal justice field is the trend toward the establishment of determinate or 'fixed' sentencing of criminal offenders" (National Advisory Commission on Criminal Justice Standards and Goals 1973).

The correctional system's failure to reduce the steadily increasing crime rate and its inability to reduce recidivism, rehabilitate offenders, or make predictive judgments about offenders' future behavior brought about public disillusionment, disappointment, and resentment. Concern also arose that wide and unfair disparities existed in sentencing based on the offender's race, socioeconomic status, and place of conviction (Petersilia 2000b). The pendulum began to swing, and by the late 1970s it seemed to have moved 180 degrees from the rehabilitative ideal to the "just deserts" approach to criminal correction.

Just Deserts
The concept that the goal of corrections should be to punish offenders because they deserve to be punished and that punishment should be commensurate with the seriousness of the offense.

Justice Model
The correctional practice based on the concept of just deserts and even-handed punishment. The justice model calls for fairness in criminal sentencing, in that all people convicted of a similar offense will receive a like sentence. This model of corrections relies on determinate sentencing and/or abolition of parole.

In contrast to the rehabilitative ideal, the **just deserts** or **justice model** changes the focus of the system from the offender to the offense. Liberals and conservatives alike embraced determinate sentencing and the abolition of parole, but for different reasons (Cullen and Gilbert 1982). The Vietnam War, the Kent State shootings, and the Attica prison uprising convinced many liberals that the state could not be trusted to administer rehabilitation in a just and humane manner. The indeterminate sentence was too vague and without due process protections to limit discretion. The just deserts approach was perceived as providing fair punishment. For conservatives, the 1974 publication by Robert Martinson (initially discussed in Chapter 1) was interpreted to mean that few correctional treatment programs worked and that the indeterminate sentence, parole, and treatment programs were too "soft" on crime. Determinate sentencing and the just deserts approach were seen as a return to a punishment-oriented correctional system (Cullen and Gilbert 1982).

FROM DISCRETIONARY PAROLE TO MANDATORY RELEASE

In 1977, nearly nine out of ten prisoners were released via a parole board. Because of the trend toward determinate sentencing and abolishing discretionary release, only about 24 to 39 percent of prisoners are now released via discretionary release, whereas mandatory release numbers have increased (Petersilia 2003). As of 2001, 15 states and the federal system had replaced discretionary release with mandatory release by abolishing parole boards for all offenses, and another five states had abolished discretionary release for violent offenses (Hughes, Wilson, and Beck 2001). From this point forward, "parole" was now split into "discretionary release" or "mandatory release."

Under discretionary release, offenders reentered society when correctional authorities and board members believed they were ready or they had improved their lives enough to earn the privilege to be released. This meant that offenders had to show they had a reentry plan and knew how they were going to stay out of trouble. Under mandatory release, offenders are released no matter how many disciplinary reports they have had or how they acted while incarcerated. Thus, many offenders under mandatory release are ill-prepared for the transition and may not have the right kind of social support when they go home (Petersilia 2003). "In the long run, no one is more dangerous than a criminal who has no incentive to straighten himself out while in prison and who returns to society without a structured and a supervised release plan" (p. 18).

First-time offenders on mandatory release serve less time on average in prison than do first timers with discretionary release. A nationwide examination concurred that this was the case for all types of offenders, except for public-order offenders (of both genders and all races) and African American offenders who were incarcerated for property and drug crimes (Hughes, Wilson, and Beck 2001). Repeat offenders convicted of two or more felonies are serving longer sentences now than repeat offenders were in 1990 (Hughes, Wilson, and Beck 2001).

Parole Today

Table 11.1 lists by state the current discretionary capability of the parole board to release prisoners. "Full" discretion means that the parole board has discretion to release all inmates, although in most states prisoners must still serve a minimum percent of their sentence. "Limited" discretion means the parole board has discretion to release only certain kinds of offenders and that parole release is completely denied to recidivists or offenders convicted of violent crimes. States that no longer

TABLE 11.1   Release Authority of Parole Boards by State

State	Discretion to Release	Indeterminate or Determinate	Comments: Who Is Eligible for Discretionary Release?
Alabama	Full	I	
Alaska	Full	I, D	
Arizona	Old cases	D	Offenses prior to 1994
Arkansas	Old cases	D	Offenses prior to 1994
California	Limited	I, D	Lifers only with concurrence of governor
Colorado	Full	I, D	
Connecticut	Full	I, D	Violent offenders have face-to-face hearings
Delaware	Old cases	D	Offenses prior to 6/30/90
Florida	Old cases	D	Capital murder/sexual batt. prior to 10/1/94
Georgia	Limited	I, D	All nonviolent offenders
Hawaii	Full	I, D	Violent off. must meet mandatory minimum
Idaho	Full	I, D	Violent off. must meet mandatory minimum
Illinois	Limited	D	Juveniles only
Indiana	None	D	
Iowa	Full	I	
Kansas	Old cases	D	Offenses prior to 7/1/93
Kentucky	Full	I, D	Violent off. must meet mandatory minimum
Louisiana	Limited	I, D	All nonviolent offenders
Maine	None	D	
Maryland	Limited	I, D	All offenders eligible except lifers
Massachusetts	Full	I	
Michigan	Full	D	All must meet minimum time first
Minnesota	Limited	I, D	Strictly controlled Hearing/Release Unit
Mississippi	Old cases	D	Offenses prior to 7/1/95
Missouri	Full	I, D	Violent must meet minimum first
Montana	Full	D	All must meet minimum time first
Nebraska	Full	D	All must meet minimum time first
Nevada	Full	I	
New Hampshire	Full	I	
New Jersey	Full	I	
New Mexico	Old cases	D	Offenses prior to 1979
New York	Full	I, D	All must meet minimum time first
North Carolina	Old cases	D	Offenses prior to 1994
North Dakota	Full	I, D	Violent must meet minimum first
Ohio	Old cases	D	Offenses prior to 7/1/96
Oklahoma	Limited	D	Governor has releasing authority
Oregon	Old cases	D	Offenses prior to 11/1/89
Pennsylvania	Full	I	With sentences of 2 years or more
Rhode Island	Full	D	All must meet minimum time first
South Carolina	Limited	I, D	Sentences must be below 20 years
South Dakota	Old cases	D	Offenses prior to 7/1/96

(Continued)

TABLE 11.1   Release Authority of Parole Boards by State (*continued*)

State	Discretion to Release	Indeterminate or Determinate	Comments: Who Is Eligible for Discretionary Release?
Tennessee	Limited	I, D	Nonviolent offenders eligible only
Texas	Full	I, D	
Utah	Full	I	
Vermont	Full	I	
Virginia	Old cases	D	Offense prior to 1995
Washington	Limited	I, D	
West Virginia	Full	D	All must meet minimum time first
Wisconsin	Old cases	D	Offenses prior to 2000
Wyoming	Full	D	All must meet minimum time first

Full = Parole board has discretion to release all inmates (though some must still serve a minimum percent of their sentence)

Limited = Parole board has discretion to release only certain kinds of offenders, whereas parole release is denied to others

Old cases = No parole discretionary release exists on current cases—only on the few cases left that were committed in the past that were under the "old law"

Indeterminate/Determinate sentence = The philosophy of sentencing practiced currently (if both are listed, determinate sentencing is usually assigned to violent or repeat offenders)

Adapted from the Association of Paroling Authorities International. 2005. Accessed: http://www.apaintl.org/content/en/pdf/2005_ParolingAuthorities_Survey.pdf

have discretionary release for anyone still honor the few cases that were committed in the past under the old law. These states are labeled "old cases." This table also classifies the current sentencing philosophies for each state as "indeterminate," "determinate," or a combination of both depending on the type of offense.

States that limit the releasing power of the parole board require that prisoners serve a flat minimum or some proportion of the maximum sentence before becoming eligible for parole. Other jurisdictions that retained discretionary release have established guidelines to reduce and structure release decision making. Both the American Probation and Parole Association and the Association of Paroling Authorities favor retaining parole boards as an important correctional institution tool. Some of the arguments in favor of discretionary release include:

- Parole boards can impose prisoner participation in treatment programs as incentives for release; with automatic release, there are no incentives for prisoners to better themselves while behind bars.
- Parole boards have improved their techniques for more objective and open decision making through parole guidelines.
- Victims can attend parole board hearings to convince the board not to release their offender, but victims have no say in mandatory or automatic release situations.
- Release from prison is a right under automatic supervision, not a privilege under discretionary parole.
- Release decisions are made by computer under automatic release, not by a human parole board that can keep prisoners in prison if it feels the offenders remain a danger to society.
- Prisoners on post-release supervision generated by automatic release can still commit crimes.
- Abolishing discretionary release does not mean that prisoners will serve their full sentence; it does not prevent prisoners from getting out, and it does not necessarily increase public safety (Burke 1995).

Joan Petersilia agrees: "While abolishing parole [discretionary release] may make good politics, it contributes to bad correctional practices—and ultimately, less public safety. . . . The public doesn't understand the tremendous power that is lost when parole is abandoned" (Petersilia 2000a, p. 32). Parole is far from completely disappearing from the correctional scene. Growth in the sheer number of releases is expected when prisoners complete the minimum terms of their sentences.

CHARACTERISTICS OF PAROLEES

According to Table 11.2, almost 825,000 people were on parole in 2007 (Bonczar 2008). This table compares the number of parolees in 2004 with those in 2007. In nearly every state, the number of people released on parole was higher. But does the higher number of parolees mean that more people are getting paroled? To control for the general growth in the U.S. population overall, the table also examines the incarceration rate and the parole rate for each state for 2007. Generally, the

TABLE 11.2   Parolee Population and Rates of Parole and Imprisonment Per 100,000

Region and jurisdiction	Parole population 2004	Parole population 2007	Number of *parolees* per 100,000 adult residents	Number of *prisoners* per 100,00 U.S. residents
United States, total	**765,355**	**824,365**	**360**	**506**
Federal	89,821	92,673	40	59
State	675,534	731,692	319	447
Northeast	**154,819**	**155,288**	**367**	**306**
Connecticut	2,552	2,177	81	410
Maine	32	32	3	159
Massachusetts	3,854	3,209	64	246
New Hampshire[a]	1,212	1,653	162	222
New Jersey	14,180	15,043	226	308
New York	54,524	53,669	360	322
Pennsylvania	77,175	78,107	807	365
Rhode Island	368	462	56	235
Vermont	922	936	190	260
Midwest	**127,840**	**136,343**	**270**	**393**
Illinois	34,277	33,354	344	371
Indiana	7,499	10,362	217	426
Iowa[b]	3,317	3,546	155	291
Kansas[b]	4,525	4,842	232	312
Michigan	20,924	21,131	277	499
Minnesota	3,872	4,744	120	181
Missouri[a]	17,400	19,849	443	506
Nebraska	805	800	60	243
North Dakota	239	342	69	221
Ohio	18,882	17,575	201	442
South Dakota	2,217	2,812	466	413
Wisconsin	13,883	16,986	395	397

(*Continued*)

TABLE 11.2   Parolee Population and Rates of Parole and Imprisonment Per 100,000 (*continued*)

Region and jurisdiction	Parole population 2004	Parole population 2007	Number of *parolees* per 100,000 adult residents	Number of *prisoners* per 100,00 U.S. residents
South	**231,994**	**243,512**	**291**	**556**
Alabama[a]	7,745	7,790	221	615
Arkansas	14,844	19,388	904	502
Delaware	539	535	81	482
District of Columbia[a]	5,318	5,569	1,169	–
Florida	4,888	4,654	33	535
Georgia	23,344	23,111	326	563
Kentucky[b]	8,006	12,741	392	512
Louisiana	24,387	24,085	746	865
Maryland	14,351	13,856	324	404
Mississippi	1,979	2,015	93	734
North Carolina	2,882	3,311	48	361
Oklahoma[a]	4,329	3,100	150	665
South Carolina	3,292	2,433	72	524
Tennessee	8,410	10,496	222	424
Texas[a]	102,072	101,748	582	669
Virginia[a]	4,392	6,850	116	490
West Virginia	1,216	1,830	128	333
West	**160,881**	**196,549**	**373**	**438**
Alaska[b]	951	1,544	305	447
Arizona	5,671	6,807	144	554
California[b]	110,261	123,764	453	471
Colorado	7,383	11,086	299	465
Hawaii	2,296	2,110	210	338
Idaho	2,370	3,114	282	483
Montana[b]	810	966	130	356
Nevada	3,610	3,653	189	509
New Mexico	2,676	3,527	238	313
Oregon	20,858	22,658	779	369
Utah	3,312	3,597	194	239
Washington[a]	120	13,017	262	273
Wyoming	563	706	176	394

[a]All data were estimated. [b]Excludes parolees in one of the following categories: absconder, out of state, or inactive.

Source: Lauren E. Glaze and Seri Palla. 2005. *Probation and Parole in the United States, 2004.* Washington, DC: U.S. Department of Justice, Bureau of Justice Statistics, p. 5; Lauren E. Glaze and Thomas P. Bonczar. 2008. *Probation and Parole in the United States, 2007.* Washington, DC: U.S. Department of Justice, Bureau of Justice Statistics, p. 4-5; Heather C. West and William J. Sabol. 2008. *Prisoners in 2007.* Washington, DC: U.S. Department of Justice, Bureau of Justice Statistics.

Southern region had the highest incarceration rates, yet the lowest parole rates. The northeast region had the opposite situation—a higher rate of parole and a lower rate of incarceration per 100,000 residents. Take a look to see how your state compares to the rest of the nation.

Table 11.3 shows how parolees have changed over time. Parolees typically served between one and two years of time on post-prison supervision, with 37 percent on

TABLE 11.3 Characteristics of Adult Parolees Over Time

	1995	2000	2007
Gender			
Male	90%	88%	88%
Female	10	12	12
Race/Ethnicity			
White	34	38	42
Black	45	40	37
Hispanic	21	21	19
American Indian/Alaska Native	1	1	1
Asian/Pacific Island/Hawaii Native	**	**	1
Status of Supervision			
Active	78	83	84
Inactive	11	4	4
Absconded	6	7	7
Supervised out of state	4	5	4
Other	**	1	2
Sentence Length			
Less than one year	6	3	4
One year or more	94	97	96
Type of Offense			
Violent	*	*	26
Property	*	*	24
Drug	*	*	37
Other	*	*	13
Adults Entering Parole			
Discretionary parole	50	37	33
Mandatory parole	45	54	48
Reinstatement	4	6	9
Other	2	2	11
Adults Leaving Parole			
Successful completion	45	43	44
Returned to incarceration	41	42	39
With new sentence	12	11	11
Other	29	31	28
Absconder[a]	*	9	11
Other unsuccessful[a]	*	2	2
Death	**	**	1
Other	10	2	3

Note: For every characteristic there were people of unknown status or type. *Not available. **Less than 0.5 percent. [a]In 1995 absconder and other unsuccessful were reported among "other."

Sources: Lauren E. Glaze and Seri Palla. 2005. *Probation and Parole in the United States, 2004.* Washington, DC: U.S. Department of Justice, Bureau of Justice Statistics; Lauren E. Glaze and Thomas P. Bonczar. 2008. *Probation and Parole in the United States, 2007.* Washington, DC: U.S. Department of Justice, Bureau of Justice Statistics, p. 6.

parole for a drug offense, 24 percent for a property offense, and 26 percent for a crime of violence. Almost half (48 percent) are on mandatory release, whereas 33 percent are on some form of discretionary parole, and the rest had their parole reinstated. Most parolees were men, but since 2000, 12 percent of offenders on parole have been women. Despite released offenders having served more time and a greater portion of their sentence before release, parole success rates have remained unchanged, with less than half of all parolees able to successfully complete their parole term (Glaze and Bonczar 2008; Glaze and Palla 2005).

FUNCTIONS OF PAROLE

The function of parole is arguably different now than it was in the past. Parole used to serve as a gradual transition from prison to the community to aid in reintegration and reduce recidivism by helping ex-offenders remain gainfully employed so they could support themselves. Williams, McShane, and Dolny (2000a) observe that the function of parole has changed:

> *[P]arole is tasked primarily with protecting the public from released offenders.* This goal is accomplished in three general objectives: (1) by enforcing restrictions and controls on parolees in the community, (2) by providing services that help parolees integrate into a noncriminal lifestyle, and (3) by increasing the public's level of confidence in the effectiveness and responsiveness of parole services through the first two activities (that is, in part a reduction in fear of crime). (pp. 45–59)

Some would argue that parole has essentially changed from being a reintegrative component of higher tolerance to merely enforcing the law with low tolerance for mistakes. This focus may be one reason why revocation rates remain so high.

Prison Population Control   Parole boards have also functioned as the "back doorkeeper" of America's prisons, often serving as the operators of safety valves to relieve crowded institutions. Some states have given legislative authority and direction to their parole boards to control prison populations. Others have done so through informal agreements among the governor, the director of corrections, and the parole board. Boards in states such as Georgia, Michigan, and Texas became actively involved in

One of the functions of parole is to provide a release valve for crowded prisons so that prison conditions do not become unconstitutional.

© Halfdark/Getty Images

prison population management out of necessity. Prison populations in those states had risen to levels that threatened the correctional authorities' ability to maintain control of their institutions (Rhine, Smith, and Jackson 1991, pp. 97–98). Federal court orders established "caps" on the prison populations in Michigan and Texas. Through a variety of formal and informal methods, parole boards in each of these jurisdictions have been utilized in efforts to reduce and maintain the prison population, with varying degrees of success.

Most authorities agree that in the long term, it is not feasible to control prison populations only by parole board action. Using parole for population control has had detrimental effects on post-release supervision because of escalating caseload sizes. Jurisdictions have increased and expanded community correctional facilities— such as halfway houses, work release centers, house arrest, electronic monitoring, and intensive supervision—to monitor the offenders who are granted release. Furthermore, in some states the continuing escalation in prison populations has had another, albeit unanticipated, effect on the ability of parole officers to revoke parole for anything other than serious criminal violations. In several states, parole officers have experienced difficulty in revoking parolees for technical violations of the conditions of supervision, even when indications exist of deteriorating behavior on the part of the parolee (this issue is discussed more in Chapter 13).

Should Terminally Ill Prisoners Be Released Early?   Parole can be a back-end release strategy for prisoners who pose minimal security risk and who would be better served in the community. Prisoners who would most likely be eligible for this category are those with terminal illnesses, particularly those with full-blown AIDS or cancer. **Medical parole,** or compassionate release, is the conditional release from prison of prisoners with a terminal illness who have been given less than one year to live and do not pose an undue risk to public safety if released.

> **Medical Parole**
> The conditional release from prison to the community of a prisoner with a terminal illness who does not pose an undue risk to public safety.

How do other people view the issue? Releasing a terminally ill prisoner to a community hospice to live out their remaining last few months does not seem to sit well with university students (Boothby and Overduin 2007) despite the repeated arguments showing it to be a more cost effective and more humane approach to hospice care for inmates and their families (Berry 2009; Rikard and Rosenberg 2007). Medical parole seems to be a politically unpopular issue, as evidenced by the much-publicized and repeated denials of Susan Atkins' request for medical parole (most recently in September 2009). The parole board cited the victim's survivors' wishes, despite the offender's pleas for mercy and evidence pointing to the fact that Atkins no longer presents a danger to the public safety. Susan Atkins, a follower of Charles Manson, was convicted nearly 40 years ago for her role in multiple slayings. At the time of her last parole hearing, Atkins was terminally ill and bedridden with brain cancer and also had one leg amputated. She died in prison on September 24, 2009.

At present, 65 percent of state and federal prison systems and 44 percent of city/county jails have a medical parole policy, but few states utilize this option (Hammett, Harmon, and Maruschak 1999). A study conducted over one decade ago found that 12 prison systems permitted compassionate release for 143 offenders, and 15 jails granted early release for an additional 171, bringing the total number to just over 300 prisoners released early nationwide in a single year for medical purposes (Hammett, Harmon, and Maruschak 1999). Since that time, the use of medical parole has declined even further, probably because of political reasons. For example, in 2007, out of the 60 requests made by federal inmates, only 10 inmates received approval. Box 11.1 presents a look at how medical parole is decided. Large-scale evaluations of medical parole have not been conducted, so its effect on public safety and how parolees receive treatment services in the community remain unknown.

BOX 11.1   COMMUNITY CORRECTIONS UP CLOSE

Should Terminally Ill Prisoners Be Paroled to a Community Hospice?

Every state has its own procedures for determining candidacy for medical parole and establishes for itself the parties (e.g., doctors, judges, parole boards, wardens, and governors) that partake in the decision-making process. In Maryland's medical parole program, inmates were initially nominated by prison nurses and doctors who worked with terminally ill prisoners with a documented diagnosis and full medical evaluation. Once the inmates were medically eligible, the warden and a case management team performed a security evaluation of the level of risk that the inmate might pose in the community. If the inmate posed a minimal risk, then an aftercare plan would be put together by a social worker. Kendig, Boyle, and Swetz (1996) found that inmates were candidates for this program if they "no longer jeopardized public safety if released" and at least one of the following three conditions existed:

1. A verifiable terminal medical condition
2. A medical condition that incapacitated the individual so that imprisonment was not required to ensure public safety
3. A medical condition that could be more appropriately treated in a community treatment facility instead of a prison (p. 22)

The researchers described the next level of scrutiny that these nominated cases undergo after they pass the inspection of prison unit employees:

These evaluations were reviewed by the DOC [Department of Corrections] medical director, the director of social work, and the assistant commissioner for inmate health care, who then recommended for or against medical parole to the commissioner of correction.

Upon review of the relevant assessments and recommendations, the commissioner of correction either ruled against medical parole or forwarded his recommendation for medical parole to the Maryland Parole Commission. . . . Inmates with life sentences or parole-restricted sentences . . . were referred by the Maryland Parole Commission with a recommendation for parole to the governor for gubernatorial approval or denial. (Kendig, Boyle, and Swetz 1996, p. 22)

The researchers reviewed all 230 cases that were submitted for medical parole from 1991 to 1994. Of those cases, 144 (62 percent) were approved for parole, but only 120 were released (some prisoners died prior to being approved or released). A follow-up of the 120 released inmates at the end of 1994 revealed that 60 inmates were still on parole in the community, 54 inmates died, two inmates had successfully completed their sentences (and were not on parole), and 4 inmates had failed parole and returned to prison. Three of the four inmates who had returned to prison committed technical violations (for example, verbally threatening staff, using illegal drugs, or moving to a new address without notifying the parole officer). One inmate violated parole by committing an armed robbery. After serving 12 months in prison for the robbery, this inmate was released and died two months later. The researchers concluded that "early release for inmates with terminal illnesses can be accomplished expeditiously and with minimal impact on public safety" (p. 25).

Source: Newton Kendig, Barbara Boyle, and Anthony Swetz. 1996. The Maryland Division of Correction Medical-Parole Program: A Four-Year Experience, 1991 to 1994. *AIDS & Public Policy Journal* *11*(1) 21–27.

Should other mechanisms be developed in place of parole? If so, what alternatives to parole are available? Some people answer this question by saying that more prison time should replace parole. The problem with this answer is that the fiscal realities and economic situations in many states have ended new prison construction and in fact, have even closed down or vacated prison units that they could not afford to operate.

SUMMARY

- Parole has its origins in the work of penal reformers in Germany, Spain, and France, and on Norfolk Island in the early decades of the 19th century.

- Walter Crofton of Ireland and U.S. prison reformer Zebulon R. Brockway studied Maconochie's work on Norfolk Island and implemented his ideas.

- Steadily increasing crime rates, the perceived failure of rehabilitation programs, and the perception that parole boards were incapable of making predictive judgments about offenders' future behavior caused the medical rehabilitation model and indeterminate sentencing philosophies of the 1930s to be replaced by the justice model and determinate sentencing in the 1970s.

- Parole is now divided into discretionary release and mandatory release. Under discretionary release, which has decreased, offenders reenter society when correctional authorities believe they have improved their lives enough to earn the privilege to be released. Under mandatory release, which has steadily increased, offenders are released regardless of disciplinary reports or their behavior while incarcerated. Thus, many offenders under mandatory release are ill prepared for the transition.

- Currently, 20 percent of all people released from prison do not receive post-prison supervision.

  Parole is focused on enforcement of conditions and public safety, and secondarily on reintegration and treatment services. Although parole is still a way to control prison crowding, medical parole is hardly used at all.

DISCUSSION QUESTIONS

1. Discuss the founders of parole and their contributions.

2. What was the English ticket-of-leave, and how did that compare with the marks system?

3. Why did England transport convicts to America and Australia? What was the connection between transportation and parole?

4. What was the significance of Alexander Maconochie's style of prison administration on the behavior of the convicts?

5. Why was Maconochie dismissed from Norfolk Island despite his success?

6. How did parole develop in the United States? Be sure to include discussions of the Irish system and the indeterminate sentence in your explanation.

7. Why did the medical model fall out of favor? What factors were associated with this phenomenon?

8. What is the justice model of corrections? What factors were associated with its emergence in the 1970s?

9. What happened to parole under the justice model? Why?

10. What role does parole play in the twenty-first century?

11. What are the pros and cons of abolishing parole?

12. How do you feel about the use of medical parole?

WEB SITES

U.S. Department of Justice Parole Statistics
http://www.ojp.usdoj.gov/bjs/pandp.htm

History of Parole in Alabama
http://www.pardons.state.al.us

History of Parole in Delaware
http://www.state.de.us/parole/default.shtml

History of Parole in New York
http://parole.state.ny.us/introhistory.html

History of Parole in Texas
http://tdcj.state.tx.us/parole/parole-history.htm

History of Parole in Utah
http://bop.utah.gov/history.html

History of Parole in Canada
http://www.npb-cnlc.gc.ca/about/parolehistory_e.htm

12

Preparing for Prisoner Reentry: Discretionary Parole and Mandatory Release

CHAPTER LEARNING OBJECTIVES

- Examine the preparations needed for the reentry process while the offender is still incarcerated.
- Discuss how reentry affects the prisoner, the victim, the community, and the prisoner's family.

- Explain mandatory supervision or discretionary parole.
- Illustrate due process in parole selection, with an emphasis on appellate court decisions.

© Raymond Alarid, Jr

Nearly 600,000 prisoners are released every year just like these two men, who are getting out on mandatory release after having each served 10 years.

CHAPTER OUTLINE

Introduction

Issues in Reentry
The Prisoner's Family
The Victim's Role in Reentry
Reentry and the Community
Community-Based Reentry Initiatives

Eligibility for Parole
Time Sheets and Eligibility Dates
Prerelease Preparation within the Institution

The Parole Board and Releasing Authority
Term and Qualifications of the Parole Board
The Parole Hearing

Parole Hearing Attendees
The Parole Board Decision

Models of Parole Release Decisions
The Surveillance Model
The Procedural Justice Model
The Risk Prediction Model

Legal Issues in Parole Hearings
No Due Process Protections
Use of Hearsay, DNA, and No Right to an Attorney

Prisoners' Perceptions of Parole Selection

Summary

KEY TERMS

reentry
reentry courts
parole board
minimum eligibility date
maximum eligibility date

good time
parole eligibility date
prerelease facility
prerelease plan
full board review

victim impact statement
salient factor score
liberty interest

Introduction

More than 95 percent of incarcerated prisoners will eventually return to their communities—nearly half within only a two-year period of time. Given that about 650,000 offenders are released *every year,* there are a substantial number of people who are making a major life transition, many of whom will do so without community supervision, and/or without having a concrete plan of employment, savings, and living arrangements. The theoretical explanation of this process originates from how offenders learn to desist from crime. In other words, it is a study of how release from prison, and all the changes that accompany it, affect how prisoners change dysfunctional behaviors into new behaviors that keep them out (Bahr, et al. 2005). Prisoner **reentry** is any activity or program dedicated to preparing and integrating parolees into the community as law-abiding citizens, using a collaborative approach with parole officers, treatment providers, and the community.

> **Reentry**
> The process of preparing and integrating parolees into the community as law-abiding citizens using a collaborative approach with parole officers and treatment providers.

Reentry into the community is a vulnerable time that affects the prisoner, his or her family, his or her employer, the victim, and the surrounding community. Box 12.1 examines what it would be like to get out of prison so you can better understand some of the needs and challenges former prisoners face when coming back to the larger community.

Issues in Reentry

Successful reentry includes prerelease planning, community referrals, and quick access to benefit programs and continuity of care so there is no gap between the care received at the institution and in the new community situation (Hammett, Roberts,

BOX 12.1   COMMUNITY CORRECTIONS UP CLOSE

What Might It Be Like to Transition from Prison to the Community?

Imagine that you've just gotten out of prison after spending three years of your life locked up in the same routine and boring life you've grown accustomed to. Now that you're out, you want to celebrate, get back with your old friends, and try to catch up on the time you lost. After all, there's a lot of catching up to do. The people and situations you remember seem different, however. You get back to your neighborhood and realize that the people who were doing well have moved on and all you see now in your neighborhood are the people who are not doing so well. They'll be glad to lend you a couple of bucks or get you drunk so you can celebrate. But those were the people and situations that helped you get yourself into this mess to begin with. What now? You burned your bridges with your brothers, who won't talk to you. Your mother will let you stay with her only until you can get on your feet again, but you don't know how long her support will last. You have a daughter who has been living with her grandmother (your mom). Your daughter is now 5 years old and doesn't even know you. You desperately want to connect with her but don't feel confident you have the skills to make the first move. You also feel guilty for not being able to pay your mom for raising your daughter and are afraid you'll never

be able to pay her back. You feel this huge sense of urgency, but at the same time, fear and depression set in, and you wonder if leaving prison early was a mistake.

Like most people who relocate to a new state, offenders need to obtain identification cards, change their address, find housing, and find a job. If relocation isn't stressful enough on its own, think of the additional challenges of finding a job with only a high school education or GED, having to explain a transient (or nonexistent) employment record, and the additional stigma of admitting your felony record. Not to mention that many people who relocate know when they are moving, while many offenders in prison do not know their exact release date very far in advance, so it presents a challenge to plan for anything other than "Who's coming to meet me at the front door to pick me up?" Other challenges include overcoming a drug or alcohol addiction, managing stress and anger, and avoiding situations that may contribute to the beginnings of bad habits. Most offenders who do not make the transition will fall short within the first six to nine months after they leave prison. The reentry process therefore starts while prisoners are incarcerated and attempts to bridge this crucial phase.

and Kennedy 2001). As Box 12.1 illustrates, a number of challenges stand between the offender and successful reentry. First, recently released offenders are indigent but still need an identification card, clothes, and bus pass; up to one-third also need medications for a physical or psychological condition (LaVigne 2006). They may not be eligible for certain benefits, and the prerelease institution may need to assist them in applying for various programs, which may take a few months for approval.

Second, there is a difference between giving offenders a list of referrals and actually making appointments for them. Given the federal regulations against openly sharing medical records and that most offenders do not leave with medical records in hand, some releasees experience a dangerous lapse between the time when their medications run out and the time when they are able to see a doctor and obtain prescription refills. Some offenders lack the initiative or the education to find a specific service provider that is right for their situation, and they will be more likely to follow through if they are expected to appear for a prescheduled appointment.

Third, parolees and other recently released offenders have other survival needs to meet, such as finding and maintaining stable employment, finding suitable housing, and staying clean of illegal drugs. They also require transportation to find employment, go to work, and attend treatment sessions. Their health care or mental health may be overlooked in light of all the other responsibilities that need their attention (Hammett, Roberts, and Kennedy 2001). In addition to the problems already mentioned, women parolees also reported the need for education and employment services, protection from abusive relationships in the community (their abuser continuing to stalk or hurt them), and child advocacy and family reunification (Richie 2001). Even after being incarcerated for as little as two months, women experienced shifts in family structure, such as separation, divorce, and where dependent children lived (Arditti and Few 2006).

The Prisoner's Family

The prisoner's family has suffered during the period of incarceration with the stigma of having a loved one behind bars. More than 1.5 million children under age 18 have at least one parent who is currently incarcerated. A significant number of prisoners' children were raised by extended family members such as grandparents, aunts, or sisters. As the years go by, prisoners with long sentences tend to receive less financial support and fewer face-to-face visits and letters. Even when prisoners are released to the community, between 24 and 54 percent have someone there to meet them at the prison or to pick them up at the bus station to take them home (Seiter and Kadela 2003; LaVigne 2006). If the prisoner was supporting dependents prior to arrest, years of financial and emotional neglect will have changed these relationships. For prisoners' families, reentry means that these ties must be reestablished or mended.

Yet, through all of this, families seem to remain supportive when prisoners are released, helping the offender find a job and a place to live. Within the life course perspective, family can affect how prisoners change their behaviors from drug use and other dysfunctional habits to healthier, socially acceptable lifestyles. Friends were less supportive of family because of the tendency to influence the offender to return to unproductive and illegal behavior (Bahr, et al. 2005). About 80 percent of prisoners lived with one or more family members upon release. As Bahr and colleagues observed, family support was empirically found to be instrumental in overall offender success and reduction of recidivism (LaVigne 2006). An example of a New York reentry program using a family case management technique is PARTNER, which stands for Parolees and Relatives toward Newly Enhanced Relationships. A team consists of a family case manager from La Bodega, a New York parole officer, the offender, and the offender's family. The case manager visits the offender's family and conducts a needs assessment prior to the offender's release. PARTNER is a model program for how communities and government agencies can work together to enhance prisoner reentry (Lehman et al. 2002).

The Victim's Role in Reentry

Most offenders know their victim as an intimate or an acquaintance. Under the philosophy of restorative justice (discussed in Chapter 10), the offender has a responsibility for repairing the harm done to both the victim and the community. Therefore, the victim's participation in the prerelease process assists in establishing special conditions at reentry. For example, some victims become active in victim impact panels or victim mediation sessions (Herman and Wasserman 2001). The parole board will be more receptive to the victim if the victim is present at the hearing. Furthermore, the community (for example, potential employers, landlords, and neighbors) will be more receptive to the offender's reentry if community members know the victim supports the reentry efforts (Lehman et al. 2002).

Even though the victim may not want to see the offender released early by the parole board, discretionary parole is viewed as safer for the victim than merely releasing offenders to the community without supervision because they have "maxed out" their sentence (Herman and Wasserman 2001).

REENTRY AND THE COMMUNITY

We know that the locations where parolees reside are *not* evenly spread within the community. Certain areas of the city receive a disproportionately larger number of parolees, and these areas have a high amount of unemployment, open drug use, and community instability and disorganization. As more and more prisoners return to the same communities, the community becomes less cohesive and more unstable, with the potential to become more criminogenic (Seiter and Kadela 2003). Some experts believe that reentry can encompass restorative justice and civic community service using a model of civic engagement if the community is willing to accept offenders returning to their communities (Bazemore and Stinchcomb 2004). Other experts say that reentry encompasses more than community acceptance:

> The reentry philosophy is based on the belief that police, courts, institutions, and community corrections all have a role in creating significant, long-term rehabilitative change for offenders. This philosophy assumes that criminal justice agencies cannot create long-lasting change for offenders without the inclusion of the family, community-based service providers, and the faith community. (Wilkinson, Rhine, and Henderson-Hurley 2005, p. 160)

This means that reentry is based on more than just criminal justice, but it must overlap with workforce development, family/social policy, and health policy to be truly successful. This is why the federal government began various community-based reentry initiatives with funding from the Department of Justice, the Department of Labor, and the Department of Health and Human Services.

Another reentry initiative allows employers who hire parolees and ex-felons to receive federal tax credits after the employee has worked a certain amount of time or has earned a certain amount of money. Since 1985, Texas has operated a statewide program called "Project RIO" that provides job training and interviews for prisoners while incarcerated to link eligible offenders with appropriate skills with employers who know their status. A study by the criminal justice policy council found that recidivism was 17 percent lower for Project RIO participants than for non participants (Solis 2006).

Inmates at the Plainfield Re-Entry Facility in Indiana work on computers during a class to provide offenders the skills needed to find employment after their release.

© AP Photo/John Harrell

COMMUNITY-BASED REENTRY INITIATIVES

The issue of reentry has been drawing more attention recently. Programs that support the reentry of criminal offenders exist in greater numbers, particularly with respect to housing, job placement, mentoring services, and faith-based initiatives (Wilkinson and Rhine 2005). Reentry partnerships have formed with faith-based organizations and grassroots community groups in neighborhoods that receive a disproportionate number of prisoners returning to the streets (Robinson and Travis 2000). Reentry partnerships do not necessarily involve more resources—they merely involve using existing resources in a smarter and more holistic way by collaborating with other agencies in criminal justice and the larger community. Let's examine a few of these as examples.

Reentry Courts   **Reentry courts** are a collaborative, team-based program that occurs after prison with the aim of improving the link between parole supervision and treatment providers. Reentry court programs initially identify and begin to work with offenders prior to release. After release, the offender has structured court appointments with the reentry team, which coordinates job training, housing, substance abuse treatment, and transportation. Reentry courts are similar to drug courts (discussed in Chapter 2) in that they use judges, court hearings, and graduated sanctions and incentives to reward positive behavior and predictably punish negative behavior. They operate on contracts that keep offenders law abiding for fear of returning to prison (Robinson and Travis 2000). Two examples are discussed below.

A Colorado reentry court has the goal of reintegrating parolees under mandatory release who have a dual diagnosis of mental illness and a substance abuse problem. The parolee initially meets with an administrative law judge within 14 days of leaving prison. The judge, together with the offender, the parole officer, and the mental health treatment provider, establishes monthly goals, and this group meets every month for one year to revisit the reentry goals (Robinson and Travis 2000).

Another reentry court in East Harlem targeted nonviolent felons who had at least two convictions. The program had three phases, which one-third of participants had successfully completed; the other two-thirds were in an earlier stage of the program. Initial evaluations of 45 participants found that 22 percent were convicted of committing a new crime while under a one-year supervision of the reentry court. The 45 participants were compared with a matched group of 90 parolees who did not attend reentry court, and the two groups had similar recidivism rates (Farole 2003). Whereas these sample sizes are too small to make any general statements about reentry courts, researchers may need to better understand factors that involve success after prison. Preliminary analyses of a reentry preparation program called Project Greenlight compared participants with a matched group of parolees and found that Greenlight participants performed no better than regular parolees (Wilson and Davis 2006). As more is learned about why ex-convicts return to prison, the increased attention to the needs of prisoners for substantial assistance with reentry has certainly been a step in the right direction.

Reentry Courts
A collaborative, team-based program that aims to improve the link between parole supervision and treatment providers to help recent parolees become stabilized.

Eligibility for Parole

The first step in the reentry process is that an offender must be eligible for parole consideration. Those permanently ineligible for release include offenders on death row, offenders serving life *without* parole, and some habitual offenders sentenced under statutes such as "three strikes and you're out."

TIME SHEETS AND ELIGIBILITY DATES

For the rest of the inmates (those with mandatory or discretionary releases), a computer keeps track of all good time earned and the number of days served to determine minimum and maximum eligibility dates. The **minimum eligibility date** is the shortest amount of time defined by statute, minus good time earned, that must be served before the offender can go before the parole board. In some states, such as Nebraska, parole boards are required to see offenders once per year even if the minimum eligibility date has not yet been met (Proctor 1999). The **maximum eligibility date** is the longest amount of time that can be served before the inmate must, by law, be released (where the offender has "maxed out" his or her sentence).

Good time (or "gain time") was originally introduced as an incentive by prison authorities for institutional good conduct. Good time reduces the period of sentence an inmate must serve before parole eligibility. Now, good time is automatically granted (in states that have it) unless the inmate commits a disciplinary infraction. That is, good time is lost for misbehavior in prison, not awarded for good behavior. Good-time credits vary greatly from state to state, ranging from five days per month to as much as 45 days per month. In recent years large amounts of good time have been awarded (for example, 120 days for every month served) by correctional authorities who are forced to temporarily increase the good time to reduce prison overcrowding and avoid a lawsuit. When jail and prison crowding subsides, good time is decreased to the usual amount.

Typically, the case manager at each prison institution submits good time earned (or in some cases submits good time lost for misbehavior) to the parole board or the division within the department of corrections that prepares status or time sheets. Offenders receive an updated time sheet every six months to one year so they know when to expect their first parole hearing.

Prisoners generally become eligible for release at the completion of their minimum sentence. The manner in which a **parole eligibility date** is established varies from state to state. Mandatory minimum states require that between 50 and 85 percent of the entire sentence be served before the prisoner first becomes eligible. Other discretionary parole states require an inmate to have served one-third of the imposed sentence to be eligible for consideration for early parole. However, most statutes allow further reductions in the eligibility date through credit for time served in jail before sentencing and good-time credits. Federal law provides mandatory parole when an offender has served two-thirds of a term of five years or longer unless the offender has serious disciplinary infractions in prison or there is a high probability of recidivism (U.S. Parole Commission 2006).

Some states credit good time to the inmate upon arrival in prison and calculate the eligibility date by subtracting credited good time from the maximum sentence. An inmate who is serving a 15-year sentence and receiving standard good time of 20 days per month (50 days' credit on his or her sentence for each 30 days served) would thus be eligible for parole consideration after 40 months. As the first parole eligibility date approaches, institutional case managers (also called institutional parole officers in some states) prepare an individualized prerelease plan for the parole board.

PRERELEASE PREPARATION WITHIN THE INSTITUTION

Some prisoners are fortunate enough to be transferred to a prerelease program within the system in preparation for their release. A **prerelease facility** is a minimum-security residential program that houses inmates who have earned this

Minimum Eligibility Date
The shortest amount of time defined by statute, minus good time earned, that must be served before the offender can go before the parole board.

Maximum Eligibility Date
The longest amount of time that can be served before the inmate must be released by law.

Good Time
Sentence reduction of a specified number of days each month for good conduct.

Parole Eligibility Date
The point in a prisoner's sentence at which he or she becomes eligible to be considered for parole. If the offender is denied parole, a new parole eligibility date is scheduled in the future.

Prerelease Facility
A minimum-security prison that houses inmates who have earned this privilege through good institutional conduct and who are nearing their release date.

privilege through good institutional conduct and are within two years of their release date. Prerelease facilities provide increased opportunities for job readiness, education, housing assistance, and furloughs. Faith-based volunteer programs (e.g., "Welcome Back" programs) educate offenders on networks of social support agencies who can assist in the release process in their locale. Texas uses "state jails" specifically for offenders who are within two years of release. Halfway houses and work release are also types of residential prerelease facilities used prior to parole. In Washington, between 30 and 40 percent of all prisoners experienced some time at a work release or prerelease center, which is considered quite high compared with most other states surveyed (Austin 2001; Fehr 2004). For those offenders who are released to the community, nonresidential programs for parolees include day reporting centers and district resource centers.

Prison institutions prepare for an inmate's release while the offender is still incarcerated through preparing a **prerelease plan.** A prerelease plan includes a summary of institutional conduct and program participation, as well as plans for housing and employment upon release. Some states have case hearing officers who interview each prisoner, prepare a case summary, and report directly to the parole board with their recommendation. Other states submit case summaries and written reports along with the case file. Having some form of prerelease plan prepared in advance of a scheduled parole hearing has three main advantages:

1. A prerelease plan increases an offender's chances of parole because it solidifies living arrangements and work opportunities.
2. A prerelease plan saves time during the parole board hearing.
3. Ties to the community will likely increase an offender's success on parole and make it less likely that the offender will return to crime.

Prerelease Plan
A case management summary of institutional conduct and program participation, as well as plans for housing and employment upon release, that is submitted to the parole board in cases of discretionary parole or to the parole officer in cases of automatic release.

An institutional case manager meets with the prisoner in an interview to document exactly where the inmate will be living, and the names of those with whom he or she will live. A different (local) field parole officer will check out the address and interview household members to ensure that the address is a valid and acceptable place for the offender to live. Positive family relations increase the likelihood of parole (Silverstein 1997). Offenders are discouraged from paroling to themselves, which means living and supporting oneself without any assistance. Because most offenders, at the time of release from prison, do not have the money required for rent and utility deposits, the vast majority must parole to an existing household of a friend or relative. In an effort to assist offenders in community reintegration, paroling some offenders to a halfway house or community residential center is helpful. Halfway houses can provide a graduated sanction that provides less supervision than prison but provides more than regular parole. This is ideal for offenders who are nearing the end of their sentences (so release is inevitable) but who pose a risk to public safety.

The institutional case manager documents the amount of money the prisoner has in savings and any job leads or specific employment plans the prisoner has. According to Petersilia (2000b), most prisoners leave prison without any savings and with few solid job prospects. The case manager then summarizes any programs the offender has attended or completed (for example, general equivalency diploma courses) while in prison and lists all disciplinary infractions (write-ups) the prisoner received during the entire period of incarceration.

Essentially, the case manager brings together official data (for example, current conviction, current age, amount of time served for the current conviction, number of prior prison incarcerations, number and type of prior convictions) and data about the offender's education level, employment history, and substance abuse history.

All of the information is scored in a systematic way, and the report is provided to the parole board for the parole hearing. The report is prepared according to predefined state parole guidelines, and the parole board uses it much like a probation officer's presentence investigation report is used by a judge at time of sentencing. Time is saved during the parole board hearing because the parole board does not have to search through offender files (many of which are fairly thick) to find the factors that measure the risk level that the offender will pose when released.

The Parole Board and Releasing Authority

The prison releasing authority is a group of individuals that have authority to release prisoners prior to completion of their sentence. Traditionally, this group has been known as the **"parole board,"** but as determinate sentencing replaced indeterminate sentencing in 16 states, the name attached to this group varied by state. This text uses the more traditional term of "parole board" to apply to any prison releasing authority regardless of its sentencing framework, for two reasons: (1) most states have a mixed sentencing structure with elements of both determinate and indeterminate sentencing; and (2) *even in states with determinate sentencing structures,* 75 percent of them still retain a releasing authority group with discretionary release (Kinnevy and Caplan 2008).

Parole Board
An administrative body empowered to decide whether inmates shall be conditionally released from prison before the completion of their sentence, to revoke parole, and to discharge from parole those who have satisfactorily completed their terms.

Parole boards have four basic functions:

1. To decide when individual prisoners should be released
2. To determine any special conditions of parole supervision
3. To successfully discharge the parolee when the conditions have been met
4. To determine whether parole privileges should be revoked or should the conditions be violated

Some parole boards have additional functions, such as granting furloughs, reviewing pardons and executive clemency decisions made by the governor, restoring civil rights to ex-offenders, and granting reprieves in death sentence cases. Each state establishes the extent of its own parole board's authority. Most parole boards are independent entities. If they are tied to an agency, it is usually to the state department of corrections. The size of the group ranges from 3 to 19 members, with an average of 7 board members. The chair of the board is typically a full-time salaried employee, and some boards have a combination of full- and part-time employees (see Table 12.1).

TABLE 12.1   Parole Board Characteristics by State

State	Discretion Type	Appointed Term (in years)	Number of Full-Time	Number of Part-Time
Alabama	Full	6	7	0
Alaska	Full	5	0	5
Arizona	Very limited	5	5	0
Arkansas	Very limited	7	6	1
California	Very limited	3	17	0
Colorado	Full	3	7	0
Connecticut	Full	4	1	12
Delaware	Very limited	4	1	4
Florida	Very limited	a	15	0
Georgia	Limited	7	5	0
Hawaii	Full	4	1	2

(continued)

TABLE 12.1   Parole Board Characteristics by State (*continued*)

State	Discretion Type	Appointed Term (in years)	Number of Full-Time	Number of Part-Time
Idaho	Full	3	0	5
Illinois	Very limited	b	6	15
Indiana	Abolished	NA	NA	NA
Iowa	Full	4	2	3
Kansas	Very limited	4	3	0
Kentucky	Full	4	7	2
Louisiana	Full	NR	NR	NR
Maine	Abolished	NA	NA	NA
Maryland	Full	6	10	0
Massachusetts	Full	5	7	0
Michigan	Full	4	10	0
Minnesota	Abolished	NA	NA	NA
Mississippi	Very limited	NR	NR	NR
Missouri	Limited	6	7	0
Montana	Full	4	0	7
Nebraska	Full	6	5	0
Nevada	Full	4	7	0
New Hampshire	Full	NR	NR	NR
New Jersey	Full	6	15	3
New Mexico	Very limited	6	0	9
New York	Limited	6	19	0
North Carolina	Very limited	4	3	0
North Dakota	Limited	3	0	6
Ohio	Very limited	NA	9	0
Oklahoma	Very limited	4	0	5
Oregon	Very limited	4	3	0
Pennsylvania	Full	6	9	0
Rhode Island	Full	3	1	6
South Carolina	Limited	6	0	7
South Dakota	Very limited	4	0	9
Tennessee	Limited	6	7	0
Texas	Full	6	7	0
Utah	Full	NR	NR	NR
Vermont	Full	NA	5	0
Virginia	Very limited	NR	NR	NR
Washington	Very limited	5	1	2
West Virginia	Full	6	5	0
Wisconsin	Very limited	NA	7	0
Wyoming	Full	6	0	7

Full = Full releasing discretion for all offenders with minor statutory limits

Limited = Releasing discretion for all offenders, except for violent or repeat felony offenders

Very limited = None or very little releasing discretion for current cases; Releasing discretion only for old cases (such as prisoners sentenced prior to 1996 or 1989)

NR = Agency not reporting/information not available

NA = Not applicable

a = 5 members serve 1 year, 5 for 2 years, and 5 for 3 years; All can be reappointed for 6 years

b = full-time serve 10 years; part-time serve 3 years

Source: Association of Paroling Authorities International. 2005. *Parole Board Survey 2005.* APAI. Retrieved from: http://www.apaintl.org/content/en/pdf/2005_ParolingAuthorities_Survey.pdf

Given that many states are large and require extensive travel, boards may be divided in half, with (for example) three members responsible for the western half of the state and the other three responsible for the eastern half. In cases like these, the release decisions require the vote of two out of three board members to grant or revoke parole for that region. Crimes of a violent or sexual nature may require a **full board review,** or the requirement that all members of the parole board review the case. If this is the case, all board members meet with the chair at a central office for a few days out of every month. A violent or sex offender is paroled if the full board decides by a majority or quorum vote that the offender should be released (Silverstein 1997). In Colorado, a quorum is defined as four of seven members who recommend release (West-Smith, Pogrebin, and Poole 2000).

Full Board Review
The statutory requirement that all members of the parole board review and vote on the early release from prison of individuals who have committed felony crimes, usually of a violent or sexual nature. Some states require this type of review on every discretionary release.

TERM AND QUALIFICATIONS OF THE PAROLE BOARD

The governor appoints members for an average of five years (ranging from one year to life appointments, depending on state statute). The gubernatorial appointment must be confirmed by the legislature. Parole board members must possess integrity, intelligence, and good judgment to command respect and public confidence. Board members should have sufficiently broad academic training and experience to be qualified for professional practice in fields such as criminology, education, psychology, law, social work, and sociology. Each member must have the capacity and the desire to learn and understand legal processes, the dynamics of human behavior, and cultural conditions contributing to crime. Ideally, parole board members have previous professional experience that has given them intimate knowledge of the human experience—situations and problems confronting offenders.

THE PAROLE HEARING

Once prisoner eligibility for release has been determined, the offender is scheduled for a parole hearing date. The parole board members have access to the entire offender case file with the summary report completed by the institutional case

A parole board asks questions to determine a prisoner's readiness for early community release.

Courtesy of Leanne Fiftal Alarid

BOX 12.2   TECHNOLOGY IN CORRECTIONS

Federal Parole Decisions Using Videoconference

The Parole Commission used to travel to more than sixty facilities all over the United States to conduct parole release and revocation hearings face to face. Prisoners facing parole release hearings saw the Commission in a prerelease facility. Prisoners facing revocation hearings (to be discussed in Chapter 13) traveled by airplane from a local jail to a central transfer facility in Oklahoma or the detention center in Philadelphia within a ninety-day period. Following their revocation hearing, they would again travel to wherever the Commission felt was best to place them.

Now, using videoconferencing, Parole Commission members can remain in Maryland because both the prisoner and the Commission can see and interact with each other from any federal facility in the United States. The technology was initially tried with parole release hearings.

The Commission found that the "video and audio transmissions are clear and the hearings are seldom interrupted by technical difficulties . . . [and] the prisoner's ability to effectively participate in the hearing has not been diminished" (U.S. Department of Justice 2005b, p.19262). Videoconferencing saves travel time and money for the Commission members as well as travel time, money, and risk involved in transferring prisoners. Videoconferencing has had such great success with parole release hearings that in 2005 the practice was extended to revocation hearings.

Source: U.S. Department of Justice. 2005b. 28 CFR Part 2: Paroling, Recommitting, and Supervising Federal Prisoners: Prisoners Serving Sentences under the U.S and D.C. Codes. *Federal Register* 70(70), April 13, 2005, p. 19262.

---

manager. As previously mentioned, some hearing examiners scrutinize the case file only without interviewing the offender, whereas other parole boards have access to both the case file and the offender in person. In the federal system, the sentencing judge, the assistant U.S. attorney, and the defense attorney may all make written recommendations to the parole board. Federal prisoners may later request a copy of their parole hearing recording under the Freedom of Information Act (U.S. Parole Commission 2006).

Parole board hearings are tape recorded and conducted in one of three ways: in person, video teleconference, and file only. Face-to-face parole board hearings are the most common of the three and take place at the prison in which the eligible prisoner is located. Hearings that are in person allow the prisoner to be in the same room with the parole board. Some boards conduct parole release hearings using videoconference technology (see Box 12.2), which has greatly reduced the need to travel to each prison, yet it allows the opportunity to ask and answer questions. File-review parole hearings have no face-to-face contact with the prisoner, and the board makes a decision based only on the submitted paperwork by prison officials.

A video or face-to-face parole hearing is attended by between one and three board members (or "hearing examiners") who represent the entire board (West-Smith, Pogrebin, and Poole 2000). In a face-to-face hearing, one hearing examiner thoroughly reviews the file and leads with the most questions. If other members are present, they review the file less thoroughly and ask supplemental questions from a different angle or ask follow-up questions to the leading parole board member's questions (Silverstein 1997). At least two signatures are required to parole a person convicted of a nonviolent crime (West-Smith, Pogrebin, and Poole 2000), but most states average three required signatures (Kinnevy and Caplan 2008).

PAROLE HEARING ATTENDEES

Parole boards consider input from other sources to assist them in making their decision. Each state varies as to who can attend the hearing and how that information may be conveyed (in person, written correspondence, telephone,

BOX 12.3   COMMUNITY CORRECTIONS UP CLOSE

The Parole Process in Oklahoma

The five-member parole board in Oklahoma meets quarterly to decide on approximately 800 cases, or about 3,200 cases per year. Half of all cases are decided based on the offender's file alone, while the others involve a face-to-face meeting with the offender at a single prison over a four-day period (about 100 face-to-face cases per day). The initial Stage 1 meeting with the offender averages about five minutes, and family supporters may attend at the same time. Three out of five parole board members must vote in favor of moving the case to a Stage 2 hearing. If the case at Stage 1 does not get the requisite number of votes, the parole date is automatically deferred.

All Stage 2 hearings take place about one month after Stage 1 hearings During Stage 2, parole opponents are invited to attend, such as the victim, the victim's family, and the district attorney who prosecuted the case. Again, the hearing at Stage 2 must obtain a voting majority by the Board. As in Stage 1, if the Stage 2 process does not receive the requisite votes, the case is deferred until later.

The third and final stage in the process is that each Board recommendation is reviewed by the governor. The governor's signature is the final step in the two-month process. Of the 3,200 cases that go up for parole, an estimated 1,000 are granted each year.

Source: Tribune Media Services. 2003. *Parole Board: Oklahoma.* [DVD–47 minutes]. Ordered through http://www.bio.com

---

or videotaped). Some states allow the offender's family at parole hearings, but most do not permit legal representation for the offender. Prosecutors, law enforcement, and victims who were directly involved in the offender's case are invited to make a statement. Relatives or potential employers may write letters or submit a videotaped statement for use at the hearing. The federal system limits each offender to one representative to make a statement on the offender's behalf (U.S. Parole Commission 2006). Box 12.3 illustrates the specific process of the parole board in the state of Oklahoma.

Victim Impact Statement
A written account by the victim(s) as to how the crime has taken a toll physically, emotionally, financially, or psychologically on the victim and the victim's family. Victim impact statements are considered by many states at time of sentencing and at parole board hearings.

Written correspondence through a victim impact statement is the most common form of accepted correspondence from victims. A **victim impact statement** mentions how the crime has taken a toll physically, emotionally, financially, or psychologically on the victim and the victim's family. Many victim impact statements cite how the victim continues to experience psychological, physical, or financial difficulties as a direct result of the actions of the offender (Bernat, Parsonage, and Helfgott 1994). States such as Alabama specify that impact statements should be confidential because of the concern that prisoners may attempt to further harm their victim(s) for opposing the offender's release. Other states are more proactive, such as Arizona and Oklahoma, because they allow victims to veto (refuse) a parole release decision if the victim requested notification of the hearing but was not given a chance to contribute his or her opinion (Bernat, Parsonage, and Helfgott 1994).

The effects of victim participation in parole hearings are noteworthy. Releasing authorities report that appearance in person was the most persuasive form of victim testimony. Parole was refused in 43 percent of cases in which victim impact statements were present, but only 7 percent of cases were denied when victim statements were absent (Bernat, Parsonage, and Helfgott 1994). Victims, particularly those who suffered injury in violent offenses, who made a statement in person had a greater impact on keeping the offender incarcerated than victims who sent in a letter (Morgan and Smith 2005; Smith, Watkins, and Morgan 1997).

The Parole Board Decision

In general, for most releasing decisions, the top three factors that releasing authorities say make an impact on their decision is crime severity, crime type, and offender criminal history. Following these three factors, the victim's input has the next level of impact, followed by the offender's family and the input from the district attorney (Kinnevy and Caplan 2008). The parole board makes a decision on each case out of three possible options: grant parole, deny parole, or defer to a later date. A decision to *grant* parole results in scheduling a conditional release before the expiration of the maximum term of imprisonment. A parole *denial* results in continued imprisonment. In the federal system, a denial of parole on a sentence less than seven years in length allows the offender to automatically go before the board again in eighteen months. A sentence longer than seven years delays the next parole board hearing for another two years (U.S. Parole Commission 2006).

A release *deferral* means that the parole board has delayed their final decision (to grant or deny) until a later time, somewhere between six months and a year. The most common reason for deferrals is that the offender has not yet completed an in-prison treatment program related to their offense. For example, a sex offender in some states must complete sex offender treatment before being considered for release, whereas a chronic drug user might have to complete an in-prison substance abuse program. The problem is not that the offender won't complete the program—the space available for treatment is limited and the offender must wait for an opening, which many times doesn't occur until after their minimum release eligibility date has already passed. The second most common reason for deferrals are administrative delays, such as the paperwork is not in order or completed by the department of corrections; the victim has not yet provided input (in the 17 states that require a victim impact statement before the board can make a decision); or the offender is at another facility and not available for the interview at the scheduled time (Kinnevy and Caplan 2008).

Models of Parole Release Decisions

In their aim to maximize both public safety and offender rehabilitation, statutes direct parole boards to base their decisions on one or more of these criteria:

- The probability of recidivism
- The welfare of society
- The conduct of the offender while in the correctional institution
- The sufficiency of the parole plan

Three models guiding parole decision making have existed over time: (1) the surveillance model, (2) the procedural justice model, and (3) the risk prediction model.

The Surveillance Model

Early parole decisions were based not on formally articulated criteria or policies but on subjective intuition of individual decision makers. Parole decision making encompassed a surveillance perspective, which was defined as an attempt to control "the dangerous classes." The surveillance approach was based on the theory that informal social controls, including positive family relations, coworkers, and friends, would help the offender by providing structure and enforcement of the rules

(Foucault 1977). Rothman (1980) reported that parole boards considered primarily the seriousness of the crime in determining whether to release an inmate on parole. However, no consensus was reached on what constituted a serious crime. Instead, "each member made his own decisions. The judgments were personal and therefore not subject to debate or reconsideration" (Rothman 1980, p. 173). The courts, to the extent that they were willing to review the parole decision at all, agreed with the contentions of paroling authorities that to impose even minimal due process constraints on the decision process would interfere with the fulfillment of their duty to engage in diagnosis and prognosis.

THE PROCEDURAL JUSTICE MODEL

In the 1970s, given the concerns about discrepant decision making, there was a movement toward the use of objective guidelines in the release decision. Parole decisions were made more visible and parole authorities were accountable for their decisions through the use of explicit parole selection policies. Known as the procedural justice or due process model, this perspective advocated fairness and emphasized legal factors such as crime severity and prior criminal record. Parole guidelines were established to make parole selection decisions more rational and consistent.

THE RISK PREDICTION MODEL

Salient Factor Score
The parole guidelines developed and used by the U.S. Parole Commission for making parole release decisions. Served as the model for parole guidelines developed in many other jurisdictions.

The risk prediction model was a "natural outgrowth of the procedural justice perspective," in that parole release decisions focused on community protection rather than due process and any potential progress the offender made while incarcerated (Silverstein 1997, p. 24). Researchers found that parole decisions could be predicted by using offense seriousness and the risk of recidivism, defined by prior criminal history. The **Salient Factor Score** (SFS) was developed to provide explicit guidelines for release decisions based on a determination of the potential risk of parole violation. The SFS measures six offender characteristics based on age and prior institutional commitments and assigns a score to each. Note in Figure 12.1 that the first offender characteristic considered in the Salient Factor Score calculation is prior convictions or adjudications. This offender characteristic has a score range of 0 to 3. Offenders with no prior convictions are assigned a score of 3; one prior conviction results in a score of 2; two to three prior convictions gives a score of 1; and four or more gives a score of 0. Each offender characteristic is scored in a similar manner, and the sum of the six items yields the predictive score. The higher the score (maximum of 10), the less likely is the probability of recidivism (Hoffman 1994). Although no prediction device is 100 percent accurate, the SFS has been able to acceptably predict different probabilities of recidivism according to a small number of known variables.

Decision makers then use guidelines to determine the customary time to be served for a range of offenses, based on the severity of the offense (see Figure 12.2). Severity is based on eight categories, ranging from the least to the most severe. For example, an adult offender whose SFS/98 score was 5 and whose offense severity was rated in Category Two would be expected to serve 12 to 16 months before being paroled.

Following the lead of the federal system, many states adopted guidelines for use in release decision making. Some states adopted an in-house matrix guideline system similar to the SFS, whereas others adopted different types of guidelines that consider factors such as criminal history, whether the current crime involved deviant sexual activity, and the offender's history of violence.

Item A. Prior Convictions/Adjudications (Adult or Juvenile) □

    None   = 3

    One   = 2

    Two or three   = 1

    Four or more   = 0

Item B. Prior Commitment(s) of More Than 30 Days (Adult or Juvenile) □

    None   = 2

    One or two   = 1

    Three or more   = 0

Item C. Age at Current Offense/Prior Commitments □

    26 years or more

        3 or fewer prior commitments   = 3

        4 prior commitments   = 2

        5 or more commitments   = 1

    22–25 years

        3 or fewer prior commitments   = 2

        4 prior commitments   = 1

        5 or more prior commitments   = 0

    20–21 years

        3 or fewer prior commitments   = 1

        4 prior commitments   = 0

    19 years or less (any number of prior commitments)   = 0

Item D. Recent Commitment-Free Period (Three Years) □

    No prior commitment of more than 30 days (adult or juvenile) or released to the community from last such commitment at least three years prior to the commencement of the current offense   = 1

    Otherwise   = 0

Item E. Probation/Parole/Confinement/Escape Status Violator This Time □

    Neither on probation, parole, confinement, or escape status at the time of the current offense; nor committed as a probation, parole, confinement, or escape status violator this time   = 1

    Otherwise   = 0

Item F. Older Offenders □

    If the offender was 41 years of age or more at the commencement of the current offense (and the total score from Items A–E above is 9 or less)   = 1

    Otherwise   = 0

TOTAL SCORE (Sum of Items A through F) □

FIGURE 12.1   Salient Factor Score (SFS/98)

Source: United States Parole Commission. 2003. *Rules and Procedures Manual,* Revised August 15, 2003, p. 58. http://www.usdoj.gov/uspc/rules_procedures/rulesmanual.htm.

Over 80 percent of releasing authorities now use some type of decision-making instrument or risk assessment that includes numeric scoring. While some risk assessments were developed in-house by each state department of corrections, others have moved to using the Level of Service Inventory-Revised (LSI-R) for all offenders or the Static-99 for sex offenders (Kinnevy and Caplan 2008). Regardless of the form that parole release guidelines take, they structure discretion.

In the age of evidence-based practices, researchers are fine-tuning parole risk prediction instruments according to other characteristics, such as gender. Using traditional instruments, female parolees have always had lower recidivism rates than male parolees, so a model was developed just for women to more accurately predict success

FIGURE 12.2 Guidelines for Decision Making: Customary Total Time to Be Served before Release

Offense Characteristics: Offense Severity (Some Crimes Eliminated or Summarized)	Offender Characteristics: (from Salient Factor Score in Figure 12.1)			
	Very Good **(10–8)**	**Good** **(7–6)**	**Fair** **(5–4)**	**Poor** **(3–0)**
Category One *Low:* possession of a small amount of marijuana; simple theft under $1,000	≤ 4 months	8 months	8–12 months	12–16 months
Category Two *Low/Moderate:* income tax evasion less than $10,000; immigration law violations; embezzlement, fraud, forgery under $1,000	≤ 6 months	10 months	12–16 months	16–22 months
Category Three *Moderate:* bribery; possession of 50 lb. or less of marijuana, with intent to sell; illegal firearms; income tax evasion $10,000 to $50,000; nonviolent property offenses $1,000 to $19,999; auto theft, not for resale	10 months	12–16 months	18–24 months	24–32 months
Category Four *High:* counterfeiting; marijuana possession with intent to sell, 50 to 1,999 lb.; auto theft, for resale; nonviolent property offenses, $20,000 to $100,000	12–18 months	20–26 months	26–34 months	34–44 months
Category Five *Very High:* robbery; breaking and entering bank or post office; extortion; marijuana possession with intent to sell, over 2,000 lb.; hard drugs possession with intent to sell, not more than $100,000; nonviolent property offenses over $100,000 but not exceeding $500,000	24–36 months	36–48 months	48–60 months	60–72 months
Category Six *Greatest I:* explosive detonation; multiple robbery; aggravated felony (weapon fired—no serious injury); hard drugs, over $100,000; forcible rape	40–52 months	52–64 months	64–78 months	78–100 months
Category Seven *Greatest II:* aircraft hijacking; espionage; kidnapping; homicide	52–80 months	64–92 months	78–110 months	100–148 months
Category Eight (parole extremely unlikely) Contract murders, murder of law enforcement officer, murder by torture, felony murder	100+ months	120+ months	150+ months	180+ months

Source: United States Parole Commission. 2003. *Rules and Procedures Manual,* Revised August 15, 2003, p. 28. Accessed: http://www.usdoj.gov/uspc/rules_procedures/rulesmanual.htm.

BOX 12.4   COMMUNITY CORRECTIONS CLOSE UP

Evidence-Based Findings about Post-Prison Release

Various ways to reduce recidivism after release from prison was comprehensively studied by a committee on law and justice that was part of the National Research Council. They determined that rates of recidivism varied widely across the U.S. in part because parolees were such a heterogeneous group. Three in-prison activities were important for success on the outside. First, was the completion of meaningful treatment interventions before release. Second, was continued contact with family members via mail, phone, or in person visits. That is related to the third factor, which was a solid prerelease plan, which included where the parolee will live and job leads.

The committee also recognized that the first few days and weeks out of prison are the most vulnerable and the riskiest time for the parolee. Factors after release that were shown to reduce recidivism:

- Cognitive-behavioral treatment programs for high-risk offenders
- Concentrated treatment services combined with parole supervision over the first few weeks of release (e.g., day reporting center)
- Strong employment ties and assistance in finding employment
- Stable relationships with significant familial others
- Assistance in obtaining identification, clothing, and medication
- Mentors who are available at time of release

Source: National Research Council. 2008. *Parole, desistance from crime, and community integration.* Washington, DC: National Academies Press.

---

and failure rates for female parolees. The researchers found that age at first arrest, age at release, release status (new release or parole violator), and number of prior arrests most accurately predicted parole failure for women (McShane, Williams, and Dolny 2002). Other generalizations about success on parole can be found in Box 12.4.

Legal Issues in Parole Hearings

There is a difference between granting probation (discussed in Chapter 7) and granting parole. While probation is administered and granted by the courts, it is a sentence in itself and therefore defendant rights must be protected. Prisoners seeking parole have already been sentenced and are seeking early release. Thus, one of the most striking aspects of the traditional parole release process has been the virtual inability to challenge parole decisions (Palacios 1994). In recent years, courts have provided some procedural protections and articulated criteria for reviewing the conditions that parole boards have set on parolees' conduct and for revoking parole and returning parolees to prison. This has to do with the courts' view that parole is a privilege and there is no expectation of due process. Below are some of the key court cases in the parole process.

No Due Process Protections

In *Menechino v. Oswald* (1971), a prisoner argued that the New York State Board of Parole's denial of parole was illegal because he had not received the right to counsel, the right to cross-examine witnesses, the right to produce favorable witnesses, and the specification of the grounds upon which the denial decision was based. The court ruled that due process was *not* an issue in parole because parole was a privilege and not a right.

A short time after the *Menechino* case, the U.S. Supreme Court directly addressed the issue of due process in parole release decision making. In *Greenholtz v. Inmates of the Nebraska Penal and Correctional Complex* (1979), the inmates of a Nebraska prison brought a class action alleging they had been unconstitutionally denied parole by the Nebraska Board of Parole. The U.S. Supreme Court reversed the decision of the court of appeals. The Court emphasized that parole boards have broad discretion in their decision making, even if it is at times imperfect.

The Nebraska procedure affords an opportunity to be heard, and when parole is denied it informs the inmate in what respect he falls short of qualifying for parole; this affords the process that is due under these circumstances. The Constitution does not require more. (p. 16)

The Court concluded that parole release and parole revocation "are quite different" because "there is a . . . difference between losing what one has and not getting what one wants" (*Greenholtz v. Inmates of the Nebraska Penal and Correctional Complex* 1979, pp. 9–10). Although the *Greenholtz* case did not extend due process as far as desired by the plaintiffs, it did establish that some due process protections were available in the parole-granting process. In summary, *Greenholtz* required reasonable notice of a parole hearing date (one month before the hearing is reasonable); an initial hearing wherein the prisoner is allowed to present the case; and, if parole is denied, written reasons for denial.

Use of Hearsay, DNA, and No Right to an Attorney

The earlier case established that there are no due process rights to be released on parole. For example, hearsay evidence may be used in parole release decisions (*Golberg v. Beeler* 1999). Parole boards have even been known to deny parole if DNA evidence informally sent by law enforcement or a crime victim matches the parole candidate for an earlier crime for which they were never prosecuted (Johnson and Willing 2008). The DNA evidence does not convict or add time to the sentence for those crimes, it just allows the parole board to deny early release for crimes for which that offender was convicted. At the same time, the parole board may not deny parole for false, insufficient, or capricious reasons (*Tucker v. Alabama Board of Pardons and Paroles* 2000), so there seems to be a fine line between what kinds of information are allowed to become part of the decision.

Prisoners seeking parole do not have the right to be represented by counsel. While a lawyer is welcome to attend in support of the prisoner, the lawyer may not represent or talk for a prisoner during a parole hearing (*Franciosi v. Michigan Parole Board* 2000). The same court one year earlier also ruled that a statement of reasons for denial of parole is not required and is not a violation of due process (*Glover v. Michigan Parole Board* 1999). Even if the parole board changes its mind about its decision, no due process rights are necessary, provided the prisoner has not actually been released from the institution (*Jago v. Van Curen* 1981).

Admitting guilt (or refusing to admit participation in a crime) can be used in some jurisdictions as a reason to deny release (*In re Ecklund* 1999; *Silmon v. Travis* 2000). Unlike sentencing, parole board decisions are not subject to judicial review if made in accordance with statutory guidelines (*Ramahlo v. Travis* 2002).

Prisoner's Perceptions of Parole Selection

The parole process has been criticized as being secretive and arbitrary and failing to provide prisoners with a clear indication of what they need to do to obtain early release. This may be because parole board hearings are truly deliberative processes, and parole board members themselves do not know the outcome of the hearing in at least 80 percent of the cases (Silverstein 1997). More often, however, prisoners feel they may have prepared themselves as much as possible for what they think will earn them release, only to be denied based on "inadequate time served," even though they have met their minimum parole eligibility date (West-Smith, Pogrebin, and Poole 2000). The renewed interest in reentry has increased the importance of the release plan and the transition from prison to the community.

Mika'il A. Muhammad (1996) interviewed 263 prisoners from the Eastern New York Correctional Facility and found that 60 percent of inmates favored a form of contract parole, "wherein the inmate negotiates with parole and correctional personnel at the beginning of the sentence a plan to address specific needs that, if met, would facilitate parole readiness and insure release on a specified date" (p. 146). Contract parole is not used at this time, but reducing uncertainty about the parole process would likely decrease prisoner stress.

Although a history of violence is important to consider, any system that reduces the importance of positive institutional behavior runs the risk of creating a nightmare for prison administrators who are supervising prisoners with "nothing to lose" and increases reentry problems in the future. Gauging what factors to consider is no easy task. Some suggest that career criminals know how to do time; that is, they can manipulate the parole board by avoiding institutional violations and participating in rehabilitation programs that look good on their record when they are reviewed for parole. Good behavior while in prison does not always predict law-abiding behavior in the community.

Although the parole board determines release and/or sets parole conditions, the day-to-day supervision of parole is left to field parole officers who work either for the parole board or for another government agency independent of the parole board, such as the parole division of a department of corrections. Parole supervision is the subject of the next chapter.

SUMMARY

- Reentry programs include those that take place in the prison setting, as well as community-based programs that follow up the transition process.

- Reentry initiatives include reentry courts and collaborations between parole agencies and grassroots community organizations or other criminal justice agencies.

- Issues in reentry affect not only the parolee but the offender's family, the victim, and the community.

- A parolee faces issues related to finding stable employment, finding suitable housing, and reestablishing contact with his or her family. Since most releasees are also on supervision, they face the pressure of being mindful of who they associate with and checking in with the parole officer.

- There are three types of release from prison—those without any supervision, those under a short period of mandatory supervision by a parole officer, and those under discretionary parole release.

- Parole boards have the power to decide whether to release prisoners who are doing sentences with the eligibility for discretionary parole.

- Parole boards determine when revocation of parole and return to prison are necessary.

- Because discretionary parole is defined as a privilege rather than a right, the courts have allowed very minimal, if any, due process.

DISCUSSION QUESTIONS

1. What issues do prisoners face in preparing for their reentry into the community?

2. What are the primary qualifications of a good parole board member? Why are these qualities important?

3. Why are good public relations between the parole board and the outside community necessary?

4. If you were a victim of a violent crime, would you take the time to write an impact statement or attend

the parole board hearing, knowing the offender would also be there? Why or why not?

5. How does prisoner reentry potentially affect the victim and/or the victim's family?

6. What issues exist with respect to prisoner reentry and the impact on the offender's family?

7. If you were a parole board member, what factors would you consider in attempting to arrive at a fair and just decision? Why?

8. If you were a prisoner, what method of release from prison would you prefer—discretionary or mandatory/automatic? Why?

9. In light of the composition of the present Supreme Court, what do you think will be the result of future decisions on parole issues?

WEB SITES

The Reentry Policy Council
http://www.reentrypolicy.org

Reentry National Media Outreach Campaign
http://www.reentrymediaoutreach.org

Reentry Trends in the U.S.
http://www.ojp.usdoj.gov/bjs/reentry/releases.htm

RAND Study: Public Health Challenges of Prisoner Reentry
http://www.rand.org/publications/RB/RB6013

Overview of Prisoner Reentry in Pennsylvania
http://www.cor.state.pa.us/

Council of State Governments Chart of Reentry Housing Options for individuals released from prison
http://tools.reentrypolicy.org/housing

U.S. Parole Commission
http://www.usdoj.gov/uspc/

Missouri Office of Victim Services: Parole Hearings
http://www.doc.missouri.gov/victims/victimparolehearings.htm

Oregon Victims' Rights at Parole Board Hearings
http://www.ncvc.org/policy/issues/parole/tables/or.html

Ohio Parole Board
http://www.drc.state.oh.us/web/parboard.htm

Tennessee Board of Parole
http://www.tn.gov/bopp/bopp_sl.htm

Texas Parole Release Guidelines
http://www.tdcj.state.tx.us/bpp/new_parole_guidelines/new_parole_guidelines.html

Parole Board, United Kingdom
http://www.paroleboard.gov.uk

CASE STUDY EXERCISE

Preparing for Prisoner Reentry

Various systems are used to make release decisions for incarcerated offenders. In states where sentences are indeterminate, a paroling authority often must make the decision to release the offender and decide when that release should occur. Sentencing laws may determine when an offender is eligible for release, but the offender is not granted a release until the parole authority approves the release.

In the following cases, the paroling authority must consider the offender cases and make a determination to release or not to release the offender to the community. Factors considered often involve probability of recidivism, victim impact, community impact, conduct of the offender in the institution, and release plan offered. Consider these cases and determine if the offender's release has merit.

CASE A

Joseph is serving a ten-to-twenty-five-year sentence for two counts of armed robbery. He has served the mandatory minimum of five years and is being considered for release for the first time; by statute he can be held in custody for thirteen years before he reaches a mandatory release date. Joseph served a previous sentence for burglary and successfully completed the release period before he committed the current crimes. The victims in both robberies were elderly gas station attendants, and very small amounts of money were obtained from the robberies. The victims remain fearful of the offender, and both indicate that their lives were significantly affected by the experience. Neither victim ever returned to work out of fear of similar future events. While incarcerated, Joseph has completed substance abuse treatment for his cocaine dependence, and the treatment summary calls for his attendance in facility Cocaine Anonymous meetings. He attends the meetings about half of the time they are offered. He has also completed an anger management program, has been assigned to several inmate jobs, and has had no rule violations while incarcerated. Joseph would like to have gone to a work release facility, but due to a waiting list, he was not able enter this program prior to being considered for release. His community plan is to return to the same community where the crimes were committed, live with his elderly aunt, seek work as a construction laborer, and attend community substance abuse aftercare. He would be under the supervision of a parole officer upon his release, if granted.

CASE B

Fred is a 39-year-old individual serving fourteen years for possession with intent to sell a controlled substance. This is his second prison term, having served a six-year sentence for sale of heroin in the 1990s. He was paroled on the first offense after four years and successfully completed parole supervision. However, he was arrested on the current charge within two months of being released from parole supervision. Law enforcement officials reported that he had been under surveillance for several months before the arrest and was suspected of dealing drugs during most of the period of his parole supervision. While under supervision, he reported regularly to his parole officer and worked steadily at a job in a warehouse owned by his brother-in-law. There were no known law violations during the period of supervision. Fred's institutional adjustment has been excellent. He attended drug counseling and is a member of the prison Narcotics Anonymous group. He attained his GED certificate and reports that he wants to attend community college when released. He will work for his brother-in-law again when released and live with his sister and her husband until he can afford to rent an apartment. The sheriff in the county to which he would be released has protested his parole release, stating that Fred is a manipulative and devious individual who maintains a façade of cooperation and honest living while continuing to sell drugs. Fred has served five years of his current fourteen-year sentence. Institutional counselors recommend his release at this time.

CASE C

Marie is a 55-year-old female who has served thirty years of a twenty years-to-life sentence for murder. She was convicted of killing her two young children (ages 2 and 4 years). She reported that her live-in boyfriend would not agree to stay with her as long as she had children. She chose to kill the children to maintain the relationship. She has maintained a near-perfect prison record and is considered by authorities to be a model inmate. She reports great remorse for her actions. The prison chaplain has counseled her for many years and states that she has been "born again" and forgiven for her crimes and sins. Marie works as a chaplain's assistant in the institution and is well thought of by both inmates and prison officials alike. If paroled, she will work for the Prison Ministries in her hometown and will be provided with a place to stay by her employers.

Parole Conditions and Revocation

CHAPTER LEARNING OBJECTIVES

- Parole conditions imposed by parole boards are subject to the same limitations as probation conditions.

- The main goal of parole is societal protection, accomplished by enforcing parolee restrictions and providing services that assist in community reintegration.

- There are certain reasons why people violate parole and/or abscond from community supervision, as well as ways to decrease this behavior.

- There are certain variables that consistently predict recidivism following release from prison.

- The parolees who violate on parole will typically do so in the first six months after release.

Parolees must meet frequently with their parole officer to report their job search progress and develop individual case plans to satisfy parole board stipulations. Motivational interviewing is used as a technique to gain compliance.

CHAPTER OUTLINE

Introduction

Prisoner Perspectives on Getting Out
California Study
Iowa Study

The Field Parole Officer
The Officer's Perspective

Conditions of Parole
Limited Rights for All Parolees
Legal Issues in Parole Conditions for Sex Offenders

Violating Parole
Warrants and Citations

Characteristics of Parole Violators
Parole Revocation Rate
Attitudes on Revocation

Parole Absconders
Why Do Parolees Leave?
Locating and Apprehending Fugitives
Predicting Absconding Behavior

Parole Effectiveness
Recidivism Studies
Predicting Parole Outcomes

Summary

KEY TERMS

parole conditions
diminished constitutional rights

preferred rights
exclusionary rule

absconder

Introduction

> **Parole Conditions**
> The rules under which a paroling authority releases an offender to community supervision.

Reentry from prison assumes that the ex-prisoner is motivated to start his or her life anew and desist from future crime. This chapter discusses the desistance process—in other words, what is it like to be on parole? While the main goal of parole is societal protection, **parole conditions** imposed determine the amount of freedom versus restrictions a parolee has. The goals are accomplished by enforcing conditions and providing services that assist in community reintegration. You will see many similarities between parole and probation, but we will be sure to point out the differences.

The length of time spent on parole averages about two years nationwide, although the amount of time is longer for violent offenders and shorter for property and drug offenders (Camp, Camp, and May 2003). The length of supervision largely depends on the laws of the state of conviction. For example, parole is limited to six months in Oregon and one year in Indiana, regardless of the type of crime. Most states allow parolees to be discharged before the full term of their sentence. Federal offenders under mandatory release are automatically discharged 180 days prior to their maximum expiration date. Offenders who remain in prison with less than 180 days left on their entire sentence are released without any community supervision whatsoever (U.S. Parole Commission 2006).

As with probation, parole revocation occurs if the parolee violates the conditions of parole. Revocation is also important to society because the parolee will once again be under the care and custody of the state, and with that comes the high cost of keeping an offender incarcerated. Much is at stake for both the parolee and the state in parole revocation.

Prisoner Perspectives on Getting Out

Few studies have examined the prisoner's perspective while on parole. Most researchers conduct studies about inmate life experiences inside prison, primarily because institutional prisoners make captive audiences. An exception to this is research conducted with prisoners recently released from prison. Craig Hemmens supervised a research team that interviewed 775 former inmates as they were waiting for the bus within a few minutes to a few hours of release from prison. Hemmens (1998) found that as prisoners age, their apprehension about reentry decreased. Less reentry apprehension also applied to prisoners who served sentences of three years or less compared with those who served sentences longer than three years. Because this study was cross-sectional, none of the prisoners were tracked to see if they succeeded. Prisoners generally have good intentions and plan on staying out of prison. Many prisoners do attempt to live a legitimate life by finding employment after release, but prisoners experience a great deal of stress and disdain during the transition period.

One such individual was Robert Grooms (1982), who wrote about the perils of release from prison and why, despite all the advantages he had over most other convicts upon release, he did not make it. When he was released, Grooms had problems finding a job, found he had nothing in common with old friends, and was uncomfortable around "square-johns." He wrote:

> I had another problem common among recently released prisoners. I wanted to make up all at once for lost time. I wanted the things that others my age had worked years to achieve, and I wanted them right away. (p. 543)

Grooms could not "sit still" and he did not want to be alone, so he began to hang around places and people where he felt comfortable. He found himself talking to ex-convicts in taverns, and they talked about what they all had in common: crime, the prison experience, and violence. Grooms concluded by saying:

> When he is released, a prisoner is in a real sense cast out into a totally alien society. Overnight he is expected to discard months and years of self-survival tactics, to change his values, to readjust to situations and circumstances that he had long forgotten, and to accept responsibility. More important, he has to overcome, in a society that rejects him, his lack of self-worth; he has to become accepted where he is not wanted. Is it any wonder that so many newly released prisoners feel out of their natural environment, that many first-time, petty offenders leave prison and find someone weak to prey on, or that the recidivism rate is so high? (p. 545)

CALIFORNIA STUDY

The most interesting thing about the reentry process for Robert Grooms and other parolees interviewed was that it has not changed. Reentry for parolees in the 1970s was similar to experiences now. A classic study interviewed 60 parolees about their experiences as they first left prison (Erickson et al. 1973). Reentry was generally a negative experience for about half of all parolees, as most of them had experienced failure on parole many times before. While on parole, offenders felt pressure to obtain a job, money, food, clothes, and a place to stay. Many parolees relied more on friends and other ex-convicts for these basic needs than they did on their own family. For example, Lloyd Nieman, age 36 with an eighth-grade education and convicted of forgery, was in the process of enrolling at a state college while on parole. Nieman explained:

> The first few days I was out were about the roughest days of this entire period. I've only been out a short time—five weeks—but the first three days were a hassle. . . . [N]o money, no transportation, no job, and no place to live. Now these things have a way of working themselves out in time, but you have to

contact the right people, and sometimes it's hard to find the right people. . . . I was lucky that I had two friends here, too, that could help me. Nick [an ex-con] gave me a place to stay, because I was out of money within four days. They [the prison] give you $60, and out of that you got to buy your own clothes. (pp. 16–17)

Shortly after his interview, Nieman absconded, leaving the state and never returning. A warrant was issued for his arrest. After one year, Nieman could not be located.

Many parolees were socially detached and many admitted to being lonely. For example, Anthony Mendez, age 46, spent the last sixteen years in prison for possession of narcotics and had been out on parole for three months when interviewed. Mendez's experience is a bit different from Nieman's. Mendez had more financial assistance from his family in Los Angeles, but he was paroled to an area of San Diego where he did not know anyone. Mendez explains his experience:

I was just kinda lost when I got out. If you've been in a while, so many things are new and different. . . . I've always gotten a lot of help [from family], so I think I've just been lucky; but I know there's a lot of other guys that didn't get the help I got. . . . I really couldn't talk to anybody, which is hard. . . . For the majority of fellows in the joint, they're so starved emotionally and so closed in, so shut off from any warmth, any friendship, that it takes a long time when you get out to break out of these bonds and be a normal person out here where you can talk to people. . . . I think that when a guy first gets out, it's a very important thing that that man go to work, if for no other reason than that eight hours is going to be occupied . . . and its not going to let him dwell on how much he's missed and much he's missing again. (Erickson et al. 1973, pp. 27–29)

One year after Mendez was interviewed, he was still on parole but had lost his job.

Through the interviews, parolees made suggestions ranging from increasing rehabilitation and vocational programs inside prison to increasing community resources on release. The lack of reentry resources has been a continual problem for parolees nationwide. For example, one parolee stated:

It just doesn't seem fair to give the convict such a little money and tell him to make it. What regular citizen today can set out in the world, with less than a high school education, no job, $50, and no close ties or other resources, and make it? That is what we are asking the parolee to do, and we will not let him forget that he is an outsider. (Erickson et al. 1973, p. 98)

One of the most innovative suggestions made in some of the interviews was that everyone released from prison be assigned a mentor in his or her area. The mentor would be a successful ex-convict who has remained out of the system, and he or she would be available to deal with emotional and social problems the parolee faces. Even though this research was conducted 30 years ago, the needs and problems of parolees remain the same today.

IOWA STUDY

Richards and Jones (1997) interviewed 30 men who were just released from prison and were sentenced to a halfway house as a form of graduated release. The researchers found that the men had not been prepared for release from prison to an environment that required them to pay rent, look for employment, sustain a job, and pay for food. One prisoner explained the pressures of getting behind in rent upon his arrival at the halfway house:

You leave the penitentiary on a Tuesday, you come here [to the halfway house], and you're broke for the whole week or two till they send your money from the penitentiary. What kind of shit is that? Ya know, I mean a man come home from the penitentiary they don't even give you gate money. They give you $5 [and] bus fare. . . . I owe for [bed] sheets, owe for bus tokens, I owe for my rent. You're automatically 2 weeks behind in rent, see what I'm saying. . . . I didn't ask to come here and be put in the hole by your all program. Ya all know that when I come here it would take a while for me to find a job. (pp. 13–14)

One of the issues likely to affect the success rate at the halfway house is financial pressures, which includes not only daily living expenses but also setting aside money for paying court costs, fees, victim restitution, and back child support that accumulated while the prisoner was behind bars. In sum, then, the intent of parolee interview research is to determine parolee needs from the prisons' point of view so that intervention programs can be designed to help address problems that ultimately lead many to fail or to sabotage themselves while on parole.

The Field Parole Officer

A field parole officer enforces the conditions of parole that are mandated by the parole board. Parole officers ordinarily manage caseloads of between 60 and 75 prisoners, although others have smaller, more specialized caseloads (numbering 25 to 50) of prisoners who need more intensive supervision. "Regular" supervision typically means about two 15-minute face-to-face contacts per month, with an annual cost of about $2,200 per parolee (Petersilia 2000b).

Parole officers are expected to perform five main functions:

1. Carry out and enforce the conditions of parole through supervision and monitoring by means of home visits, employment checks, and meeting with the parolee at the office.
2. Refer parolees to drug and alcohol treatment, anger management programs, parenting classes, and other community-based services according to their individual needs.
3. Conduct investigations, write reports, and evaluate, interpret, and report serious violations to the paroling authority.
4. Provide crime victims with information on the offender's living and working arrangements, parole conditions, and restitution payment schedule, if applicable.
5. Share applicable information with law enforcement personnel and take into custody parolees who violate their conditions.

To perform these functions, a parole officer must possess certain basic qualifications and specialized knowledge. The minimum qualifications should be a working knowledge of the principles of human behavior, knowledge of the laws of the jurisdiction in which he or she will work and of the powers and limitations of the position, and familiarity with the operation of related law enforcement agencies in the particular jurisdiction.

THE OFFICER'S PERSPECTIVE

Lynch (1998) conducted an ethnographic study of California parole officers to examine how officers managed job pressures of maintaining a specific number of contacts, having their parolees take drug tests, and filing reports within a specific time

A parole officer conducts a home visit to check curfew and drug test one of his parolees.

Courtesy of Leanne Fiftal Alarid

period. Parole officers came from a variety of backgrounds, but their "role identity" was similar in that they viewed parole more as an art than as a science. In other words, parole officers perceived that "keeping a pulse on their caseload"—knowing what their parolees were doing—through face-to-face interactions and monitoring was more important than the increased paperwork that resulted from using the computerized tracking records.

> The agents generally strove toward a very traditional law enforcement role, where they did not need to assess danger or risk or criminal activity by anything more than their own developed intuition and personal investigative skills. (Lynch 1998, p. 855)

A survey of Missouri parole officers' perceptions on the importance of their job in assisting prisoners with successful community reentry revealed that "close monitoring of behavior, assessing and referring parolees to community agencies based on their needs, helping parolees maintain employment, and holding offenders accountable for their behavior" were identified as the most important tasks (Seiter 2002, p. 53). When asked to ascertain the most important features of successful reentry programs, steady employment was mentioned by parole officers as the key element. The next three factors were that the parolee remain drug free, have positive family and peer social support systems, and have plenty of structure in daily activities. The last two were related to consistent officer monitoring and the officers' holding offenders accountable for their successes and failures. The five programs parole officers thought best assisted with parolee reentry were identified as job skills/vocational rehabilitation, substance abuse treatment, halfway houses, work release, and employment assistance (Seiter 2002).

Conditions of Parole

As in the case of probation, parole conditions may be classified into standard conditions that are mandatory for all parolees in a jurisdiction, and special conditions, which are tailored to fit the needs of an offender and therefore vary between offenders. Table 13.1 shows an example of parole conditions for the state of Oklahoma, which is fairly representative of conditions in other states. There are a number of

TABLE 13.1   Rules and Conditions of Oklahoma Parole

1. I will report to my parole officer and my employer immediately upon arrival at my destination.
2. I will obey all city, state, and federal laws. I agree to immediately report any new arrests to my parole officer.
3. I agree not to leave the State of Oklahoma without prior written permission by my officer and not leave the county without permission of my officer or his/her district office.
4. I agree to report as directed by my officer in person and in writing on the forms provided by my officer. I agree to allow the officer to visit at home, work, or other convenient places.
5. I agree to immediately report in person, in writing or by telephone any changes in residence, employment, or marital status.
6. I agree not to use or possess drugs other than those legally prescribed by a physician. I agree not to use alcohol nor go onto the premises where alcoholic beverages are served.
7. I agree not to lie or misrepresent the truth to any member of the Pardon and Parole Board, any employee of the Department of Corrections or any official of the government.
8. I agree not to associate with persons on parole/probation or persons with criminal records; I agree not to communicate with inmates of any penal institution, except members of the immediate family, unless my parole officer gives permission because of work or other good reason.
9. I agree to pay parole fees of $40 per month, payable in cashier's check or money order to the Department of Corrections Restitution and Accounting.
10. I will comply with all lawful directives issued by my supervising officer or any member of the Department of Corrections.
11. I understand that at any time or place, I am subject to search. In addition, my vehicle and any property under my control are subject to search.
12. I agree to submit to urinalysis or any other substance abuse testing procedures as required by my parole officer.
13. I agree to pay, during the term of my parole, all fines and court costs imposed by the court at the time of my conviction.
14. I understand that Oklahoma State Statute 21 § 1283(d) prohibits anyone under the supervision of the Oklahoma Department of Corrections to own or possess a firearm. I agree not to own, possess or travel in a vehicle with a firearm or explosives.
15. Sex offenders will abide by special sex offender rules.
16. I understand that violations may result in the imposition of sanctions including but not limited to:

Financial Planning	Reintegration Training	Electronic Monitoring	Day Reporting
Mental Health Counseling	Intensive Supervision	Community Service	Temporary Placement in
Attend AA	Attend N/A	Victim Impact Panel	a community correctional
Attend MRT	Curfew	Weekend Incarceration	facility or jail for up
GED Courses	Intensive Parole	Nighttime Incarceration	to 30 days Supervision

17. I agree to follow the special condition(s) listed below:

I have read these conditions and understand that I must obey them until the term of my parole expires. I understand that failure to comply with these rules and conditions may result in the imposition of intermediate sanctions or revocation of my parole. I also understand that a finding of guilt, or plea of guilty or nolo contendere will be evidence that I failed to obey the law. I will be arrested and sent back to prison to serve the remainder of my sentence plus any new sentences.

_____
WITNESS SIGNATURE AND DATE

_____
PAROLEE'S SIGNATURE AND DATE   NUMBER

Retrieved from: http://www.ppb.state.ok.us/Docket/Rules%20of%20Parole/Rules%20and%20Conditions.rtf

standard conditions for a parolee to follow—thus raising the question as to the most ideal situation for people who were previously in a very structured environment where most decisions were made for them. Are there too many conditions to follow? Not enough conditions? Is the system of conditions so rigid and strict that the parolee is destined to fail? The courts will generally uphold reasonable conditions but will strike down illegal conditions or those considered unreasonable because they are impossible to meet. As in probation, appellate courts generally allow parole boards great discretion in imposing conditions of parole (Holt 1998).

LIMITED RIGHTS OF ALL PAROLEES

An offender on parole does not lose all constitutional rights. However, as with probationers, the rights enjoyed are **diminished**, meaning that they are not as highly protected by the courts as similar rights enjoyed by nonoffenders.

Diminished Constitutional Rights
Constitutional rights enjoyed by an offender on parole that are not as highly protected by the courts as the rights of nonoffenders.

Preferred Rights
Rights more highly protected than other constitutional rights.

First Amendment Rights   Even **preferred rights** such as First Amendment rights can be limited if an offender is on parole or probation. For example, a defendant was convicted for obstructing a federal court order arising from the defendant's anti-abortion activities. The court imposed as a condition of supervision that the defendant was prohibited from "harassing, intimidating, or picketing in front of any gynecological or abortion family planning services center" (*United States v. Turner* 1995). The defendant challenged that condition, claiming it violated her rights under the First Amendment. On appeal, the Federal Court of Appeals for the Tenth Circuit held the condition valid, saying "conditions which restrict freedom of speech and association are valid if they are reasonably necessary to accomplish the essential needs of the State and public order."

Fourth Amendment Rights   As a condition of parole, parolees must allow parole officers to search their car or place of residence without a search warrant. This condition has been upheld for parole revocation hearings but not for a new criminal prosecution. A parolee's "consent" to warrantless searches by state parole agents, based on reasonable suspicion that the parolee had committed a parole violation as specified in the conditions of release, is proper under both the Fourth Amendment and the applicable provision of the Pennsylvania constitution (*Commonwealth v. Williams* 1997).

Exclusionary Rule
A rule of evidence that enforces the Fourth Amendment's prohibition against unreasonable search and seizure, whereby illegal police searches are not admissible in a court of law. The purpose is to deter police misconduct.

The **exclusionary rule** was initially used to exclude any evidence obtained or seized illegally by the police in violation of the Fourth Amendment. In the case of parolees, *Pennsylvania Board of Probation and Parole v. Scott* (1998) and probationers *(State v. Pizel* 1999), the court ruled that the exclusionary rule does not apply to parole or probation revocation hearings. The court ruled in the direction it did in part because parole officers do not need a warrant to conduct a legal search, and the burden of proof is lower in parole revocation hearings than it is in criminal court prosecutions. A different standard must be met for searches conducted for individuals under parole supervision compared with individuals not under community supervision (Hemmens, Bennett, and del Carmen 1998). Parolees and probationers have less expectation of privacy than individuals not under a correctional sentence.

LEGAL ISSUES IN PAROLE CONDITIONS FOR SEX OFFENDERS

Decisions in court cases have raised interesting legal issues involving parole conditions involving sex offenders. For example, involvement in a treatment program for sex offenders requires that offenders admit their guilt. If the crime is denied, then the offender will not be allowed to participate in treatment. Failure to participate in a treatment program is a violation of parole, and a legitimate reason for revocation. A Connecticut appellate Court noted, however, that in this situation, due process requires

BOX 13.1 TECHNOLOGY IN CORRECTIONS

How Are Internet Activities of Parolees Monitored?

With the increase in wireless capabilities in public places and across entire cities, access to the Internet is widespread, and it is virtually impossible to prohibit use as a part of probation or parole conditions. Officers have instead allowed offenders to use the Internet, but courts have upheld the right of officers to examine and control the type of Internet sites offenders visited. Officers with specialized caseloads of offenders where the Internet should be monitored can obtain free software called "Field Search" that allows them the opportunity to visit an offender's home and conduct a search of a computer hard drive for URLs that are linked to unauthorized sites (for example pornography for offenders convicted of a sexual offense). The software is so thorough that it detects deleted web addresses visited during a specific period of time—either since the last officer's visit or since the hard drive was first installed. It can be set to detect web sites, images, videos, zipped files, browser histories, cookies, and password protected files on any type of computer. Even those addresses deleted by so-called "wiping" software that claims to erase web sites off the computer can be detected, and date and time stamped as to the last time the file or image was visited. When unauthorized addresses are detected, the offender can take a polygraph test to corroborate the findings. The results from the software scan, together with a failed polygraph test, can be used as evidence for the officer to request a change in the terms of supervision or violate the supervision altogether.

National Law Enforcement and Corrections Technology Center (2009). Field Search. *TechBeat* (Winter). Accessed: http://www.justnet.org

---

that the parolee must be informed ahead of time that denial of guilt would ultimately result in revocation, and to not do so would be improper (*State v. Faraday* 2002).

Another issue involved whether paroled sex offenders must provide blood and saliva samples to create a DNA (deoxyribonucleic acid) bank. The condition was challenged as violating parolees' right against unreasonable searches and seizures. The Tenth Circuit Court of Appeals upheld the condition because of the significance of DNA evidence in solving sex offenses, the minimal intrusion on the inmate's right to privacy, and the parolee's diminished constitutional rights (*Boling v. Romer* 1996).

A sex offender on parole cannot contest a penile plethysmograph as a parole condition. The Seventh Circuit Court of Appeals upheld submission to a penile plethysmograph as a parole condition for a Michigan inmate who was convicted in federal court of kidnapping and allegedly molesting a 6-year-old boy before attempting to drown him (*Walrath v. Getty* 1995). The offender in this case objected to the condition, saying that it was fundamentally unfair and therefore denied him due process. His parole was revoked. On appeal, the Seventh Circuit ruled that "the Commission may impose or modify other conditions of parole so long as they are reasonably related to the nature of the circumstances of the offense and the history and characteristics of the parolee."

A fourth issue of monitoring a parolee's computer hard drive in their home and limiting types of Internet sites is discussed in Box 13.1.

Violating Parole

Most of the discussion in Chapter 7 on probation revocations also applies to parole revocations and won't be repeated here. Instead, this chapter focuses a short legal issues section, highlighting any *differences* between parole and probation revocations. We also discuss why people violate parole and/or abscond from community supervision, and how this behavior can be decreased. In the Field notes Ralph Garza's view as a warrant analyst was that not all parole violations result in revocation hearings.

FIELD NOTES

How Are Parole Violators and Parole Absconders Supervised?

When the officer suspects that a parolee has absconded or violated supervision, the parole officer first visits the last known residence. If there is no response at the parolee's home, then the officer reviews the local county jail bookings to determine if the parolee was arrested. Provided the parolee is not in local custody, the parole officer searches the state and national crime information centers. Then the officer calls local hospitals to determine if the offender was admitted for an illness or injury. Finally, the officer will call the local morgue and verify that the offender is not dead in the parolee's county of residence. After the parole officer has exhausted all possibilities, he or she completes a violation report and requests that a warrant be issued.

Ralph Garza *Warrant Analyst, Texas Department of Criminal Justice, Parole Division.*

Fugitive or absconder violations are time intensive for officers. When a parolee is arrested for a new offense, another series of investigations begins. First, the officer must determine if anyone was killed or injured.ext, is the offender in custody? If the parolee is in custody, this may explain why the offender could not be found and could not report. Please keep in mind that while the parole officer is dealing with one parolee, there are still 80 to 85 other parolees still on supervision that demand the officer's attention.

The parole officer will also deal with non-filed assaults. This is when the victim does not, will not or cannot go to the police and file a police report against the parolee. The parole officer attempts to gather as much evidence as possible without coercion, so that if a warrant is later issued against the parolee for the assault, then the evidence presented by the victim could result in a parole revocation for that offender.

Parolees with criminal charges are monitored by reviewing their upcoming court dates and cases. The officer will examine the parolee's case and note any changes or comments in an offender information database. If charges are pending against the parolee, then

any parole hearings are held in abeyance until the pending charges are adjudicated. The Warrant Section of the Texas Parole Division issues approximately 150 warrants a day. That is 3,000 per month or 36,000 annually. A parolee with a warrant is not automatically returned to prison. Those offenders that either have a parole hearing or waive their hearing may be continued on supervision, transferred to an intermediate punishment facility, or revoked.

Given the overcrowding in county jails and prison units, the parole officer must exercise every possible means to keep the parolee reporting and out of jail through a series of graduated sanctions. The graduated sanctions most often utilized are: warnings/admonishments, increase control, increase monitoring/programming, and modifying the special conditions pending approval by a parole panel. Warnings and admonishments consist of compliance counseling, written reprimands, and case conferences. Compliance counseling is providing guidance to the releasee to follow the rules of supervision. It is meant as a first level non-threatening sanction. A case conference means a meeting occurs between the parolee, parole officer, and unit supervisor to discuss the violations.

The next level of sanctions is for the officer to reclassify the parolee at a higher supervision level for increased control. For example, if the parolee is on minimum supervision, the parolee requires a home visit every six months. If the parolee has not reported on time or has not attended his substance abuse treatment, the officer can increase to "intensive" where the parolee will receive a home visit every month until compliance is attained. Another increase control device is having the parolee report to the District Resource Center (similar to a day reporting center), which means now the offender has to find a ride, arrive on time, and participate in substance abuse meetings for two hours. The third level involves getting the parole panel to modify the conditions. If all else fails, the last stop is back to prison.

Mr. Garza stresses that parolees are given multiple chances and options, through a process called *graduated sanctions*. Incarceration is used only as the last option after all other administrative sanctions have been exhausted.

The parole violation process is depicted in Figure 13.1 as a series of decision points. Like Mr. Garza attests, the process begins with the field parole officer, who must discover the violation and, after investigation, can decide to arrest the parolee,

FIGURE 13.1   The Parole Revocation Process.

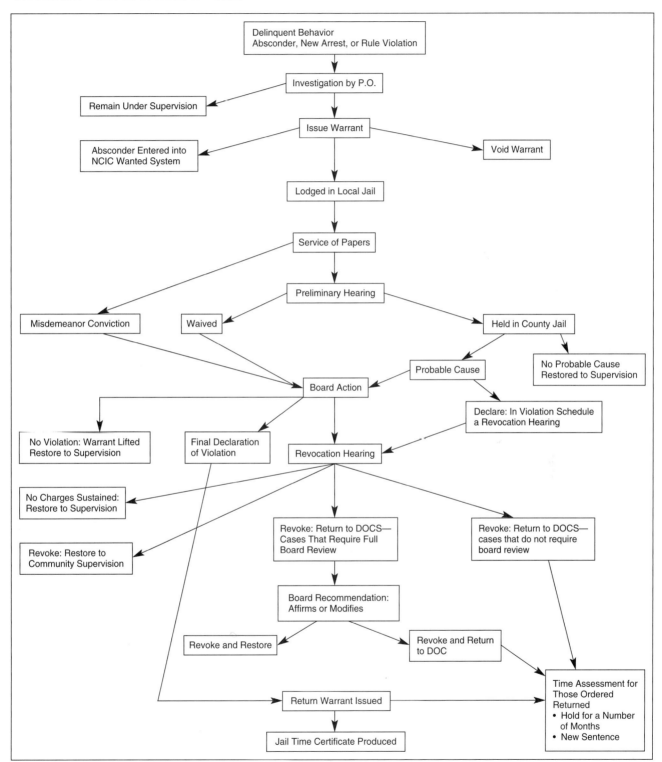

Source: Adapted from New York State Division of Parole, Office of Policy Analysis and Information. 1993. Overview of the Parole Revocation Process in New York. In *Reclaiming Offender Accountability: Intermediate Sanctions for Probation and Parole Violators,* edited by Edward E. Rhine. Laurel, MD: American Correctional Association, p. 41. Used with permission.

keep the parolee under supervision, or issue a citation to appear at a revocation hearing. When an arrest warrant is issued, the parolee is detained in the county jail until a preliminary hearing. When a citation is issued, the parolee remains in the community until a revocation hearing. The decision of whether or not to revoke parole resides with the parole board (recall that the judge revoked probation, so this is one major difference).

WARRANTS AND CITATIONS

The time it takes to revoke parole varies by jurisdiction according to case backlog and whether or not the parolee admits the allegations or requests a hearing. The time from violation detection by the officer to disposition by the parole board or the court ranged from 44 to 64 days (Burke 1997). The federal system requires that revocation hearings be held within 90 days from the time the offender is taken into custody (U.S. Parole Commission 2006). Most violators (82 percent) enter the jail booking process by a warrant, but that means that a jail bed is occupied until the hearing process ends. In order to save jail space for individuals who are a true threat to the public safety, more jurisdictions are turning to citations in place of automatic warrants for violators waiting for revocation hearings. If the violation was violent or indications exist that the parolee may abscond, then the parolee waits behind bars until the parole revocation hearing. For most parole violators, a citation allows them to continue working and supporting dependents while at the same time preparing for a possible entrance or return to jail or prison. Another distinct advantage is that citations save jail space for others.

Most states have a two-stage hearing parole revocation process. However, unlike probation revocations, a two-stage process is not required in parole revocations. Therefore, the federal system and some states merge these two proceedings into one, with a conviction for a new offense while on parole as enough evidence to revoke parole (U.S. Parole Commission 2006). This is known in the federal system as an "expedited" revocation, which now accounts for almost half of all revocations (Hoffman and Beck 2005). An expedited revocation requires the parole violator to admit wrongdoing, waive the right to a revocation hearing before the U.S. Parole Commission, and does not allow the right to appeal the revocation decision. If the offender contests the accusations, wishes to have a revocation hearing, or wishes to retain the right to appeal, he or she sits in jail waiting for the revocation hearing. Hoffman and Beck (2005) found an interesting split when they compared the outcomes of cases where offenders agreed to the expedited revocation and case outcomes of offenders who did not agree *for the same charge*. Offenders who requested a revocation hearing got the exact same decision had they just expedited their case (38.5 percent), while 31 percent received a more lenient decision and 30 percent received a harsher decision (p. 455).

Characteristics of Parole Violators

Of the parole violators who returned to state prison (most with a new sentence), more than 95 percent were men, over half were African American, and most were young or middle-aged (between 25 and 39 years of age). The most serious offense was a violent crime in 34 percent of cases, a property crime for 33 percent of violators, a drug crime in 23 percent of cases, and a public-order crime in 13 percent of cases (see Table 13.2).

TABLE 13.2   Characteristics of Parole Violators in State Prison

Characteristic	All 50 States	California	New York	Texas
Gender				
Male	95.3%	92.9%	96.7%	94.6%
Female	4.7	7.1	3.3	5.4
Race/Hispanic origin				
White non-Hispanic	27.5	30.8	11.1	23.1
Black non-Hispanic	51.8	33.4	54.2	50.3
Hispanic	18.3	31.9	33.1	26.0
Other	2.4	3.9	1.6	0.6
Age at prison release				
17 or younger	0.1	0.2	0.0	0.0
18–24	9.4	8.8	8.6	6.1
25–29	20.8	19.8	19.8	19.1
30–34	24.1	25.5	26.0	23.3
35–39	20.3	22.9	20.3	21.1
40–44	13.9	12.8	13.3	15.5
45–54	9.3	8.0	10.2	12.3
55 or older	2.0	2.0	1.8	2.5
Most serious offense*				
Violent	33.7	24.4	40.9	33.3
Property	30.1	25.3	15.6	36.8
Drug	23.1	27.1	33.6	21.3
Public order	12.9	22.9	9.4	8.6
Number of prior incarcerations				
1	42.3	28.9	52.9	44.1
2	14.0	12.6	12.6	14.1
3 to 5	26.3	27.1	26.7	28.4
6 or more	17.3	30.7	7.8	13.5

*Excludes other/unspecified offenses.

Source: Timothy A. Hughes, Doris James Wilson, and Allen J. Beck. 2001. *Trends in State Parole, 1990–2000.* Washington, DC: U.S. Department of Justice, Bureau of Justice Statistics, p. 14.

PAROLE REVOCATION RATE

Most rearrests of parolees occur in the first six months after release from prison, and within three years two-thirds of all parolees have been rearrested. If a parolee is ultimately revoked, in most cases, the revocation period is not long enough to justify a return to prison. Instead, revoked parolees remain in the community with more restrictions or they remain in the county jail for the rest of their original sentence. This puts a huge strain on county resources, especially since the rate of parole failure has increased.

Figure 13.2 shows that parole violators (for either a new crime or technical violations) constituted *35 percent of all new state prison admissions* in that year. Over time, the number of those who returned to prison with a new sentence has more than doubled since 1980 and tripled over the last 50 years. Another point: not all parolees who return to prison have necessarily committed a new offense. Of those who were returned to prison, only about 1 in 5 federal prisoners on post-release supervision and 1 in 4 state parolees were returned because they committed a new crime (Glaze and Bonczar 2008).

FIGURE 13.2   Percent of State Prisoners Who Enter Prison Because of Parole Revocation, 1930–2008.

Sources: Robyn L. Cohen. 1995. *Probation and Parole Violators in State Prison, 1991.* Washington, DC: U.S. Department of Justice, Bureau of Justice Statistics; Joan Petersilia. 2000b. When Prisoners Return to the Community: Political, Economic, and Social Consequences. In *Sentencing and Corrections: Issues for the 21st Century* [paper 9 from the Executive Sessions on Sentencing and Corrections]. Washington DC: U.S. Department of Justice; Heather C. West and William J. Sabol. 2008. *Prisoners in 2007.* Washington, DC: U.S. Department of Justice, Bureau of Justice Statistics.

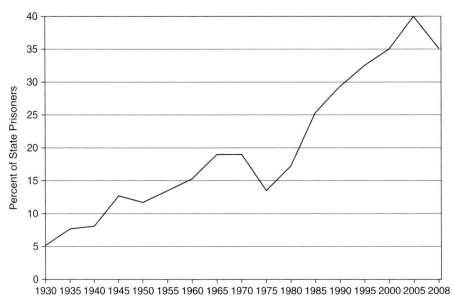

Table 13.3 provides various reasons state parolees who were sent back to state prison were revoked nationwide and compares nationwide rates with California, New York, and Texas. With the increase in rates of violations in recent years, research has been undertaken to discover the underlying causes of parole and probation revocations. One reason involves the shift in the way offenders are monitored, changing from a treatment perspective to one of control. With more emphasis placed on control and punishment, the threshold level is lowered for behaviors tolerated before a revocation occurs. Second, an increase in the average number of offenders that each parole officer has to supervise may actually mean that offenders receive less face-to-face contact. Officers spend less quality time with offenders and more time on rule enforcement and paperwork. A third reason is that parolees and probationers alike have more parole conditions, and thus more ways to violate. An increased number of conditions mean that offenders have more pressure to perform and to try to meet all those conditions. Finally, with the advances made in drug testing technology, more drug use is now detected. In addition, with the increased use of electronic monitoring in parole and probation, more hardened offenders tend to be placed in the community to avoid institutional overcrowding (Parent et al. 1994). One thing is certain—parolees who were convicted of property, drug, and public order crimes were less likely to violate their parole than offenders who went to prison for violent crimes, weapons, or immigration offenses.

An increase in revocation rates puts pressure on a number of other components in the criminal justice system. For example, parole and probation officers must devote more of their time to revocation paperwork and less time to supervising other offenders on their caseload who are functioning satisfactorily. Furthermore, while probation and parole revocators are awaiting hearings, revocation drains court resources, parole board resources, and county jail bed space (Parent et al. 1994).

ATTITUDES ON REVOCATION

The frequency of parole revocation has generated controversy. Too many parole revocations lead to prison congestion, and too few revocations lead to public apprehension about safety from convicted offenders. The implication is that parole

TABLE 13.3 Reasons for Revocation among Parole Violators in State Prison

Reason for Revocation	All 50 States	California	New York	Texas
Arrest/conviction for new offense	69.9%	60.3%	87.1%	78.8%
Drug-related violations	16.1	23.1	11.4	10.7
Positive test for drug use	7.9	12.2	5.6	4.3
Possession of drug(s)	6.6	8.9	5.6	5.6
Failure to report for drug testing	2.3	4.6	1.3	1.3
Failure to report for alcohol or drug treatment	1.7	1.1	1.9	1.2
Absconders	22.3	26.6	18.4	19.7
Failure to report/absconded	18.6	24.7	17.2	17.2
Left jurisdiction without permission	5.6	3.9	2.5	4
Other reasons	17.8	20.7	10.6	13.8
Failure to report for counseling	2.4	1.2	2	1.9
Failure to maintain employment	1.2	0.7	0.6	0.9
Failure to meet financial obligations	2.3	0.2	0	2.7
Maintained contact with known offenders	1.2	1.6	0.4	0.8
Possession of gun(s)	3.5	3.8	1.9	2.3

Excludes 37,440 parole violators who reported that their parole had not been revoked. Detail adds to more than 100% because some inmates have had more than one violation of parole.

Source: Timothy A. Hughes, Doris James Wilson, and Allen J. Beck. 2001. *Trends in State Parole, 1990–2000.* Washington, DC: U.S. Department of Justice, Bureau of Justice Statistics, p. 14.

officials are reluctant to revoke if it means adding prisoners to an already over-crowded prison system. A balance must be achieved between reintegrating offenders into society and public protection.

The public tends to view the rate of parole violation as indicative of parole success or failure. Criminal justice practitioners, in contrast, recognize that what may appear to be good parole statistical results can, in light of the quality and extent of supervision, indicate just the opposite. In truth, violation rates do not accurately measure the success or failure of parole (Parent et al. 1994).

Parole Absconders

One of the more serious, and surprisingly frequent, types of technical violations resulting in parole failure is absconding. An **absconder** is defined as an offender under community supervision who, without prior permission, escapes or flees the jurisdiction he or she is required to stay within. Official nationwide estimates report that 12.2 percent of all parolees abscond from supervision (Glaze and Bonczar 2008). The absconding rate for parolees is less than that reported for Texas probationers (18 percent) and clients at restitution centers (26 percent) (Levin 2008a). In some jurisdictions that list absconding from supervision as a criminal offense, a parole absconder can be charged with a new crime. For most parolees, leaving the area without notifying the parole officer is a technical violation.

Absconder
An offender under community supervision who, without prior permission, escapes or flees the jurisdiction he or she is required to stay within.

Why Do Parolees Leave?

Parolees who abscond do so ultimately to avoid having their parole revoked and possibly being sent back to prison. "Absconders rarely intend to run immediately, but a continuous perception of having one's opportunities stifled creates feelings of despair and ultimately . . . a long-established pattern of running from supervision" (Schwaner, McGaughey, and Tewksbury 1998, p. 48). Many parolees are uncertain about what their parole officer will do once he or she discovers a violation, and that uncertainty translates into fear. This fear leads parolees to do anything to avoid a revocation hearing. Parole absconders fall into two main categories: benign and a possible threat to community safety.

Type I Absconders: Benign   The first and most common category is absconders who have committed technical violations and do not understand the system well enough to predict what the outcome of their actions will be. The uncertainty and fear get the better of these people, and in a highly emotional state the offenders drop all responsibilities and pressures that have been building up and leaves them without thinking about the more serious consequences of escape. Ironically, the violations that led up to escape are usually less serious than the escape label that will affect the individuals for the remainder of the sentence and for any future convictions. For such persons, reasons for absconding range from drug use to financial difficulties to leaving the state to visit a dying relative. Parent substantiates the benign type of absconder by noting that "typical absconders are low-risk property offenders who remained in the community after they absconded. . . . [M]ost were not arrested for new crimes while on absconder status" (Parent 1993, p. 10).

Type II Absconders: Menace To Society   The second category of absconders includes individuals who understand the system too well. These individuals constitute a very small percentage of all absconders, and they will have committed one or more new crimes (some of which are serious) while on community supervision. They know with certainty that they will return to prison anyway. If the recent criminal behavior is serious enough, they know that they may never get out of prison again, so they take the chance of living out of prison until they are caught. This type of absconder is more likely than the first type to come to the attention of law enforcement officers and to be extradited (returned) to the original state of conviction. Type II absconders are the ones most likely to return to prison, as well as those prone to threaten community safety. Because absconders' whereabouts are not known for what could be an extended period of time, the true extent of absconder criminal activity, and whether they threaten public safety or whether they threaten the credibility of community supervision, is also largely unknown (Parent et al. 1994).

Locating and Apprehending Fugitives

Because of the large number of absconders every year, most states take a passive approach to locating and apprehending fugitives. When a parolee (or probationer) absconds from supervision, a warrant is filed with local, state, or national crime information systems. Many absconders are caught from a routine check for a traffic violation, and some are arrested because they commit a new crime. Ironically, many absconders never leave the state and could later be located through searching public utility records or other applicable databases (Parent et al. 1994). More recently, locating fugitives has been made easier by law enforcement working with parole in the use of "Fuginet" (see Box 13.2).

BOX 13.2 TECHNOLOGY IN CORRECTIONS

Finding Fugitives on the Internet through "Fuginet"

A state trooper pulls over a vehicle for speeding. Everything about the car registration and insurance checks out okay. The car is not reported stolen, and the owner has the same last name as the driver. The driver says it is his mother's car. Other than issuing a speeding ticket and seeing no valid reason to detain, the trooper lets him go, unaware that the driver is a parole violator. "Fuginet" is a more efficient way for state and local law enforcement to apprehend fugitives within their own state once a warrant is issued. The database is updated daily by parole officers and can be accessed via a secure log-in on the Internet, so the information takes less time to get processed, and there is more detailed information about each offender: parole address, family information, and vehicle information and photos. Fuginet also has facial recognition software that compares composite drawings of unidentified suspects with similar images in the database. It is anticipated that parole absconders will be arrested faster than before, and this database can also be used to help solve open investigations.

Source: National Law Enforcement and Corrections Technology Center. 2002. Fuginet'ing Parole Violators. *TechBeat* (Winter). Retrieved from: http://www.justnet.org

---

Type II absconders are pursued through more aggressive tactics because they may pose a threat to community safety. Parent and his colleagues found that states that aggressively pursue an absconder use one of three methods:

1. Their own fugitive apprehension unit
2. Receiving assistance from the Federal Bureau of Investigation (FBI)
3. Contracting out with a private apprehension unit

Many areas have fugitive units that operated in certain counties or statewide (Arizona, California, Massachusetts, Minnesota, Oklahoma, and Utah). Most locales cannot afford their own fugitive units and must seek assistance from the FBI or a private contractor. When the FBI is used, the U.S. attorney's office is made aware of the situation and agrees to extradite the absconder back to the original state of conviction from wherever the offender is captured. The state requesting the extradition must pay the extradition costs, which are about $4,000 per fugitive. The fugitive is usually accompanied by two federal officers and is transported (from long distances) by aircraft to designated airports used by the U.S. Marshall's office. At that point, the fugitive is transported by car to the home state of conviction (Parent et al. 1994).

PREDICTING ABSCONDING BEHAVIOR

The argument can be made that if absconding behavior can be predicted, then it can be prevented—or at least decreased. Shawn Schwaner (1997) compared a sample of absconders (11 percent) with nonabsconders (89 percent) in Ohio using two different data sets. Using bivariate analyses, he found that the following variables were most predictive of absconding behavior:

- Juvenile and adult felony convictions
- Arrests within five years of the current crime
- Previous adult incarcerations
- Previous probation or parole revocations

Furthermore, high-risk parole absconders were more likely to be apprehended than low-risk absconders (Schwaner 1997).

Williams, McShane, and Dolny (2000b) collected data on 863 California parolees who absconded during their first time on parole, representing 21.3 percent of their entire sample of about 4,052 parolees. This included 186 parolees (4.6 percent of the sample) who absconded two or more times in one year. The researchers found no gender differences in the absconding rate. However, individuals of Hispanic origin were less likely than people of other race or ethnic groups to abscond. Using multivariate statistical techniques, the researchers ascertained that the following seven variables contributed significantly to predicting absconding behavior (in order of highest to lowest importance):

1. Unstable living arrangements
2. Frequent unemployment
3. Previous parole violations
4. Low stakes
5. Larger number of prior arrests
6. Single marital status
7. Previous felonies

Unstable living arrangements contributed 29 percent to the explanation, making it the most powerful predictor. The bottom four variables, collectively, contributed only half as much (14 percent) to the model. Another drawback, which the researchers themselves point out, is that about 27 percent of nonabsconders also fit the absconder profile (a false positive), and thus separating absconders from nonabsconders is difficult.

To prevent absconding, parole officers must understand factors and situations leading up to an offender's decision to leave. Then, parole officers should "keep a pulse" on each person on their caseload, noting changes in behavior, to determine if a revocation pattern is occurring. Preventing absconding behavior will be more effective for the first, more benign, type of absconders. The second, more serious, type is more difficult to predict. Until more resources can be devoted to studying absconders, this behavior seems to be a casualty of community supervision.

Some jurisdictions have experimented with different methods of returning absconders to community supervision with some changes in the parole conditions. The District of Columbia's "Find and Fix" program is one such example. In Minneapolis, Minnesota, absconders were offered a brief period of amnesty. Absconders could voluntarily turn themselves in and not be reimprisoned. These programs have reported significant success (Parent et al. 1994).

Parole Effectiveness

Parole has been widely criticized as a "revolving door" to prison that reduces the impact of criminal sentences and threatens public safety. Critics claim that studies have failed to provide any assurance that paroled inmates will not continue their criminal activities while under supervision. Some public concerns are valid. For example, one study found that California parole officers "lost track of about one-fifth of the parolees they were assigned to in 1999" (Petersilia 2000b, p. 3). However, many parolees do complete their term of supervision successfully, and in fact, national parole success rates have remained the same since 1990 (Hughes, Wilson, and Beck 2001).

A study of nearly 300,000 prisoners released in 15 different states found that 67.5 percent were rearrested for a new offense and over half were returned to prison within three years (Langan and Levin 2002). These facts, however, do not fully answer the question: Is parole effective? Completion of parole without revocation may represent parole officers' failure to adequately supervise offenders. On the one hand, violations, particularly technical violations, might not come to the attention of an officer who cannot or refuses to supervise closely. On the other hand, closer supervision would probably reveal a larger number of technical violations, which could be reflected in higher recidivism statistics. Yet many of the particular offenders may not be considered failures.

To illustrate this point, consider the following examples. Which parolees are successful, and which are not?

1. Richard has not been arrested for any offense during the term of his supervision but was cited several times for technical violations, such as failure to report, failure to maintain employment, and excessive use of alcohol.
2. Vincent has no known technical violations but was arrested on two occasions for failure to pay court-ordered child support. A review of the records indicates that he got very far behind while incarcerated but has been paying regularly since being placed under supervision. He has not been able to "catch up" the delinquent balance, however, and his ex-wife regularly files charges of delinquent child support against him.
3. Josephine has no known technical violations but was arrested for driving under the influence of alcohol two months after being placed under supervision. She agreed to enter an alcohol treatment program, and there have been no further reported violations. Her alcohol treatment counselor reports that her progress is favorable.
4. David has no new crimes and no technical violations. However, he has a bad attitude and refuses to cooperate with the parole officer beyond the bare minimum required by his parole agreement.
5. Jean successfully completes five years of supervision with no arrests or technical violations. One year before she is scheduled to be terminated from supervision, she is arrested for a new offense. This is the first time in her adult life that she has gone more than six months without being arrested.
6. Jeffrey is not arrested for any new offenses, and there are no reported technical violations. However, the supervising officer has been advised repeatedly by law enforcement authorities that Jeffrey is heavily involved in narcotics trafficking.
7. Raymond was released from prison a year ago. He is working regularly and has no reported violations. One evening when returning from a movie with his wife, he is involved in a minor traffic accident. In the aftermath, he and the other driver exchange blows, and both are arrested. He is charged with simple assault and fined $200.

Which of these parolees is successful? The question cannot be answered by arrest and conviction statistics only. A strict accounting might conclude that David and Jeffrey (offenders 4 and 6) are successful. A subjective analysis might suggest that the same offenders are failures. When examining recidivism studies, pay attention to three factors:

1. How recidivism is defined (by rearrest, conviction, parole revocation, return to prison, or other form of returning to criminal behavior)
2. The duration of time that the subjects were studied (the longer the period of time subjects were followed—for example, up to three years—the better)
3. The size of the sample studied (a larger sample, or one that samples from more than one area of the country, is more generalizable)

RECIDIVISM STUDIES

Some recidivism studies are fraught with methodological problems that limit how well they can be generalized. Others, which have more methodologically sound research methods, have reported mixed findings on the impact that certain factors have on parole success. Some of these factors include:

- Race and ethnicity
- Involvement in prison education programs
- Length of time served in prison
- Behavior while incarcerated
- Current conviction type
- Parolee age

Some studies show that these factors are significant in predicting parole outcome, and other studies show no differences. For example, one study found an inverse relationship between time served in prison and parole success. Don Gottfredson and colleagues (1997) found that the less time offenders served in prison, the greater the likelihood of parole success.

Regarding type of crime, studies have consistently found that murderers have a significantly higher parole success rate (Vito, Wilson, and Latessa 1991). One study by Langan and Levin (2002) measured the rate of rearrest for state-level offenders for three years following release. With the exception of robbery, property offenders (burglars, larcenists, and other thieves) had higher rates of rearrest than offenders convicted of violent crimes. In a different study of offenders returning to the federal system between 1986 and 1997, offenders convicted of violent crimes (for example, robbery) were more likely to return to federal prison within three years than any other offender type. About 32 percent of violent offenders returned to prison as opposed to only 13 percent of drug offenders (Sabol et al. 2000).

Some of these differences stem from the different patterns of offending behavior that criminals exhibit. Some criminals begin their "criminal career" at an earlier age, accrue more arrests, and sustain criminal behavior for a long time before decelerating the rate of offending. These criminals are termed "repeat" or "habitual" offenders. Other criminals, such as murderers, do not have criminal careers per se, but they commit a serious offense, for which they get caught and serve time. These criminals are much less likely to recidivate.

Related to this idea of criminal careers and offending patterns is the relationship between age and recidivism. Research that examines this relationship has found that younger parolees, especially those under the age of 25, are more likely to recidivate than older parolees (Joo, Eckland-Olson, and Kelly 1995). One recent study of California parolees determined that gang membership should also be taken into consideration when examining different age groups. In this study, Williams and his colleagues found that younger parolees who were not gang members had rates of reoffending that were similar to those of older parolees:

In sum, the youngest parolees, as a group, are not the worst of the parolee population. There is some evidence that they may be slightly worse than the average in parolee failure, violent and serious reoffending, dangerousness, and consumption of intervention resources. But when gang membership is controlled, much of that trend is called into question. On the other hand, they are not among the best of the parolee population either. (Williams et al. 2000)

PREDICTING PAROLE OUTCOMES

The three variables that have shown more consistent findings in predicting parole outcome are gender, number of prior arrests, and supervision versus no supervision.

Gender Differences   In general, studies have shown that male parolees return to prison at higher rates than women parolees (16 percent compared with 12 percent, respectively; Sabol et al. 2000). Another research study found that women parolees are more compliant with parole conditions than are male parolees (Acoca and Austin 1996).

Number of Prior Arrests   An inverse relationship exists between prior criminal history and parole outcome. The lower the number of previous arrests, the greater the likelihood of parole success (Hughes, Wilson, and Beck 2001; Solomon 2006).

Supervision versus No Supervision   A small number of studies have been conducted comparing parolees on supervision with prisoners released unconditionally, which means they are released without any supervision whatsoever. These studies show mixed results. Two studies (Sabol et al. 2000; Sacks and Logan 1980) measured recidivism defined as a new conviction for any crime (felony or misdemeanor), and found that recidivism rates were lower for those on supervision. By the end of three years, 85 percent of the unconditional group without supervision recidivated, whereas 77 percent of parolees returned to crime (Sacks and Logan 1980). The difference was more pronounced between the two groups after just the first year, indicating that parole supervision slows down the recidivism rate and may assist some offenders in maintaining law-abiding lives. A second study of federal offenders supports this finding (Sabol et al. 2000). Of the offenders who recidivated in the federal system, offenders released on some form of community supervision were in the community for an average of 17 months before returning to prison for a new crime. Offenders released without any supervision stayed out for just over 13 months before returning to prison for a new crime (Sabol et al. 2000).

A third study by the Urban Institute measured recidivism by rearrest over a two-year period, and used Bureau of Justice Statistics data on a sample of 30,624 prisoners released from 15 states (Solomon 2006). Although the data did not factor in state-level differences in supervision, the sample was divided into three groups: unconditional (no supervision), mandatory supervised release, and discretionary parole release. The unconditional releasees served the most time behind bars and more of them had previously been arrested for violent offenses than either of the other two groups, suggesting that the unconditional releasees were significantly more disconnected from community ties than supervised parolees. Despite this difference, mandatory supervised release and unconditional releases recidivated at the same rate—61 percent and 62 percent respectively over the two-year period. A slightly lower rate—54 percent—of those released on discretionary parole by a parole board recidivated. Even when technical violators were removed from the data, those committing new crimes did not change on the three types of supervision because most rearrests were for new crimes rather than technical violations. Although technical violators are taken into custody, official statistics do not record them as "arrests." Parole supervision did benefit women and offenders with few prior convictions who were significantly less likely to recidivate while being supervised than if they were not supervised at all. In interpreting the overall recidivism findings among the three groups, Solomon (2006, pp. 31–32) says:

> "Clearly there is a value judgment being made here, in characterizing a four percentage point difference as 'relatively small,' differing 'only slightly.' . . . Because parole boards take into account factors such as a prisoner's attitude and motivation level, institutional conduct, preparedness for release and connections to the community . . . I would expect this group to be substantially, rather than marginally, less likely to recidivate. The suggestion here is that lower rearrest

rates may be largely due to who is selected for discretionary release rather than discretionary supervision itself, which is not systematically different than mandatory supervision across states."

Hughes and colleagues (2001) also used data from the Bureau of Justice Statistics and compared those on mandatory release with those who were released by a parole board (unconditional releases were not part of the sample). This data, however, spanned over a 10-year period, while the previous study by the Urban Institute was cross-sectional from releases over one year. The rates of success on discretionary parole varied between 50 and 56 percent, whereas mandatory parolees were successful only 24 to 33 percent of the time between 1990 and 1999. They concluded, "In every year between 1990 and 1999, state prisoners released by a parole board had higher success rates than those released through mandatory parole" (p. 11).

In sum, parole practices and types of supervision vary widely, and no one type of supervision (or lack of supervision) has consistently been shown to be more effective than another. The future of parole supervision involves attempting to predict the future behavior of offenders being considered for parole, as well as examining patterns of behavior that may reliably indicate when a parolee may become too much of a public safety risk to allow him or her to remain in the community. Prediction research into the causes of recidivism and subsequent revocation could be invaluable in equipping the parole officer with the tools necessary for supervision. Recall our earlier discussion of risk and needs assessment instruments in Chapter 5 when we discussed classification. It is interesting to note that the very same variables that initially classify offenders also can predict post-release behavior on parole and may lead us to a deeper understanding of why some offenders succeed and some do not (Williams, McShane, and Dolny 2000a).

Community supervision, whether it is probation or parole, is more successful with people who have less severe criminal pasts; or another way of interpreting this could be that people with a more distinctive criminal history are more likely to be revoked for the same behavior because of their past. Regardless of the type of supervision, treatment interventions and reentry assistance increase success.

SUMMARY

- Parole boards enjoy a high level of discretion when imposing parole conditions. The extent of authority and the limitations are similar to those for probation.

- Parole revocation is the formal termination of a parolee's conditional freedom, usually (but not always) resulting in a reinstatement of imprisonment.

- *Morrissey v. Brewer,* the leading case on parole revocation, held that prior to revocation parolees must be given five basic rights. However, parolees do not have a constitutional right to counsel at a revocation hearing; this right is given on a case-by-case basis.

- Parolees do not have a constitutional right to appeal a revocation, but about half of the states, by law or agency policy, allow parolees this chance.

- Parole violators constituted 40 percent of all people who returned to prison with a new sentence.

- The increase in the revocation rate is due to a shift in the way offenders are monitored; greater emphasis is placed on control and punishment, and less time is spent on treatment and reentry concerns (due to a higher caseload per officer).

- Fear and uncertainty about community supervision leads probationers and parolees who lack community ties and relationships to abscond or escape from the area.

- Computer modeling and risk prediction assessments can be used to predict parole release as well as how to respond to parole violators, making parole less of an art and more of a science.

DISCUSSION QUESTIONS

1. What problems do parolees have when they are released from prison? What ideas do you have that might assist parolees in their reintegration into society?

2. If submission to a penile plethysmograph is valid as a parole condition for sex offenders, would other devices be acceptable for use with offenders who commit other types of crimes? If so, which ones? Support your answer.

3. Discuss what this statement means: "Parolees have diminished constitutional rights." Does that statement apply to preferred rights?

4. Imagine that you are a parole officer supervising the seven parolees described in the chapter. In two or three sentences, evaluate each case as a success or as a failure.

5. If you were being accused of a series of technical violations (three times that you didn't report and one positive urine screening for cocaine) while on post-prison supervision, and you did it, would you request expedited revocation procedures or still request a hearing?

6. Would your answer change in Question No. 5 if you were being accused of a new crime (e.g., theft)? List the pros and cons of having the expedited option for taxpayers.

7. What can be done by parole officers to decrease parole absconding rates?

8. Is supervised release an effective sanction? For whom?

9. If you were considering a violent offender convicted of robbery, and you had to choose between early release with supervision versus leaving him behind bars his entire sentence with no supervision upon release, which would you choose and why?

 **WEB SITES**

U.S. Parole Commission Rules and Procedures Manual
http://www.usdoj.gov/uspc/rules_procedures/rulesmanual.htm

Connecticut Juvenile Parole Revocation Hearing Policy
http://www.dir.ct.gov/dcf/Policy/Hear22/22-9-2.htm

Georgia Parole Conditions
http://oldweb.pap.state.ga.us/parole_conditions.htm

Iowa Code for Parole Revocations
http://www.legis.state.ia.us/IACODE/2003/908/

Matthews v. NY State Division of Parole (2001) court case on revocations
http://www.law.cornell.edu/ny/ctap/comments/i01_0001.htm

CASE STUDY EXERCISE

Parole Conditions and Revocation

As indicated in this chapter, the courts have granted a great deal of leeway to paroling authorities in setting parole standard conditions and special conditions for offenders. Court rulings seem to center around whether the condition is reasonable, acknowledgment that parolees have diminished rights, and whether the condition is related to the convicted criminal behavior.

Conditions pertaining to sex offenders have received added attention in recent years. In some jurisdictions, standard conditions for sex offenders include some or all of the following:

- No contact with any minor child (including offender's minor children) if victim of sexual crime was a minor, or no contact with minors at all even if the victim(s) were adult age
- Contact with minor children approved only if parole officer approves another supervising adult to be present at the time of the contact
- No possession of sexually explicit material—written, audio, or visual
- If the offense involved the use of the Internet or a computer, cannot have a personal computer and cannot work where access to Internet is allowed, or in some jurisdictions no computer access at all even if offense did not involve computer usage
- Notification to neighbors and employers of their sexual offense history and supervision status
- Mandatory participation in sexual offender treatment or aftercare programs
- Mandatory routine polygraph exams as a part of treatment or supervision
- If offense involved filming or pictures of victims, no camera or video equipment access allowed
- Cannot work in any employment that would allow access to children or victim-aged groups; cannot be self-employed
- Cannot live within a certain distance of schools, playgrounds, public parks, or other places where minors congregate

Using the case examples below, what conditions (if any) should be imposed on the offenders if paroled? What are some of the challenges of parole supervision that these cases present?

CASE A

Steven is serving a 5- to 15-year sentence for Sexual Assault of a Minor. He has served seven and one-half years of his sentence, which is five years beyond the minimum time to be served. Because he has three prior convictions for similar offenses, he does not have to be released until he has served 10 years of his sentence. Steven spent time in prison for two of the three prior offenses against minors. Each time he was released, he successfully completed the release period of parole supervision. All of his victims have been his grandchildren; family members are strongly opposed to his release and feel he will commit similar acts upon release. Steven has completed a sexual offender treatment program during this incarceration; he always refused to participate in treatment during prior incarcerations. The prognosis by the treatment counselor is guarded, but indicates Steven has worked hard on learning his offending triggers and knows what to avoid if released. He has not had any rule violations while incarcerated and has been employed in a private prison industry. He proposes a release to a community where none of his family reside and does not want to have contact with his family. He has been accepted into a halfway house program and plans on attending community-based sexual offender aftercare groups. If released, he would be under the supervision of a parole officer.

CASE B

Gloria is being considered for parole after serving three years on her nine-year sentence for Lewd Sexual Conduct and Sexual Contact with a Minor. She was 27 years old at the time of the offense, and her victim was 16. Currently, Gloria is 30 years old and her victim is now 19 years of age and enrolled as a full-time college student in another state. This is Gloria's first felony offense, and she has no history of previous behavior on community supervision. Gloria agreed to complete a sex offender treatment program during her incarceration, but claimed during her counseling sessions that she and her victim loved each other and everything was consensual. Gloria still reports feelings for him, but the victim's family wishes to have no contact with Gloria. However, at this time, no one knows how the victim feels about the relationship because his most recent contact information was unavailable when the field officer performed her investigations. The field officer did find out that Gloria's former employer would not accept her back in her former occupation as a nurse despite Gloria's statements that the institution would. Gloria is a registered nurse who wishes to parole back to her former neighborhood and has one male child, aged 13, who has been staying with Gloria's mother over the last three years. If released, Gloria would be under the supervision of a parole officer.

PART V

Special Issues in Community Corrections

In recent years, there has been an increase in both the number of juvenile offenders and in the seriousness of the offenses they commit. Nationally, approximately 1.7 million delinquency cases occur every year, and millions of additional cases of status offenders and dependent or neglected children come to the attention of the juvenile justice system as well. Chapter 14 discusses in detail legal issues and community corrections programs to deal with juvenile delinquents.

Every adult convicted of a felony suffers additional disabilities that are not directly imposed by the court. That is, even after a person has completed serving his or her sentence for a felony crime, civil disabilities (varying by state) may disallow that person from voting in a public election, holding a public office, being employed in certain occupations, owning a firearm, or being able to parent his or her own children. Chapter 15 examines these disabilities and investigates the mechanisms by which convicted offenders may be able to restore some or all of these civil rights.

14

Juvenile Justice, Probation, and Parole

CHAPTER LEARNING OBJECTIVES

- Explain the history of the juvenile justice system.
- Understand what parens patriae means and its influences on juvenile offenders.
- Analyze the similarities and differences between the juvenile and adult justice systems.
- Describe how a juvenile offender is processed through the system.
- Identify the basics of juvenile probation and parole.

A juvenile appears with his attorney before a judge as she sentences him to 6 months probation and 80 hours community service.

CHAPTER OUTLINE

Introduction

Background and History
Juvenile Courts Created in the United States

Juvenile Justice and Adult Justice Systems Compared
Differences from Adult Courts
Jurisdiction of Juvenile Courts
Transfer from Juvenile Courts to Adult Courts

An Overview of the Juvenile Justice Process
Procedure before Adjudication
Blended Sentences

Juvenile Probation
Conditions of Probation
Change as an Integral Process

Juvenile Probation Officers as "Superheroes"
Intensive Supervision Probation
School-Based Probation
Fare v. Michael C.
Are Juvenile Records Confidential?

Juvenile Parole/Aftercare
Juvenile Parole Boards and
    Parole Officers
Revocation of Juvenile Probation
    or Parole
Evaluating Juvenile Parole Programs

The Future of Juvenile Justice

KEY TERMS

parens patriae
mens rea
juvenile delinquency
conduct in need of supervision (CINS)
transfer of jurisdiction

judicial waiver
concurrent jurisdiction
statutory exclusion
intake
adjudication

disposition
youth courts
intensive supervision probation
school-based probation

Introduction

Although the rate of juvenile crime has declined, juvenile arrests still account for 17 percent of all violent crimes and 26 percent of all property crimes each year in the U.S. (Snyder 2008). The main concern is what ought to be done to juveniles who violate laws, particularly those who commit serious and violent crimes. Answers do not come easily, partially because society wrestles with differing philosophical approaches to juvenile offending. On the one hand, there is the recognition that many acts of status offenses and delinquency originate from abusive families, unhealthy peer groups, school failure, and other deeply rooted social problems and failures of social control. The juvenile justice system seeks to do what is best for the welfare and safety of each juvenile's situation. On the other hand, the theory of just deserts advocates accountability for youth offenders based on the seriousness of the act committed and the harm done to the victim and the outlying community. There are nearly 93,000 youths incarcerated in lock-ups or residential facility placements nationwide (Sickmund, Sladky, and Kang 2008). Some would argue that as the courts have extended their reach, the result has widened the net to more incarceration and less community-based options. One observer noted

> Judges and probation officers find themselves increasingly responsible to procure, for especially hard-to-serve children who are without parental support, basic nurturance, shelter, health, and educational services that more directly qualified agencies are either unwilling or unable to provide. This responsibility is increasing in part because of statutory revisions . . . expanding the courts' formal authority over other agencies to enforce both the right to treatment and the civil liberties of children. (Jacobs 1990, p. 22):

Parens Patriae
Latin term meaning that the government acts as a "substitute parent" and allows the courts to intervene in cases in which it is in the child's best interest that a guardian be appointed for children who, through no fault of their own, have been neglected and/or are dependent.

How did we get to this point? In the beginning, children were not entitled to constitutional rights, especially at home when under the care of parents. Beginning in 1966, the concept of **parens patriae** began to decline, as due process rights and accountability for juvenile offenders were a central focus (Ward and Kupchik 2009).

IN RE GAULT: THE DECLINE OF PARENS PATRIAE

The leading due process case in juvenile justice is *In re Gault* (1967). The U.S. Supreme Court ruled that "neither the Fourteenth Amendment nor the Bill of Rights is for adults alone." In that case, a 15-year-old boy and a friend were taken into custody in Arizona as a result of a complaint that they had made lewd telephone calls. Gault's parents were not informed that he was in custody, and they were not shown the complaint that was filed against their son. The complainant never appeared at any hearing, and no written record was made of the hearing that was held. Gault was committed to a state institution as a delinquent until he reached the age of majority—a total of six years from the date of the hearing. The maximum punishment for the offense, had it been committed by an adult, was a fine of from $5 to $60 or imprisonment for a maximum of two months. Gault appealed the conviction, saying he was denied his rights during the hearing. The U.S. Supreme Court agreed.

Gault held that juveniles must be given four basic due process rights in adjudication proceedings that can result in confinement in an institution where their freedom would be curtailed. These rights are:

- Reasonable notice of the charges
- Counsel, appointed by the state if the juvenile is indigent
- The ability to confront and cross-examine witnesses
- The privilege against self-incrimination

In re Gault is significant because it was the first case decided by the U.S. Supreme Court that gave juveniles due process rights, but it was also the beginning of the decline of the pure *parens patriae* approach. *Parens patriae* is still alive in juvenile justice, but its purity has been sapped by a gradual process of "adultification" through judicial intervention. Other cases that followed the *Gault* case continued to grant rights to juveniles, but juvenile and adult proceedings still remained separate with separate bodies of law, separate courts, and separate correctional punishments (see Table 14.1).

TABLE 14.1   Major United States Supreme Court Decisions in Juvenile Justice

Cases Giving Constitutional Rights to Juveniles:

Kent v. United States (383 U.S. 541 [1966]): Juveniles must be given due process rights when transferred from juvenile to adult court. These rights are:

A hearing

Representation by counsel at such hearing

Access to records considered by the juvenile court

A statement of the reasons in support of the waiver order

In re Gault (387 U.S. 1 [1967]): Juveniles must be given four due process rights in adjudication proceedings that can result in confinement in an institution where their freedom would be curtailed. These rights are:

Reasonable notice of the charges

Counsel, appointed by the state if the juvenile is indigent

(Continued)

TABLE 14.1   Major United States Supreme Court Decisions in Juvenile Justice (Continued)

Cases Giving Constitutional Rights to Juveniles:

The ability to confront and cross-examine witnesses
The privilege against self-incrimination

In re Winship (397 U.S. 358 [1970]): Proof beyond a reasonable doubt, not simply a preponderance of the evidence, is required in juvenile adjudication hearings in cases where the act would have been a crime if committed by an adult.

Breed v. Jones (421 U.S. 517 [1975]): Juveniles are entitled to the constitutional right against double jeopardy in juvenile proceedings.

Cases That Do Not Give Constitutional Rights to Juveniles:

McKeiver v. Pennsylvania (403 U.S. 528 [1971]): Juveniles have no constitutional right to trial by jury even in juvenile delinquency cases where the juvenile faces a possible incarceration.

Davis v. Alaska (415 U.S. 308 [1974]): Despite confidentiality laws, the fact that a juvenile is on probation may be brought out by the opposing lawyer in the cross-examination of a juvenile witness.

Smith v. Daily Mail Publishing Co. (443 U.S. 97 [1979]): A state law making it a crime to publish the name of a juvenile charged with a crime is unconstitutional because it violates the First Amendment right to freedom of the press.

Schall v. Martin (467 U.S. 253 [1984]): Preventive detention of juveniles is constitutional.

Fare v. Michael C. (442 U.S. 707 [1985]): A request by a juvenile to see his probation officer is not equivalent to asking for a lawyer. Moreover, there is no probation officer-client privilege, meaning that any information a juvenile gives to a probation officer may be divulged in court even if the information was given by the juvenile in confidence.

New Jersey v. T.L.O (469 U.S. 325 [1985]): Public school officials need reasonable grounds to search students; they do not need a warrant or probable cause.

Juvenile Justice and Adult Justice Systems Compared

Juvenile justice and adult justice are similar in many ways. Both represent efforts by the state to preserve public order and at the same time protect the basic constitutional rights of offenders. Despite the presence of *parens patriae*, the government is the offended party in juvenile cases and is represented by the prosecutor. In both juvenile and adult proceedings, the offender provides his or her own lawyer, except when indigent. When an offender is found to have committed the offense charged, the punishment in both proceedings includes deprivation of liberty by the state, through the use of jails or state institutions.

DIFFERENCES FROM ADULT COURTS

Despite the growing similarity between juvenile and adult criminal proceedings, some differences persist, the most notable being the role of the juvenile court judge. First, a juvenile court judge takes a more active part in the proceedings. He or she is expected to act as a wise parent rather than as an impartial arbiter, which is the judge's role in adult criminal cases. The juvenile court judge may initiate the questioning of the alleged offender, cross-examine witnesses, bring up a juvenile's background, or actively admonish or counsel an offender:

> In many jurisdictions, the juvenile court judge is the direct administrator of the juvenile probation department and/or court staff. When operating in this capacity, the juvenile court judge can assure coordination of services between the court and the probation department and may also take on the burden of fiscal management (Kurlychek, Torbet, and Bozynski 1999, p. 2).

A second difference between juvenile and adult justice, however, is the severity of the punishment imposed. For instance, juveniles spend limited time in institutions because they are released upon reaching a maximum age specified by state law. In contrast, adult criminals can be made to spend life in prison, a sanction that cannot be administered to juveniles unless they are tried as adults through a waiver or certification process.

A third difference is in the imposition of the death penalty as an ultimate sanction. Back in the late 1980s, the U.S. Supreme Court allowed the death penalty to be administered for juveniles if the crime was committed when the juvenile was 16 or 17 years old (*Stanford v. Kentucky* 1989). However, that opinion was overruled when the Court said in *Roper v. Simmons* (2005) that it is unconstitutional to execute juveniles who committed their crime before the age of 18. So whereas adult offenders can be given the death penalty, offenders under 18 years of age can no longer be given a death sentence regardless of the seriousness or nature of the crime. The differences that exist are summarized below (del Carmen, Parker, and Reddington 1998, p. 9):

Adult Proceedings	Juvenile Proceedings
1. Arrested	1. Taken into custody by police
2. Charged	2. Prosecutor petitions court
3. Accused of crime under the penal code	3. Violation comes under the juvenile code or family code
4. Trial	4. Adjudication
5. Formal, public trial	5. Usually a private, informal hearing
6. Judge is neutral	6. Judge acts as wise parent
7. Found guilty of a criminal offense by an impartial judge or jury	7. Found to have engaged in delinquent conduct
8. Disposition	8. Sentenced if found guilty
9. Committed to a state facility	9. Sent to jail or prison for juveniles
10. Judge or jury determines length of incarceration	10. Youth detention authorities determine when to release
11. Serves sentence for definite term, subject to parole law	11. Committed for an indeterminate amount of time, but usually released upon reaching age of majority
12. Purpose is mainly punishment	12. Purpose is rehabilitation
13. Released on parole, if eligible	13. Released on aftercare
14. A criminal case	14. A civil or quasi-civil case
15. Adults can be given the death penalty	15. Juvenile can no longer be given the death penalty (*Roper v. Simmons* 2005)

In reality, the above differences are more terminological than substantive and are, therefore, more symbolic than real. They have minimal impact on the process because the procedures are similar regardless of the term used. For example, adults who are arrested and juveniles who are taken into custody are deprived of liberty and are under the control of the justice system. Neither is there much difference between the adult suspect being charged and the prosecutor petitioning the court for the juvenile to be adjudicated because both processes lead to hearings. Sentencing and disposition both subject the offender to lawfully prescribed sanctions, including incarceration. Whether an adult is on parole or a juvenile is in aftercare, the degree of supervision and the results in case of violation are similar.

JURISDICTION OF JUVENILE COURTS

The types of cases that go to juvenile courts are defined by state law. Jurisdiction, or the authority to try cases in juvenile courts, varies from state to state. Such jurisdiction is usually based on the *age* of the offender and the *act* committed.

Based on Age   Criminal liability is based on the concept of **mens rea**, which is the Latin term for "a guilty mind" (Garner 2009, p. 1006). Without intent, an act is generally not considered criminal. A guilty mind implies that the actor knows what he or she is doing; therefore, the act is punishable because the actor intended for the injury to occur. Children below a certain age, however, are presumed by law to be unaware of the full consequences of what they do. Absent *mens rea,* they should not and cannot be punished like adults.

Mens Rea
Latin term meaning "guilty mind" that addresses level of mental intent to commit a crime.

During the latter part of the eighteenth century, children younger than 7 years old were deemed incapable of *mens rea* and exempt from criminal liability. Those above 7 years of age could be prosecuted and sentenced to prison or given the death penalty if found guilty (Snyder and Sickmund 1995). No state in the United States at present punishes juveniles so severely at such a young age, but the minimum age for juveniles to come under the jurisdiction of juvenile courts varies from state to state.

In contemporary juvenile cases, there is an upper and lower age limit, as determined by state law. Wide variations exist among states—from a youngest age of 6 years (when a juvenile court can assume jurisdiction) to an oldest age of 24 (when a juvenile is released). Most states, however, have a youngest age of 10 years and an oldest age of 17 years for juvenile court jurisdiction (see Table 14.2). Juveniles aged below the lowest limit who commit criminal acts are usually processed informally by the police or placed in the care of state social welfare services. Offenders above the oldest age are processed as adult criminals. The youngest and oldest ages apply to the time the act was committed, not when the offender was caught or tried in court. Despite these ages, some states provide that the juvenile can be kept in a juvenile institution or supervised until he or she is older (18, 21, or 24), particularly in juvenile delinquency cases when state authorities see the need for continued supervision.

Based on Acts Committed   Juvenile acts that trigger court intervention are of three types: **juvenile delinquency cases, conduct in need of supervision (CINS)**, and juveniles as victims. About six in ten of all juvenile justice cases are delinquency proceedings, which center on criminal actions committed by juveniles that would also be considered criminal if committed by adults. Another two in ten are for conduct in need of supervision, which otherwise include status offenses that would not be illegal if committed by an adult. The remaining 20 percent are from child victims of abuse (Roberts 2004).

Each state, by law, determines what acts come under each category. In general, juvenile delinquents are those who commit acts that are punishable under

Juvenile Delinquency
Acts committed by juveniles that are punishable as crimes under a state's penal code.

Conduct In Need of Supervision (CINS)
Acts committed by juveniles that would not have been punishable if committed by adults; status offenses.

TABLE 14.2   Minimum and Maximum Ages for Delinquency Cases

Youngest age for original juvenile court jurisdiction in delinquency matters:

Age	State
6	North Carolina
7	Maryland, Massachusetts, New York
8	Arizona
10	Arkansas, Colorado, Kansas, Louisiana, Minnesota, Mississippi, Pennsylvania, South Dakota, Texas, Vermont, Wisconsin

Oldest age for original juvenile court jurisdiction in delinquency matters:

Age	State
15	Connecticut, New York, North Carolina,
16	Georgia, Illinois, Louisiana, Massachusetts, Michigan, Missouri, New Hampshire, South Carolina, Texas, Wisconsin
17	Alabama, Alaska, Arizona, Arkansas, California, Colorado, Delaware, District of Columbia, Florida, Hawaii, Idaho, Indiana, Iowa, Kansas, Kentucky, Maine, Maryland, Minnesota, Mississippi, Montana, Nebraska, Nevada, New Jersey, New Mexico, North Dakota, Ohio, Oklahoma, Oregon, Pennsylvania, Rhode Island, South Dakota, Tennessee, Utah, Vermont, Virginia, Washington, West Virginia, Wyoming

Oldest age for which the juvenile court may retain jurisdiction in delinquency cases:

Age	State
18	Alaska, Iowa, Kentucky, Nebraska, Oklahoma, Tennessee
19	Mississippi, North Dakota
20	Alabama, Arizona, Arkansas, Connecticut, Delaware, District of Columbia, Georgia, Idaho, Illinois, Indiana, Louisiana, Maine, Maryland, Massachusetts, Michigan, Minnesota, Missouri, Nevada, New Hampshire, New Mexico, New York, North Carolina, Ohio, Pennsylvania, Rhode Island, South Carolina, South Dakota, Texas, Utah, Vermont, Virginia, Washington, West Virginia, Wyoming
21	Florida
22	Kansas
24	California, Montana, Oregon, Wisconsin
*	Colorado, Hawaii, New Jersey

* Until full term of disposition.

Source: Snyder, Howard N. and Melissa Sickmund (2006). *National Report Services Bulletin: Juveniles in Court.* Washington, DC: Office of Juvenile Justice and Delinquency Prevention, p. 103.

the state's penal code. Examples are murder, robbery, burglary, and any act considered criminal in that state. Every year, juvenile courts in the United States handle an estimated 1.7 million juvenile delinquency cases (Sickmund 2009). Most delinquency cases (82 percent) were referred by law enforcement agencies to the court. Sanctions imposed for juvenile delinquents are often more severe than those for conduct in need of supervision. Juvenile delinquents can be confined in a state institution, whereas conduct in need of supervision merely results in probation or referral to juvenile programs in the community. Nothing prevents a state, however, from imposing severe penalties even on juveniles who commit lesser offenses, as long as the penalty is not greatly disproportionate to the offense.

In contrast, CINS (also known in some jurisdictions as CHINS—children in need of supervision), MINS (minors in need of supervision), or JINS (juveniles in need of supervision) are juveniles who commit acts that would not be punishable if committed by adults. These are usually status offenses (meaning they are punished because of their status, in this case, their age) and include such categories as truancy, ungovernability, running away from home, tobacco use, inhalant abuse, curfew violation, and underage drinking (Snyder and Sickmund 2006). Law enforcement agencies refer fewer CINS cases to court than delinquency cases—just over half of all CINS cases were referred to juvenile courts by police. The rest reached the courts through reports from social services agencies, victims, probation officers, county attorneys, schools, or parents (Snyder and Sickmund 2006).

TRANSFER FROM JUVENILE COURTS TO ADULT COURTS

For the most serious and violent juvenile cases, all states have provisions for the **transfer of jurisdiction** from juvenile courts to adult courts. Transfer provisions gained popularity in the 1990s with the public's response to the problem of violent juvenile crime. Transfer (also known as "waiver" or "certification") provisions may be classified into one of three general categories (Sickmund 2003):

- **Judicial Waiver.** Authority to transfer the case to criminal court is given to the juvenile court judge who certifies, remands, or binds over for criminal prosecution.
- **Concurrent Jurisdiction**. Original jurisdiction is shared by both criminal and juvenile courts, and the prosecutor has discretion to file in either court. This process is also known in some states as prosecutorial waiver, prosecutor discretion, or direct file.
- **Statutory Exclusion**. State legislative statutes automatically exclude certain juvenile offenders from juvenile court jurisdiction.

Of the three categories, judicial waiver is the most commonly used, but the two other approaches are also available in some states. The transfer decision follows the intake decision, or the initial decision to formally file a case before the court. The decision to transfer is made based on the severity of the offense, prior juvenile record, prior responses the juvenile has had to supervision and treatment in the juvenile justice system, and level of dangerousness the juvenile may pose in the future. Once transferred, the juvenile ceases being a juvenile and virtually becomes an adult for all purposes, including the trial proceedings and the sentence. Adult sanctions are imposed if a juvenile is tried in adult court; hence, much is at stake for the juvenile and the public.

Wide variation exists among states on judicial waivers, with some states making waivers mandatory and others considering them discretionary. Twenty-two states and the District of Columbia have at least one provision for transferring juveniles to the criminal court for which no minimum age is specified. Although judicial waivers are widely available, the number of juvenile cases that go through this procedure is rare—only about 0.5 percent of all delinquency cases (Sickmund 2009). Surprisingly, about half of all cases waived were for non-violent crimes. Of the 6,900 cases waived in one year, 51 percent were for violent crimes of person, 27 percent for property crimes, 12 percent for drugs, and 10 percent for public order crimes (Sickmund 2009).

Transfer of Jurisdiction
The transfer of a juvenile from juvenile court to adult court for trial.

Judicial Waiver
Transferring a juvenile case from a juvenile court to an adult court.

Concurrent Jurisdiction
Original jurisdiction for certain juvenile cases is shared by both criminal and juvenile courts, with the prosecutor having discretion to file such cases in either court.

Statutory Exclusion
The automatic exclusion of certain juvenile offenders from juvenile court jurisdiction by state statute, requiring the case to be filed directly with the adult criminal court.

As some juveniles are arrested for serious crimes, a small percentage of them are transferred into the adult system to be tried just like an adult.

Not all waived juveniles end up doing prison time. In fact, about half of the waived cases are supervised on adult probation or in a community-based facility, which is comparable to what they would have received in the juvenile justice system (Butts and Mears 2001). The other half of waived juveniles who are found guilty are sentenced to confinement. Of the nearly 4,000 youths in prison in an adult facility, 51 percent are in maximum security, 38 percent in medium, and 11 percent in minimum custody (U.S. Department of Justice, Bureau of Justice Statistics, 2003). While waivers are indeed a symbol of "get tough" policies, the reality is that few youths are receiving the most serious sanctions for fear of widening the net too broadly to youths who will age out of crime (Butts and Mears 2001).

An Overview of The Juvenile Justice Process

We have discussed general differences between juvenile justice and the adult criminal justice systems thus far. Table 14.3 shows more explicitly the finer details of those commonalities and differences for each stage of the process.

PROCEDURE BEFORE ADJUDICATION

The civil or quasi-civil process of juvenile justice casts a wider net than that of the adult system. Juvenile behavior that sets the process in motion may come to the attention through the general public, probation officers, victims, parents, neighbors, school authorities, or the police. Most state statutes encourage police officers to release juveniles to a parent or guardian. In practice, police officer decisions can include release, warning, referral to community agency for services, referral to a "citizen hearing board," or referral to court intake.

TABLE 14.3   Juvenile Justice and Adult Criminal Justice Systems Compared

JUVENILE JUSTICE SYSTEM	COMMON GROUND	ADULT CRIMINAL JUSTICE SYSTEM
Intake-Prosecution		
• Juvenile court intake decides what cases to file based on social and legal factors. • A significant portion of cases are diverted from formal case processing. • Intake or the prosecutor diverts cases from formal processing to other programs or services	• Probable cause must be established. • The prosecutor acts on behalf of the State.	• Plea bargaining is common. • The prosecution decision is based largely on legal facts. • Prosecution exercises discretion to withhold charges or divert offenders.
Detention-Jail/lockup		
• Juveniles may be detained for their own protection or the community's protection. • Juveniles may not be confined with adults unless there is "sight and sound separation."	• Accused offenders may be held in custody to ensure their appearance in court. • Detention alternatives such as electronic monitoring are used.	• Accused individuals have the right to apply for bond/bail release.
Adjudication-Conviction		
• Juvenile court proceedings are "quasi-civil" (not criminal) and may be confidential • If guilt is established, the youth is adjudicated delinquent regardless of offense. • Right to jury trial is not afforded in all States.	• Standard of "proof beyond a reasonable doubt" is required. • Rights of attorney, to confront witnesses, and to remain silent are afforded. • Appeals are allowed. • Specialized courts (i.e., drug courts, mental health courts).	• Defendants have a constitutional right to a jury trial. • Guilt must be established on individual offenses charged for conviction. • All proceedings are open.
Disposition-Sentencing		
• Disposition decisions are based on individual and social factors, offense severity, and youth's offense history. • Philosophy includes a significant rehabilitation component. • Dispositions cover a wide range of community-based and residential services. • Disposition orders may be directed to include parents or guardians. • Disposition based on progress demonstrated by the youth.	• Decisions are influenced by current offense, offending history, and social factors. • Decisions hold offenders accountable. • Decisions may give consideration to victims (e.g., restitution and "no contact" orders). • Decisions may not be cruel or unusual.	• Sentencing decisions are bound primarily by the severity of the current offense and by the offender's criminal history. • Sentencing philosophy is based largely on proportionality and punishment.
Aftercare-Parole		
• Function combines surveillance and reintegration activities (e.g., family, school, work).	• Violation of conditions can result in reincarceration.	• Function is primarily surveillance and reporting to monitor illicit behavior.

Source: Howard H. Snyder and Melissa Sickmund (1999). *Juvenile Offenders and Victims; 1999 National Report*. Washington, DC: OJJDP, pp. 95–96.

FIGURE 14.1 Case flow of delinquency cases after arrest.

Source: Sickmund, Melissa. 2009. *Delinquency cases in juvenile court, 2005.* Washington, DC: Office of Juvenile Justice and Delinquency Prevention, p. 4.

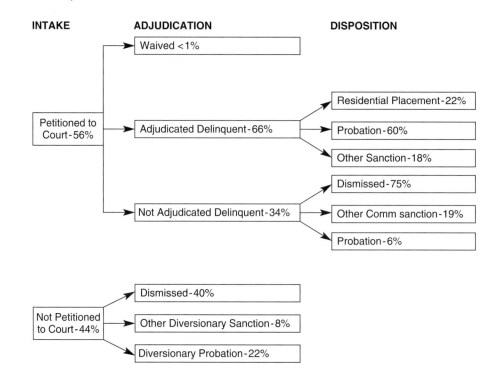

INTAKE   ADJUDICATION   DISPOSITION

Waived <1%

Petitioned to Court-56%

Adjudicated Delinquent-66%

Residential Placement-22%

Probation-60%

Other Sanction-18%

Not Adjudicated Delinquent-34%

Dismissed-75%

Other Comm sanction-19%

Probation-6%

Not Petitioned to Court-44%

Dismissed-40%

Other Diversionary Sanction-8%

Diversionary Probation-22%

Intake
The process whereby a juvenile is screened to determine if the case should proceed further in the juvenile justice system or whether other alternatives are better suited for the juvenile.

The Intake Stage Figure 14.1 details the three stages of the juvenile justice process: intake, adjudication, and disposition. A juvenile taken into custody by the police usually goes through the **intake** process, considered by some to be "one of the most crucial case processing points in the juvenile justice system" (Juvenile Probation Officer Initiative Working Group 1993, p. 32). Intake is a term unique to juvenile justice to describe a case screening process that determines if the juvenile should proceed further into the juvenile justice system or whether other diversion alternatives are better suited for the offender. A probation officer, intake officer, or prosecutor usually handles the intake. Binder, Geis, and Bruce (1997, p. 260) summarize the functions of the intake process as follows:

- Determine whether the circumstances of the case bring it within the jurisdiction of the juvenile court.
- Determine whether the evidence is sufficient to warrant a court hearing.
- Decide whether the case is serious enough to require a court hearing.
- Arrange for a process of informal supervision if that alternative seems desirable.

If the case will be handled formally, a petition is filed to request either an adjudicatory hearing (where the case goes through the juvenile courts) or a waiver hearing (where the case is further screened to see if it should go through the adult courts). If the case will be handled informally through diversion, a petition will not be filed.

Slightly less than half of all juvenile cases were either dismissed or diverted from the system at intake (Sickmund 2009). Cases dismissed at intake were handled in this way because of lack of evidence. The diverted cases were documented in a written agreement known as a consent decree. Juvenile diversion works identical to adult diversion (diversion was discussed in Chapter 2) and includes a period of supervision with such conditions as school attendance, community service, drug counseling, curfew, and restitution if applicable. Diverted cases that were successfully completed resulted in later dismissal (Sickmund 2003).

The intake process is considered to be highly subjective, involving very little collateral investigation or checking of sources. The intake process has been criticized for its lack of formal guidelines and the possibility of inconsistency from one intake officer to another (Lindner 2008). As a result, prosecutors have replaced probation officers in some jurisdictions in an attempt to correct these inconsistencies.

Intake may also involve detention screening, crisis intervention, or other procedures if mandated by the court. A juvenile may be detained by the police, but only for a limited time. The laws in all 50 states now dictate that a detention hearing must be held within a few days (generally within 24 hours) after a juvenile is taken into custody (Snyder and Sickmund 2006). Federal law provides that juveniles be separated from adult offenders by "sight and sound." This assures that juveniles are detained in facilities separate from those used for adults. The U.S. Supreme Court has held that preventive detention of juveniles, due to the likelihood that they will commit other offenses, is constitutional (*Schall v. Martin* 1984).

If the intake officer decides to refer the case to court, the prosecutor petitions the court for the juvenile to be adjudicated. A summons is issued directing the juvenile to appear before the court at a specified time and place for an initial appearance on the petition. An arraignment is then held, and the juvenile is given the opportunity to admit or deny the allegations.

The Adjudication Stage   **Adjudication** is the equivalent of a trial in adult criminal cases. However, it is less formal, and the judge takes a more active part in the hearing—including asking questions of juveniles, their parents or guardians, and witnesses. Originally no lawyers were allowed, formal rules of evidence were waived, and the juvenile enjoyed no legal or constitutional protections. That has changed considerably. Now the features of the original juvenile courts become more like adult courts with lawyers and rules of evidence, but juveniles still do not have the right to a jury trial or to bail. This is because the purpose of an adjudication hearing is to establish responsibility (*mens rea*) for the criminal act. You can see in Figure 14.1 that about 66 percent of cases that go to court are adjudicated delinquent, which is the same as a finding of guilt. The other 34 percent of cases *not* adjudicated delinquent will be dismissed unless the youth and his or her parents can be convinced to voluntarily take part in a sanction (Sickmund 2009).

> **Adjudication**
> Juvenile justice equivalent of a trial in adult criminal cases.

The Disposition Stage   If a juvenile is found to have engaged in the conduct alleged in the petition, the disposition stage follows. **Disposition** is the equivalent of sentencing in adult cases, but the juvenile court judge wields greater discretion than do judges in adult criminal trials. Because most states consider rehabilitation an integral part of juvenile corrections, the judge typically has a wide choice of available dispositions, including oral reprimand, probation, drug court, mental health court, community service, residential placement, and even confinement in a state institution. Most adjudicated delinquency cases (60 percent) resulted in formal probation, 22 percent were sent to residential placement, such as a training school, treatment center, boot camp, drug treatment, or private group home (Sickmund 2009). Status offenders are typically placed on probation as the maximum sanction. If probation is revoked, however, the juvenile may then be classified as a delinquent because of a violation of a court order. The current trend has been to decrease the percentage of youths in an institutional "placement" and find other alternatives for them. Some promising strategies are teen courts, juvenile drug courts, and youth mental health courts.

> **Disposition**
> Juvenile justice equivalent of sentencing in adult cases.

Youth Courts
Community-based programs in which youth sentence their peers for minor delinquent and status offenses. Also known as teen, peer, and student courts.

Most states have established **youth courts** to respond to youth who have no prior record and who have been involved in delinquency, such as vandalism/graffiti, theft, disorderly conduct, assault, possession of marijuana, and minor in possession of alcohol. The philosophy behind teen courts is to tap into the primary group of influence for young kids—other peers. The thinking here is that youth who have made bad choices are more likely to listen to other youth than to their parents or other people they view as authority figures. Youth volunteers act as a panel or as jurors, usually under the supervision of an adult coordinator or adult judge (Butts and Buck 2000). The National Youth Court Association reported that youth courts are most often tied to the juvenile courts (42 percent), sponsored by a school (36 percent) or by a private community agency (22 percent). Through these leadership roles, the teen court concept also allows prosocial youth the opportunity to become involved as positive mentors in their community and learn about legal principles and its application.

Youth courts are a good example of restorative justice because many of the creative sentences involve the youth offender taking responsibility for his or her behavior and restoring harm to the victim and the community. The most frequent disposition given in youth court is community service, written apology/essay, or restitution. Some youths are sentenced to serve as jurors for other peers that come before the youth court, while others are engaged in victim offender mediation (Butts and Buck 2000). The effectiveness of teen courts remains unclear, as most evaluations have not included a comparison group. The National Youth Court Association was established in 2007 to be the central clearinghouse of information related to programs and studies of youth courts (see www.youthcourt.net).

BLENDED SENTENCES

The trend in many states toward a more punitive treatment of juveniles has led to the passage of blended sentencing laws. These laws authorize courts to impose juvenile or adult punishment on young offenders, thus creating a "middle ground" between traditional juvenile and adult sanctions. Blended sentences give judges the power to choose from a wider assortment of punishments and impose one that best fits the offense committed. It also narrows the gap between juvenile and adult punishments. As of the end of legislative sessions for 2004, 15 states had blended sentencing laws that authorized juvenile courts to impose criminal sentences on certain juvenile offenders (Snyder and Sickmund 2006).

Juvenile Probation

As it is with adults, probation is the disposition most often used by judges when formally adjudicating juvenile delinquency cases. Juvenile probation can be formal or informal. Formal probation takes place through court action after an adjudication hearing where the juvenile is found to have committed a delinquent act. Informal probation occurs when a juvenile, with prior consent from him or his parents, agrees to be placed on probation even prior to adjudication. If the juvenile adheres to the conditions imposed, the charges are dropped and nothing appears in the juvenile's record.

In 2005, more than 373,400 juveniles were placed on formal probation, which is nearly twice the number from 20 years ago (Livsey 2009). Compared to 1985, the number of formal probation cases grew, while the number of informal probation cases decreased, reflecting a trend toward formal juvenile case processing. This is likely because there were more person, drug, and public order offenses on probation in 2005 than in 1985 (Livsey 2009). The gender split of youths on probation is 75 percent male and 25 percent female, with youths aged 14 to 16 accounting for the largest share of probationers.

CONDITIONS OF PROBATION

Judges Have Much Discretion   Juvenile court judges have considerable discretion when imposing probation conditions because very few states specify the conditions that should be imposed. Instead, setting conditions is left to the sound discretion of the juvenile court, usually upon recommendation of the probation officer, and acting as a wise parent. Typically, conditions include provisions designed to control as well as rehabilitate the juvenile (Sickmund 2003). These dual goals make the imposition of conditions more challenging for the court but, at the same time, assure wide discretion in that just about any condition of probation can be justified as rehabilitative and contributing to behavior control.

Types of Conditions   Juvenile probation conditions are usually of two types: mandatory or discretionary. Both may be specified by law or left to the discretion of the juvenile court judge or to the releasing authority in the case of aftercare. Only a few states impose mandatory conditions, and where imposed, they vary from one jurisdiction to another. Mandatory conditions usually include the following rules (Juvenile Probation Officer Initiative Working Group 1993, p. 16):

- Probationers may not commit a new local, state, or federal delinquent act.
- Probationers must report as directed to their probation officers.
- Probationers must obey all court orders.
- Discretionary conditions also vary from one jurisdiction to another. As an example, the New Jersey Juvenile Statutes list the following discretionary conditions:
- Pay a fine.
- Pay restitution.
- Perform community service.
- Participate in a work program.
- Participate in programs emphasizing self-reliance.
- Participate in a program of academic or vocational education or counseling.
- Be placed in a suitable residential or nonresidential program for the treatment of alcoholic or narcotic abuse.
- Be placed in a nonresidential program operated by a public or private agency, providing intensive services to juveniles for specified hours.
- Be placed in any private group home with which the Department of Correction has entered into a purchase of service contract.

CHANGE AS AN INTEGRAL PROCESS

Changing attitudes and behaviors is a difficult and sometimes painstaking process. The change process is the essence of juvenile probation and its most effective tool for rehabilitation.

> The common thread that runs through all approaches to supervision is utility; that is, that juvenile justice intervention must be designed to guide and correct the naturally changing behavior patterns of youth. Unlike adult probation, juvenile supervision views a young offender as a developing person, as one who has not yet achieved a firm commitment to a particular set of values, goals, behavior

patterns, or lifestyle. As such, juvenile justice supervision is in the hopeful position of influencing that development and thereby reducing criminal behavior (Juvenile Probation Officer Initiative Working Group 1993, p. 79).

The important part of change is the realization that it is a process that has some minor victories and also some setbacks. Change is not like a light switch that can be turned on and off at will; rather, change occurs over time. A frequently asked question about change process is whether change can be forced or if it is completely up to each individual. If change is self-induced, when does it occur and how do people know when they've changed? Box 14.1 addresses this very important question from a former director of a boys ranch for at-risk youth.

FIELD NOTES

When you worked as a program director at a boy's ranch, when did youth offenders begin to make changes in their lives and who was instrumental in that process?

In juvenile corrections success is measured by the future behaviors of the youth. As program director my charges were urban youth who were knockin' on prisons' door due to repeated offenses and probation violations. To succeed I needed to learn how to create the conditions where most of the boys would make the decision to change and how to make that happen as early as possible.

To help learn what worked I conducted an exit interview with every boy that successfully finished the program and tracked recidivism. The most significant discovery was boys that changed could always discuss when they made the decision! They could easily talk about what was happening at the time, who was helpful to them in deciding to make the change, and how they went about it. These decisions were usually made alone, thinking about their situation and deciding to try a technique taught in a skills group on anger management, problem solving, or assertiveness. The usual time frame for making the decision was 3 to 5 months. There were some 30-day wonders and some hardheads at 9 to10 months, but they were not the norm.

After hearing about their decision to change, my focus in the interview shifted to asking if there was anything we could have done to get them to make the decision earlier. The short answer is that resistance to change varies widely between individuals. When asked if the reason for such a late decision was "on us" or "on you," the latter was the case. The usual answer was, "It was on me because I wasn't ready to change."

Mark Masterson, *M.Ed., NCC*
Director of Corrections,
Sedgwick County, Kansas

The interviews helped me realize that reducing resistance to change first requires feeling safe in your environment. That doesn't happen fast in a juvenile offender facility. For this reason I sequenced programming to include cognitive skills curricula on problem solving, anger management, and refusal skills during the first three months. It worked well and was like "planting seeds" to grow when the time was right.

Decisions to change ingrained antisocial thinking, attitudes and behaviors are hard work and most likely to be made during times of pain and frustration. Each setback or crisis translates into an opportunity for self-reflection and supportive intervention. Interestingly, not a single youth reported making the decision during a scheduled counseling session. For this reason all direct care staff needed to be trained to watch for and effectively use these moments and to be included as members of the treatment teams.

The conditions for change are ripe when the youth is "tired of being tired" of the risks and consequences of their behavior and they decide to reach out to a staff member they feel cares about them. I found maximizing these opportunities was the key for youth to make a decision to change in less time. Staff members that are able to connect with youth and make themselves available at these times are critical to the change process. Many times when told of their helpfulness, the staff member did not realize the significance of the moment for the youth. It was their usual practice of doing their jobs, having a caring attitude, being approachable and then available to the youth that separated the most effective staff from the rest. This became a cornerstone of our training program and helped improve youth success and reduce recidivism.

JUVENILE PROBATION OFFICERS AS "SUPERHEROES"

The job of a juvenile probation officer is often more demanding than that of an adult probation officer. Playing the roles of a hard-nosed cop, a confessor, a teacher, a problem solver, a crisis manager, and a community resource specialist, this officer has a difficult job made even more challenging by changing system philosophies, programs that won't accept particular youth, and an increasingly high-risk clientele.

> The probation officer is expected to fulfill many different roles, often 'taking up the slack' after judges, attorneys, social agencies, parents, and so on have met what they see as their own clearly defined responsibilities in the case and have expressed an unwillingness to extend themselves beyond these limits (Juvenile Probation Officer Initiative Working Group 1993, pp. 119–120).

In his book titled, *Screwing the System and Making It Work,* Mark Jacobs (1990) observed the drama and genuine passion that juvenile probation officers put forth in their job as advocates for youth who never had anyone else stand up for them. Jacobs describes some of the barriers as unsupportive parents and sometimes the system itself that has such narrow criteria, with agencies often screening out the youth who most need help. The paperwork situation is frustrating, along with the inordinate amount of time spent in court appearances, investigations, and necessary documentation that takes away from counseling and helping functions. Despite all of this, juvenile probation officers remained optimistic, believing that change is possible. Termed by Jacobs as modern day "superheroes," these officers display a noteworthy creativity and sacrifice in their jobs despite the system barriers (Jacobs 1990). The juvenile probation officer is the last hope of rehabilitation for the juvenile, a situation validated by workers who prioritize rehabilitation as part of system accountability (Ward and Kupchik 2009).

It is recommended that probation departments "consider the converging interests of the juvenile offender, the victim, and the community at large in developing individualized case plans for probation supervision" (Juvenile Probation Officer Initiative Working Group 1993). To reconcile conflicting goals (such as rehabilitation

School-based probation and police/probation partnerships are common to keep kids mainstreamed in school and avoid problems with truancy and excessive absences.

© A. Ramey/Photo Edit

versus punishment, treatment versus control, and public safety versus youth development), probation "must endeavor to not only protect the public and hold the juvenile offender accountable, it must also attempt to meet his needs" (p. 79). Thus, the ideal form of juvenile probation supervision aims more at rehabilitation than merely meting out punishment. Standards proposed by several organizations recommend that a needs assessment be conducted and a service plan be developed before a juvenile is placed on probation (p. 44).

These standards further suggest that the probation officer, in conjunction with the juvenile and the family, assess needs in the following areas: medical problems, proximity of the program to the youth, the capacity of the youth to benefit from the program, and the availability of placements. In addition, the standards place strong emphasis on the "availability of supplemental services to facilitate the youth's participation in a community-based program" (p. 53).

INTENSIVE SUPERVISION PROBATION

Intensive Supervision Probation
A form of probation that stresses intensive monitoring, close supervision, and offender control.

Intensive supervision probation (ISP) is a type of supervision used in both juvenile and adult probation (recall our discussion in Chapter 9). ISP is defined as a program of intensive surveillance of and contact with an offender and is aimed at reducing criminal conduct by limiting opportunities to engage in it. Strategies vary from one state to another, but there are some common features in intensive supervision for juveniles:

- A greater reliance is placed on unannounced spot checks. These may occur in a variety of settings including home, school, known hangouts, and job sites.
- Considerable attention is directed at increasing the number and kinds of collateral contacts made by staff, including family members, friends, staff from other agencies, and concerned residents in the community.
- Greater use is made of curfew, including both more rigid enforcement and lowering the hour at which curfew goes into effect.
- Surveillance is expanded to ensure seven-day-a-week, 24-hour-a-day coverage. (Juvenile Probation Officer Initiative Working Group 1993, p. 87)

Contrary to popular belief, intensive probation is usually not designed to deal with violent juvenile offenders. The majority of juveniles placed on intensive supervision are "serious and/or chronic offenders who would otherwise be committed to a correctional facility but who, through an objective system of diagnosis and classification, have been identified as amenable to community placement" (p. 65).

One random assignment experiment examined the effectiveness of ISP compared to institutional placement for over 500 young boys. Both groups were followed for two years. The group assigned to ISP committed more delinquent acts, more status offense, and more technical violations than the group that was incarcerated. However, the institutional group had overall committed more serious offenses than the ISP group. The researchers concluded that the ISP group was not significantly different than the institutionally placed group (Barton and Butts 1990).

School-Based Probation
A type of probation where probation officers move out of traditional district offices into middle, junior high, and high school buildings and supervise their caseloads right in the schools.

SCHOOL-BASED PROBATION

A comparatively new but increasingly popular concept in juvenile probation supervision is **school-based probation**. Truancy is a serious problem in primary and secondary education that is also linked to delinquency. School-based probation supervision has emerged within school districts, partnering probation with local law enforcement officers, in a team effort to enforce probation conditions and prevent future delinquency (Alarid, Sims, and Ruiz, 2010). Griffin and Torbet (2002) indicate that "in recent years, juvenile probation officers in jurisdictions across the country have been moving out of traditional district offices, into middle, junior high, and high school buildings—and supervising their caseloads right in the schools" (p. 92). They list the benefits of school-based probation as follows:

- *More contact.* More direct contact with probationers—in some cases daily contact—can lead to better relationships and more awareness of school, home, and peer problems.
- *Better monitoring.* Closer monitoring of juvenile offenders and better observation of their behavior and interactions can lead to more effective and immediate responses to problems.
- *Focus on school success.* Juveniles with school-based probation officers may have more incentive to attend regularly, try hard, and refrain from misconduct, increasing their overall chances of succeeding as students.

A study of school-based probation in the State of Pennsylvania (see Table 14.4) found that "school-based probation officers, school administrators, and students on school-based probation strongly believed that the program was effective in boosting attendance and academic performance and reducing misbehavior in school" (Griffin and Torbet 2002, p. 92). Alarid and her colleagues (2010) found that home visits and court hearings were effective at reducing student truancy and tardiness, with strong leadership, information sharing, and involvement of parents as three contributors to program success.

FARE V. MICHAEL C.

The only case ever to be decided by the U.S. Supreme Court on juvenile probation supervision is *Fare v. Michael C.* (1985). This important California case helps define the relationship between a probation officer and a probationer during probation supervision. Michael C., a juvenile, was taken into police custody because he was

TABLE 14.4 School-Based Probation Agreements

School-based probation program arrangements and procedures should be formalized via a written agreement between the juvenile court/probation department and the participating school district. At a minimum, such an agreement should contain the following:

- A statement of the philosophy, goals, and objectives of school-based probation.
- A clear definition of the role of the probation officer within the school environment.
- A clear definition of the role of the school district administration and staff in supporting the probation officer.
- A list of probation officer responsibilities, including participation in any student assistance or pupil services team involving a probationer.
- If probation officers are permitted to carry firearms, the procedure for carrying and storing that firearm while on school property.
- A list of the school district's responsibilities, including the provision of a telephone line and office space affording privacy within the school for the probation officer.
- Procedures assuring probation officers' access to probationers' student records, including attendance, discipline, grading, and progress reports.
- Provisions for meetings between probation department administrations and school administrators to discuss ongoing program issues.

Source: Pennsylvania Juvenile Court Judges' Commission, "Standards Governing School-Based Probation Services," as printed in *Desktop Guide to Good Juvenile Probation Practice*, (2002) by Patrick Griffin and Patricia Torbet (eds.), Washington, DC: Office of Juvenile Justice and Delinquency Prevention, p. 93.

suspected of having committed a murder. He was advised of his *Miranda v. Arizona* (1966) rights. When asked if he wanted to waive his right to have an attorney present during questioning, he responded by asking for his probation officer. He was informed by the police that the probation officer would be contacted later but that he could talk to the police if he wanted.

Michael C. agreed to talk and during questioning made statements and drew sketches that incriminated himself. When charged with murder in juvenile court, Michael C. moved to suppress the incriminating evidence, alleging it was obtained in violation of his *Miranda* rights. He said that his request to see his probation officer was, in effect, equivalent to asking for a lawyer. However, the evidence was admitted at trial, and Michael C. was convicted.

On appeal, the U.S. Supreme Court affirmed the conviction, holding that the request by a juvenile probationer during police questioning to see his or her probation officer, after having received the *Miranda* warnings, is not equivalent to asking for a lawyer and is not considered an assertion of the right to remain silent. Evidence voluntarily given by the juvenile probationer after asking to see his probation officer is therefore admissible in court in a subsequent criminal trial.

The *Michael C.* case is significant because the Supreme Court laid out two principles that help define the supervisory role of a juvenile probation officer. First, the Court stated that confidentiality of communication between the probation officer and a juvenile probationer is not equivalent to lawyer–client privilege. This means that information given by a probationer to the probation officer may be disclosed in court, unlike the information given to a lawyer by a client—which cannot be revealed to anyone unless the right to confidentiality is waived by both the client and the lawyer. Said the Court:

> A probation officer is not in the same posture [as a lawyer] with regard to either the accused or the system of justice as a whole. Often he is not trained in the law, and so is not in a position to advise the accused as to his legal rights. Neither is he a trained advocate, skilled in the representation of the interests of his client before police and courts. He does not assume the power to act on behalf of his client by virtue of his status as advisor, nor are the communications of the accused to the probation officer shielded by the lawyer–client privilege.

Second, the *Fare v. Michael C.* case is also significant because the Court emphasized that a probation officer's loyalty and obligation is to the state, despite any obligation owed to the probationer. The Court said:

> Moreover, the probation officer is the employee of the State which seeks to prosecute the alleged offender. He is a peace officer, and as such is allied, to a greater or lesser extent, with his fellow peace officers. He owes an obligation to the State notwithstanding the obligation he may also owe the juvenile under his supervision. In most cases, the probation officer is duty bound to report wrongdoing by the juvenile when it comes to his attention, even if by communication from the juvenile himself.

This statement defines where a probation officer's loyalty lies. Professionalism requires that the officer's loyalty must be with the state and not with the probationer, regardless of the sympathy the officer might have for the juvenile.

ARE JUVENILE RECORDS CONFIDENTIAL?

One traditional characteristic of juvenile proceedings is confidentiality. Although the criminal and probation records of adults are public and can be accessed by just about anybody, juvenile records are either confidential or can be disclosed only to certain individuals. A member of the public does not have access to the probation record of a juvenile. The exception is if such records are made public by state law. Probation records contain such data as the offense for which a juvenile is on probation, the length of probation, and probation conditions. But whereas probation records are generally closed to the public, the fact that a juvenile is on probation is a matter of public record. Court personnel can disclose the fact that a juvenile is on probation, but not much more beyond that (such as the offense committed, the conditions and length of probation, and the treatment programs prescribed) because the details of juvenile probation are shielded from public scrutiny.

The confidentiality of juvenile records, however, is not a constitutional right and may be lifted by state law or agency policy. Over the years, confidentiality has gradually diminished. One publication notes, "juvenile codes in 42 states allow names (and sometimes pictures and court records) of juveniles involved in delinquency proceedings to be released to the media." In 16 states, juvenile court records or proceedings (including probation records) are now public. In 27 states, the identity of the juvenile in delinquency cases may be released, but only in cases involving certain crimes and/or repeat offenders. In 11 states, media access to juvenile courts is allowed, but with a court order" (Snyder and Sickmund 1999). The general rule, however, still is that in the absence of state law or agency policy allowing disclosure, juvenile records are confidential.

Juvenile Parole/Aftercare

Juveniles who are confined in a state institution are released on aftercare, which is the equivalent of parole. The release decision is left to the discretion of institutional officials, with the exception of a few states that have juvenile parole boards. If released on aftercare, the juvenile is supervised after he or she reaches the age of majority—generally 18.

> Juvenile aftercare is not a new idea. Its foundations date to the 18th century, when youth were released to "masters" for additional training. Today youth are released to their families or guardians and monitored by the court. . . . Thus aftercare today is concerned with creating a smooth transition from institution to community, identifying community support systems and resources for youth, assisting in the development of positive peer interaction, and monitoring youth's progress (Gordon 2003, pp. 5–6).

In some jurisdictions, juvenile probation and parole are administered by the same agency and officers supervise juvenile probationers and parolees. The conditions of probation and parole are the same in many jurisdictions, the most common being not committing violations of the law, getting gainful employment, curfew, electronic monitoring, drug testing, reporting regularly, and allowing home visits.

JUVENILE PAROLE BOARDS AND PAROLE OFFICERS

As of 2004, five states had a separate juvenile parole board (California, Colorado, New Jersey, South Carolina, and Utah) whose memberships vary from five to nine members. Some members serve full time, others serve part time; most are appointed by the governor, others are elected; some are paid, others are unpaid. (Frendle 2004, p. 2).

One state lists the characteristic duties and responsibilities of juvenile parole officers as follows: (State of New Hampshire, Human Resources)

- Conducts predispositional and other investigations as directed by the court or Juvenile Parole Board concerning juvenile delinquents and/or children in need of services

- Prepares written reports and recommendations for the court or Juvenile Parole Board, including reporting alleged violations of conditional release and juvenile parole
- Supervises juveniles on conditional release or juvenile parole in order to ensure compliance with the terms of conditional release or parole, or other conditions set forth by the court or Juvenile Parole Board
- Takes into custody juveniles who violate conditional release or juvenile parole, and prepares case information for prosecution before the court or Juvenile Parole Board
- Coordinates with court officials, law enforcement agencies, community-based agencies, state agencies, family members, and the public to assist the court in making dispositional determinations in matters of juvenile delinquency and children in need of services
- Provides family-centered intervention to families and caretakers to help maintain the family unit
- Coordinates suitable out-of-home care to meet a specific need of the juvenile and family, including facilitating transportation
- Manages cases to ensure case plan is carried out and court and administrative reviews under state and federal laws are completed in a timely manner

Another state lists the duties and responsibilities of juvenile parole officers as similar to those of probation officers, which are as follows: correctional case planning, case management, community resource development, report writing, and other miscellaneous duties (State of Oregon, Department of Administrative Services, Juvenile Parole and Probation Officer). It then adds that the job requires basic knowledge of:

- Legal codes, regulations, and court procedures
- Procedures for arrest, investigations, and rights of juveniles
- Resources available to diagnose and treat maladjusted adolescents and young adults
- Techniques and methods used in individual and group counseling
- Techniques and methods of investigation and evidence presentation
- Methods of report writing

REVOCATION OF JUVENILE PROBATION OR PAROLE

Violation of probation or parole conditions leads to revocation, and the process works the same way as discussed in Chapters 7 and 13. Revocation can result in the juvenile probationer or parolee being sent to an institution for juveniles. Probation revocation is similar to a finding of juvenile delinquency in that the juvenile may now be given the same sanctions as a juvenile delinquent, which include being deprived of freedom and confinement in a juvenile institution. Unlike adult probationers who must serve the jail or prison term originally imposed (subject to parole law), juveniles are kept in state institutions only until they reach the age of majority (adulthood). The release of a juvenile on parole prior to reaching the age of majority is determined by the juvenile authorities who run the state institution, not by the judge. In some cases, certain types of juveniles are kept beyond the age of majority by special laws that mandate harsher sanctions. For example, some states allow detention of parole violators or other serious offenders in state institutions until they are 24 years old.

EVALUATING JUVENILE PAROLE PROGRAMS

One source noted that juvenile aftercare has been unsuccessful, attributing the lack of success to the following: "(1) a lack of communication between institutional staff and aftercare staff during the transitional period, (2) the inability to identify appropriate service providers for youth, (3) large caseload sizes for aftercare workers, and (4) selection of inappropriate youth for aftercare" (Gordon 2003, p. 4). A study that evaluated five different juvenile aftercare programs around the country (including programs in Pennsylvania Michigan and Maryland) concluded that "the overall picture is mixed" (OJJDP 1999). Recommendations were that aftercare programs" must be preceded by parallel services in the corrections facility and must include careful preparation for the aftercare to follow," and that these programs be funded and staffed at levels that would enable them to provide enhanced service delivery (p. 2).

The Future of Juvenile Justice

The juvenile justice system is over 100 years old, and in that time, it has undergone a huge transformation into the system we have today. While the future of the juvenile court as a separate entity from the adult system is still debated, the juvenile system we have now seems to be more balanced with elements of both rehabilitation and punishment. There are a wider range of community-based and graduated sanctions than in the past. There are diversion options such as drug courts and mental health courts to keep children out of the system, and yet, options exist for youth who may be better served in the adult system. The use of assessment tools is important for the prevention and early intervention of youth with substance abuse and mental health problems. The emphasis on restorative justice is ideal to facilitate a stronger family unit and increase institutions of social control back in schools, peer groups, and communities. Evidence-based practices and use of technology to increase data gathering and information sharing have filtered into juvenile agencies. We believe the future of juvenile justice looks bright.

SUMMARY

- Juvenile justice in the United States is heavily influenced by *parens patriae* and the concept of diminished *mens rea*.

- Juvenile courts are an American creation and have jurisdiction based on age and acts committed. Minimum and maximum ages for juveniles vary from state to state.

- Juvenile delinquency refers to acts that if committed by adults are punishable under the state's penal code; conduct in need of supervision comprises acts committed by juveniles that if committed by adults would not be punishable at all.

- Juveniles may be transferred for trial from a juvenile court to an adult court. Once transferred to an adult court, the juvenile ceases to be a juvenile and is tried and punished like an adult.

- An important juvenile law case decided by the United States Supreme Court is *In re Gault* (1967), which held that a juvenile is entitled to due process if charged with an offense that can result in being sent to a juvenile institution.

- After a juvenile is taken into custody, the processing sequence for juveniles consists of intake, adjudication, and disposition.

- Probation is the disposition that judges use most often in delinquency cases.

- Juvenile probation through schools is a mechanism by which youths can be effectively supervised.

- No conclusive data or study establishes that juvenile probation or parole is more effective than other approaches to corrections.

DISCUSSION QUESTIONS

1. How does *parens patriae* influence the way juveniles offenders are processed?

2. Do you think that the juvenile justice system should become more like the adult justice system? If so, for which types of offenses? If not, why not?

3. Provide examples assessing the main difference between juvenile delinquents and conduct in need of supervision. Can a juvenile be both?

4. In the traditional juvenile justice system, do the intake, adjudication, and disposition stages unfairly label children as delinquent?

5. Do you think the idea of the youth court should be expanded to other crimes?

6. Pick one effective method of supervising a juvenile in the community and discuss the characteristics of the program, concluding with why you believe it to be effective.

7. Is school-based probation an effective means of supervision? Why or why not?

8. What did the Court say in the case of *Fare v. Michael C.*? Why is that case important for probation officers?

9. In the juvenile justice cases that have been decided by the U.S. Supreme Court, what general trend or directions are noteworthy?

10. If you could change anything about the juvenile justice system, what would it be and how would your change make an improvement?

 ## WEB SITES

American Bar Association Juvenile Justice Center
http://www.abanet.org/dch/committee.cfm?com=CR200000

Juvenile Justice Clearinghouse
http://www.fsu.edu/~crimdo/jjclearinghouse

National Council on Crime and Delinquency
http://www.nccd-crc.org

The National Youth Court Association
http://www.youthcourt.net

National Youth Gang Center
http://www.iir.com/nygc

A Bibliography of Gangs
http://www-lib.usc.edu/~anthonya/gang.htm

South Dakota Juvenile Aftercare
http://doc.sd.gov

Texas Youth Commission
http://www.tyc.state.tx.us

CASE STUDY EXERCISE

Juvenile Justice, Probation, and Aftercare

You are a juvenile probation officer who is attempting to decide what to do with each of the court referrals before you, so that you can make recommendations to the judge. Should the case be dismissed? Should the case be diverted to another program (for example, to teen court)? Should the case be adjudicated? If so, should the case be adjudicated within the juvenile justice system, or should the case be waived to adult court?

CASE A

Brian is a 13-year-old male who has come to the attention of the court for the offense of vandalism. He and a friend "tagged" a school building with graffiti and broke several windows in the school gymnasium. The school principal estimated the total damage and cleanup costs to be approximately $1,300. Brian resides with both natural parents and two younger siblings. The family income is $65,000 annually. Brian admits the offense but refuses to identify his co-offender to authorities. The family has agreed to pay complete restitution. Brian has no prior juvenile record although he has been disciplined several times in school in the past year for minor violations of school rules. His grades, which were formerly As and Bs, have fallen off to Cs and Ds.

CASE B

Quint is a 17-year-old male who has been referred to the court for aggravated robbery. Quint is accused of robbing a convenience store and assaulting the clerk. Quint is a high school dropout with a lengthy history of arrests including robbery, burglary, car theft, and larceny. He was adjudicated delinquent for burglary 10 months before the current offense and placed on probation. His probation officer reports that he has been uncooperative and hostile toward supervision. He lives off and on with his mother and three younger siblings. His mother reports that she has little control over his behavior and that he spends many nights away from home. She suspects that he is using drugs.

CASE C

Carlos is a 15-year-old male who was referred to the court for truancy. Carlos has missed 34 school days in the past 90 days. He is failing in all his classes. His parents report that they send him to school every day but he never stays. Even when they take him to the front door of the school, he leaves immediately after they do. Carlos is of average intelligence and relates well to his peers. He has no other involvement with illegal activity, and until this past school year he did well in school and attended regularly. His parents have no explanation for the change in his behavior.

CASE D

Cathy is a 14-year-old female who has been referred to the court for running away. Cathy's parents report that she is a chronic runaway, having left home on more than 10 occasions since age 12. She is in the seventh grade. She has been "left back" twice and is thus two grade levels behind her peers. Cathy was diagnosed with attention deficit disorder at age 7. She is currently taking Ritalin under a physician's supervision. Her parents have attempted to get help for Cathy on many occasions, but nothing seems to be effective. She has been referred once for shoplifting, three times for truancy, and three times previously for running away.

Collateral Consequences of Conviction, Pardon, and Restoration of Rights

CHAPTER LEARNING OBJECTIVES

- Identify how civil and political rights differ.
- Explain how civil disabilities vary from one state to another.
- Describe how rights are lost as a result of conviction.
- Summarize passed sex offender registration and notification laws and provide for the involuntary commitment of sexual predators.
- Discuss lost rights and the loss of good moral character.
- Define expungement and its importance.

in the past ten years other than misdemeanors and summary offenses?

Yes ☐   No ☐

If yes, explain circumstances and disposition of matter below.

Job applications that ask about prior convictions create a tough situation for felons who are court-ordered to find employment. How do we balance the need of employers to screen applicants in some jobs with the need for felons to follow court orders and/or desire to become productive societal members?

CHAPTER OUTLINE

Introduction
Civil and Political Rights Defined
Background of Civil Disabilities

Civil Disabilities Today
Differences by State
Rights Lost Through Discretion

Civil and Political Rights Commonly Affected by Conviction
Loss of Right to Vote
Loss of Employment-Related Rights
Loss of Right to Own or Possess a Firearm
Loss of Welfare Benefits
Loss in Court
Loss of Right to Hold Public Office
Problems with Civil Disability Laws
Loss of Parental Rights

Effects of Conviction for Sex Offenders
Sex Offender Registration Laws
Community Notification Laws

Residency Restrictions
Involuntary Civil Commitment of
  Sexual Predators

Pardon
The Power to Pardon
Kinds of Pardon
Procedure for Obtaining a Pardon
Legal Effects of a Pardon
Effects of a Pardon on Occupational
  Licensing

Restoration of Rights
Restoration upon Application
Automatic Restoration
Restoring Good Moral Character
Expungement of Arrest and Conviction Records
Sealing of Records Not Resulting
  In a Conviction

Summary

KEY TERMS

civil rights	moral turpitude	rehabilitation certificate
political rights	public offices	automatic restoration of rights
outlawry	surety bond	certificate of discharge
attainder	pardon	expungement
good moral character	conditional pardon	sealing of records

Introduction

Conviction of a crime carries direct and collateral (indirect) consequences. Direct consequences are penalties such as a fine, probation, and commitment to jail or prison. Collateral consequences are civil disqualifications or deprivations that have roots in Greek, Roman, and English civilizations. The initial purpose of the loss of civil penalties at that time was for social disapproval and to disallow family members from inheriting all property of guilty offenders. This chapter discusses collateral consequences and how the rights lost might be restored.

The distinctions between the direct and collateral consequences of conviction may be summarized as follows:

Direct Consequences	**Collateral Consequences**
Criminal penalties, as specified in the state or federal penal code	Civil consequences, as specified in various state or federal laws or by administrative agencies, local agencies, or private employers
Includes fines, probation, jail, or prison	Includes loss of right to vote, disqualification for jury service, loss of good moral character, and so on

| Lasts only during the time specified in the sentence | Can last after probation, jail or prison time, or for a lifetime |
| Time served cannot be restored | Can be restored by legislation, court decision, or agency decision |

Collateral consequences may include the following:

- Loss of the right to vote
- Loss of right to serve on a jury
- Loss of credibility as a witness
- Occupational license restrictions
- Loss of capacity to be bonded
- Loss of right to own or possess a firearm
- Denial of welfare benefits
- Loss of parental rights
- Grounds for divorce
- Barred from serving in the armed forces
- Dishonorable discharge from the armed forces
- Cannot serve as union officer
- Loss of pension rights
- Restrictions on holding some public offices
- Cannot serve as a notary public
- Registration with local law enforcement (sex offenders)
- Denial of federal financial aid for higher education (felony drug offenders)
- Denial of Section 8 housing (felony drug offenders)
- Denial of Social Security, Medicare, and/or Medicaid payments to prisoners while incarcerated
- Aliens ineligible for naturalization

As discussed later in this chapter, civil rights lost may be restored in various ways. Some rights, however, are more difficult to restore than others and are often lost forever because the offender is unaware of restoration procedures.

CIVIL AND POLITICAL RIGHTS DEFINED

Black's Law Dictionary defines **civil rights** as "individual rights of personal liberty guaranteed by the Bill of Rights and by the 13th, 14th, 15th, and 19th Amendments, as well as by legislation such as the Voting Rights Act" (Garner 2009, p. 263). Examples are freedom of speech, freedom of the press, freedom from discrimination, and freedom of assembly. **Political rights** are "the right to participate in the establishment or administration of government, such as the right to vote or the right to hold public office" (Garner 2009, p. 1348.). Civil rights are broader in scope and include political rights, which are also guaranteed by the Constitution. The two categories of rights vary, however, in that civil rights are broader and usually enjoyed by all people within the borders of a country. On the other hand, the exercise of political rights is limited to citizens of a state. Thus, anybody in the United States (citizens, aliens, legal residents, or illegal residents) enjoys freedom of speech, association, or assembly, but only U.S. citizens enjoy the right to vote.

Civil Rights
Rights that belong to a person by virtue of citizenship.

Political Rights
Rights related to the participation in the establishment, support, or management of government.

BACKGROUND OF CIVIL DISABILITIES

Civil disabilities as a consequence of crime go way back to ancient Greece (Damaska 1968). The Greeks called the disability *infamy,* a word that found its way into Anglo-American criminal law in the term *infamous crimes.* Infamous crimes carried severe

Outlawry
In old Anglo-Saxon law, the process by which a criminal was declared an outlaw and placed outside the protection and aid of the law.

Attainder
At common law, the extinction of civil rights and capacities that occurred when a person received a sentence of death or outlawry for treason or another felony. The person's estate was forfeited to the Crown.

Good Moral Character
The totality of virtues that form the basis of one's reputation in the community.

Moral Turpitude
An act of vileness, or socially offensive behavior, that is contrary to justice, honesty or the public's accepted moral standards.

penalties as well as the additional sanctions of outlawry and attainder. **Outlawry** considered a person outside the protection of the law and, in effect, established an open season on the offender, who could then be hunted down and killed by any citizen. This person, considered "an outlaw," lost all civil rights and forfeited all property to the Crown through **attainder,** which is defined in common law as "the act of extinguishing a person's civil rights when that person is sentenced to death or declared an outlaw for committing a felony or treason" (Garner 2009, p. 137). The justification for both outlawry and attainder was that the offender had declared war on society by committing an infamous crime, and therefore the community had the right to retaliation and retribution against the offender.

Much of the U.S. common law heritage was borrowed from the English except for outlawry, bills of attainder, and forfeiture of all property. Outlawry as a form of punishment is not allowed in the United States, by virtue of Article l of the U.S. Constitution that forbids "bills of attainder." In comparison to English society, the framers of the U.S. Constitution relaxed civil punishments. Another example is forfeiture—instead of losing all property, forfeiture now refers to property or assets gained or used directly from or with the crime.

Many collateral consequences flow from the assumption that a convicted offender lacks "**good moral character**" and therefore fails to satisfy the requirement to vote, to be a credible witness, to obtain and retain many occupational licenses, to hold a public office, or to be a member of certain professions. A criminal act involving **moral turpitude** is defined as "conduct that is contrary to justice, honesty, or morality" (Garner 2009, p. 1030). In some cases, state laws provide for loss of good moral character only if the criminal act involves moral turpitude. Most states, however, provide for loss of good moral character if a person is convicted of any criminal act, or at least of a felony.

Civil Disabilities Today

Buckler and Travis (2003) identify reasons for retaining collateral consequence statutes. Some civil rights are removed from offenders to maintain public confidence in government operations, such as running for public office, serving as a notary public, witness credibility on the stand, and juror restrictions. A second reason involves a cutback on government benefits—narrowing the benefits to the law abiding and not providing to those who break the law in the areas of welfare, pension, student financial aid, or federal employment opportunities, and disallowing naturalization privileges to aliens who break the law. These cutbacks further separate people socioeconomically. More recently, certain rights have been denied offenders based on increasing public safety and protecting children from harm. The rights included here involve firearms restrictions, sex offender registration, and loss of parental rights.

Differences by State

States differ in the way civil rights are removed or restricted. Some statutes deprive the criminal of all or almost all civil rights while he or she is serving a prison sentence (Buckler and Travis 2003). The trend has been toward finding ways to restore rights. For example, in Florida, offenders convicted of all felonies (except crimes of violence) who complete their sentences successfully and who pay all of their restitution will get all of their rights automatically restored, except for possessing a firearm, which will still be prohibited. All felony offenders convicted of violent crimes must appear before a board after sentence completion for an individual case review.

For some rights, loss of rights exists only within a particular state; in other cases, the loss extends to other states if the offender relocates (Kuzma 1998). What happens if the laws of the state where the offender was convicted differ from those of the state where the offender relocates? To illustrate, some states define a felony as an offense punishable by incarceration of one year or more; other states designate a crime as a felony or a misdemeanor without regard to amount of time served. For example, assume that Jeff was convicted of misdemeanor theft and served the maximum sentence of 18 months in a county jail. The conviction state designates this theft a misdemeanor, but Jeff moved across state lines into another state that defines any criminal act that carries a sentence of more than 12 months a felony, which carries civil disabilities. Does Jeff lose his civil rights? The answer is usually determined by the laws of the state where the crime was committed; therefore, Jeff in this case does not lose his civil rights. However, there are states that provide for such loss even if the crime was committed elsewhere. In this case, Jeff loses his civil liberties while he is in that state.

Another issue involves military offenses. While committing a crime in the military can result in a dishonorable discharge, military crimes are technically not classified as either felonies or misdemeanors, and some military crimes do not constitute a crime under civilian law. Given this situation, do people convicted of a military crime lose their rights as civilians? Susan Kuzma (1998), of the Office of the United States Pardon Attorney, discusses both the relocation issue and the resolution of military crimes, saying: "Some states' laws permit resolution of such interpretational problems by providing that the disability applies only when the conduct would constitute a felony under the law of the state imposing the disability (the state of residence)" (p. 72).

RIGHTS LOST THROUGH DISCRETION

Other differences exist. For example, some rights can be lost through judicial or administrative discretion. A judge may decide in a particular case that the offender loses a certain civil right. This is valid as long as the loss is related to the offense committed. For example, a judge might deny welfare benefits to a person convicted of a conspiracy to defraud the government. The loss may also be caused by an administrative decision of governmental agencies. Licensing agencies may decide to deny a license to an individual who commits an offense, provided that such denial is related to the offense committed. To illustrate, an agency that licenses bartenders might deny a license to an applicant who has been convicted of DWI even if state laws do not provide for such denial. Moreover, private employers are not bound by the provisions of the Bill of Rights and may deny offenders certain rights to which they are otherwise entitled if employed by public agencies. Private employers may refuse to hire an individual who applies for work if he or she refuses to disclose an arrest record.

In some states, a conviction must be followed by incarceration for a specified period before rights are lost. The right is not lost if conviction is followed by probation or if the sentence to probation is not considered a conviction, as in the case of deferred adjudication or informal probation. Some rights are permanently lost and cannot be restored; others are automatically restored upon completion of the sentence or may be restored by action of the executive or a court. To determine the status of a particular convicted offender's rights, one must examine the statutory provisions, judicial decisions, administrative rulings and practices, and actions of individuals in both the state of conviction and the state in which a particular right is sought to be enforced (Office of the Pardon Attorney 1996). Because of variations, the extent of civil disabilities in a state, or even within a local jurisdiction, is difficult to ascertain.

Collateral consequences may amount to a complete denial of a right, or may merely impose restrictions and conditions on its exercise. In some jurisdictions, the right to vote and the right to hold public office are denied for life unless restored by a pardon or a certificate. A conviction generally does not completely disqualify the offender from serving as a witness, but if the witness's prior criminal record becomes public, it can result in diminished credibility.

Civil and Political Rights Commonly Affected by Conviction

As previously noted, many privileges and rights are restricted or removed following conviction of a crime. This section discusses eight commonly restricted rights, which are: voting, serving on a jury, credibility as a witness, holding public office, employment limitations, possessing a firearm, welfare benefits, and parental rights.

LOSS OF RIGHT TO VOTE

The U.S. Supreme Court held that it is constitutional for a state to deprive ex-felons of the right to vote, thus giving states a lot of authority to disenfranchise offenders, if they so desire (*Richardson v. Ramirez* 1974). Limiting the right to vote is widely practiced, the assumption being that the votes of offenders somehow dilute the purity of the voting process, and therefore the denial of that right of citizenship is justifiable. An organization called the Sentencing Project keeps an update on the current state of voting disenfranchisement. The impact of felony disenfranchisement is quite significant (p. 1):

- "An estimated 5.3 million Americans, or one in 41 adults, have currently or permanently lost their voting rights as a result of felony conviction.
- "2.1 million disenfranchised people are ex-offenders who have completed their sentences.
- "1.4 million African American men, or 13 percent of black men, are disenfranchised, a rate seven times the national average. Given current rates of incarceration, three in 10 of the next generation of black men can expect to be disenfranchised at some point in their lifetime. In states that disenfranchise ex-offenders, as many as 40 percent of black men may permanently lose their right to vote.
- "An estimated 676,730 women are currently ineligible to vote as a result of felony conviction."

The Sentencing Project reports that in 48 states and the District of Columbia, felony inmates *while incarcerated* are prohibited from voting. At this time, Maine and Vermont allow inmates to vote (usually through the mail). A number of states also prohibit felons from voting while they are on parole (36 states) or probation (31 states). Most states allow the restoration of voting rights after the sentence is complete: "Each state has developed its own process of restoring voting rights to ex-offenders but most of these restoration processes are so cumbersome that few ex-offenders are able to take advantage of them. . . . three states deny the right to vote to all ex-offenders who have completed their sentences" (p. 1).

In the last decade, it seems as though the public sentiment on this issue is turning. Eighteen states made changes to their felony disfranchisement laws, resulting in enfranchising over 700,000 individuals. Three states in particular are worthy of note. California restored voting rights to probationers who were in jail. Probationers have the right to vote, but prisoners do not, so the court clarified that even though incarcerated, probationers retain this right (*League of Women Voters of California vs. McPherson* 2006). Louisiana enacted a bill requiring the Department of Public Safety and Corrections to provide them with voter registration applications when they leave prison. Florida and Kentucky have both made it easier for felons to have their voting rights restored.

The right to vote in the United States for federal, state, or local offices is then left to the states with some limitations. For example, the ACLU is challenging a practice in Alabama that prohibits people convicted of felony crimes from voting. The current Alabama state constitution denies voting rights to individuals who have been convicted of felonies involving moral turpitude, but also states that only the legislature can decide which felonies qualify under this category. The Alabama legislature defined 15 felonies that fit the moral turpitude definition for disenfranchisement, including murder, impeachment, treason, rape, and various sex related offenses. In 2005, the Attorney General (instead of the legislature) added 16 more felony offenses to the list. The ACLU seeks to block those 16 offenses saying they were added inappropriately. In other words, the state is allegedly disfranchising felons under a much broader category of convictions than is permissible under the constitution.

Some state courts have recently decided cases involving the voting rights of convicted felons. In Pennsylvania, the State Supreme Court overturned a disenfranchisement clause passed as part of the Pennsylvania Voting Rights Act of 1995 (*Mixon v. Commonwealth of Pennsylvania* 2001). Other state courts are in the process of addressing legal issues related to felons' disenfranchisement (Uggen and Manza 2004). Table 15.1 shows the current situation of voting restrictions for felons in the U.S.

TABLE 15.1   Voting Restrictions

No Restrictions	Cannot Vote While Incarcerated	Cannot Vote While Incarcerated or on Parole	Cannot Vote Until Completion of Sentence	Lifetime Bar That Can Be Lifted
Maine	Hawaii	Alaska	Arizona	Alabama
Vermont	Indiana	California	Arkansas	Delaware
	Illinois	Colorado	Florida	Iowa
	Massachusetts	Connecticut	Georgia	Kentucky
	Michigan	New York	Idaho	Maryland
	Montana	Wisconsin	Kansas	Mississippi
	New Hampshire		Louisiana	Nebraska
	North Dakota		Minnesota	Nevada
	Ohio		Missouri	Tennessee
	Oregon		New Jersey	Virginia
	South Dakota		New Mexico	Washington
	Utah		North Carolina	Wyoming
			Oklahoma	
			Pennsylvania	
			Rhode Island	
			South Carolina	
			Texas	
			West Virginia	

Source: Legal Action Center. 2004. After Prison: Roadblocks to Reentry: A Report on State Legal Barriers Facing People with Criminal Records, p.14. http://www.lac.org/roadblocks.html; Updated May 2009.

LOSS OF EMPLOYMENT-RELATED RIGHTS

The risk of reoffending decreases the more time that has passed since the last arrest. One study found that *after seven years*, the risk of reoffending was nearly identical to that of a person who had never committed a crime (Kurlychek, Brame, and Bushway 2007). Ironically, the issues related to employment of former convicts are broad restrictions on occupational licenses, loss of good moral character, limitations in public and private employment, and the restriction on an individual's capacity to be bonded. Without even counting the common application question: "Have you ever been convicted of a felony?" the licensing restrictions make future job prospects very limiting to former felons. However, in the licensing section the argument stands that the limitations in place now are perhaps too restrictive and need to be reexamined.

Private Employment   A job applicant with a criminal record faces almost insurmountable barriers to private employment. This is because job applicants with a felony conviction are not protected from discrimination if they are hired by private employers. With more employers (45 percent) conducting background checks prior to the job offer, using Internet companies to perform background checks can help employers with the right to know about an applicant's history. Employers can avoid lawsuits for negligence in the hiring process, at the same time considering for employment those applicants who have a criminal past. While some employers do just that, others seem to use the criminal record as part of the reason for not hiring. Companies that were required to conduct background checks were more reluctant to hire former offenders than companies where the check was optional (Stoll and Bushway 2008). When asked, 60 percent of all employers were reluctant to hire anyone with a criminal record, regardless of the offense (Holzer 1996). For this reason, states like Florida and Hawaii allow employers to consider convictions only after a conditional offer of employment has been made (Haw. Rev. Stat., Section 378-2.5).

Some business and trade organizations and private employers provide jobs to convicted offenders. The Solution to Employment Problems (STEP) program of the National Association of Manufacturers is one such effort. In this program, employers provide equipment and instructors to train offenders while they are in prison and then guarantee them jobs upon their release. In the absence of laws specifically prohibiting it, private employers may discriminate on the basis of prior conviction, claiming risk and lack of good moral character as justifications.

Public Employment   Paid employment within a federal, state, or local governmental agency constitutes public *employment* because the pay or salary comes from the public coffers. Public *office* refers to government positions that involve policy making. Thus, a janitor in the office of a police chief is a public employee, but not a public officer because he or she does not have policy-making responsibilities. On the other hand, a police chief is both a public officer and a public employee.

Most state statutes permit public employment for people convicted of a felony. Some statutes allow employment after completion of a sentence. A felony conviction may not be the sole grounds for denial of public employment unless the offense bears a direct relationship to the position sought. In addition, a small number of states apply a direct relationship test and consider other factors such as rehabilitation, the time lapse since offense, the offender's age at the time of conviction, and the nature and seriousness of the offense. No statutory restrictions are placed on public employment of convicted people in the District of Columbia, Maine, Utah, or Vermont.

TABLE 15.2   Examples of Occupations That Require a License

Accountant/CPA	Acupuncturist	Aircraft Dispatcher/Mechanic/Pilot
Alarm Systems	Alcohol Server	Appraiser, Real Estate
Architect	Asbestos Removal	Athletic Trainer
Attorney/Lawyer	Auctioneer	Audiologist
Banking	Barber/Hairdresser	Boiler Operator
Building Codes	Bus Driver, School	Charter Boat Operator
Child Care Provider	Chiropractor	Collection Agency Operator
Commercial Fisher	Commercial Vehicle Operator	Concert Promoter
Contractor	Cosmetologist	Counselor/Therapist
Customs Broker	Dentist/Dental Hygienist	Dietician/Nutritionist
Electrician	Electrology	Emergency Medical Technician
Engineer	Explosives Handler	Forester
Freon Technician	Funeral Director/Services	Geologist
Hearing Aid Dealer	Home Inspector	Insurance Occupations
Investment Broker/Dealer	Land Surveyor	Law Examiner
Locksmith	Long-Term Health Care	Massage
Medical Examiner	Midwife	Mortician
Naturopath	Nursing (LPN, RN)	Occupational Therapist
Optician	Optometrist	Osteopath
Painter	Paramedic	Pastoral Counselor
Pesticide Applicator	Pharmacist/Technician	Physical Therapy
Physician/Surgeon	Plumber	Podiatrist
Psychologist	Real Estate	Refrigeration
Residential Builder	Respiratory Care	Sanitarian Examiner
Security Guard	Social Worker	Speech-Language Pathologist
Tattooing	Taxidermist	Teacher
Therapeutic Recreation	Veterinarian	Water Systems Operator

Sources: Illinois Department of Professional Regulation (http://www.dpr.state.il.us/); North Carolina Secretary of State Occupational Boards (http://www.secretary.state.nc.us/blio/occboards.asp); South Carolina Department of Labor, Licensing, and Regulation (http://www.llr.state.sc.us/pol.asp); Washington State Department of Licensing (http://www.dol.wa.gov)

Occupational License Limitations   Federal, state, and local governments throughout the United States restrict entry into more than 800 occupations and professions through licensing requirements (see Table 15.2 for examples). The number of occupations that require licenses has doubled in the last 30 years. As of 2005, "thirty-three states have general laws that prohibit a refusal to hire and/or issue a professional or occupational license to a person 'solely' because of their criminal record, or otherwise limit consideration of a conviction in connection with employment or licensing" (Love 2005, p. 10).

State licensing boards denied ex-convicts an occupational license if the conviction was related to the occupation or if the conviction was too recent. For example, an offender who has served time for robbery may be denied a license to be a bank teller, but not to be a land surveyor. For some occupations, such as attorneys, any felony conviction is cause for suspension or revocation of an existing certification, or may disqualify an applicant from obtaining a license. Other occupations require that a license may be issued only to "people of good moral character," which could exclude convicted individuals. The exact provisions of licensing statutes vary from state to state, from occupation to occupation, and even within occupations.

Increasingly, more occupations are restricted, and the disqualification may not have anything to do with the crime or how long ago it occurred. One source found that a company called the "Private Security Bureau" regulates 16 different occupations that are considered "security-related" (e.g., armed guards, locksmiths, alarm system staff, etc.) apart from the state board. One difference was that ". . . the Private Security Bureau checks the criminal backgrounds of applicants. But unlike virtually every other such agency, the bureau doesn't then evaluate whether applicants' past behavior has any relevance to their current work, how long ago the crime occurred or whether they have tried to rehabilitate themselves. Instead, applicants with a record sullied by most crimes above a traffic ticket are automatically rejected" (Dexheimer 2007, p. 1). It seems that 20 years must pass after the conviction for an applicant to become eligible again. A criminal record that disqualifies may be for a felony conviction, a misdemeanor conviction, or only certain types of crimes. The lack of uniformity in the laws and practices of the various states and localities makes it difficult for people with criminal records to determine where they might be allowed to apply their training and skills, whether they acquired them in or out of prison. The ironic part is that ex-offenders are expected to remain out of prison and in legitimate jobs, but then they are limited in the kinds of jobs they can obtain.

Loss of Capacity to be Bonded   Jobs in which employees handle money or merchandise may require the employee to be bonded. For example, banks, warehouses, truck-driving companies, collection agencies, bookkeepers, ticket takers, and vendors may require a bond before the employee will be allowed to work. A bond protects the employer or the company from losses caused by dishonest employees. The bonded employee is known as the principal. He or she signs and pays the fee to obtain a simple bond. A **surety bond** is signed by the principal and by one or more third parties, known as sureties, who promise to pay money in the event that the assured, the party in whose favor the bond is written, suffers damage because the principal failed to perform as agreed. The decision to write or deny a bond rests with the insurance company, which carefully investigates all people who request bonds and refuses to bond people it considers poor risks. A person with a felony criminal record is considered a poor risk by the company issuing the bond.

Surety Bond
A certificate signed by the principal and a third party, promising to pay in the event the assured suffers damages or losses because the employee fails to perform as agreed.

   The McLaughlin Company, through the Employment and Training Administration of the U.S. Department of Labor, offers fidelity bonding coverage for job applicants. The coverage is available to people who cannot obtain suitable employment because they have police, credit, or other records that preclude their being covered by the usual commercial bonds. Ex-offenders are eligible for the bonds if they are qualified and suitable for the job and are not commercially bondable under ordinary circumstances. The applicant applies for the bond through a state employment office. The bond becomes effective when the applicant begins work and the manager of the local employment service office or other authorized representative of the state agency has certified the bond. Unfortunately, few ex-offenders take advantage of this program and instead refrain from applying for jobs that require bonding. Since employers and prospective employees seem to lack information about the bonding that is available through state employment agencies, we highlight this option in Box 15.1.

Loss of Good Moral Character   The statute requiring that the licensee possess *good moral character* is another obstacle to obtain gainful employment. It is usually assumed that a person who has been convicted of a criminal offense is not of good moral character. The obstacles created by the provisions and assumptions about good moral character are all the more serious because a convicted person has a difficult time proving or restoring his or her good moral character. Moreover, few

BOX 15.1   COMMUNITY CORRECTIONS UP CLOSE

How Can At-Risk Job Applicants Become Bonded?

Commercially purchased bond insurance serves to protect the employer against employee dishonesty or for loss of money or property through theft, forgery, larceny, and embezzlement. These companies refuse coverage to persons considered "at risk," such as former offenders, recovering substance abusers, people who have declared bankruptcy, poor credit score, dishonorable discharge from the military or employees who have behaved in a manner that questions their credibility or honesty. As a result, applicants who are "at risk" are routinely denied employment because they cannot be bonded.

The U.S. Department of Labor (USDOL) created the Federal Bonding Program in 1966 as an incentive for employers to hire employees who are "at risk." The bonds issued by the Federal Bonding Program were

". . . designed to reimburse the employer for any loss due to employee theft of money or property with no deductible amount to become the employer's liability (i.e., 100% bond insurance coverage). . . . Bond issuance can apply to any job at any employer in any State, and covers any employee dishonesty committed on or away from the employer's work facility. Any full or part-time employee paid wages (with Federal taxes automatically deducted from pay) can be bonded, including persons hired by "temp agencies." However, self-employed persons cannot be covered by these Fidelity Bonds."

Most public or private companies must be preapproved or "certified" to use Fidelity Bonds. Once certified,

- Bonds are issued free-of-charge effective the day that the applicant is scheduled to start work and are self-terminating after 6 months
- The bond insurance ranges from $5,000 to $25,000 coverage for the initial 6-month period with no deductible;
- When the initial 6-month bond coverage expires, continued bond coverage can be purchased by the employer if the worker demonstrated job honesty during that time period.

"At-risk" job applicants seeking bonding services should call 1.877.872.5627 for the nearest workforce office and the state bonding coordinator for the appropriate state of residence.

Source: U.S. Department of Labor. 2009. *The Federal Bonding Program*. Retrieved from: http://www.bonds4jobs.com/index.html

---

procedures for restoring civil rights erase a conviction or adjudication of delinquency, and therefore, "good moral character" is seldom, if ever, restored. As a practical matter, licenses are refused or revoked according to the various meanings that licensing agencies place on such terms. In general, however, a licensing agency regards a conviction as conclusive evidence of bad character, and the courts have not yet overruled this long-standing decision (*Peterson v. State Liquor Authority* 1973).

LOSS OF RIGHT TO OWN OR POSSESS A FIREARM

For some individuals, the right to own a firearm continues to be the most restrictive of all civil disabilities lost by conviction. Federal law prohibits convicted felons from possessing, shipping, transporting, or receiving any firearms or ammunition (18 U.S.C., sec. 921(a)(20)). It also prohibits the possession of guns by anybody convicted in any court of domestic violence, which is a misdemeanor crime (18 U.S.C. sec. 922(g)(9)). According to Buckler and Travis (2003), 37 states restrict both firearm possession and ownership for people convicted of a felony crime, and seven additional states restrict just the possession of all firearms. Twenty-one states allow firearms restrictions to be restored (12 through passage of time from completion of sentence and nine through restoration of rights proceedings). Seven states have no such firearms restrictions whatsoever (Massachusetts, Missouri, New York, Ohio, Pennsylvania, Tennessee, and Vermont.)

The issue of the loss of the right to own a firearm has been litigated in a number of cases. In *Beecham v. United States* (1994), the U.S. Supreme Court held that "federal felons remain subject to the federal firearms disability until their civil rights are restored through a federal, not a state, procedure." This means "federal felons who have had their civil rights restored by state law or procedure nonetheless are still prohibited by federal law from possessing firearms."

In another case, defendant Fowler was charged with possessing a .25 caliber semiautomatic handgun in 1997 after having been convicted of a felony in 1972 for second degree burglary. In 1975, the Alabama Board of Pardons and Paroles granted Fowler a certificate to restore "all his civil and political rights" although the certificate did not expressly name which rights those were. Fowler was initially convicted for violating federal law, but the court reversed Fowler's conviction when it decided that a certificate restoring "all civil and political rights without reservation" *permits* the defendant to carry a firearm (*U.S. v. Fowler*, 1999).

A Massachusetts defendant received a certificate restoring his civil and political rights, but this certificate allowed (by Massachusetts law) the defendant to possess rifles and shotguns, while restricting the defendant from carrying any handguns. The defendant was arrested for the possession of six shotguns in violation of the Federal firearm law. The U.S. Supreme Court said that the "possession of firearm" clause in a certificate to restore civil rights is an all or nothing clause, in that when a certificate bars only one type of firearm, it bars all types of firearms where the federal firearm statute is concerned. Thus, even though Massachusetts state law permitted the defendant to possess the rifles, the defendant's restriction of handguns invoked the "unless clause" since a handgun is a type of firearm, and thus, the defendant was not allowed to possess any firearm—not a rifle, shotgun, or a handgun (*Caron v. U.S.*, 1998). In effect, the Court said that federal law prevails over state law in case of conflict concerning firearms regulation.

Loss of Welfare Benefits

Withholding welfare benefits is the most recent form of collateral consequence for convicted drug offenders. When the government overhauled the welfare system with its Welfare Reform Act, the former Aid to Families with Dependent Children (AFDC) was replaced with a program called "Temporary Assistance for Needy Families." The federal Welfare Reform Act denied food stamps and benefits to anyone convicted of possession or sale of controlled substances. Buckler and Travis (2003) report that "of the 42 states that deny eligibility for welfare benefits, 22 states deny benefits entirely, 10 states partially deny welfare benefits, and 10 states have enacted statutes stipulating that the denial of welfare benefits is contingent upon drug treatment" (p. 444).

Loss of Parental Rights

About one and a half million children under age 18 had at least one parent serving time in prison. Of the 48 states that allow parental rights to be terminated for felony offenders, 18 states may terminate a parent's rights for long-term prison confinement, "which deprives the child of a normal home life or produces negative effects on the parent-child relationship" (Buckler and Travis 2003, p. 442). Most states (37) will terminate parental rights for a serious felony conviction against one or more children in the household, which includes murder/manslaughter or felonious assault/battery. In Indiana, if it can be shown to the court that a continuation of the parent-child relationship will pose a threat to the child's well-being, any conviction will result in the termination of parental rights (Buckler and Travis 2003).

LOSS IN COURT

To sustain the integrity of the court system, two common rights that are limited for felons are the right to serve on a jury and the ability to be viewed as a credible witness in any future court proceedings.

Right to Serve on a Jury   The exclusion of convicted people from jury service has its origin in common law. The federal rule is that citizens are not competent to serve on a federal grand or petit (trial) jury if they have been convicted of a crime punishable by imprisonment for more than one year and if that person's civil rights have not been restored (28 U.S.C. sec. 1865). Felons are deprived of the right to serve on a jury except in four states (Alaska, Illinois, Maine, and Missouri). Eleven states and the District of Columbia permit felons to serve on juries after they complete their sentences. On the other hand, others suspend the right only until the offender is released from incarceration, or through the passage of time (Buckler and Travis 2003). The right to serve on a jury may be restored through a pardon or expungement (Office of the Pardon Attorney 1996) in most states, except eight, which offer no restoration mechanisms for this right.

Loss of Credibility as a Witness   Absolute disqualification to be a witness in court applies to people convicted of (telling a lie under oath) or subornation of perjury (inducing another person to take a false oath). The justification for absolute disqualification for those convicted of perjury is that a person who has been convicted of a crime cannot be trusted to give truthful testimony. The usual situation, however, is that a person who has been convicted of a crime other than perjury or subornation of perjury is permitted to testify, but the fact of the conviction may be used to discredit a witness's testimony, the court or jury being allowed to take the conviction into account. The witness can be asked if he or she has been convicted of a felony or other crime and must answer truthfully. Opposing counsel may then argue, and usually does, that because the witness is a convicted offender the testimony should not be believed. Whether a witness who is an ex-offender is entitled to full credibility or no credibility at all is up to the judge or jury.

LOSS OF THE RIGHT TO HOLD PUBLIC OFFICE

Elective positions in federal, state, and municipal governments, as well as some appointive positions, are generally regarded as **public offices.** A public office does not have to carry any compensation; examples are positions on a school board or a municipal council. Federal statutes and the U.S. Constitution contain provisions that exclude some offenders from holding certain positions in the government of the United States. Congress may bar ex-felons from holding any nonconstitutional public office for offenses that include falsifying, destroying, or removing public records or documents; receiving compensation in matters affecting the government; rebellion; and treason (Office of the Pardon Attorney 1996, p. 7). Conviction for treason disqualifies the defendant from holding "any office under the United States."

A total of 40 jurisdictions limit or restrict felons from holding public office. Twelve states restrict the right to hold public office after a felony conviction, unless the convicted person receives a pardon. Fifteen states return the right to hold public office after discharge from probation, parole, or prison. Four states restrict this right to felons until a mandatory period of time has elapsed following the completion of their sentence, ranging from 3 to 15 years. Nine states permanently restrict this right and do not allow any means of restoration (Buckler and Travis 2003).

Public Offices
Elective positions in federal, state, and municipal governments as well as appointive positions.

PROBLEMS WITH CIVIL DISABILITY LAWS

Civil disability laws create a number of problems for offenders, which are summarized by Margaret Colgate Love as follows: "In almost every U.S. jurisdiction, offenders seeking to put their criminal past behind them are frustrated by a legal system that is complex and unclear and entirely inadequate to the task. Categorical disqualifications are generally overbroad, and discretionary decision-making is often unfair and unreliable" (Love 2005, p. 92). Some of the main research findings in the same publication are:

- "In every U.S. jurisdiction, the legal system erects formidable barriers to the re-integration of criminal offenders into a free society.
- "These legal barriers are always difficult and often impossible to overcome. . . .
- "While every jurisdiction provides at least one way that convicted persons can avoid or mitigate the collateral consequences of conviction, the actual mechanisms for relief are generally inaccessible and unreliable, and are frequently not well understood even by those responsible for administering them" (Love 2005, pp. 4–5).

The constitutionality of civil disability laws has been challenged on the ground that they violate the provisions on due process and equal protection, and constitute cruel and unusual punishment. Challengers allege that these laws serve none of the objectives of modern correctional theory and impede offenders' rehabilitation, both within the correctional institution and in the community. Recommendations to remedy these conditions include the following:

- Elimination of unnecessary restrictions, such as those on voting
- Reasonable application of necessary restrictions
- Greater participation by the sentencing court in determining the civil disabilities to be imposed on the individual defendant
- Automatic restoration of rights and privileges five years after the convict's release into the community, provided the offender has lived a crime-free life during that time

Effects of Conviction for Sex Offenders

Sex offenders face an enormous number of limitations that affect their civil liberties and integration well after conviction. These include being required to register with local law enforcement, community notification of the offender's residence, residency restrictions, and the possibility of civil commitment for sexual predators.

SEX OFFENDER REGISTRATION LAWS

All 50 states and the District of Columbia require that sex offenders, both on and off supervision, register with the local authorities, usually within one month following release or completion of their sentence. Sex offender registration statutes (stemming from Megan's Law and the Adam Walsh Child Protection and Safety Act) were enacted to protect the public and improve the competence of the police to investigate sex crimes. Registration with the local police is required through the Dru Sjodin National Sex Offender Public Website (NSOPW) operated by the U.S. Department of Justice.

Washington was the first state to actively require registration of all sex offenders in 1990. California actually enacted the first registration statute in 1947, but it wasn't used much and didn't catch the nation's attention quite like Washington's statute did (Tewksbury 2002). When states began developing their databases, the information reported was vastly different and the number of years required for registration of offenders varied greatly. Enforcing the updates is difficult as insufficient information was found on a significant number of listed sex offenders in one state (Tewksbury 2002).

The Adam Walsh Child Protection and Safety Act of 2006 creates an organized and consistent national sex offender registry whereby every state provides the same information about each offender. Information requested includes name, address, date of birth, convicted offenses, and a recent photo. The database also organizes sex offenders into three risk tiers, with Tier 3 defined as the most serious. Tier 1 offenders (which includes minors as young as 14 years of age) update their whereabouts every year for 15 years. Tier 2 offenders update their whereabouts every six months for 25 years. Tier 3 offenders must update their whereabouts every three months for the rest of their lives. Failure to register and update information is a felony.

There are 100,000 registered sex offenders just in Texas and California alone. So an estimate of 400,000 registered sex offenders throughout the United States is likely conservative. In the federal system, offenders are required to register for all federal sex offenses that occurred on or after November 26, 1998 or a military conviction for a sex crime on or after September 1, 1997 (Administrative Office of the United States Courts 2003). Moreover, the registered offenders are not all adults. In Texas, for example, 8.5 percent of all sex offenders were juveniles, most of whom were considered higher risks than many of the adults, due to the juvenile having committed more sex crimes total and more sex crimes of an aggravated nature (Craun and Kernsmith 2006).

When legally challenged, the U.S. Supreme Court said that the public posting of a sex offender registry does not violate the due process clause of the Fourteenth Amendment (*Connecticut Department of Public Safety et al. v. Doe* 2003). In this case, Connecticut law required that upon their release into the community, sex offenders provide their name, address, photograph, DNA samples, and notification of any change in residence. Connecticut law requires sex offenders to register for 10 years, but those convicted of sexually violent offenses must register for life. The offender in this case alleged that this law was unfair because he was no longer "currently sexually dangerous," and therefore it violated his due process rights. The Court disagreed, saying that the defendant had to register because he was a sexual offender, not because he continued to be dangerous. The Court said that the law was constitutional, even if no prior opportunity is given to prove that the defendant is not dangerous.

In another case, also decided that same year, the Court said that a sex offender registration and notification law that is not punitive does not violate the ex post facto clause of the Constitution (*Smith v. Doe* 2003). In this case, the Alaska Sex Offender Registration Act required a registration system and a notification system that were both retroactive, meaning they applied to offenders who were convicted even before the law was passed. Defendants challenged its constitutionality, saying its retroactive application violated the ex post facto clause (the clause that prohibits punishment without prior trial) of the Constitution. The Court upheld the Alaska law, saying that the Alaska Offender Act regulates rather than punishes; therefore, its retroactive application does not violate the ex post facto clause. The Court reasoned that what Alaska wanted to do with the statute was to "regulate" instead of "punish" conduct. Since the law was primarily regulatory instead of punitive, the ex post facto clause does not apply. Critics of this decision contend that registries have had a significant impact on sex offenders finding a place to live, work, and be accepted back into the community.

Community Notification Laws

In contrast to registries, community notification statutes "either make information about sex offenders available on request to individuals and organizations or authorize or require probation and parole departments, law enforcement agencies, or prosecutor offices to disseminate information about released offenders to the community at large" (Finn 1997, p. 1). Notification statutes assume ". . . that registration alone is inadequate to protect the public against released sex offenders and that better notification provides the public with a better means of protecting itself" (Finn 1997, p. 1). As with the registry, there are three tiers of risk, with each tier having its own set of notification procedures.

Sex offenders are believed to pose different levels of risk to the community, depending on the nature and prevalence of their crimes as well as their choice of victim. The third tier permits or requires proactive dissemination (knocking on doors, flyers, and so on) and the other lower tiers permit information dissemination only in response to individuals who seek out that information (see Table 15.3 for a sampling of states). Notifying the community about the presence of ex-offenders is up to each individual jurisdiction.

One study examined whether community notification of sex offenders reduced recidivism and whether the program aided law enforcement in offender apprehension. The study used a treatment and a matched control group, and found that after 54 months there was no statistically significant difference between the two groups on the rate of arrest. However, the offenders who participated in the notification program were arrested more quickly than members of the control group (Finn 1997).

Offenders who are convicted of a sexual crime have been met with the most community resistance. The signs pictured here are protesting a proposed group home for sex offenders in Phelan, California.

© AP Photo/Francis Specker

TABLE 15.3 Principal Features of Seven Sex Offender Notification Statutes

State	Year Statute Went Into Effect	How Long Offenders Remain Subject to Notification	Notification Mandatory or Discretionary	Notification Proactive or Only in Response to Request	Sex Offenses Covered by Statute	Implementing Agency	Immunity Explicitly Provided to Implementers	Who May be Notified	Retroactivity	Information That May be Disseminated
Alaska	1994	*for life:* 2 or more convictions *15 years:* 1 conviction	mandatory by administrative regulation	upon request	all offenses	State Dept. of Public Safety	provided	anyone	retroactive	limited by statute
Connecticut	1996	10 years after end of probation or parole	discretionary	proactive	selected offenses	probation	not provided	anyone	not retroactive	unrestricted
Louisiana	1992	10 years after release	mandatory	proactive	all offenses	offenders-supervised by probation	provided	limited by statute	retroactive to June 1992	limited by statute
New Jersey	1994	indefinitely, but may petition for relief 15 years after release	mandatory	proactive	selected offenses	prosecutor and police	provided	people likely to encounter the offender	retroactive	not specified
Oregon	1993, 1995	for life; may petition for waiver after 10 years	varies[1]	proactive and upon request	selected offenses	probation and police	not provided	anyone	retroactive	unrestricted
Tennessee	1995	10 years minimum; then may petition for relief	discretionary	proactive	all offenses	Tennessee Bureau of Investigation	provided	not specified	retroactive	"relevant" information
Washington	1990	for life, 15 years, or 10 years depending on seriousness of offense	discretionary	proactive and upon request	all offenses	police	provided	not specified	retroactive	not specified

[1]Mandatory if under supervision; discretionary if not.

Source: Peter Finn, *Sex Offender Community Notification,* (Washington, DC: U.S. Department of Justice, February 1997), p. 4.

Zevitz and Farkas (2000) investigated the impact of community notification on the workloads of Wisconsin probation and parole officers who supervise sex offenders. Because Wisconsin is a state that has authorized proactive information dissemination, the researchers found much effort went into dealing with the community itself. Overall results indicated that sex offender supervision takes an extraordinary amount of training, time, and resources to find suitable housing, conduct home and employment visits, and monitor sex offenders to the rising community expectations. Yet, the community reported feeling more *fearful* rather than safer with the knowledge of where the offender lived (Beck and Travis 2004).

RESIDENCY RESTRICTIONS

In addition to registration and community notification, 22 states have added residential restrictions affecting where sex offenders live within the community. The assumption here is to reduce opportunity for sex offenders by prohibiting them from living within 1,000 feet of school property (some states specify up to 2,500 feet). Critics point out the flawed logic in this assumption, saying that this restriction is based on the assumption that most sex offenders victimize children they don't know. This is simply not the case since sex offenders primarily victimize children already known to them. Restricting where sex offenders live is unlikely to decrease recidivism and opportunity (Levenson, Zgoba, and Tewksbury 2007).

How well is this restriction adhered to? In one county in Ohio, a spatial analysis mapped the locations of 1,095 sex offenders in relation to the 345 schools in the area and found that 45 percent (494 offenders) were living within 1,000 feet of school property—including buildings, parking lots, and open fields on school property (Grubesic, Mack, and Murray 2007). The researchers found that if this restriction was strictly adhered to, it reduces housing choices by 50 percent; in this particular county, half of all residents lived within 1,000 feet of a school. In more densely populated counties, the percentage is likely higher. Another argument against this restriction is that it is more difficult to monitor an offender when you know the offender's address than when he or she is homeless because of having no place to live (Levenson, Zgoba, and Tewksbury 2007). We can conclude that what works with sex offenders is treatment completion and a positive social support system—both of which significantly decreased recidivism.

INVOLUNTARY CIVIL COMMITMENT OF SEXUAL PREDATORS

Convicted sex offenders are also subject to possible involuntary civil confinement following incarceration. The sex offender may be subject to involuntary civil confinement if the following requirements are present: he or she poses a continuous and dangerous threat to public safety, that threat is related to the sex offender's lack of control over their own behavior, and the offender has a severe mental illness or disorder that requires treatment. Since involuntary commitment is a civil statute, the commitment decision does not constitute double jeopardy (*Seling v. Young* 2001). The attorney general's office for each state screens the cases, but the lack of written guidelines affords authorities wide discretion as to who should be committed.

The Adam Walsh Child Protection and Safety Act requires offenders with any history of sex offenses to be screened prior to release to determine whether they are sexually dangerous. If they are deemed as such, they remain in the custody of the federal or state prison system until a court hearing is held to determine whether by "clear and convincing evidence" the sex offender should be civilly committed or released. The commitment process is private and confidential. However, Mansnerus (2003) was allowed to attend six hearings with special permission. She reports:

> The hearings are roughly modeled on commitments for the mentally ill, but with a key difference. In a regular civil commitment, the focus is on the patientís current state of mind; crimes committed long ago are usually not considered relevant. In the hearings at Kearney, however, criminal records are considered critical evidence of the patient's thoughts, behaviors and possibility of committing future crimes . . . almost any information about him is admissible . . . like hearsay evidence, evaluations written years ago by the police or psychiatrists, statements to therapists and the patient's own writings. (p. 2)

In *Kansas v. Hendricks* (1997), the Supreme Court decided that a Kansas statute that permits the potentially indefinite commitment of sexually violent predators is constitutional. The Kansas Sexually Violent Predator Act authorizes the civil commitment of people who are likely to engage in predatory acts of sexual violence due to a mental or personality disorder. Defendant Hendricks had an extensive history of sexually molesting children and was scheduled for release from prison. But the state filed a petition to commit him under this act. The Court said that the Kansas law did not violate the prohibition against double jeopardy. However, five years later, in *Kansas v. Crane* (2002), the Supreme Court held that the civil commitment of a dangerous sex offender is not permitted without proof of serious difficulty in controlling behavior. It added, however, that total inability to control behavior is not required. Rather, the state must show that an offender has difficulty controlling that behavior and that the lack of control is related to the serious mental illness. Taken together, the *Hendricks* and *Crane* cases say that the civil commitment of dangerous sex offenders is constitutional, but the state must prove prior to a civil commitment that the offender is unable to control his behavior (del Carmen, Ritter, and Witt 2005, p. 321).

Pardon

Pardon is defined as "the act or an instance of officially nullifying punishment or other legal consequences of a crime" (Garner 2009, p. 1144). Operating as a distinct subsystem of the criminal justice process, a **pardon** is an act of forgiveness or mercy. One author notes: "Pardon is assigned a central role in overcoming the legal barriers to reintegration of criminal offenders in almost every U.S. jurisdiction, and in most jurisdictions it is the only mechanism by which adult felony offenders can avoid or mitigate collateral penalties and disabilities" (Love 2005, p. 7). But despite its importance to a well-balanced system of justice, pardon has received little scholarly attention. This lack of study has led to misunderstandings about its nature and function.

Pardon
An executive act of clemency that serves to mitigate or set aside punishment for a crime.

Courts differ on the issue of a pardon's legal effect. Some jurisdictions hold that a pardon wipes out the crime as though it never happened; thus, the offender is a "new person." Other jurisdictions hold that for some purposes, a pardon does not wipe out the fact of a conviction. Under this view, the recipient of a pardon is regarded not as a "new person" but as a convicted criminal. This happens, for example, when the pardoned criminal takes the stand as a witness in a trial. His or her testimony may be impeached and credibility is diminished because of the previous conviction even though a pardon has been granted. Again, states differ on how the results of a pardon are viewed.

The Power to Pardon

Historically, the power to pardon belonged to the king or sovereign. Because a crime was considered to be an offense against the king, he was deemed to have the power to forgive it. In early American law, the power to pardon was given to the legislature. When it was granted to the executive, it was severely restricted. By the time the U.S. Constitution was written, the older rule was again followed. The president was given the power of pardon in all federal cases except that of impeachment (*In re Bocchiaro* 1943). The Office of the Pardon Attorney in the Department of Justice receives applications from all over the country, and the Pardon Attorney is responsible for making recommendations to the president.

In most states today, the power to pardon state felony cases belongs to the governor, acting alone or in conjunction with some official or board of pardons. When granted to the governor, the power may be either restricted or unrestricted. In some states, the governor's power to pardon does not extend to treason and impeachment. In these states, those guilty of these acts or proceedings may be pardoned by the legislature. The power to pardon usually does not extend to violations of municipal ordinances; it extends only to offenses against the state because the power to pardon belongs to a state official. In some states, pardon can be given at any time after the person is charged or indicted, but in other states pardon can be granted only after conviction. Other states forbid pardon until the minimum sentence or a certain length of sentence has been served or until a specific number of years of successful parole have been completed. Where state law so provides, both absolute and conditional pardons may be given.

Kinds of Pardon

Pardons are either absolute (full) or conditional. An absolute pardon freely and unconditionally absolves an individual from the legal consequences of his or her conviction. Absolute pardon does not require that the prisoner or offender accept or reject it since no conditions whatsoever are attached (*Biddle v. Perovich* 1927). An absolute pardon, once delivered, cannot be revoked, and it restores citizenship rights. By contrast, a **conditional pardon** does not take effect until certain conditions are met or until after the occurrence of a specified event. For example, a public officer who commits an offense while in office and is convicted may be pardoned if he or she shows remorse, apologizes to the public, and resigns from public office. A conditional pardon generally does not restore the full civil rights of the offender unless express language to that effect is stated in its proclamation. This type of pardon may be revoked for violation of the conditions imposed. A prisoner may prefer to serve out his or her sentence rather than accept the conditions attached to the pardon, which the offender may deem burdensome or onerous. Some courts restrict the right of the governor to revoke a conditional pardon by prohibiting revocation without a determination that the person pardoned has violated the conditions.

Conditional Pardon
A pardon that becomes operative when the grantee has performed some specific act(s) or that becomes void when some specific act(s) transpires.

Procedure for Obtaining a Pardon

The procedure for obtaining a pardon is fixed by statute or by regulations of the pardoning authority. Generally, the convicted person must apply for a pardon, and time must elapse after release from confinement or discharge on parole before the offender may apply. When the offender applies, he or she is required to notify certain people, typically the prosecuting attorney, the sheriff, and the court of conviction. Posting (meaning the publication of a public notice) may be required. There may be limitations on repeated applications for pardon, such as a minimum time interval between applications. In most cases, the pardoning authority conducts an investigation. A public hearing on the application may be held in some states.

LEGAL EFFECTS OF A PARDON

An absolute pardon restores most, but not all, civil rights that were lost upon conviction. For federal offenses, one publication notes that "a presidential pardon restores civil rights lost as a result of a federal conviction, including the rights to vote, to serve on a jury, and to hold public office, and generally relieves other disabilities that attach solely by reason of the commission or conviction of the pardoned offense" (Federal Statutes Imposing Collateral Consequences Upon Conviction 2000, p. 13). For federal offenders, the Supreme Court has held that only federal law can nullify the effect of a federal conviction through pardon, expungement, or restoration of civil rights (*Beecham v. United States* 1994).

There are two points of view on the issue of whether a pardon wipes out guilt. The classic view, which represents the minority position today, was expressed by the U.S. Supreme Court over a century ago when it said:

> A pardon reaches both the punishment prescribed for the offense and the guilt of the offender; and when the pardon is full, it releases the punishment and blots out the existence of the guilt, so that in the eyes of the law the offender is as innocent as if he had never committed the offense. (*Ex parte Garland* 1867)

The opposite and majority view states that a pardon is an implied expression of guilt and that the conviction is not obliterated (*Burdick v. United States* 1915). Each state determines which view it upholds. State law, a court decision, or the state pardoning authority defines the procedures and determines the effects of a pardon for state felony convictions. These determinations are binding only in that state. For example, a pardon given in one state may be used to increase the punishment of a subsequent offense in that state (*State v. Walker* 1983), but not in other states. An absolute pardon usually restores eligibility for public office, but will not restore a person to any public office he or she held at the time of conviction. By contrast, a conditional pardon usually does not restore rights or remove disqualifications for office (*Ex parte Lefors* 1957). Generally, a conviction for which a witness has been conditionally pardoned can nonetheless be used for witness impeachment in some courts.

EFFECTS OF A PARDON ON OCCUPATIONAL LICENSING

A pardon does not automatically restore an occupational license that has been revoked as a result of a criminal conviction. Although loss of a professional license is a penalty, some court decisions hold that the proceedings to revoke a license are not penal in nature (*Marlo v. State Board of Medical Examiners* 1952; *Murrill v. State Board of Accountancy* 1950). A professional license that is lost through conviction is usually not restored by a pardon because licenses are issued by licensing authorities or boards that have their own power and are independent from the pardoning authority. In California, the law provides that a pardon shall:

> operate to restore to the convicted person all the rights, privileges, and franchises of which he has been deprived in consequence of said conviction. . . . [N]othing in this article shall affect any of the provisions of the Medical Practices Act, or the power or authority conferred by law on the Board of Medical Examiners therein, or the power or authority conferred by law upon any board which permits any person or persons to apply his or their art or profession on the person of another. (Cal. Penal Code, sec. 4853)

Restoration of Rights

Restoration of rights may be done in two ways: by application or by automatic restoration. Most states provide for automatic restoration because it is easier to administer and is less discriminatory toward certain types of offenders. In Table 15.4, you will see how each state allows offenders to regain voting rights—some of which are automatic and others which must be accepted through an application process.

RESTORATION UPON APPLICATION

Some states, by statute, provide procedures the offender can initiate to remove the disabilities that follow a conviction. Typically, a certificate is furnished upon completion of the proceedings that specifies the rights that are restored. An ex-offender must possess one of these certificates to apply for a job or a license barred by virtue of a criminal conviction. These certificates and the order of the court usually restore the ex-offender to such political rights as the right to vote and provide him or her with a document that establishes good conduct since release from custody. Nonetheless, they are not binding and do not prevent a prospective employer or a licensing agency from taking the conviction into account in deciding whether to give the offender a job or a license.

Rehabilitation Certificate
A certificate that allows former offenders to obtain a license or work in certain occupations that have barred felons upon conviction.

Six states (Arizona, California, Illinois, Nevada, New Jersey, and New York) offer **rehabilitation certificates** (or certificates of good conduct) that allow former offenders to obtain a license or work in certain occupations that have barred felons

TABLE 15.4 Discretionary Restoration of the Vote after a Felony Conviction

State	Right to Vote Lost upon Conviction, Restored upon Completion of Sentence	Right to Vote Lost upon Conviction, Restored after Additional Waiting Period	Right to Vote Lost upon Conviction, Restoration Discretionary
Alabama			felony offenses involving moral turpitude must obtain executive restoration of rights or pardon
Arizona	first offenders only		recidivists must obtain pardon or judicial restoration
Delaware		five years, except for certain serious offenses	pardon required for certain serious offenses
Florida			executive restoration of rights or pardon
Kentucky			pardon
Maryland	first offenders only	three years for recidivists	pardon required if two or more violent felonies
Mississippi			for all constitutionally specified offenses, pardon or legislative restoration
Nevada	first offenders only		pardon or judicial restoration
Tennessee			pardon or judicial restoration
Virginia			executive restoration of rights or pardon
Wyoming		five years for first-time nonviolent offenders	executive restoration or pardon for violent offenders and recidivists

Source: Margaret Colgate Love, Relief from the Collateral Consequences of a Criminal Conviction, July 2005 (Accessed: http://www.sentencingproject.org/rights_restoration/table8.html)

upon conviction. These certificates typically cover an unlimited number of misdemeanors and only up to one or two felonies. Other states have some form of administrative pardon system that offers a similar form of relief to enter occupations and obtain licensing (Alabama, Connecticut, Georgia, Nebraska, and South Carolina).

AUTOMATIC RESTORATION

The Office of the United States Pardon Attorney has published a state-by-state survey titled *Civil Disabilities of Convicted Felons*. The study reported that 33 states have laws for **automatic restoration of rights** upon completion of sentence. The remaining states require some affirmative action on the part of the offender (Office of the Pardon Attorney 1996).

A New Hampshire statute, which provides automatic restoration by virtue of a **certificate of discharge,** reads, in part,

> the order, certificate, or other instrument of discharge, given to a person sentenced for a felony upon his discharge after completion of service of his sentence or after service under probation or parole, shall state that the defendant's rights to vote and to hold any future public office of which he was deprived by this chapter are thereby restored and that he suffers no other disability by virtue of his conviction and sentence except as otherwise provided by this chapter. (N.H. Rev. Stat. Ann., sec. 607-A:5)

The laws of the other states that grant automatic restoration of rights are basically similar, but the provisions differ somewhat. The Illinois Unified Code of Corrections, for example, contains this language:

> On completion of sentence of imprisonment or on a petition of a person not sentenced to imprisonment, all license rights and privileges granted under the authority of this State which have been revoked or suspended because of conviction of an offense shall be restored unless the authority having jurisdiction of such license rights finds after investigation and hearing that restoration is not in the public interest. (Illinois Unified Code of Corrections, sec. 1005-5-5(d))

Most courts consider the effect of automatic restoration of rights as equivalent to a pardon. A certificate of good conduct and/or an automatic restoration of rights retains the conviction. Thus, the conviction remains on record as a prior conviction for purposes of increasing a future sentence if the offender is ever convicted again of another offense. The ex-offender is not restored to eligibility to receive an occupational or professional license and still must report the conviction on job application forms.

RESTORING GOOD MORAL CHARACTER

None of the methods and procedures for removing or reducing the collateral consequences of a criminal conviction discussed in this chapter restores good moral character to the ex-offender. Licensing statutes almost universally require that the holders of a professional or occupational license be of good character, and many private employers of nonlicensed workers impose the same requirement. This closes the door for many convicted people in job markets that require a license. The lack of a generally accepted standard is one of the problems with determining good moral character. The Supreme Court in *Konigsberg v. State Bar* (1957) noted that

> the term [good moral character] by itself is unusually ambiguous. It can be defined in an almost unlimited number of ways, for any definition will necessarily reflect the attitudes, experiences, and prejudices of the definer. Such a vague

Automatic Restoration of Rights
Reinstatement of some or all civil rights upon completion of sentence. The extent of restoration varies by state and by offense type.

Certificate of Discharge
Official written document signifying that an offender has completed his or her sentence.

qualification, which is easily adapted to fit personal views and predilections, can be a dangerous instrument for arbitrary and discriminatory denial of the right to practice law.

Yet, the rule remains as it was when announced by the Supreme Court in 1898:

[The state] may require both qualifications of learning and of good character, and if it deems that one who has violated the criminal laws of the state is not possessed of sufficient good character, it can deny to such a one a right to practice medicine, and further, it may make the record of a conviction conclusive evidence of the fact of the violation of the criminal law and of the absence of the requisite good character (*Hawker v. New York* 1898).

This rule has been generally followed in subsequent legislation and court decisions (*De Veau v. Braisted* 1960). When good moral character is required for occupational licensing, courts or enforcement agencies can disqualify an applicant based on differing perceptions of what that term means; thus, the term becomes subjective. Conviction of any offense may be good enough for disqualification in some courts or agencies, but other jurisdictions require conviction of only certain types of serious offenses for good moral character to be lost.

EXPUNGEMENT OF ARREST AND CONVICTION RECORDS

Expungement
An erasure. Process by which the record of a criminal conviction (or juvenile adjudication) is destroyed or sealed after expiration of time.

Expungement (erasing or destroying a record) and sealing (closing an existing record) are two ways to limit public availability to arrest records and conviction records. Whendiscussing expungement and (later) the act of sealing, a distinction must be made between *arrest* records and court records that did *not lead to conviction* versus court records of *conviction*. The arrest records are defined and handled by law enforcement officers according to the number of police contacts that resulted in an arrest, regardless of case outcome (e.g., dismissal, diversion, plea of guilty, trial, etc.). A record of conviction is one in which the defendant pled guilty or was found guilty and was formally sentenced by the court. Each state deals with expunging and sealing arrest and conviction records differently. We will differentiate between expunging and sealing the two terms in a general sense, but please note that some jurisdictions use the terms interchangeably, so it becomes quite confusing.

Forty states allow people to expunge or seal *arrest* records and if the applicant is successful, 30 of those same states also allow the denial that these arrest records exist. Less than half the number of states allows expungement for convictions, however. For felony offenses, one source reports 21 states that have expungement procedures (Legal Action Center 2004, p. 6), while another source says 26 states, District of Columbia, Puerto Rico, and the Virgin Islands (Bureau of Justice Statistics, 2004). However, in all but 10 of these states, even if the record is expunged, the information is still accessible to law enforcement, courts, and other government agencies. The meaning of the word can be misleading, because some expungement statutes only remove the court decision, but not evidence of the case itself, so if allowable, a defendant must specify the expungement of both the arrest records and the conviction records, or must first expunge the decision, and then seal the rest of the record. Others do not automatically remove the legal action from the public criminal record. Four states are featured below to provide examples of expungement statutes.

Expungement in Washington   Washington's equivalent of expungement is called "vacating a conviction." An applicant must wait between 3 years (misdemeanors) and up to 10 years (Class B felonies) from the time they completed their sentence. Vacating a record in Washington takes the conviction off of the record and gives the person the right to say they do not have a criminal record; however, the arrest records or other court records of that case without a finding of guilt remains. Once a conviction is vacated, it cannot be used as a part of one's criminal history for purposes of determining a sentence in any future conviction. For all purposes, including responding to questions on employment or housing applications, a person whose conviction has been vacated may state that he or she has never been convicted of that crime. An expunged conviction also results in having all civil rights restored for that conviction, except for owning a firearm.

Expungement in Ohio   In Ohio, after a period of three years for nonviolent first-time felonies, and after one year for misdemeanors, offenders pay a fee of $50 to be considered. If the judge agrees to expunge the records, at least 13 agencies must be notified, which makes it quite difficult to actually clear a person completely. Such expunged records include complaints, arrests, warrants, institutional commitments, photographs, fingerprints, judicial docket records, and presentence reports. In addition, the records are sealed rather than destroyed, and state law still permits sealed records to be viewed by some employers, such as agencies that work with children or the elderly (Horn 2000).

Expungement in Oregon   In Oregon, the applicant must pay an applicant fee of $80 and not be currently on any form of supervision. After a waiting period of one year from an arrest or three years or more for any misdemeanor or Class C Felony conviction, only one conviction can be expunged every ten years. Dismissed cases do not have to wait to apply for expungement. Traffic cases, Class B felonies, and Class A felonies are ineligible (Or. Rev. Stat. §137.225(1) through (12)).

Expungement in New Jersey   In New Jersey, a person may apply to expunge an "indictable offense" after 10 years, a "disorderly people" offense or a juvenile adjudication five years later, a municipal ordinance two years later, and a possession of a controlled substance charge as a juvenile one year after the sentence is completely served. Types of offenses that cannot be expunged include murder, manslaughter, kidnapping, sexual assault, crimes against children, arson, perjury, robbery, motor vehicle offenses, sale or distribution of large quantities of drugs, and occupational crimes committed by people holding public office. Even after records are expunged, certain occupations such as law enforcement, the judicial branch, and corrections agencies, still require applicants to report in detail information about any expunged arrests and/or convictions (Stewart Law Firm 2000).

SEALING OF RECORDS NOT RESULTING IN A CONVICTION

A more significant issue is the easy access to criminal records on the Internet. Defendants in some jurisdictions who have had their conviction expunged complain that evidence of the offense still appears (e.g., the offense appears with no decision or verdict leaving employers to question it). Extra steps may still need to be taken by the defendant to ensure that the expunged information is not disclosed in public databases. In some states, this may require an additional step known in some areas as sealing or a petition for nondisclosure. A **petition for nondisclosure** is a court order prohibiting public disclosure of the defendant's criminal history record. Other states call this **sealing of records;** it is the act or practice of officially preventing

petition for nondisclosure
A court order prohibiting public disclosure of the defendant's criminal history record

Sealing of Records
The legal concealment of a person's criminal (or juvenile) record such that it cannot be opened except by order of the court.

access to particular (esp. juvenile-criminal) records, in the absence of a court order (Garner 2009, p. 1377). Sealing differs from expungement in that in expungement the record is erased, whereas in sealing, specifically defined records are closed. Sealing of records usually applies to juvenile proceedings or adult diversion proceedings that have not resulted in a conviction.

As with expungement, the sealing process must be initiated by the offender. The applicant must establish that his or her desire to seal the records outweighs the right of the public to have access to that information. Sealed records restrict public access to everyone (including the person who wants the records sealed), and the person is not obligated to disclose any information to any employer, governmental agency, or any official. Legally, the applicant who has his or her records sealed can say no such records exist. Note that sealed records are retained and not physically destroyed. The only way sealed records can be examined is if the original applicant or a prosecutor files a court order and that order is granted by the court to unseal the record if public interest outweighs the original justification to seal.

In some states with sealing statutes (an example is Colorado), criminal records may be sealed only for crimes where a person was not charged, the case was dismissed, or the defendant was acquitted. Sealing may include the following records: fingerprint cards, arrest records, photos, the indictment, the prosecutorial information, competency hearing, a disposition, pretrial custody, correctional institution records while in custody, and any probation or parole records. No information involving a conviction may be sealed (Colorado Revised Statutes 1998, § 24-72-308).

It seems that in Washington state, convictions must first be vacated, and then the applicant may be able to apply to request that the record be sealed. Washington's sealing law was designed primarily to petition the court to seal arrest records or court records that have not led to a conviction. Record sealing is an option for dismissed cases, but is more difficult for deferrals and convictions (Washington Law GR-15, Chapter 10.97.060).

Although expungement and sealing are available procedures, their use is infrequent. As one writer notes: "[A]s more and more people have a criminal record, relief from the collateral consequences of conviction has never seemed more elusive in most of the states and for federal offenders. It would seem that if rehabilitation of criminal offenders is a desirable social goal, it would be helpful to begin serious discussion of the growing contrary pressures that seem to consign all persons with a criminal record to the margins of society, and to a permanent outcast status in the eyes of the law" (Love 2005, p. 12).

The removal of civil disabilities remains an open question. On the one hand, rehabilitated ex-offenders have a right to start their lives over with the tools that they have been given through treatment efforts. Conversely, however, the public has a right to know of the previous criminal record to protect itself against the recidivist offender. Kuzma (1998) points out the importance of achieving some kind of balance within these two competing perspectives:

> [Restrictions] . . . require careful consideration and reflection about whether the rigidity and severity of such an approach is justified by identifiable societal gains in protecting the community. . . . It's a tough issue for society as a whole to resolve. When has an offender paid his debt to society? The price for crime can't be too cheap, lest no one follow the law. Yet, do we achieve another bad result by making it impossible to stop paying for having committed a crime? (p. 72)

SUMMARY

- Collateral consequences, which are in the form of civil disabilities, can deprive a person of civil and political rights and may make finding or holding a job difficult.

- The types of civil disabilities for conviction vary from one state to another and are governed by federal and state laws.

- Some of the civil and political rights that are lost after conviction are the right to vote, serve on a jury, hold public office, own and possess a firearm, receive welfare benefits, and exercise parental rights.

- Private and public employers may discriminate against offenders unless such is prohibited by law.

- All 50 states and the District of Columbia have sex offender registration laws; most states also have sex offender notification laws.

- In some states, sexual predators may be civilly committed.

- Pardon is an act of grace and is available for offenders, but it is hard to obtain.

- The effects of a pardon vary from one state to another. In some states it erases guilt; in others it does not.

- Rights lost may be restored through various ways.

- Criminal records may be expunged or sealed, but their use is infrequent.

DISCUSSION QUESTIONS

1. If you were an employer, would you hire a former felon who has stayed out of trouble for five years? Support your answer.

2. Identify and discuss the variations in the type and extent of loss of civil rights of offenders.

3. "Former felons have the same rights and credibility as other witnesses in civil and criminal trials." Is that statement true or false? Explain your answer.

4. In your opinion, what are the arguments for and against sex offender registration laws?

5. Should the residents be notified about the presence of a sex offender in a neighborhood? Discuss this issue from the perspective of the residents and then from the perspective of the offender.

6. Assume you are an offender and are given a choice between an absolute pardon and a conditional pardon. Which would you prefer and why?

7. Are you in favor of restoring some, all, or none of the rights of ex-offenders discussed in this chapter? If you were a state legislator or a judge, which rights, if any, would you want restored and why?

8. Should an ex-felon be allowed to own or possess a firearm? Argue both sides of this issue.

9. Assume you are given a choice between expungement and sealing of a conviction. Which would be more appropriate and why?

10. Should ex-felons be given the right to vote? Explain why or why not.

WEB SITES

The Sentencing Project Discussion on Felony Disenfranchisement
> http://www.sentencingproject.org/Advocacy.aspx?IssueID=4

Federal Statutes Imposing Collateral Consequences Upon Conviction
> http://www.usdoj.gov/pardon/collateral_consequences.pdf

Felony Disenfranchisement
> http://www.sentencingproject.org/IssueAreaHome.aspx?IssueID=4

A discussion of eligibility for Federal housing for people who have been incarcerated
> www.mentalhealthcommission.gov/papers/CJ_ADACompliant.pdf

Dru Sjodin National Sex Offender Public Website (NSOPW) operated by the U.S. Department of Justice.
> http://www.nsopw.gov

State Sex Offender Registry Websites (Federal Bureau of Investigation)
> www.fbi.gov/hq/cid/cac/registry.htm

Special Issues in Community Corrections

Code Amber Sex Offender Registries by State
http://codeamber.org/sor.html

Resources from the Office of the Pardon Attorney
http://www.usdoj.gov/pardon/readingroom.htm

Pardon and Clemency in the United States
http://en.wikipedia.org/wiki/Pardon

Resources from the Office of the Pardon Attorney
http://www.usdoj.gov/pardon/readingroom.htm

Office of the Pardon Attorney Presidential pardons, 1945–2001
http://www.usdoj.gov/pardon/actions_administration.htm

Automatic Restoration of Rights
http://www.aclu.org/votingrights/exoffenders/index.html

The Pardon Resource Center: Twelve steps to a federal pardon
http://www.silicon-valley.com/pardonme/index.html

Expungement and Sealing Laws in Various States
http://www.recordclearing.org/states.htm

CASE STUDY EXERCISE

Should the Rights Lost Be Automatically Restored, or Should the Offender Apply for This Privilege?

This chapter presents controversial issues on the loss of rights as a result of conviction for a crime. States differ on what specific rights are lost upon conviction, the duration or the loss, and whether the rights lost should automatically be restored after the sentence is served or whether the right is restored only upon application by the ex-offender. There are no authoritative national answers to these hypothetical case studies because laws, court decisions, agency rules, and practices in the private sector vary. The aim of these case studies is to make the reader think about what he or she would do if given the final decision on what the law, court, agency chief, or private employer should say or would do in these cases. Each decision must be justified based on the reader's personal opinion instead of on what established law or practice says. In sum, disregard the law in these cases and simply give your well-considered opinion.

1. THE RIGHT TO VOTE: Assume that Citizen A, the head of a prominent investing firm in your community for many years, was charged, tried, and convicted of defrauding investors in his company. Prior to that, A was an active citizen in civic and humanitarian activities as well as in political circles. He was a member of the Rotary Club and was president of that organization for five years. He is sentenced to 10 years in prison. Assuming your state has no law governing this issue: (a) Should Citizen A be allowed to vote while he is in prison? (b) If your answer is no, should he be allowed to vote after he gets out of prison and is back in the community? and (c) if Citizen A were an ordinary member of the community, without any previous involvement or influence, would your answer be different?

2. THE RIGHT TO HOLD PUBLIC OFFICE: B, a current prominent member of your city council is charged, tried, and convicted of sexually harassing her male secretary while she was in office. She was convicted because she threatened to fire her male secretary if he did not engage in intimate relations with her. The secretary refused and was fired. Assume that kind of conduct by B is criminal in your state. B was placed on probation for two years, which she successfully served. She now wants to run for the same office, saying she has "learned her lesson," is now married, and promises to be on her best behavior if elected. You are in her district and voted for her in previous elections. Questions: (a) Should she be allowed to hold public office again? and (b) Will you vote for her again?

3. THE RIGHT TO PUBLIC EMPLOYMENT: C served time in city jail for one year because he was convicted of beating up his wife, which resulted in her confinement in a hospital for two days. He is now divorced from his wife and is jobless. He has served time in jail with good behavior and is applying for a job as a janitor at the community college where you are a student. Questions: (a) Are you in favor of hiring him for the job or not? (b) Assume that C in fact is a former professor in the community college and, after having served time for the same crime, is now reapplying for the same job as professor. Do you think

he should be rehired as professor? and (c) Assume C is a professor and was convicted of reckless homicide of a student because he recklessly drove one evening on campus while drunk. Would your answer be the same or different?

4. THE RIGHT TO AN OCCUPATIONAL LICENSE: D, a medical doctor in the community where you reside, was convicted of shooting one of his neighbors after they had a big fight. The fight ensued because D had an affair with his neighbor's wife, which the neighbor later discovered. D was placed on probation for five years on a plea bargain after pleading to the charge. Assume you are a legislator and are asked the following questions by reporters: (a) Should D be allowed to practice medicine while he is on probation? and (b) Should D be denied an occupational license if he violates the terms of his probation and serves time in prison for two years for the offense?

5. THE WISDOM OF A PRIVATE EMPLOYER: You are the owner of a big grocery store in town and run a successful business. One day, an applicant comes to you and applies for any job he could get in your store. He says he did not finish high school and did drugs. He further tells you that he was confined in a state institution for juveniles when he was 16 years old because he took part in a robbery with other members of a gang. He is now 20 years old, is no longer a member of a gang, uses drugs occasionally, and is in a rehabilitation program for drug users. As sole owner of the store, you have the final decision to hire or not to hire. What will you do and why?

6. THE RIGHT TO OWN A FIREARM: Citizen E is an avid hunter and a member of the local gun club. He has all kinds of firearms in his house, which he uses to hunt. One night, he had a serious quarrel with one of his neighbors. In a fit of great anger, he went inside the house, pulled out one of his guns, and shot and seriously injured the neighbor. This was his first offense ever involving a firearm. He was tried, convicted, and sentenced to serve 12 years in a state prison. While in prison, he was a model prisoner, and he was released on parole after eight years. Assume that both state and federal laws provide for C to be deprived of his right to own a firearm. Do you agree with these laws? Suppose C was convicted instead of shooting a burglar who broke into his home and was sentenced to serve time in jail for three months. Would your answer be the same? Suppose C was convicted of a misdemeanor using his firearm to threaten his wife and was given probation for that offense? Should he be allowed to keep his firearms?

7. PROVISIONS FOR SEX OFFENDER REGISTRATION AND NOTIFICATION: F, an immigrant carpenter who had a wife and three young children, was charged with and pleaded guilty to molesting the child of a rich couple for whom he worked occasionally. He did not want to plead guilty and claimed innocence all throughout the proceedings. But he pleaded guilty after spending almost a year in jail because he could not afford to post bail and could not support his family any longer while he was in jail (this is known in law as an Alford plea, a plea where a defendant pleads guilty for practical reasons even though he or she continues to maintain innocence). Assume that the state where F works provides for sex offender registration and notification. Should there be exceptions in those laws for offenders like F? Does it make any difference to your answer if you truly believe F is innocent?

8. THE RIGHT TO A PARDON: G, one of your former classmates, was convicted of rape while he was under the influence of drugs based mainly on the testimony of three witnesses who claimed to have been at the same fraternity party when the crime was committed. G is currently serving a 10-year sentence in a state prison. New DNA evidence now shows that G did not commit the offense and

that somebody else at the party did it, as proved by the DNA test results. The same three witnesses, however, say that they stand by their court testimony and that for them nothing has changed. Should G be pardoned as soon as possible by the governor (who is the only person authorized in the state to grant a pardon)? If the pardon is given, should it restore G's good moral character and all other rights he may have lost as a result of conviction?

9. THE DECISION TO EXPUNGE OR SEAL: J, a juvenile who was 15 years old when he committed a burglary, served time in a juvenile state institution. He had a string of offenses before that, including robbery and sale of drugs. He is now 18 years old and wants his juvenile records expunged and sealed. Assume you are the juvenile court judge before whom J's request is made. Assume further that your state law gives you, the judge, the discretion to expunge and seal juvenile records. Will you grant J's request? Does it make sense for you to grant J's motion to seal his record, but not grant expungement? Or vice versa? Will your decision be the same or different if J's only offense was that burglary and he had an exemplary record while in the juvenile state institution?

Glossary

absconder   An offender under community supervision who, without prior permission, escapes or flees the jurisdiction he or she is required to stay within.

absolute immunity   Protection from legal action or liability unless workers engage in discretion that is intentionally and maliciously wrong.

active GPS   A real-time GPS system that transmits data through wireless networks continuously at a rate of once or twice per minute. A phone line continually calls a reporting station to update the offender's location, which is tracked by a computer.

adjudication   Juvenile justice equivalent of a trial in adult criminal cases.

Alexander Maconochie   A British naval captain who served as governor of the penal colony on Norfolk Island, who instituted a system of early release that was the forerunner of modern parole. Maconochie is known as the "father of parole."

amercement   A monetary penalty imposed arbitrarily at the discretion of the court for an offense.

attainder   At common law, the extinction of civil rights and capacities that occurred when a person received a sentence of death or outlawry for treason or another felony. The person's estate was forfeited to the Crown.

automatic restoration of rights   Reinstatement of some or all civil rights upon completion of sentence. The extent of restoration varies by state and by offense type.

bail   Monetary payment deposited with the court to ensure the defendant's return for the next court date in exchange for the defendant's release.

boot camp   A form of shock incarceration that involves a military-style regimen designed to instill discipline in young offenders.

brokerage of services   Supervision that involves identifying the needs of probationers or parolees and referring them to an appropriate community agency.

caseload   The number of individuals or cases for which one probation or parole officer is responsible.

casework   A community supervision philosophy that allowed the officer to create therapeutic relationships with clients through counseling and directly assisting in behavior modification to assist them in living productively in the community.

certificate of discharge   Official written document signifying that an offender has completed his or her sentence.

civil disenfranchisement   The loss of the right to vote for felony offenders.

civil rights   Rights that belong to a person by virtue of citizenship.

classification   A procedure consisting of assessing the risks posed by the offender, identifying the supervision issues, and selecting the appropriate supervision strategy.

clear conditions   Conditions that are sufficiently explicit so as to inform a reasonable person of the conduct that is required or prohibited.

clemency   An act of mercy by a governor or the president to erase consequences of a criminal act, accusation, or conviction.

cognitive-behavioral therapy   A therapeutic intervention of helping a person change, that is a blend of two different types of therapies: cognitive therapy which prepares the mind, and behavioral change which conditions the body.

collateral consequences   Disabilities that follow a conviction that are not directly imposed by a sentencing court—such as loss of the right to vote, serve on a jury, practice certain occupations, or own a firearm.

collateral contact   Verification of the probationer or parolee's situation and whereabouts by means of the officer speaking with a third party who knows the offender personally (such as a family member, friend, or employer).

community corrections   A nonincarcerative sanction in which offenders serve all or a portion of their sentence in the community.

Community Corrections Act   Formal written agreement between the state government and local entities for the state to fund counties to implement and operate community corrections programs on a local level.

community justice   A philosophy of using the community to control and reduce crime through community policing, community courts, restorative justice, and broken-windows probation.

community resource management team (CRMT) model   A supervision model in which probation or parole officers develop skills and linkages with community agencies in one or two areas only. Supervision under this model is a team effort, each officer utilizing his or her skills and linkages to assist the offender.

community service   Unpaid labor for the public to compensate society for harm done by the offense of conviction.

commutation   Shortening sentence length or changing a punishment to one that is less severe, as from a death sentence to life in prison without parole.

completion rates   Individuals who are favorably discharged from drug court as a percentage of the total number admitted and not still enrolled.

concurrent jurisdiction   Original jurisdiction for certain juvenile cases is shared by both criminal and juvenile courts, with the prosecutor having discretion to file such cases in either court.

conditional pardon   A pardon that becomes operative when the grantee has performed some specific act(s) or that becomes void when some specific act(s) transpires.

conduct in need of supervision (CINS)   Acts committed by juveniles that would not have been punishable if committed by adults; status offenses.

conviction   A judgment of the court, based on a defendant's plea of guilty *or nolo contendere*, or on the verdict of a judge or jury, that the defendant is guilty of the offense(s) with which he or she has been charged.

day fines   Fines that are calculated by multiplying a percentage of the offender's daily wage by the number of predefined punishment units (the number of punishment units depend on the seriousness of the crime).

day reporting centers   Nonresidential programs typically used for defendants on pretrial release, for convicted offenders on probation or parole, or as an increased sanction for probation or parole violators. Services are provided in one central location, and offenders must check in daily.

delegated release authority   Statutory authority that allows pretrial services officers to release the defendant before the initial court appearance in front of the judge.

determinate sentence   A sentencing model that establishes a narrow range of punishment for a specific crime, taking previous criminal convictions into consideration.

determinate sentencing   A sentencing philosophy that focuses on consistency for the crime committed, specifying by statute or sentencing guidelines an exact amount or narrow range of time to be served in prison or in the community, which mandates the minimum amount of time before the offender is eligible (if at all) for release. Also known as a presumptive, fixed, or mandatory sentence.

diminished constitutional rights   Constitutional rights enjoyed by an offender on parole that are not as highly protected by the courts as the rights of nonoffenders.

disclosure   The right of a defendant to read and refute information in the presentence investigation report prior to sentencing.

discretionary release   Conditional release because members of a parole board have decided that the prisoner has earned the privilege while still remaining under supervision of an indeterminate sentence.

disposition   Juvenile justice equivalent of sentencing in adult cases.

diversion   An alternative program to traditional criminal sentencing or juvenile justice adjudication that provides first-time offenders with a chance or addresses unique treatment needs, with the successful completion resulting in the dismissal of the current charges.

drug courts   A diversion program for drug addicts in which the judge, prosecutor, and probation officer play a proactive role and monitor the progress of clients through weekly visits to the courtroom, using a process of graduated sanctions.

due process   Laws must be applied in a fair and equal manner. Fundamental fairness.

dynamic factors   Correlates of the likelihood of recidivism that can be changed through treatment and rehabilitation (drug and alcohol abuse, anger management, quality of family relationships, and so forth).

early termination   Termination of probation at any time during the probation period or after some time has been served.

electronic monitoring   A correctional technology used as a tool in intensive supervision probation, parole, day reporting, or home confinement, using a radio frequency or satellite technology to track offender whereabouts using a transmitter and receiver.

evidence-based practice   Integrating into everyday practice the correctional programs and techniques that have been shown to be the most effective with offenders using evaluation results from systematically evaluated research studies.

exclusion zones   Exact locations the offender is prohibited from being in or near.

exclusionary rule   A rule of evidence that enforces the Fourth Amendment's prohibition against unreasonable search and seizure, whereby illegal police searches are not admissible in a court of law. The purpose is to deter police misconduct.

expungement of record   An erasure. Process by which the record of a criminal conviction (or juvenile adjudication) is destroyed or sealed after expiration of time.

failure to appear   A situation in which a defendant does not attend a scheduled court hearing.

fee   A monetary amount imposed by the court to assist in administering the criminal justice system by the offender's repayment of debt accrued by the investigation, prosecution, and supervision of the case.

field contact   An officer's personal visit to an offender's home or place of employment for the purpose of monitoring progress under supervision.

filing   A procedure under which an indictment was "laid on file," or held in abeyance, without either dismissal or final judgment in cases in which justice did not require an immediate sentence.

final revocation hearing   A due process hearing that must be conducted before probation or parole can be revoked.

fine   A fixed monetary sanction defined by statute and imposed by a judge, depending on the seriousness of the crime.

forfeiture   A government seizure of property that was illegally obtained, was acquired with resources that were illegally obtained, or was used in connection with an illegal activity.

full board review   The statutory requirement that all members of the parole board review and vote on the early release from prison of individuals who have committed felony crimes, usually of a violent or sexual nature. Some states require this type of review on every discretionary release.

full pardon   A pardon without any attached conditions.

global positioning system   A system that uses 24 military satellites orbiting the earth to pinpoint the offender's exact location intermittently or at all times.

good moral character   The totality of virtues that form the basis of one's reputation in the community.

good time   Sentence reduction of a specified number of days each month for good conduct.

halfway house   The oldest and most common type of community residential facility for probationers or parolees who require a more structured setting than would be available if living independently.

hearsay evidence   Information offered as a truthful assertion that does not come from the personal knowledge of the person giving the information but from knowledge that person received from a third party.

home-based electronic monitoring   An intermittent or continuous radio frequency signal transmitted through a land line telephone or wireless unit into a receiver that determines whether the offender is or is not at home.

house arrest   A community-based sanction in which offenders serve their sentence at home. Offenders have curfews and may not leave their home except for employment and correctional treatment purposes. Also called home detention or home confinement.

inclusion zones   Exact locations, such as employment, school, or an appointment, where the offender is required to be at a certain time.

indeterminate sentence   A sentencing philosophy that encourages rehabilitation and incorporates a broad sentencing range where discretionary release is determined by a parole board based on the offender's remorse, insight into his or her mistakes, involvement in rehabilitation, and readiness to return to society.

in-service training   Periodic continuing education training for seasoned officers.

institutional corrections   An incarcerative sanction in which offenders serve their sentence away from the community in a jail or prison institution.

intake   The process whereby a juvenile is screened to determine if the case should proceed further in the juvenile justice system or whether other alternatives are better suited for the juvenile.

intensive supervision probation   A form of probation that stresses intensive monitoring, close supervision, and offender control.

intermediate sanctions   A spectrum of community supervision strategies that vary greatly in terms of their supervision level and treatment capacity, ranging from diversion to short-term duration in a residential community facility.

interstate compact   An agreement signed by all states and U.S. territories that allows for the supervision of parolees and probationers across state lines.

Interstate Compact for Adult Offender Supervision   A formalized decree granting authority to a commission to create and enforce rules for member states for the supervision of offenders in other states.

Irish System   Developed in Ireland by Sir Walter Crofton, the Irish system involved graduated levels of institutional control leading up to release under conditions similar to modern parole. The American penitentiaries were partially based on the Irish system.

John Augustus   A Boston bootmaker who was the founder of probation in the United States.

just deserts   The concept that the goal of corrections should be to punish offenders because they deserve to be punished and that punishment should be commensurate with the seriousness of the offense.

justice model   The correctional practice based on the concept of just deserts and even-handed punishment. The justice model calls for fairness in criminal sentencing, in that all people convicted of a similar offense will receive a like sentence. This model of corrections relies on determinate sentencing and/or abolition of parole.

juvenile delinquency   Acts committed by juveniles that are punishable as crimes under a state's penal code.

law violations   Violations of probation or parole conditions that involve the commission of a crime.

liberty interest   Any interest recognized or protected by the due process clauses of state or federal constitutions.

mandatory release   Conditional release to the community under a determinate sentence that is automatic at the expiration of the minimum term of sentence minus any credited time off for good behavior.

marks system   A theory of human motivation organized by Maconochie that granted credits for good behavior and hard work, or took away marks for negative behavior. Convicts used the credits or marks to purchase either goods or time (reduction in sentence).

maximum eligibility date   The longest amount of time that can be served before the inmate must be released by law.

medical model   The concept that, given proper care and treatment, criminals can be cured into productive, law-abiding citizens. This approach suggests that people commit crimes because of influences beyond their control, such as poverty, injustice, and racism.

medical parole   The conditional release from prison to the community of a prisoner with a terminal illness who does not pose an undue risk to public safety.

mental health courts   A diversion program for mentally ill defendants in which the judge, prosecutor, and probation officer play a proactive role and monitor the progress of clients through weekly visits to the courtroom.

mens rea   Latin term meaning "guilty mind" that addresses level of mental intent to commit a crime.

minimum eligibility date   The shortest amount of time defined by statute, minus good time earned, that must be served before the offender can go before the parole board.

moral turpitude   An act of vileness, or socially offensive behavior, that is contrary to justice, honesty or the public's accepted moral standards.

motion to quash   An oral or written request that the court repeal, nullify, or overturn a decision, usually made during or after the trial.

motivational interviewing   A communication style in which the community supervision officer creates a positive climate of sincerity and understanding that assists the offender in the change process

negligence   The failure of an officer to do what a reasonably prudent person would have done in like or similar circumstances.

neighborhood-based supervision   A supervision strategy that emphasizes public safety, accountability, partnerships with other community agencies, and beat supervision.

net widening   Using stiffer punishment or excessive control for low-risk offenders who would have ordinarily been sentenced to a lesser sanction.

Norfolk Island   The notorious British supermax penal colony 1,000 miles off the coast of Australia that housed the most incorrigible prisoners.

offender-based presentence report   A presentence investigation report that seeks to understand the offender and the circumstances of the offense and to evaluate the offender's potential as a law-abiding, productive citizen.

offense-based presentence report   A presentence investigation report that focuses primarily on the offense committed, the offender's culpability, and prior criminal history.

outlawry   In old Anglo-Saxon law, the process by which a criminal was declared an outlaw and placed outside the protection and aid of the law.

pardon   An executive act of clemency that serves to mitigate or set aside punishment for a crime.

parens patriae   Latin term meaning that the government acts as a "substitute parent" and allows the courts to intervene in cases in which it is in the child's best interest that a guardian be appointed for children who, through no fault of their own, have been neglected and/or are dependent.

parole   Early privileged release of a convicted offender from a penal or correctional institution, under the continual custody of the state, to serve the remainder of his or her sentence in the community under supervision.

parole board   An administrative body empowered to decide whether inmates shall be conditionally released from prison before the completion of their sentence, to revoke parole, and to discharge from parole those who have satisfactorily completed their terms.

parole conditions   The rules under which a paroling authority releases an offender to community supervision.

parole d'honneur   French for "word of honor," from which the English word parole is derived.

parole eligibility date   The point in a prisoner's sentence at which he or she becomes eligible to be considered for parole. If the offender is denied parole, a new parole eligibility date is scheduled in the future.

passive GPS   A GPS system that temporarily stores location data that is downloaded through a landline phone once every 24 hours or at specific times when the offender is home.

Peace Officer State Training   Specialized and standardized training that officers are required to complete before they may carry a firearm on the job.

penile plethysmograph   A device that measures erectile responses in male sex offenders to determine level of sexual arousal to various types of stimuli. This device is used for assessment and treatment purposes.

petition for nondisclosure   A court order prohibiting public disclosure of the defendant's criminal history record.

political rights   Rights related to the participation in the establishment, support, or management of government.

postsentence report   A report written by a probation officer after the defendant has pled guilty and been sentenced in order to aid probation and parole officers in supervision, classification, and program plans.

preferred rights   Rights more highly protected than other constitutional rights.

preliminary hearing   An inquiry conducted to determine if there is probable cause to believe that the offender committed a probation or parole violation.

preponderance of the evidence   A level of proof used in a probation revocation administrative hearing, in which the judge decides based on which side presents more convincing evidence and its probable truth or accuracy, and not necessarily on the amount of evidence.

prerelease facility   A minimum-security prison that houses inmates who have earned this privilege through good institutional conduct and who are nearing their release date.

prerelease plan   A case management summary of institutional conduct and program participation, as well as plans for housing and employment upon release, that is submitted to the parole board in cases of discretionary parole or to the parole officer in cases of automatic release.

prerelease program   A minimum-security community-based or institutional setting for offenders who have spent time in prison and are nearing release. The focus of these programs includes transitioning, securing a job, and reestablishing family connections.

presentence investigation   An investigation undertaken by a probation officer for the purpose of gathering and analyzing information to complete a report for the court.

presentence investigation (PSI) report   A report submitted to the court before sentencing describing the nature of the offense, offender characteristics, criminal history, loss to the victim, and sentencing recommendations.

preservice training   Fundamental knowledge and/or skills for a newly hired officer in preparation for working independently.

presumptive sentence   A statutorily determined sentence that offenders will presumably receive if convicted. Offenders convicted in a jurisdiction with presumptive sentences will be assessed this sentence unless mitigating or aggravating circumstances are found to exist.

presumptive sentencing grid   A narrow range of sentencing guidelines that judges are obligated to use. Any deviations must be provided in writing and may also be subject to appellate court review.

pretrial release   A defendant's release in the community following arrest as an alternative to detention while the defendant prepares for the next scheduled court appearance.

pretrial supervision   Court-ordered correctional supervision of a defendant who has not yet been convicted whereby the defendant participates in activities such as reporting, house arrest, and electronic monitoring to ensure appearance at the next court date.

principles of effective intervention   Eight treatment standards that, if practiced, have been shown to reduce recidivism above that of other methods and constitute a theory behind evidence-based correctional practices.

prisoner reentry   Any activity or program conducted to prepare ex-convicts to return safely to the community and to live as law-abiding citizens.

private service provider   Any for profit or non-profit private organization that contracts with county-level or state-level government to provide probation supervision, independent probation treatment services, or both probation supervision and treatment.

private probation   An agency that is owned and operated by a private business or nonprofit organization, and contracts with the state, local, or federal government to supervise clients convicted of a misdemeanor.

probation   The community supervision of a convicted offender in lieu of incarceration under conditions imposed by the court for a specified period during which the court retains authority to modify the conditions or to resentence the offender if he or she violates the conditions.

public employment   Paid employment at any level of government.

public office   Uncompensated, elected or appointed government position.

qualified immunity   Protection from liability in decisions or actions that are "objectively reasonable."

real-time access   Instant and immediate access via a supervising officer's internet connection to pinpoint the exact location of offenders on GPS monitoring with a 30-second delay.

reasonable conditions   Probation conditions that the offender can reasonably comply with.

receiving state   Under the interstate compact, the state that undertakes the supervision.

recidivism   The repetition of or return to criminal behavior, variously defined in one of three ways: rearrest, reconviction, or reincarceration.

recognizance   Originally a device of preventive justice that obliged people suspected of future misbehavior to stipulate with and give full assurance to the court and the public that the apprehended offense would not occur. Recognizance was later used with convicted or arraigned offenders with conditions of release set.

reentry   The process of preparing and integrating parolees into the community as law-abiding citizens using a collaborative approach with parole officers and treatment providers.

reentry courts   A collaborative, team-based program that aims to improve the link between parole supervision and treatment providers to help recent parolees become stabilized.

reflective justice   Each defendant's case is considered in total according to its subjectivities, harms, wrongs, and contexts, and then measured against concepts such as oppression, freedom, dignity, and equality.

Rehabilitation Certificate   A certificate that allows former offenders to obtain a license or work in certain occupations that have barred felons upon conviction.

relapse   When an offender with a substance abuse problem returns to using alcohol or drugs.

remote location monitoring   When a supervising officer uses a hand-held remote receiver to wirelessly verify an offender's physical location.

reprieve   Postponing or interrupting a sentence (for example, a prison term or an execution).

residential community corrections facilities   A sanction in the community in which the convicted offender lives at the facility and must be employed, but can leave the facility for a limited purpose and duration if preapproved. Examples include halfway houses, prerelease centers, restitution centers, drug treatment facilities, and work release centers.

restitution   Court-ordered payment by the offender to the victim to cover tangible losses that occurred during or following the crime.

restitution center   A type of residential community facility specifically targeted for property or first-time offenders who owe victim restitution or community service.

restorative justice   Various sentencing philosophies and practices that emphasize the offender taking responsibility to repair the harm done to the victim and to the surrounding community. Includes forms of victim offender mediation, reparation panels, circle sentencing, and monetary sanctions.

retention rates   The combined total of the successful completers and those actively enrolled compared to the total number admitted to drug court.

revocation   The process of hearings that results when the probationer is noncompliant with the current level of probation. Results of a revocation are either modifying probation conditions to a more intensive supervision level, or the complete elimination of probation and sentence to a residential community facility, jail, or prison.

risk assessment   A procedure that provides a measure of the offender's propensity to further criminal activity and indicates the level of officer intervention that will be required.

role ambiguity   The discretion that exists in the role of the probation and parole officer to treat clients fairly and consistently and according to individual circumstances.

role conflict   The two functions of a probation and parole officer, that of enforcing the rules and laws, and providing support and reintegration, that are sometimes contradictory and difficult to reconcile.

Salient Factor Score   The parole guidelines developed and used by the U.S. Parole Commission for making parole release decisions. Served as the model for parole guidelines developed in many other jurisdictions.

school-based probation   A type of probation where probation officers move out of traditional district offices into middle, junior high, and high school buildings and supervise their caseloads right in the schools.

sealing of records   The legal concealment of a person's criminal (or juvenile) record such that it cannot be opened except by order of the court.

security for good behavior   A recognizance or bond given the court by a defendant before or after conviction conditioned on his or her being "on good behavior" or keeping the peace for a prescribed period.

sending state   Under the interstate compact, the state of conviction.

sentencing   The postconviction stage, in which the defendant is brought before the court for formal judgment pronounced by a judge.

sentencing commission   A governing body that monitors the use of the sentencing guidelines and departures from the recommended sentences.

shock incarceration   A brief period of incarceration followed by a term of supervised probation. Also called shock probation, shock parole, intermittent imprisonment, or split sentence.

Sir Walter Crofton   An Irish prison reformer who established an early system of parole based on Alexander Maconochie's experiments with the mark system.

special conditions   Conditions tailored to fit the needs of an offender.

standard conditions   Conditions imposed on all offenders in all jurisdictions.

standard of proof   The level of proof, measured by the strength of the evidence, needed to render a decision in a court proceeding.

static factors   Correlates of the likelihood of recidivism that (once they occur) cannot be changed (age at first arrest, number of convictions, and so forth).

statutory exclusion   The automatic exclusion of certain juvenile offenders from juvenile court jurisdiction by state statute, requiring the case to be filed directly with the adult criminal court.

subornation of perjury   the criminal act of persuading another person to commit perjury.

supervision   The oversight that a probation or parole officer exercises over those in his or her custody.

surety   An individual who agrees to become responsible for the debt of a defendant or who answers for the performance of the defendant should the defendant fail to attend the next court appearance.

surety bond   A certificate signed by the principal and a third party, promising to pay in the event the assured suffers damages or losses because the employee fails to perform as agreed.

suspended sentence   An order of the court after a verdict, finding, or plea of guilty that suspends or postpones the imposition or execution of sentence during a period of good behavior.

technical violations   Multiple violations that breach one or more noncriminal conditions of probation.

therapeutic community   A type of residential community facility specifically targeted for drug offenders, offenders who are alcoholics, and/or drug addicts who are amenable to treatment.

ticket-of-leave   A license or permit given to a convict as a reward for good conduct, which allowed him to go at large and work for himself before his sentence expired, subject to certain restrictions and revocable upon subsequent misconduct. A forerunner of parole.

transfer of jurisdiction   The transfer of a juvenile from juvenile court to adult court for trial.

transportation   The forced exile of convicted criminals. England transported convicted criminals to the American colonies until the Revolutionary War and afterward to Australia.

unconditional release   A type of release from prison without correctional supervision because the full sentence has been served behind bars. Also known as "maxing out" or "killing your number."

victim compensation fund   A state fund that dispenses compensation to victims of violent crime and is paid for by offenders who are convicted.

victim impact statement   A written account by the victim(s) as to how the crime has taken a toll physically, emotionally, financially, or psychologically on the victim and the victim's family. Victim impact statements are considered by many states at time of sentencing and at parole board hearings.

widening the net   When an individual who should have received probation is sentenced to a harsher intermediate sanction only because that sanction is available, not because the offender requires more intensive supervision.

work ethic camp   A 120-day alternative to prison that teaches job skills and decision making using a cognitive–behavioral approach, followed by intensive supervision probation.

work release   A program in which offenders who reside in a facility (a community facility, jail, or prison) are released into the community only to work or attend education classes or both.

youth courts   Community-based programs in which youth sentence their peers for minor delinquent and status offenses. Also known as teen, peer, and student courts.

Zebulon R. Brockway   The American prison reformer who introduced modern correctional methods, including parole, to the Elmira Reformatory in New York in 1876.

References

Abadinsky, Howard. 1978. Parole history: An economic perspective. *Offender Rehabilitation* 2(3): 275–278.

Acoca, Leslie, and James Austin. 1996. *The crisis: The woman offender sentencing study and alternative sentencing recommendations project: Women in prison.* Washington, DC: National Council on Crime and Delinquency.

Adams, Devon B. 2002. *Summary of state sex offender registries, 2001.* Washington, DC: U.S. Department of Justice, Bureau of Justice Statistics.

Administrative Office of the U.S. Courts. 2003. *The supervision of federal defendants* [Monograph 111]. Washington, DC: Administrative Office of the U.S. Courts.

Administrative Office of the U.S. Courts. 2005a. *The pretrial services investigation and report* [Monograph 112]. Washington, DC: Administrative Office of the U.S. Courts.

Administrative Office of the U.S. Courts. 2005b. *The presentence investigation report for defendants sentenced under the Sentencing Reform Act of 1984* [Monograph 107]. Washington, DC: Administrative Office of the U.S. Courts.

Administrative Office of the U.S. Courts. 2006. Gang member supervision growing part of job for probation officers. *The Third Branch* 38(2): 1–3. Retrieved from: http://www.uscourts.gov/ttb/02-06/gangsupervision/index.html.

Administrative Office of the U.S. Courts. 2007. *The supervision of federal offenders* [Monograph 109]. Washington, DC: Administrative Office of the U.S. Courts.

Alarid, Leanne F., and Paul Cromwell. 2006. *In her own words: Women offenders' views on crime and victimization.* Los Angeles, CA: Roxbury.

Alarid, Leanne F., Leslie A. Hernandez, and Christine S. Schloss. 2009. Utilization of community-based programs: Which sanctions do attorneys recommend?" *The Criminal Law Bulletin,* 45 (5): 847–860.

Alarid, Leanne F., and Carlos D. Montemayor. 2009. Legal and Extralegal Factors in Attorney Recommendations of Pretrial Diversion. An unpublished manuscript.

Alarid, Leanne F., and Carlos D. Montemayor. (forthcoming). "Attorney Perspectives and Decisions on the Presentence Investigation Report: A Research Note." *Criminal Justice Policy Review.*

Alarid, Leanne F., and Christine S. Schloss. 2009. Attorney views on the use of private agencies for probation supervision and treatment. *International Journal of Offender Therapy and Comparative Criminology* 53 (3):278–291.

Alarid, Leanne F., Barbara A. Sims, and James Ruiz. 2010. School-Based Juvenile Probation and Police Partnerships for Truancy Reduction. An unpublished manuscript.

Albonetti, Celesta A., and John R. Hepburn. 1997. Probation revocation: A proportional hazards model of the conditioning effects of social disadvantage. *Social Problems* 441: 124–137.

Alexander, Melissa, Scott W. VanBenschoten, and Scott T. Walters. 2008. Motivational interviewing training in criminal justice: Development of a model plan. *Federal Probation* 72 (2), 61–66.

Allen, Frederick G., and Harvey Treger. 1994. Fines and restitution orders: Probationers' perceptions. *Federal Probation* 58(2): 34–40.

Alonso, Alfonso. 2009. *Best practices for drug courts.* An unpublished Master's thesis. University of Nevada Reno.

Altschuler, David M. 1999. Trends and issues in the adultification of juvenile justice. In *Research to results: Effective community corrections,* edited by Patricia M. Harris. Lanham, MD: American Correctional Association, pp. 233–271.

American Bar Association. 1994. *Standards for criminal justice, sentencing,* 3rd ed. Sec. 18–3.16f.

American Friends Service Committee. 1971. *Struggle for justice.* New York: Hill and Wang.

American Probation and Parole Association. n.d. APPA position statement: Community justice. Retrieved from: http://www.appa-net.org/about%20appa/communityjustice_1.htm.

———. 1994. APPA position statement: Weapons. Retrieved from: http://www.appa-net.org/about%20appa/weapons.htm.

———. 2006. *APPA adult and juvenile probation and parole national firearm survey 2005–2006.* Lexington, KY: APPA. Retrieved from: http://www.appa-net.org/information%20clearing%20house/survey.htm.

Anderson, David C. 1998. *Sensible justice: Alternatives to prison.* New York: New Press.

Anderson, James F., Laronstine Dyson, and Jerald Burns. 1999. *Boot camps: An intermediate sanction.* Lanham, NY: University Press of America.

Andrews, Don A., and James Bonta. 1998. *The psychology of criminal conduct,* 2nd ed. Cincinnati, OH: Anderson.

Andrews, Don A., James Bonta, and J. Stephen Wormith. 2006. The recent past and near future of risk and/or need assessment. *Crime and Delinquency* 52(1): 7–27.

Andrews, Sara and Linda S. Janes. 2006. Four-point strategy reduces technical violations of probation in Connecticut. *Topics in Community Corrections: Effectively Managing Violations and Revocations.* Longmont, CO: National Institute of Corrections.

Annison, Jill, Tina Eadie, and Charlotte Knight. 2008. People first: Probation officer perspectives on probation work. *Probation Journal* 55 (3): 259–271.

Aos, Steve, Marna Miller, and Elizabeth Drake. 2006. *Evidence-based adult corrections programs: What works and what does not.* Olympia, WA: Washington State Institute for Public Policy. Retrieved from: http://www.wsipp.wa.gov/rptfiles/06-01-1201.pdf

Arditti, Joyce A., and April L. Few. 2006. Mothers' reentry into family life following incarceration. *Criminal Justice Policy Review* 17(1): 103–123.

Armstrong, Gaylene and Beth Freeman. 2009. *GPS monitoring of sex offenders in Maricopa county, Arizona.* Paper presented at the annual meeting of the Academy of Criminal Justice Sciences, Boston, MA.

Associated Press. 2006. The truth is out with second autopsy: Boy's boot-camp death now said to be result of beating. *The Kansas City Star,* March 17, A7.

Association of Paroling Authorities International. 2005. *Parole Board Survey 2005.* APAI: Association of Paroling Authorities International. Retrieved from: http://www.apaintl.org/content/en/pdf/2005_ParolingAuthorities_Survey.pdf

Augustus, John. 1939. *First probation officer.* New York: National Probation Association.

———. 1972. *A report of the labors of John Augustus, for the last ten years, in aid of the unfortunate.* Montclair, NJ: Patterson Smith. (Originally published 1852)

Austin, James. 2001. Prisoner reentry: Current trends, practices, and issues. *Crime and Delinquency* 47(3): 314–334.

Bahr, Stephen J., Anita Harker Armstrong, Benjamin Guild Gibbs, Paul E. Harris, and James K. Fisher. 2005. The reentry process: How parolees adjust to release from prison. *Fathering* 3(3): 243–265.

Barklage, Heather, Dane Miller and Gene Bonham. 2006. Probation conditions versus probation officer directives: Where the twain shall meet. *Federal Probation* 70(3):37–41.

Barthwell, Andrea G., Peter Bokos, J. Bailey, Miriam Nisenbaum, Julien Devereux, and Edward C. Senay. 1995. Interventions/Wilmer: A continuum of care for substance abusers in the criminal justice system. *Journal of Psychoactive Drugs* 27(1): 39–47.

Barton, William, and Jeffrey A. Butts. 1990. Viable options: Intensive supervision programs for juvenile delinquents. *Crime and Delinquency* 36(2): 238–256.

Barton, William, and Cheryl Justice. 2000. The John P. Craine House: A community residential program for female offenders and their children. Paper presented at the annual meeting of the American Society of Criminology, San Francisco, California, November 14–17.

Baumer, Eric P., Ian O'Donnell, and N. Hughes. 2009. The porous prison. *The Prison Journal* 89(1): 119–126.

Bayens, Gerald, Michael Manske, and John Ortiz Smylka. 1998. The attitudes of criminal justice workgroups toward intensive supervised probation. *American Journal of Criminal Justice* 22(2): 189–206.

Bazemore, Gordon, and Jeanne Stinchcomb. 2004. A civic engagement model of reentry: Involving community through service and restorative justice. *Federal Probation* 68(2): 14–24.

Bazemore, Gordon, and Mark Umbreit. 2001. A comparison of four restorative conferencing models. *Juvenile Justice Bulletin* (February). Washington, DC: U.S. Department of Justice, Office of Juvenile Justice and Delinquency Programs.

Beck, Allen J. 2000. *Prisoners in 1999.* Washington, DC: U.S. Department of Justice, Bureau of Justice Statistics.

Beck, V.S. and Lawrence F. Travis. 2004. Sex offender notification and fear of victimization. *Journal of Criminal Justice* 32 (5): 455–463.

Bennish, Steve. 2008. Technology helps gangs go hi-tech. *Dayton Daily News,* February 18.

Berk, Jillian. 2008. Does work release work? Retrieved from: http://client.norc.org/jole/SOLEweb/8318.pdf

Bernat, Frances P., William Parsonage, and Jacqueline Helfgott. 1994. Victim impact laws and the parole process in the United States: Balancing victim and inmate rights and interests. *International Review of Victimology* 3(1/2): 121–133.

Berry, William W. 2009. Extraordinary and compelling: A re-examination of the justifications for compassionate release. *Maryland Law Review* 68 (4), 115–141.

Beto, Dan Richard. 2000. Reinventing probation: A history of the national movement and the Texas initiative. *Criminal Justice Mandate* 8(1): 9–13.

Bexar County Diversion Program. 2006. Providing jail diversion for people with mental illness. *Psychiatric Services* 57 (10): 1521–1523.

BI Inc. 2009. BI products and services. Retrieved from: http://www.bi.com

Binder, Arnold, Gilbert Geis, and Dickson D. Bruce. 1997. *Juvenile delinquency,* 2nd ed. Cincinnati, OH: Anderson.

Bloom, Barbara, and Anne McDiarmid. 2000. Gender-responsive supervision and programming for women offenders in the community. In *Topics in community corrections annual issue 2000: Responding to women in the community.* Longmont, CO: LIS, Inc. and National Institute of Corrections.

Bonczar, Thomas P. 1997. *Characteristics of adults on probation.* Washington, DC: U.S. Department of Justice.

Bonczar, Thomas P., and Lauren E. Glaze. 1999. *Probation and parole in the United States, 1998.* Washington, DC: U.S. Department of Justice, Bureau of Justice Statistics.

Bonta, James, S. Wallace-Capretta, and J. Rooney. 2000. A quasi-experimental evaluation of an intensive rehabilitation supervision program. *Criminal Justice and Behavior* 29(June): 312–329.

Boothby, Jennifer L. and Lorraine Y. Overduin. 2007. Attitudes regarding the compassionate release of terminally ill offenders. *The Prison Journal* 87(4), 408–415.

Bosco, Robert J. 1998. Connecticut probation's partnership with the private sector. In *Topics in community corrections: Annual issue 1998: Privatizing community supervision.* Longmont, CO: National Institute of Corrections, U.S. Department of Justice, pp. 8–12.

Bottcher, Jean, and Michael E. Ezell. 2005. Examining the effectiveness of boot camps: A randomized experiment with a long-term follow-up. *Journal of Research in Crime and Delinquency* 42(3): 309–332.

Bouffard, Jeffrey and Lisa R. Muftic. 2007. The effectiveness of community service sentences compared to traditional fines for low-level offenders. *The Prison Journal* 87 (2):171–194.

Bourque, Blair B., Mei Han, and Sarah M. Hill. 1996. *A National Survey of Aftercare Provisions for Boot Camp Graduates*. NCJ 157664. Washington, DC: National Institute of Justice.

Brady, Brian. 2008. Prisoners to be chipped like dogs. *The Independent*, January 13. Retrieved from: http://www.independent.co.uk/news/uk/politics/prisoners-to-be-chipped-like-dogs-769977.html

Braithwaite, John. 1989. *Crime, shame, and reintegration*. Cambridge, NY: Cambridge University Press.

Brame, Robert, and Doris Layton MacKenzie. 1996. Shock incarceration and positive adjustment during community supervision: A multisite evaluation. In *Correctional boot camps: A tough intermediate sanction*, edited by Doris L. MacKenzie and Eugene E. Hebert. Washington, DC: U.S. Department of Justice.

Brown, Kelly L. 2007. Effects of supervision philosophy on intensive probationers. *Justice Systems Journal* 4 (1):1–18.

Buckler, Kevin G., and Lawrence F. Travis. 2003. Reanalyzing the prevalence and social context of collateral consequence statutes. *Journal of Criminal Justice* 31: 435–453.

Bureau of Justice Assistance. 1996. *How to use structured fines day fines as an intermediate sanction*. Washington, DC: U.S. Department of Justice, Bureau of Justice Assistance.

_____. 1998. *Critical elements in the planning, development, and implementation of successful correctional options*. Washington, DC: U.S. Department of Justice, Bureau of Justice Assistance.

Burke, Peggy B. 1995. *Abolishing parole: Why the emperor has no clothes*. Lexington, KY: American Probation and Parole Association, and California, MO: Association of Paroling Authorities, International.

_____. 1997. *Policy-driven responses to probation and parole violations*. Washington, DC: U.S. Department of Justice, National Institute of Corrections (March).

Burton, Velmer S., James Marquart, Steven J. Cuvelier, Leanne Fiftal Alarid, and Robert J. Hunter. 1993. A study of attitudinal change among boot camp participants. *Federal Probation* 57(3): 46–52.

Butts, Jeffrey A., and Janeen Buck. 2000. *Teen courts: A focus on research*. Washington, DC: Office of Juvenile Justice and Delinquency Prevention.

Butts, Jeffrey A., and Adele V. Harrell. 2003. Delinquents or criminals: Policy options for young offenders. Retrieved from: http://www.urban.org/.

Butts, Jeffrey A., and Daniel P. Mears. 2001. Reviving juvenile justice in a get-tough era. *Youth and Society* 33(2): 169–198.

Byrne, James and Jacob Stowell. 2007. The impact of the Federal Pretrial Services Act of 1982 on the release, supervision, and detention of pretrial defendants. *Federal Probation* 71(2): 31–38.

Byrne, James M., and Faye S. Taxman. 1994. Crime control policy and community corrections practice. *Evaluation and Program Planning* 17: 227–33.

Cadigan, Timothy P. 2003. Average length of pretrial supervision. *News and Views* 28 (23): 1–2.

Cadigan, Timothy P. 2007. Pretrial services in the federal system: Impact of the Pretrial Services Act of 1982. *Federal Probation* 71(2): 10–15.

Cameron, Angela. 2006. Stopping the violence: Canadian feminist debates on restorative justice and intimate violence. *Theoretical Criminology* 10(1):49–66.

Camp, Camille Graham, and George M. Camp. 1999. *The corrections yearbook: 1999*. Middletown, CT: Criminal Justice Institute.

Camp, Camille Graham, George M. Camp, and Bob May. 2003. *The 2002 corrections yearbook: Adult corrections*. Middletown, CT: Criminal Justice Institute, Inc.

Caputo, Gail A. 2005. Community service in Texas: Results of a probation survey. *Corrections Compendium* 30(2): 8–9, 35–37.

Carey, S., and Michael Figgin. 2004. A detailed cost analysis in a mature drug court setting. *Journal of Contemporary Criminal Justice* 20(3): 315–334.

Carter, Madeline M. (Ed.). 2001. *Responding to Parole and Probation Violations: A Handbook to Guide Local Policy Development*. Prepared for the National Institute of Corrections, U.S. Department of Justice (Washington, DC).

Carter, Madeline M., and Ann Ley. 2001. Making it work: Developing tools to carry out the policy. In *Responding to parole and probation violations: A handbook to guide local policy development*, edited by Madeline M. Carter. Washington, DC: National Institute of Corrections, U.S. Department of Justice.

Castillo, Eladio D., and Leanne F. Alarid. 2009. *Supervision Options for Offenders with Mental Illness*. Paper presented at the annual meeting of the Academy of Criminal Justice Sciences, March 11–15, Boston, MA.

Center for Community Corrections. 1997. *A call for punishments that make sense*. Washington, DC: Bureau of Justice Assistance. Retrieved from: http://www.communitycorrectionsworks.org/art4web-ccc/pdfs%20of%20booklets/punishments.pdf

Chasnoff, Brian. 2006. Unarmed probation officers fret. *San Antonio Express News*, October 21, 1A.

Clark, Cherrie L., David W. Aziz, and Doris L. MacKenzie. 1994. *Shock incarceration in New York: Focus on treatment*. Washington, DC: National Institute of Justice (August).

Clark, John, and D. Alan Henry. 2003. *Pre-trial services programming at the start of the 21st century: A survey of pretrial services programs*. Washington, DC: Bureau of Justice Assistance (July).

Clark, Michael D. 2005. Motivational interviewing for probation staff: Increasing the readiness to change. *Federal Probation* 69(2): 22–28.

Clear, Todd, R., and Ronald Corbett. 1997. Community corrections of place. Retrieved from: http://www.corrections.com/njaca/Fact_Sheets/Fact_sheets_start.htm.

Cohen, Neil P. 2005. *The law of probation and parole*, 2nd ed. St. Paul, MN: West Group. (2005 supplement).

Cohen, Robyn L. 1995. *Probation and parole violators in state prison, 1991*. Washington, DC: U.S. Department of Justice, Bureau of Justice Statistics.

Cohen, Thomas H., and Brian A. Reaves. 2006. *Felony defendants in large urban counties, 2002.* Washington, DC: U.S. Department of Justice.

Cook, Kimberly J. 2006. Doing difference and accountability in restorative conferences. *Theoretical Criminology* 10(1): 107–124.

Cooprider, Keith W., Rosemarie Gray, and John Dunne. 2003. Pretrial services in Lake County, Illinois: Patterns of change over time, 1986–2000. *Federal Probation* 67(3): 33–41.

Corbett, Ronald P. Jr. 2000. Juvenile probation on the eve of the next millennium. *Perspectives* (Fall): 22–30.

Council of State Governments. 2008. *Mental health courts: A primer for policymakers and practitioners.* Washington, DC: Bureau of Justice Assistance.

Craddock, Amy. 2009. Drug reporting center completion. *Crime and Delinquency* 55 (1): 105–133.

Crank, John. 1996. The construction of meaning during training for probation and parole. *Justice Quarterly* 13(2): 265–290.

Craun, Sarah W. and Poco D. Kernsmith. 2006. Juvenile sex offenders and sex offender registries. *Federal Probation* 70 (3): 45–49.

Cullen, Francis T., John E. Eck, and Christopher T. Lowenkamp. 2002. Environmental corrections: A new paradigm for effective probation and parole supervision. *Federal Probation* 66(2): 28–37.

Cullen, Francis T., Bonnie S. Fisher, and Brandon K. Applegate. 2000. Public opinion about punishment and corrections. In M. Tonry (ed.), *Crime and justice: A review of research.* Chicago: University of Chicago Press.

Cullen, Francis T., and Paul Gendreau. 2000. Assessing Correctional Rehabilitation: Policy, Practice, and Prospects. pp. 109–175 in J. Horney (ed.) *Criminal Justice 2000: Volume 3—Policies, Processes, and Decisions of the Criminal Justice System.* Washington, DC: U.S. Department of Justice, National Institute of Justice.

Cullen, Francis T., and Karen E. Gilbert. 1982. *Reaffirming rehabilitation.* Cincinnati, OH: Anderson.

Cushman, Robert, and Dale Sechrest. 1992. Variations in the administration of probation supervision. *Federal Probation* 56(3): 19–29.

Czuchry, Michael, Tiffiny L. Sia, and Donald F. Dansereau. 2006. Improving early engagement and treatment readiness of probationers. *The Prison Journal* 86(1): 56–74.

Daly, Kathleen, and Julie Stubbs. 2006. Feminist engagement with restorative justice. *Theoretical Criminology* 10(1): 9–28.

D'Angelo, L. 2002. Management note—Women and addiction: Challenges for drug court practitioners. *The Justice System Journal* 23(3): 385–400.

Dannerbeck, A., Paul Sundet, and Kathy Lloyd. 2002. Drug courts: Gender differences and their implications for treatment strategies. *Corrections Compendium* 27(12): 1–9.

Davidson, Janet T., Richard Crawford, and Elizabeth Kerwood. 2008. Constructing an EBP post-conviction model of supervision in United States probation, district of Hawaii: A Case Study. *Federal Probation* 72 (2): 22–28.

Davis, Robert C., Barbara Smith, and Susan Hillenbrand. 1992. Restitution: The victim's viewpoint. *Justice System Journal* 15 (3): 746–756.

del Carmen, Rolando V. 2003. *Criminal procedure: Law and practice,* 6th ed. Belmont, CA: Wadsworth.

del Carmen, Rolando, Maldine Beth Barnhill, Gene Bonham, Lance Hignite, and Todd Jermstad. 2001. *Civil liabilities and other legal issues for probation/parole officers and supervisors,* 3rd ed. National Institute of Corrections: U.S. Department of Justice.

del Carmen, Rolando V., Mary Parker, and Francis P. Reddington. 1998. *Briefs of leading cases in juvenile justice.* Cincinnati, OH: Anderson.

del Carmen, Rolando, Sue E. Ritter, and Betsy A. Witt. 2005. *Briefs of Leading Cases in Corrections,* 4th ed. Cincinnati, OH: Anderson.

Deschenes, Elizabeth Piper, Susan Turner, and Joan Petersilia. 1995. A dual experiment in intensive community supervision: Minnesota's prison diversion and enhanced supervised release programs. *The Prison Journal* 75(3): 330–356.

Dexheimer, Eric. 2007. Locked out of their livelihoods. *Austin American-Statesman,* February 18. Retrieved from: http://www.statesman.com.

Diggs, David, and Stephen Pieper. 1994. Using day reporting centers as an alternative to jail. *Federal Probation* 58: 9–12.

DiMascio, William M. 1997. *Seeking justice: Crime and punishment in America.* New York: Edna McConnell Clark Foundation.

Domurad, Frank. 1999. So You Want to Develop Your Own Risk Assessment Instrument. *Topics in Community Corrections: NIC Annual Report 1999: Classification and Risk Assessment.* Longmont, CO: National Institute of Corrections.

Drake, Elizabeth. 2007. *Does participation in Washington's work release facilities reduce recidivism?* Olympia, WA: Washington State Institute for Public Policy. Retrieved from: http://www.wsipp.wa.gov/rptfiles/07-11-1201.pdf

Durose, M. R., & Langan, Patrick A. 2007. *Felony sentences in state courts, 2004.* Washington, DC: Bureau of Justice Statistics.

Eisenberg, Michael, and Tony Fabelo. 1996. Evaluation of the Texas correctional substance abuse treatment initiative: The impact of policy research. *Crime & Delinquency* 42(2): 296–308.

Ely, John F. 1996. Inside-out: Halfway house staff management of punishment and empathy on the ambiguous boundary between prison and the outside [Unpublished Ph.D. dissertation]. University of California-Santa Barbara.

English, Kim, Suzanne Pullen, L. Jones, and M. Kruth. 1996. *Managing adult sex offenders: A containment approach.* Lexington, KY: American Probation and Parole Association.

Erickson, Rosemary J., Wayman Crow, Louis A. Zurcher, and Archie V. Connett. 1973. *Paroled but not free.* New York: Behavioral Publications.

Evjen, Victor H. 1975. The federal probation system: The struggle to achieve it and its first 25 years. *Federal Probation* 39(2): 3–15.

Farole, Donald. 2003. The Harlem parole reentry court evaluation: Implementation and preliminary impact. New York: Center for Court Innovation. Retrieved from: http://www.courtinnovation.org/_uploads/documents/harlemreentryeval.pdf.

Farrall, Stephen. 2003. J'accuse: Probation evaluation-research epistemologies, part one: The critique. *Criminal Justice* 32: 161–179.

Federal Statutes Imposing Collateral Consequences upon Conviction. 2000. Retrieved from: http://www.sentencingproject.org/pubs_05.cfm.

Fehr, Larry M. 2004. Washington female offender reentry programs combine transitional services with residential parenting. *Corrections Today* (Oct): 82–84.

Festervan, Earlene. 2003. *Women probationers: Supervision and success.* Lanham, MD: American Correctional Association.

Finn, Peter. 1997. *Sex offender community notification.* Washington DC: National Institute of Justice.

Fischer, Brenda. 2003. "Doing good with a vengeance": A critical assessment of the practices, effects and implications of drug treatment courts in North America. *Criminal Justice* 3(3): 227–248.

Fogel, David. 1979. *. . . We are the living proof . . . The justice model for corrections,* 2nd ed. Cincinnati, OH: Anderson.

Forst, Brian. 1995. Prosecution and sentencing. In *Crime,* edited by James Q. Wilson and Joan Petersilia. San Francisco, CA: Institute for Contemporary Studies, pp. 363–386.

Foucault, Michel. 1977. *Discipline and punish.* New York: Pantheon Books.

Frendle, Julie Wesley. 2004. *An overview of juvenile parole boards in the United States.* Prepared for the New Mexico Sentencing Commission.

Galaway, Burt. 1992. Restitution as innovation or unfilled promise? In *Towards a critical victimology,* edited by Ezzat A. Fattah. New York: St. Martin's Press, pp. 347–371.

Galloway, Alyson L., and Laurie A. Drapela. 2006. Are effective drug courts an urban phenomenon? *International Journal of Offender Therapy and Comparative Criminology* 50(3) 280–293.

Garner, Bryan A. 2009. *Black's Law Dictionary,* 9th ed. St. Paul, MN: West Group.

Geerken, Michael R., and Hennessey D. Hayes. 1993. Probation and parole: Public risk and the future of incarceration alternatives. *Criminology* 31(4): 549–564.

Gendreau, Paul. 1996. The principles of effective intervention. In *Choosing correctional options that work: Defining the demand and evaluating the supply,* edited by A.T. Harland. Thousand Oaks, CA: Sage.

Gendreau, Paul. 1998. Keynote speech: What works in community corrections: Promising approaches in reducing criminal behavior. In *Successful community sanctions and services for special offenders,* edited by B. J. Auerbach and T. C. Castellano. Lanham, MD: American Correctional Association, pp. 59–74.

General Accounting Office: Harris, DC, Charles Michael Johnson, Barry J. Seltser, Douglas M. Sloane, David P. Alexander, Stuart M. Kaufman, Pamela V. Williams, Thelma Jones, George H. Quinn, Katherine M. Wheeler, Jena Sinkfield, Jan B. Montgomery, and Ann H. Finley. 1997. *Drug courts: Overview of growth, characteristics, and results.* Washington, D.C., United States General Accounting Office.

Glaser, Daniel. 1969. *The effectiveness of prison and parole systems.* Indianapolis, IN: Bobbs-Merrill.

Glaser, Daniel. 1995. *Preparing convicts for law-abiding lives: The pioneering penology of Richard A. McGee.* Albany, NY: State University of New York Press.

Glaze Lauren E. and Thomas P. Bonczar. 2008. *Probation and Parole in the United States, 2007.* Washington, DC: Bureau of Justice Statistics, U.S. Department of Justice.

Glaze, Lauren E., and Seri Palla. 2005. *Probation and parole in the United States, 2004.* Washington, DC: Bureau of Justice Statistics, U.S. Department of Justice.

Goldapple, Gary C., and Dianne Montgomery. 1993. Evaluating a behaviorally based intervention to improve client retention in therapeutic community treatment for drug dependency. *Research on Social Work Practice* 31: 21–39.

Golden, Lori S., Robert J. Gatchel, and Melissa A. Cahill. 2006. Evaluating the effectiveness of the National Institute of Corrections' 'thinking for a change' program among probationers. *Journal of Offender Rehabilitation* 43 (2), 55–73.

Goldkamp, John S., and Michael D. White. 1998. *Restoring accountability in pretrial release: The Philadelphia pretrial release supervision experiments* [NCJ 189164]. Washington, DC: U.S. Department of Justice.

Goodwin, Catharine M. 2001. Looking at the law: Update on selected restitution issues. *Federal Probation* 65(1): 54–62.

Gordon, Jill. 2003. Aftercare. In *Encyclopedia of Juvenile Justice,* edited by McShane, Marilyn D. and Frank P. Williams III. Thousand Oaks, CA: Sage Publications.

Gordon, Jill A., Christina M. Barnes, and Scott W. VanBenschoten. 2006. The dual treatment rack program: A descriptive assessment of a new in-house jail diversion program. *Federal Probation* 70 (3): 9–17.

Gottfredson, Denise C., and M. Lyn Exum. 2002. The Baltimore city drug treatment court: One- year results from a randomized study. *Journal of Research in Crime and Delinquency* 39(3): 337–356.

Gottfredson, Denise C., Brook W. Kearley. Stacy S. Najaka, and Carlos M. Rocha. 2007. How drug treatment courts work: An analysis of mediators. *Journal of Research in Crime and Delinquency* 44(1): 3–35.

Gottfredson, Denise C., Stacy S. Najaka, and Brook Kearley. 2003. Effectiveness of drug treatment courts: Evidence from a randomized trial. *Criminology & Public Policy* 2(2): 171–196.

Gottfredson, Don, Michael Gottfredson, and James Garofalo. 1997. Time served in prison and parolee outcomes among parolee risk categories. *Journal of Criminal Justice* 5: 1–12.

Gowen, Darren. 2000. Overview of the federal home confinement 1988–1996. *Federal Probation* 64(2): 11–18.

———. 2001. Remote location monitoring—A supervision strategy to enhance risk control. *Federal Probation* 65(2): 38–41.

Gray, M. Kevin, Monique Fields, and Sheila Royo Maxwell. 2001. Examining probation violations: Who, what and when. *Crime and Delinquency* 47(4): 537–557.

Greek, Cecil E. 2002. The cutting edge: Tracking probationers in space and time: The convergence of GIS and GPS systems. *Federal Probation* 66(1):51–53.

Griffin, Patrick, and Patricia Torbet (Eds.). 2002. *Desktop guide to good juvenile probation practice.* Washington, DC: National Center for Juvenile Justice.

Grooms, Robert M. 1982. Recidivist. *Crime and Delinquency* 28: 541–545.

Grubesic, Tony H., Elizabeth Mack, and Alan T. Murray. 2007. Spatial analysis for evaluating the impact of Megan's law. *Social Science Computer Review* 25: 143–162.

Hammett, Theodore M., Patricia Harmon, and Laura M. Maruschak. 1999. *1996–1997 update: HIV/AIDS, STDs, and TB in correctional facilities.* Washington, DC: National Institute of Justice, Bureau of Justice Statistics, and Centers for Disease Control and Prevention.

Hammett, Theodore M., Cheryl Roberts, and Sofia Kennedy. 2001. Health-related issues in prisoner reentry. *Crime and Delinquency* 47(3): 390–409.

Hanley, Dena. 2002. *Risk differentiation and intensive supervision: A meaningful union? An unpublished doctoral dissertation,* University of Cincinnati, Cincinnati, OH.

Hansen, Christopher. 2001. The cutting edge: A survey of technological innovation: Where have all the probation officers gone? *Federal Probation* 65(1): 51–53.

Hansen, Chris. 2008. Cognitive-Behavioral interventions: Where they come from and what they do. *Federal Probation* 72 (2): 43–49

Harries, Keith. 2003. Using geographic analysis in probation and parole. *National Institute of Justice Journal* 249: 32–33.

Harris, M. Kay. 1996. Key differences among community corrections acts in the United States: An overview. *The Prison Journal* 76(2): 192–238.

Hartmann, David J., Paul C. Friday, and Kevin I. Minor. 1994. Residential probation: A seven year follow-up study of halfway house discharges. *Journal of Criminal Justice* 22(6): 503–515.

Hemmens, Craig. 1998. Life in the joint and beyond: An examination of inmate attitudes and perceptions of prison, parole, and self at the time of release [Unpublished Ph.D. dissertation]. Sam Houston State University.

Hemmens, Craig, Kathryn Bennett, and Rolando del Carmen. 1998. The exclusionary rule does not apply to parole revocation hearings: An analysis of *Pennsylvania Board of Probation and Parole v. Scott. Criminal Law Bulletin* 35(4): 388–409.

Henry, Thomas. 2007. Reflections on the 25th anniversary of the pretrial services act. *Federal Probation* 71(2): 4–6.

Hensley, Denise Bray. 1995. One Boy's Life. *Houston Chronicle* (September 17).

Herman, Susan, and Cressida Wasserman. 2001. A role for victims in offender reentry. *Crime and Delinquency* 47(3): 428–445.

Hill, Brian J. 2006. Four-point strategy reduces technical violations of probation in Connecticut. *Topics in Community Corrections: Effectively Managing Violations and Revocations.* Longmont, CO: National Institute of Corrections.

Hindman, Jan, and James M. Peters. 2001. Polygraph testing leads to better understanding adult and juvenile sex offenders. *Federal Probation* 65(3): 8–15.

Hoffman, Peter B. 1994. Twenty years of operational use of a risk prediction instrument: The United States Parole Commission's Salient Factor Score. *Journal of Criminal Justice* 22(6): 477–494.

Holsinger, Alex M., Arthur J. Lurigio, and Edward J. Latessa. 2001. Up to speed: Practitioners' guide to understanding the basis of assessing offender risk. *Federal Probation* 65(1): 46–50.

Holt, Norman. 1998. The current state of parole in America. In *Community corrections: Probation, parole, and intermediate sanctions,* edited by Joan Petersilia. New York: Oxford University Press, p. 36.

Holzer, Harry J. 1996. *What employers want: Job prospects for less-educated workers.* New York: Sage.

Horn, Dan. 2000. Offenders find records hard to erase. *Cincinnati Enquirer,* December 18.

Hudson, Barbara. 2006. Beyond white man's justice: Race, gender, and justice in late modernity. *Theoretical Criminology* 10(1), 29-47.

Hughes, John M. 2008. Results-based management in federal probation and pretrial services. *Federal Probation* 72 (2), 4–14.

Hughes, Timothy A., Doris James Wilson, and Allen J. Beck. 2001. *Trends in state parole, 1990–2000.* Washington, DC: U.S. Department of Justice, Bureau of Justice Statistics.

International Community Corrections Association. 2009. Retrieved from: http://www.iccaweb.org/history.htm

Jacobs, Mark D. 1990. *Screwing the system and making it work: Juvenile justice in the no-fault society.* Chicago: University of Chicago Press.

Jeffrey, R., and S. Woolpert. 1974. Work furlough as an alternative to incarceration. *Journal of Criminology* 65 (3), 405–415.

Jenuwine, Michael J., Ronald Simmons, and Edward Swies. 2003. Community supervision of sex offenders— Integrating probation and clinical treatment. *Federal Probation* 67(3): 20–27.

Johnson, Kevin and Richard Willing. 2008. New DNA links used to deny parole. *USA Today,* February 7. Retrieved from: http://www.usatoday.com/news/nation/2008-02-07

Johnson, Richard. 2001. Intensive probation for domestic violence offenders. *Federal Probation* 65(3): 36–39.

Jones, Mark. 1995. Predictors of success and failure on intensive probation supervision. *American Journal of Criminal Justice* 19: 239–254.

Jones, Mark, and John J. Kerbs. 2007. Probation and parole officers and discretionary decision-making: Responses to technical and criminal violations. *Federal Probation* 71(1):9–15.

Jones, Mark, and Darrell L. Ross. 1997. Electronic house arrest and boot camp in North Carolina. *Criminal Justice Policy Review* 8(4): 383–403.

Joo, Hee-Jong, Sheldon Ekland-Olson, and William Kelly. 1995. Recidivism among paroled property offenders released during a period of prison reform. *Criminology* 33(3): 389–410.

Juvenile Probation Officer Initiative Working Group. 1993. *Desktop guide to good juvenile probation practice.* Washington, DC: National Center for Juvenile Justice, Office of Juvenile Justice and Delinquency Prevention.

Kalfrin, Valerie. 2008. Ankle device foils boat burglar's plan, police say." *The Tampa Tribune*, January 9.

Karp, David R. 1998. *Community justice: An emerging field.* Lanham, MD: Rowman and Littlefield.

Karp, David R., and Todd R. Clear. 2002. *What is community justice*? Thousand Oaks, CA: Pine Forge Press.

Karuppannan, Jaishankar. 2005. Mapping and corrections: Management of offenders with geographic information systems. *Corrections Compendium* 30(1): 7–9, 31–33.

Keller, Oliver J., and Benedict S. Alper. 1970. *Halfway houses: Community-centered correction and treatment.* Lexington, MA: D.C. Heath.

Kelly, Brian J. 2001. Supervising the cyber-criminal. *Federal Probation* 65(2): 8–10.

Kelly, Phaedra Athena O'Hara. 1999. The ideology of shame: An analysis of first amendment and eighth amendment challenges to scarlet-letter probation conditions. *North Carolina Law Review* 77(2): 783–864.

Kempinen, C.A., and Megan C. Kurlychek. 2003. An outcome evaluation of Pennsylvania's boot camp: Does rehabilitative programming within a disciplinary setting reduce recidivism? *Crime and Delinquency* 49(4): 581–602.

Kendig, Newton, Barbara Boyle, and Anthony Swetz. 1996. The Maryland Division of Correction medical-parole program: A four-year experience, 1991 to 1994. *AIDS & Public Policy Journal* 11(1): 21–27.

Kenney, J. Scott and Don Clairmont. 2009. Using the victim role as both sword and shield: The interactional dynamics of restorative justice sessions. *Journal of Contemporary Ethnography* 38(3): 279–307.

Kilgour, D., and S. Meade. 2004. Look what boot camps done for me: Teaching and learning at Lakeview Academy. *Journal of Correctional Education* 55: 170–185.

Kim, Dae-Young, Cassia Spohn, and Mark Foxall. 2007. An evaluation of the DRC in the context of Douglas County, Nebraska. *The Prison Journal* 87 (4): 434–456.

Kim, Dae-Young, Hee-Jong Joo, and William P. McCarty. 2008. Risk assessment and classification of day reporting center clients. *Criminal Justice and Behavior* 35 (6): 792–812.

Kinnevy, Susan C., and Joel M. Caplan. 2008. *Findings from the APAI international survey of releasing authorities.* Center for Research on youth and social policy. Retrieved from: http://www.apaintl.org/pdfs/final_apai_survey_10222008.pdf

Kittrie, Nicholas N., Elyce H. Zenoff, and Vincent A. Eng. 2002. *Sentencing, sanctions, and corrections: Federal and state law, policy, and practice,* 2nd ed. New York: Foundation Press.

Klein-Saffran, Jody. 1992. *Electronic monitoring versus halfway houses: A study of federal offenders* [Unpublished Ph.D. Dissertation]. University of Maryland.

Klockars, Carl B. Jr. 1972. A theory of probation supervision. *Journal of Criminal Law, Criminology and Police Science* 63(4): 550–557.

Krauth, Barbara, and Larry Linke. 1999. *State organizational structures for delivering adult probation services.* Longmont, CO: LIS, Inc. for the National Institute of Corrections.

Kurlychek, Megan C., Robert Brame and Shawn D. Bushway. 2007. Enduring risk? Old criminal records and predictions of future criminal involvement. *Crime and Delinquency* 53(1): 64–83.

Kurlychek, Megan, Patricia Torbet, and Melanie Bozynski. 1999. Focus on accountability: Best practices for juvenile court and probation. *JAIBTG Bulletin* (August).

Kuzma, Susan M. 1998. Civil disabilities of convicted felons. *Corrections Today* (August): 68–72.

Kyckelhahn, Tracey and Thomas H. Cohen, 2007. *Felony Defendants in Large Urban Counties, 2004.* Washington, DC: Bureau of Justice Statistics, Table 29. Retrieved from: http://www.ojp.usdoj.gov/bjs/stssent.htm#scps

Langan, Patrick. 1994. Between prison and probation: Intermediate sanctions. *Science:* 791–793.

Langan, Patrick A., and Mark Cunniff. 1992. *Recidivism of felons on probation, 1986–1989.* Washington, DC: U.S. Department of Justice, Bureau of Justice Statistics (February).

Langan, Patrick A., and David J. Levin. 2002. *Recidivism of prisoners released in 1994.* Washington, DC: U.S. Department of Justice, Bureau of Justice Statistics (June).

Latessa, Edward J., and Alexander Holsinger. 1998. The importance of evaluating correctional programs: Assessing outcome and quality. *Corrections Management Quarterly* 2(4): 22–29.

Latessa, Edward J., and Lawrence Travis. 1992. Residential community correctional programs. In *Smart sentencing: The emergence of intermediate sanctions,* edited by J. M Byrne, A. J. Lurigio, and J. Petersilia. Newbury Park, CA: Sage.

Lattimore, Pamela K. 2006. Reentry, reintegration, rehabilitation, recidivism, and redemption. *The Criminologist* 31(3): 1–6.

La Vigne, Nancy G. 2006. Prisoner reentry: Taking stock and moving forward. *Austin/Travis County Reentry Roundtable Annual Community Forum.* The Urban Insititute.

LeClair, D. P. and Susan Guarino-Ghezzi. 1991. Does incapacitation guarantee public safety? Lessons from the Massachusetts furlough and prerelease programs. *Justice Quarterly* 8(1), 9–36.

Legal Action Center. 2004. After prison: Roadblocks to reentry: A report on state legal barriers facing people with criminal records. Retrieved from: http://www.lac.org/roadblocks.html.

Lehman, Joseph, Trudy Gregorie Beatty, Dennis Maloney, Susan Russell, Anne Seymour, and Carol Shapiro. 2002. *The three r's of reentry.* Washington, DC: Justice Solutions.

Lehnerer, Melodye. 1992. Becoming involved: Field research at a halfway house for ex-offenders [Unpublished Ph.D. dissertation]. York University.

Lerner, Kenneth, Gary Arling, and S. Christopher Baird. 1986. Client Management Classification Strategies for Case Supervision. *Crime and Delinquency* 32 (3): 254–271.

Levenson, Jill, Kristen Zgoba and Richard Tewksbury. 2007. Sex offender residence restrictions: Sensible crime policy or flawed logic? *Federal Probation* 71(3): 2–9.

Levin, Marc A. 2008a. Work release: Con job or big payoff for Texas? *Texas Public Policy Foundation Policy Perspective* (April). Retrieved from: http://www.texaspolicy.com

———. 2008b.Five technological solutions for Texas' correctional and law enforcement challenges. *Texas Public Policy Foundation Policy Perspective* (June). Retrieved from: http://www.texaspolicy.com

Leznoff, JoAnne. 1998. Privatization of community supervision as a public safety issue. In *Topics in community corrections: Annual issue 1998: Privatizing community supervision*. Longmont, CO: National Institute of Corrections, U.S. Department of Justice, pp. 19–24.

Lilly, J. Robert. 2006. Issues behind empirical EM reports. *Criminology & Public Policy* 5(1): 93–102.

Lilly, J. Robert, Richard A, Ball, G. David Curry, and Richard Smith. 1992. The Pride, Inc., program: An evaluation of 5 years of electronic monitoring. *Federal Probation* (December): 42–47.

Lindner, Charles. 2007. Thacher, Augustus, and Hill: The path to statutory probation in the United States and England. *Federal Probation* 71(3):36–41.

Lindner, Charles. 2008. Probation intake: Gatekeeper to the family court. *Federal Probation* 72(1): 48–53.

Lindner, Charles, and Margaret R. Savarese. 1984a. The evolution of probation: Early salaries, qualifications, and hiring practices. *Federal Probation* 48(1): 3–10.

———. 1984b. The evolution of probation: The historical contributions of the volunteer. *Federal Probation* 48(2): 3–10.

———. 1984c. The evolution of probation: University settlement and the beginning of statutory probation in New York City. *Federal Probation* 48(3): 3–12.

———. 1984d. The evolution of probation: University settlement and its pioneering role in probation work. *Federal Probation* 48(4): 3–13.

Linke, Larry, and Barbara Krauth. 2000. *Perspectives from the field on the interstate compact on juveniles: Findings from a national survey* [NIC-016491]. Longmont, CO: National Institute of Corrections.

Lipton, Douglas, Robert Martinson, and J. Wilks. 1975. *The effectiveness of correctional treatment.* New York: Praeger.

Listwan, Shelley Johnson, Jody L. Sundt, Alexander M. Holsinger, and Edward J. Latessa, 2003. The effect of drug court programming on recidivism: The Cincinnati experience. *Crime and Delinquency* 49(3): 389–411.

Livsey, Sarah. 2009. *Juvenile delinquency probation caseload, 1985–2005*. Washington, DC: Office of Juvenile Justice and Delinquency Prevention.

Locke, Hubert G. 1998. Closing comments. In *Successful community sanctions and services for special offenders,* edited by B. J. Auerbach and T. C. Castellano. Lanham, MD: American Correctional Association, pp. 253–259.

Love, Margaret Colgate. 2005. Relief from the collateral consequences of a criminal conviction: A state by state resource guide. The Sentencing Project. Retrieved from: http://www.sentencingproject.org/rights-restoration.cfm.

Lowenkamp, Christopher T., and Kristin Bechtel. 2007. The predictive validity of the LSI-R on a sample of offenders drawn from the records of the Iowa Department of Corrections data management system. *Federal Probation* 71 (3): 25–29.

Lowenkamp, Christopher T., Richard Lemke, and Edward Latessa. 2008. The development and validation of a pretrial screening tool. *Federal Probation* 72(3): 2–9.

Lowenkamp, Christopher T., and Edward J. Latessa. 2005. Increasing the effectiveness of correctional programming through the risk principle: Identifying offenders for residential placement. *Criminology & Public Policy* 4(2): 263–290.

Lubitz, Robin L., and Thomas W. Ross. 2001. Sentencing guidelines: Reflections on the future. In *Sentencing and corrections: Issues for the 21st century* (No. 10, June). Washington, DC: U.S. Department of Justice.

Lurigio, Arthur J., and Robert C. Davis. 1990. Does a threatening letter increase compliance with restitution orders? A field experiment. *Crime & Delinquency* 364: 537–548.

Lutjen, Karen. 1996. Culpability and sentencing under mandatory minimums and the federal sentencing guidelines: The punishment no longer fits the criminal. *Notre Dame Journal of Law, Ethics, and Public Policy* 10(1): 389–466.

Lutze, Faith E., and David C. Brody. 1999. Mental abuse as cruel and unusual punishment: Do boot camp prisons violate the eighth amendment? *Crime and Delinquency* 45(2): 242–255.

Lutze, Faith E., R. Peggy Smith, and Nicholas P. Lovrich. 2004. A practitioner-initiated research partnership: An evaluation of neighborhood based supervision in Spokane, Washington. An unpublished manuscript.

Lynch, Mona. 1998. Waste managers? The new penology, crime fighting, and parole agent identity. *Law and Society Review* 32(4): 839–869.

Mack, Julian W. 1909. The juvenile court. *Harvard Law Review* 23: 102–109.

MacKenzie, Doris L. 2000. Evidence-based corrections: Identifying what works. *Crime and Delinquency* 46(4): 457–472.

MacKenzie, Doris L., Robert Brame, D. McDowall, and Claire Souryal. 1995. Boot camp prisons and recidivism in eight states. *Criminology* 33(3): 327–357.

MacKenzie, Doris L., Angela R. Gover, Gaylene Styve Armstrong, and Ojmarrh Mitchell. 2001. A national study comparing the environments of boot camps with traditional facilities for juvenile offenders. *National Institute of Justice Research in Brief*. Washington, DC: U.S. Department of Justice.

MacKenzie, Doris L., and Eugene E. Hebert (Eds.). 1996. *Correctional boot camps: A tough intermediate sanction.* Washington, DC: U.S. Department of Justice.

MacKenzie, Doris L., and Claire Souryal. 1995. Inmates' attitude change during incarceration: A comparison of boot camp with traditional prison. *Justice Quarterly* 12(2): 325–354.

MacKenzie, Doris L., David B. Wilson, and Gaylene S. Armstrong. 2001. The impact of boot camps and traditional institutions on juvenile residents: Perceptions, adjustment, and change. *Journal of Research in Crime and Delinquency* 38(3): 279–313.

Maher, Richard J. 1994. Community service: A good idea that works. *Federal Probation* 58(2): 20–23.

———. 1997. Community service: A way for offenders to make amends. *Federal Probation* 61(1): 26–28

Maidment, MaDonna R. 2002. Toward a woman-centered approach to community-based corrections: A gendered analysis of electronic monitoring in eastern Canada. *Women and Criminal Justice* 13(4): 47–68.

Mair, George. 1995. Day centers in England and Wales. In *Intermediate sanctions in overcrowded times,* edited by Michael Tonry and Kate Hamilton. Boston, MA: Northeastern University Press.

Mair, George, and Claire Nee. 1992. Day centre reconviction rates. *British Journal of Criminology* 32: 329–339.

Mansnerus, Laura. 2003. Questions rise over imprisoning sex offenders past their terms. *New York Times,* November 17: 1–6. Retrieved from: http://www.nytimes.com.

Martin, Christine, Arthur J. Lurigio, and David E. Olson. 2003. An examination of rearrests and reincarcerations among discharged day reporting center clients. *Federal Probation* 67(1): 24–30.

Martin, Jamie S., Kate Hanrahan, and Teah M. Travers. 2008. *Probation officers' assessment of electronic monitoring as an intermediate sanction.* Paper presented at the annual meeting of the Academy of Criminal Justice Sciences, March 11–15, 2008. Cincinnati, OH.

Martinson, Robert. 1974. What works? Questions and answers about prison reform. *Public Interest* 35(Spring): 22–35.

Maruna, Shadd and Anna King. 2008. Selling the public on probation: Beyond the bib. *Probation Journal* 55(4), 337–351.

Maxfield, Michael G., and Terry L. Baumer. 1990. Home detention with electronic monitoring: Comparing pretrial and postconviction programs. *Crime and Delinquency* 36(4): 521–536.

Maxwell, Gabrielle and Allison Morris. 1996. Research in family group conferences with young offenders in New Zealand. Pp. 88–110 in *Family group conferences: Perspectives on policy and practice,* edited by Joe Hudson, Allison Morris, Gabrielle Maxwell, and Burt Galaway. Monsey, NY: Criminal Justice Press.

Mawhorr, Tina L. 1997. Disabled offenders and work release: An exploratory examination. *Criminal Justice Review* 22(1): 34–48.

Mayzer, Roni, and M. Kevin Gray. 2000. Probation absconders. Paper presented at the annual American Society of Criminology meeting, San Francisco, California, November 15–18.

McDonald, Douglas, Judith Greene, and Charles Worzella. 1992. *Day fines in American courts: The Staten Island and Milwaukee experiments.* Washington, DC: U.S. Department of Justice, National Institute of Justice.

McKay, Brian. 2002. The state of sex offender probation supervision in Texas. *Federal Probation* 66(1): 16–20.

McManus, Patrick D., and Lynn Z. Barclay. 1994. *Community Corrections Act: Technical assistance manual.* College Park, MD: American Correctional Association.

McShane, Marilyn, Frank P. Williams, and H. Michael Dolny. 2002. Do standard risk prediction instruments apply to female parolees? *Women and Criminal Justice* 13(2/3): 163.

Michigan Judicial Institute. 2003. Case review and probation revocation in designated case and automatic waiver proceedings. In *Juvenile Justice Benchbook* (Revised edition), pp. 457–467.

Milligan, Jessie. 2001. Blood, sweat, and fears. *Fort Worth Star Telegram Sunday Magazine,* March 18, 2001.

Minor, Kevin I., James B. Wells, and Crissy Sims. 2003. Recidivism among federal probationers: Predicting sentence violations. *Federal Probation* 67(1): 31–36.

Miyashiro, Carol M. 2008. Research 2 results (R2R): The pretrial services experience. *Federal Probation* 72(2):80–86.

Moreland, D.W. 1941. History and prophecy: John Augustus and his successors. *National Probation Association Yearbook.* Presentation delivered at the 35th Annual Conference of the National Probation Association, Boston, Massachusetts, May 29, 1941.

Morgan, Kathryn D. 1994. Factors associated with probation outcome. *Journal of Criminal Justice* 22: 341–353.

———. 1995. Variables associated with successful probation outcome. *Journal of Offender Rehabilitation* 22(3/4): 141–153.

Morgan, Kathryn, and Brent L. Smith. 2005. Victims, punishment, and parole: The effect of victim participation on parole hearings. *Criminology & Public Policy* 4(2): 333–360.

Morris, Norval. 2002. *Maconochie's gentlemen: The story of Norfolk Island and the roots of modern prison reform.* New York: Oxford University Press.

Morris, Norval, and Michael Tonry. 1990. *Between prison and probation: Intermediate punishments in a rational sentencing system.* New York: Oxford University Press.

Moscicki, Ronald W. 1996. If you don't take responsibility, you take orders. In *Juvenile and adult boot camps,* edited by American Correctional Association. Lanham, MD: American Correctional Association.

Muhammad, Mika'il A. 1996. Prisoners' perspectives on strategies for release. *Journal of Offender Rehabilitation* 23: 131–152.

Mumola, Christopher J. 2000. *Incarcerated parents and their children.* Washington, DC: U.S. Department of Justice, Bureau of Justice Statistics.

Mumola, Christopher J., with Thomas P. Bonczar. 1998. *Substance abuse and treatment of adults on probation, 1995.* Washington, DC: U.S. Department of Justice, Bureau of Justice Statistics.

National Advisory Commission on Criminal Justice Standards and Goals. 1973. *Report on corrections.* Washington, DC: U.S. Department of Justice.

National Institute of Corrections and the Council of State Governments. 2002. *Interstate compact for adult offender supervision: State officials guide.* Longmont, CO: National Institute of Corrections, U.S. Department of Justice.

National Institute of Justice. 1994. *Program Focus Shock Incarceration in New York.* Washington, DC: U.S. Department of Justice, National Institute of Justice.

National Law Enforcement and Corrections Technology Center. 2002. Fuginet'ing Parole Violators. *TechBeat* (Winter). Retrieved from: http://www.justnet.org

National Law Enforcement and Corrections Technology Center. 2006. The eyes have it. *TechBeat* (Fall). Retrieved from: http://www.justnet.org

National Law Enforcement and Corrections Technology Center. 2009. Field search. *TechBeat* (Winter). Retrieved from: http://www.justnet.org

National Research Council. 2008. *Parole, desistance from crime, and community integration.* Washington, DC: National Academies Press.

Neff, Tom. 2006. *Chances: The women of Magdalene.* Video documentary, The Documentary Channel, February 26, 2006.

Nellis, Mike. 2006. Surveillance, rehabilitation, and electronic monitoring: Getting the issues clear. *Criminology & Public Policy* 5(1): 103–108.

Nelson, William F. 2004. Prostitution: A community solution alternative. *Corrections Today* (October): 88–91

Newville, Lanny L. 2001. Cyber crime and the courts: Investigating and supervising the information age offender. *Federal Probation* 65(2): 11–17.

New York State Division of Parole, Office of Policy Analysis and Information. 1993. Overview of the Parole Revocation Process in New York. In *Reclaiming Offender Accountability: Intermediate Sanctions for Probation and Parole Violators,* edited by Edward E. Rhine. Laurel, MD: American Correctional Association.

Nielsen, Amie L., Frank R. Scarpitti, and James Inciardi. 1996. Integrating the therapeutic community and work release for drug-involved offenders: The CREST program. *Journal of Substance Abuse Treatment* 13(4): 349–358.

Nieto, Marcus. 1996. *The changing role of probation in California's criminal justice system.* Sacramento, CA: California Research Bureau.

Norman, Michael D., and Robert C. Wadman. 2000. Probation department sentencing recommendations in two Utah counties. *Federal Probation* 64(2): 47–51.

North Carolina Sentencing and Policy Advisory Commission. 1994. *Structured sentencing for felonies-training and reference manual.* Raleigh, NC: Author.

OJJDP. 1999. Reintegration, Supervised Release, and Intensive Aftercare. *Juvenile Justice Bulletin.* Retrieved from: http://ojjdp.ncjrs.org/jjbulletin/9907_3/contents.html.

Office for the Victims of Crime. 2002. *Victims' rights and services.* Washington, DC: U.S. Department of Justice, Office for Victims of Crime.

Office of the Pardon Attorney. 1996. *Civil disabilities of convicted offenders.* Washington, DC: U.S. Department of Justice.

Ogden, Thomas G., and Cary Horrocks. 2001. Pagers, digital, audio, and kiosk: Officer assistants. *Federal Probation* 65(2): 35–37.

Olson, David E., Brendan Dooley, and Candice M. Kane. 2004. The relationship between gang membership and inmate recidivism. *Illinois Criminal Justice Information Authority Research Bulletin* 2(12): 1–12.

Olson, David E., and Gerard F. Ranker. 2001. Crime does not pay, but criminals may: Factors influencing the imposition and collection of probation fees. *Justice Systems Journal* 22: 29–46.

O'Malley, Pat. 2008. Theorizing fines. *Punishment and Society* 11(1): 67–83.

Ostermann, Michael. 2009. An analysis of New Jersey's day reporting center and halfway back programs: Embracing the rehabilitative ideal through evidence-based practices. *Journal of Offender Rehabilitation* 48: 139–153.

Ostrom, Brian J., Matthew Kleiman, Fred Cheesman, Randall M. Hansen, and Neal B. Kauder. 2002. *Offender risk assessment in Virginia.* Williamsburg, VA: National Center for State Courts.

Outlaw, M.C., and R. Barry Ruback. 1999. Predictors and outcomes of victim restitution orders. *Justice Quarterly* 16: 847–869.

Padgett, Kathy G., William D. Bales, and Thomas G. Blomberg. 2006. Under surveillance: An empirical test of the effectiveness and consequences of electronic monitoring. *Criminology & Public Policy* 5(1): 61–92.

Palacios, Victoria J. 1994. Go and sin no more: Rationality and release decisions by parole boards. *South Carolina Law Review* 45: 613.

Palmer, Ted. 1992. *The re-emergence of correctional intervention.* Newbury Park, CA: Sage.

———. 1994. *A profile of correctional effectiveness and new direction for research.* Albany, NY: State University of New York Press.

Palumbo, Dennis, Mary Clifford, and Joann K. Snyder-Joy. 1992. From net-widening to intermediate sanctions: The transformation of alternatives to incarceration from benevolence to malevolence. In *Smart sentencing: The emergence of intermediate sanctions,* edited by James M. Byrne, Arthur J. Lurigio, and Joan Petersilia. Newbury Park, CA: Sage.

Panzarella, Robert. 2002. Theory and practice of probation on bail in the report of John Augustus. *Federal Probation* 66(3): 38–42.

Paparozzi, Mario A., and Paul Gendreau. 2005. An intensive supervision program that worked: Service delivery, professional orientation, and organizational supportiveness. *The Prison Journal* 85(4): 445–466.

Parent, Dale. 1990. *Day reporting centers for criminal offenders: A descriptive analysis of existing programs.* Washington, DC: U.S. Department of Justice.

———1993. Structuring policies to address sanctions for absconders and violators. In *Reclaiming offender accountability: Intermediate sanctions for probation and parole violators,* edited by Edward E. Rhine. Laurel, MD: American Correctional Association.

———. 1995. Day reporting centers. In *Intermediate sanctions in overcrowded times*, edited by Michael Tonry and Kate Hamilton. Boston, MA: Northeastern University Press.

———. 1996. Boot camps and prison crowding. In *Correctional boot camps: A tough intermediate sanction*, edited by Doris L. MacKenzie and Eugene E. Hebert. Washington, DC: U.S. Department of Justice.

———. 2003. *Correctional boot camps: Lessons from a decade of research*. Washington, DC: National Institute of Justice.

Parent, Dale, Jim Byrne, Vered Tsafaty, Laua Valade, and Julie Esselman. 1995. *Day reporting centers*, vol. 1. Washington, DC: U.S. Department of Justice, National Institute of Justice.

Parent, Dale, Terence Dunworth, Douglas McDonald, and William Rhodes. 1997. *Key legislative issues in criminal justice: The impact of sentencing guidelines*. Washington, DC: U.S. Department of Justice, National Institute of Justice.

Parent, Dale G., Dan Wentworth, Peggy Burke, and Becky Ney. 1994. *Responding to probation and parole violations* Washington, DC: U.S. Department of Justice.

Parisi, Nicolette. 1981. A taste of the bars. *Journal of Criminal Law and Criminology* 72: 1109–1123.

Payne, Brian K., and Matthew DeMichele. 2008. Warning: Sex offenders need to be supervised in the community. *Federal Probation* 72 (1): 37–42.

Payne, Brian K., and Randy R. Gainey. 2002. The influence of demographic factors on the experience of house arrest. *Federal Probation* 66(3): 64–70.

———. 2004. The electronic monitoring of offenders released from jail or prison: Safety, control, and comparisons to the incarceration experience. *The Prison Journal* 84(4): 413–435.

Petersilia, Joan. 1993a. *Evaluating intensive supervised probation/parole: Results of a nationwide experiment* [NCJ 141637]. Washington, DC: U.S. Department of Justice, National Institute of Justice.

———. 1993b. Intensive probation and parole. In *Crime and justice: A review of research*, vol. 17, edited by Michael Tonry. Chicago: University of Chicago Press.

———. 1995. A crime control rationale for reinvesting in community corrections. *The Prison Journal* 75(4): 479–496.

———. 1998a. Probation in the United States, part 1. *Perspectives* 22(Spring): 30–41.

———. 1998b. *Community corrections: Probation, parole, and intermediate sanctions*. New York: Oxford University Press.

———. 2000a. Parole and prisoner reentry in the United States, part 1. *Perspectives* 24(Summer): 32–46.

———. 2000b. When prisoners return to the community: Political, economic, and social consequences. In *Sentencing and corrections: Issues for the 21st century* [paper 9 from the Executive Sessions on Sentencing and Corrections]. Washington DC: U.S. Department of Justice (November).

———. 2002. *Reforming probation and parole in the 21st century*. Lanham, MD: American Correctional Association.

———. 2003. *When prisoners come home*. New York: Oxford University Press.

Peterson, Liz Austin. 2009. A potential at ease: Harris County youth boot camp may replace rigorous drills with therapy. *Houston Chronicle*, January 28.

Phillips, Kirby. 2001. Reducing Alcohol-Related Crime Electronically. *Federal Probation* 65(2): 42–44.

Pollock, Jocelyn. 1999. *Criminal women*. Cincinnati, OH: Anderson.

Prendergast, Michael, Jean Wellisch, and Mamie Mee Wong. 1996. Residential treatment for women parolees following prison-based drug treatment: Treatment experiences, needs and service, outcomes. *The Prison Journal* 76(3): 253–274.

President's Commission on Law Enforcement and Administration of Justice. 1967. *The challenge of crime in a free society*. Washington, DC: U.S. Government Printing Office.

Proctor, Jon L. 1999. The new parole: An analysis of parole board decision making as a function of eligibility. *Journal of Crime and Justice* 22(2): 193–217.

Purkiss, Marcus, Misty Kiefer, Craig Hemmens, and Velmer S. Burton. 2003. Probation Officer Functions—A Statutory Analysis. *Federal Probation* 67(1): 12–23.

Quinn, Frederick. 2002. *The courthouse at Indian Creek*. Santa Ana, CA: Seven Locks Press.

Rainey, James. 2002. Probation cadets see job from behind bars. *Los Angeles Times*, February 8, p. A3.

Ransom, George, and Mary Ellen Mastorilli. 1993. The Massachusetts boot camp: Inmate anecdotes. *The Prison Journal* 73(3/4): 307–318.

Reddington, Frances P., and Betsy Wright Kreisel. 2000. Training juvenile probation officers: National trends and practice. *Federal Probation* 64(2): 28–32.

———. 2003. Basic fundamental skills training for juvenile probation officers: Results of a nationwide survey of curriculum content. *Federal Probation* 67(1): 41–45.

Reichel, Philip, and Billie Sudbrack. 1994. Differences among eligibles: Who gets an ISP sentence? *Federal Probation* 58(4): 51–58.

Reinventing Probation Council [Manhattan Institute]. 1999. Broken windows probation: The next step in fighting crime. *Civic Report* 7 (August).

Reske, Henry J. 1996. Scarlet letter sentences. *ABA Journal* 82: 16–17.

Reuell, Peter. 2008. High-tech device knows when you're not sober. *The Metrowest Daily News*, February 10. Retrieved from: http://www.metrowestdailynews.com/multimedia/

Rhine, Edward E. 2002. Why "what works" matters under the "broken windows" model of supervision. *Federal Probation* 66(2): 38–42.

Rhine, Edward E., William R. Smith, and Ronald W. Jackson. 1991. *Paroling authorities: Recent history and current practice*. Laurel, MD: American Correctional Association.

Richards, Stephen C., and Richard S. Jones. 1997. Perpetual incarceration machine: Structural impediments to post-prison success. *Journal of Contemporary Criminal Justice* 13(1): 4–22.

Richie, Beth E. 2001. Challenges incarcerated women face as they return to their communities: Findings from life history interviews. *Crime and Delinquency* 47(3): 368–389.

Rikard, R.V., and Ed Rosenberg. 2007 Aging inmates: A convergence of trends in the American criminal justice system. *Journal of Correctional Health Care* 13 (3): 150–162.

Roberts, Albert. 2004. *Juvenile Justice Sourcebook: Past, Present, and Future.* Oxford: Oxford University Press.

Roberts, Julian V., and Mike Hough. 2002. *Changing attitudes to punishment: Public opinion, crime and justice.* United Kingdom: Willan.

Robinson, Laurie, and Jeremy Travis. 2000. Managing prisoner reentry for public safety. *Federal Sentencing Reporter* 12(5) (March/April).

Roman, John, Wendy Townsend, and Avinash Singh Bhati. 2003. *Recidivism rates for drug court graduates: Nationally based estimates.* NCJ 201229. Washington, DC: U.S. Department of Justice.

Roscoe, Thomas, David E. Duffee, Craig Rivera, and Tony R. Smith. 2007. Arming probation officers: Correlates of the decision to arm at the departmental level. *Criminal Justice Studies* 20 (1), 43–63.

Rotman, Edgardo. 1995. The failure of reform. In *The Oxford history of the prison,* edited by Norval Morris and David Rothman. New York: Oxford University Press, pp. 71–197.

Roy, Sudipto. 1994. Adult offenders in an electronic home detention program: Factors related to failure. *Journal of Offender Monitoring* 7: 17–21.

———. 1997. Five years of electronic monitoring of adults and juveniles in Lake County, Indiana: A comparative study on factors related to failure. *Journal of Crime and Justice* 20: 141–60.

Roy, Sudipto, and Jennifer N. Grimes. 2002. Adult offenders in a day reporting center—A preliminary study. *Federal Probation* 66(1): 44–50.

Ruback, R. Barry, and Mark H. Bergstrom. 2006. Economic sanctions in criminal justice: Purposes, effects, and implications. *Criminal Justice and Behavior* 33(2): 242–273.

Ruback, R. Barry, Stacy N. Hoskins, Alison C. Cares, and Ben Feldmeyer. 2006. Perception and payment of economic sanctions: A survey of offenders. *Federal Probation* 70(3):27–31.

Ruback, R. Barry, Gretchen R. Ruth, and Jennifer N. Shaffer. 2005. Assessing the impact of statutory change: A statewide multilevel analysis of restitution orders in Pennsylvania. *Crime and Delinquency* 51(3): 318–342.

Ruddell, Rick, Brian Roy, and Sita Diehl. 2004. Diverting offenders with mental illness from jail: A tale of two states. *Corrections Compendium* 29(5): 1–5, 38–42.

Sabol, William J., William P. Adams, Barbara Parthasarathy, and Y. Yuan. 2000. *Offenders returning to federal prison, 1986–1997.* Washington, DC: U.S. Department of Justice, Bureau of Justice Statistics.

Sabol, William J., and Heather Couture. 2008. *Prison inmates at midyear 2007.* Washington, DC: U.S. Department of Justice, Bureau of Justice Statistics.

Sabol, William J., and Todd D. Minton. 2008. *Jail inmates at midyear 2007.* Washington, DC: U.S. Department of Justice, Bureau of Justice Statistics.

Sachwald, Judith, Ernest Eley, and Faye S. Taxman. 2006. Four-point strategy reduces technical violations of probation in Connecticut. *Topics in Community Corrections: Effectively Managing Violations and Revocations.* Longmont, CO: National Institute of Corrections.

Samenow, Stanton E. 1984. *Inside the criminal mind.* New York: Times Books.

Sandhu, Harjit S., Richard A, Dodder, and Minu Mathur. 1993. House arrest: Success and failure rates in residential and nonresidential community-based programs. *Journal of Offender Rehabilitation* 19(1/2): 131–44.

Scharr, Timothy M. 2001. Interactive video training for firearms safety. *Federal Probation* 65(2): 45–51.

Schloss, Christine S., and Leanne F. Alarid. 2007. Standards in the privatization of probation services: A statutory analysis. *Criminal Justice Review* 32(3): 233–245.

Schultz, E.J. 2007. Female inmates: Jammed behind bars? Sacramento Bee, July 9. Retrieved from: http://www.november.org/stayinfo/breaking07/Jammed.html

Schwaner, Shawn. 1997. They can run, but can they hide? A profile of parole violators at large. *Journal of Crime and Justice* 20(2): 19–32.

Schwaner, Shawn L., Deanna McGaughey, and Richard Tewksbury. 1998. Situational constraints and absconding behavior: Toward a typology of parole fugitives. *Journal of Offender Rehabilitation* 27(1/2): 37–55.

Seiter, Richard P. 2002. Prisoner reentry and the role of parole officers. *Federal Probation* 66(3): 50–54.

Seiter, Richard P., and Karen R. Kadela. 2003. Prisoner reentry: What works, what does not, and what is promising. *Crime and Delinquency* 49(3): 360–388.

Sentencing Accountability Commission and the Statistical Analysis Center. 2005. First Year Assessment of the 2003 Probation Reform Law's Impact on the Administration of Justice in Delaware (Senate Bill 50 & 150). Retrieved from: http://www.state.de.us/budget/sac/publications/sb50.pdf.

Sentencing Project. 1998. *Felony Disenfranchisement Laws in the United States.* Retrieved from: http://www.hrw.org/reports98/vote/usvot98o.htm.

Settles, Tanya. 2004. *Financial management and strategic planning in a non-profit service organization: Crosspoint, Inc. of San Antonio.* Packard Foundation.

Shelden, Randall G. 1999. *Detention diversion advocacy: An evaluation.* Washington, DC: Office of Juvenile Justice and Delinquency Prevention.

Shepherd, Robert E. Jr. 1999. The juvenile court at 100 years: A look back. In *Juvenile justice: An evolving juvenile court, 100th anniversary of the juvenile court, 1899–1999.* Washington, DC: National Center for Juvenile Justice, Office of Juvenile Justice and Delinquency Prevention.

Sickmund, Melissa. 2003. *Juveniles in court.* Washington, DC: Office of Juvenile Justice and Delinquency Prevention.

Sickmund, Melissa. 2009. *Delinquency cases in juvenile court, 2005*. Washington, DC: Office of Juvenile Justice and Delinquency Prevention.

Sickmund, Melissa, T.J. Sladky, and Wei Kang. 2008. *Census of juveniles in residential placement databook*. Washington, DC: Office of Juvenile Justice and Delinquency Prevention. Retrieved from: http://www.ojjdp.ncjrs.org/ojstatbb/cjrp/

Siedschlaw, Kurt D., and Beth A. Wiersma. 2005. Costs and outcomes of a work ethic camp: How do they compare to a traditional prison facility? *Corrections Compendium* 30(6): 1–5, 28–30.

Silverstein, Martin. 1997. Doing justice: National parole board decision making [Unpublished Ph.D. dissertation]. Arizona State University, Tempe.

Sims, Barbara, and Mark Jones. 1997. Predicting success or failure on probation: Factors associated with felony probation outcomes. *Crime and Delinquency* 43: 314–327.

Skeem, Jennifer L., Paula Emke-Francis, and Jennifer Eno Louden. 2006. Probation, mental health, and mandated treatment. *Criminal Justice and Behavior* 33(2): 158–184.

Slate, Risdon N. 2003. From the jailhouse to Capitol Hill: Impacting mental health court legislation and defining what constitutes a mental health court. *Crime and Delinquency* 49(1): 6–29.

Slate, Risdon N., Richard Feldman, Erik Roskes, and Migdalia Baerga. 2004. Training federal probation officers as mental health specialists. *Federal Probation* 68(3): 9–15.

Slate, Risdon N., and W. Wesley Johnson. 2008a. *The criminalization of mental illness: Crisis and opportunity in the justice system*. Durham, NC: Carolina Academic Press.

Slate, Risdon, and W. Wesley Johnson. 2008b. *A comparison of federal and state probation officer stress levels*. Paper presented at the annual meeting of the Academy of Criminal Justice Sciences, Cincinnati, OH.

Slate, Risdon N., W. Wesley Johnson, and Terry L. Wells. 2000. Up to speed: Probation officer stress: Is there an organizational solution? *Federal Probation* 64(1): 56–59.

Slate, Risdon N., Erik Roskes, Richard Feldman, and Migdalia Baerga. 2003. Doing justice for mental illness and society: Federal probation and pretrial service officers as mental health specialists. *Federal Probation* 67(3):13–19.

Sluder, Richard, Robert Shearer, and Dennis Potts. 1991. Probation officers' role perceptions and attitudes toward firearms. *Federal Probation* 55: 3–11.

Small, Shawn E., and Sam Torres. 2001. Arming probation officers: Enhancing public confidence and officer safety. *Federal Probation* 65(3): 24–28.

Smith, Brent L., Erin Watkins, and Kathryn Morgan. 1997. The effect of victim participation on parole decisions: Results from a southeastern state. *Criminal Justice Policy Review* 8(1): 57–74.

Smith, Michael E. 2001. What future for "public safety" and "restorative justice" in community corrections? *Sentencing and corrections: Issues for the 21st century* (No. 11, June). Washington, DC: U.S. Department of Justice.

Smith, Michael E., and Walter J. Dickey. 1999. Reforming sentencing and corrections for just punishment and public safety. *Sentencing and corrections: Issues for the 21st century* (No. 4). Washington, DC: U.S. Department of Justice.

Snyder, Howard. 2008. *Juvenile arrests 2006*. Washington, DC: Office of Juvenile Justice and Delinquency Prevention.

Snyder, Howard, and Melissa Sickmund. 1995. *Juvenile offenders and victims: A national report*. Washington, DC: Office of Juvenile Justice and Delinquency Prevention.

———. 1999. *Juvenile offenders and victims: 1999 national report*. Washington, DC: Office of Juvenile Justice and Delinquency Prevention.

———. 2006. *Juvenile offenders and victims: 2006 national report*. Washington, DC: Office of Juvenile Justice and Delinquency Prevention.

Solis, Dianne. 2006. Convicts get help going straight to work. *Dallas Morning News*, September 24.

Solomon, Amy L. 2006. Does parole supervision work? Research findings and policy opportunities. *Perspectives* (Spring): 26–37. Retrieved from: http://www.urban.org/uploadedpdf/1000908_parole_supervision.pdf.

Stageberg, Paul, and Bonnie Wilson. 2005. *Recidivism among Iowa probationers*. Iowa Division of Criminal and Juvenile Justice Planning. Retrieved from: http://www.state.ia.us/government/dhr/cjjp/images/pdf/recidivism%20among%20Iowa%20probationers.pdf#.

State of New Hampshire, Human Resources. 2006. Retrieved from: http://nh.gov/hr/classpec_j/5462.htm.

State of Oregon, Department of Administrative Services, Juvenile Parole and Probation Officer. Retrieved from: http://www.hr.das.state.or.us/hrsd/class/6634.HTM.

Steiner, Benjamin. 2004. Treatment retention: A theory of post-release supervision for the substance-abusing offender. *Federal Probation* 68(3): 24–29.

Stewart Law Firm. 2000. Expungement under the New Jersey Code of Criminal Justice. Retrieved from: http://home.pro-usa.net/rstewart/lexpunge.htm.

Stickels, John. 2007. A study of probation revocations for technical violations in Hays County, Texas, USA. *Probation Journal* 54(1): 52–61.

Stinchcomb, Jeanne B., and Daryl Hippensteel. 2001. Presentence investigation reports: A relevant justice model tool or a medical model relic? *Criminal Justice Policy Review* 12(2): 164–177.

Stoll, Michael A., and Shawn D. Bushway. 2008. The effect of criminal background checks on hiring ex-offenders. *Criminology and Public Policy* 7(3): 371–404.

Storm, John P. 1997. What United States probation officers do. *Federal Probation* 61(1): 13–18.

Stottmann, Jonathan O. 2007. Presentence restitution: When opportunity knocks. *News and Views* 32 (19): September 10.

Stowe, Michael L. 1994. Professional orientation of probation officers: Ideology and personality [Unpublished Ph.D. dissertation]. University of Pittsburgh.

Taxman, Faye. 2002. Supervision—Exploring the dimensions of effectiveness. *Federal Probation* 66(2): 14–27.

Taxman, Faye S. 2008. No illusions: Offender and organizational change in Maryland's proactive community supervision efforts. *Criminology and Public Policy* 7 (2): 275–302.

Taxman, Faye S., and Jeffrey A. Bouffard. 2003. Drug treatment in the community—A case study of system integration issues. *Federal Probation* 67(2): 4–14.

Taylor, Scott and Ginger Martin. 2006. Four-point strategy reduces technical violations of probation in Connecticut. *Topics in Community Corrections: Effectively Managing Violations and Revocations.* Longmont, CO: National Institute of Corrections.

Tewksbury, Richard. 2002. Validity and utility of the Kentucky sex offender registry. *Federal Probation* 66(1): 21–26.

Texas Department of Criminal Justice. 1999. Community corrections facilities outcome study. Retrieved from: http://webarchive.org/web/2000081165233/http://www.tdcj.state.tx.us/publications/cjad/ccfout~1.pdf

Texas Legislative Budget Board. 2005. Statewide criminal justice recidivism and revocation rates. Retrieved from: http://www.lbb.state.tx.us/pubsafety_crimjustice/3_reports/recidivism_report_2005.pdf

Tonry, Michael. 1997. *Intermediate sanctions in sentencing guidelines.* Washington, DC: U.S. Department of Justice, National Institute of Justice (May).

———. 1998. Evaluating intermediate sanction programs. In *Community corrections: Probation, parole and intermediate sanctions,* edited by Joan Petersilia. New York: Oxford University Press.

———. 1999a. Parochialism in U.S. sentencing policy. *Crime and Delinquency* 45(1): 48–65.

———. 1999b. Reconsidering indeterminate and structured sentencing. *Sentencing and corrections: Issues for the 21st century.* Washington, DC: U.S. Department of Justice.

Travis, Jeremy. 2000. But they all come back: Rethinking prisoner reentry, *Sentencing and corrections: Issues for the 21st century.* Washington, DC: U.S. Department of Justice.

Turner, Susan, Jesse Janneta, James Hess, Randy Myers, Rita Shah, Robert Werth, and Alyssa Whitby. 2007. *Implementation and early outcomes for the San Diego high risk sex offender GPS pilot program* (Working paper). Center for Evidence-Based Corrections, University of California, Irvine.

Turner, Susan, and Judith Greene. 1999. The FARE probation experiment: Implementation and outcomes of day fines for felony offenders in Maricopa County. *The Justice System Journal* 21 (1): 1–19.

Turner, Susan, and Joan Petersilia. 1996a. *Day fines in four jurisdictions.* Santa Monica, CA: RAND Corporation.

———. 1996b. Work release in Washington: Effects on recidivism and correctional costs. *The Prison Journal* 76(2): 138–164.

Twill, Sarah E., Larry Nackerud, Edwin Risler, Jeffrey Bernat, and David Taylor. 1998. Changes in measured loneliness, control, and social support among parolees in a halfway house. *Journal of Offender Rehabilitation* 27(3/4): 77–92.

Uggen, Christopher. 2004. Disenfranchisement and the civil reintegration of convicted felons. Retrieved from: http://www.soc.umn.edu/~uggen

Ulrich, Thomas E. 2002. Pretrial diversion in the federal court system. *Federal Probation* 66(3): 30–37.

Umbreit, Mark S. 1999. Restorative justice: What works. In *Research to results: Effective community corrections,* edited by Patricia M. Harris. Lanham, MD: American Correctional Association.

Umbreit, Mark S., and Robert B. Coates. 1993. Cross-site analysis of victim–offender mediation in four states. *Crime and Delinquency* 39: 565–585.

Umbreit, Mark S., Robert B. Coates, and Betty Vos. 2001. The impact of victim–offender mediation: Two decades of research. *Federal Probation* 65(3): 29–35.

U.S. Bureau of Prisons. 2008. *Guidelines Manual* (November 1, 2008). Section 7B1.4, p. 488.

U.S. Department of Justice. 1974. *Attorney general's survey of release procedures.* New York: Arno.

———. 2005. 28 CFR Part 2: Paroling, recommitting, and supervising federal prisoners: Prisoners serving sentences under the U.S and D.C. codes. *Federal Register* 70(70), April 13, 2005: 19262.

———. 2008. *Compendium of federal justice statistics, 2004.* Washington, DC: U.S. Department of Justice. Accessed at: http://www.ojp.usdoj.gov/bjs/pub/pdf/cfjs0407.pdf

U.S. Department of Justice, Bureau of Justice Statistics. 1995. *Correctional Populations in the United States 1994.* Washington, DC: U.S. Department of Justice.

U.S. Department of Justice, Bureau of Justice Statistics. 2003. *Census of state and federal correctional facilities, 2000.* Washington, DC: U.S. Department of Justice.

U.S. Department of Labor. 2006. *Occupational outlook handbook, 2006–07 edition.* Probation officers and correctional treatment specialists, Bureau of Labor Statistics. Retrieved from: http://www.bls.gov/oco/ocos265.htm.

U.S. Department of Labor. 2009. *The Federal Bonding Program.* Retrieved from: http://www.bonds4jobs.com/index.html

U.S. Parole Commission. 2003. *Rules and procedures manual.* Washington, DC: U.S. Parole Commission. Retrieved from: http://www.usdoj.gov/uspc/rules_procedures/rulesmanual.htm.

———. 2006. Answering your questions. Retrieved from: http://www.usdoj.gov/uspc/questionstxt.htm.

U.S. Sentencing Commission. 2002a. *2001 Sourcebook of federal sentencing statistics.* Washington, DC: U.S. Sentencing Commission.

U.S. Sentencing Commission. 2002b. *Federal Sentencing Guidelines* Chapter 3603, 1–10:1001–1002. Retrieved from: http://www.ussc.gov/2002guid/TABCON02.htm

VanBenschoten, Scott. 2008. Risk/needs assessment: Is this the best we can do? *Federal Probation* 72 (2): 38–42.

Van Ness, Daniel, and Karen Strong. 1997. *Restoring justice.* Cincinnati, OH: Anderson.

VanNostrand, Marie and Gena Keebler. 2007. Our journey toward pretrial justice. *Federal Probation* 71(2): 20–25.

Vigorita, Michael S. 2002. Fining practices in felony courts: An analysis of offender, offense, and systemic factors. *Corrections Compendium* 27(11):1–5, 26.

Vollum, Scott, and Chris Hale. 2002. Electronic monitoring: A research review. *Corrections Compendium* 27(7): 1–4, 23–27.

von Hirsch, Andrew. 1976. *Doing justice: The choice of punishments.* New York: Hill and Wang.

von Zielbauer, Paul. 2003. Court treatment system is found to help drug offenders stay clean. *New York Times, November 9.Health section.* Accessed at: www.nytimes.com.

Vose, Brenda, Francis T. Cullen, and Paula Smith. The empirical status of the level of service inventory. *Federal Probation* 72 (3), 22–29.

Waldo, Gordon P., and Theodore G. Chiricos. 1977. Work release and recidivism: An empirical evaluation of a social policy. *Evaluation Quarterly* 1 (1), 87–108.

Walker, Donald R. 1988. *Penology for profit.* College Station, TX: Texas A&M University Press.

Walker, Lorenn. 2002. Conferencing: A new approach for juvenile justice in Honolulu. *Federal Probation* 66(1): 38–43.

Walker, Lorenn and Leslie A. Hayashi. 2007. Pono Kaulike: A Hawaii criminal court provides restorative justice practices for healing relationships. *Federal Probation* 71(3): 18–24.

Walsh, C. L., and S. H. Beck. 1990. Predictors of recidivism among halfway house residents. *American Journal of Criminal Justice* 15(1): 137–156.

Ward, Geoff and Aaron Kupchik. 2009. Accountable to what? Professional orientations towards accountability-based juvenile justice. *Punishment and Society* 11(1): 85–109.

Weisburd, David, Tomer Einat, Matt Kowalski. 2008. The miracle of the cells: An experimental study of interventions to increase payment of court-ordered financial obligations. *Criminology and Public Policy* 7(1):9–36.

Wells, Terry, Sharla Colbert, and Risdon N. Slate. 2006. Gender matters: Differences in state probation officer stress. *Journal of Contemporary Criminal Justice* 22(1): 63–79.

West, Heather C. and William J. Sabol. 2008. *Prisoners in 2007.* Washington, DC: U.S. Department of Justice, Bureau of Justice Statistics.

West-Smith, Mary, Mark R. Pogrebin, and Eric D. Poole. 2000. Denial of parole: An inmate perspective. *Federal Probation* 64(2): 3–10.

Wicharaya, Tamask. 1995. *Simple theory, hard reality: The impact of sentencing reforms on courts, prisons, and crime.* New York: State University of New York Press.

Wilkinson, Reginald A., and Edward E. Rhine. 2005. The international association of reentry: Mission and future. *Journal of Correctional Education* 56(2): 139–145.

Wilkinson, Reginald A., Edward E. Rhine, and Martha Henderson-Hurley. 2005. Reentry in Ohio corrections: A catalyst for change. *Journal of Correctional Education* 56(2): 158–172.

Williams, Frank P. III, Marilyn D. McShane, and H. Michael Dolny. 2000a. Developing a parole classification instrument for use as a management tool. *Corrections Management Quarterly* 4(4): 45–59.

———. 2000b. Predicting parole absconders. *The Prison Journal* 80(1): 24–38.

Williams, Frank P. III, Marilyn D. McShane, Lorraine Samuels, and H. Michael Dolny. 2000. The youngest adult parolees: Do they have different parole experiences? Paper presented at the annual meeting of the American Society of Criminology, San Francisco, California, November 14–17.

Wilson, David B., Doris L. MacKenzie, and Fawn Ngo Mitchell. 2005. Effects of Correctional Boot Camps on Offending. A Campbell Collaboration systematic review, available at: http://www.aic.gov/au/campbellcj/reviews/titles.html

Wilson, James A., and Robert C. Davis. 2006. Good intentions meet hard realities: An evaluation of the Project Greenlight reentry program. *Criminology & Public Policy* 5(2): 303–338.

Wines, Fredrick H. 1919. *Punishment and reformation: A study of the penitentiary system.* New York: T.Y. Crowell.

Wolf, Thomas J. 1997. What United States pretrial services officers do. *Federal Probation* 61(1): 19–24.

Wright, Martin. 1996. *Justice for victims and offenders: A restorative response to crime,* 2nd ed. Winchester, England: Waterside Press.

Wright, Ronald. 1998. *Managing prison growth in North Carolina through structured sentencing.* Washington, DC: National Institute of Justice Program Focus

Zevitz, Richard, and Mary Ann Farkas. 2000. The impact of sex-offender community notification on probation/parole in Wisconsin. *International Journal of Offender Therapy and Comparative Criminology* 44(1): 8–21.

CODES

California Interstate Compact on Juveniles, Cal. Welf. and Inst. Code, secs. 1300–1308 (West).

California Penal Code, sec. 1203, 4853 (West).

Colorado Revised Statutes 1998, sec. 24-72-308.

Community Corrections Act, Oregon Revised Statutes 423.505 (Oregon Laws 1995).

Federal Rules of Criminal Procedure, Art. 3564.

Federal Criminal Code and Rules, 2004. Belmont, CA: West.

Illinois Unified Code of Corrections, sec. 1005–5–5(d).

Indiana Juvenile Code Title 31, Article 6, Chapter 9, Section 31–6–9–4(a).

Model Penal Code, sec. 7.07 (5); sec. 301.2.

N.H. Rev. Stat. Ann. sec. 607–A:5.

New York Penal Law, sec. 65.00–1 (McKinney).

Texas Code of Criminal Procedure, Article 42.12, Sec. 7, Sec. 11(1), Sec. 20, Sec. 22(a)(1). (Vernon).

III. Unified Code of Corrections sec. 1005–6–5(2).

United States Codes, Title 10, U.S.C., sec. 504; Title 11, U.S.C.A., sec. 1328 (a)(3); Title 18 U.S.C. sec. 921 (a)(20); sec. 922g1; sec. 3561; sec. 3563(a)(2); sec. 3563 (b)(11); sec. 3583 (e) (3); sec. 3606; sec. 5037 (c)(1); sec. 5037 (c)(2); Title 28 U.S.C. sec. 235(a)(1)(B)(ii)(IV); sec. 1865 (b)(5); Title 29 U.S.C., sec. 405.

U.S. Constitution, Article 1.

Wis. Stat. Ann. sec. 57.078.

COURT CASES

Ballenger v. State, 436 S.E.2d 793 (Ga. App. 1993).

Bearden v. Georgia, 461 U.S. 660 (1983).

Beecham v. United States, 511 U.S. 368 (1994).

Belk v. Purkett, 15 F.3d 803 (8th Cir. 1994).

Benton v. State, 2003 WL 22220501, Ala. Crim. App. (2003)

Best v. State, 264 A.D.2d 404, 694 N.Y.S.2d 689 (2d Dep't 1999).

Biddle v. Perovich, 274 U.S. 480, 47 S. Ct. 664, 71 L. Ed. 1161 (1927).

Boling v. Romer, 101 F.3d 1336 (10th Cir. 1996).

Breed v. Jones, 421 U.S. 517 (1975).

Bruggeman v. State, 681 So.2d. 822 (1996).

Burdick v. United States, 236 U.S. 79, 59 L. Ed. 476 (1915).

Cabell v. Chavez-Salido (1982) 454 U.S. 432

Cabla v. State, 6 S.W.3d 543 (Tex. Crim. App.1999).

Caron v. United States, 524 U.S. 308 (1998).

Commonwealth v. Chase, in Thacher's Criminal Cases, 267 (1831), recorded in vol. 11 of the Records of the Old Municipal Court of Boston, 199.

Commonwealth of Massachusetts v. Talbot, 444 Mass. 586, 830 N.E.2d 177 (2005).

Commonwealth v. Williams, 1997 Pa. LEXIS 786 (1997).

Connecticut Department of Public Safety et. al. v. Doe, 538 U.S. 1 (2003).

Davis v. Alaska, 415 U.S. 308 (1974).

De Veau v. Braisted, 363 U.S. 144, 80 S. Ct. 1146, 4 L. Ed. 2d 1109 (1960).

Eddings v. Oklahoma, 455 U.S. 104 (1983).

Ex parte Garland, 71 U.S. 333, 18 L. Ed. 366 (1867).

Ex parte Lefors, 303 S.W.2d 394 (Tex. Crim. App. 1957).

Ex parte United States, 242 U.S. 27, 37 S. Ct. 72, 61 L. Ed. 129 (1916).

Fare v. Michael C., 442 U.S. 707 (1985).

Fields v. State, 2002 WL 126972, Ala. Crim. App. (2002)

Franciosi v. Michigan Parole Board, 461 Mich. 347 (2000).

Fuller v. Oregon, 417 U.S. 40 (1974).

Gagnon v. Scarpelli, 411 U.S. 778 (1973).

Glover v. Michigan Parole Board, 460 Mich. 511 (1999).

Golberg v. Beeler, 82 F.Supp.2d 302 (1999).

Goldschmitt v. State, 490 So.2d 123 (Fla. Dist. Ct. App. 1986).

Greenholtz v. Inmates of the Nebraska Penal and Correctional Complex, 442 U.S. 1, 99 S. Ct. 2100, 2107, 60 L. Ed. 2d 668 (1979).

Griffin v. Wisconsin, 483 U.S. 868 (1987).

Hampton v. State, 786 A.2d 375 (R.I. 2001).

Hawker v. New York, 170 U.S. 189, 18 S. Ct. 573, 42 L. Ed. 1002 (1898).

Hawkins v. Freeman, 166 F.3d 267 (1999).

Higdon v. United States, 627 F.2d 893 (9th Cir. 1980).

Inouye v. Kemna, 06-15474 (9th Cir. 2007), DC No. CV-04-00026-DAE

In re Bocchiaro, 49 F. Supp. 37 (W.D.N.Y. 1943).

In re Ecklund, 139 Wash. 2d 166 (1999).

In re Gault, 387 U.S. 1 (1967).

In re Winship, 397 U.S. 358 (1970).

Jago v. Van Curen, 454 U.S. 14 (1981).

Jones v. State, 916 S.W.2d 766 (Ark. App. 1996).

Kansas v. Crane, 534 U.S. 407 (2002).

Kansas v. Hendricks, 521 U.S. 346 (1997).

Kent v. United States, 383 U.S. 541 (1966).

King v. Simpson, 189 F.3d 283 (2d Cir. 1999).

Konigsberg v. State Bar, 353 U.S. 252, 77 S. Ct. 722, 1 L. Ed. 2d 810 (1957).

Lay v. Louisiana Parole Board, 741 So.2d 80 (La. Ct. App. 1st Cir. 1999).

Marlo v. State Board of Medical Examiners, 112 Cal. App. 2d 276, 246 P.2d 69 (1952).

Matter of J.B.S., 696 S.W.2d 223 (Tex. App. 1985).

McKeiver v. Pennsylvania, 403 U.S. 528 (1971).

McKune v. Lile 536 U.S. 24 (2002), 224 F. 3d. 1175.

Mempa v. Rhay, 389 U.S. 128, 88 S. Ct. 254, 19 L. Ed. 2d 336 (1967).

Menechino v. Oswald, 430 F.2d 403, 407 (2d Cir. 1970), cert. denied, 400 U.S. 1023, 91 S. Ct. 588, 27 L. Ed. 2d 635 (1971).

Miller v. District of Columbia, 294 A.2d 365 (D.C. App. 1972).

Miranda v. Arizona, 384 U.S. 436 (1966).

Mixon v. Pennsylvania, 783 A.2d (2000).

Moore v. United States, 571 F.2d 179 (3rd Cir. 1978).

Morrissey v. Brewer, 408 U.S. 471 (1972).

Murrill v. State Board of Accountancy, 97 Cal. App. 2d 709, 218 P.2d 569 (1950).

Newsom v. State, 2004 WL 943861, Miss. Ct. App. (2004).

New Jersey v. T.L.O., 469 U.S. 325 (1985).

Pennsylvania Board of Probation and Parole v. Scott, 524 U.S. 357 (1998).

People v. Colabello, 948 P.2d 77 (Colo. App. 1997).

People v. Heckler, 16 Cal. Rptr. 2d 681, 13 C. A. 4th 1049 (1993).

People v. Letterlough, 655 N.E. 2d 146 (N.Y. 1995).

People v. Meyer, 176 Ill. 2d 372, 680 N.E. 315 (1997).

People v. Price, 24 Ill. App. 2d. 364 (1960).

People v. Ramos, 48 CrL 1057 (Ill.S.Ct.) (1990).

People v. Sweeden, 116 Cal. App. 2d. 891 (1953).

Perry v. State, 778 So. 2d 1072 (Fla. Dist. Ct. App. 5th Dist. 2001)

Peterson v. State Liquor Authority, 42 A.D. 2d 195, 345 N.Y.S. 2d 780 (1973).

Ramahlo v. Travis, 737 N.Y.S.2d 160 (3d Dep't 2002).

Reyes v. Tate, 91 Ohio St. 3d 84, 742 N.E.2d 132 (2001).

Richardson v. New York State Executive Department, 602 N.Y.S.2d 443 (1993).

Richardson v. Ramirez, 418 U.S. 24, 94 S. Ct. 2655, 41 L. Ed. 2d 551 (1974).

Rodriguez v. State, 378 So.2d 7 (Fla. Dist. Ct. App. 1979).

Roper v. Simmons, 543 U.S. 551 (2005).

Scarpa v. United States Board of Parole, 477 F.2d 278, 281 (5th Cir. 1972), vacated as moot; 414

U.S. 809, 94 S. Ct. 79, 38 L. Ed. 2d 44 (1973).

Schall v. Martin, 104 S. Ct. 2403 (1984).

Seling v. Young, 531 U.S. 250 (2001).

Silmon v. Travis, 95 N.Y.2d 470 (2000).

Smith v. Daily Mail Publishing Co., 443 U.S. 97 (1979).

Smith v. Doe, 538 U.S. 84 (2003).

Soliz v. State, 171 Tex. Crim. 376 (1961).

Spaulding v. Nielsen, 599 F.2d 728 (5th Cir. 1979).

Stanford v. Kentucky, 109 S.Ct. 2969 (1989).

State v. Bourrie, 190 Or. App. 572, 80 P.3d 505 (2003).

State v. Faraday, 69 Conn. App. 421 (2002).

State v. Graham, 30 P.3d 310 (Kan 2001).

State v. Gropper, 888 P.2d 12211 (Wash. App. 1995).

State v. Pizel, 987 P.2d 1288 (Utah Ct. App. 1999).

State v. Walker, 432 So.2d 1057 (La. Ct. App. 1983).

Summers v. State, 817 So. 2d 950 (Fla Dist. Ct. App. 2d Dist. 2002).

United States v. Allen, 13 F.3d 105 U.S. (4th Cir. December 1993).

United States v. Angulo, 864 F.2d 504 (7th Cir. 1988).

United States v. Bachsian, 4 F.3d 288 (1993).

United States v. Balon, 384 F.3d 38 (2d Cir. 2004).

United States v. Booker, 125 S. Ct. 738, 160 LED 2d 621 (U.S. 2005).

United States v. Caron, 524 U.S. 308 (1998).

United States v. Dougherty, 810 F.2d 763 (8th Cir. 1987).

United States v. Fowler, U.S. (11th Cir. 1999).

United States v. Gordon, 4 F.3d 1567 U.S. (10th Cir. September 1993).

United States v. Knights, 534 U.S. 112 (2001).

United States v. Laney, 189 F.3d 954 (9th Cir. 1999).

United States v. Lasky, 592 F.2d 5670 (9th Cir. 1979).

United States v. Lockhart, 58 F.3d 86 (4th Cir. June 1995).

United States v. McCormick, 54 F.3d 214 U.S. (5th Cir. 1995).

United States v. Pettus, 303 F.3d 480 (2d Cir. 2002).

United States v. Porotsky, 105 F.3d 69 U.S. (2nd Cir. 1997).

United States v. Rivera, 96 F.3rd 41 (2nd cir. September 1996).

United States v. RLC, 503 U.S. 291 (1992).

United States v. Salerno, 481 U.S. 739 (1987).

United States v. Thurlow, 44 F.3d 46 U.S. (1st Cir. 1995).

United States v. Trevino, 89 F.3d 187, U.S. (4th Cir. July 1996).

United States v. Turner, 44 F.3d 900 (10th Cir. 1995).

United States v. Washington, 11 F.3d 1510 U.S. (10th Cir. November 1993).

United States v. Wolff, 90 F.3d 191 (7th Cir. 1996).

Walrath v. Getty, 71 F.3d 679 (7th Cir. 1995).

Warner v. Orange County Department of Probation, 115 F3d 1068 (2nd Cir 1997).

Williams v. New York, 337 U.S. 241 (1949).

Williams v. Oklahoma, 358 U.S. 576 (1959).

Williams v. State of New Jersey, 2006 NJ Lexis 389, (2006).

Young v. Harper, 520 U.S. 143 (1997).

Table of Cases

B

Ballenger v. State (1993), 50
Bearden v. Georgia (1983), 169, 247
Beecham v. United States (1994),
    360, 369
Belk v. Purkett (1994), 168
Benton v. State (2003), 168
Best v. State (1999), 151
Biddle v. Perovich (1927), 368
Boling v. Romer (1996), 305
Breed v. Jones (1975), 327
Bruggeman v. State (1996), 166
Burdick v. United States (1915), 369

C

Cabell v. Chavez-Salido (1982), 139
Cabla v. State (1999), 240
Commonwealth v. Chase (1830), 80
Commonwealth v. Williams (1997), 304
Commonwealth of Massachusetts v. Talbot
    (2005), 60
Connecticut Department of Public Safety
    et al. v. Doe (2003), 363

D

Davis v. Alaska (1974), 327
De Veau v. Braisted (1960), 327

E

Ex parte Garland (1867), 369
Ex parte Lefors (1957), 369
Ex parte United States 242 U.S. 27
    (1916), 80

F

Fare v. Michael C. (1985), 327,
    341–342
Fields v. State (2002), 168
Franciosi v. Michigan Parole Board
    (2000), 292
Fuller v. Oregon (1974), 250

G

Gagnon v. Scarpelli (1973), 167–168
Glover v. Michigan Parole Board (1999), 292
Golberg v. Beeler (1999), 292
Goldschmitt v. State (1986), 50

Greenholtz v. Inmates of the Nebraska
    Penal and Correctional Complex
    (1979), 291–292
Griffin v. Wisconsin (1987), 51

H

Hampton v. State (2001), 167
Hawker v. New York (1898), 372

I

In re Bocchiaro (1943), 368
In re Ecklund (1999), 292
In re Gault (1967), 326–327
In re Winship (1970), 327
Inouye v. Kemna (2007), 51

J

Jago v. Van Curen (1981), 292

K

Kansas v. Crane (2002), 367
Kansas v. Hendricks (1997), 367
King v. Simpson (1999), 150
Konigsberg v. State Bar (1957),
    371–372
Kent v. United States (1966), 326

L

League of Women Voters of California vs.

M

McPherson (2006), 355
Marlo v. State Board of Medical Examiners
    (1952), 369
McKeiver v. Pennsylvania
    (1971), 327
McKune Warden v. Lile (2002), 51
Menechino v. Oswald (1971), 291
Mempa v. Rhay (1967), 168
Miranda v. Arizona (1966),
    60, 341
Mixon v. Commonwealth of Pennsylvania
    (2001), 355
Moore v. United States (1978), 59
Morrissey v. Brewer (1972), 167
Murrill v. State Board of Accountancy
    (1950), 369

N

New Jersey v. T.L.O (1985), 327
Newsom v. State (2004), 168

P

Pennsylvania Board of Probation and
    Parole v. Scott (1998), 304
People v. Colabello (1997), 169
People v. Heckler (1993), 50
People v. Letterlough (1995), 50
People v. Meyer (1997), 50
People v. Ramos (1990), 212
Perry v. State (2001), 167
Peterson v. State Liquor Authority
    (1973), 359

R

Ramahlo v. Travis (2002), 292
Reyes v. Tate (2001), 168
Richardson v. Ramirez (1974), 354
Roper v. Simmons (2005), 328

S

Schall v. Martin (1984), 327, 335
Seling v. Young (2001), 366
Silmon v. Travis (2000), 292
Smith v. Daily Mail Publishing Co.
    (1979), 327
Smith v. Doe (2003), 363
Soliz v. State (1961), 167
Spaulding v. Nielsen (1979), 150
Stanford v. Kentucky (1989), 328
State v. Bourrie (2003), 49
State v. Faraday (2002), 305
State v. Graham (2001), 168
State v. Gropper (1995), 169
State v. Walker (1983), 369
State of Missouri v. Anthony Williams, 54
Summers v. State (2002), 166

T

Tucker v. Alabama Board of Pardons and
    Paroles (2000), 292

U

United States v. Allen (1993), 60
United States v. Angulo (1988), 250

United States v. Bachsian (1993), 240
United States v. Balon (2004), 221
United States v. Booker (2005), 47
United States v. Dougherty (1987), 250
United States v. Fowler, (1999), 360
United States v. Gordon (1993), 60
United States v. Knights (2001), 51, 102
United States v. Laney (1999), 239
United States v. Lasky (1979), 59
United States v. Lockhart (1995), 59
United States v. McCormick (1995), 168

United States v. Pettus (2002), 166
United States v. Porotsky (1997), 49
United States v. Riviera (1996), 59
United States v. RLC (1992), 169
United States v. Salerno (1987), 23
United States v. Thurlow (1995), 49
United States v. Trevino (1996), 58
United States v. Turner (1995), 304
United States v. Washington
    (1993), 60
United States v. Wolff (1996), 247

W

Walrath v. Getty (1995), 305
*Warner v. Orange County Department of
    Probation* (1997), 51
Williams v. Oklahoma (1959), 58
Williams v. New York (1949),
    52, 58
Williams v. State of New Jersey
    (2006), 146
Wooden v. State (2001), 240

Name Index

A

Abadinsky, Howard, 262
Alarid, Leanne F., 31–32, 55, 58, 113, 151–153, 184, 189, 194
Albonetti, Celesta A., 171
Alexander, Melissa, 106
Alonso, Alfonso, 33–34
Alper, Benedict S., 182
Anderson, James F., 189
Andrews, Don A., 98
Andrews, Sara, 164
Annison, Jill, 148
Applegate, Brandon K., 10
Arling, Gary, 101
Armstrong, Anita Harker, 277
Armstrong, Gaylene, 111, 193, 216–218, 221
Atkins, Susan, 271
Augustus, John, 81–83, 85
Aziz, David W., 188–189

B

Baerga, Migdalia, 193–195
Bahr, Stephen J., 277
Bailey, J., 199
Baird, S. Christopher, 101
Bales, William D., 221
Barclay, Lynn Z., 88
Barklage, Heather, 160–161
Barnes, Christina M., 37
Barnhill, Maldine Beth, 150
Barthwell, Andrea G., 199
Barton, William, 200–201
Baumer, Eric P., 205
Baumer, Terry L., 213
Bechtel, Kristin, 98
Beck, Allen J., 264, 308–309, 311, 317, 318
Beck, V.S., 7
Bennish, Steve, 112
Bentham, Jeremy, 83, 246
Bergstrom, Mark H., 241, 246–250
Berk, Jillian, 204
Bernat, Jeffrey, 184
Beto, Dan Richard, 91
Bhati, Avinash Singh, 37
Binder, Arnold, 84, 334
Blomberg, Thomas G., 221
Bloom, Barbara, 196
Bokos, Peter, 199
Bonczar, Thomas P., 4, 7, 186, 195, 267, 269–270

Bonham, Gene, 150, 160–161
Bonta, James, 98, 211
Bosco, Robert J., 152
Bouffard, Jeffrey A., 33, 245
Bourque, Blair B., 189
Boyle, Barbara, 272
Brady, Brian, 219
Braithwaite, John, 232–233
Brame, Robert, 192
Brody, David C., 192
Bazemore, Gordon, 233–236
Brockway, Zebulon R., 262
Brown, Kelly L., 210–211
Bruce, Dickson D., 84, 334
Buckler, Kevin G., 352, 359–361
Burke, Peggy B., 163, 165–167
Burnham, L. P., 85
Burns, Jerald, 189
Burton, Velmer S., 189
Butts, Jeffrey A., 85
Byrne, James, 26–28, 223–224

C

Cadigan, Timothy P., 26–28
Cahill, Melissa A., 106
Camp, Camille Graham, 10, 103, 110, 137, 141, 144, 180, 183, 214, 298
Camp, George M., 10, 103, 110, 137, 141, 144, 180, 183, 214, 298
Caputo, Gail A., 243–244
Carey, S., 35
Carter, Madeline M., 159, 161
Chasnoff, Brian, 148
Castillo, Eladio D., 31–32, 194
Cheesman, Fred, 31
Clark, Cherrie L., 188–189
Clark, John, 23–25, 27–28
Clark, Michael D., 106
Clear, Todd R., 9
Clifford, Mary, 213
Cohen, Robyn L., 310
Cohen, Thomas H., 26–27, 28
Colbert, Sharla, 149
Cook, Rufus R., 85
Coolidge, Calvin, 84
Cooprider, Keith W., 24, 27–28
Corbett, Ronald, 9
Couture, Heather, 180
Craddock, Amy, 221–222, 224–226
Crank, John, 142

Crawford, Richard, 104
Crofton, Sir Walter, 261
Cromwell, Paul, 113
Cullen, Francis T., 10, 98, 104
Cuniff, Mark, 170
Cushman, Robert, 154
Cuvelier, Steven J., 189

D

D'Angelo, L., 35
Dannerbeck, A., 34–35
Davidson, Janet T., 104
del Carmen, Rolando, 150
DeMichele, Matthew, 111
Deschenes, Elizabeth Piper, 210
Devereux, Julien, 199
DiMascio, William M., 13, 15, 179
Dodder, Richard A, 213
Dolny, H. Michael, 270, 314, 316
Dooley, Brendan, 112
Donnell, Ian, 205
Drake, Elizabeth, 203
Drapela, Laurie A., 33, 37
Dyson, Laronstine, 189
Duffee, David E., 144, 146
Dunne, John, 24, 27–28

E

Eadie, Tina, 148
Eck, John E., 104
Eisenberg, Michael, 199
Eley, Ernest, 164
Ely, John F., 185
Emke–Francis, Paula, 194
Eng, Vincent A., 52–53, 57, 58
Esselman, Julie, 223–224
Evjen, Victor H., 84
Exum, M. Lyn, 36

F

Fabelo, Tony, 199
Farkas, Mary Ann, 50, 366
Farrall, Stephen, 171
Feldman, Richard, 193–195
Festervan, Earlene, 113, 204
Fields, Monique, 163–164, 171
Figgin, Michael 35
Fisher, Bonnie S., 10
Fisher, James K., 277
Fischer, Brenda, 36
Flower, Lucy L., 85

Fogel, David, 8
Forst, Brian, 7, 8
Freeman, Beth, 111, 216–218, 221
Friday, Paul C., 186

G

Galileo, 211
Galloway, Alyson L., 33, 37
Garofalo, James, 316
Garza, Ralph, 305–306, 308
Gatchel, Robert J., 106
Geerken, Michael R., 170
Geis, Gilbert, 84, 334
Gendreau, Paul, 16, 104, 106, 211
Gibbs, Benjamin Guild, 277
Glaser, Daniel, 182
Glaze, Lauren E., 4, 258, 269–270
Goldapple, Gary C., 198
Golden, Lori S., 106
Goldkamp, John S., 29–30
Gordon, Jill A., 37
Gottfredson, Denise C., 36–37
Gottfredson, Don, 316
Gottfredson, Michael, 316
Gowen, Darren, 216–218, 220
Gray, M. Kevin, 163–164, 171
Gray, Rosemarie, 24, 27–28
Greek, Cecil E., 215–216, 218
Griffin, Patrick, 340–341
Grooms, Robert, 299
Guarino–Ghezzi, Susan, 203

H

Hale, Chris, 205
Han, Mei, 189
Hanley, Dena, 98, 210–11
Hansen, Christopher, 57, 105
Hansen, Randall M., 31
Harrell, Adele V., 85
Harries, Keith, 109
Harris, M. Kay, 88
Harris, Paul E., 277
Hartmann, David J., 186
Hebert, Eugene E., 187
Hayes, Hennessey D., 170
Hemmens, Craig, 299, 304
Henry, D. Alan, 23–25, 27–28
Hensley, Denise Bray, 191
Hepburn, John R., 171
Hignite, Lance, 150
Hill, Brian, 164
Hill, Matthew Davenport, 83
Hill, Sarah M. 189
Hindman, Jan, 111
Hippensteel, Daryl, 53
Hoffman, Peter B., 308
Holsinger, Alexander M., 18, 33, 37, 96
Horrocks, Cary, 102
Hough, Mike, 10
Hudson, Barbara, 44
Hughes, N., 205

Hughes, Timothy A., 264, 309, 311, 314, 317, 318
Hunter, Robert J., 189

I

Inciardi, James, 205

J

Jacobs, Mark, 339–340
Janes, Linda S., 164
Jeffrey, R., 203
Jenuwine, Michael J., 110
Jermstad, Todd, 150
Johnson, Richard, 211
Johnson, Shelley, 33, 37
Johnson, W. Wesley, 37, 149
Jones, Mark, 160–161, 171, 211
Jones, and Richard S., 300–301
Justice, Cheryl, 200–201

K

Kalfrin, Valerie, 217
Kane, Candice M., 112
Karp, David R., 16
Kauder, Neal B., 31
Kearley, Brook W., 36–37
Keebler, Gena, 23, 26
Keller, Oliver J., 182
Kelly, Brian J., 56
Kelly, Phaedra Athena O'Hara, 16–17, 50
Kendig, Newton, 272
Kennedy, Robert F., 182
Kerbs, John J., 160–161
Kerwood, Elizabeth, 104
Kilgour, D., 189
King, Anna, 9, 10
Kittrie, Nicholas N., 52–53, 57, 58
Kleiman, Matthew, 31
Klockars, Carl, 137–138
Knight, Charlotte, 148
Krauth, Barbara, 154
Kreisel, Betsy Wright, 140, 142
Kuzma, Susan, 353, 374

L

Langan, Patrick A., 180, 316
Latessa, Edward J., 18, 25, 31, 33, 37, 96, 182–183, 186
LeClair, D. P., 203
Lehnerer, Melodye, 185
Lemke, Richard, 25, 31
Lerner, Kenneth, 101
Levin, David J., 316
Levin, Marc A., 204, 217–219
Ley, Ann, 159
Leznoff, JoAnne, 153
Lindner, Charles, 81, 83, 85–86
Linke, 154
Lipton, Douglas, 8
Listwan, Listwan, 33, 37

Lloyd, Kathy, 35
Locke, Hubert G., 8
Louden, Jennifer Eno, 194
Love, Jack, 214
Love, Margaret Colgate, 357, 362, 367, 370, 374
Lovrich, Nicholas P., 110
Lowenkamp, Christopher T., 25, 31, 96, 98, 104, 186
Lubitz, Robin L., 44
Lutze, Faith E., 110
Lynch, Mona, 301–302

M

Mack, Julian W., 85–86
MacKinzie, Doris L., 18, 187–189, 192–193
Maconochie, Alexander, 83, 259–260
Maher, Richard J., 245
Mair, George, 225
Mansnerus, Laura, 367
Manson, Charles, 271
Mathur, Minu, 213
Marquart, James, 189
Marsangy, Bonneville de, 258
Martin, Ginger, 160
Martinson, Robert, 7–8, 264
Maruna, Shadd, 9, 10
Masterson, Mark, 338
Mastorilli, Mary Ellen, 191
Mawhorr, Tina L, 203
Maxfield, Michael G., 213
Maxwell, Sheila Royo, 163–164, 171
May, Bob, 10, 103, 110, 137, 141, 144, 298
Mayzer, Roni, 163
McDiarmid, Anne, 196
McKay, Brian, 112
McManus, Patrick D., 88
McShane, Marilyn D., 270, 314, 316
Meade, S., 189
Mears, Daniel P., 85
Mendez, Anthony, 300
Miller, Gene, 160–161
Milligan, Jessie, 192
Minor, Kevin I., 171
Minton, Todd D., 201–202
Mitchell, Fawn Ngo, 189, 192
Miyashiro, Carol M., 22
Montemayor, Carlos D., 31, 55, 58
Montesinos, Manuel, 258–259
Montgomery, Dianne, 198
Moore, Joel R., 84
Moreland, John, 83
Morgan, Kathryn, 170–171
Morris, Norval, 179, 260–261
Moscicki, Ronald, 187
Muftic, Lisa R., 245
Muhammad, Mika'il A., 293
Mumola, Christopher J., 195, 200

N

Nackerud, Larry, 184
Najaka, Stacy S., 36–37
Neff, Tom, 200
Nelson, William F., 200
Newville, Lanny L., 24
Nielsen, Amie L., 205
Nieman, Lloyd, 299–300
Nieto, Marcus, 145
Nisenbaum, Miriam, 199
Norman, Michael D., 52, 57

O

O'Malley, Pat, 247
Obermaier, Georg Michael, 259
Ogden, Thomas G., 102
Olson, David E., 112, 250
Ostrom, Brian J., 31

P

Padgett, Kathy G., 221
Palla, Seri, 258, 269–270
Palumbo, Dennis, 213
Panzarella, Robert, 83
Paparozzi, Mario A., 211
Parent, Dale, 193, 223–225
Payne, Brian K., 111
Peel, Sir Robert, 83
Prendergast, Michael, 199
Peters, James M., 111
Petersilia, Joan, 9, 52, 106, 171, 203, 210, 263–264, 267, 281, 310
Peterson, Liz Austin, 189
Phillips, Kirby, 219
Pollock, Jocelyn, 200
Potts, Dennis, 146
Price, Teressa, 147

Q

Quinn, Frederick, 52, 103, 148

R

Rainey, James, 144
Ranker, Gerard F., 250
Ransom, George, 191,
Reaves, Brian A., 26–27, 28
Reddington, Frances P., 140, 142
Reske, Henry J., 16–17, 50
Reichel, Philip, 210
Reuell, Peter, 219
Rhine, Edward E., 307
Richards, Stephen C., 300–301
Rigueti, Honore–Gabriel (Comte de Mirabeau), 258
Risler, Edwin, 184
Rivera, Craig, 144, 146
Roberts, Julian V., 10
Rocha, Carlos M., 36–37
Roman, John, 37
Rooney, J., 211
Roscoe, Thomas, 144, 146

Roskes, Erik, 193–195
Ross, Darrell L., 211
Ross, Thomas W., 44
Rothman, David, 288
Rotman, Edgardo, 79
Roy, Sudipto, 214, 220, 225–226
Ruback, R. Barry, 240–242, 246–250
Russell, Richard V., 107–109

S

Sabol, William J., 180, 201–202
Sachwald, Judith, 164
Salinas, Abel, 197
Samuels, Lorraine, 270, 316
Sandhu, Harjit, 213
Savarese, Margaret R., 81, 83, 85–86
Scarpitti, R., 205
Scharr, Timothy M., 146–147
Schloss, Christine S., 151–153
Schultz, E. J., 183
Schwaner, Shawn, 312, 313
Schwitzgebel, Robert, 214
Sechrest, Dale, 154
Senay, Edward C., 199
Settles, Tanya, 180, 182, 183
Shearer, Robert, 146
Shelden, Randall G., 31
Shepherd, Jr., Robert E., 85
Sickmund, Melissa, 325, 329–331, 333–337, 343
Siedschlaw, Kurt D., 204
Simmons, Ronald, 110
Sims, Barbara, 171
Skeem, Jennifer L., 194
Slate, Risdon N., 37, 38, 149, 193–195
Sluder, Richard, 146
Small, Shawn E., 146
Smith, Paula, 98
Smith, R. Peggy 110
Smith, Tony R., 144, 146
Snyder, Howard N., 325, 329–331, 333, 335–336, 343
Snyder–Joy, Joann K., 213
Solomon, Amy L., 317–318
Spear, John Murray, 81
Stageberg, Paul, 170
Steiner, Benjamin, 137, 195–196, 210
Stickels, John, 169
Stinchcomb, Jeanne B., 53
Storm, John P., 55–57, 98
Stottmann, Jonathan O., 241
Stowell, Jacob, 26–28
Strong, Karen, 16
Sudbrack, Billie, 210
Sundet, Paul, 35
Sundt, Jody L., 33, 37
Swetz, Anthony, 272
Swies, Edward, 110

T

Taxman, Faye S., 33, 102, 104, 106, 107, 164
Taylor, David, 184
Taylor, Scott, 160
Thacher, Peter Oxenbridge, 80
Tonry, Michael, 7, 179–180
Torbet, Patricia, 340–341
Torres, Sam, 146
Townsend, Wendy, 37
Travis, Lawrence, 182–183, 186, 352, 359–361
Tsafaty, Vered, 223–224
Turner, Susan, 203, 210, 218, 221
Twill, Sarah E., 184

U

Ulrich, Thomas E., 31, 37
Umbreit, Mark S., 16, 233–237, 242

V

Valade, Laua, 223–224
Van Ness, Daniel, 16
VanBenschoten, Scott W., 37, 98, 106
VanNostrand, Marie, 23, 26
Vollum, Scott, 215
von Hirsch, Andrew, 8
von Zielbauer, Paul, 37
Vose, Brenda, 98

W

Wadman, Robert C., 52, 57
Walker, Donald R., 235
Walters, Scott T., 106
Wallace–Capretta, S., 211
Wellisch, Jean, 199
Wells, Terry, 149, 182, 184
Wells, James B., 171
White Michael D., 29–30
Wicharaya, Tamask, 44
Wiersma, Beth A., 204
Wilks, Judith, 8
Williams III, Frank P., 270, 314, 316
Wilson, Bonnie, 170
Wilson, David B., 189, 192, 193
Wilson, Doris James, 264, 309, 311, 314, 316–318
Wines, Enoch, 83
Wines, Frederick H., 258–259
Wolf, Thomas J., 24
Wong, Mamie Mee, 199
Woolpert, S., 203
Wormith, J. Stephen, 98
Wright, Martin, 16
Wright, Ronald, 45

Z

Zenoff, Elyce H., 52–53, 57, 58
Zevitz, Richard, 50, 366

A

absconders, 306, 311–314
absolute immunity, 150
active GPS, 216–217
Adam Walsh Child Protection and
Safety Act, 362–363, 366–367
adjudication, 335
adult basic training, 141–142
Aggression Replacement Training
(ART), 105
Alaska Offender Act, 363
Alcoholics Anonymous (AA), 33, 51, 184
amercement, 79
American Bar Association, 247
American Correctional Association, 142
American Friends Service Committee, 8
American Probation and Parole
Association (APPA), 4, 104,
144–145, 148, 266
Antabuse, 196, 224
Arkansas sentencing guidelines, 47
Association of Paroling Authorities, 266
attainder, 352
Australia, 260–261
automatic restoration of rights, 371
Axis I disorders, 38

B

bail amounts, 25–26
bail bond offices, 23
bail decision, 12–13
Bail Reform acts, 23
bankruptcy, 240
blended sentences, 336
bonds, 25, 259, 358
See surety bond
boot camp, 186–193
criticisms of, 192
evaluations of, 192–193
perspectives on, 189–192
brokerage of services, 90

C

California
and "banked probation," 103
and community service, 243
and electronic monitoring, 221
firearm guidelines, 145
gender-based drug court programs, 35
and halfway houses, 183
and house arrest, 211
and ISP, 209–210
officer citizenship, 138, 139

parole officers, 301–303
and probation law, 86, 87
reentry study, 299–300
therapeutic communities, 199
Canada, 232, 236, 237
Carlie's law, 162
case plan, 98, 101
caseload, 103
casework, 90
cellular communication, 216
certificate of discharge, 371
characteristics of parolees, 267–270
chat rooms, 112
Children's Aid Society of
Pennsylvania, 84
children in need of supervision
(CHINS), 331
circle sentencing, 235–236
civil disabilities, 351–362
background of, 351–352
contemporary, 352–362
problems with laws, 362
civil rights, 351, 354
classification, 96–98
clear conditions, 49
Client Management Classification
(CMC), 97, 101
cognitive-behavioral therapy,
105–106
collateral consequences, 350–354
collateral contact, 102
Colorado
corrections costs, 11
and full board reviews, 284
reentry court, 279
community corrections, 3–6
benefits of, 1
conditions of, 47–51
and correctional budgets, 10–11
and correctional goals, 14–17
definition of, 3
evidence-based practices, 17–19
and pretrial and bail, 12–13
and probation, 5–7
public perceptions of, 9–10
and reentry, 13–14
referral to, 12–14
and sentencing, 13
statistics on, 4, 6
Community Corrections Acts (CCAs),
88–90
community justice, 16, 231
See restorative justice

community notification laws, and sex
offenders, 364–366
community resource management
team (Crmt) model, 90
community service, 242–246
definition of, 242
effectiveness of, 244–246
experience of, 245
English model of, 243
history of, 243
prevalence of, 243
purpose of, 243
completion rates, 36
Comprehensive Crime Control Act
(1984), 84
concurrent jurisdiction, 331
conditional pardon, 368
conditional release, 25
conditions of parole
See parole conditions
conduct in need of supervision (CINS),
329–331
conviction, 80
correction, definition of, 13
correctional
budgets, 10–11, 15
dilemma, 3–9
goals, 14–17
paradox, 9–12
roles, 12–14
treatment, 15
Correctional Offender Management
Profiles for Alternative Sentences
(COMPAS), 97
corrections, role of, 12–14
Corrections Program Assessment
Inventory (CPAI), 16, 104
court costs, 249–250
Council of State Governments, 154
CREST program, 205
criminal procedure, 79
cybercriminal, 56

D

Dade County, Florida, 33
day fines, 248
day reporting centers (DRCs), 221–226
completion rates, 225
day in the life of, 223
definition of, 221
evaluations of, 224–225
failure predictors, 225–226
and itineraries, 244

day reporting centers (DRCs) *(cont.)*
    supervision-oriented, 224–225
    treatment-oriented, 224–225
decision to revoke, 161–164
"deferred adjudication," 169
delegated release authority, 25
Delaware
    and the merit system, 139
    probation reform law, 171
    sentencing guidelines, 47
determinate sentencing, 8–9
deterrence through shaming, 16–17
    See shaming
diminished constitutional rights, 304
direct consequences, 350–351
disclosure, 58–59
discretion, 12
discretionary release, 257, 264
discretionary conditions, 49
disposition, 335
diversion, 30–39
    candidates for, 31–32
    criticisms of, 39
    definition of, 30
    and drug courts, 32–33
    and risk assessment instruments, 31
driving under the influence (DUI), 215
drug abuse
    and probation, 82–83
    RCCFs, 195–200
    and rehabilitation, 15–16
    and mental illness, 38
    and urine testing, 219, 224
drug courts, 32–37
    characteristics of, 33
    chart, 36
    definition of, 32–33
    evaluating, 35–37
    and gender, 34–35
due process, 167, 291–292
dynamic factors, 97
early termination of probation, 159
education of probation officers, 140–141

E

Eighth Amendment, 17, 50, 192, 248
electronic monitoring (EM), 213–221
    advances in, 216
    definition of, 214
    and DRCs, 224
    evaluations of, 220–221
    and gender, 221
    history of, 214–215
    long-term effects of, 221
    problems of early homebound
        EM, 215
    and public opinion, 220
employment assistance, 106–107
employment-related rights, 356
England
    and criminal law, 79, 80
    and community service, 243

See transportation
evidence-based practices (EBP), 17–19
    effectiveness of, 18
    principles of, 104–105
exclusion zones, 217
exclusionary rule, 60
expungement, 372–373

F

failure to appear (FTA), 28–30
family group conferencing, 234–235
Federal Bonding Program, 259
Federal Bureau of Investigation
    (FBI), 313
Federal Bureau of Prisons (FBP), 84, 187
Federal Court of Appeals, 49
federal parole, *See* U.S. Parole
    Commission
Federal Pretrial Services Act
    (1982), 23
federal probation, 48, 84
federal probation officers, 107–109, 141
    duties of, 141
Federal Sentencing Reform Act
    (1984), 81
fees, 249–250
female offenders, 4, 34–35
    electronic monitoring, 221
    and parole, 317
    and probation, 171
    and RCCFs, 200–201
    and recidivism, 289–290
    and rehabilitation, 182
    and restitution centers, 204
    and substance abuse, 196, 199
    and supervision, 113
field contact, 101
field parole officer, 301–303
Fifth Amendment rights, 51
filing, 79
final revocation hearing, 167
Financial Assessment Related
    to Employability (FARE)
    program, 249
fines, 246–249
    day fines, 248
    definition of, 246
    and forfeitures, 248
    increasing, 247–248
    prevalence of, 246–247
    and revocation of probation,
        247–248
firearms policies for probation officers,
    144–148
Firearms Training System (FATS), 148
First Amendment, 50, 51, 304
Freedom of Information Act, 285
"flight risk," 26–27
Florida
    drug courts, 33
    and electronic monitoring, 220–221
    and house arrest, 211–212

and officer telecommuting, 57
    work release centers, 204
forfeiture, 248
Fourteenth Amendment, 139, 247,
    326, 363
Fourth Amendment, 51, 60, 304
"Fuginet," 312–313
full board review, 284

G

gang members, 112–113
gender
    and electronic monitoring, 221
    and parole outcomes, 317
    and substance abuse, 196
    and supervision, 113
    See female offenders
General Accounting Office (GAO), 36
Geneva Convention (1949), 261
Geographic information system
    (GIS), 109
Georgia
    and boot camps, 186
    and house arrest, 211
    prison population control, 270–271
    and private probation, 152
    and probation detention centers, 166
Germany
    and fines, 246
    and parole, 259
"getting lost," prisoner's perspective on,
    298–301
global positioning systems (GPS), 111,
    216–221
    evaluations of, 220–221
    limitations of, 218
    offender type, 218
    and public opinion, 220
    and satellite technology, 218
    and zones, 217
good moral character, 352, 358–359
good time, 280
graduated sanctions, 306
group monitoring, 216

H

halfway houses, 181–186
    definition of, 181–182
    and DRCS, 224
    evaluation of, 185–186
    levels system, 183–184
    as prerelease facility, 281
    program components, 183–185
    punishment and treatment role
        orientations, 185
    U.S. history of, 182
    and work release, 202
    worker perspectives, 184–185
good conduct, 262
Harris County, Texas, 222–223
"hearing examiners," 285
hearsay evidence, 59–60

"high quality" treatment programs, 16
home-based electronic monitoring, 214
house arrest, 211–213

I

Illinois
    and community corrections act, 89
    DRCs, 225–226
    and juvenile court, 84–85
    and "tolled" probation, 170
Illinois Criminal Justice Authority,
    225–226
Illinois Juvenile Court Act (1899),
    84–85
immigration cases, 26
immunity, 150
implementing the supervision case plan
    caseload standards, 103
    supervision levels, 103
    surveillance, 101
    treatment, 104–107
    workload standards, 104
in-house administrative options before
    filing a revocation, 159–161
in-service training, 144
incarceration, 6
inclusion zones, 217
indeterminate sentencing, 7–8, 53
    and parole, 262
Indiana
    and DRCs, 222, 225
    and indigent offenders, 240
    RCCFs, 200–201
Individual Treatment and Supervision
    Plans (ITSPs), 222
infamy, 351
informal social controls, 107
institutional corrections, 14
intake, 334–335
intensive supervision probation (ISP),
    181, 209–11
    and DRCs, 222
    evaluations of, 210
    and juveniles, 340–341
    and specialized caseloads, 209, 211
intermediate sanctions, 179
    definition of, 13, 179
    and rehabilitation, 15
International Community Corrections
    Association, 183
International Halfway House
    Association, 183
Interstate Compact for Adult
    Offender Supervision, 154–155
interstate compacts on probation,
    154–155
involuntary civil commitment of sexual
    predators, 366–367
Iowa reentry study, 300–301
iris recognition technology, 202
the Irish system, 261–262
Isaac T. Hopper Home, 182

J

jail-based work release, 201–202
John P. Craine House, 200–201
judicial waiver, 331
just deserts, 264
justice model, 91, 264
juvenile courts, 84–86, 329
juvenile delinquency, 329–330
juvenile justice system
    compared to adult justice system,
        327–332
    and constitutional rights, 326–327
    courts, 84–86, 329
    future of, 345
    overview of process of, 332–336
    parole/aftercare, 343–345,
    preservice training, 142
    probation, 84–88, 169, 189, 336–343
    probation officer (JPO), 147
    probation revocation, 169
    and records, 342–343
    and reparation bonds, 234–235
    restorative justice, 232–237, 239,
        241–242
    victim-offender mediation, 233–234,
        241–242
    See boot camps
juvenile justice process, 332–336
    adjudication, 335
    blended sentences, 336
    disposition, 335
    intake, 334–335
    procedure before adjudication, 332
juveniles in need of supervision (JINS),
    331
juvenile parole/aftercare, 343–345
juvenile parole boards, 343–344
juvenile probation, 84–88, 169, 189,
    336–343
    change as integral process, 337–338
    conditions of, 337
    intensive supervision probation, 340
    JPOs as "superheroes," 339–340
    revocation of, 344
    school-based probation, 340–341
juvenile probation officer (JPO), 147,
    339–340, 343–344
juvenile records, 342–343

K

Kansas Sexually Violent Predator
    Act, 367
"Killits" case, 80–81
kiosk machines, 102

L

Law Enforcers, 138
law violations, 162–163
Level of Service Inventory-Revised
    (LSI-R), 97–98, 289
levels of supervision, 103

loss of capacity to be bonded, 358
losses eligible for compensation, 239
Lutze, Faith E., 192

M

"Magdalene" program, 200
Maine, and determinate sentencing, 8–9
mandatory minimums, 9
mandatory release, 257
Manhattan Bail Project, 23
Manhattan Court Employment
    project, 30
Maricopa County, Arizona, 222
marks system, 260
Maryland
    caseload standards, 104
    and principles of effective
        intervention,104
Massachusetts
    boot camps, 189
    and DRCs, 222
    and halfway houses, 182
    and probation, 81–84, 86
maximum eligibility date, 280
media, 9–10
medical parole, 263, 271–272
mens rea, 329, 335
mental health courts, 37–38
mental illness, and
        deinstitutionalization,214
mental illness RCCFs, 193–195
merit system, of probation officers,
    138, 139
Michigan
    gender-based drug court programs, 35
    and mandatory revocation, 162
    prison population control, 270–271
    and probation supervision, 163
Milwaukee, Wisconsin, and day fines, 249
minimum eligibility date, 280
Minnesota
    community corrections act, 88
    and parole absconders, 314
    RCCFs, 200
    and restitution, 236–237, 242
    sentencing guidelines, 47
Minnesota Restitution Center, 242
minors in need of supervision
    (MINS), 331
Miranda warnings, 60, 341–342
Missouri
    firearm guidelines, 146
    parole officers, 302
    and private probation, 153
    sentencing guidelines, 47
    Mobile Community Supervision
        Techniques, 102
    models of parole release decisions,
        287–291
Moral Reconation Therapy (MRT), 105
moral turpitude, 352
motion to quash, 80

motivational interviewing, 106
Multnomah County, Oregon, 35, 195

N

Narcotics Anonymous, 33
National Advisory Commission on
 Criminal Justice Standards and
 Goals (1973), 90
National Association of Pretrial
 Services, 24
National Institute of Corrections (NIC),
 155
National Probation Act, 84
Native Americans, and restorative
 justice, 232
National Sex Offender Public Website
 (NSOPW), 362
National Youth Court Association, 336
Nebraska parole procedure, 291–292
negligence, 150
neighborhood-based supervision
 (NBS), 91, 107, 109–110
New Jersey
 caseload standards, 104
 expungement, 373
 firearm guidelines, 146
New York
 boot camps, 188–189
 and day fines, 249
 and DRCs, 222
 gender-based drug court programs,
  35
 and halfway houses, 182
 and juvenile probation, 84
 and mental illness, 195
 and parole, 261–262
 and parole denial, 291–292
 prison boot camps, 188
 and probation law, 81, 86, 87
 and qualified immunity, 151
 reentry court, 279
 reentry program, 277
New York Children's Aid Society, 84
New Zealand, 232, 235, 237
Norfolk Island, 259–261
North Carolina
 community corrections act, 89
 corrections costs, 11
 and DRCs, 222
 presumptive sentencing grids, 45
 sentencing guidelines, 45–46
 training requirements, 141–143
North Dakota training requirements,
 141

O

O-track system, 165
occupational licenses
 effects of pardon on, 369–370
 examples of, 357
 limitations, 357–358
offender-based presentence report, 53

Offender Inventory Assessment
 (OIA), 97
offense-based presentence report, 53
officer salary, 144
Ohio
 community corrections act, 89
 corrections costs, 11
 expungement, 373
Oklahoma
 parole conditions, 303
 parole process, 286
 victim impact statement, 286
Oregon
 community corrections act, 89
 drug courts, 35
 expungement, 373
 and house arrest, 211
 and mental health services, 195
Oregon Community Corrections
 Act, 89
outlawry, 352

P

pardons, 367–369
parens patriae, 85, 326–327
parental rights, 360
parole, 6–7, 14
 absconders, 311–314
 characteristics of parolees, 267–270
 conditions of, 303–305
 cost reduction of, 262
 definition of, 14, 257
 development of in the U.S., 261–264
 discretionary release, 264
 effectiveness, 314–318
 eligibility, 279–282
 functions of, 270
 and good conduct, 262
 and indeterminate sentence, 262
 justifications for, 261–262
 and mandatory release, 264
 medical model of, 263
 origins of, 258–261
 outcomes, predicting, 316–318
 philosophical change in model,
  263–264
 post-release supervision, 262
 and prison population control,
  270–271
 release decisions, models of, 287–291
 revocation, 309–311
 selection, and prisoner perceptions,
  292–293
 statistics on, 6–7
 and technology, 109
 and terminally ill prisoners, 271–272
 today, 264–272
 violators, 308–311
parole absconders, 306, 311–314
parole board, 7, 266
 characteristics by state, 282–283
 decision, 287

definition of, 282
 functions of, 282
 and parole hearing, 284–286
 as releasing authority,
  282–287
 terms and qualifications of, 284
 violating, 305–308
Parole Commission
 See U.S. Parole Commission
parole conditions, 298, 303–305
 definition of, 298
 limited rights of all parolees, 304
 for sex offenders, 304
parole d'honneur, 258
parole effectiveness, 314–318
parole eligibility, 279–282
 and prerelease preparation,
  280–281
 and time sheets, 280
parole eligibility date, 280
parole hearings, 284–286
 attendees, 285–286
 legal issues in, 291–292
 and due process, 291–292
 and hearsay, DNA, and right to an
  attorney, 292
parole officer, perspective of,
  301–303
parole outcomes, 316–318
Parole and Probation Compact
 Administrators' Association
 (PPCAA), 155
parole release decisions, models of,
  287–291
 procedural justice model, 288
 risk prediction model, 288–289, 291
 surveillance model, 287–288
parole revocation
 attitudes on, 310–311
 rate, 309–310
 table, 310
parole selection, prisoner's perceptions
 of, 292–293
parole violations, 306, 308–311
parole violators, characteristics of,
  308–309
parolees, 267–270, 305
PARTNER (Parolees and Relatives
 toward Newly Enhanced
 Relationships), 277
passive GPS, 217
Peace Officer State Training (POST),
  137, 142
Pennsylvania
 and halfway houses, 182
 and parole, 262
 presumptive sentencing grids, 45
 and restitution, 242
 voting rights act, 355
petition for nondisclosure, 373
Phoenix, Arizona, and day fines, 249
placing out, 84

penile plethysmograph, 111
political rights, 351, 354
polygraph tests, 111
post-booking diversion
    See diversion
postsentence report, 53
power to arrest probationers, 166
power to suspend sentence, 80–81
"pre-plea report," 55
preferred rights, 304
preliminary hearing, 167
preponderance of the evidence, 168
prerelease facility, 280
prerelease plan, 281
prerelease program, 14
presentence investigation, 53
presentence investigation report (PSI),
    52–60
    definition of, 52
    disclosure of, 58–59
    contents of, 53–54
    for cybercriminals, 56
    errors in, 150
    evaluative summary, 56–57
    and exclusionary rule, 60
    hearsay in, 59–60
    inaccuracies in, 58
    initial interview, 55–56
    investigation and verification, 56
    legal issues concerning, 57–60
    and LSI-R, 98
    and *Miranda* warnings, 60
    preparing, 55–58
    purposes of, 52–53
    right to a lawyer during, 60
    sentence recommendation, 57
    and telecommuting, 57
presentence investigation report (PSI)
    interview, 55–56, 61
preservice training, 142, 144
President's Commission on Law
    Enforcement and Administration of
    Justice (1967), 13
presumptive sentence, 8
presumptive sentencing grids, 44–45
pretrial, 12–13
pretrial release, 22–24
pretrial release decision, 24–27
pretrial services, 22–30
pretrial services officer, 24–25
pretrial supervision, 13, 27–28
principles of effective intervention, 104
prior arrests, and parole, 317
prison population control, 17,
    270–271, 280
Prison Boot Camps, 187–188
prisoner perspectives
    on getting lost, 298–301
    on parole selection, 292–293
private employment, 356
private probation, 151–153
privilege against self-incrimination, 51

probation, 3–6, 77
    conditions, 159–161
    definition of, 3
    demographics, 91–93
    departments, 86–91
    early legislation, 86
    federal, 84
    founders of, 81–83
    and Geographic information system
        (GIS), 109
    interstate compacts on, 154–155
    outcomes, 170–173
    precursors to, 79–86
    private, 151–153
    procedures related to, 80–81
    purpose of, 5–6
    recidivism rates, 170–171
    and sentencing, 44
    and shaming, 50
    statistics on, 6
    success rates, 171
    supervision, 90–91
    See juvenile probation
probation conditions, modifying,
    159–161
probation departments, 86–91
probation demographics, 91–93
probation officers, 52–57
    a day in the life of, 107–109
    education of, 140–141
    firearms policies, 144–148
    job stress, 148–151
    qualifications and training, 139–144
    salary of, 144
    sample job advertisements, 142
    selection and appointment of,
        138–139
    training program, 143
    U.S. citizen requirement, 139
probation outcomes, 170–173
probation recidivism rates, 170–171
probation supervision, 90–91
Probation/Jail Boot Camps, 188
probationers versus parolees,
    171–172
procedural justice model of parole
    release, 288
"programming," 15
Project Greenlight, 279
"Project MUSTER" (Must Earn
    Restitution), 248
"Project RIO" (Re-Integration of
    Offenders), 278
prostitution, 200
Providence Community
    Corrections, 152
public employment, 356
public office, 361
public perceptions, 9–10
public protection, 15
public shaming, *See* shaming
punishment, 5, 8

Q
qualified immunity, 150–151

R
reasonable conditions, 49
Reasoning and Rehabilitation
    (R&R), 105
recidivism
    definition of, 18–19
    and drug programs, 37
    and electronic monitoring, 221
    and family-group counseling, 235
    and indeterminate sentencing, 7–8
    and mental illness, 195
    and post-prison release, 291
    and probation, 170–171
    studies, 316
    and victim-offender mediation, 234
receiving state, 154
    recognizance, 80
"redeemability," 10
reentry
    and the community, 278–279
    community-based initiatives, 279
    decision, 13–14
    definition, 14, 257, 275
    experiences of, 276, 291, 299–301
    issues in, 275–282
    and prisoner's family, 277
    prisoner's perceptions of parole
        selection, 292
    victim's role in, 277
reentry courts, 279
reentry decision, 13–14
reflective justice, 44
registration laws, for sex offenders,
    362–363
rehabilitation
    and correctional goals, 14–16
    definition of, 15–16
    and indeterminate sentencing, 7–8
rehabilitation certificate, 370
reintegration, 13
reintegrative shaming, 232
    See shaming
relapse, 199
Relapse Prevention Therapy (RPT), 105
released on their own recognizance
    (ROR), 23, 25
remote location monitoring, 216
reparation bonds, 234
residency restrictions, of sex offenders,
    366
residential community corrections
    facilities (RCCFs), 180–185
    evaluations of, 185
    and the mentally ill, 193–195
    specialized caseloads, 193–201
    and substance abusers, 195–200
    and women offenders, 200–201
    See halfway houses

restitution, 237–242
    amount, 240
    and bankruptcy, 240
    before sentencing, 241
    collection rates, 241
    collecting, 241
    definition of, 237
    determining amount of, 240
    effectiveness of, 242
    in history, 237–238
    increasing collection rates, 241
    indigent offenders, 240
    losses eligible for compensation,
        239
    problems associated with,
        239–240
    in restorative justice, 238–239
restitution centers, 203–204
restoration of rights, 370–374
restorative justice, 16, 231–237
    circle sentencing, 235–236
    effectiveness of, 236–237
    family group conferencing, 234–235
    forms of, 233
    principles of, 232–237
    reparation bonds, 234
    roots of, 232
    victim-offender mediation, 233–234
retention rates, 36
retribution, 10
revocation, 158–159
    after probation term expires,
        169–170
    attitudes on, 310–311
    decision-making process, 161–164
    for inability to pay, 169
    of juvenile probation or parole, 344
    and parole, 309–311
    procedure, 164–166
    rights of probationers and parolees,
        167–170
Rhode Island
    caseload standards, 103
    and community corrections
        act, 89
    merit system, 139
    and probation law, 86, 87
right
    to bear firearm, 359–360
    to a hearing, 167–168
    to hold public office, 361
    to a lawyer, 168
    to serve on jury, 361
    to vote, 354–355
rights
    affected by conviction, 354–362
    lost through discretion, 353–354
risk assessment, 97–100
risk assessment instruments, 31
risk prediction model of parole release,
    288–289, 291
Risk Prediction Index (RPI), 24

role ambiguity, 149
role conflict, 149–150

S

Sacramento Intelligence Unit
    (SIU), 112
Safe Streets Act (1968), 183
salary, of probation officers, 144
Salient Factor Score, 97, 288–289
"scarlet letter" conditions,
    49–50
school-based probation,
    340–341
SCRAM® (Secure Continuous Remote
    Alcohol Monitoring), 219
sealing of records, 373–374
searches and seizures, 51
security for good behavior, 79
sending state, 154
sentencing
    commissions, 47
    decision, 13
    definition of, 43
    determinate, 8–9
    factors affecting, 43–44
    grids, 44–45
    guidelines, 9, 44–47
    indeterminate, 7–8
Seventh Circuit Court of
    Appeals, 247
sex offenders, 110–112
    community notification laws, 364–366
    effects of convictions, 362–367
    involuntary civil commitment of
        sexual predators, 366–367
    and parole, 304–305
    registration laws, 362–363
    residency restrictions, 366
    treatment, 111
shaming, 16–17, 49–50, 199, 232–233,
    235, 237
shock incarceration, 186–193
    See boot camp
Sixth Amendment, 60
Solution to Employment Problems
    (STEP) program, 356
Spain, 258–259
special conditions, 49
specialized caseloads, 110–113
    and ISP, 209–210
    moving to, 211
standard conditions, 47
standard of proof, 168
Staten Island, New York, and day
    fines, 249
static factors, 97
Static-99, 289
"status hearing," 38
statutory exclusion, 331
Strategies for Self-Improvement and Change
    (SSC), 105
stigmatization, 232, 233, 237

supervision, 101–102
    and the Constitution, 51
    of gang members, 112–113
    levels, 103–104
    and parole, 317–318
    of sex offenders, 110–112
    and technology, 109
    "treatment retention" model,
        195–196
    of women offenders, 113
    of working offenders, 201–205
supervision case plan, 98–110
supervision levels, 103–104
supervision-oriented DRCs, 224–225
surety, 80
surety bond, 25–26, 28, 358
surveillance, 101
surveillance model of parole release,
    287–288
suspended sentence, 80
Synthetic Officers, 138

T

tables
    Adults on Probation, on Parole, in Jail,
        and in Prison: (1980–2007), 6–7
    Annual Costs per Person for
        Selected Forms of Correctional
        Supervision, 11
    Case flow of delinquency cases after
        arrest, 334
    Comparing Therapeutic
        Communities and Drug
        Courts, 198
    Characteristics of Adult Parolees
        Over Time, 269
    Characteristics of Adults on
        Probation Over Time, 92–93
    Characteristics of Federal
        Probationers Terminating
        Supervision, 172
    Characteristics of Parole Violators in
        State Prison, 309
    Daily Schedule for Offenders in
        New York Shock Incarceration
        Facilities, 188
    Differences for Each Supervision
        Level, 103–104
    Discretionary Restoration of the
        Vote after a Felony Conviction,
        370
    Electronic Monitoring Techniques
        for Various Offender Risk
        Levels, 218
    Examples of Occupations That
        Require a License, 357
    Failure-to-Appear Follow-up by
        Pretrial Programs, 29
    Failure to Appear and Rearrest Rates
        for Federal Defendants, 29
    Federal Release and Detention
        Rates, 27

Federal Revocation Table Determining Imprisonment Months, 162

Firearms Policies for Probation and Parole Officers, 144–145

Flowchart of Two Drug Court Approaches, 32–33

Guidelines for Decision Making: Customary Total Time to Be Served before Release, 290

How Electronic Monitoring is Used, 215

Most Common Probation Conditions

Juvenile Justice and Adult Criminal Justice Systems Compared, 333

Major United States Supreme Court Decisions in Juvenile Justice, 326–327

Minimum and Maximum Ages for Delinquency Cases, 329–330

Most Common Probation Conditions Received by Sentenced Felony Defendants, 244

Number of States with Firearms Policies for Probation and Parole Officers, 145

Organizational Structure of Adult and Juvenile Probation/Parole Services, 87–88

Parole Board Characteristics by State, 282–283

The Parole Revocation Process, 307

Parolee Population and Rates of Parole and Imprisonment Per 100,000, 267–268

Percent of State Prisoners Who Enter Prison Because of Parole Revocation, 1930–2008, 310

Pie chart of Private Treatment Services, 152

Principal Features of Seven Sex Offender Notification Statutes, 365

Probation Violation Decision Guidelines, 161

Probation/Parole Officer Basic Training Program Course Topics and Hours, 143

Reasons for Revocation among Parole Violators in State Prison, 311

Release Authority of Parole Boards by State, 265–266

Releases from State Prison, by Method of Release, 1980–2003, 258

Roots of Restorative Justice in U.S., 232

Rules and Conditions of Oklahoma Parole, 303

Salient Factor Score (SFS/98), 289

School-Based Probation Agreements, 341

Typology of Restorative Justice Sanctions, 238

Typology of Work Styles, 138

Voting Restrictions, 355

technical violations, 162–163

technology
    iris recognition, 202
    and parole, 109
    and revocations, 165
    and surgical microchips, 219
    tissue spectroscopy, 219
    and urine testing, 219
    See electronic monitoring; global positioning systems

Tennessee, and therapeutic communities, 200

terminally ill prisoners, 271–272

Texas
    bankruptcy, and restitution, 240
    and community service, 243–244
    and DRCs, 222–223
    juvenile probation boot camps, 189
    prerelease facilities, 281
    prison population control, 270–271
    and probation user fees, 249
    reentry program, 278
    restitution centers, 204
    work release programs, 204

Therapeutic Agents, 138

therapeutic community (TC), 196–199

Thinking for a Change (T4C), 105

three strikes laws, 9

ticket-of-leave, 260–261

Time-Servers, 138

"tolled" probation term, 170

transfer of jurisdiction, 331

transportation, 259–261
    of English Prisoners to America, 259–260
    of English prisoners to Australia, 260–261

Treatment Alternatives to Street Crime (TASC), 30

treatment needs, 98

treatment-oriented DRCs, 224–225

"truth in sentencing" laws, 9

Type I Absconders, 312

Type II Absconders, 312–313

U

unconditional release, 257

U.S. citizen requirement, for parole officers, 139

U.S. Parole Commission, 261, 285

U.S. sentencing guidelines, 45, 47

unsecured bond, 25

V

Vermont
    community corrections act, 89
    and probation, 86
    and work release, 204

victim compensation fund, 246

victim impact statement, 54, 286

victim-offender mediation (VOM), 233–234, 242

violating parole
    See parole violations

Virginia sentencing guidelines, 47

Virtual Community Supervision Techniques, 102

vocational training, 15

voice verification monitoring, 216

Volstead Act, 84

voting restrictions, 355

W

warrants and citations, 308

Washington
    and expungement, 372–373
    and sex offenders, 362–363
    and work release programs, 203–204, 281

Washington, D.C.
    "Find and Fix" program, 314
    and juvenile courts, 85

welfare benefits, 360

Welfare Reform Act, 360

widening the net, 18, 180, 210, 234

Wisconsin Client Management Classification, 97

Wisconsin Risk and Needs sheet, 99–100

Wisconsin, and sex offenders, 366

witness credibility, 361

work ethic camp, 204–205

work release, 201–203, 281

work styles, 138

"workload standard," 104

writ of habeas corpus, 167

Y

youth courts, 336